EU

By the late 1960s, in a Europe divided by the Cold War and challenged by global revolution in Latin America, Asia, and Africa, thousands of young people threw themselves into activism to change both the world and themselves. This new and exciting study of "Europe's 1968" is based on the rich oral histories of nearly 500 former activists collected by an international team of historians across fourteen countries. Activists' own voices reflect on how they were drawn into activism, how they worked and struggled together, how they combined the political and the personal in their lives, and the pride or regret with which they look back on those momentous years. Themes explored include generational revolt and activists' relationship with their families, the meanings of revolution, transnational encounters and spaces of revolt, faith and radicalism, dropping out, gender and sexuality, and revolutionary violence. Focussing on the way in which the activists themselves made sense of their revolt, this work makes a major contribution to both oral history and memory studies. This ambitious study ranges widely across Europe from Franco's Spain to the Soviet Union, and from the two Germanys to Greece, and throws new light on moments and movements which both united and divided the activists of Europe's 1968.

Robert Gildea is Professor of Modern History at the University of Oxford. He was a Lecturer at King's College London (1978–79) and Fellow and Tutor in History at Merton College Oxford (1979–2006). He is a Fellow of the British Academy.

James Mark is Professor of History at the University of Exeter.

Anette Warring is Professor of Modern History at Roskilde University. She is a Fellow of the Royal Danish Academy of Sciences and Letters, and was Chairman of the Danish Council for Independent Research/Humanities in 2011–13.

Europe's 1968

Voices of Revolt

Edited by
ROBERT GILDEA
JAMES MARK
ANETTE WARRING

OXFORD

UNIVERSITY PRESS

Great Clarendon Street, Oxford, OX2 6DP,
United Kingdom

Oxford University Press is a department of the University of Oxford.
It furthers the University's objective of excellence in research, scholarship,
and education by publishing worldwide. Oxford is a registered trade mark of
Oxford University Press in the UK and in certain other countries

Published in the United States of America by Oxford University Press
198 Madison Avenue, New York, NY 10016, United States of America

British Library Cataloguing in Publication Data
Data available

Library of Congress Cataloging in Publication Data
Data available

ISBN 978–0–19–958751–3 (Hbk.)
ISBN 978–0–19–880102–3 (Pbk.)

Foreword

Sheila Rowbotham

Doing history is always beset by anxiety. How to capture what happened? How to interpret what you have not known? Historians, like those be-whiskered Victorian butterfly-hunters, head off intent on an elusive prey. Then, as the years advance, history has this habit of catching up on you, becoming the times you remember. While trying to avoid being the elderly grump expostulating, 'But it wasn't like that', it is exasperating to be served up the complicated past you recollect in bland superficial packages. In contrast, when Robert Gildea asked me to participate in the second workshop of the Around '68 project, I was intrigued by the spirit of open enquiry, along with the geographical scale of investigation. At last, I decided, here were people seeking to find out the thoughts and views of a wide range of participants in social movements.

The Around '68ers invited me to comment on the interviews they were conducting as a participant and as a remembering historian. This double role was not new for me. From the late 1960s, and in defiance of the chiliastic temper of the times, I had been aware of the need to chronicle the networks and movements in which I participated, hoarding letters, notes, leaflets, pamphlets, magazines, journals, and posters. These found their way subsequently into Ron Heisler's Collection of radical ephemera at Senate House Library and my own archive in the Women's Library. Over the decades I also wrote many short articles and was interviewed. Then, in 1998, stung by taking part in an especially shallow radio programme, I started to write a memoir of the 1960s. Working on *Promise of a Dream* taught me how memories could lie dormant and then suddenly flare through reading an old letter or looking at a diary. I experienced too those tricks of time—the unsettling, momentary collision between time present and time past that leaves you reeling.

But my chronicling and memoir writing had been individual rather than collective. So when I attended the Around '68 workshops, I did feel a little uncertain about etiquette. What, I wondered, was appropriate behaviour for a living document? Just how oral was I meant to be? No one seemed too bothered, and as they kept asking me to turn up again, I played it by ear. For much of the time I became so interested in listening I would remain silent, encompassed by that intense, absorbent characteristic of the oral interviewer. It was like eavesdropping on oral history.

I found myself being roused to speak up usually on nuance and content. Remembering is to possess a consciousness of several dimensions of time. You recall the time before what is being discussed, as well as the time after. Being aware of the time before makes you alert to the influences at work, as well as what was being reacted against. So 'around '58' could be said to be moving within and against 'around '68'. Moreover, having been there, you are dealing with the known, and consequently aware of what seemed so obvious at the time that no one bothered to mention it. Taken-for-granted attitudes are the ones that evade historians.

Of course, when the past is not just 'out there' to be discovered and apprehended, but involves interpreting what you remember, there is a problem of entanglement. I was in my twenties during the 1960s and early 1970s and the startling sense of newness and discovery I associate with those years beams through my memories. Emotionally I am unable to infer whether this can be taken as characteristic of the era or simply a reflection of my age at the time. Intellectually I can conclude it is a bit of both. And, because 1968 is a historical trigger-point around which layers of supposition have accrued, and because I recall it retrospectively, it can be hard to extricate myself from impressions that have cohered into patterns of assumption. Familiarity can be illuminating as long as you avoid being wrapped up by it.

Attending the workshops enabled me to experience a cooperative search to understand events I had lived through. The material from the oral interviews was remarkable and often surprising. The researchers were following so many trails at once, sharing their findings and disputing their meanings. So much had been found, so much was being interpreted from differing perspectives. The mix of known and unknown induced a feeling of wonder.

I have attended so many meetings in my life that an allergic resistance has set in; I am inclined to wriggle, grow restless and drift off. Instead, I found myself concentrating intently and learning in every workshop as information and ideas went bouncing around the room. I was able to see my particular impressions from many angles and heard much that I had never realized at the time. Our discussions stimulated and enhanced my own memories, providing me with a wider context for my own knowledge of the period.

The cooperative exchange of ideas in a democratic manner has always been a source of the deepest delight for me. I have learned to value this indefinable state of grace that can be nurtured, but is so easily devastated. The Around '68 workshops were like floating into an historian's heaven, especially blissful because I did not have to face the daunting responsibility of writing it all up. As we gathered year after year, I began to marvel at the manner in which they combined their research. Collaborative research is a severe discipline and I could see how hard it was for them to get a balance between the cherished, revealing, individual quote and the shared analysis.

The creative result is a book that no individual could have written. It is in the most profound sense a *collection*. It has not been patched together, it is the result of fusion, painful and enriching. It is going to open up countless new ways of seeing the years around 1968.

Contents

PART III. MAKING SENSE OF ACTIVISM

Acknowledgements

We are very grateful to the Arts and Humanities Research Council (AHRC) and the Leverhulme Trust, together with the British Academy, which funded the 'Around 1968: Activism, Networks, Trajectories' project between 2007 and 2011. Anna von der Goltz would like to thank Magdalen College, Oxford for allowing her to suspend a fellowship to work on this project. Piotr Osęka expresses his gratitude for the support of the National Programme for the Development of Humanities, established by the Polish Ministry of Science and Higher Education. We are grateful to Gabi Maas for compiling the bibliography. Finally, we all wish to record our heartfelt thanks to those who took the time to tell us about their experiences of activism. Without their generosity and trust, this book would not have been possible. Their rich and complex life stories were the foundation of this project, and opened up for us new ways of seeing the history of this period.

List of Abbreviations

ACLI	Associazioni Cristiane Lavoratori Italiani/Association of Italian Christian Workers
AKE	Antifasistiko Kinima Elladas/Anti-fascist Movement of Greece
AST	Alternativa Sindical de Trabajadores/Alternative Union of Workers
BDM	Bund deutscher Mädel/League of German Girls
CAL	Comités Action Lycéens/High School Action Committees
CFDT	Confédération Française Démocratique du Travail/French Confederation of Democratic Workers
CGT	Confédération Générale du Travail/General Confederation of Workers
CIA	Central Intelligence Agency
CISL	Confederazione Italiana Sindacati Lavoratori/Italian Confederation of Workers' Trade Unions
CND	Campaign for Nuclear Disarmament
CVB	Comités Vietnam de Base/Vietnam Base Committees
CVN	Comité Vietnam Nationale/National Vietnam Committee
DKP	Danish Communist Party
DNL	Dimokratiki Neolaia Lambraki/Lambrakis Democratic Youth
EAM	Ethniko Apeleftherotiko Metopo/National Liberation Front
EDA	Eniaia Dimokratiki Aristera/United Democratic Left
EKKE	Epanastatiko Kommounistiko Kinima Elladas/Revolutionary Communist Movement of Greece
ELAS	Ellinikos Laikos Apeleftherotikos Stratos/Greek People's Liberation Army
FDJ	Freie Deutsche Jugend/Free German Youth
FGCI	Federazione Giovanile Comunista Italiana/Italian Communist Youth Federation
FHAR	Front Homosexuel de Libération Révolutionnaire/Revolutionary Homosexual Liberation Front
FLN	Front de Libération National/National Liberation Front
FLP	Frente de Liberación Popular/Popular Liberation Front
FRAP	Frente Revolucionario Antifascista y Patriota/Revolutionary Antifascist and Patriotic Front
FTP	Francs-Tireurs et Partisans/Free Shooters and Partisans
FUA	Front Universitaires Anti-fasciste/Anti-fascist University Front
GARI	Groupes d'action révolutionnaire internationalistes/Internationalist Revolutionary Action Groups
GDR	German Democratic Republic
GOP	Gauche Ouvrière et Paysanne/Peasant and Worker Left
GP	Gauche Prolétarienne/Proletarian Left

IMG	International Marxist Group
IRA	Irish Republican Army
IS	International Socialists

JAC	Jeunesse Agricole Chrétienne/Young Christian Farmers
JCR	Jeunesse Communiste Révolutionnaire/Revolutionary Communist Youth
JEC	Jeunesse Étudiante Chrétienne/Young Christian Students
JOC	Jeunesse Ouvrière Chrétienne/Young Christian Workers

KISZ	Kommunista Ifjúsági Szövetség/Communist Youth League
KKE	Kommounistiko Komma Elladas/Communist Party of Greece
KOR	Komitet Obrony Robotników/Committee for Workers' Defence
KPD	Kommunistische Partei Deutschlands/Communist Party of Germany
KPD(AO)	Kommunistische Partei Deutschlands (Aufbauorganisation)/Communist Party of Germany (Organizational Structure)

LSE	London School of Economics

MIL	Movimiento Ibérico de Liberación/Iberian Liberation Movement
MLAC	Mouvement pour la Liberté de l'Avortement et de la Contraception/Movement for Free Abortion and Contraception
MSI	Movimento Sociale Italiano/Italian Social Movement
MTA	Mouvement des Travailleurs Arabes/Arab Workers' Movement

NATO	North Atlantic Treaty Organization
NICRA	Northern Ireland Civil Rights Association
NRP	Nouvelle Résistance Populaire/New Popular Resistance

OAS	Organisation de l'Armée Secrète/Secret Armed Organization
ORT	Organización Revolucionária de Trabajadores/Revolutionary Organization of Workers

PAK	Panellinio Apeleftherotiko Kinima/Panhellenic Liberation Movement
PCE	Partido Comunista de España/Spanish Communist Party
PCF	Parti Communiste Français/French Communist Party
PCI	Partito Comunista Italiano/Italian Communist Party
PD	People's Democracy
POW	prisoner of war
PRL	Polska Rzeczpospolita Ludowa/People's Republic of Poland
PSU	Parti Socialiste Unifié/United Socialist Party
PUWP	Polska Zjednoczona Partia Robotnicza/Polish United Workers Party

QUB	Queen's University Belfast

RAF	Rote Armee Fraktion/Red Army Faction

SDLP	Social Democratic Labour Party
SDS	Sozialistischer Deutscher Studentenbund/Socialist German Student League
SPD	Sozialdemokratische Partei Deutschlands/Social Democratic Party of Germany

List of Abbreviations

SED	Sozialistische Einheitspartei Deutschlands/Socialist Unity Party of Germany
SMOG	Samoe Molodoe Obshestvo Geniev/The Youngest Organization of Geniuses
UDI	Unione Donne Italiane/Union of Italian Women
UEC	Union des Étudiants Communistes/Union of Communist Students
UNEF	Union Nationale des Étudiants de France/French National Union of Students
UJC(ml)	Union des Jeunesses Communistes (marxiste-léniniste)/Union of Marxist-Leninist Communist Youth
VLR	Vive la Révolution/Long Live Revolution
ZMS	Związek Młodzieży Socjalistycznej/Socialist Youth Association

List of Contributors

Apor, Péter Research fellow at the Institute of History, Research Center for the Humanities, Hungarian Academy of Sciences. He conducted research at the London at the School of Slavonic and East European Studies as a Fellow in Hungarian Studies (2007), the Central European University, Budapest (2003 and 2011) and at the University of Exeter (2008–09). His main research interests include the politics of history and memory, the social and cultural history of the socialist dictatorships and the history of historiography. His publications include: *Fabricating Authenticity in Soviet Hungary: The Afterlife of the First Hungarian Soviet Republic in the Age of State Socialism* (2014) and *Past for the Eyes: East European Representations of Communism in Cinema and Museums after 1989* (with Oksana Sarkisova, 2008).

Černá, Marie Researcher at the Institute of Contemporary History, Prague. She has worked extensively on cadre policy and practices in Czechoslovakia under Communist rule and has co-edited a work on vetting and purges: *Prověrky a jejich místo v komunistickém vládnutí. Československo 1948–1989* (2012). Most recently, she has worked on the presence of the Soviet Army in Czechoslovakia between 1968 and 1991 and its impact on society.

Clifford, Rebecca Associate Professor in History, University of Swansea. Her publications include *Commemorating the Holocaust: The Dilemmas of Remembrance in France and Italy* (2013). She is currently working on a Leverhulme Trust-funded project on Child survivors and Holocaust memory.

Davis, John Associate Professor in History, University of Oxford, has published widely on the history of London in the nineteenth and twentieth centuries. He is the author of *A History of Britain, 1885–1939* (1999).

Fürst, Juliane Senior Lecturer in History, University of Bristol. Her publications include (ed.) *Late Stalinist Russia: Society between Reconstruction and Reinvention* (2006) and *Stalin's Last Generation: Soviet Post-war Youth and the Emergence of Mature Socialism* (2010). She is currently working on an AHRC-funded project on 'Dropping out of society: Alternative lifestyles in Eastern Europe, c. 1960–1990' and writing *Flowers through the Concrete: The World of Soviet Hippies* (forthcoming 2018).

Gildea, Robert Professor of Modern History, University of Oxford. Publications include *Children of the Revolution: The French, 1799–1914* (2008), *Marianne in Chains: In Search of the German Occupation* (2002) and *Fighters in the Shadows: A New History of the French Resistance* (2015). He is currently directing a Leverhulme Trust-funded project, 'A Transnational Approach to Resistance in Europe, 1936–1948' and writing *Empires of the Mind: Legacies of French and British Colonialism* (forthcoming 2018).

Jóhannesson, Gudni Research Fellow, Reykjavík Academy. Publications include *Troubled Waters. Cod War, Fishing Disputes, and Britain's Fight for the Freedom of the High Seas, 1948–1964* (2007), *Collapse: Iceland on the Brink of Bankruptcy and Disintegration* (2007) and *The History of Iceland* (2013). He was elected President of Iceland in 2016.

Mark, James Professor of History, University of Exeter. He is the author of *The Unfinished Revolution. Making Sense of the Communist Past in Central-Eastern Europe* (2010) and

Che in Budapest: Global Revolution in the Socialist Bloc (forthcoming). He is currently directing a Leverhulme Trust-funded project '1989 after 1989: Rethinking the Fall of State Socialism in Global Perspective' and an AHRC-funded project 'Socialism Goes Global: Cold War Connections Between the "Second" and "Third" Worlds'.

Osęka, Piotr Associate Professor at the Institute of Political Studies, Polish Academy of Sciences. He has published *Rytuały stalinizmu (Rituals of Stalinism)* (2007), *Marzec '68 (March '68)* (2008), *Whitewashing: The Cases of Propaganda in Poland* (2010) and *We, People of March: Self-portrait of the Generation '68* (2015).

Reynolds, Chris Reader in French and European Studies at Nottingham Trent University. His publications include *Memories of May '68: France's Convenient Consensus* (2011) and *Sous les pavés... The Troubles: France, Northern Ireland and the European Collective Memory of 1968* (2014).

Townson, Nigel Senior Lecturer in History at the Complutense University of Madrid. He is the author of *The Crisis of Democracy in Spain* (2000) and ed. *Is Spain Different? A Comparative Analysis* (2012).

Voglis, Polymeris Associate Professor in History, University of Thessaly. He has published *Becoming a Subject. Political Prisoners during the Greek Civil War* (2002), *Greek Society under the Occupation, 1941–1944* (2010, in Greek) and *The Unfeasible Revolution. The Social Dynamics of the Greek Civil War* (2014).

von der Goltz, Anna Assistant Professor of German History, Georgetown University. She is the author of *Hindenburg: Power, Myth, and the Rise of the Nazis* (2009) and editor of *'Talkin' 'bout my Generation': Conflicts of Generation Building and Europe's '1968'* (2011) and *Inventing the Silent Majority in Western Europe and the United States: Conservatism in the 1960s and 1970s* (forthcoming, 2017).

Warring, Anette Professor of History, Roskilde University. Her books include *Tyskerpiger— under besættelse og retsopgør (German Girls—During Occupation and Postwar Purge)* (1994), *Besættelsestiden som kollektiv erindring (The Years of Occupation as Collective Memory)* (with Claus Bryld, 1998), *Historie, magt og identitet (History, Power and Identity)* (2004), ed. *Fortider tur/retur. Reenactment og historiebrug (Roundtrips to Pasts. Reenactment and Uses of Pasts)* (2015), *1968* (forthcoming, 2018).

Introduction

Robert Gildea and James Mark

The late 1960s and early 1970s marked a moment of political and cultural radicalism during which the authority of governments, institutions and ways of thought were challenged across Europe. From Paris to Prague, and from Athens to Copenhagen, a diverse set of newly assertive activisms arose in universities, factories and public spaces. Conflicts across a continent divided by the Cold War were at once similar and different. In the West, activists criticized the shallowness of their liberal democracies and were far more likely to attack the norms of the nuclear family, traditional gender roles and moral conformism, and to engage with communal living, sexual liberation, feminism and gay rights. In southern European right-wing authoritarian systems, the struggles of communists, worker-priests, Maoists or anarchists were often directed as much at the immediate goal of toppling their regimes as they were at changing their societies. East of the Iron Curtain, activists often sought new spaces for radical and reformist projects under socialist dictatorship: here, many who revolted came from progressive family traditions and held to the belief that a better socialism was still possible; some, however, used the opportunity to express anti-regime and anti-communist positions. That said, activists across Europe often had the sense of being part of a revolt that went beyond their own groups, country or region: many saw themselves as part of a common anti-authoritarian revolt for greater democracy, inspired by anti-imperialist politics globally. Moreover, new forms of cultural protest—such as new artistic and musical happenings—and new spaces in which protest had hitherto generally been absent—in schools, churches and rural life, for instance—were to be found across the continent. Many of these movements have come to be referred to through the shorthand '1968'[1]: in fact, they were disparate in form and erupted with varying chronologies in different countries.

---

[1] On the growth of this shorthand, see Anna von der Goltz, 'Introduction. Generational belonging and the "68ers" in Europe' in idem (ed.) *'Talkin' 'bout my Generation': Conflicts of Generation Building and Europe's '1968'* (Göttingen, 2011), 7–28; Detlev Claussen, 'Chiffre 68', in Dietrich Harth and Jan Assmann (eds) *Revolution und Mythos* (Frankfurt am Main, 1992), 219–28; Beate Fietze, '1968 als Symbol der ersten globalen Generation', *Berliner Journal für Soziologie* 3 (1997), 365–86; Sarah Waters, 'Introduction: 1968 in memory and place', in Ingo Cornils and Sarah Waters (eds) *Memories of 1968. International Perspectives* (Bern, 2010), 8–10; Richard Vinen, 'The poisoned madeleine: The autobiographical turn in historical writing', *Journal of Contemporary History* 46 (2011), 549–50.

This work is based on the stories of a diverse range of these activists whose political and cultural radicalism animated the European politics of this period. Many—although not all—were born around or during the Second World War and had early memories of its privations. They were then brought up in the shadow of the Cold War and what they considered the ossification of conventional politics. Many were shaped by radical left-wing ideology, but were nevertheless alienated by the betrayal of an authentic progressive politics under the eastern European 'People's Democracies' or the remnants of Stalinism in some western European communist parties. Others emerged from progressive Catholic milieux inspired by the reformism of Vatican II but at odds with the conservative hierarchy. Still others came from organized workers', populist or peasant radical traditions, or from nationalist backgrounds. Many were inspired by the wave of anti-colonial and anti-imperialist revolts that swept across Latin America, Africa and Asia from the 1950s onwards, directed against the declining colonial powers of western Europe, and the imperialism of the United States and Soviet Union in the present. These revolts included that of Algerian nationalists against the French, of Egyptians and Cypriots against the British, of Cubans and North Vietnamese against the Americans, and of the Chinese against Soviet imperialism. Some espoused the ideology of the leaders of these revolts—Fidel Castro and Che Guevara, Mao Tse-Tung and Ho Chi Minh—and wanted to bring them home to Europe. Many also looked to renew European struggles, viewing themselves as fighting or refighting the Second World War battles of their parents. In order to overcome the confines of contemporary morality, or the sclerotic and authoritarian elements of educational, medical and political institutions that the postwar settlement had done little to address, some saw themselves resuming a resistance against Nazism and fascism that had remained unfinished, or taking up a struggle that their parents' generation had failed to engage in at the time.

The radicalism of 1960s and 1970s had a formative influence for those who became activists in these years. Yet the public and confrontational aspects of their revolt soon went into decline with, variously, state-directed clampdowns on politically threatening projects in both the east and west of the continent from 1968 onwards; activists' own declining faith in the 'Third World' socialist regimes whose progressive experiments had once inspired them but now seemed to have exhausted themselves or led to their own bloodbaths; the Reagan-Thatcher experiment in economic liberalism; and, eventually, the collapse of state socialist regimes in eastern Europe in 1989. Moreover, from the 1980s onwards, politicians and commentators increasingly attacked what was now labelled the '1968 generation' for their attraction to political violence and cultural hedonism. Activists' own experience of revolt, however, would shape the rest of their lives. Some kept their leftist dreams alive, despite the risk of seeming naïve or dangerous. Others remade their politics and rejected the leftism of their youth for liberalism or neo-conservatism. Many more, however, reinvented their activism, channelling it into the cultural sphere or into their professional lives.

A EUROPEAN 1968?

One of our central questions is whether, over and above the simultaneous or staggered outbreak of protests and movements from one end of Europe to the other, it is possible to talk about a common 'European 1968'.[2] Despite the so-called 'transnational turn' in historical studies, and the popularity of presenting 1968 as a transnational political and cultural moment par excellence, there has been little interest in a sustained comparison of the revolts in different parts of the European continent. Although increasingly globalized accounts incorporate the experience of the Far East or Latin America into the story of 1968, the legacy of dominant historical interpretations that presented western Europe as the core of events, and other stories as peripheral, is still strong. Many historical accounts of 1968 focussed on what has traditionally been seen as the epicentre of revolt in France, West Germany and Italy, with a bridge across the Atlantic.[3] Some works deal only with West Germany and the USA.[4] Other surveys are global, adding Japan, China, Mexico and other places into the mix.[5] Because Europe remained divided until 1989, the true '1968' was seen essentially as a western phenomenon. When events in East Berlin and Prague are dealt with they are often written up as nationally specific accounts, and presented as 'other '68s'.[6]

---

[2] For broad assessments of commonalities, see Charles S. Maier, 'Conclusion: 1968—did it matter?', in Vladimir Tismaneanu (ed.) *Promises of 1968: Crisis, Illusion, and Utopia* (Budapest and New York, 2011), 407–9; Gábor Gyáni, 'Keleti és nyugati hatvannyolc: különbözőség és egység', *Mozgó világ* 8 (2008), 29–34.

[3] These include Ronald Fraser, *1968. A Student Generation in Revolt* (London, 1988), which looks at France, West Germany, Italy, Great Britain and the USA; Arthur Marwick, *The Sixties. Cultural Change in Britain, France, Italy and the United States, c. 1958–c. 1974* (Oxford and New York, 1998); Ingrid Gilcher-Holtey (ed.) *1968. Vom Ereignis zum Gegenstand der Geschichtswissenschaft* (Göttingen, 1998), together with her *Die 68er Bewegung. Deutschland-Westeuropa-USA* (Munich, 2001) and (ed.) *1968. Vom Ereignis zum Mythos* (Frankfurt am Main, 2008); Gerd-Rainer Horn, *The Spirit of '68. Rebellion in Western Europe and North America, 1956–1976* (Oxford, 2008); Hans Righart, 'Moderate versions of the "Global Sixties": A comparison of Great Britain and the Netherlands', *Journal of Contemporary European Studies* 6/13 (1998), 82–96.

[4] Martin Klimke, *The Other Alliance: Student Protests in West Germany and the United States in the Global Sixties* (Princeton, 2010); Belinda Davis, Wilfried Mausbach, Martin Klimke and Carla MacDougall, *Changing the World, Changing Oneself: Political Protest and Collective Identities in West Germany and the US in the 1960s and 1970s* (New York and Oxford, 2010); Jeremy Varon, *Bringing the War Home: The Weather Underground, the Red Army Faction, and Revolutionary Violence in the Sixties and Seventies* (Berkeley, CA and London, 2004).

[5] Here the pioneer was David Caute, *Sixty-Eight. The Year of the Barricades* (London, 1988). He has been joined by Carol Fink, Philipp Gassert and Detlef Junker (eds) *1968. The World Transformed* (Cambridge, 1998) and Martin Klimke and Philipp Gassert (eds) *1968: Memories and Legacies of a Global Revolt* (Washington, DC, 2009).

[6] See Martin Klimke, Jacco Pekelder and Joachim Scharloth (eds) *Between Prague Spring and French May: Opposition and Revolt in Europe, 1960–80* (New York and Oxford, 2011); Gerd-Rainer Horn (eds) *1968 und die Arbeiter: Studien zum 'proletarischen Mai' in Europa* (Hamburg, 2007); Jürgen Danyel, 'Das andere "1968" des Ostens. Prag und Ostberlin', in Martin Sabrow (ed.) *Mythos '1968'* (Leipzig, 2009), 75–94; Jakub Patočka, Jacques Rupnik and Aleksander Smolar, 'L'autre 1968 vu aujourd'hui de Prague et de Varsovie. Table ronde', *Esprit* 5 (2008).

After the fall of the Berlin Wall and the political reunification of Europe, many came to connect the fight for greater democracy in eastern Europe in 1968 with the collapse of communist dictatorship in 1989: this historical turn enabled the development of the perception of a common European struggle for democratization in 1968.[7] Certainly, since the 1990s, it has become possible to ask whether '1968' is a powerful site of memory that has the potential alongside or instead of the Holocaust to define a common European memory after decades of political division during the Cold War.[8] For promoters of European integration, stressing the commonalities in historical experience, despite the political division of Europe for over four decades, has been an important factor in a search for unity in the present. Others have been more sceptical, however, claiming that the eastern revolt was fundamentally different from the violent, hedonistic, overly idealistic rebellion of their western compatriots.[9]

This public debate, which came to a head at the 40th anniversary of 1968 in 2008, has nevertheless only had a limited effect on scholarship. Although the eastern European experience was increasingly included in collected or synthetic works on the 1960s revolt, and there was an increased interest in looking for cultural convergence across the blocs, the Prague Spring or the 'Polish March' were still by and large presented as 'other 1968s' or nationally specific phenomena.[10] The northern European and Iberian countries are often presented as places where the movements of 1968 were bypassed, although this impression is increasingly being challenged.[11] There has been little attempt to integrate the eastern, southern or northern European story into a broader account. More often than not, when they are compared, the different cases are placed side by side by virtue of their simultaneity, rather than examined in terms of actual transfers and cross-fertilizations across borders.[12] One of the aims of our approach is to create a comparative—and in some cases transnational—history of Europe's 1968, which addresses both the degree to which particular forms of revolt were nationally or locally specific, while also uncovering the levels of solidarity and networking across borders.

[7] See e.g. Vladimir Tismaneanu, 'Introduction', in idem (ed.) *Promises of 1968*, 8, 16–18.
[8] Étienne François, Matthias Middell, Emmanuel Terray and Dorothee Wierling (eds) *1968- Ein europäisches Jahr?* (Leipzig, 1997); Jürgen Danyel, *Crossing 68/89* (Berlin, 2008).
[9] György Konrád, 'Hatvannyolcasok. A nagyvárosi aszfalt utópiát virágzott', *Magyar Lettre Internationale* 70 (2008).
[10] Gerd-Rainer Horn and Padraic Kenney, *Transnational Moments of Change. Europe 1945, 1968, 1989* (Lanham, MD and Oxford, 2004); Martin Klimke and Joachim Scharloth (eds) *1968 in Europe. A History of Protest and Activism, 1956–1977* (Basingstoke, 2008).
[11] For a critique of the absence of a Scandinavian 1968, see Tor Egil Førland, 'Introduction to the special issue on 1968', *Scandinavian Journal of History*, 33/4, especially 323. For how to 'Europeanise' the northern 1968, see Thomas Ekman Jørgensen, 'The Scandinavian 1968 in European perspective', *Scandinavian Journal of History* 33/4 (2008), 326–38.
[12] Klimke and Scharloth, *1968 in Europe*; see also Klimke et al. (eds) *Between Prague Spring and French May*. For an outline of the cultural transfers across Europe, and in particular the place of a southern European 1968, see Kostis Kornetis, 'Everything links?' Temporality, territoriality and cultural transfer in the '68 protest movements', *Historein* 9 (2009), 34–45.

A COLLABORATIVE PROJECT

In order to answer these questions, our project was designed as an international collaborative project that was capable of telling a broad and complex story of European activism. This was a challenging enterprise and one for which few precedents exist.[13] The team set itself the task of locating over a hundred activist networks of different kinds scattered across fourteen European countries (see Appendix). Networks here are understood as the fluid groups that served as vehicles for activists both to change the world and to change themselves. It should be noted that they were not clearly bounded, often involved informal links between individuals and shifted rapidly over time. We focussed on an average of seven networks for each country and selected them according to three criteria. The first was that they should illustrate the range and depth of the radical projects and experiments that took place around 1968. This process affected nearly every part of society, from the university and the factory to the Church, neighbourhoods and households. Some of these networks were overtly political and took up the banner of various forms of Marxism, while others had a more cultural thrust and provided new spaces for artistic innovation, new forms of community living, changed gender roles or sexual preferences. Some networks, such as the New Society in Denmark, attempted with more or less success to combine political and cultural experimentation, while in the communist bloc experimental groups such as Orfeo in Budapest, the Holy Cross School of Pure Humour without Wit in Prague and the Yellow Submarine Commune in Leningrad necessarily constituted a political challenge as well as a cultural one.

The second criterion was that, while revisiting some of the better-known networks, such as the French Maoists or the Socialist German Student League (SDS), we should study a large number of networks that had not publicized their activities and received little attention from historians. In Italy, for example, extra-parliamentary movements such as Lotta Continua and Potere Operaio have been well studied, so the Il Manifesto network and in particular one of its cultural circles was selected. Fiat workers, likewise, have received considerable attention, but not the petrochemical workers of the Porto Marghera complex outside Venice. While the Catholic activists of the Isolotto neighbourhood in Florence have an almost iconic status, radical Catholic activism in France, Spain and Hungary is a dimension of 1968 that has been seriously understudied. In Denmark, Italy and France

---

[13] Examples of comparative oral history include Ronald Fraser, *1968. A Student Generation in Revolt* (London, 1988); Mercedes Vilanova, 'Oral history and democracy: Lessons from illiterates', in Donald Ritchie (ed.) *Oxford Handbook of Oral History* (New York and Oxford, 2011), which compares illiterates in Baltimore, Barcelona and Nazi death camps. For a project on wartime forced labour that used interviews from England, France, Germany, Israel, the Czech Republic and Ukraine, see Alexander von Plato, Almut Leh and Christoph Thonfeld (eds) *Hitler's Slaves. Life Stories of Forced Labourers in Nazi-Occupied Europe* (Oxford, 2010). For a comparative analysis of this material, see Christoph Thonfeld, 'Memories of former World War Two forced labourers. An international comparison', *Oral History* 39 (2011), 33–48.

women's groups received a high priority but the emergence of men's groups was also explored.

A third consideration was to 'decentre' 1968 away from the traditional epicentres of Paris, Milan and West Berlin. First, this meant exploring regional and peripheral locations that contributed in very significant ways to the diversity of revolt.[14] For France, for instance, Paris is of course impossible to ignore; however, we also studied activism in Nantes, new forms of protest in the Lip watch factory of Besançon near the Swiss border, and the anti-militarist struggle that was waged on the Larzac plateau of the Massif Central. In West Germany, much has been written on Berlin students so these were complimented by studies of the anti-nuclear protesters of Wyhl near the Swiss border and the Bremen protesters who clustered around the Lila Eula jazz club. Second, this meant a 'decentring' on a European scale, moving away from the traditional 'western core' to study activism in a much wider range of European contexts. These included Great Britain but also Northern Ireland, which has only slowly been incorporated in a transnational account of 1968; the Nordic region in the shape of Denmark and Iceland; the Mediterranean dictatorships—the Greece of the Colonel's Regime (1967–74) and General Franco's Spain; and the socialist bloc countries—Poland, Czechoslovakia, Hungary, the German Democratic Republic and the Soviet Union. In these cases, we often placed greater emphasis on more 'mainstream' forms of revolt—such as the Commandos in Poland, the Communist Youth Reform Movement in Hungary, the Frente de Liberación Popular (FLP, 'Felipe') and Organización Revolucionária de Trabajadores (ORT) in Spain, or the young activists in the Eniaia Dimokratiki Aristera (EDA) in Greece—since their stories have hitherto not been incorporated into broader European accounts of activism.

The collaboration of an international team also made possible a serious examination of both transnational and comparative questions.[15] First, it enabled us not only track cross-border networks and encounters between activists from different parts of Europe, but also to ask whether these interactions had a transformative effect on politics on either side. Here, for instance, we traced the transnational linkages of the Greek emigration across Europe, the extent of activists' interactions across the Iron Curtain[16] or over the Franco-Spanish border, or the different ways in which those living under dictatorship, and those in western democracies, made contact with sites of the anti-imperialist struggle in Algeria, Cuba or Vietnam. Our

[14] On the necessity of addressing the regional '68, see Sofia Serenelli-Messenger, '1968 in an Italian province: Memory and the everyday life of a new left group in Macerata', in Cornils and Waters (eds) *Memories of 1968*, 348–51.

[15] Recent attempts at a transnational approach to 1968 are Paulina Bren, '1968 East and West' in Horn and Kenney, *Transnational Moments of Change*, 119–35; Parts I and III of Klimke and Scharloth (eds) *1968 in Europe*; and Belinda Davis, 'A whole world opening up: Transcultural contact, difference and the politicization of new left activists', in Davis et al. (eds) *Changing the World, Changing Oneself*, 255–73.

[16] On the importance of studying such links, see Michael David-Fox, 'The implications of Transnationalism', *Kritika: Explorations in Russian and Eurasian History* 12/4 (2011), 887. See Chapter 5 for a broader discussion.

focus on the individual and the network also enabled a nuanced approach to the transfer of political and cultural concepts across borders: here we addressed, for example, the ways in which revolutions aboard—whether in the decolonizing world outside Europe or in Paris—were imagined, mediated and put to use, often in very different ways, by various activist groupings across Europe.[17]

Second, this approach allowed us to assess the extent we can talk of a 'European 1968'. On one hand, it enabled us to compare the different ways in which similar issues—such as the nature of revolutionary change, communal living, the relationship between faith and radicalism, or the appropriateness of violence—played out in different national settings and political contexts. On the other, it evidenced the extent to which activists in different parts of the continent imagined that they were part of an international revolution. It explored ways in which they understood—or often misunderstood—each other, and how their developing perceptions of solidarity or difference affected their capacity to work together, or to gain a sense of generational affinity.[18]

Third, this collaboration made it possible to examine ways in which the idea of 1968 as a European event has been constructed in the years since. 1968 as a global revolt has often been linked unproblematically to growth of new transnational social movements, and even to the eventual political unification of the continent with the accession of post-communist countries into the European Union.[19] This project has elicited a more nuanced view, enabling us to examine those whose activism led them into new transnational linkages alongside those whose activism remained separate, national and refused linkages with wider European movements. It also allowed us to trace differences between 'triumphalist' narratives of democratization according to which the promise of 1968 was fulfilled with the reunification of the continent after 1989, and those that regard the eventual shutting down of political alternatives after 1968 as a defeat.

THE ORAL HISTORY APPROACH

The source material of the project was, to a large extent, created by the team itself. Nearly 500 life history interviews were conducted between 2007 and 2011, telling

---

[17] On reception and mediation, see e.g. Eckhardt Fuchs and Benedikt Stuchtey (eds) *Across Cultural Borders: Historiography in Global Perspective* (Lanham, MD, 2002); Astrid Erll and Ann Rigney (eds) *Mediation, Remediation, and the Dynamics of Cultural Memory* (Berlin, 2009). On the importance of transnational 'cultural brokers', see e.g. Simon Schaffer, Lissa Roberts, Kapil Raj and James Delbourgo, *The Brokered World: Go-Betweens and Global Intelligence, 1770–1820* (Sagamore Beach, 2009). On cultural hegemony and its impact on the translation of ideas between cultures, see Joan W. Scott, Cora Kaplan and Debra Keates (eds) *Transitions, Environments, Translations: Feminisms in International Politics* (London, 1997).

[18] On the transformative function of transnational encounters see Michael Werner and Bénédicte Zimmermann, 'Beyond comparison: *Histoire croisée* and the challenge of reflexivity', *Theory and History* 45 (2006), 30–50; on the importance of networks, and of misunderstanding and suspicion alongside meaningful exchange, see e.g. Patricia Clavin, 'Defining transnationalism', *Contemporary European History* 14/4 (2005), 421–4.

[19] See e.g. Jürgen Danyel, *Crossing 68/89*, 6, who states explicitly that we need to 'accomplish a joint history of 1968 . . . if we want to take the well-led formula of a "common European memory" seriously'.

the story of revolt through the voices of those who participated in movements across Europe. This personal testimony allowed us to analyse the ways in which these individuals themselves made sense of how they came to be activists, how they navigated their way through activism and how they reflect on the impacts this activism had had both on themselves and on the world around them.

From this perspective, our project can be conceived of as a form of 'collective biography' of the various groups across Europe whose activism was forged around 1968. It should be noted that we do not claim to tell a fully representative story— an unmanageable task for any project that adopts in-depth interviewing and the careful and considered uncovering of the experience of particular groups. The range of countries, networks and individuals nevertheless makes possible a much more diverse account than has previously been attempted. The collective biography follows a tradition of research that uses multiple life histories in order to tell the story of a collective who travelled through similar institutions, localities or eras.[20] Such an approach began as early as the 1930s, with the rise of prosopography, a methodology that has been applied, for instance, to the profiling of members of institutions with a fixed membership, such as parliamentary or local assemblies, interleaving data on family background, education, career, marriage alliances, fortunes and political connections in order to explain, for example, how particular political cultures evolved.[21] This method was less useful to us, since we were often dealing with rapidly shifting groups that lacked clear boundaries and were addressing activists' subjectivity. Rather, we drew on two other approaches. First, the 'collective life history' of, for example, the sociologist Daniel Bertaux: his work explored the membership of more informal networks or groups, and emphasized the decisions and processes by which individuals become members of networks and the dynamic relationship or transactions between members of the group.[22] Second, we engaged with the work of those—such as Natalie Zemon Davies in her *Women at the Margins*[23]—who tell the story of era by both comparing multiple (and sometimes unconnected) biographies, and examining the way in which identities are complex, often contradictory, and shift over time in changing social and cultural contexts.[24]

[20] For a brief analysis see Paul Sturges, 'Collective biography in the 1980s', *Biography* 6/4 (1983), 316–32.

[21] This approach was pioneered by Ronald Symes in his 1939 study of Roman élites, which analysed the families, offices and political ties of members of the ruling class: *The Roman Revolution* (Oxford, 1939). For later examples, see Timothy Tackett, *Becoming a Revolutionary. The Deputies of the French National Assembly and the Emergence of a Revolutionary Culture, 1789–1790* (Princeton, 1996); Werner Eck (ed.) *Prosopographie und Sozialgeschichte: Studien zur Methodik und Erkenntnismöglichkeit der kaiserzeitlichen Prosopographie* (Cologne, 1993).

[22] Daniel Bertaux, *Biography and Society: The Life History Approach in the Social Sciences* (Beverly Hills, 1981). See e.g. his work on Parisian bakers: *Le Récit de vie* (Paris, 1997, 2005).

[23] Natalie Zemon Davis, *Women at the Margins. Three Seventeenth-century Lives* (Cambridge, MA, 1995). This study develops three case-studies of women—one German, one French, one Dutch— who existed at the edges of seventeenth-century society yet forged powerful and highly individual careers.

[24] This last characteristic is a feature of the so-called 'new biography': Jo Burr Margadant (ed.) *The New Biography. Performing Femininity in Nineteenth-Century France* (Berkeley, Los Angeles, 2000),

This collective biography approach was undertaken through oral history. It should be emphasized that we are not the first to use this method to study '1968'. Indeed, the democratizing anti-authoritarian instincts of this era gave a boost to the development of oral history in the West. In Britain, for example, oral historians often came from a cohort of academics and students who had been involved in radical movements around 1968, motivated by the democratizing claims of a methodology that could provide access to voices 'from below'. At this time Paul Thompson—a former Campaign for Nuclear Disarmament (CND) activist and social historian from the new University of Essex, which had been at the forefront of the student occupations of 1968—was collecting oral testimony the length and breadth of the UK for what became *The Edwardians*.[25] Raphael Samuel—a tutor at the trade-unionist Ruskin College, where the first British feminist conference would be held in 1970—was interviewing stone-quarryers on the outskirts of Oxford, for what became *Miners, Quarrymen and Saltworkers*.[26] In Italy too, a key figure, Alessandro Portelli—who was interviewed for this volume—began his interest in capturing the sound of less-privileged voices, recording folk songs for long-playing records (in December 1969) and then the voices of people from the Roman slums involved in housing occupation and protest (in 1970–1).[27] Later, he wrote that he regarded oral history as the product of the *sensibilità* of 1968 because it sought:

> to open up public space both to speak and to listen to people who have difficulty speaking in public, specifically because they are not considered public figures, and as such their stories do not seem 'extraordinary' or 'unique enough' to be told to others.[28]

Some of the pioneers of oral history methodology who later critiqued this positivist search for 'everyday experiences' also emerged from the revolt around 1968. In Italy, Luisa Passerini, alongside Portelli, came to stress the role of subjectivity and memory in the creation of testimony. These intellectual developments were in many ways the product of the cultural turn in leftist academic thought that followed the perceived defeat of the political 1968.

1–32. Examples of the 'new biography' include Catherine Steedman, *Landscape for a Good Woman* (London, 1986); Stephen Greenblatt, *Will in the World. How Shakespeare became Shakespeare* (London, 2004); Alison Light, *Mrs Woolf and the Servants* (London, 2007); and Sheila Rowbotham, *Edward Carpenter. A Life of Love and Liberty* (London, 2008).

[25] Paul Thompson, *The Edwardians: The Remaking of British Society* (London, 1975).
[26] Raphael Samuel (ed.) *Miners, Quarrymen and Saltworkers* (London, 1977).
[27] Interview with Alessandro Portelli, conducted by RC, Rome, 12 December 2008. Indeed, the growth of oral history in Italy is linked to ethnomusicology, particularly through the Istituto Ernesto de Martino in Milan, which focussed on collecting political folk music and, in a broader sense, of creating a sound archive that would represent everyday, working-class approaches to left-wing politics.
[28] See also Alessandro Portelli, 'Introduction', in Francesca Cerocchi et al. (eds) *Un anno durato decenni. Vite di persone comuni prima, durante e dopo il '68* (Rome, 2006), 5. See also idem, *Death of Luigi Trastulli and other Stories: Form and Meaning in Oral History* (New York, 1991), 41, 295 (n2).

Within twenty years, interviews were being used to write histories of '1968'. Indeed, practitioners soon spotted the fit between a methodology that gave voice to people 'from below' and histories of groups who were challenging convention, institutions and power.[29] For the most part, however, these early works did not foreground their subjects' voices or explore the links between their stories and identities. Hamon and Rotman's *Génération* was based on interviews with the 'mountain crest' of 1968 activists in France, predominantly Maoists, but the actual voices of respondents were not used as the authors 'wrote over' the interviews in their own words.[30] In post-socialist Hungary, Ervin Csizmadia interviewed those who became activists from the late 1960s and then went into dissidence; in his published work, separate volumes divide the activists' own words from the scholarly account.[31] Ronald Fraser's *1968. A Student Generation in Revolt* was based on interviews with 230 people undertaken in 1984–5 by nine historians, including Daniel Bertaux and Luisa Passerini.[32] It was a path-breaking work but it used oral testimony to add local colour to the historians' narrative of dramatic events rather than to explore ways in which respondents talked about how they became activists, about being activists and what sense they made later of their activism. Passerini subsequently came to regret the absence of an examination of the way in which radicals constructed their identities by telling stories about themselves, and made very different use of the oral testimony she had collected in Italy in her *Autobiography of a Generation*, which she described as 'a history of subjectivity'.[33] By this she meant a study of the revolt from the viewpoint of the participants themselves that addresses how they construct themselves as activists, with all the ambivalences and contradictions that involves.

The oral history approach in this volume has benefitted from these and other practitioners of oral history. In the first place, it takes seriously oral history's longer-term democratizing and diversifying claims by recovering the voices of groups whose experiences would have otherwise been lost. This methodology enables us to provide a different perspective from the 'panoramic' accounts of 1968 that lose individuals in crowds of demonstrators, or that highlight the viewpoint of a small number of celebrity activists.[34] Here, the 'mountain crest' has been complemented by much less well-known, unsung activists, some of whom have not left a written record of their activities. Voices of 'other '68s' less well represented in the literature—activists

---

[29] See for example Daniel Cohn-Bendit's interviews with former leaders across Europe in *Nous l'avons tant aimée, la révolution* (Paris, 1986).

[30] Hervé Hamon and Patrick Rotman, *Génération 1. Les Années de rêve. II. Les Années de poudre* (Paris, 1987–8). The notion of 'mountain crest' is at II, 10.

[31] Ervin Csizmadia, *A magyar demokratikus ellenzék (1968–1988)* vols 1–3 (Budapest, 1995).

[32] Ronald Fraser, *1968. A Student Generation in Revolt* (London, 1988).

[33] Luisa Passerini, *Autobiography of a Generation: Italy 1968* (Hanover and London, 1996), 21.

[34] Recent examples of the panoramic view are Jean-François Sirinelli, *Mai 68. L'Événement Janus* (Paris, 2008); Norbert Frei, *1968: Jugendrevolte und globaler Protest* (Munich, 2008); and Wolfgang Kraushaar, *Achtundsechzig: Eine Bilanz* (Berlin, 2008). Recent examples of the celebrity memoir are Daniel Cohn-Bendit, *Forget 68* (Paris, 2008); Alain Geismar, *Mon mai 1968* (Paris, 2008); Peter Schneider, *Rebellion und Wahn—Mein '68. Eine autobiographische Erzählung* (Cologne, 2008); and Rainer Langhans, *Ich bin's—Die ersten 68 Jahre* (Berlin, 2008).

involved in cultural rather than political activism, radical Christian alongside Marxist activists, men's groups alongside women's, workers as well as students, rural as well as urban activists—play a major role here.

Our approach also follows the Passerini-Portelli argument that oral testimonies are not simply repositories of facts, but are constructed stories that, in this instance, can be interpreted as the activists' narrative expression of their radical identity. Subjectivity, memory and story are closely linked here. Portelli underlines that 'autobiographical discourse...is always about the construction and expression of one's subjectivity'.[35] Subjectivity suggests an account of 1968 from the perspective of the activists themselves: how they present and explain themselves as activists, how they create meaning out of their experience, how they historicize themselves. This subjectivity relies on memory, on what Sheila Rowbotham calls in her Foreword 'the unsettling, momentary collision between time present and time past'.[36] To make sense of that memory, however, a story has to be told. As Luisa Passerini makes clear, 'What attracts me is memory's insistence on creating a history of itself'.[37]

Subjectivity was placed in the foreground of our interviewing methodology and analysis. The life history interview, in which respondents provide a broadly chronological account of their lives, provided the backbone of the project. This was based on an interview schedule with a range of topics to be covered. A first set of questions inquired about the interviewee's family, upbringing and education. A second set dealt with the interviewee's engagement with politics, or politicization, perhaps as a result of a conflict with authority or joining a political campaign, and about their involvement with cultural and political activism in the 1960s and 1970s. A third set of questions was designed to elicit stories about their political, professional and personal trajectory after these years and invited them to reflect on their experience of 1968 from a present-day perspective. Much of the interview process was deliberately only 'semi-structured': although we wanted certain areas covered, we also wished to grant respondents as much scope as possible to shape the form of their own life narratives. In this sense, the focus was placed on exploring subjectivity as we sought to uncover of the forms the interviewees gave to the stories they told to make sense of their lives.

This approach was central in framing the questions we asked of our interview material. For instance, we wanted to trace the ways in which a broad range of individual activists subjectively constructed themselves and their paths into activism, moving constantly between the personal and the political.[38] Did they, for example,

---

[35] Alessandro Portelli, 'Philosophy and the facts', in idem, *The Battle of Valle Giulia. Oral History and the Art of Dialogue* (Madison, Wis., 1997), 79–80.

[36] See above, p. v.

[37] Luisa Passerini, *Autobiography of a Generation: Italy 1968* (Hanover and London, 1996), 23. The original Italian has 'storia' for 'history'.

[38] See Bronwyn Davies and Susanne Gannon (eds) *Doing Collective Biography: Investigating the Production of Subjectivity* (New York, 2006); Mary Jo Maynes, Jennifer L. Pierce and Barbara Laslett (eds) *Telling Stories: The Use of Personal Narratives in the Social Sciences and History* (Ithaca, 2008), especially ch. 2.

construct a generational identity against their own parents, or against society at large? Did they understand their radical activism as the result of some personal clash with authority, or did they see themselves as part of continuing historic struggles that went back, for instance, to the Russian Revolution, wartime resistance or the Greek and Spanish civil wars, or as a response to anti-colonial resistance movements in the so-called Third World? What sort of life stories did they create for themselves to make sense of the activist life—often confrontational and difficult—they had chosen? In addition, this interest in subjectivity moulded some of our analysis, especially with regard to issues of performance, fluency and silence. Of particular interest were interviews that threw up examples of topics that were difficult for interviewees to narrate, or about which they were reluctant to talk. For instance, there were those respondents—such as female Muslim activists, or certain public male political figures—who were much less prepared to talk about their private life, or their family origins, and their relationship to activism. For others, however, the political and personal were interwoven, and little distinction between these worlds was drawn. Rather than seeing these differences as impediments to comparative analysis, they were considered indicative of important aspects of activists' subjectivity, a telling introduction to how respondents viewed the public and private in the expression of their politics. In other cases, we noted the difference between those activists who provided a rehearsed and polished performance against those who offered an interview with greater spontaneity in which they 'brought to consciousness' aspects of their lives, sometimes for the first time.[39] These differences could be indicative of both political and personal processes, illustrating which stories had retained relevance for the individual and society, and which had become a liability to utter in the contemporary world, or perhaps had been hidden away as too painful to contemplate.

Interviews also demonstrated aspects of 'intersubjectivity':[40] they were dialogues between respondents and a group of historians with a range of different relationships to their subjects. Some came from the same culture, some from outside; all were younger than their interviewees, most by a generation. Thus the interview was a process through which former activists not only tried to make sense of their lives to themselves, but also sought to make their experiences meaningful to those who were socialized in other cultures and in other generational units. Scholars have written about intersubjectivity mostly in the context of power relations, addressing how the interviewee performs for a scholar who represents 'authority', and the responsibilities of the oral historian in this context.[41] In our comparative project

---

[39] Ronald Grele 'Private memories and public presentation: the art of oral history', in idem (ed.) *Envelopes of Sound* (New York, 1991), 254–60.

[40] On intersubjectivity in the interview, Lynn Abrams, *Oral History Theory* (Abingdon and New York, 2010), ch. 4; Maynes et el. (eds) *Telling Stories,* ch. 4; Michael Frisch, *A Shared Authority: Essays on the Craft and Meaning of Oral and Public History* (Albany, NY, 1990). Intersubjectivity can be conceptualized in broader terms, as the process of narrative construction in response to all the different audiences the interviewee imagines, and within which the interviewer is only one of many imagined recipients.

[41] On the importance of feminist thinking on unequal power relations in interviewing, see Abrams, *Oral History Theory*, 71–4; on the need to make the interview a more collaborative process, see Frisch, *A Shared Authority*.

involving multiple interviewers, a central issue was the different ways in which interviewees related to their questioners, and the impact of this diversity of interaction on testimony. One particular concern for us was the effect of an interviewer's status on the interviewee's preparedness to relate an in-depth story of their own socialization and politicization. In some cases, the issue was the 'outsider position' of the interviewer, which sometimes prompted the interviewee to offer generic accounts in which they envisaged themselves as the representative not of their own personal story, but rather their nation's or generation's, narrated to a figure who stood outside this community. In a few cases, where interviewers were closer in age and politics to the respondent, interviewees wanted the interviewer to be more explicit about their own beliefs, and to engage in debate over the meaning of the past, rather than play the role of 'neutral historian'.[42] Interviewers thus had to develop certain approaches to ensure comparable and in-depth material necessary for a collective project. Some 'outsider' historians found it useful to insert themselves into domestic debates, by relating other, often controversial, voices they had heard, in order to encourage the interviewee to engage in a dialogue with their own group or culture. Such an effect could also be achieved through dual or group interviews, where multiple participants in a particular movement would recreate debates over the meaning of their activism from within their own environment. In the 'insider case' related above, the historian had to think carefully about the ways in which to present their politics that weighed up their responsibility to respect the interviewee against the extent to which such a revelation would shape the type of testimony gathered. In fact, as many practitioners have recognized, the interviewer is never regarded as a neutral presence; rather, therefore, issues of perception and the shaping of testimony need to be embedded in the analysis itself.[43]

Our approach also addresses questions concerning the relationship between individual and collective memory. The accounts of individual activists were not entirely personal but were framed by the memory shared by individuals who experienced events within the same group;[44] they were also formed in relation to public memory elaborated by politicians, journalists and commentators both nationally and internationally.[45] Rather than rejecting the aspects of narratives shaped by

---

[42] On the question of revealing one's politics to an interviewee, see Alessandro Portelli, 'Research as an experiment in equality', in his *The Death of Luigi Trastulli: Form and Meaning in Oral History* (New York, 1991), 31.

[43] This is of course true of nearly all sources that are constructed with an audience in mind; the oral historian has the advantage that they often know much more about that audience.

[44] On collective memory, see Maurice Halbwachs, *On Collective Memory* (Chicago, 1992 [1950]); on oral history and its relationship to collective memory, see Paula Hamilton and Linda Shopes, 'Introduction: Building partnerships between oral history and memory studies', in idem (eds) *Oral History and Public Memories* (Philadelphia, PA, 2008), xii–xvii.

[45] See Susan Crane, 'Writing the individual back into collective memory', *American Historical Review* 102/4 (1997), 1372–85; Anna Green, 'Individual remembering and collective memories: Theoretical presuppositions and contemporary debates', *Oral History* 32/2 (2004), 35–44; Anna Green, 'Can memory be collective?' and Alistair Thomson, 'Memory and remembering in oral history', in Donald Ritchie (ed.) *Oxford Handbook of Oral History* (Oxford, 2011), 77–95 and 96–111; Jeffrey K. Olick and Joyce Robbins, 'Social memory studies: From collective memory to the historical sociology of mnemonic practices', *Annual Review of Sociology* 24 (1998), 105–40.

these later forces for their ahistoricism, they were rather incorporated into the analysis itself as evidence of the way in which individuals create and recreate their identities by continually 'working on' their life histories. Responding to two particularly powerful narratives of 1968—one that celebrates it as a moment of individual and cultural liberation, the other that demonizes it for the excesses of private hedonism, political violence or totalitarian ideologies to which it was said to have given rise—activists' accounts often navigated between these forms of memory, seeking to defend the identity and reputation of the groups in which they participated, and embracing or contesting the narratives dominant in the collectivities to which they have belonged. This feature of testimony may have been amplified due to the fact many of the interviews were conducted around the fortieth anniversary of 1968 in 2008, a moment at which such debates over 1968 regained public prominence. In the final chapter 'Reflections', the manner in which activists reconsider the meaning of their life stories for the present—an act that some interviewees believed vital to maintain the relevance of their politics and ideals—is brought to the fore.[46] In other chapters, we focus on the 'closing down' of activist language, addressing why certain discourses that were prominent 'around 1968' can no longer be uttered unproblematically. In 'Inspirations', for example, we examine the loss of a language of anti-fascism to describe revolt in some countries. In 'Violence', we address the tensions inherent in masculine representations of conflict, exploring how some male activists simultaneously need to show a preparedness to engage in conflict alongside a desire to condemn force in anything but a symbolic form, for a world whose attitudes towards non-state violence have been shaped by the 'War on Terror'.[47]

Life histories were not only valued for their insights into the diversity of ways in which individuals made sense of their pasts: they also offered us evidence of the collectivities in which activists came together to forge new forms of politics. From this perspective, the life history interview allowed us to go beyond much academic writing in the 1980s and 1990s, which defined 1968 in macro-sociological terms as a social agitation that then fed into a succession of 'new social movements'.[48] This approach tended to impose rather rigid boundaries on activism based on recruitment, forms of organization, political goals and tactics, growth and decline, and its relation to formal political systems, and viewed one movement leading to another in a schematic and chronological way. Our approach is more

---

[46] On the importance of storytelling for activism, see Francesca Polletta, *It Was Like a Fever: Storytelling in Protest and Politics* (Chicago, 2006).

[47] See also Rebecca Clifford, 'Emotions and gender in oral history: Narrating Italy's 1968', *Modern Italy* 17/2 (2012), 215–17.

[48] See for example Joachim Raschke, *Soziale Bewegungen. Ein historisch-sytematischer Grundriss* (Frankfurt and New York, 1985); Andrew Jamison, *Social Movements: A Cognitive Approach* (Cambridge, 1991); Ruud Koopmans, *Democracy from Below. New Social movements and the Political System in West Germany* (Boulder, San Francisco and Oxford, 1995); Dieter Rucht, Barbara Blattert and Dieter Rink, *Soziale Bewegungen auf dem Weg zur Institutionalisierung. Zum Strukturwandel 'alternativer' Gruppen in beiden Teilen Deutschlands* (Frankfurt and New York, 1997); and Ron Eyerman and Andrew Jamison, *Music and Social Movements: Mobilizing Traditions in the Twentieth Century* (Cambridge, 1998).

micro-historical, focussing on networks that were often informal and short-lived bundles of activism, based on the peer group, comradeship, locality or emotional and erotic ties. Moreover, starting with the life stories of individuals who made up those networks, we trace trajectories through, between and out of the networks with which they were associated, thus providing a dynamic account that demonstrates the complex evolutionary paths from one form of activism to another. Such an approach also enables us to observe the diversity of the ways in which new forms of collective activism were born: our networks were variously linked by ideology, by institutional setting (e.g. a factory, church, asylum or university), or by locality (e.g. around a neighbourhood, commune or rural spaces). Moreover, this approach allowed us to explore in depth the different environments in which groups formed in various political settings: in western democracies, for instance, networks might express new forms of extra-parliamentary political activity in solidarity committees, and were more frequently constructed across borders; to the east of the Iron Curtain, by contrast, networks more often emerged in semi-tolerated spaces within official communist youth organizations.

THE STRUCTURE OF THE BOOK

The structure of the book is shaped by the format of the life history interview itself. Part 1, 'Becoming an Activist', charts respondents' accounts of their journeys into activism. Part 2, 'Being an Activist', explores their understandings of the nature of their revolt. Part 3, 'Thinking about Activism', follows activists' trajectories, and their attempts to make sense of their activism in the years since.

'Becoming an Activist' examines, in three chapters, how family background, life experiences and political context shaped the engagement of activists. Chapter 1, 'Awakenings', presents the diverse ways in which they make sense of their journeys into activism across Europe. Here, the focus is on how many factors—the legacies of the Second World War, the Cold War context, encounters with poverty or exclusion, confrontations with institutional authority, and moral, political or sexual crises—are bound up together, in varying combinations, in the biographical self-understanding of activists. Speakers have a fundamental task: to make sense of the beginning of their revolt by bringing the individual life and the collective struggle together in a narrative, justifying the decision or commitment to become an activist, and explaining the pathway into revolt in relation to broader life experience.

Chapter 2, 'Families', focusses on the ways in which activists make sense of their family backgrounds and upbringing in their journeys into revolt. For many, the legacies of the war and of Nazism or fascism within their families were paramount: some suggest a generational conflict between activists and their parents, particularly when the latter were seen to have been too close to authoritarian or imperialist regimes. Others suggest a greater continuity with the activism of their parents, who resisted Nazism and fascism in the Second World War, although often felt a disappointment that the postwar generation had given up the struggle for a better world. Others' journeys into activism were shaped by the shame of seeing their parents cave in before Nazi persecution, or suffering defeat in the Spanish or Greek civil wars.

'Inspirations' (Chapter 3) uses oral history to uncover the range of political models that activists drew upon as inspiration for their own struggles. It examines the extent to which the tradition of the anti-fascist struggle of the 1930s and 1940s remained, or regained, importance in the socialization of activists of this generation, and ways in which new exemplars drawn from the revolutions against imperialism and colonialism in Latin America, Africa or Asia supplanted earlier models. Testimony is drawn from southern European dictatorships, the communist bloc and democratic west of Europe to compare ways in which, in very different political contexts, anti-fascism and anti-imperialism were harnessed to motivate and legitimate revolt.

The middle section of the book—'Being an Activist'—explores how they make sense of different forms of activism. Chapter 4, 'Revolutions', examines the varying forms in which activists conceived of revolution, whether in political terms, above all as a Marxist proletarian revolution, or in cultural or lifestyle terms, challenging the nuclear family and conventional morality through sexual liberation, gender equality and artistic innovation. It investigates how the 'May '68' Parisian model of revolution was received and reacted to in very different parts of Europe. It also traces how revolutionary strategies were reinvented after the authorities clamped down on the main wave of unrest in the summer of 1968, with activists variously going underground to pursue political revolution, moving the emphasis to cultural and lifestyle revolution, or looking to the community rather than class as the vehicle of radical social change.

Chapter 5, 'Encounters', examines the extent to which the Cold War divided activists between western and eastern Europe, exploring not only the impact of physical separation and mutual misunderstanding, but also ways in which the experiences of 1968 transcended these barriers. It addresses the encounter in terms of actual linkages and 'imagined solidarities', not only around 1968, but also in the years since. It presents those who rejected the internationalism of these years alongside others—such as western activists whose break with Marxism in the later 1970s led them into the arms of eastern European anti-communist dissidence—for whom '1968' was a starting point for an ever more entangled relationship across the Iron Curtain.

Chapter 6, 'Spaces', explores ways in which different locations were used to construct and communicate revolt and became laboratories of new kinds of politics. It focusses on sites in both western Europe and the communist bloc, and contrasts the opportunities that existed for protesters to challenge the state offensively in 1968, contesting public spaces within universities or on the streets, or forging links between students, intellectuals and workers. It highlights the contrasts between different countries based both on nationally specific historical repertoires of protest, and on the ideological nature of the state concerned. In a second phase after 1968, following state repression, protesters retreated into new spaces that were often far from seats of power and not easily controlled by the authorities: a mental asylum, a sheep-farming plateau or an abandoned chapel. These enabled a new kind of politics that was democratic and subversive, simultaneously local and transnational in its reach.

Chapter 7, 'Drop-outs', examines two experiments in communal living in very different political contexts—London and Leningrad. It explores the creation of intimate spaces on the margins of conventional society in which freedom could be explored in its various forms. It asks whether dropping out was purely cultural, escapist and hedonistic, or the pursuit of a new kind of politics. Within these micro-societies in West and East it explores different and contradictory attitudes to imperialism, capitalism, property, democracy and sexual relations, the tensions these communities faced during their short lives, and their enduring legacy.

Chapter 8, 'Faith', challenges the dominance of secular activism in accounts of '1968' by exploring the ways in which individuals were inspired by or converted to Christian activism in order to fight for a more just and spiritual society. It returns to the idea of encounter with difference, especially with poverty and deprivation, as a shaper of activism. It addresses the impact of the teaching of Vatican II and the dialogue between Christianity and Marxism, as activists attempted to reduce the distance between clergy and laity and to develop much more egalitarian 'base communities' as vehicles for faith and action. Taking Mediterranean and eastern bloc Catholicism and as its foci, it examines the different thinking and practice of radical Christianity in different political contexts.

'Gender and Sexuality' (Chapter 9) investigates the tensions between the desire to change the world and the desire to change oneself, or what has been called the politicization of the personal. It analyses the tension in the accounts of activists between the desire for sexual liberation and the persistence of sexual inequality. It explores the utopia of political and personal liberation and whether activists thought it possible to campaign for both at the same time. It asks whether men and women could work together towards greater sexual equality, for example in communes, or whether this had to be done separately, through feminist movements and men's groups. Lastly it considers under what circumstances female separatism implied lesbianism and sexual liberation involved gay liberation.

Chapter 10, 'Violence', explores the tension between alternative role models available to activists, whether as confrontational heroic revolutionaries or as nonviolent campaigners. It examines both the way in which the rhetoric of violence was used by activists to distinguish themselves from conventional politics, and how the fear of being delegitimized as terrorists in later contexts shaped their *post hoc* justifications. It explores differences in the language of violence from one part of Europe to another and replays internal debates over violence and non-violence between activists in the same country.

While the relationship between past and present in oral history is noted throughout the book, it is brought to the fore in Part III, 'Making Sense of Activism'. A single long chapter examines how interviewees across the continent made sense of their former radicalism as they became parents, took up careers, changed their politics or attempted to reinvigorate their political engagement. It examines how they related their own experiences to wider social memories or narratives that either celebrated the utopian goals of activism or demonized its sexual and brutal excesses. It addresses the multiple ways in which activists celebrated, apologized for, rejected or reworked aspects of their pasts. Indeed, these different approaches could often be found alongside each other in a single life history: former activists could simultaneously view themselves as agents of a process of democratization in Europe, while atoning for a past in which they had sailed too close to violence, had supported Soviet communism or succumbed to the 'totalitarian temptation'. The chapter demonstrates how the powerful but contradictory memories of 1968 resonate even today.

PART I

BECOMING AN ACTIVIST

1

Awakenings

Rebecca Clifford, Robert Gildea and James Mark

May '68 is clear for me: it was at 4.20 pm on 3 May because I had a class at the Sorbonne at 4 o'clock...I left [my father] at his cinema and tried to get into the Sorbonne, but it was surrounded by the CRS [Compagnies Républicaines de Sécurité, the riot police]. I had a very brutal awakening because I had the idea that in a liberal democracy the police are not the Gestapo, and I was very shocked to see the Sorbonne cordoned off...I protested with everyone else and I don't know what happened. The first tear-gas canisters went off, everyone scattered. I did the same and then saw the students returning to the charge and I followed them, even though I was frightened to death and violence isn't my thing. I remember fleeing from the CRS and jumping onto a passing bus, telling people about the scandalous use of violence and having the idea that we must tell the press, that the public had to know.[1]

There are as many stories of journeys into activism as there are activists themselves. The routes of those in the eastern bloc were not the same as those of activists in western Europe, those of individuals who were involved in lifestyle experimentation not the same as those who engaged in political activism, while the stories of activists who went underground in the face of repression differed from the stories of those who 'marched through the institutions' and never fully broke with legality. And yet patterns emerge in all these accounts. Their life stories invariably seek to explain how they became *engagés* or involved in activism, the struggle to change the world and also to change themselves. It is a story of transformation—from private life to political life, and from individual concerns to a collective project. Across Europe, activists told stories that wove together, with varying combinations and emphases: their upbringing; the influence of their families' pasts and presents; their encounters with the limits of contemporary morality, institutional sclerosis or class division; the unresolved legacies of the Second World War; the Cold War environment that—in East and West, North and South—placed stifling boundaries on political expression; and the inspirations of new revolutionary movements in the decolonizing world. Through these complex stories of 'awakening', activists demonstrated how they had come to re-imagine the self in relation to the political and cultural world around them: they sought to bring the individual life and the

---

[1] Interview with Françoise Picq, conducted by RG, Paris, 27 April 2007.

collective struggle together in a cohesive narrative, to justify the decision to become *engagé*, to explain the pathway into activism in relation to broader life experience, and to make comprehensible a step into the political that fundamentally changed their lives. The story of the journey into activism often formed the starting point in interviewees' own life history narratives and hence it starts our book too.

THE SEARCH FOR AN ALTERNATIVE POLITICS

Many of those who would challenge the political and moral order of the 1960s were brought up in left-wing or communist milieux; nevertheless, they were unhappy with the rigidities of Soviet communism alongside their disdain for capitalism and the conventional democratic parties that emerged or re-emerged after 1945. Germano Mariti (b. 1937), for instance, participated in the iconic workers' movement at the Porto Marghera factory complex in Venice, which was one of the first industrial areas to radicalize during the wave of worker protests—the so-called 'hot autumn'—that brought Italian production to a near standstill in 1968–9.[2] Workers at Porto Marghera mobilized in the summer of 1968, demanding that an equal production bonus be paid to all workers regardless of their seniority or level of skill.[3] University students, particularly from Venice's prestigious school of architecture, rallied alongside workers at the factory complex, and groups from the extra-parliamentary left (radical left-wing political organizations that formed in the late 1960s in Italy, characterized by their opposition to the Communist Party and drawing in large numbers of student activists) attempted to help workers organize while themselves joining in the conflict. Mariti was involved in the new factory council that privileged direct, rather than representational, contact between workers and bosses.[4] In joining the Porto Marghera protest movement, he found himself caught up in a network that drew together skilled and unskilled workers, students, intellectuals and sympathetic members of the broader community. The political alternatives that were explored in this environment were novel to Mariti, and exhilarating.

These stood in sharp contrast to the political environment in which he was brought up. Mariti's father and uncles had fought in the Italian resistance during the Second World War, and his family had long been active in the local Italian Communist Party (PCI) headquarters. He begins his story by describing the roots of his rebellion in his rejection of his family's own communist political outlook:

> [My family] began to take me to Communist Party meetings from the time I was a child, but from a very young age I didn't feel comfortable, I didn't feel free...I was a bit

---

[2] On the 'hot autumn', see in particular Bruno Trentin, *Autunno caldo: Il secondo biennio rosso 1968–1969* (Rome, 1999), and Alessandro Pizzorno et al., *Lotte operaie e sindacato: Il ciclo 1968–1972 in Italia* (Bologna, 1978). For overviews in English, see Gerd-Rainer Horn, *The Spirit of '68: Rebellion in Western Europe and North America, 1956–1976* (Oxford, 2008), 111–8; and Robert Lumley, *States of Emergency: Cultures of Revolt in Italy from 1968 to 1978* (London, 1990), 167–269.

[3] On the period of industrial action in Porto Marghera, see in particular Cesco Chinello, *Sindacato, Pci, movimenti negli anni sessanta. Porto Marghera-Venezia 1955–1970*, vol. 2 (Milan, 1996).

[4] On the factory councils, see Lumley, *States of Emergency*, 260–4.

rebellious with regards to these ideological concepts, and I preferred to go out dancing with my friends here and there, rather than going to those *feste dell'Unità* [festivals organized by the PCI, originally intended to increase readership of the party's newspaper, *l'Unità*], as was the fashion for certain Italian youth. You either went to church or you were in the Communist Party—there weren't many alternatives. And between these two choices, well, it didn't work for me, I didn't like it.[5]

Mariti's rebellious streak began to sharpen into an interest in alternative politics when he began working in the electroplating shop of a zinc factory in Porto Marghera at the age of nineteen. When he entered the factory, he was astounded to discover a 'mega-structure' in which individuals were stripped of their identities and dehumanized. The fact that workers were referred to by number, rather than by name, reminded him of a concentration camp. The shock of this early experience of the factory led him towards his first moments of political awakening, as he joined a group of anarchists who were operating in the metalworks:

> When I entered the factory I was given a number, 821. And I started to realize that in this mass of people—well, I realized something that scared me: I'd entered into a mechanism that had destroyed my subjectivity, my personality. Inside I was a number: 821. I wasn't Germano Mariti, I was 821, and this made me gradually think—you make connections, like, I don't know, you think of concentration camps, don't you?...It wasn't possible to be human, to live life in those conditions. You started looking for something new. Unlike some of my colleagues who turned to the Communist Party, I couldn't grow politically within the Party, but I met a little group of anarchists who taught me a lot with respect to power, the power of the state, the power of the bosses, the power of the political parties, that sort of thing.[6]

Mariti's leap into direct activism came in 1968–9. He was inspired first by the student movement, and made contact with students from the architecture school who had begun to distribute leaflets and newspapers at the gates of the Porto Marghera factories. Many of these students were also members of Lotta Continua ('Continuous Struggle'), the largest and most ideologically experimental of the extra-parliamentary left organizations, and one that actively sought to link students' and workers' concerns.[7] The involvement of these students enabled Mariti to feel part of a wider activist world that reached to France and the US, and which transformed his politics from the bread-and-butter concerns of the metalworkers to a much greater desire for freedom and equality. In 1969, his co-worker Gianni Sbrogiò, who was active in the extra-parliamentary organization Potere Operaio ('Workers' Power'), suggested that he go along to observe the workings of the new factory council that workers had established in the Porto Marghera petrochemical

---

[5] Interview with Germano Mariti, conducted by RC, Porto Marghera, 16 March 2009.
[6] Mariti interview.
[7] Anna Bravo, *A colpi di cuore. Storie del sessantotto* (Rome, 2008), 106–7. Bravo observes that, while there were real ideological differences between the groups of the extra-parliamentary left, membership in the three most powerful organizations can be broadly characterized (and perhaps stereotyped) as follows (here she quotes an anonymous former member of Lotta Continua): 'those who were spontaneous [went into] Lotta Continua, the extremists [went into] Potere Operaio, and the intellectuals [went into] Il Manifesto'.

complex. Mariti was motivated to begin building a similar council in his own workplace:[8]

> I met some students who were in Lotta Continua, and I began bringing their newspaper into the factory to spread the word, to help myself and others to learn about these new things. This is why the student movement was fundamental, at least in my opinion, in this early phase. I finally felt that I wasn't alone and isolated. I was part of a wider circle, America, France, Italy: students were on the move and I recognized myself in that environment. When Gianni [Sbrogiò] started working in the factory, we began discussing things, and he said 'look, Germano, there's this factory council that's already up and running at the petrochemical factory complex—why don't you go to their meeting and see what they're saying?'. I accepted happily and I went along, and...I discovered that their objectives were goals that I shared—this idea of equality.[9]

The challenge for Tiennot Grumbach (b. 1939) was to find a form of politics that responded to the escalation of revolution in the Third World and to the difficult legacies of the Second World War. With Alsace Jews on his father's side, and the Portuguese Jewish community in Bordeaux on his mother's, he was one of the Jewish children hidden during the war by the good offices of French rescuers. He does not, however, use this as a possible explanation of his activism; rather he highlights the fact that he is the nephew of Pierre Mendès-France, who played a leading role in the French Resistance against Nazism and as prime minister in the mid-1950s was responsible for France's withdrawal from Vietnam, Tunisia and Morocco:

> My mother was the sister of Pierre Mendès-France, as you probably know...I said that I became politically active at the age of fourteen, partly because my uncle—my mother's brother—was a politician. That matters. He fought for peace and was an important player in the struggle for peace in Vietnam and then looked favourably on the liberation of the North African peoples.[10]

As well as asserting this bloodline of activism, Grumbach was keen to demonstrate that he himself became politically active at a very young age, during protests against his own government's actions in their attempts to subdue Algerian nationalists who wanted independence. The precise event that drove him onto the streets in protest was the French bombing of Sakiet Sidi Youssef in Tunisia, which was being used by the Algerian National Liberation Front (FLN) as a base, killing scores of civilians: 'In my memory it was my first demonstration, when we left the *lycée* and joined a student demonstration in the Latin Quarter.'[11] He argues that his long campaign against the Algerian War and the methods used by the French—the torture of rebels,

---

[8] On the role of Potere Operaio in Porto Marghera, see Egidio Pasetto and Giuseppe Pupillo, 'Il gruppo "Potere operaio" nella lotta di Porto Marghera: Primavera '66–primavera '70', *Classe* 3 (1970), 95–119. Gianni Sbrogiò's older brother Italo was among the founders and leaders of the Porto Marghera branch of Potere Operaio.

[9] Mariti interview.

[10] Interview with Tiennot Grumbach, conducted by RG, Paris, 18 April 2008.

[11] Grumbach interview.

collective reprisals and bombings—was fundamental in his political apprenticeship, and prepared him to become the one of the leaders of France's 1968:

> It sounds horrible, but I have often said that we were lucky to have had a long Algerian War which shaped us politically. We had seven years of rebellion, consciousness-raising, study, research, indignation, demonstrations, learning how to become activists. Then there was the unity, the possibility of joining forces with people who thought in the same way and had the same objective—peace for the Algerian people.[12]

Grumbach went on a long journey of discovery of 'Third World' revolutions: first to Algeria after its independence in 1962 to help build a new socialist society, where he met Che Guevara; then with Che to Castro's Cuba, which was becoming the showcase of Third World revolution; finally to China, which had broken from the tutelage of the USSR and was demonstrating the possibilities of 'revolution within the revolution'. He was one of the young communists who broke from the Union des Étudiants Communistes (UEC) in 1967 and set up the Union des Jeunesses Communistes (marxiste-léniniste) or UJC(ml), which was inspired by Mao Tse-Tung's Cultural Revolution. He recalls the thinking behind the Maoist idea that students and intellectuals must not lecture the masses but work among them and learn from them:

> I have always cherished a quote from Chairman Mao which I still like and retell. It is, 'There are those who cross the field and do not see the roses, there are those who stop their horse to look at the roses, and there are those who get down from their horse to smell the perfume of the roses'. That was our idea, to smell the roses' perfume. For us the roses were the workers, the working class, the people. The essential thing was to live among the people, to work with the people.[13]

Increased alienation from the values of contemporary left-wing politics was also a feature of many activists' histories to the east of the Iron Curtain. For Hungarian György Pór (b. 1944), the rejection of both family and the political traditions of the postwar period were central to his journey into activism. Like many other unofficial or semi-official leftist activists who emerged in Hungary's elite educational establishments in this period, Pór had been brought up in the 'spirit of socialism' within a family that regarded itself as part of an anti-fascist revolutionary workers' tradition. He remembers the impact of this early education:

> I read the history of the Soviet Communist Bolshevik Party at the age of eleven... I was fascinated by the story inspired by the revolutionary struggle of the working class, the workers' movement of the 19th and 20th centuries, so I had those childhood heroes like Marx—who to me was not a German philosopher but almost like a personal friend. I read novels of his life and things like that so that was a kind of emotional education. It all came from my father. And of course all that triggered my fascination for... the anti-fascist movement, and not only the workers' movement, but in more general terms every revolutionary movement became

---

[12] Grumbach interview.
[13] Grumbrach interview.

something very attractive to me that I wanted to learn more about. So, Spartacus's revolt against Rome, or I read a book I still remember about Benjamin Franklin and the American Revolution. So...I wanted to become a revolutionary from about ten or eleven.[14]

He still remained a supporter of the regime after the suppression of the 1956 uprising, even though his father had taken part in the name of 'reformed socialism'. Rather, aged twelve, he broke with his father and accepted the idea that 1956 was a counter-revolution made up of right-wingers who were enemies of true socialism; a position he held until the early 1970s:

> In 1956 when I was only twelve years old but, you know, old enough to remember shooting, the big noises because we lived just three blocks away from the Soviet embassy in Budapest...I was raised in the 'spirit of socialism'...I saw my father changing sides and he joined the revolutionaries, but through the education that he had been giving me they looked more like counter-revolutionaries. So my first understanding of '56 was not an independent intellectual one, I was just an indoctrinated twelve year old who held the official Party line against my father who joined the revolution... I just had that position that anyone that wants to eliminate the socialist system and bring back an older mode of social organization, the capitalist system, that is counter-revolution. That was to turn back the clock of history.[15]

Pór's activism, as for many elsewhere in the eastern bloc, was formed within official activist movements, in his case the Communist Youth (in Hungary, KISZ). Here he quickly became disillusioned with the 1960s socialist state, which, for him, had become overly obsessed with consumerism, materialism and stability, and had abandoned its revolutionary goals. Yet it was his exposure to the struggles of the less-developed world—both through the solidarity movements encouraged by the Communist Youth and the public reporting of global struggles—that gave him access to a breadth of socialist alternatives in a system where domestic political divisions were usually not publicly articulated. Like Grumbach, he was inspired by the revelation of the 'authentic struggle' of the Chinese revolution, with its popular mobilization, its seeming support for workers and its anti-bureaucratism. While Grumbach actually visited communist China, however, Pór only read about it in the communist press:

> I told you about the influence of Karl Marx's thinking and life on my 'childhood fantasies'. And so that influence deepened when I started studying his writings, and experienced the sharp contrast between what he envisioned [and]...the Hungarian reality...Lenin spoke about the dictatorship of the proletariat—the reality in Hungary was in fact a dictatorship of a ruling elite over the proletariat and over the people. So that was the first conscious articulation of my opposition to the system...in '64 *Népszabadság* [the mouthpiece of the party until 1989] published the long letter of the Chinese Communist Party's Central Committee to the Central Committee of the Communist Party of USSR. And that was very influential for me because it ac-

---

[14] Interview with György Pór, conducted by JM, Brussels, 13 March 2009.
[15] Pór interview.

cused the Soviet bloc of betraying communism, and that coincided with my own observations from reading Marx and Lenin.[16]

Pór went on to organize unofficial protests against both US imperialism and insufficient Soviet and Hungarian commitment to the anti-imperial struggle, working within the structures of the Communist Youth movement to found a 'semi-tolerated' Vietnamese Solidarity Committee at Eötvös Loránd University in Budapest. He helped to create a small underground movement called the Hungarian Revolutionary Marxist-Leninist Party that organized study circles and considered how the political system could be changed. Thrown out of university in 1966, he went to work in the Ganz factory in Budapest, before being arrested in spring 1968 and put on trial for organizing a Maoist 'anti-state conspiracy', a charge and label that Pór rejected.

CROSSING THE LINE

In many activists' accounts, moments of awakening were provoked by crossing a line, either geographical, social or based on gender or sexual identity. These moments are often related in terms of an encounter with something 'other', whether a different country, class or social role. They reveal the troubling existence of social inequality, injustice or oppression. These encounters are seen as transformative in that they exposed individuals to different conditions and cultures, which caused them to reflect on and break with previous ideas or modes of behaviour. They also introduced them to like-minded individuals on the other side of those boundaries and to a radical politics that was transnational or interclass, or that subverted gender and sexual norms. Very often these moments provoked a crisis in relations with their own family, whose attitudes and lifestyle they were questioning, if not an outright break with their parents.

The most significant boundary crossing was often an encounter with events and people in other countries. This might be virtual or imagined, such as seeing dramatic pictures on television. Equally important, however, were genuine encounters with different people and first-hand interactions with a foreign culture.[17] Jean-Pierre Duteuil (b. 1944), one of the founders of the subversive 22 March movement at the University of Nanterre in 1968, recalls that his first significant encounter with far-off events was via television pictures of the Soviet invasion of Hungary when he was twelve:

The first political image I have . . . I was very young, the first television pictures were in 1956, I was twelve—was the toppling of Stalin's statue in Budapest, with people

---

[16] Pór interview.

[17] Belinda Davis, 'A whole world opening up: Transnational contact, difference and the politicization of "New Left" activists', in idem (ed.) *Changing the World, Changing Oneself* (New York and Oxford, 2010), 255–73, looks at this question from the point of view of West German activists.

shouting all around. There were some pictures on the television of the beginning of
the uprising...To see people rise up really affected me.[18]

Although at school in a comfortable suburb of Paris, Duteuil found that the Algerian War was being fought in his neighbourhood and school, as anti-fascists confronted so-called 'fascists' who in 1960–2 were resorting to violence in defence of
French Algeria. These included repatriated French settlers from Algeria, the so-
called *pieds noirs*, some of whom were enrolled in the Organisation de l'Armée
Secrète (OAS), which used bombs in pursuit of its ends:[19]

> Afterwards, when I was at the *lycée*, it was the Algerian War. For me that meant more
> than getting involved, because I was quickly in favour of an independent Algeria...In
> my *lycée*...there was an Anti-fascist University Front (FUA), which was based in
> Paris and had some branches in the *lycées*. Sometimes I skived off lessons to take part
> in demonstrations organized by the FUA. Things were very tense because there were
> quite a lot of young *pieds noirs*, who were supporters of a French Algeria...It was also
> a neighbourhood in which there were OAS attacks on the Lycée La Fontaine. There
> were bombs, little bombs, which wounded people. The whole climate drove me to
> become involved (*m'engager*), and in any case to become very political. From that
> time I felt and said that I was an anarchist.[20]

Having been exposed to different political cultures at home, Duteuil then discovered these more radically abroad, initially almost by accident. As a result of being
too involved in politics he failed his *baccalauréat* twice and decided to do a retake
on his own. Needing a foreign language, he went to Italy in 1962 to learn Italian,
fell in with a group of anarchists and became familiar with the struggles of the
labour movement:

> I stayed there for a time. I met some Italian anarchists in Venice. A group of artists,
> potters, painters, and a female singer, who had an anarchist bookshop...I began to
> read the history of the labour movement and the theoretical texts. I turned to social
> anarchism, that is, the history of social struggles, the Commune, anti-militarism. I was
> really in the anti-militarist movement.

From here he became involved with anarchists and CND activists in Britain and
met Spanish republicans exiled after the triumph of Franco at anarchist camps in
Switzerland. In 1964 he went to the new University of Nanterre outside Paris, where
he set up an anarchist group, and in 1965, at an anarchist camp in the Alps, he met
Gabriel Cohn-Bendit, the older brother of Dany Cohn-Bendit. Duteuil is quietly
keen to assert his seniority over Dany, who became the star of the 22 March movement at the University of Nanterre, and of Paris's May 1968 in general, by relating
that Gaby asked him to mentor Dany when the latter became a student:[21]

[18] Interview with Jean-Pierre Duteuil, conducted by RG, Paris, 27 May 2008.
[19] See Todd Shepard, *The Invention of Decolonization. The Algerian War and the Remaking of France*
(Ithaca and London, 2008) and Olivier Dard, *Voyage au coeur de l'OAS* (Paris, 2011).
[20] Duteuil interview.
[21] See J. Sauvageot, A. Geismar, D. Cohn-Bendit and J.-P. Duteuil, *La Révolte étudiante. Les animateurs parlent* (Paris, 1968). Duteuil's accounts, *Nanterre, 1965-66-67-68. Vers le Mouvement du*

My first political action was to invade a France–Scotland rugby match, to protest at nuclear rearmament. Why France–Scotland? Because it was on television, it was being broadcast…Four or five of us ran onto the pitch with banners against nuclear weapons. I started going back to London from time to time, at Easter time when there were the traditional anti-nuclear marches in England, CND. I also went on trips to Switzerland, where you met lots of Spanish exiles, Spanish refugees and deserters from the Algerian War who had fled to Switzerland…There was an anarchist camp in 1965, the summer of '65, in the Alps, organized by the Spanish republicans in exile, which was attended by young French people. I was there with two mates from Nanterre and I met Gaby [Cohn-Bendit], the brother. We linked up politically and then Gaby said, 'My brother is going to France next academic year. Could you look after him a bit, guide him?'[22]

While Duteuil encountered anarchism by travelling to Italy, Alessandro Portelli (b. 1942), born and raised in Italy, first encountered political activism as an exchange student in Los Angeles in 1960. Portelli would later become active in a cultural circle associated with the extra-parliamentary left organization Il Manifesto, founded in 1969 by a group of young intellectuals who were expelled from the Italian Communist Party after demanding that, in the wake of the invasion of Czechoslovakia, the Party rethink its relationship with the Soviet Union.[23] He would also come to use his burgeoning interest in sound recordings and oral history to document working-class protest in Rome. He was brought up in a 'normal middle-class family' by parents who were 'basically middle-of-the-road people politically…apolitical'. His mother, an English teacher, helped him to understand the lyrics to American rock songs and cultivated in him an interest in American culture that has remained with him throughout his life. Like Duteuil, it was television that introduced him to far-flung events, in his case 'the images from Little Rock, those little black girls' protesting as part of the civil rights movement. From the Italian school system, where political issues were avoided in the classroom in a country still struggling to come to grips with the legacy of fascism, he was pitched at the age of eighteen into a Californian high school in the grip of a presidential campaign:

You know, I've always said, being eighteen in 1960 in Los Angeles was being in the right place at the right time. And that's when I really discovered politics, in a number of ways. One is that as I arrived,…we were in the middle of the Kennedy-Nixon campaign, and one thing about the Italian school system was the teaching of history stopped at 1919…so no politics at all…The moment that I stepped into this high school, they were running mock elections and…I was asked 'are you for Kennedy or Nixon?'. And, you know, I think I was for Kennedy because somehow

---

22 mars (La Bussière, 1988) and *Mai 68. Un Mouvement politique* (La Bussière, 2008), are silent on his own autobiography. See also Daniel Cohn-Bendit, *Nous l'avons tant aimée, la révolution* (Paris, 1986) and *Forget 68* (Paris, 2008).

[22] Duteuil interview.

[23] Historians have written little about Il Manifesto, but for a brief overview see Marco Bascetta et al. (eds) *Enciclopedia del '68* (Rome, 2008), 256–7.

I knew that he had some connection with the civil rights movement, but that's where I discovered... it was only at the end of the school year when I was getting ready to leave that I realized that all my friends I made, and girls I went out with, were from the liberal Jewish community.[24]

In the politically charged environment of this American high school, Portelli was forced to reconsider where he placed himself. In 1956 he had been on an anti-communist demonstration against the Soviet invasion of Hungary, in the company of fascists, but confronted by the extreme anti-communism of Cold War America and constant references to America as the champion of the free world, he had to think again about his views on communism as he knew it in Italy. In the high school in Los Angeles:

We were all supposed to read *Time* magazine and do a current events report each week for our history class. So that was the turning point, which was: one day I wrote a current events report criticizing an article in *Time* which said, you know, that, I still remember the words, that the USSR 'exacts a precious pound of propaganda' for each bit of help it gives to the Third World... I was asked to report to the class and... and one of the kids in the class asked, 'but why are there so many communists in Italy?'... And my reply was 'because it's a free country'. And, you know, you could see the wave of shock running through the class, because I'd only been there a couple of months and I was already fed up with this idea that America's the only free country in the world and... I couldn't take the arrogance... So that was, you know, an instant cure for anti-communism.[25]

The boundary crossing for Maren Sell (b. 1945), born into post-war western Germany, was the discovery of France in the wake of May 1968. This made it possible for her to break away from the Nazi past that was not discussed in her family and from the Americanization that German society indulged in to bury that past.[26] Her father, an engineer, had built airports for the Third Reich, but as a child, Sell fantasized that her parents were not as close to the Nazis as she feared:

My parents were not Nazis, they did not belong to the party. My father tried—not with a huge amount of courage—to remain on the outside of all that. As for my mother, I had a fantasy which turned out that... I wasn't the only one to have these fantasies about our German guilt. Because we lived in Breslau, near Auschwitz, I imagined or rather hoped... that my mother had sheltered a German deserter, a soldier. I wrote that in my book but it wasn't true... I imagined that I was the daughter of a resister. We had ideas like that. Or else to trace our Jewish origins, to discover that we were on the right side.[27]

---

[24] Interview with Alessandro Portelli, conducted by RC, Rome, 12 December 2008.

[25] Portelli interview.

[26] For conflicts over German memory, see Jeffrey Herf, *Divided Memory: The Nazi Past in the Two Germanys* (Cambridge, MA, 1997); and Alon Confino and Peter Fritzsche, *The Work of Memory: New Directions in the Study of German Society and Culture* (Urbana, 2002).

[27] Interview with Maren Sell, conducted by RG, Paris, 21 April 2008. The book she refers to is her memoir, *Mourir d'absence* (Paris, 1978).

For Sell, a resistance identity was something that had to be invented. A student at Freiburg, she returned to her home town of Zweibrücken in the Palatinate in 1966, hoping to break out of the straitjacket of family silence and express a liberating anti-Nazism. Interestingly, she names the German chancellor as Henry instead of Kurt Georg Kiesinger, thinking perhaps of Henry Kissinger, as if to elide Nazism with the protection former Nazis allegedly enjoyed under American occupation:

> I remember my first demonstration, I don't know, it was possibly in '66. Our Chancellor at the time, Henry Kiesinger, left Baden-Württemberg to visit the little town of Zweibrücken, where we were living...He was welcomed by the mayor, there were flowers and music, but he was an ex-Nazi. So we went back to the village and stood in the front line and shouted, 'Kiesinger ist ein fascist!'. I found that very liberating. I started out on the path that was liberating for me...The family was like an iron collar, sealed by silence. People, our parents, didn't want to do any thinking. It was the time of the German miracle, people strove after more and more wealth...Instead of undertaking a work of conscience about what they had done wrong they identified immediately with the Americans.[28]

Sell's conversion came when French activist missionaries of May 1968 came to lecture German students in Frankfurt the following September and she made the contact that led her to Paris and to activist circles there:

> Jean-Marcel Bouguereau, who edited the paper *Action*, spoke to us about the different currents of '68. I remember going to see him after the lecture and chatting with German friends. He said, 'Maren, you are studying romance languages. You ought to go to Paris and see'. And he gave me his telephone number and address. That was my first contact in Paris. When I arrived in October I contacted him. Through him, straight away, I met Guy Hocquenghem, Henri Weber, all the leaders of the movements in France...I became a Maoist.[29]

Encountering difference could mean discovering social inequality, injustice and exploitation either at home or abroad. One of the key encounters with working-class life was that of worker-priests in the Catholic Church who rejected the hierarchy's charitable approach to poverty and thought that priests should throw away their clerical garb, labour in factories alongside industrial workers and become directly involved in their sufferings and struggles. Sometimes they initially 'discovered' poverty in the Third World, only to find on their return that it existed in Europe as well. The Church hierarchy attempted to ban this fraternization with workers on the grounds that priests were abandoning their sacerdotal mission and becoming seduced by communist ideas of class struggle.[30] Worker-priests were

---

[28] Sell interview.
[29] Sell interview.
[30] On the worker-priests, see Oscar L. Arnal, *Priests in Working-Class Blue: The History of the Worker-Priests, 1943–1954* (New York, 1990); Emile Poulat, *Les Prêtres-ouvriers: naissance et fin* (Paris, 1999); José Centeno García, Luis Díez Maestro and Julio Pérez Pinillos (eds) *Curas obreros: Cuarenta y cinco años de testimonio 1963–2008* (Barcelona, 2009); Julio Pérez Pinillos, *Los Curas Obreros en España* (Madrid, 2004); and Esteban Tabares, *Los Curas Obreros, su compromiso y su espíritu* (Madrid, 2005).

followed by New Left or Marxist activists, for whom 'the masses' were the vehicle of the proletarian revolution they had read about only in books, since many came from middle-class backgrounds and had rarely encountered the working-class world. The discovery of shanty towns or factory life was often transformative, a key moment in the political apprenticeship of an activist.

Miguel González González (b. 1939) went to work as a parish priest in a rural area of Spain upon leaving the seminary in the mid-1960s. His real first encounter with poverty came in 1968, when he went to Argentina with two fellow priests. They decided to live near the city of Rafaela in what the Argentines call a 'misery town' or a slum. They lived in a shack and were joined by the left-wing bishop. González González recalls that 'We had to make a "black hole" because there were no sewers, so there we were with the bishop digging holes'. He decided to become a worker-priest, and took a succession of manual jobs, in a cheese-making factory, as a bread delivery man and in an adobe [mud brick] factory. He explains that 'our principal motive was to be with the common people, with the most humble, the lowest, that is to say. Not to be a burden on anyone'. Having encountered extreme poverty in Latin America, he returned to Spain in 1973. It was 'perfectly clear' to him that he would continue as a worker-priest. He became a bricklayer but was also employed in a left-wing Catholic bookshop and publishers, which printed titles such as *Socialist Autonomy* and *Socialist Movement*. He lived in a shanty town to the south of Madrid where he became involved in an assembly movement and a neighbourhood association that was active, alongside the Communist Party, in oppositional politics that challenged Franco's regime:

> When we lived in the shacks, we formed a group of Christian people, no? But we were committed to the area, and just there in San Fermín—because the shacks were right next to San Fermín—the neighbourhood association also included the shacks. Later, we created our own neighbourhood association, there in the shacks...With the neighbourhood association we began to hold our own meetings as a, we can say, socialist movement, but a bit 'from below'. I remember that we coincided in the area with the PCE [Spanish Communist Party], which was pretty strong, and there was the Communist Movement—not many—and one or two from the ORT [a Maoist group]. And then there was us, the Christians.[31]

The path trodden by worker-priests was later followed by students and other militants in Europe's radical left movements. In France, Maoist activists were at the forefront of this encounter with the working classes, so much so that they were sometimes referred to as 'red priests'. For some Maoists, the revolutionary impulse might in fact be a transposition of the Christian impulse to know suffering and effect redemption. Anne Victorri, née Lorenceau (b. 1949), became a Maoist, joining the UJC(ml) just before May 1968 and one of its successors, the Gauche Prolétarienne, after 1968.[32] In her account of her activist awakening she battles with

---

[31] Interview with Miguel González González, conducted by NT, Madrid, 6 May 2010.
[32] On French Maoists see Richard Wolin, *The Wind from the East: French Intellectuals, the Cultural Revolution and the Legacy of the 1960s* (Princeton, 2010).

the contradictions of her background. Her father had been in the French resistance and Communist Party, but had also graduated from elite schools into the French establishment. Anne was sent to the Lycée Victor Duruy, attended by the daughters of ministers and high civil servants, and had a Catholic background, but she was very conflicted and steadily through new sets of friends and a change of school she was exposed to more radical ideas:

> I had this thirst to get involved. I was a very shy, reserved girl. I could equally have got involved in something Catholic, for example, it was the same…I have always been completely atheist but I was on a kind of warhorse and if I had been Catholic I would have joined something with the same passion. It lasted for two or three years, and then there was the Vietnam War…At the *lycée* I had a friend who was already pro-Chinese in '66–'67 and she started to make me doubt things. She came from a rather ordinary background and had met this guy…All this time I was in love with a fervent Catholic, who didn't live in Paris and was an activist in the JEC [Young Christian Students]. He supported the Americans in Vietnam. I still have whole letters about this…The debate on Vietnam left me completely confused. Until I went to [the Lycée] Lakanal and met a group of boys who had joined the UJC(ml), this was in '67–'68, and they were in the CVB, the Comités Vietnam de Base, and so I wanted to join the UJC(ml) just at the time it was being dissolved.[33]

At this *lycée* in 1967–8 she tried to resolve the tension between her middle-class background and her desire to go to the people and promote a fairer society by espousing Maoism. She broke away from her family with its high ideals but comfortable lifestyle, and in the wake of 1968 ran away with Bernard Victorri, a Maoist mathematics student at the École Normale Supérieure, to stir up the proletariat in industrial northern France:

> Well, I was selling a newspaper called *La Cause du Peuple*, door to door, in the shanty towns of Massy. It was quite an experience…I had a desire to live like the poor, to know the poor. I felt as though I was confined in a milieu, despite the intellectual commitment of my parents. I was torn between the 7th *arrondissement* and the 14th. I had read all sorts of things when I was young which gave me a social vision, which made me want to know the world in all its wretchedness. I think that was one of the sources of my activism. I was profoundly shocked by the fact that my parents had lots of grand ideas and good sentiments but in their daily life they lived entirely apart from all that.[34]

For working-class labour activists, the 'other' they encountered was the brutal and depersonalizing reality of factory life. They were often torn between the desire to become good workers and the urge to protest against injustice, exploitation and the threat of being laid off. This involved building contacts with other workers through traditional trade unions or with action committees that grouped unionized and non-unionized workers, and developing tactics of resistance over many years. Around 1968, students arrived on the scene, wanting to make common

---

[33] Interview with Anne and Bernard Victorri, conducted by RG, Paris, 28 May 2007.
[34] Victorri interview.

cause. In the case of Germano Mariti, the link between workers and students was perceived as a positive one; in other cases, however, young workers discovered their own radical bent, with little need for (and, indeed, some scepticism towards) student agitation.[35]

Fatima Demougeot (b. 1949) was a young worker who took part in the strike and occupation of the Lip watch factory at Besançon, near the Swiss border, in 1973. Of Algerian origin, Demougeot explains that her awakening as an activist, as someone who took responsibility and was prepared to speak out, was part of a long process that dated back to her coming to France as a refugee from Algeria after independence in 1962—her father had fought alongside the French—and finding herself the oldest child of nine in a refugee camp in south-west France:[36]

> I think it was again because of our immigration, which was very hard, because I was the oldest in a family of nine children. I had an older brother who had been adopted by my parents but I was biologically the eldest child, and like many oldest children, as I learned later, who had younger children, I had to take on responsibilities, I had to think about responsibilities from a very young age, so that when I arrived at Besançon I was someone who was very visible, who already had a plan, even if it wasn't worked out.[37]

She left her family in 1967 at the age of eighteen and went to find work at the opposite end of the country, in Besançon. Finding accommodation in a girls' home, she found herself able to articulate the girls' frustration with the strict living conditions in the climate of 1968, and found herself elected to the home's management committee to change them. At the same time, at Lip, she felt that she had the 'seeds of trade unionism' within her, and joined the non-communist CFDT union, which was dominant among workers who came from a very Catholic part of France. During the 1973 strike and occupation Demougeot was a key member of the Action Committee of younger, dynamic workers, who challenged the trade-union leadership of older, highly skilled male workers to take more radical action, such as restarting the factory under workers' control and paying all workers the same wage:[38]

> When the conflict of 1973 arrived there was already a team of young people which was conscious and organized. You can call it what you want—it was called a strike committee in 1968, I remember—...It started in '73, in April '73 when we decided to occupy the factory...If we young people...were more anti-authoritarian, it's because our political awakening was recent, fresh, because we had just discovered democracy

[35] On the relationship between students and workers in Italy, see Giuseppe Carlo Marino, *Biografia del sessantotto* (Milan, 2005), 356–67; and on France, Xavier Vigna, *L'Insubordination ouvrière dans les années 68. Essai d'histoire politique des usines* (Rennes, 2007).

[36] On the *harkis* (Algerians who fought for France) see Fatima Besnaci-Lancou, *Les Harkis dans la colonisation et ses suites* (Paris, 2008).

[37] Interview with Fatima Demougeot, conducted by RG, Besançon, 21 May 2007.

[38] On Lip see Charles Piaget, *Lip: Charles Piaget et les Lip racontent* (Paris, 1973); Monique Piton, *C'est possible!* (Paris, 1975); Jeannette Colombel, *Les Murs de l'école* (Paris, 1975), 252–305; Claude Neuschwander, *Patron, mais...* (Paris, 1975); Jean Divo, *Lip et les catholiques de Franche-Comté* (Yens-sur-Morges, 2003); and Jean Raguénès, *De mai 68 à Lip: Un Dominicain au coeur des luttes* (Paris, 2008).

and debate, because we had also discovered another way of struggling, of shaking up the unions.[39]

In addition to crossing geographical and social boundaries, some activists had their moment of political awakening when they crossed the line that separated 'acceptable' from transgressive gender roles or sexuality. Giovanna Pala (b. 1933), was a former Miss Europe and an actress who starred in nearly a dozen films in the 1950s before launching herself into the women's movement in Rome in the early 1970s. As a feminist, she was particularly involved in the mass movement to legalize abortion, a campaign that spawned a huge wave of activism in Italy in 1975–6.[40] She explains her trajectory from 'objectified' film star to committed feminist by highlighting the importance of her discovery and acceptance of her lesbianism. The decision to acknowledge her attraction to women ripped her established life apart, and propelled her towards participation in the emerging women's movement.

The account of her journey into activism is nested within the story of her family and of the loss of her mother, who died after an illegal abortion:

> So my family history is a bit delicate, because my mum died from an abortion, she died from an abortion and I didn't know, I was little...I was not yet even two years old. And...my mother had had to marry my father because she got pregnant, she had three children with my father whom she hated, but my grandmother was very Catholic and forced them to get married...So what did [my mother] do? She went to a *mammana* in the village and had an abortion.[41]

By the time she was a teenager, she had lost her entire family: her father went off to fight in the war and 'I didn't see him again for years and years', her grandfather was murdered by the occupying German forces as they withdrew from the region where she lived in October 1944,[42] and the grandmother who raised her died when she was fifteen. Left to her own devices, she was swept up in the postwar cinema industry after winning first a national beauty contest and then the 'Miss Europe' pageant in 1950. She framed her pathway into activism by recounting the sense she had of being used and manipulated during her time as an actress. She contrasted the bizarre, empty world of commercial film production with the atrocities she witnessed during the war:

> This actress period was terrible, my stomach was awful, I had stomach pains because I felt objectified, really objectified because I wasn't really an actress, I was always in swimming costumes, they always put me...when I was on the set everyone around would come to stare...it was something really, it wasn't for me, I hated it, and then, well, I had seen all those things during the war, right? Even though I was small,

[39] Demougeot interview.
[40] On the abortion campaign in Italy, see Robert Lumley, *States of Emergency*, 321–5.
[41] Interview with Giovanna Pala, conducted by RC, Rome, 2 December 2008.
[42] The village where Pala grew up, Vergato, was close to the village of Marzabotto, where the Waffen SS murdered more than 700 civilians (possibly many more; the numbers have never been established) in the autumn of 1944—the worst massacre of civilians committed by the Germans in Italy during the war.

I remember it all: I saw people crushed against the wall after a bombing, I saw a little girl dead in the middle of the street, I saw terrible things. And then I found myself with all these people completely lacking in…well, in this negative environment, right? And as well, women in Rome were really considered stupid then. You were beautiful, but stupid, you didn't count. You were cancelled out, your brain didn't exist, what can I tell you? There was no freedom.[43]

Pala married a film producer, a person she describes as 'a lovely person, very kind, very gentle', and had a daughter, but soon realized the full implications of something she had always suspected about herself: she was attracted to women. After falling in love with another woman and having a brief affair that 'went horribly', Pala left her husband and began to search for alternative models of femininity. The experience of crossing the line between socially acceptable and subversive behaviour for women propelled her towards a passionate interest in women's lives, and onwards towards activism in the emerging women's movement:

I always read everything that had to do with women, but…at the time no one talked about these things. There was the UDI [Unione Donne Italiane, Italy's largest women's organization[44]], but the UDI was all about the family, children, maternity, right? It was a type of feminine expression that didn't work for me, because I thought that we weren't only [about] family, children, and…well, at this point, everything fell apart. I was separated, and when I heard that the Radical Party was holding a conference on women's rights, I went straight down there, and there was a woman there from the Lega Italiana Divorzio [Italian Divorce League, attached to the Radical Party] and she said to me 'over there are those crazy women who are holding meetings without men', they had come to the conference and they were angry with men and they had decided to go it alone. So I said to myself, I have to see these crazy women, because this is really what I'm looking for. I'm one of the crazy women![45]

Pala got in touch with the group of women who had formed what would become the largest feminist network in Rome, the Roman Feminist Movement, and began to attend their meetings. She quickly jumped into an all-consuming activism within the group:

from that moment onwards, my life totally changed. I put everything at their disposition; I lived for feminism. I opened my house to women who had run away from home or who had come to Rome to have an abortion. My house became a sort of public space.[46]

A similar transgressive moment leading to activism was described by gay activist Jean Le Bitoux (1948–2010). Le Bitoux was brought up in a very repressive household, and had a cold and distant relationship with his naval-officer father. He explains that:

---

[43] Pala interview.
[44] Founded in 1944 and associated with the Communist Party, the UDI had an uncomfortable relationship with the feminist movement in the early 1970s. See Yasmine Ergas, 'Tra sesso e genere', *Memoria. Rivista di storia delle donne*, 19–20 (1987), 11–18.
[45] Pala interview.   [46] Pala interview.

My father was educated in a private boarding school by Jesuits…The regime was extremely strict, he did not really have a family life as a boy or adolescent. His life was militarized from the start. I don't think he knew what a tender family life was in which he could watch the kids grow up. When I was fourteen or fifteen he treated me like a sailor on his ship rather than as his son. He spoke to me very little. He was a distant figure and very quickly I disagreed with him…When he was at home I moved to a different room at once.[47]

In 1968, while at the *lycée* of Nice, Le Bitoux confesses that he was afraid of paving stones being thrown. His moment came in April 1971 when he came across the taboo-breaking twelfth edition of *Tout!* magazine, guest-edited by the Revolutionary Homosexual Action Front (FHAR):

I discovered an incredible thing, a convergence of my revolutionary convictions and my secret. That is, the emergence or revolt of something as intimate as your sexual preferences which are not those of others. Incredible. I remember it exactly. I opened—I bought the whole *gauchiste* press as one would say today—and bang!—a double-page spread on homosexuality, 'Stop slinking along the walls'. It was sublime. At the bottom was a little insert which said, 'The FHAR meets every Thursday at 8:30 at the Beaux Arts'. Amazing. I waited two or three months as I was still very fearful. Then I wrote to them saying that I was interested and could I do something in Nice. The contact told me that someone in Nice had written the same thing and gave me his address. We met and agreed to set up the FHAR in Nice. I discovered an activist friendship. Until then I had not had sex, I did not even know how to masturbate. I think that I only just avoided psychiatric hospital or suicide.

ENCOUNTERS WITH AUTHORITY

For some activists, interactions with authority were at the heart of their stories of awakenings. Here, clashes both physical (with police) and intellectual and moral (with figures of authority and with institutions) represented historical processes beyond the encounter itself. These stories were often used by interviewees to explain how the unresolved legacies of Nazism or fascism, the stifling effects on liberty of Cold War politics across the continent, or the conservatism of a Catholic Church as yet unreformed by the Vatican Council, shaped their young lives. For Massimo Taborri (b. 1953), born and raised in a working-class family in Rome, it was his encounter with the remnants of fascism in postwar Italy. His story of his journey into activism begins with a description of the distress he felt when he moved from the working-class world of his elementary school into the elite world of the *liceo*, and encountered fascist sympathizers for the first time. As a result, he became involved very early in clashes between students and the administration at his grammar school:

[47] Interview with Jean Le Bitoux, recorded by RG, Paris, 10 April 2008. See also his memoir, *Citoyen de la Seconde Zone* (Paris, 2003).

I was from that generation of children of working-class families who were able to enter the *liceo* [elite grammar school] for the first time…When I arrived at the school, I experienced a sort of trauma, let's call it that, because even then you could really see that a part of the teaching body had been there during the '30s and '40s, and some of them were more or less openly fascist nostalgists. For example, the headmaster of the institute was very authoritarian, and this authoritarianism really shaped the character of the school…But in '68 there was a sort of caesura, a watershed, it was the year in which the climate around the school changed in a radical way. It was a radical event that led to a rapid change…inside the institution, it led the students to want to participate, and the very first thing they demanded was the right to hold assemblies.[48]

As pupils in his school began to test the limits of the institution's power structure, Taborri was drawn into his first radical political act: along with other students, he occupied the school to demand the right to free assembly. The occupation, which lasted for several days, was a defining moment for Taborri in terms of both his activist and personal development: 'that's where I met my first girlfriend; there was an important element of maturation involved, in a broad sense'.[49]

If the authoritarian elements of the state school system were frustrating and confining in western democracies, they were even more so for those living under eastern European or Mediterranean dictatorships. Milan Knížák (b. 1940), a Czech artist who was the founder of the Aktual art group and director of the Fluxus East collective of artists and musicians, is keen to relate that he has always been sensitive to the abuse of power. He traces this back to his experience in school, where the Communist Party's corruption was in strong evidence, and where he set up his first 'anti-state cell':

We had a schoolmistress who was relatively young, but she seemed old to me, she was such a disgusting giant woman. She cheated because she wanted her class to be the best. This is a typical communist way of doing things, to present oneself as the best using any means…Because I was the best pupil in the class, they put me next to the son of a communist, so that he could copy from me, or so that I would have a good influence on him. At that time, I was interested in aviation, and I had read in a book that the fastest plane was an American one. I told this to this boy, and he repeated it at home. The regional [party] committee became concerned about this. They were concerned about the way that I was being brought up, that I should tell the son of, I don't know, the regional party secretary, that American planes were best when, of course, the best planes were the Soviet ones…The times were so weird. We founded, me and my friends, an anti-state cell; we thought it was necessary. It was funny, of course, we didn't do anything.[50]

Knížák's confrontation with corrupt authority at school as a child was reinforced by more direct confrontations with the state as a young man. He recalls that he

---

[48] Interview with Massimo Taborri, conducted by RC, Rome, 11 December 2008.
[49] Taborri interview.
[50] Interview with Milan Knížák, conducted by MC, Prague, 3 July 2008.

attracted the attention of the police because of his appearance, and in 1966, during the Fluxus exhibition in Prague, he was arrested and his hair was forcibly cut:

> I refused to hide my hair when I went into town. No one has right to restrict me in this. Policemen checked my papers all the time. All the time! Three hundred, four hundred times, maybe more, I don't know. Any time I went out, they checked me... They often took me to the police station, and I spent several hours there; sometimes they released me after a while, sometimes not. Sometimes they cut my hair. It was like that in Prague.[51]

Such anti-authoritarian routes into activism within the socialist bloc might, however, be more ambiguous. In Poland, for example, many of those who would become student leaders, protesting for the democratization of universities and societies in 1968, came from leftist families. They often regarded themselves as inheritors of a struggle for the democratization of the system that had begun in 1956 with mass strikes and rallies, and in which Warsaw students had played their roles alongside the largest factories in the capital. Indeed, many continued to believe in the possibility of a more democratic form of state socialism well into the 1970s. Moreover, they often found their way into activism through official state structures such as the Socialist Youth, which they used for their own ends, setting up ideologically subversive discussion clubs within the system itself.[52] Teresa Bogucka (b. 1947), who uncharacteristically for such an activist came from a non-communist family of progressive Catholic intelligentsia, in which she was brought up to value social altruism and sensitivity to human poverty and suffering, went to the University of Warsaw, where she became a leader of the so-called Commando group. Here, she recalls how she and her fellow activists used the Socialist Youth for their own ends: to improve socialism, to further justice and to compel the authorities to deliver on their promises given years ago in 1956:[53]

> There was a ceaseless pressure on those mechanisms of power, to push them towards reason, to rescue something, not to squander things, to exploit a good opportunity. It amounted to persuading Party members that it was in their interest, in Poland's interest, that if they do it, then ho, ho, it would turn out to be very important [i.e. both to further Polish socialism and their own careers]. One stage was the takeover of the Socialist Youth Association (ZMS). The organization was totally dead, because even those who had belonged to it in secondary school had not renewed their membership as it didn't serve any purpose. So in our circle we had the idea of retaking Socialist Youth organizations. For this reason I joined ZMS, and for the first time in my life and at that first meeting I was elected head of propaganda. The first meeting we held was on 'What is left of '56?'[54]

---

[51] Knížák interview.

[52] There were of course some activists from anti-Communist families involved, but their number was smaller; see Chapter 2, especially pp. 56–7, for some of their voices.

[53] This is quite different from many Hungarian activists of the late 1960s, who related that they did not think about the struggles of 1956 in the late 1960s, and only 'discovered' these linkages in the 1970s.

[54] Interview with Teresa Bogucka, conducted by PO, Warsaw, 21 January 2009.

In Greece, a country caught between the Civil War (1946–9) and the later Colonels' Dictatorship (1967–74), activism was often shaped by confrontation with the police. Despoina Maroulakou (b. 1939) traces her radicalism to the arrest of her parents in the Civil War. Both were involved in the National Liberation Front in Athens during the German Occupation and for that reason they were persecuted as leftists. When they were imprisoned, she lived with her grandmother but searched for her mother by going from police station to police station. The first place she went was the Security Police Headquarters in Athens, where police officers initially denied that they were holding her mother. Other arrestees, however, informed Maroulakou that her mother was indeed there, so she returned and made her first defiant gesture to authority:

> I went to the Security Police, angry this time…I went there and I said to [the guard], 'It is impossible. I've been all over the place, she can't be anywhere else. She is here! Look!'. And he replied 'Wait, kid'. He went to Rakintzis [the director of the Security Police]. Rakintzis said to him, 'Tell the kid to come here'. I went inside. It was an office with photographs of handguns [on the walls]. Obviously to intimidate the people who were interrogated there. I don't know. I looked at them. He said 'What's going on, kid? Your mother is here. And since she is here, she is not in danger'. He couldn't believe that I was doing all this on my own. He thought that someone was with me…I did something then, I made a face at him.[55]

Having very good relations with her parents ('I admired them', 'I looked up to them'), their arrest came as a shock. It bred her enmity towards the state at a very young age and taught her to be assertive. 'I knew that my parents were fighting for something good and they were being punished for that reason, for the good they were fighting for. I knew that very well. That's why I was so brave, so to speak'. After the right-wing colonels took power in 1967, the police came to her parents' home to search, and her husband was arrested, as well as her brother-in-law and many of her friends, although they were released after a short time. Her 'work' was to find places where those who went underground could stay for a few days or weeks. When it became too risky to continue doing this, she opted to move to Paris with her husband in July 1967. Their Parisian flat was an 'open house' for Greek students, as her parents' house had been for leftists before the Civil War. She was active in the movement against the dictatorship, but did not become a member of any political group. She feared that if she identified her personal life with politics, she might lose all her friends as her parents had, or, even worse, be separated from her child, as she had been from her mother. Her motto was 'no groups, only help'.[56]

In both democracies and dictatorships, some speakers first encountered inflexible authority when they were obliged to do military service. Conflicts with military authorities could quickly precipitate moral crises when speakers were asked to do something they found unjust or ethically questionable. Finding the courage to

---

[55] Interview with Despoina Maroulakou, conducted by PV, Athens, 6 December 2008.
[56] Maroulakou interview.

stand up to military authorities or to speak out against injustice was a starting point for many speakers on the road to activism. In France during the Algerian War, students could postpone military service until they had finished their studies, but workers were drafted for eighteen months at the standard age of twenty. Yves Rocton (b. 1938), the leader of the occupation of the Sud-Aviation factory at Nantes in 1968, speaks about his hostility to colonial war and torture in the same language used by student activists:

> I was called up in July 1958 and came back in October 1960. I spent two years there...Algeria did nothing for my character, the more so because I was a difficult guy. I remember having denounced torture in the Djebel, which was quite risky. I went to see my commanding officer and I said, 'I am not here to torture or to see it done. I don't agree with it'. I was summoned to the hierarchical superior to whom I said the same thing, as intelligently as I could, that I was there to make peace, that we were there to make peace and not to...to which I was told that the other side tortured, to which I said, 'I am against them torturing too'...So I was sent to a disciplinary battalion.[57]

Returning to the Sud-Aviation factory with a hostility to military authority, Rocton then had a problem with the powerful communist-run General Confederation of Workers (CGT) trade union. He became a Trotskyist, an ideological stance that he considered most effectively expressed opposition within communism—and clashed with its leadership over the miners' strike of 1963, which he wanted to develop into a fully-fledged general strike. He was expelled from the CGT and subsequently joined the non-communist union Force Ouvrière as an entryist, in order to develop Trotskyist militancy:

> I organized a vote in the factory's CGT union to the effect that we take part in a general strike with the miners. I got a majority...The general secretary said, 'I refuse to forward the motion'. It was the beginning of war. It had already been war a little because coming back from Algeria I wasn't following the line. There were demonstrations, I was settling accounts, memories, I wanted answers. So there was already trouble between the union leadership and me. '63 was the beginning of my expulsion.[58]

On the other side of the Iron Curtain, military service could also bring future activists into conflict with authorities, although the issues that prompted dissent could be very different. Although a fully-fledged Party member, Petr Uhl (b. 1941) was held back from promotion in the army because he questioned the nature of elections in communist Czechoslovakia. In theory, people had the right to vote, and elections were secret; in practice, however, people were expected to vote for the official candidates of the parties and other organizations that had been approved by the state and that were united in the so-called National Front.[59] As there were no alternatives to the official candidates, the only possibility 'choice' was to cross off

[57] Interview with Yves Rocton, conducted by RG, Fenioux (Deux-Sèvres), 14 May 2008.
[58] Rocton interview.
[59] Roman Chytilek and Jakub Šebo (eds) *Volební systémy* (Brno, 2004), 186–9; Zákon o volbách do Národního shromáždění a do národních výborů, č. 34/1964 Sb.

the names of some candidates. This was perceived as an unwelcome expression of dissent. In the army, where the stress on unity and control was much stronger, such a gesture was even more subversive:

> I was not allowed to pass the officers' exam with the explanation that my health was not good enough. The actual reason was that during the election in '64, I did not vote for the candidates of the National Front. I participated, the others were very surprised, in all pre-election meetings and I asked 'candidates'—in quotation marks because for every post there was only one candidate—questions about who they were, and I erased half of them. In order to do that I went behind the screen...everyone from the committee was looking at me—a major and a colleague of mine were sitting there. When I came out from behind the screen I told my colleague: 'Víťa, there is no pencil there!'. He went pale and said: 'Comrade major, there is no pencil there'. He took a pen and I altered the candidates' list. The next day when the results for the various candidates were announced there was one voice against. Everyone was looking at me. So these were the secret elections of the old regime.[60]

Some activists locate their moment of awakening to a struggle with religious hierarchies, and in particular with the Catholic Church. They saw the Church as the guardian of doctrines and of morality that were out of line with the contemporary world. Some broke with the Church at adolescence, rejecting the faith and the institutions it sanctified. Other activists, however, negotiated some sort of compromise with faith, if not with the official Church itself. Gioietta Torricini (b. 1937), born and raised in Florence, came from a Catholic household and was deeply religious as a child. Her very enthusiasm brought her into conflict with Church authorities, as she began to discover that there was little place for intelligent, driven women within the hierarchies of the Church. She eventually joined a group of dissident Catholics in the Isolotto, a working-class suburb of Florence; after trying to open up their church from within the world of official Catholicism, the Isolotto group succeeded in breaking away from the Vatican to form Italy's first non-aligned, radical Catholic base community.[61] In tracing the trajectory of her own journey into activism, Torricini recalls her disillusionment at discovering that women were barred from all but the simplest roles within Church hierarchies:

> I was very pious; I remember that when I was little I used to say that when I grew up I would be a priest, without realizing that within the Catholic Church this wasn't possible, but I would recite the mass and all that...The priest wouldn't let me touch the vessels on the altar because that was the boys' prerogative. And, slowly, this lively faith that I had, that was enough to...I did the drills, I behaved well and I studied and I tried to be worthy of...well, slowly it began to...I began to have my doubts.[62]

As Torricini entered adolescence, her questioning of Church rules sharpened to a challenge. She recalls that her sometimes-provocative questioning was supported by figures such as her religious education teacher, who was the personal confessor

---

[60] Interview with Petr Uhl, conducted by MČ, Prague, 17 May 2008.
[61] See Chapter 8, 'Faith', for a more detailed discussion of the Isolotto case.
[62] Interview with Gioietta Torricini, conducted by RC, Florence, 5 May 2008.

of famed dissident priest Lorenzo Milani (whose book *Letters to a Schoolteacher*, which criticized the state school system in Italy, was one of the pivotal works of Italy's 1968). The fact that she had some support from a mentor she looked up to honed her sense of entering a religious 'crisis':

> When I entered the *liceo classico* I was sixteen years old, and I had the good fortune to have a priest—we had to take religious education classes—but this priest, Monsignor Bensi, was Don Milani's confessor, and so he was quite a bit more open...And we discussed things in class as kids of sixteen or seventeen do, and I remember one day as I was leaving, I was a bit famous for my eccentricity, and as I was leaving I said 'in my opinion, if Jesus had been around today, he would have joined the Communist Party'. Roars from the class, who teased me, but Monsignor Bensi, on the other hand, said 'no, no, Gioietta is right, because effectively the true essence of Christianity is the same as the true essence of Marxism, although the aims have been somewhat unfulfilled on both sides'. And that's where my crisis began.[63]

In the communist bloc, by contrast, the expression of religious belief could itself be a gesture of dissent and provoke conflict with the authorities. In Czechoslovakia, for example, the right to practise religion was enshrined by the constitution, but from the 1950s onwards the communist regime fought to reduce the influence of the Catholic Church, closing religious orders and church schools, nationalizing church property, making civil marriage compulsory, and developing propaganda that suggested that religion was backwards and destined to disappear under communism.[64]

Věra Jirousová (b. 1944), an art historian who graduated from Prague's Philosophy Faculty and was a member of the School of Pure Humour without Wit, an informal community of non-conformist artists who met in Prague's pubs, recalls that she cultivated a secret passion for religion in the face not only of the communist regime, but also of her father, who was until 1968 dedicated to communism:

> My parents wanted me to study electrical engineering, but I already knew why I did not want to...I spent a lot of time in the church pews looking at beautiful pictures and sculptures; they were telling stories I had never heard. At that time I knew only about Jesus Christ's birth in Bethlehem, the adoration of the Three Magi and the Crucifixion. During the '50s, almost all sacred symbols were removed from Prague, and only churches, chapels and sculptures remained in the city. In spite of this, I found stories about the Virgin Mary and later other stories about saints in a second-hand bookshop...My father found out somehow and he stopped me from going, he did not want me to learn about God. I had to find my way on my own...I read religious books in secret, and then I discovered the forbidden book of the Bible. I did not understand everything, but I discerned the internal connections in the succession of images that the stories were based on. I was always interested in reading things I did not understand.[65]

---

[63] Torricini interview.

[64] Karel Kaplan, *Stát a církev v Československu v letech 1948–1953* (Brno, 1993); Jaroslav Cuhra, 'KSČ, stát a římskokatolická církev', *Soudobé dějiny* 2–3 (2001).

[65] Interview with Věra Jirousová, conducted by MČ, Prague, 1 January 2009.

CONCLUSION

What do these stories tell us about the myriad reasons why individuals felt compelled to join collective protest movements? First and perhaps foremost, these stories are windows into the subjective experience of discovering a political consciousness: they tell us how it felt to become involved in collective radicalism, how this moment of awakening is remembered forty years on, and why the journey into activism is often recalled as a pivotal moment in the construction of individual identity. It is clear that, in many cases, these stories are the fruit of a long process of thinking and rethinking, reflecting the importance of the moment of awakening to the speaker's life history as a whole; occasionally, however, the narrative assumes a spontaneous quality: the journey into activism is being plumbed for meaning even as the interviewee speaks. Between the practised and the spontaneous aspects of the narrative, there are layered stories that are made richer by their contradictions: they can reveal at one and the same time an awareness both of belonging and of marginality, a feeling of liberation tied to a moment of personal crisis, or a sense of always having been different coupled with the memory of a dramatic moment of conversion. As the speaker peels back the layers of his or her own narrative, we see that the story of awakenings is couched within other stories concerning family, neighbourhoods, education, class, and gender.

These stories also tell us much about the communal experience of the journey into activism, as we see patterns that are shared by speakers both within geographical areas, and across regional and national divides. The shock of coming face-to-face with social injustice and class divides, the clash between a rhetoric of democracy and equality delivered from on high and the reality of rigid and authoritarian institutions, the trauma of encountering police violence or state repression first hand, the stifling impact of religious conformity or official atheism: these moments of rupture, experienced by so many former activists, frame the collective experience of 1968 in Europe. The patterns that emerge in these individual narratives remind us that, while '1968' had its liberating, celebratory and hedonistic aspects, the path into activism could start from a moment of conflict, crisis or caesura that is often remembered as difficult, even traumatic.

The commonalities in these stories, in turn, tell us much about the memory of the Cold War as it was experienced by young people growing up in postwar Europe. Whether it is overt in the narrative or present only as a subtext, this Cold War context links and shapes all the stories in this book. Across Europe, many activists remember the shock of discovering that, underneath promises of political democracy and economic prosperity, there were deep pools of poverty, inequality and institutional sclerosis. Some present their journeys into radical politics as shaped by the legacies of fascism and Nazism, whether in their schools or their families. Across Europe, many activists were brought up in communist milieux but confronted the Party over its insufficient commitment to revolutionary change or its betrayal of the anti-fascist struggle: in the West, some discovered radicalism outside the Party, in protest movements or New Left groups. In the East, many were socialized into activism through Party structures, but came to reject these and struggled in their search for new forms of political expression within a tightly controlled political system. In the right-wing dictatorships of the Mediterranean, these stories bear the imprint of confrontation with authoritarian power structures, and activists recall that their moment of awakening grew out of a context in which a lack of political freedom was often accompanied by grinding economic hardship. Behind the Iron Curtain, young people were confronted by the propaganda of a triumphant revolutionary regime that accorded little value to alternative thought; in these circumstances, activism often emerged out of the need to create a space for reflection and creativity independent of the Party's dictates. These diverse Cold War contexts shape the stories of activists in different ways. Yet while the details of the journey into activism in North and South, East and West are different, the basic premise underlying these stories is remarkably similar. Young activists across Europe were spurred on by a sense that there was a fundamental hypocrisy present at the heart of postwar European society, and these stories of political awakening are the tales of individual and communal efforts to struggle against this.

2

Families

Piotr Osęka, Polymeris Voglis and Anna von der Goltz

When asked about their views of the societies in which they had grown up, former activists interviewed for this project frequently conveyed the sense that they had embarked on a 'new' project in 1968, and, by doing so, had severed some of the ties to the histories of their families and to the pasts of their countries. Many activists, be they German, French or Polish, had thought that 'we were a new generation that was seizing power',[1] and explained that 'we had this feeling that the main opponent was the generation of our parents',[2] or that 'we no longer wanted to have anything to do with this world [of our parents]'.[3] They often conveyed a sense of the strange conservative morality of the societies in which they had grown up and emphasized their desire to 'break free' from this world.

In doing so, interviewees invoked one of the most popular notions to explain the protests of the late 1960s that had originated in the social sciences at the time—the 'generation gap'.[4] Many scholarly studies written since then have equally turned to the idea of 'generational change' to explain why much of Europe's youth began to protest two decades after the end of the Second World War.[5] Such interpretations typically identified postwar economic growth and the baby boom as the underlying socio-economic factors that determined the behaviour and experiences of a generation of protesters: while their parents had lived through the economic crisis of the 1930s and the Second World War and its consequences—violent death, political repression, food shortages, forced migration and the establishment

---

[1] Interview with André Senik, conducted by RG, Paris, 3 April 2007.

[2] Interview with Marek Zwoliński, conducted by PO, Warsaw, 25 November 2009.

[3] Interview with Klaus Hartung, conducted by AvdG, Berlin, 5 January 2010. Hartung's statement echoes Luisa Passerini's observation that the activists of 1968 'chose to be orphans' in the sense that they sought to create a new subjectivity of their own. Luisa Passerini, *1968: Autobiography of a Generation: Italy 1968* (Middletown, CT, 1996), 22–36.

[4] Margaret Mead, *Culture and Commitment: A Study of the Generation Gap* (New York, 1970).

[5] Much recent scholarship has rightly emphasized that 'generational change' does not provide a clear-cut explanation for the wider social, political and cultural upheavals of the decade: Detlef Siegfried, 'Understanding 1968: Youth rebellion, generational change and postindustrial society', in Axel Schildt and Detlef Siegfried (eds) *Between Marx and Coca-Cola: Youth Cultures in Changing European Societies* (Oxford, 2006), 59–81; on generational discourse and '1968' across Europe, see Anna von der Goltz (ed.) *'Talkin' 'bout my Generation': Conflicts of Generation Building and Europe's '1968'* (Göttingen, 2011).

of communist regimes—the 'first postwar generation' had experienced the benefits of peace instead: relative political stability, economic growth, the expansion of education, and upward social mobility. Because they had felt less need to 'play it safe', they had allegedly been prone to rebel.[6]

This notion may have left strong traces in many of our interviewees' accounts, but interpretations of 1968 that centre on 'generational change' often overemphasize rupture and succession and underplay the complex and powerful ways in which members of the 'first postwar generation' remained bound to the recent histories of their countries.[7] For all their emphases on 'new beginnings' and 'breaking free', listened to more closely, the stories our interviewees related comprised both rupture *and* continuity with reference to the histories of their families.

In social and cultural terms, the 1940s and 1950s, a period during which many of those who would become active around 1968 had grown up, indeed acted as a hinge between the authoritarian and traditional past and the more pluralistic, liberal and leisure-orientated consumer society of the second half of the twentieth century, especially in western Europe.[8] Families played a vital role in creating and sustaining the ties between past and present. As the first socializing institution they mediated between individuals and the wider societies into which they had been born. Crucially, activists from all the countries dealt with in this chapter—and indeed in this project overall—grew up in families that had experienced the Second World War, the greatest outpouring of violence in human history.[9] Those who became active in the late 1960s and early 1970s had been raised in families with vastly divergent—and in many ways nationally specific—experiences of the war.[10] Although they had mostly not experienced the war consciously, it often remained a powerful presence in their lives. Memories of the war and its aftermath, the atmosphere in which they grew up, and the accounts about their families' recent pasts they were told as children had a profound impact on how future activists would view the world around them.

This chapter investigates the stories activists from both German states, Poland, France and Greece, told to make sense of the links between their family backgrounds, their upbringing and their political awakenings. Numerous differences existed between these national cases: German activists, some of whom

[6] Ronald Fraser, *1968: A Student Generation in Revolt* (New York, 1988), 5; Ronald Inglehart, *The Silent Revolution: Changing Values and Political Styles among Western Publics* (Princeton, NJ, 1977).

[7] On the manifold ways in which the war and postwar remained embedded in the consciousness of Europeans who had lived through it, as well as their offspring, see Norman Naimark, 'The persistence of the "postwar": Germany and Poland', in Frank Biess and Robert Moeller (eds) *Histories of the Aftermath: The Legacies of the Second World War in Europe* (New York and Oxford, 2010), 13–29; on private memories of the past in the two Germanies, see Dorothee Wierling, 'Generations as narrative communities: Some private sources of public memory in postwar Germany', in ibid., 102–22.

[8] Dominik Geppert, 'Introduction', in idem (ed.) *The Postwar Challenge: Cultural, Social, and Political Change in Western Europe, 1945–58* (Oxford, 2003), 2.

[9] cf. Richard Bessel and Dirk Schumann, 'Introduction: Violence, normality, and the construction of postwar Europe', in idem. (eds) *Life after Death: Approaches to a Cultural and Social History of Europe during the 1940s and 1950s* (Cambridge, 2003), 1–14.

[10] cf. Frank Biess, 'Introduction', in Biess and Moeller (eds) *Histories of the Aftermath*.

had experienced the destruction of wartime as young children, grew up in the knowledge that the country in which they lived had committed an unprecedented genocide, waged an expansionist war and occupied much of Europe in the not too distant past—even if their parents and grandparents often sought refuge in silence or stories of German wartime suffering and victimhood, especially in the West;[11] French, Polish and Greek activists, by contrast, had to contend with often painful and difficult family experiences of occupation—clashes between resisters and collaborators, German reprisals, food shortages and family members who were prisoners of war. Childhood and family experiences of Europe's postwar regularly surfaced in our interviewees' narratives as well: the persecution of leftists in Greece, of non-communists or other critics of the regimes in Poland and East Germany, of de-Nazification and reconstruction in the Federal Republic, and the legacy of colonialism in France.

In spite of these divergent experiences, activists drew connections between their families and the process of their political awakening in broadly comparable terms: they commonly charted their life stories as journeys. The frequency of such a form of autobiographical narrative was in part a reflection of our own methodology: we asked our interviewees explicitly and early on in the interview to tell us about their family background and upbringing. Our technique thus required respondents to make their lives comprehensible, to tell us a *story* with a beginning and an end. At the same time, the weight these narratives accorded to their family backgrounds and upbringing was in itself a product of the period in which they had come of age. The focus on family life had been a common feature of postwar European societies that had emerged from the horrors of the Second World War and had desperately sought to rebuild 'normal' life.[12]

Tales of childhoods and family backgrounds are thus important milestones in the narratives of activists of 1968; they mark the starting point that set them on a particular path. Activists often relate their journeys into activism as natural progressions, as building on particular family traditions, or they tell a story that centres on struggle—one that involved rejecting specific elements of their upbringing, such as religious or social values, or their parents' politics altogether.

GROWING UP WITH A NAZI PAST IN THE FEDERAL REPUBLIC OF GERMANY

The popular notion that 1968 had arisen out of a 'conflict between the generations' leaves particularly strong traces in the oral testimonies of former West German activists. So widely spread is the notion of the '68ers' as a generation that rejected its parents that even those who had not been students or teenagers at the

---

[11] Robert Moeller, *War Stories: The Search for a Usable Past in the Federal Republic of Germany* (Berkeley, CA, 2001).

[12] Bessel and Schumann, 'Introduction'.

time appropriate it to make sense of their politicization. Wolfgang Schiesches (1931–2010), a radical Protestant pastor from Bremen, who was already in his mid-thirties when he got heavily involved in the 'tram riots' against a planned increase in public transport fares and in the pupils' movement in this north-western German city, described 1968 as a 'world puberty'.[13] He and his younger peers had been conscious:

> that we could not simply copy what our elders had demonstrated. That was definitely wrong, we had to think for ourselves. And this was the basic idea of the 68ers . . . it was a generation that stood in opposition to its parents.[14]

Whereas Schiesches talks about rejecting the older generation in rather broad terms; interviewees whose parents had been Nazis often describe rejecting their specific family background as the driving force of their political involvement. One female activist (b. 1945), who had been part of the anti-nuclear protests in Wyhl and the women's movement in the early 1970s, remembered her family upbringing decidedly in such terms. 'We wanted to be different from our parents', she said. During the war, her father, a doctor, worked in a clinic with close ties to the SS. The female physician, who had aided her mother during her birth, was later convicted during the doctors' trials at Nuremberg:

> I think that it played a very large role for all of my later political activism (*engagement*), that I had a lot to deal with. The first thing I had to deal with was my father's past as a doctor, which was not discussed . . . I think that this was a strong motif for me: wanting to know, to do research [She became an academic], to look . . . beneath the surface of things, to find out what happened.
>
> I later went into therapy and at one point the therapist said to me: 'You don't have to carry your parents' guilt on your shoulders'. I had problems with my hands and the therapist said: 'Your father, as a surgeon or orthopaedist, has a reason to feel pain in his hands, but not you'.[15]

Although this is a deeply personal story of emotional scars left by her strictly authoritarian upbringing and her father's suspected crimes, the interviewee situates her memories into a collective framework of experience and interprets the activism of her whole 'generation', not just her personal story, as a collective struggle for 'restitution':

> [T]his whole generation was of course anxious and angry about what our parents had backed. Angry about the fact that one did not deal with it openly and that they did not tell us about what had happened. And also very eager to restore something. I think that my generation asked quite a lot of itself.

---

[13] On 1968 in Bremen and the 'tram riots' in particular, see Detlef Michelers, *Draufhauen, Draufhauen, Nachsetzen! Die Bremer Schülerbewegung, die Straßenbahndemonstrationen und ihre Folgen 1967/70* (Bremen, 2002); and Olaf Dinné, Jochen Grünwaldt and Peter Kuckuck (eds) *Anno dunnemals: 68 in Bremen* (Bremen, 1998).

[14] Interview with Wolfgang Schiesches, conducted by AvdG, Bremen, 23 February 2010.

[15] Interview with anonymous respondent, conducted by AvdG, Bremen, 13 November 2008.

For K.D. Wolff (b. 1943), a literary publisher and one-time chairman of the West German SDS, his activism had been equally bound up with the relationship to his parents. Both had been members of the Nazi party and Wolff had argued with them, particularly with his father, a local judge in his native Northern Hesse, about politics from an early age. In the late 1950s, at the age of seventeen, Wolff returned from a student exchange to the US, where he had been exposed to the ideas of the burgeoning civil rights movement. 'In many ways I was very confused... I had just started arguing with my father properly'. Within two months, however, his father was run over and killed by a drunk driver. Wolff returns to this incident throughout the interview. In Freiburg, where he became active at university, he started covering the trial of a high-ranking police officer, who had been involved in large-scale atrocities against Polish Jews on the Eastern Front, for the student newspaper. 'Of course this was a way of indirectly dealing with my father', Wolff explains. For a long time afterwards, he was haunted by feelings of guilt for having 'killed' his father with his criticism. 'When this kind of conflict unfolds with the father there are murderous impulses. And suddenly he is dead. That is horrible, you know'.[16] It was only when he underwent psychoanalysis many years later that he dared to read his parents' detailed wartime correspondence and realized that his mother, not his father, had been the more committed Nazi. Nevertheless, for Wolff, the meaning of his activism had remained tied up with his father's politics and premature death.

Opposition to and distance from parents—however direct or vocal—did not just manifest themselves in strictly political terms. Rather than describing conflicts that evolved around tangible political ideas, many West German interviewees highlight the generally repressive atmosphere in which they had grown up and describe their desire to 'break free' from this as much in corporeal as in political terms.

Jörg Streese (b. 1947), now a documentary filmmaker, was politicized at school, and took part in the Bremen 'tram riots' of 1967. His parents separated shortly after he had been born and Streese was raised by his grandparents. From his early teens, he felt that he would 'go to waste' unless he escaped the confines of Adenauer's Germany and, worse still, his grandparents' imperial German values:

> The era of Adenauer was a totally repressed period... People really thought that if we were nice and tidy and clean, world history would accept and welcome us back. And that's what the houses looked like, and dishevelled hair was considered terrible and was fought with all available familial instruments of power... The whole society was restrained and this was experienced on an individual level in one's own family... To the outside world, a neat boy had to leave the front door. And the girls really put on their makeup at the tram stop and took it off again at the tram stop before they came back, otherwise there would have been trouble at home.[17]

---

[16] Interview with K.D. Wolff, conducted by AvdG, Berlin, 28 May 2008.

[17] Interview with Jörg Streese, conducted by AvdG, Bremen, 27 February 2010. While Streese invokes an image of the 1950s as a period of 'restoration', much recent scholarship has painted a more complex picture of this decade. See Axel Schildt and Arnold Sywottek (eds) *Modernisierung im Wiederaufbau: Die westdeutsche Gesellschaft der 50er Jahre* (Bonn, 1993).

The urge to leave the stifling atmosphere of their homes behind and to break free from their families no doubt motivated countless West German activists. Yet, as contemporary sociological studies showed, many of them, particularly leading members of the SDS and other organizations that made up the core of the extra-parliamentary opposition, did not come from families with a right-wing or particularly conservative outlook.[18] However firmly the notion of generational conflict may be established in popular memory, many activists—in Germany and elsewhere—did not experience such a political conflict within their own families. Instead they rebelled against the older generation at large—against their 'abstract parents' rather than their actual ones, as one interviewee phrased it.[19] Consequently, one can detect manifold narratives of intergenerational relations in interviews.[20] Indeed, many activists came down on the same side politically as their parents and jointly attended demonstrations with older family members.[21] Even in West Germany, in a society that had helped to sustain the Nazi regime through active participation and consent until 1945, the natural view of the world of many activists who joined groups of the revolutionary left around 1968 was an extension of the world in which they had grown up.

Katja Barloschky (b. 1954), for one, who took part in the Bremen protests of high school pupils as a teenager, had been raised to 'think politically' by her radical democrat parents. Both were teachers who sought to offer their three children a classically educated middle-class upbringing, but also encouraged them to be non-conformist in order to overcome Germany's authoritarian traditions. Today Barloschky thinks that this was an inherent contradiction. She explains vividly that her parents had been convinced that:

> Naturally our daughter, if not our sons, has to learn to play an instrument! And naturally we virtually devour literature at home! But naturally we are also radically different! As teachers, we wear denim suits and go to school barefooted! … Naturally we don't spend money on a television… on cars and such things. A person does not need much, one lives ascetically, and we only put butter on our bread on Sundays, but the red wine always flows freely.[22]

Barloschky and her two brothers had witnessed lively debates from an early age, and she attended her first ever demonstration (against the military coup in Greece) in Bremen with her mother in 1967. The whole family also joined one of the largest demonstrations against the controversial emergency legislation in Bonn on

[18] As contemporary sociological studies showed, a large number of leading student activists came from left-wing parental homes. Klaus Allerbeck, *Soziologie radikaler Studentenbewegungen* (Munich, 1973), 121.
[19] Fogt, *Politische Generationen*, 144 and 147; interview with Tissy Bruns, conducted by AvdG, Berlin, 18 December 2009.
[20] cf. Belinda Davis, 'New leftists and West Germany: Fascism, violence, and the public sphere, 1967–1974', in P. Gassert and A.E. Steinweis (eds) *Coping with the Nazi Past: West German Debates on Nazism and Generational Conflict 1955–1975* (New York and Oxford, 2006), 210–37.
[21] Interview with Carola Bury, conducted by AvdG, Bremen, 22 June 2010; interview with Christian Semler, conducted by AvdG, Berlin, 29 August 2008.
[22] Interview with Katja Barloschky, conducted by AvdG, Bremen, 21 June 2010.

11 May 1968. Even though she fell on the same side politically as her parents, the
Nazi past still left a strong imprint on her childhood, illustrating the complex ways
in which family background and wider societal conditions interacted in this period.
As committed leftists, her parents had imbued her with anti-fascist convictions
from her infancy, but had always made her feel that she might have been susceptible to Nazi ideology had she been born earlier:

> This question ...: what would I have done? What would have happened to me? This
> question—I was confronted with it already when I was eight, when I was nine, when
> I was ten. I was being compared to my aunt [who had sympathized with Nazism]:
> blond, blue-eyed, and [they would say] 'You, with your pigtails, and unstable as you
> are and emotional!'... So the lesson I cut my teeth on was that I would have been in
> danger, in grave danger and probably would have been a fervent BDM [Bund deut-
> scher Mädel, League of German Girls] girl... and would have become a perpetrator.

Proving her anti-fascist credentials, both generally, and to her parents in particular,
became an impetus of Barloschky's political work. She felt heavily drawn to the
'other Germany' of the Weimar Republic and the communist resistance.[23] She saw
her very 'first communist' at the 1967 demonstration against the Greek coup. Her
mother pointed out an older woman, Maria Kröger, who was a member of the
illegal Communist Party (KPD) and had been part of the communist resistance
movement during the Nazi years. It was then that Barloschky, who would join the
Communist Party once it was re-founded as the DKP in 1968, realized that:

> These were the anti-fascists! These were the ones who were upright! These were the
> ones who did not give up and these were the ones who ended up in concentration
> camps. These were the heroes of the resistance against fascism! And I was deeply im-
> pressed that they still existed! They were not merely these historical figures, but: she
> [Maria Kröger] is just walking around here!

DISAPPOINTED IDEALISM AND NARRATIVES OF ANTI-FASCISM IN POLAND AND EAST GERMANY

While Katja Barloschky had to seek out underground members of the communist resistance to find role models in a Cold War West Germany ripe with anti-
communism, across the Iron Curtain, in Poland and East Germany, activists had
grown up with officially sanctioned narratives of anti-fascism that presented the
young with a heroic activist model to emulate. Polish interviewees from socialist
families, in particular, stated explicitly that they had sought to remain faithful to

---

[23] See also the interview with Tissy Bruns (b. 1951) who says that for her the DKP had a particularly strong allure in the early 1970s, because there were many 'renowned resistance fighters' and
'concentration camp survivors' in its ranks. On this point see further, Claus-Dieter Krohn, 'Die westdeutsche Studentenbewegung und das "andere Deutschland"', in Axel Schildt, Detlef Siegfried and
Karl-Christian Lammers (eds) *Dynamische Zeiten, Die 60er Jahre in den beiden deutschen Gesellschaften*
(Hamburg, 2000), 695–718.

the ideals of their parents and to fulfil their dreams. They explained that in 1968 the young were finally given the chance to prove themselves worthy of their parents' wartime activism against the Nazi occupiers. In an article published in the Polish underground press in 1981, Jan Walc (b. 1948) argued that political demonstrations of 'March 1968' finally offered young Poles the chance to write themselves into the heroic narrative of the national struggle:

> For the authorities back then March was a demonstration of contempt for values, but for my generation it was a moment of exceptionally strong commitment to values. It was a moment when we felt that we were going down in the history of our country. Indeed, our time had come and we didn't have to be jealous of our parents' generation any longer, in that they, during the war, had had a chance to prove themselves, a chance we'd been denied.[24]

This was particularly the case for the 'Commandos', an informal group set up at the University of Warsaw in the mid-1960s that got its name from its members' frequent disrupting of meetings held by the official socialist youth organization. Its members had often been raised by parents who had been communist activists since the interwar period and were now critical of contemporary state socialism.

In 1962 Adam Michnik (b. 1946), then a pupil at secondary school, set up a discussion circle called the 'Club of Contradiction Seekers'. Many of its members came from communist families and some of the members' parents belonged to the party elites. Michnik described this circle thus:

> We started out with a dozen or so people. Thereafter we were like a magnet attracting iron filings, or like fly-paper. A wide variety of young people were drawn to us, people who were interested in politics, history, ideology... The language of our debates was critical of our reality, but it drew upon socialist ideology, even communist ideology, as well as upon the symbolism and value system of the revolutionary left. Our group attracted a unique type of person, one who had grown up in a communist environment.[25]

The 'Contradiction Seekers' soon discovered that although their own acquaintance was quite recent, their parents had known each other for decades. Thus the younger ones discovered that they had unintentionally imitated their predecessors, and a feeling of intergenerational affinity emerged on both sides. Marta Petrusewicz (b. 1946), the daughter of a former deputy minister and a well-known scientist, recalls:

> We became——me and my colleagues [from the Club of Contradiction Seekers] ——...one team, one group. They started to visit my place. And my father was profoundly moved when he saw them, because many were the kids of his prewar friends and comrades... Generally speaking, my father was glad to see us in the opposition. He pretended to be against it, saying we are loony yet actually he was quite pleased because under his eyes the youth was growing up in a similar fashion to the way he had. And

---

[24] Jan Walc, *Marzec 68. Referaty z sesji na Uniwersytecie Warszawskim w 1981 roku* (Warsaw, 2008), 75.

[25] A. Michnik, J. Tischner and J. Żakowski, *Między Panem a Plebanem* (Kraków, 1995), 81.

the approach of my friends' parents was not much different. They were impressed with our activity and bravery—despite the fact that they often belonged to the very establishment we were struggling against.[26]

Polish activists—many from socialist homes—often did not distance themselves from the choices of their parents, even if they acknowledged that the system these had established was far from perfect. Many of them more or less literally declared that in 1968 their aim was to 'continue the mission'—to help build the just world the preceding generation had failed to create. Stefan Bekier (b. 1946), a participant in the protests at the main school of planning and statistics in Warsaw, who would become a member of the Trotskyist movement in France, explains:

> My mother survived my father, and after many years, as she passed away at 93...But, sadly, she told me that she'd wasted her life in the defence of a mistaken cause...There were some very serious conversations at the end of her life...[S]he once said 'my generation was the manure of history'...It was really sad...So by getting involved in '68...together with my friends I was trying to give her some hope, to show her that it wasn't all for naught. To show that, true, they hadn't built what they wanted to, the system they had once dreamt of—but their efforts had not been for naught, and that the next generations had learnt what not to do.[27]

Bekier was not the only one who felt closely attached to his family history and elaborated it to make his own life path meaningful. One of his peers, Adam Ringer (b. 1949), a businessman who had also been a member of the Trotskyist movement, studied the history of his family very carefully and interprets his activism as something akin to an intergenerational project. He discovered that the biographies of his forebears had been shaped by a combination of their Jewish background, leftist views and desire to assimilate into Polish culture. Ringer defended his father's life choices, stressing that his joining the communist movement had not been a betrayal of Poland (as the myth of 'Jewish communists' alleged), but an attempt to reinforce his Polish identity:

> My father spent a long time in prison before the war. And he went over to this movement of the Jewish left with Haszomer Hacair [a scouting organization of Polish Jews] and from there it was a natural road. And it's clear that for my father that road to the Communist Party was a road to things Polish. This is very important in the sense that it was a Polish party...Today it's hard to understand how it all developed. I gathered interviews with people from that generation. I conducted interviews with them, people from the generation of my parents, and I read a lot on the topic.[28]

---

[26] Joanna Wiszniewicz, *Życie przecięte. Opowieści pokolenia Marca* (Wołowiec, 2008), 313–14.

[27] Interview with Stefan Bekier, conducted by PO, Warsaw, 23 June 2009.

[28] Interview with Adam Ringer, conducted by PO, Warsaw, 25 July 2009. Although Ringer did not address this issue directly, one should note that Jewish identity was awakened in Poland in 1968—triggered through pressure from the state. In response to the student strikes of March 1968, the authorities unleashed an unprecedented anti-Semitic campaign (barely and clumsily disguised under the banner of 'anti-Zionism'), which was accompanied by a nationwide purge and followed by a wave of forced emigration. The official socialist media were especially prone to highlighting the invented or real Jewish origins of those who led the protests.

Anna Dodziuk (b. 1947), a student at Warsaw University in 1968 with close ties to the core of the Commandos, was even more explicit about being on an intergenerational mission when she admitted half-jokingly that throughout her adult life she had unconsciously imitated her father. Asked whether her father had ever been imprisoned, she answers:

> Yes, yes. He did ten years [in Poland before 1939]. He did ten years and actually, if you ask about my political involvement, it had this very result that all my husbands, and there were three of them, were political prisoners in the People's Republic of Poland (PRL). So to say, I did eventually realize—it occurred during my last informal marriage with Piotrek Niemczyk [a member of Solidarity], and I realized when he started to talk with my father and it turned out they were charged under the same article. What my father had before the war, Piotrek had after the war—the article about 'an attempt to overthrow the system forcibly'. So I thought 'Wow!', and looked back at my marriages and I thought 'Well, well, this is something for Doctor Freud'.[29]

Some parents, however, including members of the communist establishment, did not want their children to get involved in politics. In such families conflicts often erupted that involved the course of children's education: future activists sought to study philosophy, sociology or history while their parents wanted them to chose politically safe careers as engineers or physicians. Some of those who had experienced Stalinism were anxious for their children and wanted to spare them the brutality of politics in communism. Michnik's father had been a communist activist since the 1930s, but was disappointed with the system after 1945:

> When I was a child, father was notorious for arguing with everyone, attacking the regime...As far as the system was concerned he had no illusions. However—and this was the very difference between us—he didn't believe that any kind of political activity against this regime was possible at all. He had Soviet experiences and in the Soviet Union no opposition was allowed to exist. According to him it wouldn't have been allowed in Poland either. He didn't believe in any sort of significant defiance nor in anti-Soviet dissidence...Father was perfectly aware of what real socialism was, its vileness and filth, yet at the same time was absolutely convinced that any active protest against this vileness was tantamount to suicide. This is why for many years he tried to persuade me to emigrate.[30]

Other parents sought to spare their children political difficulties and to protect them through silence. Karol Modzelewski (b. 1937) recalled his childhood in Stalinist Warsaw as a time when adults avoided the subject of politics—even when they were among the key architects of the postwar political order. His father had perished in the Soviet Union during the Great Purge while his stepfather became the minister of foreign affairs in communist Poland after being released from the Gulag:

> [I]n my presence no one talked about political matters. There was a dead silence. If one of our friends disappeared, and there were such cases, I was told he had

---

[29] Interview with Anna Dodziuk, conducted by PO, Warsaw, 7 September 2009.
[30] A. Michnik, J. Tischner and J. Żakowski, *Między Panem a Plebanem* (Kraków, 1995), 53.

gone abroad on a business trip. When in Moscow, I got the same answer to the
question 'where is my daddy?'... Only afterwards I learned everything. And those
whose parents had strong anti-communist beliefs talked to kids much less, because they had enough of an instinct of self-preservation and concern for their
children not to do that. It was a time when one could be imprisoned just for listening to Radio Free Europe, if a neighbour denounced you to the police... Well,
it was simply that fear would sit at the table along with the family and prevented
everyone from talking.[31]

While young Poles from socialist families made up the core of the Commandos,
numerous activists who took part in the student protests of March 1968 actually
came from non-communist or even anti-communist homes. The Commandos had
been decisive in preparing the central rally at Warsaw University, but the nationwide student strikes that followed were organized by people with no direct connection to this network. Many of these other activists had been shaped by values that
can hardly be described as Marxist or even leftist. Their parents had sometimes
experienced severe repression from the communist state; some had been prisoners
in the Soviet Gulag. These interviewees often described the atmosphere in which
they had been brought up as one of utter distrust or animosity against the system
and explained that their own politicization owed much to their parents' opposition. As Bernard Bujwicki (b. 1946), one of the strike leaders at Kraków Polytechnic, explains, '[In my family home] one gossiped about politics a lot. [In 1940] my
mother's family was deported to Siberia. Seven persons perished there, their bones
remained there'.

During the war, Bujwicki's father had belonged to the Home Army (a clandestine organization loyal to the Polish government in exile) and then to the anti-
communist partisans:

So things remained this way. There was always [in my family] an anti-commie atmosphere, to defy commies because commies were suppressing us in every possible
manner. So this [my involvement in the protests of 1968] was simply an extension
of this.[32]

Those activists whose parents had not been involved in anti-communist resistance,
sometimes came from families who suffered from the lack of personal and economic
freedom in the postwar communist order. Jan Wyrowiński (b. 1947), a member of
the Polish parliament who had been active in the protests at Gdańsk Polytechnic in
1968, relates how his family was targeted by the communist regime's economic
policies designed to facilitate the transformation to a planned economy:

Before the war my father was a merchant. After the war he also ran a shop for year and
a half, yet soon fell victim to 'the Battle for Trade' [an operation against small private
enterprises begun by the state in 1947] along with tens of thousands of people
harmed by Hilary Minc [the minister of industry] and that new reality... Although
my family's attitude toward the system was not overtly expressed, in a closed family

[31] Interview with Karol Modzelewski, conducted by PO, Warsaw, 18 March 2009.
[32] Interview with Bernard Bujwicki, conducted by PO, Białystok, 17 July 2010.

group we were talking about the system in an utterly negative way. This was true both for my father's family and my mother's.[33]

Many Polish activists of 1968 now see themselves as part of a generational collective formed *by* the protests. However, they seldom claim that the rejection of their parents' politics was what drove them to become active in the first place.[34] Only a small number of the Polish activists interviewed for this project spoke of a clear intergenerational conflict. Włodzimierz Witaszewski (b. 1949), an architect and later participant in KOR (Committee for Workers' Defence), was one of them. He mentioned that he had charged his father—a party dignitary responsible for supervising the security apparatus—thus: 'What you are doing has nothing in common with socialism' and gave him the example of Mao's Cultural Revolution.[35] Later, in 1968, it was none other than Witaszewski—the father—who directed the operations of the *milicja* in their crushing of the student strikes whose leader (at Warsaw's Politechnika) was Witaszewski, the son.

According to the journalist Piotr Rachtan (b. 1949), 'There's a certain natural conflict between generations. Me, I didn't care too much for the churchiness, as it were, of my family—that religious patriotism didn't suit me'.[36] While Rachtan only hints at conflicts revolving around his parents' social conservatism, the broader rebellion against the generation of the parents was the leitmotif of two interviews with participants of the Polish hippie movement—Marek Zwoliński and Jerzy Illg. The hippie movement did not develop fully until the 1970s, yet 1968 was a pivotal moment in its history as the first major rallies took place in Mielno and Duszniki, which attracted several thousand participants.

Marek Zwoliński's (b. 1949) life story centres on his disappointment with the general attitude, materialism and lack of idealism of his parents, whose marriage had always been on the brink of a divorce (he was partly brought up by his grandmother). He blamed them for their inability to build a happy family and for their 'high level of consumption', which he considered excessive. They were mostly absent at home, because they were working hard in pursuit of luxury goods, such as a car or television set. This experience led him to reject his parents' generation more broadly and to hark back to much older historical traditions to make sense of his activism:

... the basis of my reluctant attitude toward the authorities was that, first of all, they had resorted to such brutal methods, and secondly because they were from the older generation. I had a strong generational identity then...The point was to create a cultural revolution, not a youth culture...well, the point was to create a culture that would be created by the young and would be a repudiation or rejection of the culture of our parents' generation. Here I have to confess that I'd always had

[33] Interview with Jan Wyrowiński, conducted by PO, Warsaw, 8 July 2010.
[34] On this aspect see further: Piotr Osęka, 'The people of March', in Anna von der Goltz (ed.) *Talkin' 'bout my Generation*, 137–62, which uses some of the same material as this chapter.
[35] Interview with Włodzimierz Witaszewski, conducted by PO, Warsaw, 30 April 2010.
[36] Interview with Piotr Rachtan, conducted by PO, Warsaw, 24 June 2009.

this feeling that our grandparents' generation was closer to us. After all, in my generation we were eager to draw upon models that were very old, even a millennium, right? You know, the experiences of early Christianity, of Hinduism, Buddhism... Yeah, we had this feeling that the main opponent was the generation of our parents.[37]

Jerzy Illg (b. 1950) also had ambiguous feelings toward his parents. They both came from the intelligentsia and he grew up in a home filled with books. On one hand he acknowledged his parents' broad outlook, yet on the other he deemed them to be 'representatives' of adult life with all its rigours and prohibitions that existed to hamper his innate freedom:

> On one hand I had something to draw on, a kind of tradition, yet on the other hand, I had something to defy as well. Certainly I put my parents to a great deal of trouble, since from the very beginning I had such an instinct to wrench myself towards freedom. I still can't understand why a seven-year-old boy brought to school was resisting so desperately, dragging his legs along the pavement. My mother on one side and grandfather on the other were hauling me to the first class. And I had this terrible awareness that this was the end of my freedom, that after that the treadmill had begun and was going to last forever: first school, then secondary school, studies and finally— work; and 'farewell to my freedom'.[38]

The narratives of Polish activists of 1968 shared some traits with those of activists across the country's western border, in the German Democratic Republic. Some of the young East Germans, who engaged in various forms of political and cultural opposition around this time, had adopted their anti-regime attitude directly from their families. This was especially true in the Protestant milieu that spawned a significant number of East German dissidents.[39]

Rainer Eckert (b. 1950), a historian and director of a well-known institute and museum of contemporary history in Leipzig, the Zeitgeschichtliches Forum, protested against the Warsaw Pact's invasion of Czechoslovakia and was involved in an oppositional circle in his native Potsdam. He described his father, who died when Rainer was five years old, as a diehard communist. His father had been so hostile to the 'class enemy' that he had refused to cross the territory of West Berlin on his way to work, instead rising daily at 5 am to catch a slow train that circled the western enclave. His mother, by contrast, had leaned more towards social democracy and had been a committed Protestant. Her own wartime experiences instilled in Eckert a deep hostility towards the Soviet-controlled GDR:

> When she fled [the German Empire's eastern territories] in 1945, she was raped by Soviet soldiers and taken to a work camp from which she escaped. She didn't tell me this for a long time. But she was always scared when she saw a Soviet soldier. When we went for a walk in the forest and a Soviet soldier passed she would drag me behind a bush and push me to the floor. So that was an influence that was decisive and it was

---

[37] Zwoliński interview.
[38] Interview with Jerzy Illg, conducted by PO, Warsaw, 17 February 2010.
[39] Ehrhart Neubert, *Geschichte der Opposition in der DDR 1949–1989* (Berlin, 1997).

an anti-communist one...Also anti-Soviet and at the same time Protestant, pugnaciously Protestant.[40]

Klaus Behnke (b. 1950), one of Eckert's closest peers at the time, was also from a family with strong Christian traditions that had fled westwards at the end of the war. His mother's side of the family had lost its land and started from scratch after 1945. His father owned a private haulage business that was constantly threatened with expropriation by the socialist authorities. Behnke, a psychotherapist who would dedicate much of his adult life to researching the brutal methods of East Germany's infamous security service, the Stasi, relates that he became familiar with the regime's repressive side at a very young age.[41] Invoking a stereotypical image of Stasi agents, one episode, in particular, stuck in his mind:

> My first negative political memories were of my parents trembling on a particular day when some gentlemen in leather coats turned up and of their great joy afterwards when nothing had happened. That was a very early contact with the Stasi and the Party.[42]

As we can see, the anti-regime attitude of activists such as Behnke and Eckert had developed relatively naturally in families with experiences of Soviet brutality or political repression in the early years of the GDR. However, much as in neighbouring Poland, some of the most prominent East German activists of 1968 were the children of committed socialist parents and leading functionaries of East Germany's state party, the Socialist Unity Party (SED). Like their Polish peers from socialist homes, these young East Germans had often been as deeply committed to the socialist project as their parents, but increasingly began to question the reality of life in the GDR. They frequently tell stories of disappointed idealism to make sense of their search for alternative types of socialism.

Burkhard Kleinert (b. 1948), a former East German Trotskyist first arrested for oppositional activities in 1969, had been politicized at home from a young age. His father had been a Soviet prisoner of war and was won over to the communist cause at an 'anti-fascist school' in captivity. A former member of the National Committee for a Free Germany, a German organization that had opposed the Nazis from Soviet territory during the war, Kleinert's father rose through the ranks of the SED to become a leading socialist cadre after the foundation of the GDR. In 1958, however, he was purged for 'liberalist convictions' in one of the last innerparty purges following Stalin's death. While Kleinert does not claim that he sought to emulate his father's activism directly, he describes his politicization as the natural outcome of both the politics of his family and the repression his father had experienced. He thus became aware of the system's shortcomings and contradictions early on:

[40] Interview with Rainer Eckert, conducted by AvdG, Leipzig, 24 June 2010.
[41] Klaus Behnke and Jürgen Fuchs, *Zersetzung der Seele: Psychologie und Psychiatrie im Dienste der Stasi* (Hamburg, 1995); Klaus Behnke, *Stasi auf dem Schulhof: Der Missbrauch von Kindern und Jugendlichen durch das Ministerium für Staatssicherheit* (Berlin, 1998).
[42] Interview with Klaus Behnke, conducted by AvdG, Berlin, 3 May 2010.

Our father's chequered story naturally did not pass us children by. I have to say for myself that I was politicized very early, already as a child. Because my father talked about things very openly at home... So we had access to a lot of internal party information. But he also told us about Khrushchev's speech at the twentieth party congress... We also watched western television and father was convinced that if you could not bear this, you could never be a good communist. [laughs] And therefore in a political sense we were socialized relatively openly.[43]

The anti-Stalinism instilled in him by his father following the purge is a central thread of Kleinert's narrative that divorces GDR reality from alternative socialist ideals, which he continues to espouse. The 'cultural revolution' of the 1960s and the general climate of wanting to 'question authority' then fell on fertile ground, turning Kleinert into a Trotskyist activist and communard, who nevertheless managed to pursue a successful career as an economist in East Germany and remains committed to 'democratic socialism' to this day.

Like Kleinert, Bettina (b. 1947) and Claudia Wegner (b. 1942) were raised by dedicated communist parents and amid lively political discussion. Bettina, a well-known political songwriter who was eventually forced to leave for the West, explains:

...my parents were wonderful, we did not have to repeat things in a parrot-fashion if we saw anything. They always said 'We can discuss anything'. So I was not raised to say 'yes' all the time. And of course that quickly created problems. Not with my parents, but with the institutions, school, it started at school.[44]

Her arrest for distributing leaflets against the Warsaw Pact's invasion in Czechoslovakia in August 1968 was extremely tough on her parents who did not oppose the intervention:

They thought what I had done was awful. They suffered like pigs, because of course their party comrades came and said they should distance themselves from me, and they said they could not...[They said:] 'The child made a mistake!'... They suffered because of my mistake, but also...because someone like me was sent to prison. It shattered something in them, too. And they said they would never distance themselves from me.

Her older sister Claudia explains that the regime's officially sanctioned anti-fascism had gone a long way towards binding young people to the socialist project. Until she finally turned her back on the regime after her sister's arrest in 1968, she had aspired to emulate her parents' example:

Because they weren't hypocrites. They really were honest communists. My father and mother put up leaflets in '33, against Hitler. And my father deserted during the war with a group of very young soldiers...Of course they were role models for us. After all, not everybody from that time can say that their parents were anti-fascists...[T]hey had a bonus. But this didn't last forever. At some point it was used up.[45]

43 Interview with Burkhard Kleinert, conducted by AvdG, Berlin, 27 April 2010.
44 Interview with Bettina Wegner, conducted by AvdG, Berlin, 2 May 2010.
45 Interview with Claudia Wegner, conducted by AvdG, Berlin, 24 June 2010.

While her activism in the wake of 1968 led to severe clashes at home, she had not been driven towards opposition to the system by political conflicts within her family. Instead, she explains, her open anti-socialist stance would have been impossible without having grown up in such an open and supportive atmosphere:

> I have to say that my old communist parents ... —whom my sister and I argued with massively, whom we always had huge rows with, who hated us; I would have loved to push my father down the stairs for his Stalinist sentences! [laughs]—but, in reality, it was also them who brought us there through their conviction that you have to stand up for what you believe in and should not be hypocritical.

Even when East German activists from socialist families experienced political conflicts at home, they seldom framed their stories as generational rebellion.

COLLABORATION, RESISTANCE AND 'DEFEAT SYNDROME' IN FRANCE AND GREECE

Despite the shortcomings of 'really existing socialism' in eastern Europe, the ideal of socialism had not lost its clout in postwar 'free' Europe. In postwar France, the cult of the French Resistance was very powerful, especially its Gaullist dimension, although its communist strand had suffered marginalization in the face of Cold War anti-communism. Young activists could—and did—readily build on social and family traditions of resistance—much more so than activists in neighbouring West Germany were able to do. However, like the East German or Polish children of socialist functionaries, French activists often combined approval for their parents' political commitment with a sense of disappointment, either because their parents had left the Communist Party after the Soviet invasion of Hungary in 1956, just as young people became active over the Algerian War, or because they felt that their parents' high ideals had not endured the test of time.

Jean-Pierre Le Dantec (b. 1943) traces his radicalism back to the fact that his parents were among the primary school teachers (*instituteurs*) who were seen as the apostles of the anti-clerical Third Republic and who went into the communist resistance—the Francs-Tireurs et Partisans (Free Shooters and Partisans or FTP)— and then the Communist Party. Even more influential was his aunt, whose story added the heroic dimension of deportation to Nazi camps:

> My father and mother were *instituteurs*, both of them ... brought up in a sort of secular religion, known as the 'black hussars of the Republic', and in the socialist milieu before the war. During the Resistance they joined the FTP ... I went to Paris for the first time at the age of eight, to stay with my father's sister, who had married a communist militant who had returned from Buchenwald ... There was a sort of family truth in my activism (*engagement*), in the sense that I had for my parents if not admiration, at least filial piety; I thought they were right.[46]

---

[46] Interview with Jean-Pierre Le Dantec, conducted by RG, Paris, 24 April 2007. See also his *Les Dangers du Soleil* (Paris, 1978).

Alongside the powerful place that the Resistance held in French collective memory in the postwar decades,[47] many French activists tell stories that pivot on familial conflict. In these cases, the struggle often arose because the parents had not offered any resistance to Nazism; either because the father had been absent in a prisoner of war (POW) camp, or because the family had sympathized with Vichy, or—in the case of Jewish families—because they had gone into hiding to avoid deportation. This struggle often continued in school and in church against the same values espoused by the parents, and the incubation of radical ideas was often painful and lonely.

Dominique Grange (b. 1940) moved towards revolt through conflict with her family and its values. While she worshipped her grandfather, a veteran of the Great War, she despised her father, who had spent the war and her childhood in a German POW camp. She also had a difficult relationship with her absent mother, who suffered from tuberculosis (TB). Sent away to convent school she found herself confronting another source of authority, the Catholic Church, and traces her sense of revolt back to that period of loneliness and oppression:

> My father was taken prisoner by the Germans. So we did not see much of him until the end of the war... this father who returned and wanted immediately to affirm his authority at once because we grew up without him during our first years. There were many conflicts with my father's authority... No, I did not have a happy childhood because right after the war my mother became ill. She had TB and had to go away to a sanatorium... My sister and I were sent to a convent school for seven years. It was not a happy time. I think it was a period when I found the seeds of my sense of revolt—against the rules that people wanted to impose on me, against rigid religious thought, against belief, and also a revolt against solitude because at that age one needs love and I didn't have much of that.[48]

Michel-Antoine Burnier (b. 1942) was also pitted against his father in a struggle that could not be offset by maternal love because his mother had died in childbirth. He was hostile to his father and father's generation, which had failed to stop the rise of fascism in the 1930s, suffered defeat in 1940 and the German occupation, and was generally sympathetic to the Vichy regime. Like Dominique Grange he received a highly reactionary Catholic education at the hands of ageing priests. It was 'a very Catholic education, an almost totalitarian Catholicism, a nineteenth-century Catholicism'. Only his steady shift to radicalism—through reading rather than relationships—was natural. Burnier read Voltaire, lost his faith at the age of fifteen, and found a new political hero in Jean-Paul Sartre: 'The Enlightenment saved me from this closed, brutal Christianity. It was a sort of liberation. I searched for how to understand the world, and... Sartre launched me on a political career'.[49]

---

[47] Pieter Lagrou, *The Legacy of Nazi Occupation: Patriotic Memory and National Recovery in Western Europe, 1945–1965* (Cambridge, 2000), 30–1 and 38–47.

[48] Interview with Dominique Grange, conducted by RG, Paris, 10 May 2007.

[49] Interview with Michel-Antoine Burnier, conducted by RG, Paris, 11 May 2007. Among his autobiographical writings see *A ma fille. Histoire d'un père de cinquante ans qui ne voulait pas avoir d'enfant* (Paris, 1993) and *L'adieu à Sartre* (Paris, 2002).

As a student at the Sorbonne and Sciences-Po, Burnier became involved with clandestine networks during the Algerian War, hiding deserters and FLN militants, and opposing the extreme-right defenders of French Algeria. This was a generational struggle, he explained, to make up for the failings of his parents' generation in the war:

> We were clear that that our parents had not risen up immediately against fascism, which they should have done in 1933 or 1934, and fascism arrived. We saw fascism arriving in Algeria and we got going at once. We fought straight away and those who trained us were the generation of the Resistance.

Unlike his West German peers who rejected their Nazi parents, French activists whose parents had supported Vichy could still look towards alternative national models. While activists in the Federal Republic of Germany had to hark back to the years of the Weimar Republic to find any visible national tradition of left-wing politics worth emulating, French activists could forge links—real and imagined— with the wartime Resistance. Through his activism Burnier came into contact with Emmanuel d'Astier de la Vigerie (1900–69), the founder of the Libération-Sud Resistance movement. He explains that the heritage of the Resistance not only overcame generational conflict but provided him with an ideal father he could admire:

> Really, there was no conflict of generations. We were happy to serve adults who had such a glorious past...I dropped everything to follow D'Astier...I took his wife for my mother, his sons for my brothers, I took him as my father.

The struggle of André Senik (b. 1938) went back to what he saw as the shame of belonging to a family of Polish-Jewish immigrants to Paris who had been forced to go into hiding during the German occupation of France. With his brother he had been separated from his parents for two years, hidden by the Red Cross, and when he reached adolescence he clashed with his Zionist father and elders about the way forward. While they wanted him to go to work on a kibbutz and build Israel, he wanted to espouse communism to build the new world order. Although Stalinism was anathema to east European activists, for Senik it was a way to carve out his independence:

> I was in a Zionist movement and at fifteen you had to decide to go to Israel. So at the age of fourteen my friend and I had a crisis of conscience. We said, 'We are revolutionaries, we are Marxists, what should we do?'. We asked the leaders of this Zionist organization what to do and they refused to answer and we debated it for a year. There were other reasons that decided it for us in reality. Perhaps we just wanted to leave our families and a certain life. So at fourteen my friend and I decided to leave the Zionist movement and to join the Communist Youth.[50]

Senik joined the Young Communists and the French Communist Party. In 1957, despite the controversy over the Soviet suppression of the Hungarian revolt, he went

---

[50] Interview with André Senik, conducted by RG, Paris, 4 April 2007.

to the Festival of Youth in Moscow and laid a wreath at the tombs of Lenin and Stalin. He was a student at the Sorbonne and member of the Union of Communist Students when debate raged about Khrushchev's Secret Speech in 1956 denouncing certain evils of Stalinism. While the French Communist Party refused to follow the new line, the Italian Communist Party did and Communist students who embraced this line were dubbed the 'Italians':

> We were going to liquidate Stalinism, socialism was going to be wonderful and we were part of the movement. Without knowing it we were a new generation that was seizing power. With hindsight I realize that in a way it was a struggle with the father, because we had declared war on the French Communist Party... We hated them, we called them murderers, dogs, because suddenly they had revealed what we did not want to know about, that there were concentration camps in the Soviet Union, the full horror.

The 'Italians' were driven out of the Union of Communist Students in 1965 and in 1968 Senik was a young philosophy teacher in a Paris *lycée*, encouraging protest among his students. Asked why he became involved in 1968 he returned to the humiliation of having to hide as a Jewish boy:

> As a young man the important thing was not to be like our parents. Above all not to be a timid and fearful little Jewish boy. Being revolutionary for Jews was thus a paradoxical and rather aggressive way of becoming part of society instead of having to hide. Finally there was a demonstration in which everyone was shouting, 'We are all German Jews!'. For us it was a way of settling our accounts with parents who told us not to raise our voices, not to say that we were Jewish, to take care that people didn't think ill of us because we were Jewish.[51]

Narratives that conveyed such a clear sense of generational rebellion were scarcer in the case of Greece. Some Greek activists nevertheless considered their political rebellion to be bound up with rejecting their upbringing and the surrounding atmosphere. They described their experiences in terms of conflict with the school, the police and, sometimes, with their family.

Most Greek activists came from leftist or liberal families and thus followed in their footsteps. Of particular importance was their experience of the Greek Civil War (1946–9), in which the left was defeated and persecuted in the years that followed. These traumas were reflected in the way in which families brought up their children. Some family members influenced their children directly and introduced them to politics. Petros Kounalakis (b. 1937), a leading cadre of the Unified Democratic Left in West Germany in the 1960s, had been 'instructed' by his uncle who had moved from Athens to Herakleion on the island of Crete to take over his sister's business when Kounalakis was eleven:

> So my uncle, who had been in the EPON [Unified Panhellenic Organization of Youth], came and I became leftist. My first instructor was my uncle. [laughs] He gave me books, Russian literature, and he talked to me about the left all day long. So at the age of twelve,

---

[51] Senik interview.

thanks to my uncle, I had a leftist consciousness without having any kind of contact with a party or a political group. Anyway, things were tough then.[52]

Policemen frequently harassed his uncle and this is how Kounalakis came to witness the violence of the Civil War. One of the memories from his childhood was that one evening, when he was sitting in a coffee shop with his uncle, a group of policemen showed up. They carried the head and arm of a famous guerrilla whom they had just killed and they shook the dead man's arm in front of his uncle's face, yelling 'Here is your friend'. In spite of the atmosphere of terror and police brutality against the left, Kounalakis continued to socialize with the radicals of Herakleion as a young boy. On several occasions, he witnessed police brutality against his leftist friends, although he was not victimized himself because of his family's social standing. In the mid-1950s, a time of demonstrations for the independence of Cyprus, he was arrested after an attack on the British consulate in Herakleion:

> We went and we ruined the place. They arrested me and some other guys, all high-school students. Our fathers came to protest and the police set us free. That's how it was in Crete, when you came from a bourgeois family and your father was not a leftist, you enjoyed 'immunity'. The guys from lower classes paid the price, those who had nothing, no back-up, no protectors.

Precisely because 'things were tough then' and only a small number of people could rely on their class background to avoid persecution, very few did what Kounalakis's uncle did and 'instructed' their children in political matters. Most of the leftist parents did not want their children to go through what they had experienced in the Civil War years. Much as in communist Poland, where anti-communist parents often sought to shield their children from persecution, silence became a form of protection for their children. They simply did not talk about their political beliefs or their experiences during the wartime resistance and the Civil War that followed, and the children often only discovered their parents' past later on. Christina Stamatopoulou (b. 1946) did not know that her father had been leftist, that he had been dismissed from the bank where he worked because of his political beliefs, or that the family had had to change residence as a result of police harassment. She did not even know that her father had been banished to a remote island from 1946 until 1948. Stamatopoulou did not remember the absence of her father until the moment that she found out about it by accident:

> CS: My father carefully hid it [his political past] because he went through all these things. He was afraid that his kids might take the same path…I started to learn what happened, to read history, that there was a Civil War. I didn't know anything, I had no idea. Once I was reading a book by Lountemis [a popular leftist novelist] in which he described life in exile…I don't know how it occurred to me but I said that's where my father must have been. I was sure that my father was there. I started searching in the chests at home [laughs] and eventually I found some letters of my

---

[52] Interview with Petros Kounalakis, conducted by PV, Athens, 21 October 2009.

father and my mother. They corresponded and she sent him pictures. I had always
been puzzled because in the pictures were the three of us... I had never thought it
before, but in the pictures we were always my mother, my brother and me. I found
some of the pictures that my mother had hidden away, in which she wrote on the
back 'look how pretty we have become... and the kids'. I found letters as well... I said
to him, 'Why didn't you tell us anything?'.

PV: Did you ask him, did you talk about that?

CS: Yes, yes. I was leftist by that time and he said to me 'I didn't want you to get
involved with the party mechanisms' etc. [laughs][53]

Stamatopoulou laughs because in spite of her father's intentions and his efforts
to keep politics out of his home (she discovered years later that he had brought
the leftist newspaper *Avgi* home, but had hidden it from his children), she was
heavily involved in politics in the 1960s. As a student at the medical school in
Athens, she briefly joined the Lambrakis Democratic Youth in 1964.[54] Soon she
found out that she was more attracted by a Maoist student group, the Progressive
All-Student Union Front; after the Colonels' coup in 1967 she fled to Paris to
meet her boyfriend, Giorgos Karambelias, and both were active in the movement
against the dictatorship. However, her father wanted to keep her not just out of
politics in general, but out of the internal politics of the Communist Party in
particular. Many leftists of the Resistance era distanced themselves from the
Communist Party because of the impact that the Civil War had had on society
at large and their personal lives as well.

Then there were the children of faithful party members. Anna Filini (b. 1945) is
the daughter of Kostas Filinis, a leading member of the Resistance Youth organization (EPON) during the Axis occupation and a prominent figure of the Greek left.
When the Greek Communist Party was banned in 1947, her father went underground. She saw her father again eight years later, in 1955, when he was arrested.
She continued to visit prisons and court rooms in order to see her father until
1966, when he was released (only to be arrested again in 1967 after the coup):

I remember there was a small window, a small window with thick bars. I was relatively
tall for a little kid... He came along, I remember he held a cigarette, and he was doing
t-t-t-t [he couldn't speak] I remember that, he was trembling... My father was
coming [to Athens] because he had several less important trials. So I went to see him
in the trial or I was going to prison. It was in '59 or '60 that I made my first long trip
to Corfu together with two aunts. I had the opportunity to visit my father alone several times. We talked a lot. The main subject we discussed most was his relation to my
mother, why they separated. I was very worried about it; they were worried as well
about this thing.[55]

---

[53] Interview with Christina Stamatopoulou, conducted by PV, Athens, 2 November 2007. On the
Greek political prisoners, see Polymeris Voglis, *Becoming a Subject: Political Prisoners during the Greek
Civil War* (New York, 2002).

[54] After the assassination of the MP of EDA Grigoris Lambrakis in Salonica on 22 May 1963, the
youth organization of the EDA (Neolaia EDA) was dissolved and a front youth organization the
Lambrakis Democratic Youth (Dimokratiki Neolaia Lambraki, DNL) was established in 1964.

[55] Interview with Anna Filini, conducted by PV, Athens, 29 February 2008.

Many leftist families experienced the consequences of the Civil War and family relations were severely tested. However, activists from these families generally do not criticize their parents for their choices despite the heavy price they sometimes paid. Filini describes the relationship to her father as 'very close' despite the fact that she actually grew up without him. As a student she took part in the United Democratic Left (EDA) and organized campaigns for the release of political prisoners—her father was one of them. She recalls how upset she felt when a cadre of the EDA pointed out to her in 1965 that the question of political prisoners was not among the priorities of the party at the time. She claims that the attitude of the party 'marked' her not only because she was the daughter of a political prisoner but also because she thought that the party line on this issue was 'right-wing' and 'opportunistic'. A few years later and after the Colonels' coup, Filini's criticism of the 'opportunism' of the established left led her to set up a new and more radical party, the Epanastatiko Kommounistiko Kinima Elladas (Revolutionary Communist Movement of Greece).

Activists did not criticize their families because they did not associate the hardships they experienced with their parents' choices but with the policies of a hostile and repressive state. After 1958, when the EDA gained almost 25 per cent in the elections, the police repression of Karamanlis' government escalated. A special branch of the security police that monitored students' activities was established, a militant right-wing student group (EKOF) emerged that attacked leftist students, and 190 citizens were sent to exile in the second half of 1958.[56] The wave of terror culminated in the rigged elections of 1961 when two members of the Youth of the EDA were murdered.

Sometimes activists experienced the vindictiveness of the state at a very young age. Klearchos Tsaousidis (b. 1947) still remembers that he was severely beaten by the police at the age of fourteen; his uncle was a political refugee who lived in East Berlin and the police thought that he had contact with him:

> I don't know why [I was beaten]...At school we were involved in things...they pointed the finger at me. It probably isn't a coincidence that one year later I was expelled from school. But...it is not a paradox. Then it was usual. You didn't ask [the police] many questions and your only concern was to leave. That was the point. I remember I returned home crying from the beatings and I asked my father 'Who is he [the uncle]?'. He explained to me. After that he talked to me about everything I asked, because I had many questions, some of his friends showed up out of the blue, we hadn't seen them before and we didn't see them ever again. Such things happened then, you know, and children shouldn't know because they were the most vulnerable, right? I mean, with one slap you would collapse.[57]

While Greek activists do not talk about a clear conflict between the generations, they highlight one important difference between themselves and their parents: young

---

[56] Ioanna Papathanasiou, *I neolaia Lambraki sti dekaetia tou 1960. Arheiakes tekmirioseis kai autoviografikes katatheseis* (Athens, 2008), 57–8.
[57] Interview with Klearchos Tsaousidis, conducted by PV, Thessaloniki, 25 May 2009.

people did not carry with them a 'defeat syndrome'. Their parents, who had been involved in the resistance movement in the 1940s, carried the burden of defeat after the liberation and, most importantly, their defeat in the Greek Civil War. This sense of defeat was often combined with feelings of guilt, betrayal, fear and power-lessness. The next generation had to confront this legacy.

Theodoros Paraskevopoulos (b. 1946) describes this confrontation with the legacy of the previous generation as a 'political rebellion'—a rebellion that proved difficult to accomplish in his case. Both his parents had been in the National Liberation Front during the occupation, and in high school he had contacts with the Youth of the EDA. When Paraskevopoulos finished high school, he thought it was time to follow his own path, away from his family and its political culture:

> When I sought to set myself free from my parents, I sought to break free from the United Democratic Left. On the left, of course, but not in the United Democratic Left, the Greek Communist Party. But I did nothing, not with any other organization. The mentality of the United Democratic Left and of the Greek Communist Party were already deep inside me, so I didn't.[58]

In 1963 he followed his mother to West Germany, where she had emigrated to work, and moved to Hamburg, the city where she lived. He worked for two years as an unskilled worker at a large electronics company, before moving further north to Kiel to study. While he was in Hamburg he socialized in the Greek immigrant community in which the EDA was very active. After a while he became a member of the EDA in West Germany, showing how difficult it was to break with one's own past.

Venios Aggelopoulos (b. 1943) also came from a leftist middle-class family. His mother, a teacher, was on the left but not organized, while his father, a doctor, had been in the Communist Youth in the interwar period and a member of the Resistance during the wartime occupation. In 1948 his father was banished on an island for his political beliefs and Aggelopoulos did not see him for five years. He had very different experiences from his father since he graduated from an elite high school and went to study at the École Polytechnique in Paris. He was not seriously involved in student politics before the Colonels' coup of 1967. This became the turning point in his life; after the coup he embraced radical ideas. He became one of the founding members of the Movement 29 May, which advocated the violent overthrow of the Greek dictatorship. The idea of violence, which the Greek left had repudiated after the defeat in the Civil War, became a credo among several far-left groups as a way to overcome the defeat syndrome of their parents' generation. Aggelopoulos emphasizes that his generation had not been crushed as had his parents', and therefore could still believe in the idea of revolution:

> Don't forget that we were neither sent to Makronisos Island nor tortured. These things had happened to our fathers in the Civil War. But we hadn't experienced this, we had not been beaten like this. We didn't have the fear of the Occupation and the defeat

---

[58] Interview with Theodoros Paraskevopoulos, conducted by PV, Athens, 30 September 2009.

syndrome, that anything we did was doomed to fail. We didn't have it. It was something that they could not pass on to us. It was a matter of experience. They were saying 'Don't be too risky. I know better, I've had it', but it didn't always work. Especially at a time when around the world the spirit was to overthrow the existing system, capitalism to say it properly.[59]

However, the bitter experiences of leftist families were not the whole story; other Greek activists came from liberal or right-wing families. These families had also had traumatic experiences in the 1940s, especially when they were targeted by the left in the Civil War. The different civil wars in the 1940s (the clashes between resisters and collaborators during the Occupation, the battle of Athens in December 1944, and the Civil War between 1946 and 1949) divided society deeply between left and right and made indelible marks on most Greek families.[60] Activists who came from right-wing families confronted that traumatic family past and challenged the political beliefs of their parents. They had to start their 'revolution' at home.

Giorgos Glynos (b. 1946) came from a right-wing family, marked by the Civil War—his father's brother had been killed by the communists. It was also a practising Christian family; his grandmother was especially devout, and he went to church regularly as a child. Moreover, he attended a private French school run by Catholic *frères*. All this, however, did not prevent him from espousing radical ideas while he was a high-school student. He felt, as he says:

fascination with the forbidden left, ideas challenging the establishment and everything that happened around me. I began having arguments first with my grandmother, and then with my dad and mum, that is at home. Like people used to say later, you start the revolution at home and then you move outwards.[61]

In 1965 Glynos joined the Lambrakis Democratic Youth (DNL), the youth wing of the EDA. After a while he found that the DNL was very moderate and left it to join a Trotskyist group, the Kommounistiko Diethnistiko Komma Elladas. Together with other student comrades he published the journal *Spoudastikos Logos* (*Students' Word*), something that upset his parents, as he still remembers with pride:

I remember that we had to put down a name of whom would be the editor of the journal, so I put my name, 'Journal editor,' I don't recall how it was exactly written, Giorgos Glynos. I also put down my home phone number. When my parents saw it, they had a nervous breakdown, 'You brought communism to our home!', and so forth. There was a bloody mess at home. Anyway we published it. We printed two issues and then the dictatorship came.

[59] Interview with Venios Aggelopoulos, conducted by PV, Athens, 2 December 2008.
[60] On the impact of the Civil War upon Greek society, see for instance Mark Mazower (ed.) *After the War was Over: Reconstructing the Family, Nation and State in Greece, 1943–1960* (Princeton, 2000); and P. Carabott and T. Sfikas (eds) *The Greek Civil War: Essays on a Conflict of Exceptionalism and Silences* (Aldershot, 2004).
[61] Interview with Giorgos Glynos, conducted by PV, Athens, 18 May 2009.

However, seen from a different perspective, there was no sharp contrast between left-wing and right-wing families in the way they brought up their children in 1950s Greece. Although there were differences concerning the role of religion in family life, both left-wing and right-wing families were traditional in their values and morality, and conservative when it came to their daughters. Girls' roles were strongly circumscribed in the patriarchal institution of the family, and after finishing school they had to get married. For young Greek women, studying at university not only paved the road to a career but was also a means to escape their gendered 'fate': to be under either their father's or their husband's sway.

Maria Kavvadia (b. 1948) grew up in a close-knit leftist family. Apart from her parents and her sister, their grandparents lived in the same apartment. Two uncles and one aunt also lived in the same building. Kavvadia took part in a student demonstration for the first time when she was thirteen. It was one of the many 'spontaneous' demonstrations of the early 1960s: university students outside the school gate called the high-school students to leave the classrooms and join them in a demonstration demanding an increase in public spending for education. When she returned home and her parents found out where she had been, her father beat her up. The beating was just one (violent) instance of a suffocating and authoritarian environment at home. She saw studying at university and getting involved in politics as a way of escaping her family rather than rebelling against it:

> My family was like a stranglehold, especially my father, and for that reason I'd wanted to leave since I was a kid. I had thought of becoming a hostess, a missionary, a radio operator on a ship, to go away, literally. All this when I was a kid. When I finished high school, I said to myself: 'What am I going to do now? How can I go away from my family? University.' I had in mind to get organized in a political group. I told myself: 'Now I am a student, I am a citizen, my father cannot influence me any more or restrict me'. And eventually, when I got into university, I left my home in the morning and returned at night.[62]

As a student Kavvadia approached the main leftist youth organization Lambrakis Democratic Youth but she did not become a member because she realized that the power relations were similar to those she had experienced at home. 'I didn't like it very much', she says, 'I thought that it was too bureaucratic and ... It was the way power functioned, someone was superior, the other inferior. "Now you will talk" or "It is none of your business"'.

After the coup of 21 April 1967 she was briefly involved in the Dimokratikes Epitropes Antistaseos, an opposition group led by Trotskyists. Being critical of the way political groups functioned in general, she eventually joined an underground group of communal living in which she could practise radicalism in her everyday life.

---

[62] Interview with Maria Kavvadia, conducted by PV, Athens, 12 May 2009.

CONCLUSION

The 'generation gap', a concept that was regularly invoked to explain the protest movements of the time as a revolt of the young against their parents and everything they represented, had great traction around 1968. As such, it left significant traces in the accounts of some of our interviewees, who framed the stories of their politicization as a rebellion against the 'adult world' or the politics and conduct of the previous generation as a whole. Predictably, this narrative was especially pronounced among West German activists who sought to distance themselves from the country's Nazi past. Most of our interviewees, however—including German ones—told more nuanced and multi-layered stories that often acknowledged positive familial influences while being critical of specific elements of their upbringing or their parents' way of life, which often did not match their radical ideas.

While activists usually explained their politicization as a natural progression or as the result of a struggle at home, few activists emulated or rejected their parents unequivocally. Some, like the young East German and Polish activists from socialist homes, set out to 'continue the mission' by emulating their parents' heroic example of anti-fascist activism, but found themselves in opposition to their beliefs once they began to criticize 'really existing socialism' and their parents' failure to build a more perfect society. Others initially fought hard to 'break free' from their families' politics, but later found themselves following in their footsteps. Overall, even those who were initiated into activism through family traditions still found themselves confronted with societal institutions that they rejected.

Activists were especially critical of their families when these embodied the consent to, or accommodation with, fascism, Nazism or Stalinism. By contrast, families with a history of resistance against these regimes had a 'bonus'. In this sense the life stories of our interviewees reflected the powerful legacies of these regimes in postwar Europe. The protests of the 'first postwar generation' did not happen in a historical vacuum but were linked in complex ways to the recent histories of their countries: the legacies of Nazism, the Second World War, occupation, colonialism and its end, and the establishment of communist or right-wing regimes. European societies experienced and were transformed by historical developments; ordinary people participated in and were affected by the changes that the Second World War and the postwar era wrought, and activists' parents and other family members represented 'living history'. Seen from this angle, the activism of 1968 was less of a historical caesura than being firmly embedded in the broader history of twentieth-century Europe. The way activists related the stories of their politicization to the history of their families and to their upbringing provides insights into how they wrote themselves into the broader histories of their countries. Continuity was as much a part of these stories as rupture.

3

Inspirations

James Mark, Nigel Townson and Polymeris Voglis

In recounting their journeys into the political struggle, European radicals inevitably placed themselves in relation to other revolutionaries, both past and present. Some regarded their work as the continuation of their parents' resistance to fascism during the Second World War, while for others this struggle had been superseded by the revolutions in Algeria, Cuba and Vietnam, which provided them with a paradigm for heroic action that was either lacking or tainted in their own domestic anti-fascist traditions. Oral history provides insights into the ways in which activists from across the continent related to these inspirations. Not only do individual testimonies demonstrate how activists constructed themselves as inheritors of, participants in, or in solidarity with, struggles of the past and present, but they also reveal how anti-fascist and anti-imperialist ideas were *transmitted* within families, through emerging political networks, or in public debate, and how they came to shape activists' political identities. Radicals who were fighting the dictatorships in southern Europe, seeking to reform the sclerotic bureaucratism of eastern European socialism, or seeking revolution or democratization in the West, were all shaped by their encounters with both the anti-fascism of their parents' generation and the anti-imperialism of their own, and they all sought to make sense of, and engage with, these two traditions.

THE SURVIVAL OF ANTI-FASCISM?

In the 1960s anti-fascism as a source of ideological and moral inspiration for radical activists in Europe underwent a wholesale transformation. It had been a vital leftist tradition in Europe after the war: many radicals-to-be grew up in families whose parents had been part of underground communist movements under right-wing interwar regimes, had participated in resistance movements to Nazi occupation in the Second World War, or had fought against 'counter-revolutionary' forces in civil wars. For some activists, the anti-fascism of the 1930s and 1940s had bequeathed a weak or at least ambiguous legacy; in countries where the leftist 'anti-fascist' forces had been beaten in civil wars, such as Greece (1946–9) and Spain (1936–9), anti-fascism was associated with defeat and consequently might be forgotten. Even where leftist struggles had been successful, anti-fascism was increasingly seen as a tired ideology, exploited both by communist parties in western Europe that were committed to the status quo and by communist regimes in the East to justify the suppression of progressive alternatives. Yet among some groups the memories of the struggle against fascism resurfaced as new right-wing authoritarian circles took power in Greece (1967–74) and threatened in Italy, where radicals looked back to the struggles of their leftist parents in the Second World War. In western European democracies too, young radicals often pinned the problems of the state on the unresolved legacies of fascism and viewed themselves as continuing an unfinished struggle.

THE DEFEATED REVOLUTION: ANTI-FASCISM OF CIVIL WARS

As elsewhere in Europe, the late 1960s in Greece and Spain saw the emergence of new radical leftist revolutionaries influenced by Maoism, Trotskyism and the new left. Although they shared many of the ideological traits of activists elsewhere in Europe, their activism was shaped by a different political context: the struggle against right-wing dictatorship, which had survived in Spain since 1939 and was established in Greece in 1967. Moreover, unlike radicals elsewhere in Europe, who were heirs to a victorious anti-fascist resistance, both the Spanish and the Greek radicals of the 1960s were the inheritors of a left that had been defeated in civil wars by the right.[1]

The anti-fascist tradition in Spain was embodied in the greatest anti-fascist struggle of the 1930s, the Spanish Civil War.[2] However, three decades later, most Spanish radicals felt that the Civil War was 'a long time ago for us'.[3] For Francisco Pereña, an activist in the FLP (or 'Felipe'), one of the two leading student groups, 'the Civil War always seemed to me to have been in the Middle Ages'.[4] One reason why the anti-fascism of the Civil War appeared so distant was that there was little political continuity between the 1930s and the anti-Francoist opposition. The Republican forces that had fought in 1936–9 had been devastated or destroyed altogether by exile and the postwar repression.[5] Another was that the activists of the 1960s

---

[1] On the radical left in Spain, see Hartmut Heine, 'La contribución de la "Nueva Izquierda" al resurgir de la democracia española, 1957–1976', in Josep Fontana (ed.) *España bajo el franquismo* (Barcelona, 2000), 142–59; Consuelo Laiz, *La lucha final: los partidos de la izquierda radical durante la transición española* (Madrid, 1995); and José Manuel Roca (ed.) *El proyecto radical. Auge y declive de la izquierda revolucionaria en España (1964–1992)* (Madrid, 1993). On the Frente de Liberación Popular in particular, see Julio Antonio García Alcalá, *Historia del Felipe (FLP, FOC y ESBA). De Julio Cerón a la Liga Comunista Revolucionaria* (Madrid, 2001).

[2] For a thoughtful reflection on the impact of the anti-fascist tradition on the left under Franco, see Javier Muñoz Soro, 'La reconciliación como política: memoria de la violencia y la guerra en el antifranquismo', *Jerónimo Zurita* 84 (2009), 113–33.

[3] Interview with José Sanroma Aldea, conducted by NT, Madrid, 1 June 2010.

[4] Interview with Francisco Pereña García, conducted by NT, Madrid, 26 May 2010.

[5] On the exile, see José Luis Abellán, *De la guerra civil al exilio republicano (1936–1977)* (Madrid, 1983), and idem (ed.) *El exilio español de 1939*, 6 vols (Madrid, 1976–8), as well as Louis Stein,

knew very little about what had happened thirty years earlier. Dictatorial censorship and rejection of the official discourse on the Civil War naturally played their
part, but so too did the self-censorship that operated within families that were fearful of passing down their memories of the conflict.[6]

'Felipe' activist Manuel Garí (b. 1947) was born into a professional family in
1947. During the Civil War, his father fought in the republican army, rising to the
rank of 'captain or commandant', before being detained in a concentration camp
following the cessation of hostilities:

> NT: How long did he spend in the concentration camp?
> MG: Well, it's that, these are parts of the past that aren't... In my family, as in so many
> families, not everything was transmitted. We're talking about the dictatorial years,
> in which there was also a certain secretiveness, on the part of the victims in this
> case...
> NT: Did he speak of the Civil War?
> MG: Yes, but only anecdotes.
> NT: And at home did one talk of politics?
> MG: Very little, very little.[7]

The great majority of the 1960s generation of radical activists therefore felt a
great distance from the anti-fascism of the 1930s. For José Sanroma (b. 1947),
secretary-general of the Maoist ORT:

> There had taken place, I believe, a very important generational rupture. We didn't see
> ourselves as continuing with that. Rather, we only had to defeat Franco. To defeat
> Francoism... This, in a sense, linked us to the past. But our connection was not prin-
> cipally with the [earlier] forces that had fought against Francoism.[8]

The collective memory of the Civil War therefore played a remote role in the activism of many of the radical groups of the 1960s and 1970s. This was certainly the
case for Juan Aranzadi (b. 1949):

> In my experience as a left-wing activist, the memory of the Civil War and the
> memory of the political parties in the Civil War and the anti-fascist struggle was,
> in reality, a memory, or historiographical knowledge, [but] as an interest, very, very
> little.[9]

Underpinning all of these reasons for the circumscribed appeal of the anti-fascism
of the 1930s was the fact that the Spanish Civil War had resulted in the defeat of

---

Beyond Death and Exile: The Spanish Republicans in France, 1939–1955 (Cambridge, MA, 1979). On
the repression, see Santos Juliá (ed.) *Víctimas de la Guerra Civil* (Madrid, 1999); Paul Preston, *The
Spanish Holocaust: Inquisition and Extermination in Twentieth Century Spain* (New York, 2012); and
Julius Ruiz, *El terror rojo* (Madrid, 2012) and *Franco's Justice: Repression in Madrid after the Spanish
Civil War* (Oxford, 2005).
   [6] On the silences within Spanish society, see also Paloma Aguilar, *Memory and Amnesia: The Role of
the Spanish Civil War in the Transition to Democracy* (Oxford, 2000) and Santos Juliá (ed.) *Memoria de
la guerra y del franquismo* (Madrid, 2006).
   [7] Interview with Manuel Garí Ramos, conducted by NT, Madrid, 4 June 2010.
   [8] Sanroma Aldea interview.
   [9] Interview with Juan Aranzadi Martínez, conducted by NT, Madrid, 21 April 2010.

the Republic by the counter-revolutionary forces under General Franco.[10] As the revolution was defeated, the Civil War was largely irrelevant to radical activists in the 1960s, which is precisely why they did not regard it as their cause.

That said, some radical groups, particularly those of the far left who embraced the 'armed struggle', *were* inspired by the revolutionary tradition of the Civil War. An outstanding example is the Catalan Movimiento Ibérico de Liberación (MIL), or Movement for the Liberation of Iberia, immortalized in the film *Salvador*, which concerns the execution by *garrote vil* of MIL activist Salvador Puig Antich in 1974.[11] The MIL militants saw themselves as direct heirs of the *maquis*, the 'anti-fascist' guerrilla fighters that defied the Franco dictatorship for over twenty years after the Civil War ended.[12] When the MIL was established in 1970, relates Jordi Solé Sugranyes (b. 1951), brother of founder Oriol Solé Sugranyes:

> Seven years previously they had killed the last *maquis*. We considered ourselves *maquis*. We had the arms of Sabaté, of Quico Sabaté, the most famous of the Catalan *maquis*. All these arms that we had at the end were from the *maquis* of the Civil War. The last *maquis* was killed in '63.[13]

Jordi and Oriol met the French activist Jean-Marc Rouillan (b. 1952) in Toulouse in southern France, headquarters of the Spanish exile, and established contact with the anarcho-syndicalist CNT.[14] There they met the legendary figures of the 1930s, but they were also horrified by the lack of young people among the movement's activists and by the perception that the latter 'were thinking that we were their salvation'. Instead, the Solé Sugranyes brothers and Rouillan linked up with former comrades of Sabaté, the celebrated guerrilla leader, and some dissident anarchists, the two '1st May' groups. Later, the MIL galvanized the '1st May' activists, many of whose parents were refugees from the conflict of 1936–9, into carrying out joint operations:

> Two years before we arrived there was a big round up. And almost all of them were scattered, the ones from the two '1st May' groups. So—now with us—they began to organize again. They organized themselves and they participated too in a kidnapping, the kidnapping of Baltasar Suárez, a kidnapping that we carried out of a director from the Banco de Bilbao in Paris. And they participated actively. They became organized again because many of them had been expelled from Belgium, others were in jail.

The MIL's linkage with the Civil War was therefore twofold: the revolutionary example of the anarchists and the continuation of the armed struggle in the shape of the *maquis*.

---

[10] For two recent reappraisals of the Civil War, see Stanley G. Payne, *Civil War in Europe, 1905–1949* (Cambridge, 2011) and Michael Seidman, *The Victorious Counterrevolution: The Nationalist Effort in the Spanish Civil War* (Madison, WI, 2011).

[11] See Antoni Segura and Jordi Solé Sugranyes, *El FONS MIL. Entre el record i la historia* (Barcelona, 2006).

[12] On the *maquis*, see Eduardo Pons Prades, *Guerrillas españolas, 1936–1960* (Barcelona, 1977); Secindino Serrano, *Maquis: historia de la guerrilla antifranquista* (Madrid, 2001); José Antonio and Vidal Sales, *Maquis: la verdad histórica de la 'otra guerra'* (Madrid, 2005).

[13] Interview with Jordi Solé Sugranyes, conducted by NT, Barcelona, 16 May 2010.

[14] On the CNT during the Franco years, see Ángel Herrerín, *La CNT durante el franquismo. Clandestinidad y exilio (1939–1975)* (Madrid, 2004).

As in Spain, the Civil War in Greece (1946–9) was a difficult memory as it brought to mind the 'mistakes' of the Stalinist leadership and the defeat of the communist movement, as well as being a deeply divisive conflict in social and political terms that was, as a result, difficult to justify.[15] Consequently, the dominant memory of the Civil War, for the left, was not one of heroism but of victimization and defeat. The emblematic figure of the Civil War was not the courageous fighter but rather the defeated political prisoner in the Makronisos island camps. When a right-wing coup took place in 1967, the left did not look back to the Civil War to provide inspiration for a new struggle; rather, the event was regarded as the 'second defeat of the left'. Sabbetai Matsas (b. 1947), a Greek of Jewish origin who was a student at the medical school in Athens and became one of the leading figures of the Trotskyite movement in Greece, recalls that the relation between the Civil War defeat and the coup framed his initial reaction in 1967:

> When this thing happens in 1967, the big question for all the people, and especially my generation which was younger, was the following: how come less than twenty years after the previous defeat in '49, a new one comes about in '67?[16]

Activists in the late 1960s took up the fight against the military junta in order to overcome the 'pacifism' of the left. Above all, they did not want to be burdened with the 'defeat syndrome' that had afflicted leftists of their parents' generation. Greek radicals of the 1960s nevertheless had another tradition of anti-fascism that they could draw upon—the memory of the wartime anti-fascist Resistance against the German occupation. Yet even here the surfacing of memory—and its impact on a young generation—was problematic. Knowledge of the left's wartime resistance to the German occupation had in fact been repressed after its defeat in the Civil War: not only were the left-wing resistance organizations, such as the National Liberation Front and the Communist Party, outlawed, but also references to the Resistance were penalized as they were associated with the threat of communism. This was backed up by the harsh repression of the 1950s. As in Spain, faced with this top-down official repression of memory, erstwhile resisters exercised a form of self-censorship as they were fearful of the consequences for themselves and their families. Despite this, some interviewees recalled the importance of a comic-strip magazine, *The Little Hero*, about the adventures of a company of children during the Occupation, in maintaining a positive image of resistance among children. Dimosthenis Dodos (b. 1948) recalls:

---

[15] David Close (ed.) *The Greek Civil War, 1943–1950: Studies of Polarization* (London, 1993); Mark Mazower (ed.) *After the War was Over: Reconstructing the Family, Nation and State in Greece, 1943–1960* (Princeton, 2000); John O. Iatrides and Linda Wrigley (eds) *Greece at the Crossroads: The Civil War and its Legacy* (University Park, PA, 1995); Philip Carabott and Thanasis Sfikas (eds) *The Greek Civil War: Essays on a Conflict of Exceptionalism and Silences* (London, 2004). On memory, see R.V. Boeschoten, T. Vervenioti, E. Voutyra, V. Dalkavoukis and K. Mbada (eds) *Mnimes kai lithi tou ellinikou emfyliou polemou* (Thessaloniki, 2008).

[16] Interview with Sabethai Matsas, conducted by PV, Athens, 26 January 2009. The interviewee is best known in Greece by his pseudonym Savvas Mihail.

What was this popular magazine doing? It gave you a sense that the Resistance, the type of resistance it described anyway, was something good. The Resistance was not bad, which was the official viewpoint. It opened a window and you said, there were these guys and what they did was a good thing.[17]

Greece was different from Spain, despite this common postwar repression of the anti-fascist tradition. From the late 1950s, as we shall see below, a revival of stories of anti-Nazi resistance, promoted by the Communist Party and permitted in an atmosphere of increased political liberalization, provided young radicals with access to stories of heroic wartime struggle that they would later draw upon in their fight against the regime of the Greek colonels after 1967.

THE REVOLUTION BETRAYED

It was not only the association of anti-fascism with distant defeats that made it problematic as a source of inspiration for a new generation of radicals; for those living in countries where anti-fascism had been victorious in the Second World War and had provided the ideological underpinning for the political order—both in the liberal democratic West and the state-socialist East—these earlier mobilizing myths of anti-fascist resistance that had once seemed urgent and meaningful in countries liberated from Nazi rule now appeared degraded, either by their instrumentalization to justify an increasingly stale dictatorship in the communist bloc, or, in countries such as France, by their proponents' use of colonial power to put down movements of national liberation outside Europe.

This critique was particularly important for those who were to become attracted to Maoism or Trotskyism. Many such radicals had been brought up in leftist families, with anti-fascist traditions, and had grown up with stories of wartime resistance or the struggle against 'reaction' on the right. Although many stressed this continuity with the leftism of their parents, the public invocation of anti-fascism seemed increasingly hollow and unable to speak to the concerns of the present. Hungarian activist Tibor Gáti (b. 1945) had been brought up by his mother, who, in the interwar period, had been involved in the Szalmás Piroska People's choir, a legal organization closely associated with the then illegal Communist Party. His uncle, who had been involved in union activity and with the Social Democrats, had also provided a powerful left-wing presence in his family. He states that he was brought up in this left-wing world like 'Candide', to believe that everything around him in the communist system was the best it could possibly be. His first important political memories were from the 1956 Uprising when he was eleven years old: he remembers intense family discussions in which they responded as good and proper communists, understanding the revolt not as a legitimate popular protest but as a fascist counter-revolution, and were glad that the Soviets had come in to put an end to it. He then continues:

---

[17] Interview with Dimosthenis Dodos, conducted by PV, Thessaloniki, 23 February 2008.

'56—from here on I was formed politically, because out of this I became a 'conscious communist'. Everybody had been a 'little drummer' or a 'pioneer' before 1956, and we sang the Internationale, but then I didn't understand what these words really meant. But from 1956 I was among the first to sign up to be a pioneer...I was a pioneer leader by my eighth school year...from September 1957 Russian was introduced as a compulsory language...I loved Russian.[18]

For Gáti—unlike reform socialists who had taken part in the Uprising and saw its suppression as the great betrayal of anti-fascist progressive traditions—the ideological crisis was provoked by the so-called 'bourgeois realities' of 1960s statesocialist Hungary that had departed from its Marxist-Leninist foundations and had become 'stale'. In particular, radical leftists such as Gáti believed that the post-'56 elite were introducing capitalism into the system, and had become obsessed with the provision of consumer goods.[19] Eventually, at university, this criticism led him to form a secret Marxist-Leninist organization in 1966, inspired by both the Chinese Cultural Revolution ('there was no true socialism [here]...we saw China as somewhere with real socialism') and the purer anti-fascist traditions and the revolutionary romance of the interwar Hungarian communist underground. Its cells would eventually be broken up, and some of its members accused of Maoist deviation at a trial in June 1968.

Some of those Italian activists attracted to the new radical leftist politics of the late 1960s saw the same tension as these Hungarians did: on the one hand, they noted that their parents and/or grandparents were anti-fascists, and felt that they were carrying on the tradition. On the other hand, they believed that traditional forms of anti-fascism did not lead to a dynamic active engagement. Maria Paola Fiorensoli (b. 1947), who was involved in student politics at the University of Turin and then in the women's movement in Rome, recollects that:

> One thing that I've always had in my family is both anti-fascism and an interest in politics. There isn't a single person in my family, both my nuclear and my extended family, who isn't completely impassioned by politics, even though they have completely different ideas. This is a legacy that is almost hereditary, that's it.[20]

Anti-fascism could engender both continuity and rupture within the same family. Activists might embrace their parents' anti-fascist values, but be disappointed by their lack of engagement. By taking up activism, such people were endeavouring to return to, or take forwards, the 'real' anti-fascism of the wartime partisan movement. Pietro De Gennaro (b. 1953) and his cousin Massimo Taborri (b. 1953) were both active in the Italian Communist Youth Federation (FGCI) before becoming

[18] Interview with Tibor Gáti, conducted by PA, Budapest, 20 October 2008.
[19] On broader social responses and fears, in the mid-1960s, of the 'individualization' that would result from the market reforms, see Iván T. Berend, *The Hungarian Economic Reforms 1953–1988* (Cambridge, 1990), 149–51.
[20] Interview with Maria Paola Fiorensoli, conducted by RC, Rome, 11 December 2008.

involved with the extra-parliamentary organization Il Manifesto. They recollect in a joint interview that:

PG: We have a rich history from a political point of view, because our grandfather was politically involved in the fascist period. He was a construction worker who in the early years of fascism was... because he opposed the regime, sent into internal exile... for five years, on an island, Ustica, in Sicily—an island that had also seen the presence of Antonio Gramsci... I don't want to go into this too deeply, but his experience guided us in certain ways. It guided me, even if it was a political approach that was only marginal for a twelve- or thirteen-year-old. Thus in '68 first [Massimo] then I joined the Young Communists.

MT: Our parents, while they were communists, weren't particularly involved in political activity, not with the same militant spirit as our grandfather, for example. To be communist had become with time something a bit different, less active (*impegnata*; as in the French *engagé*). They voted for the Communist Party and sometimes they went to the local Party headquarters... and read the newspapers of the Communist Party, but this was it. And so let's say that the *impegno militante* was lost a bit in our family... However, with the grandchildren of our grandfather, that is to say *us*, this activism was taken up again, and it certainly helped that we were from a communist family. But it was rediscovered and reborn when we joined the Young Communists, we didn't do it because we came from a communist family, we did it because we were new to events that were part of this huge explosion of young student protest.[21]

The idea that the Communist Party had lost its revolutionary vanguard role, and had betrayed the anti-fascist struggle, was also important for radicals living under the right-wing dictatorship in Spain. Some recalled that it was the Spanish Communist Party (PCE) that claimed a monopoly on the anti-fascist memory of the Civil War, and that the role of other groups, such as those of the anarcho-syndicalist movement, and the Socialist Party and its trade union, had been largely forgotten or repressed. Yet the Communist Party had appeared to turn its back on the anti-fascist cause of the 1930s by adopting a policy of 'National Reconciliation' in a declaration of 1956 and at the IV Congress of 1960.[22] Many anti-Francoist radicals felt little but contempt for this 'revisionism' and 'opportunism' of the PCE.

Spanish radicals therefore turned elsewhere for inspiration in response to their disillusionment with Soviet and Spanish communism. As Juan Aranzadi, founder of the El Comunista group, out of which many members of the Maoist ORT emerged, insists:

The PCE, throughout my life as an activist, never enjoyed even the most minimal prestige. What's more, I would say to you that even between '67 and '75 the main representative, for me, of what was a conservative organization of order was the PCE. The other was taken for granted: the fascists did not even represent 'order', the fascists

[21] Interview with Pietro De Gennaro and Massimo Taborri, conducted by RC, Rome, 11 December 2008.
[22] See Santos Juliá, *Historias de las dos Españas* (Madrid, 2006); Pablo Lizcano, *La generación del '56: La Universidad contra Franco* (Madrid, 2006); and Muñoz Soro, 'La reconciliación como política', 121–2.

were a band of assassins. The Spanish right are social and human scum in relation to which I don't even give a thought. The conservatives, 'order', are the PCE. The revolution begins to its left.[23]

Some Spanish radicals sought to revive a dynamic anti-fascist tradition from the Spanish Civil War that the Communist Party had abandoned. The Frente Revolucionario Antifascista y Patriota (FRAP), or Revolutionary Antifascist and Patriotic Front, was established in 1973 with a view to violently overthrowing the Franco dictatorship and installing a revolutionary socialist regime. The FRAP explicitly rejected the communist policy of national reconciliation on the grounds that 'reconciliation with a regime that after thirty odd years still practises the same fascist behaviour that gave rise to the war is really absurd'. Moreover, the FRAP could even boast a direct personal continuity with the 1930s insofar as one of its founders and honorary president was Julio Álvarez del Vayo, a minister of foreign affairs during the Civil War. As Álvarez del Vayo declared at a meeting in Rome in 1974, 'despite all the years that have passed, I maintain the same combative spirit that I had during the Spanish war'.[24]

The idea of a betrayal of anti-fascist and revolutionary traditions was also commonly found in France too. The Parti Communiste Français (PCF), emerged from the war as the largest political party, basking in its claim to have sacrificed most in the Resistance as the party of the '75,000 *fusillés*' executed under the German occupation. Briefly in government until the onset of the Cold War in 1947, it reasserted its patriotic credentials by supporting the socialist government's taking of emergency powers to deal with the beginning of Algeria's struggle for independence in 1956.[25] Young men resisting the draft or young people demonstrating against France's war to keep hold of Algeria found no help in the Communist Party. Moreover, both the French and Soviet communist parties seemed to do too little to support the anti-colonialist and anti-imperialist movements developing in Latin America, Africa and Asia, which were being more aggressively championed by the USSR's emerging rival, communist China.

Yves Cohen (b. 1951) was torn between the anti-fascist and communist legacy of his parents and his hostility to the French Communist Party of the 1960s. His parents were solidly communist and had survived the war although his mother had been deported to Auschwitz in 1943, on account of her communism rather than Judaism. He was brought up a young communist but soon revolted against it; sent to a communist summer camp in East Germany, he was horrified by the poverty he discovered. He did not want to follow his older brother, who espoused orthodox communism. He was inspired by the Chinese Cultural Revolution as the revolution proper, and later joined the Maoist Gauche Prolétarienne (GP), or Proletarian Left. Out of respect for his parents, however, he tried in his activism to separate the

[23] Aranzadi Martínez interview.
[24] Muñoz Soro, 'La reconciliación como política', 132. See also the interviews with Julio Álvarez del Vayo in Miguel Herberg, *La guerra de España y la resistencia española (Entrevistas con Julio Álvarez del Vayo, 1974)* (Madrid, 2009).
[25] See Daniele Joly, *The French Communist Party and the Algerian War* (Basingstoke, 1991).

positive story of communist wartime resistance from the negative one of postwar Stalinism:

> I hated the Communist Party, whereas I was immediately enthusiastic, when I started to find out about it, about the Chinese [Cultural] Revolution. To return to the question of not breaking away from my parents, I am sure that it was because they were resisters and my mother had been deported... On the one hand there was a rejection of something parental, an adolescent revolt against my parents, but there was also... a constant homage rendered to my parents who had been resisters. That was crucial in the line we followed in the GP, where we played resisters against collaborators, inventing the same enemies in our imaginary space.[26]

'ANTI-FASCISM LIVES!'

Although anti-fascism was in some ways a 'wounded ideology' that failed to motivate activists, it did enjoy a renaissance among certain radicals in the 1960s. On the one hand, this was the product of what radicals perceived to be the 'revitalisation of fascism' in the strengthening of right-wing authoritarianism in southern Europe: alongside Franco's Spain and Salazar's Portugal, a 'fascist contagion' engulfed Greece with the Colonels' Dictatorship (1967–74) and appeared to threaten Italy too. On the other hand, in western Europe, it was also a product of the way in which a new generation understood their 'superficially' democratic systems, which were regarded as being tainted by the unresolved legacies of the fascist era. Comparisons between the violence of French forces in Algeria in the late 1950s and the methods of the Gestapo in the Second World War, between the 'unlearnt lessons of the Holocaust' and the bombing of Vietnam, along with the entry of neo-fascists into government in Italy in 1960 and the re-emergence in the early 1970s of the issue of French collaboration with the Germans, highlighted for young radicals the connections between the fascist past and the supposedly democratic present.[27] In order to fight the 'revival of fascism' in the south of Europe and the perceived legacies of fascism in the West, radicals often sought to forge new forms of anti-fascist struggle by looking to heroic figures of resistance or by reinvigorating the anti-fascist traditions of their families. Yet these new forms

---

[26] Interview with Yves Cohen, conducted by RG, 9 May 2008.

[27] The ways in which this discourse on fascism emerged has been most extensively studied for western Germany, see Hans Kundnani, *Utopia or Auschwitz: Germany's 1968 Generation and the Holocaust* (London, 2009); Wilfried Mausbach, 'America's Vietnam in Germany—Germany in America's Vietnam: On the relocation of spaces and the appropriation of history', in Belinda Davis, Wilfried Mausbach, Martin Klimke and Carla MacDougall (eds) *Changing the World, Changing Oneself: Political Protest and Collective Identities in West Germany and the US in the 1960s and 1970s* (New York, 2010), 41–64; Holger Nehring, 'Generation, modernity and the making of contemporary history: Responses in West European Protest Movements around "1968"', in Anna von der Goltz (ed.) '*Talkin' 'Bout my generation': Conflicts of Generation Building and Europe's '1968'* (Göttingen, 2011), 79–80; on France, see Henri Rousso, *The Vichy Syndrome: History and Memory in France since 1944* (Cambridge, MA, 1991).

of anti-fascism were also moulded by the contemporary politics of anti-imperialism: fascism could now be understood as the product of a global system, spearheaded by the Americans, who sought to prevent political instability or to repress the left through the installation of authoritarian right-wing regimes, and used barbarous techniques— as Vietnam made plain—which echoed the Nazi barbarity of the 1940s.

In Greece, at the time of the right-wing coup in 1967, radicals remember interpreting their activism through the anti-fascist tradition, viewing their struggle against the Colonels' Dictatorship as the continuation of the Resistance of the Second World War, as embodied in the heroic image of guerrilla fighters such as Aris Velouchiotis (1905–45). To explain this, one needs to return to the decision of the communists to embrace the memory of the Resistance in the late 1950s, together with the liberalization of politics in the first half of the 1960s that permitted the recognition and celebration of the opposition to the Nazi invasion for the first time since the war. The left had a vested interest in highlighting the fight against German occupation, and in converting it into a leading narrative of national history, as the communists had led the anti-Nazi struggle, while the right not only played a minor role in the Resistance but also many of its supporters were alleged to have been collaborators of the Germans. It was therefore only in the 1960s that many students 'discovered' the anti-fascist past of their parents. The Occupation and the Resistance became part of public discussion as novels and memoirs about the Resistance excited the imagination of young people.[28] The myth of the Resistance thereby became a part of these activists' political imagination and bred a corresponding hostility towards the post-Civil War regime that had persecuted rather than honoured those who had fought the Nazis.[29]

Once the military junta came to power in 1967, radical activists therefore had access to a set of imagined histories that immediately allowed them to draw parallels between the Resistance of the 1940s and the new struggle against the US-backed dictatorship. In both cases, an authoritarian regime had been imposed through the intervention of a foreign nation: the Germans in the 1940s and the Americans in the 1960s. In consequence, the struggle against the junta was, as in the 1940s, one for the liberation of the country. The myth of the Resistance thereby lent legitimacy to the anti-dictatorial opposition by reviving the relative inclusivity and moral fervour of the cause that had vanquished the Nazis. The German occupation and the military junta were regarded as episodes in the same national narrative: the fight of 'the people' for freedom and democracy against the self-

---

[28] Books that were published between the Liberation in 1944 and the outbreak of the Civil War two years later, and which then became out of print, were republished in the 1950s and 1960s. Some of the most popular Resistance memoirs and accounts in the 1960s were Sotoris Patatzis, *Matomena Chronia* (Athens, 1946); Stefanos Sarafis, *O ELAS* (Athens, 1946); Gerasimos Avgeropoulos, *To Chroniko tou Agona, St'Armata, St'Armata. Istoria tis Ethnikis Antistasis* (Athens, 1950); and Nikiforos Dimitriou, *Andartis sta youna ris Roumelis Chroniko 1940–1944* (Athens, 1965).

[29] Nonetheless while the Resistance was present in the discourse of the left in the 1960s, it was less so in the activists' narratives forty years on. Interviewees emphasized their parents' participation in the Resistance or the Civil War as a way to construct an intergenerational continuity rather than to explain how they were involved in radical politics.

serving interests of the ruling classes and their foreign backers. This patriotic framing was reflected in the name of major opposition groups such as the Patriotiko Antidiktatoriko Metopo (PAM) or Patriotic Anti-dictatorial Front, and Panellinio Apeleftherotiko Kinima (PAK) or Panhellenic Liberation Movement.

The fusion of the patriotic and anti-fascist causes led young activists in the 1960s to see themselves as heirs of the 1940s tradition. When the news of the dictatorship's establishment reached Anna Filini (b. 1945), who was studying architecture in Italy and in 1969 was among the founders of the EKKE (Epanastatiko Kommounistiko Kinima Elladas—Revolutionary Communist Movement of Greece), one of the leading far-left organizations of the early 1970s, her life changed:

> When the coup happened it was…a shock to many people. We freaked. I mean this thing was totally overwhelming; it took me by surprise, and I realized that none of all the things I did before really mattered…Studies, academic work, nothing. We had to go back [to Greece]. Gradually after a couple of months this idea took shape…We were ready to take to the mountains. With guns and the rest, say, to make the new EAM! Or rather, the new ELAS.[30]

The ELAS (Greek People's Liberation Army) was the military wing of the EAM (National Liberation Front). The ELAS was very popular with students in the 1960s and one of its outstanding guerrilla leaders, Aris Velouchiotis, became a 'cult' figure for them. His life and death—he refused to disarm after liberation in 1945 and committed suicide rather than surrender to the monarchist paramilitary group that chased him—'led to his canonization by [Communist] Party dissidents as a figure of uncompromising and relentless struggle'.[31] Not surprisingly, one of the 'armed resistance' groups to the Colonels was dubbed 'Aris'.

The fight against the military junta of 1967–74 was therefore viewed by radical activists as a continuation of that against 'fascism'. Just as the Nazis and collaborators were denounced in the 1940s as 'fascists' and the governments that followed as 'monarchofascist', so the Colonels' regime was vilified as 'fascist'. Anti-fascism thereby created a sense of continuity with the past, a long-standing confrontation between 'the people' and their 'fascist oppressors'. Nikos Tsiokos (b. 1944) came from a leftist family. His father was involved in the Resistance and his family was thus persecuted in the Civil War and fled to Athens. Tsiokos got involved in politics at a very young age; in 1955 he was in contact with cells of the youth of the illegal Communist Party and in 1957 he joined the Youth of the EDA. When he was arrested on 2 July 1967, the continuity with his family history was immediately drawn:

> They took me to the police station in Egaleo. I went down the stairs and the moment I was going down, my late mother showed up, saying 'Nikos, what happened? What shall we do?'. I said, 'The police came, they want something …'. And she said, 'Just

[30] Interview with Anna Filini, conducted by PV, Athens, 29 February 2008.
[31] Kostis Kornetis, 'Student resistance to the Greek military dictatorship: Subjectivity, memory and cultural politics', PhD thesis, European University Institute, Florence (2006), 117.

like then, with the Germans, eh?'. And I said to her, 'Just like then, with the
Germans'.[32]

As in Greece, many activists in eastern and western Europe regarded the Colonels'
regime as a revival of reactionary authoritarinism that represented a threat to democracy across Europe. They believed that, as in Spain and Portugal, Greece had
fallen into the grip of fascism. If the peoples of Europe did not react promptly,
fascism would spread throughout the continent. From this perspective, anti-fascism created a basis for solidarity and internationalism across Europe. At the same
time it created a new idea about Europe: Europe was identified with democracy
and therefore its mission was to defend democracy. Damianos Vasileiadis (b. 1937)
was in Munich and, as a member of the PAK, sought to raise awareness among the
German students in relation to the threat that the dictatorship represented. He
underlines that:

> We showed that the Greek people passively and non-passively, with open resistance if
> they could, had not settled for the junta, that if that regime spread to other European
> countries, like Italy... because other countries, like Spain and Portugal had a junta... If
> democratic Europe didn't react, then there was a danger that the fascist cancer would
> spread to other European countries.[33]

Activists from other countries recalled the power of the Greek Colonels' regime to
reinforce their leftist radicalism. In Hungary, the notion that fascism was on the
rise again, and that the anti-fascist struggle of the Greeks needed to be supported,
became a part of both official socialist and less official, radical cultures. For some
activists, the military junta was regarded as proof that bourgeois democracy was
a hollow façade that merely camouflaged elite, anti-democratic interests, and as a
result it was always vulnerable to dictatorial tendencies. Hence the socialist version of democracy had to be maintained at home. János Atkári (b. 1946), one of
the leaders of the Communist Youth reform movement at Eötvös Loránd University in Budapest, and later, after 1989, deputy mayor of Budapest, attended a
Cambridge summer school in 1969. There he argued that the collapse of bourgeois democracy in Greece was a much graver development than the Soviet invasion of Czechoslovakia:

> I went with the same old prejudices, [the British students] immediately asked me
> about Czechoslovakia, I however asked about Greece—that was the time of the Greek
> putsch... [I argued] that bourgeois democracy could not defend itself against its own
> destruction. I judged bourgeois democracy very poorly... I was a rather empty, pre-
> tentious activist. I knew what to say in the right company. It doesn't sound very nice
> today.[34]

The Greek case was also used by radicals who were critical of official communism
and sought out more 'authentic' anti-fascist progressive movements distinct from

---

[32] Interview with Nikos Tsiokos, conducted by PV, Athens, 24 June 2009.
[33] Interview with Damianos Vasileiadis, conducted by PV, Athens, 22 December 2007.
[34] Interview with János Atkári, conducted by JM, 12 November 2008.

those propagated by the state. Greek radical culture thus played an important role in these milieux in the late 1960s: the Hungarian Communist Youth promoted radical folk resistance music, especially the songs of Theodorakis.[35] Dissident groups such as Gáti and Pór's underground organization mentioned above formed connections with Greek radicals who had been exiled to Hungary during both the period of both the Civil War and 1967 dictatorship.[36] The radical Maoist-influenced Orfeo cultural collective built the culture of Greek protest into their own leftist radicalism directed at the stale anti-fascism of the communist state. One of its members-to-be designed protest posters against the dictatorship in 1967 during his student days at the Academy of Fine Arts.[37] After the foundation of Orfeo in 1969, the culture of anti-fascist resistance in southern Europe nurtured its art. In oral history interviews, these struggles were presented as authentic fights that were distinct from the compromised domestic traditions: the stories and songs of the Spanish Civil War and resistance against both Franco and the Greek military dictatorship were exploited to provoke audiences into thinking about genuine ideological commitment, revolutionary radicalism, and the appropriateness of violence against a bureaucratic, undynamic socialist system in need of reform.[38] István Nemes (b. 1953), singer in Orfeo's folk group, explains the range of political influences on their choice of songs:

> The other source, that we worked from, was the Italian musician Sergio Liberovici, who had collected loads of songs from the underground in Franco's Spain. Songs of resistance. And we sang those, along with those from Chile from the group Quilapayún, and other Latin American songs, and a few Greek ones too, of resistance to the extreme military junta.[39]

For leftist radicals in this period, it was not only the strengthening of right-wing authoritarianism in southern Europe that inspired a new anti-fascism: it was also the fear that aspects of fascism were returning to—or had never properly been purged from—postwar liberal democracies. For Italian leftists, the fascism of the 1940s appeared to be very much alive in the postwar period: the Republic was democratic but vestiges of fascism remained in the institutions and laws of the state; the fascist party was banned and yet the neo-fascist MSI (Italian Social Movement) existed on the political fringes; the Italian Communist Party emerged from the war rejuvenated in terms of its mass following, and yet it was banned from government. The 'Tambroni affair' of 1960—when Prime Minister Tambroni had

---

[35] See for example the magazine, *Ifjúkommunista* [Communist Youth], 1967/10.
[36] The Greek exile community in Hungary numbered 4800 in 1975; Eleni-Nelly Psarrou, 'The Greek diaspora in eastern Europe and the Former Soviet Union', in J. Blaschke (ed.) *Immigration and Political Intervention, Vol II. Diasporas in Transition Countries* (Berlin, 2004).
[37] Interview with Mihály Kiss, conducted by JM, Budapest, 29 January 2009.
[38] The radical Maoist-influenced cultural collective Orfeo also performed the play *Étoile* based on Semprun's novel *At the end of the War*: it reinterpreted debates over resistance to Franco's dictatorship to address the Paris student revolt and questions of political action under the Hungarian socialist state in the early 1970s. Interview with Tamás Fodor, published in István Nánay, 'Az Orfeo-ügy. Fodor Tamás és Malgot István visszaemlékezésével', *Beszélő*, 1998/3.
[39] Interview with István Nemes, conducted by JM, Budapest, 24 January 2009.

to turn to the neo-fascist party for votes in order to secure a parliamentary majority, provoking riots in several cities—scared the left with the spectre of fascist re-
cidivism, and encouraged a rebirth of vigilant anti-fascism. Maurizio Lampronti
(b. 1950) was an activist as a secondary-school student and then at university, in
the extra-parliamentary left organization Lotta Continua. He insists that:

> The fascists were fascists then as they are now, in the sense that they were inspired by
> Mussolini's regime, and often by the Social Republic [the RSI, the puppet government
> set up in Salò after 1943]. We ended up fighting both with the police and the fascists.
> In addition, but this is a bit later, in 1968 and perhaps a bit in 1969 as well, there were
> fascists in the universities and we didn't stop them from speaking in the assemblies.
> But then there was a political rupture, in the sense that, at a certain point it was de-
> cided that we wouldn't let them speak any more, and to stop them from speaking we
> would either throw them out or beat them up.[40]

The fascist threat to Italy's relatively fragile democracy became a very immediate
one during the period of the 'strategy of tension' from 1969 into the 1970s. Neo-
fascist groups, with assistance from the American secret services (Operation
Galdio), tried to provoke so much public and political terror of the left that a right-
wing coup would come about. Gualtiero Bertelli (b. 1944), a well-known com-
poser of protest songs in the 1960s who became involved in the iconic workers'
protests in Porto Marghera in the summer of 1968, describes the meaning of anti-
fascism during this crucial period in Italy's recent history:

> In that period we were strongly anti-fascist; some people say today 'it was useless', but
> it isn't true…There was the Cold War, and Italy was a frontier country, where the
> American secret service was active, and the Russians too, probably. So…so it was a
> truly unstable country, in which every democratic victory had to be won with a strug-
> gle, even things like [the right to] divorce, right? Fundamental rights, they were bat-
> tles, they were real, proper battles. Equal salaries for men and women, the right to
> study, all these things were struggles…To be anti-fascist then meant guarding against
> the return [of fascism], as there had been attempts at a coup in Italy. We weren't
> against the return of the fascist party, but rather against fascist infiltration into the
> state…Anti-fascism meant that we were guarding against backsliding, not only con-
> cerning the neo-fascist party but really against this continual, powerful infiltration by
> the right and the secret services.[41]

Anti-fascism was incredibly important for Italian radicals—perhaps more so than
in nearly all other European countries. In the 1960s and 1970s they regularly
fought the neo-fascist youth, who were led in many instances by 'old guard' fascists
from the war, such as Giorgio Almirante (who for some time headed the neo-fascist
MSI). All the major extreme-left organizations, such as Lotta Continua or Potere
Operaio, created a *servizio d'ordine* (a group of stewards) to deal with attacks from
neo-fascist youth (the stewards would head marches, for example, to protect
marchers and head off fascist attacks).

---

[40] Interview with Maurizio Lampronti, conducted by RC, Florence, 17 April 2008.
[41] Interview with Gualtiero Bertelli, conducted by RC, Mira, 19 March 2009.

In France too, a revival of anti-fascism was fundamental to the student and new left protests of the 1960s. Extreme-right groups that had been influential in the struggle to keep Algeria French sprang up again around 1968, not least in order to attack leftists campaigning for a victory of the communists in Vietnam. Jean Bijaoui (b. 1946), an economics student of Tunisian Jewish origin at the Paris Law Faculty, describes how the pro-Vietcong leftists attacked a pro-American exhibition organized by the extreme right in Paris's rue de Rennes in April 1968. He is critical too of the French Communist Party for failing to undertake this sort of campaign:

> We attacked on a Sunday morning, in a quasi-military fashion, to smash everything up. The fascists, who were beaten, were mad with rage... That kind of action had been completely forgotten by the left and had become the preserve of the fascists. Smashing things up, fighting took place in the '30s, but not after that. The PCF never did things like that except against the *gauchistes* to keep their own house in order, which they knew how to do... The fascists said that they would get their revenge and that the Bolsheviks had better leave the Latin Quarter. Fascist groups started to attack students randomly, seeing them as Bolsheviks, or assaulted known individuals from the left.[42]

French *gauchistes* were initially handicapped in their desire to resurrect anti-fascist rhetoric and the legends of French resistance to German occupation because De Gaulle, the acknowledged leader of the French wartime Resistance, was still in power. This changed in 1969 when he resigned and was replaced as president by Georges Pompidou. Pompidou not only had no resistance credentials but he pardoned a notorious leader of the collaborationist Militia, Paul Touvier, while clamping down heavily on leftist agitators. At the same time Ophuls' film *Le Chagrin et la Pitié*, which showed how widespread collaboration had been in France, was banned from French television. This made it possible not only for *gauchistes* to lay claim to the Resistance myth but for some heroes of the wartime Resistance to embrace the *gauchistes*. Jean-Pierre Le Dantec (b. 1943), who was editor of the Gauche Prolétarienne's *La Cause du Peuple*, was sent to prison in 1970 for inciting violence. On his release he was praised by Resistance hero Maurice Clavel, the so-called 'liberator of Chartres cathedral'. They both perceived the anti-fascist project of postwar France to be incomplete as the shadow of Nazi collaboration still hung over the country. The cult of the Resistance thus became a weapon with which to beat the regime. Le Dantec recalls that Clavel:

> Had an almost religious image of us. He thought that we were the bearers of ideals of altruism and generosity which for him were the ideals of the Resistance. That echoed our idea that at the time we were undertaking a new Resistance, because the process of resistance had never been completed in France... They were men of action, who did not like Pompidou. For them Pompidou had never been a Gaullist. He had never undertaken a single act of resistance during the war.... The great scandal for Maurice Clavel was when Pompidou said that the quarrels of the Resistance and Occupation were finished and should not be talked about any more... and

---

[42] Interview with Jean Bijaoui, conducted by RG, Paris, 12 April 2008.

that the state would not do anything about the Militia chief Touvier, who has since
been tried, because people had to forget that episode.

From the above we can see how a new form of 'authentic' anti-fascism was revived
in the 1960s in western democracies, the communist bloc and in Greece, whether
to protect Europe from the spread of right-wing authoritarianism in the south of
the continent, to criticize the absence of an authentic progressive politics in socialist states, or to warn against the remnants of fascism that were still held to exist
within western European liberal democracies.

THE DISCOVERY OF ANTI-IMPERIALISM

While anti-fascist traditions in certain countries still retained some ideological
power for a postwar generation of radicals who had not themselves directly experienced the struggle against fascism, these were increasingly displaced, or at the very
least complemented by, a new set of seemingly victorious revolutionary struggles
against contemporary imperialism in Egypt, Cyprus, Cuba and Algeria in the
1950s, or Vietnam and Latin America in the 1960s.[43] In some cases, anti-fascism
could be combined with the anti-imperialist politics of the 1960s: thus Second
World War resistance fighters were now placed alongside the anti-imperialist fighters of the decolonizing world in Africa, Asia and Latin America. For instance, the
martyred Greek wartime partisan fighter Aris Velouchiotis became a 1960s icon
alongside Che Guevara and Ho Chi Minh in clandestine magazines under the
Colonels' regime. In other cases, the anti-colonial fighters of the less-developed
world became much more vital exemplars for a generation for whom the struggles
of decolonization, the imperialism of both the Americans and the Soviets, and the
perceived bureaucratic obsolescence of the European communist parties were
major factors in their political socialization. This new form of anti-imperial or
'Third Worldist' politics became important for activists across Europe, whether in

---

[43] The most developed literature on anti-imperialism and Third Worldism concerns France: Christoph
Kalter, *Die Entdeckung der Dritten Welt* (Frankfurt am Main, 2011); Kristin Ross, *May '68 and its
Afterlives* (Chicago and London, 2002), especially 80–99; Robert Frank, 'Imaginaire politique et fig-
ures symboliques internationales: Castro, Hô, Mao et le "Che"' and Geneviève Dreyfus-Armand and
Jacques Portes, 'Les interactions internationales de la guerre du Viêtnam et Mai 68', in Geneviève
Dreyfus-Armand et al. (eds) *Les Années 68. Le temps de la contestation* (Paris, 2000, 2008), 31–68;
Julien Hage, 'Sur les chemins du tiers monde en lutte: Partisans, Révolution, Tricontinental', in
Philippe Artières and Michelle Zancarini-Fournel (eds) *68. Une Histoire collective, 1962–1981* (Paris,
2008), 86–93. On West Germany see Quinn Slobodian, *Foreign Front: Third World Politics in Sixties
West Germany* (Durham, NC and London, 2012); Ingo Juchler, *Die Studentenbewegungen in den
Vereinigten Staaten und der Bundesrepublik Deutschland der sechziger Jahre. Eine Untersuchung hinsichtlich ihrer Beeinflussung durch Befreiungsbewegungen und theorien aus der Dritten Welt* (Berlin, 1996);
for the communist bloc, see David Engerman, 'The Second World's Third World', *Kritika* 12/1
(2011), 183–211; Young-Sun Hong, 'The benefits of health must spread among all: International solidarity, health, and race in the East German encounter with the Third World', in Katherine Pence and
Paul Betts (eds) *Socialist Modern: East German Everyday Culture and Politics* (Ann Arbor, 2008), 183–210;
for Greece, see Ioannis Stefanidis, *Stirring the Greek Nation: Political Culture, Irredentism and Anti-
Americanism in Post-war Greece, 1945–1967* (Aldershot, 2007).

liberal democratic western Europe, the communist East or the right-wing dictatorships of the South. Yet—as oral testimony demonstrates—radicals' common anti-imperialism was discovered through different causes in different countries, and 'brought home' to inspire their domestic struggles in diverse ways.

The moment of discovery of anti-imperialist politics was an important feature of many activists' biographies across Europe. For both Greek and Spanish radicals who would come to the forefront of the struggle against the southern European dictatorships in the 1960s, the sense of being the victims of the western imperialism of the Cold War was vital in their socialization. In Spain, it was the support of the western powers for Franco's dictatorship as a result of its anti-communist credentials—a backing made clear and powerful by Franco's new Concordat with the Vatican in August 1953 and then, much more importantly, by the Pact of Madrid with the US one month later—that led them to give up on their remaining hopes that the dictatorship might be brought down with outside help.[44] Anti-imperialism in Spain began as a critique of the backing of the Franco dictatorship by the US.[45] Francisca Suquillo (b. 1943), a student activist in the early 1960s and later a founder member of the Maoist ORT, recalls that: 'I believe that everything negative about the United States was related to the support which it gave Spain...We understood that the problems of Spain came from the support which it gave to the United States'.[46]

Still, this anti-Americanism was soon placed by left-wing activists within a much broader context. For instance, the Popular Liberation Front (FLP) was created in 1956, its name partly reflecting the ideological diversity of the organization, but above all it was inspired by the liberation fronts that, in the words of founder member José Ramón Recalde, had been formed 'to fight against the colonial powers'.[47] The FLP activists viewed their struggle against the US-backed Franco regime as part of a series of fronts challenging imperialism across the world.

The struggles of the Greek left were increasingly understood in a broader anti-imperial context too. Although many activists were too young to have been directly politically socialized by the role that the British, and then the American, 'imperialists' played in defeating the left in the Greek Civil War of the 1940s, foreign intervention in support of the right nevertheless nurtured a culture of anti-imperialism on the left that would later come alive for the postwar generation of radicals over the Cyprus question. In 1955, the armed struggle for the liberation of Cyprus from British control was unleashed and a series of rallies and demonstrations were held throughout Greece in solidarity. For the right, the

---

[44] See Charles Powell, *El amigo americano. España y Estados Unidos: de la dictadura a la democracia* (Barcelona, 2011) and his briefer analysis, 'The United States and Spain: From Franco to Juan Carlos', in Townson (ed.) *Spain Transformed*, 227–47.

[45] This was despite the fact that Spain had been condemned as a 'fascist' regime in 1946 by the United Nations. On the disillusionment of the anti-Francoist opposition and its early anti-Americanism, see A. Seregni, *El antiamericanismo español* (Madrid, 2007), 177–8 and 186.

[46] Interview with Francisca Suquillo Pérez, conducted by NT, Madrid, 1 September 2009.

[47] Prologue to García Alcalá, *Historia del Felipe*, 16.

Cypriot struggle was that of the Greek people against British rule and symbolized the last stage of Greek irredentism. For the left, the fight of the Cypriots for
national independence from Britain was comparable to anti-colonial conflicts in
other parts of the world, such as that between Britain and Egypt over the Suez
Canal in 1956. The (still illegal) Greek Communist Party reacted to the Suez
Crisis by declaring that 'the dark conspiracy against Egypt provoked the indignation of the Greek people who demand: the invaders out of Egypt', and connected
the struggle of the Egyptians with that of the Cypriots for self-determination.[48]
Yet for the left it was also a way of undermining the right's claims to represent
the Greek nation, as they accused the right-wing government of Konstanti-
nos Karamanlis of being insufficiently supportive of the Cypriots' right to self-
determination (due to its desire to maintain good relations with Britain). Between
1955 and 1956 a multitude of rallies and meetings were held, some of which
ended in violence, as in the demonstration of 9 May 1956 in Athens, when three
civilians and a policeman were killed. This nationwide campaign was not organized by political parties but by student unions and professional associations.
Among these students was Elias Katsoulis (b. 1936), who would later become
general secretary of the Greek Students and Scientists Union of West Germany.
He came from a liberal family and his political awakening occurred during the
campaign on behalf of Cyprus. His brother was a teacher on the island and
member of the main nationalist Cypriot organization. He admits that when he
was a student:

> there were some weird situations then, ultra nation-centered, and all of us, eighteen–
> nineteen-year-old guys, we were nationalists. We believed what we were told about the
> particularity of the Greek civilization, that we taught the rest of the world.[49]

Now critical of his encounters with nationalism in the 1950s, he remembers that:

> I spent the whole day, from the morning till night, in the streets. For Cyprus only.
> From 1955–6 what moved us and made us take to the streets was the question of
> Grivas, of Cyprus, of Makarios, of the Union [between Greece and Cyprus] ... All
> these created a nation-centered consciousness, right?[50]

Nationalism, as Katsoulis points out, was a driving force behind anti-imperialism
in the 1950s. In the anti-communist climate of the time, it was the only legitimate
framework within which to express social and political discontent. Despoina
Maroulakou (b. 1939) was a law student at the University of Athens who came
from a leftist family that had experienced state repression during the Civil War. As
she explains, the Cyprus question was a way for the left to come out because 'it is
a national question, and it is not easy to slander you and put you in jail'. The demonstrations for Cyprus became a showcase for the opposition to the right-wing

[48] 'On the side of the Egyptian people who fight for independence', 31 October 1956, *Communist
Party of Greece, Official Texts, 1956–1961* (Athens, 1997), 111–12.
[49] Interview with Elias Katsoulis, conducted by PV, Athens, 18 January 2008.
[50] Katsoulis interview.

government and a breeding ground for the radicalism of the 1960s. Like many other Greek activists, she emphasizes the 'spontaneity' of those demonstrations. At the same time, she downplays the importance of nationalism, as it did not have a major impact on her personal story (she moved to Paris in 1965 and became involved in radical left circles there):

> I believe that it was something spontaneous. It is not that we weren't interested in Cyprus, we were interested. But we didn't know exactly what was going on down there. I think that young people took to the streets because it was one of the few things that they allowed us to do. It was like...a way to blow off steam.[51]

Within the communist bloc, by contrast, identification with anti-colonial liberation movements was not necessarily a feature of anti-establishment radicalism. Even where it later led to subversive activism, oral histories reveal how anti-imperialism was more commonly discovered as part of the official state sponsorship of 'Third World' liberation. Warsaw Pact countries in eastern Europe followed the lead of the Soviet Union, which, by the late 1950s, was questioning both the dominant late Stalinist idea that there was only one pattern for the development of socialism that had to be followed by all countries, and its earlier, racially inflected thinking that indicated that development might not be available to Africa or Asia. Instead, Soviet elites increasingly presented the peoples of the Third World as capable of carrying out their own revolutions, and, as imperialism was broadly associated with capitalism, hoped that elites in newly independent countries would naturally be attracted to socialism to ensure their rapid development.[52] Within socialist Hungary, for instance, solidarity with the global anti-imperial struggle was propagated through the organs of the Communist Youth League (KISZ) and, from the early 1960s, was employed in an attempt to mobilize the enthusiasm of a younger generation that had not experienced Nazism and hence might not find accounts of the wartime anti-fascist struggle sufficiently inspiring. László Trencsényi (b. 1947), who was to become an important figure in the KISZ reform movement, recalls the absence of inspiring domestic role models and the contrasting appeal of the officially sponsored solidarity movements with the Cuban Revolution organized at school:

> The Cuban crisis...there was this time when the classroom door suddenly opened, and the class above us came in through the door...and they said that we would go on a protest: 'Stop the clocks! There's going to be a protest against the blockade of Cuba'. And all of us young ones streamed out. At last there was some kind of revolutionary situation, there was something happening to us. Yes, I had been an upstanding pioneer in December 1957, defending the honour of my red necktie, but now, at last, here was the revolution! And from our language lesson we pushed and shoved our way out into the hallway, where we had to condemn American imperialism, which we did happily, clapping with abandon, 'Out of Cuba, Yankees no!' as we went.[53]

---

[51] Interview with Despoina Maroulakou, conducted by PV, Athens, 6 December 2008.
[52] Odd Arne Westad, *The Global Cold War: Third World Interventions and the Making of our Times* (Cambridge, 2005), 166–7.
[53] Interview with László Trencsényi, conducted by PA, Budapest, 15 January 2009.

THE APPEAL OF THIRD WORLDISM

By the early 1960s in Europe, under liberal democratic, communist and right-wing authoritarian regimes, the figure of a new freedom fighter—from Algeria, Egypt or Cuba—was beginning to exert a powerful hold over the revolutionary imagination of activists. This was to develop further in the 1960s as a new form of leftist politics emerged that was not tied to the politics of communist parties and that allowed radicals to transcend the binaries of the Cold War, and what they perceived as imperialism on both sides.

In countries with strong communist parties, which were often viewed by radicals as insufficiently committed to radical social change or revolutionary ambition, a new identification with Third Worldist movements provided the inspiration for novel forms of politics outside of traditional party structures.[54] In France, the trajectories of some interviewees illustrates this shift: in 1961, Jean-Paul Dollé (1939–2011), joined the UEC within which there was opposition to what was perceived as a 'Stalinist' leadership unsympathetic to Third World struggles. After Algeria, Dollé recalls, 'There was Cuba. We were mad about Cuba. There was everything happening in the Third World... In 1962, 1963, people started to say "Third Worldist", there was Frantz Fanon, all that'.[55]

Within the UEC, Dollé joined a small group of 'pro-Chinese' who delighted in the Chinese Communist Party's support for Third World struggles for national liberation which the USSR had seemingly sacrificed to its own policy of 'peaceful coexistence' with the West. In 1964, Dollé was expelled from the UEC, and was among the founders of the first Maoist network in France.

Solidarity with the Third World increased dramatically in France during the Vietnam War. Maoists and Trotskyists who opposed the war and had been expelled from the Communist Party established the National Vietnam Committees (CVNs) and Vietnam Base Committees (CVBs) located in neighbourhoods and university faculties. These new organizations were dedicated initially to meetings and demonstrations, then to street-fighting against the extreme-right groups who supported the Americans and 'their stooges' in Vietnam. Economics student Jean Bijaoui (b. 1946), who was active in the CVB of the 14th *arrondissement*, recollects that: 'For us the Vietnam War was the popular war par excellence, full of lessons for activists. Not for throwing bombs or hiding in the forest but on questions of propaganda, building bridges to the people, the mass line'.[56]

Third Worldism as an expression of dissatisfaction with domestic policies and the lack of a genuine solidarity with oppressed peoples of the decolonizing world was even a feature of radical politics within the communist bloc where anti-colonial solidarity was part of official state ideology. In May 1966, for instance, the official

[54] See Robert Gildea, James Mark and Niek Pas, 'European radicals and the "Third World". Imagined solidarities and radical networks 1958–73', *Cultural and Social History* 8/4 (2011), 449–71.

[55] Interview with Jean-Paul Dollé, conducted by RG, Paris, 15 May 2007.

[56] Interview with Jean Bijaoui, conducted by RG, Paris, 10 April 2008.

Hungarian Communist Youth League established *Vádoljuk az imperializmust!* (Let's indict imperialism!), a movement devoted to organizing anti-colonial solidarity meetings, exhibitions[57] and 'pol-beat' events that often focussed on the plight of the Vietnamese people.[58] The socialist state held annual 'Solidarity weeks' to collect funds for Vietnam.[59] In Hungary, as in France, it was those attracted to the Chinese Cultural Revolution who established alternative Third Worldist solidarity movements. According to Gábor Révai (b. 1947), socialist regimes appeared to have abandoned their revolutionary instincts of the postwar years and settled into a more materialist and less dynamic form of socialism, and were thus incapable of expressing real solidarity. Semi-official Vietnam Solidarity Committees were formed in 1965 at the Eötvös Loránd University and the University of Economics in Budapest. These demonstrated against not only western imperialism in Asia, but also the insufficient Soviet and Hungarian support provided to the North Vietnamese:[60]

> We became politicized within KISZ, it was '67, Vietnam, they [i.e. the socialist bloc] were critical of America… [but] in our opinion, it was the socialist countries that also needed to be sharply criticized… Their [i.e. official] solidarity was just a formal thing, it wasn't enough, so we tried to organize some solidarity movement, very similar to that in Berlin… we wanted to do something… everybody was just standing by, we organized Vietnamese Sundays (*vietnámi vasárnapok*), tons of university students came out to collect money.[61]

In Hungary, unofficial forms of Third Worldism could be invoked to criticize the lack of revolutionary ambition at home too. Che Guevara in particular was presented as the embodiment of a form of authentic and romantic revolutionary intent that could no longer be found in a socialist state in which an increasingly aged bureaucracy ruled, and where the Party was experimenting with new forms of marketization, competition, wage differentiation and consumerism. Indeed, Guevara himself had been critical of those socialist experiments in Hungary and Poland that were employing market incentives, characterizing them as steps back towards

---

[57] It put together over forty-three exhibitions with titles such as 'Children in the War', 'Solidarity with Vietnamese Youth' and 'Under Vietnamese Skies'. PIL [Politikatörténeti és Szakszervezeti Levéltár, Budapest] 289/3/245. On the relationship between the Hungarian communist state and the Vietnamese war, see Zoltán Szöke, 'Magyarország és a vietnami háború, 1962–1975', *Századok* 144/1 (2010), 47–98.

[58] KISZ Intéző Bizottság Report, 24 May 1966: PIL 289/3/193; Sándor Révész (ed.) *Beszélő évek: a Kádár-korszak története* (Budapest, 2000), 452.

[59] Official solidarity movements for Vietnam continued to exist until the mid-1970s.

[60] Protests against American aggression in Vietnam also occurred in Poland (see below), the Soviet Union, eastern Germany (see Chapter 5) and Czechoslovakia: here see Jaroslav Pažout, *Mocným navzdory* (Prague, 2008), 164–7, on student marches e.g. from Brno to the American embassy in Prague in February 1968. On East German official solidarity, see Günter Wernicke, 'The World Peace Council and the antiwar movement in East Germany', in Andreas W. Daum, Lloyd C. Gardner and Wilfried Mausbach (eds) *America, the Vietnam War, and the World* (Cambridge and New York, 2003), 299–320.

[61] Interview with Gábor Révai, conducted by PA, Budapest, 8 October 2008.

capitalism. For radicals such as György Pór (b. 1944)—who read Guevara's *Bolivian Diary* in prison following his prosecution in June 1968 for involvement in a supposed 'Maoist conspiracy'—Che represented authentic radical struggle:

> Being a minister in a communist government in Cuba and then dropping the whole thing and going to organize guerrillas, that was the embodiment of authenticity. And so he was already our hero in the solidarity movement when we had a strong sympathy with Cuba.[62]

These unofficial Third Worldist cults of the Cuban Revolution and Che Guevara could exist because their objects of fascination were viewed by the state as useful revolutionary exemplars for a new generation that did not remember the anti-Nazi liberation and the postwar struggles to build socialism, and which, if used carefully, could be used to mobilize support for the contemporary socialist project.[63] Thus the Hungarian state did not openly denounce Che Guevara but sought to reconcile his message with its policy of the 'revolution of the everyday', in which the young were encouraged to identify with socialism through engagement in small-scale, day-to-day acts of work rather than grandiose revolutionary projects. According to Minister of Culture György Aczél, speaking at a Communist Youth Central Committee debate on youth politics on 17 March 1970, Che, 'was heroic, demonstrated that the impossible was possible, but he could have been a bigger hero if he had devoted himself to thirty years of small-scale everyday revolutionary work'. Lenin was then presented as the real hero of socialist construction for his commitment to the slow, grinding work of building socialism.[64]

Likewise, Spanish radicals also turned to the 'Third World' in response to their disillusionment with Soviet communism. Manuel Garí of the Marxist FLP did not find the literature that was sent from Soviet Union to be uplifting:

> The manuals from the Soviet Union which some friends from the PCE passed us fell to the floor, they were so boring. It was because they had nothing to do with reality... For us it was not a model.[65]

Rather than look to the Soviet Union, radicals turned to the Third World in search of revolutionary socialist inspiration. For Aranzadi and members of the ORT, the principal source was communist China:

> The idea that we had of the Cultural Revolution was that of a reaction against the increasingly bourgeois nature of the Soviet bureaucracy... China was simply the place where there had been a revolution within the revolution and which had maintained the purity of the revolution in the face of the renunciations that Khrushchev and the twentieth congress of the CPSU [Communist Party of the Soviet Union] represented.[66]

---

[62] Interview with György Pór, conducted by JM, Brussels, 13 March 2009.
[63] 'The intellectual youth', *Magyar Ifjúság*, 30 January 1970, 3–4.
[64] KISZ Central Committee debate on youth politics, 17 March 1970. Lajos Méhes's report 182–3: PIL 289/2/55.
[65] Garí Ramos interview.
[66] Aranzadi Martínez interview.

Moreover, China appeared to be at the very heart of the anti-imperialist struggle in the Third World. For José Sanroma, secretary-general of the ORT, the appeal of communist China was not just that it represented a renewal of Marxism but also that it:

> supported the revolutionary movements in the Third World, what was then considered the Third World, the weak link in what we considered the imperialist chain. A shift of revolutionary thought from the European countries to the Third World. And a more determined support for this struggle.[67]

For the Marxist FLP, the Third World model of revolutionary socialism was not communist China but Cuba. José María Mohedano Fuertes (b. 1948) remembers that:

> The country that was closest to our utopia was Cuba. Note what a great mistake. But, undeniably, it was Cuba. Around here I have articles that I wrote even, about Che Guevara, Fidel Castro, etc. And about Cuba itself… But yes, it was our dream, our utopia.[68]

Inevitably related to the disillusionment with Soviet-style socialism was an urge to supersede the stale polarities of the Cold War. Third Worldism therefore became a means of criticizing not just US imperialism but also Soviet 'social-imperialism'. For a Maoist such as José Sanroma, anti-imperialism was not just anti-American—because of its support for the Franco dictatorship—but also anti-Soviet, especially as its policy of peaceful, Cold War coexistence meant that it gave insufficient support to liberation movements in the Third World and practised its own form of imperialism in eastern Europe:

> The Soviet Union became a country that invaded Czechoslovakia—Hungary [referring to the suppression of reform socialism in 1956] was distant for us, we didn't know it. This was the negative factor. United, moreover, to a policy of peaceful coexistence that was exercised then with American imperialism, which was the principal support—exterior and very powerful—of the Francoist dictatorship.[69]

A fellow activist, José Molina (b. 1946), also emphasizes the way that the Soviets, following their interventions in Hungary in 1956 and Czechoslovakia in 1968, had also become identified as imperialists as much as the Franco-supporting USA:

> We evaluated the subject of Stalin, critically. We valued his role in the Second World War, although afterwards, really, with all that we've come to know, it's enough to have given ourselves a good beating. And we understood that the Soviet Union had sold out the Spanish Republic, a bit. That we did understand. Later, everything that it did with Czechoslovakia, with Hungary and so on, we didn't like at all. That is to say, we thought that it was a form of bureaucratic state that was repressive and, so, another great power. It's true that when you fight against NATO [North Atlantic Treaty

[67] Sanroma Aldea interview.
[68] Interview with José María Mohedano Fuertes, conducted by NT, Madrid, 7 June 2010.
[69] Sanroma Aldea interview.

Organization] it seems that you're in favour of the Warsaw Pact, but that's not true. We understood that NATO was our enemy because we had American bases in Spain. And because there was repression in Latin America and Spain.[70]

That said, Spanish left-wing radicals inevitably felt a greater hostility to the US than to the USSR, as Manuel Garí explains:

At that time, the greatest concern was Latin America. I felt very close to the Latin American revolution. And the Indochina factor. I felt very close to the Vietnam revolution. So, clearly, the United States was, given its aims, 'The Great Beast', to put it one way, in two revolutionary processes.[71]

Thus the victorious radicalism of Third World revolutionaries was not only a stick with which to beat the conservatism of the communist states in eastern Europe, in addition to the domestic communist movements in western and southern Europe, but also a means of developing new political paradigms that eschewed the ossified polarities of the Cold War, of rejecting the imperialism of 'both sides'.

ANTI-IMPERIALISM AND INTERNATIONALISM

Anti-imperialism's power for radicals lay also in its internationalism: they understood their own domestic activism as part of a much broader 'anti-imperialist front'. Many interviewees recalled the debates over how their own struggle related to global ones. In Spain, the fight against the Franco dictatorship was often placed in this context: if José Sanroma of the ORT felt that his organization was part of a 'world revolutionary process',[72] then Manuel Garí of the FLP was equally convinced that 'at a global level, I felt part of an anti-imperialist front'.[73] The fundamental question, as Juan Aranzadi stresses, was:

Where do I carry out the revolution? In the Basque country, only? Or in Spain, as part of the world revolution? Well, the broadest thing that I had was Spain, and so I said, 'yes, in Spain, globally'. But the perception was that 'we form part of an international movement whose triumph is imminent'.[74]

Seeing themselves as part of a broader struggle against imperialism, some radicals attempted to reach out to anti-colonial movements beyond Europe's borders. For example, the French radical Tiennot Grumbach (b. 1939) travelled to Algeria. He had been involved in the campaign against the Algerian War and in particular the torture methods used by the French army, both while at school and when studying economics at the Paris Law Faculty. He became an ardent Third Worldist and went to Algeria

[70] Interview with José Molina Blázquez, conducted by NT, Madrid, 1 June 2010.
[71] Garí Ramos interview.
[72] Sanroma Aldea interview.
[73] Garí Ramos interview. See also Manuel Garí, 'El "Felipe": una historia por escribir', in Roca, *El proyecto radical*, 123–32.
[74] Aranzadi Martínez interview.

to collaborate, following independence in 1962, as one of the *pieds rouges* who replaced the *pieds noirs* or French colonial settlers, who now fled back to France. He explains how a site in newly independent Algeria became a training ground for Europeans who would return to their continent and play a large role in 1968:

> I went to Algeria for three days with medical supplies and stayed for three years. My political education was there. I had the luck to meet Che Guevara there. I went to Cuba with Che. It was a whole history. We learned about workers' control in industry, peasants' control...We were very enthusiastic. There was Cuba, Algeria. I thank heaven for that. For three or four years, including part of '68, we thought we could make a revolution. We were very happy...I organized a [youth] camp at Sidi Ferruch through which all the young people who made 'May '68' passed—Italians you will find in Lotta Continua, together with German students.[75]

British radical John Hoyland (b. 1941), a CND activist and founder of the 'guerrilla' art group Agitprop, as well as a journalist at *Black Dwarf*, remembers the importance of visiting Cuba to his political socialization, and how he sought to bring aspects of Cuban public commemoration back to London:

> in '66 I'd gone to Cuba...I shook hands with Fidel Castro...I'd decided I wanted to write a book...about South America...I went to Cuba in the summer of '66 while England was watching the World Cup...I was very politicized by the whole South American experience, and I knew which side I was on. There was no doubt whatsoever...there was an art school event in Trafalgar Square where we did a performance based on a big rally in the stadium I'd seen in Cuba in the July '66 celebrations, there were about 10,000 people in the stadium, and all along one side were children, and each one...had six, half a dozen or so, placards. And every now and again they'd hold these up in front of them, so you could no longer see the children, all you could see was each placard was, as it were, a pixel...of an immense picture, or slogan. And one of the slogans I remember was 'Vietnam, Cementério del Imperialismo' right. 'Vietnam, Cemetery of Imperialism'. And I thought this was terrific, and so we...we actually [laughs] did our own little version of this...we had these big placards with a dragon that represented imperialism, and [from then] the street theatre group—the 'Agitprop Street Players' and then—'Red Ladder' took off.[76]

Within the communist bloc, networks of solidarity were officially sponsored. In Hungary, for instance, exchange programmes with elite factories in Vietnam were organized[77] and associations such as the Cuban-Hungarian Friendship Society enabled trusted intellectuals to travel to the Third World. Younger radicals who were critical of official socialism, by contrast, seldom got the opportunity to travel.

---

[75] Interview with Tiennot Grumbach, conducted by RG, Paris, 18 April 2008. See also Catherine Simon, 'Les pieds-rouges, hors de l'histoire officielle', in Artières and Zancarini-Fournel (eds) *68. Une Histoire collective*, 158–65.

[76] Interview with John Hoyland, conducted by JD, London, 25 May 2010.

[77] In the late 1960s, twinning between Hungarian and Vietnamese 'sister factories' took place: Budapest's 'Red Csepel' was paired with the Trang Hung Dao machine factory of Hanoi, for instance, and exchanges took place in 1968 and 1970. Open Society Archive (OSA), Budapest, HU OSA 300-40-2-Box 53.

Nevertheless, some recall attempting it: the one-time radical Gábor Révai (b. 1947), a member of an unofficial student movement, relates that:

> we had such a young, romantic spirit that we applied voluntarily to go out and fight in Vietnam...we sent our application to the party's political committee, and we got a very 'polite' reply, saying, 'we are pleased to receive this, and if it becomes necessary later, then you can go as volunteers to Vietnam' ...[78]

In Spain, some radicals looked outwards not only to support Third Worldist movements, but also to obtain direct support from new regimes emerging from those struggles for their own struggle against the Francoist regime. On the one hand, José Luis de Zárraga (b. 1941) of the FLP affirms that in relation to Cuba and Algeria:

> We identified with them. If it had been necessary, we would have helped them. If it had been possible, we would have helped them. We believed in international solidarity...We read what they wrote and their things with interest, although it was so distant from our reality.[79]

On the other hand, the FLP had previously sent a delegation to Tunisia to ask for military support from the Algerians, but none was forthcoming. Once Algeria became independent, an FLP delegation again tried to win military and propaganda help, but the Algerian president refused to meet the FLP representative. Still, the FLP managed to arrange a meeting there with Che Guevara and in Paris the FLP representatives approached Cuban diplomats with a view to securing backing for the group's envisaged guerrilla operations. But Cuba only provided some money and reading material.[80] Altogether, the contacts with the Third World proved disappointing. As De Zárraga concludes:

> The FLP II [1960–2] had contacts above all with those of the Third World: with Cuba, with Algeria, and with Yugoslavia. In fact, a substantial part of the leaders of the FLP II were trained in Yugoslavia... there were certain attempts to reach an agreement with the Cubans, so that they would give us arms and so on, but this was an ephemeral thing.[81]

The Maoists of the ORT had somewhat greater success with the Chinese communists. As Secretary-General Sanroma relates:

> For us, the essential thing was to establish contact with the Communist Party of China. We considered that the situation of the European Maoists was not very close to ours...They [the Chinese] opened an embassy here in Madrid at the beginning of the '70s. We began to take them our propaganda. We also did it in Paris. In Paris and here in Madrid. Above all in Paris. We created an 'Association of Friendship with the Chinese People'.[82]

[78] Interview with Gábor Révai, conducted by PA, Budapest, 8 October 2008.
[79] Interview with José Luis de Zárraga Moreno, conducted by NT, Madrid, 2 June 2010.
[80] García Alcalá, *Historia del Felipe,* 285–7.
[81] De Zárraga Moreno interview.
[82] Sanroma Aldea interview.

Sanroma made a total of three trips to China between 1975 and 1979. The Chinese were extremely reluctant to finance the Spanish group on account of their previous experiences with European Maoists. Nevertheless, the Chinese were prepared to back a company to sell not only foreign-language editions of the works of Mao Tse-Tung, but also petrol to the Spanish government. As Sanroma recalls:

> They were prepared to help us—and that's what we did—to create a company to enable commerce between the two countries. We did it, but there was very little time. We did it in '79 and in '80 we closed it. We created a society for export and import.[83]

Anti-imperialism was important for radicals not only because it connected their own struggles with those of the 'Third World', but also due to the fact that it created a shared revolutionary outlook that could bind radicals together in both real and imagined forms of solidarity across Europe. This was particularly important for activists living under dictatorships of the right and left, whose Third Worldism gave them common cause with activists in the liberal democratic west of the continent. In Hungary, some anti-imperialist activists saw themselves as part of a wider Third Worldism that united radicals on both sides of the Iron Curtain. This identification with anti-imperialism led radicals to look for contacts with western European activists who shared their concerns. The Hungarian Gábor Révai developed a close relationship and correspondence with Rudi Dutschke, whom he got to know on his visit to Budapest in 1966. Dutschke encouraged him to view the struggle in Hungary as the vanguard of a global one alongside Greece, southern Europe and the 'revolutionary centres' of Africa, Asia and Latin America.[84] Indeed, other students alongside Révai joined Maoist cells falsely believing that these were part of a pan-European anti-imperialist network, and only later did they become disabused at the so-called 'Maoist trial' of spring 1968, in which it became clear that the network was limited to elite universities in Budapest.

For Greek radicals who were exiled following the establishment of the Colonels' Dictatorship in 1967, anti-imperialist solidarity gave them the sense of belonging to a wider European and global struggle and of sharing a common language of protest. Some Greek exile activists remembered their attempts to make common cause with exiled Viet Cong and French 68ers in the protests against the US in Paris.[85] An anonymous respondent was a student in mathematics who arrived in Paris in 1970 to research his doctorate. Abandoning his studies, he became a member of both the Greek Maoist group Antifasistiko Kinima Elladas (AKE) (Anti-fascist Movement of Greece) and worked for the Maoist journal, *La Cause du Peuple*. He gave up on returning to Greece and instead became a very mobile

[83] Sanroma Aldea interview.
[84] Correspondence dated 30 October 1966; reproduced in 'Rudi Dutschke és Révai Gábor lev-élváltása', *2000* (2008), 7–8.
[85] Interview with Christina Stamatopoulou, conducted by PV, Athens, 2 November 2007.

activist, dubbing himself the 'famous agent Inter-revolution', and travelling to the protests on the Larzac plateau, in the LIP factory and to occupied houses in West Germany. Part of his 'revolutionary world' were the demonstrations for Vietnam, Chile or Cambodia that, as for many Greek radicals, signalled their shift away from an understanding of anti-imperialism as a Greek national struggle against its oppressors, to a new internationalism and global solidarity.[86] In fact the demonstration that he remembers most vividly was the one before the signing of the Paris Peace Accords (January 1973) that ended the US involvement in the Vietnam War:

> AR: I remember certain moments, like the big demonstration for Vietnam we had in Paris. When I talk about demonstrations, I have this demonstration in mind.
> PV: Why?
> AR: Because it was...you felt like you were in a city in uprising. I mean you weren't alone, for the first time in my life we were the majority. Or, at least that's how it looked like. [laughs] Obviously we weren't the majority but you felt that you owned the streets, that you were winning...You had it your way, they were afraid of you, they were on retreat. After a few days the war was over. It's not that the demonstration in Paris ended the war. They had already started to give way and...this was it, the war was over. [87]

ANTI-IMPERIALISM AND NATIONAL STRUGGLE

Régis Debray, the French revolutionary who had fought with Guevara in Bolivia, when reflecting back in 1977 on this era of anti-imperialism noted, 'all the revolutionaries I have known personally were ardent patriots whose "internationalism" was generally a national messianism...in Cuba and Vietnam being a revolutionary...means being a nationalist'.[88] Anti-imperialism was powerful not only because it fostered internationalism, solidarity and new forms of international protest; it could simultaneously be deployed as a defence of national sovereignty against American or Soviet imperialism, and through it activists might understand their work as linked to longer-term struggles for national independence at home.[89]

The parallels between the struggles for national sovereignty in the 'Third World' against American imperialism and their own resistance to Soviet imperialism were drawn by activists in the communist bloc. In Poland, the leftist

---

[86] See also Kostis Kornetis, 'Everything links?' Temporality, territoriality and cultural transfer in the '68 protest movements', *Historein* 9 (2009), 35.

[87] Interview with anonymous respondent, conducted by PV, Athens, 9 October 2007.

[88] Régis Debray, 'Marxism and the national question', *New Left Review* (September–October 1977), 25. Régis Debray, who had gone to Cuba with Roland Castro in 1961, left his teaching post and returned to Cuba in 1965 at the invitation of Fidel Castro. He published a study of guerrilla warfare in Cuba and Latin America, *La Révolution dans la Révolution* (Paris, 1967) and then went to report on the activities of Che Guevara in Bolivia.

[89] See also Samuel Moyn, *The Last Utopia* (Cambridge, MA, 2010), ch. 3.

Commandos group—some of whose members would play a pivotal role in the opposition to the state socialist regime that was to break out at Warsaw University in March 1968—were firm supporters of the Vietnamese struggle against American imperialism in 1967 insofar as they used it to critique Soviet imperialism in Poland. They scattered leaflets around Warsaw University that stated:

> This is not the first time that... the tanks of the world's superpowers shape the existing social order... Vietnamese fighters struggle for the cause which is our cause as well: they struggle for the right to carry our revolution which is going to abolish... national bondage; they struggle for freedom from exploitation, from internal dictatorship and from dictatorship of superpowers over small nations... We can't keep silent because we remember the consequences of [the] Munich Treaty... because we remember the foreign intervention which suppressed the Hungarian revolution... because of the cause for which Che Guevara gave his life, for which thousands of people are dying every day in Latin America and in Vietnam, is the cause of freedom of every small country confronted with a superpower—the struggle for an independent and socialist Vietnam is the struggle for an independent and socialist Poland. To all those who are going to trample on the sovereignty of working people, in whichever country, one should respond with the slogan of Spanish antifascists: No pasarán.[90]

Jan Lityński (b. 1946), one of the prominent Commandos, explains how Vietnam, a symbol of superpower aggression, was invoked alongside the suppression of the Hungarian Uprising in 1956 in order to criticize Soviet rather than American imperialism, and to assert the necessity of Polish independence: 'we talked about Vietnam in order to actually talk about the Soviet Union, just as we talked about Hungary [i.e. the suppression of the 1956 Uprising by Soviet tanks]... to highlight the imperial politics of the Soviet Union'.[91]

In Hungary, too, Third Worldism could be interpreted as an ideology of national self-determination by activists, and parallels were drawn between Hungary's past struggles for independence and those against the Soviet imperialism of the present. Radical leftists sometimes critiqued Soviet dominance in this way with reference back to 'anti-imperial' progressive national movements of 1848. Judit Gáspár (b. 1943), who was expelled from university and worked at the Csepel factory in Budapest, recalls that 'we were 1848ers in our souls, absolutely, 1848 was a real living tradition'.[92] In the late 1960s and early 1970s, Third Worldist heroes such as Che Guevara were

---

[90] Franciszek Dąbrowski, Piotr Gontarczyk and Paweł Tomasik (eds) *Marzec 1968 w dokumentach MSW. Tom 1: Niepokorni* (Warszawa, 2008), 822. It should be noted here that anti-imperialism is mixed with the anti-fascist inspiration still drawn from the Spanish Civil War; this may be because some of the Commandos were formerly part of the *Walterowcy*, the independent (but legal) scout organization established by Jacek Kuroń, which was devoted to upholding the internationalist traditions of the Russian Revolution and Spanish Civil War.

[91] Interview with Jan Lityński, conducted by PO, Warsaw, 25 November 2009. Another Commando, Seweryn Blumsztajn (b. 1946), noted that the 'Vietnamese flyer [didn't mean] I was engaged in the Vietnam cause at all... the anti-American aspects I didn't fancy at all... it was about the Soviet Union' (interview with Seweryn Blumsztajn, conducted by PO, Warsaw, 5 January 2010).

[92] Interview with Judit Gáspár, conducted by PA, Budapest, 11 March 2009.

compared with Sándor Petőfi, the radical Hungarian poet who had fought for Hungarian independence during the revolutions of 1848. Indeed, their shared martyrdom—one (probably) at the hands of the Russian army in 1849 and the other in the jungles of Bolivia in 1967—made them popular figures of revolutionary romanticism and symbols of the national fight against Soviet domination.[93] A police report from 1971 stated that Che's image was painted onto the 'communist trinity' of Marx-Engels-Lenin on Petőfi Street in Budapest, further demonstrating the linkages that could be made.[94]

This was part of the attraction of Third Worldism to Hungarian populists who represented the 'national peasantry' and who had viewed communism as a form of occupation, but who had nevertheless made their peace with the regime after the experience of the 1956 revolution, often viewing western forms of individualistic capitalism as a greater threat to rural Hungary and the state socialist status quo as the lesser evil. Sándor Csoóri, a prominent young populist, became a passionate Third Worldist, visiting Cuba in the 1960s.[95] For him, the Cuban Revolution could be celebrated both for its anti-capitalism and as a moment of national independence. This wave of Latin American liberation struggles echoed Hungary's attempt to gain independence in the nineteenth century, and, by implication, to throw off Soviet dominance in the twentieth:

> Fidel Castro and Che Guevara were in my eyes the relatives of the young revolutionaries of 1848. The twentieth-century relatives of Petőfi, Vasvári, Lenkey. I met twice with Che, once in our hotel another time during the march on José Martí square. It was like being in a Jókai[96] novel in which I was the main character. Of course we didn't have the faintest idea that the Soviet Union would entrench itself politically in this once 'liberated island'... So I saw Cuba when it was a free, independent country, ruled by courageous young people... who cared about the poor.[97]

Greek radicals also often placed their contemporary struggle against the Colonels' Dictatorship, supported by the US, into a longer-term narrative concerning the fight of the Greek people against foreign intervention. Nikos Tsiokos (b. 1944), for many decades a member of the Greek Communist Party, states:

> They [the Americans] wanted to control Greece. It was proven, there were hints and suspicions that the coup on the 21 April 1967 was directed by the American intelligence agencies to break democracy in Greece... The way I see it is the following... I mean, I've studied Greek history and I am not wrong. From a historical point of view, if we go back, the Civil War was due to the foreigners. The 'Minor Asia disaster', what was it? It was to benefit the foreigners.[98]

---

[93] Indeed, Régis Debray saw Guevara as the successor to the national freedom fighters of 19th century Latin America.

[94] CURT Report, 'Hungary Youth Turns to Mao, Che Credos', HU OSA 300-40-2 Box 21.

[95] For a romantic diary account of these experiences, see Sándor Csoóri, *Kubai napló* (Budapest, 1965).

[96] 19th century Hungarian romantic nationalist novelist.

[97] Sándor Csoóri, 'Közel a szülőföldhöz', *Kortárs*, 2004/4.

[98] Tsiokos interview. The 'Minor Asia Disaster' refers to the Greek-Turkish War that ended in 1922 with the defeat of the Greek army and the expulsion of the Greek populations from Asia Minor.

Indeed, despite the fact that interviewees refer to this very little today, the connections between the wars for national independence and the struggles of the 1960s were made clear at the time by the practice of naming dissident groups after 19th century Greek intellectuals and revolutionaries. One armed opposition group named itself after Yiannis Makrygiannis (1797–1864), a general from the Greek Revolution of 1821, while the youth wing of the reformist Communist Party took the name of Rigas Feraios (1757–98), a late eighteenth-century intellectual whose struggles foreshadowed those of the Greek Revolution of 1821. For these groups, the struggle against the US-backed Colonels' regime went hand in hand with the idea of an incomplete struggle for national independence dating back to the late eighteenth century.

CONCLUSION

Anti-fascism as a source of revolutionary inspiration in Europe appeared to be on the wane by the 1960s. For many radicals, especially in eastern Europe, the anti-fascist tradition was synonymous with the distinctly unrevolutionary achievements of stale stultifying and bureaucratic communist parties and states. The violent opposition of the French Republic to decolonization was also seen by many radicals as a betrayal of the anti-fascist tradition, while in Greece and Spain anti-fascism was tarnished by defeat in civil war. Nonetheless, anti-fascism was revived during the course of the 1960s, fired by the perception that western liberal democracies had still not expunged the remnants of fascism from their political systems, and by the resurgence of right-wing authoritarianism in southern Europe. Accordingly, the conviction that fascism had not been completely destroyed by the Second World War became increasingly powerful among activists, especially in France, Italy and Greece. However, the anti-fascist tradition was in other ways replaced—or at least complemented—by the revolutionary examples provided by anti-imperialist struggles in Algeria, Cuba, Vietnam and elsewhere. Anti-imperialism proved to be remarkably elastic in framing and inspiring radical activism within Europe. It could be invoked by activists who regarded themselves as challenging the oppressive 'colonialism' of their own governments as well as by those who saw themselves as fighting for the nation against an occupying power. Furthermore, anti-imperialism gave radical activists a sense that their own particular cause formed an integral part of a much wider, even global, anti-capitalist movement. Whether in the liberal democracies, the communist bloc states or in the dictatorships of southern Europe, anti-imperialism, like anti-fascism, proved to be a potent source of inspiration to radical activists.

PART II

BEING AN ACTIVIST

4

Revolutions

Marie Černá, John Davis, Robert Gildea and Piotr Osęka

Prisca Bachelet (b. 1940), a philosophy graduate from the Sorbonne, like many leaders of France's May 1968, had been a member of the UEC, the student branch of the French Communist Party, before it exploded under the pressure for more radical Marxist forms of revolution in the mid-1960s. She describes how meetings were a forum for passionate debate about what revolution might be like:

> There was the UEC which quickly became a huge space, a sort of philosophical club of I don't know how many people—three, four hundred—where we discussed political ideas in turn... It was a bit like being at university, not in a post-revolutionary sense because all the talk was about how to make the revolution, but it was nothing to do with the politics of politicians. Everyone was there, the Trotskyists, the future JCR [Revolutionary Communist Youth], workers, control people (*conseillistes*), the Italians, who were Gramscians... The pro-Chinese arrived right at the end.[1]

Prisca herself was uneasy with the Marxist groups who thought only in terms of political revolution, an uprising of the proletariat and seizure of power with the help of students and intellectuals. She described herself as a 'communist libertarian', a bit of an anarchist, and believed that revolution should also be cultural, shaped by the ideas and emotions that made up what might be called 'revolutionary subjectivity', a desire for revolution. She was inspired not only by Rosa Luxemburg but by the pop singer and lyricist Évariste and the sexologist Wilhelm Reich:

> For me Rosa Luxemburg's *Mass Strike, Party and Trade Unions* was very important. I was always interested in workers' democracy, giving voice to the base, broadening the revolutionary process to something more than the economy... So we were happy in '66–'67 when the first texts of Évariste were in circulation, and he said, 'we have the objective contradictions but we must create the subjective conditions of revolution'. For us the goal was revolutionary subjectivity... We wanted an autonomous movement of youth, we had read Reich, we had psychological references too. We were in favour of sexual liberation, the struggle against the family, all that.[2]

---

[1] Interview with Prisca Bachelet, conducted by RG, Paris, 27 May 2008. The Jeunesse Communiste Révolutionnaire (JCR) was a branch of the Trotskyist movement in France, founded in April 1966. The 'pro-Chinese' later became the Maoist Union des Jeunesses Communistes Marxiste-Léniniste, or UJC(ml), founded in December 1966. See Christophe Bourseiller, *Les Maoïstes. La Folle histoire des gardes rouges français* (Paris, 1996), and Richard Wolin, *The Wind from the East: French Intellectuals, the Cultural Revolution and the Legacy of the 1960s* (Princeton, 2010).

[2] Bachelet interview.

Having broken with the UEC in 1965, Prisca devoted her energies to the student movement as vice-president of the French Student Union (UNEF) and was working at the communist town hall of Nanterre when the students occupied the administrative building of Nanterre university on 22 March 1968, giving rise to the playful and subversive movement of the same name.[3]

Ole Vind (b. 1944), a Danish student at the University of Copenhagen, specialized in maths and physics but was also interested in philosophy and spirituality, engaging in 'an exploration of life and the world'. He was involved in the Campaign for Nuclear Disarmament (CND) in the early 1960s and was in France in the wake of May 1968. In the autumn of 1968 he was one of the founders of the New Society, which for three years was an important centre for the complex milieu of Danish youth rebels, especially on the Copenhagen scene. The student movement was divided between revolutionary socialists on the one hand and anarchistic hippies and so-called 'cultural radicals' on the other.[4] The aim of the New Society was to bring these groups together, to provide a centre for free debate, and to combine politics and ethics, and politics, music and happenings to encourage new forms of social life, new ways of being together and new forms of expression in the creation of a new society. 'Certainly are we going to destroy capitalism', wrote Ole Vind in the underground magazine *Superlove* in 1969, 'but it is not only an attack on those in power; it is also an attack on the deepest structures within ourselves'.[5] He contrasted different figures such as Pilgrims and Samaritans, Warriors and Freaks, Activists and Drop Outs, echoing Arthur Koestler's distinction between the Yogi who wants to revolutionize the inside through self-contemplation and the commissar who wants to organize a political party and carry out radical changes from above.[6] Vind himself went in search of a philosophy of revolution that went beyond the political:

> And I suppose I felt that those revolutionary groups and things like that were very busy planning something strategic. I had a hard time taking that seriously and it's linked to smoking pot and the religious and historical perspective... The core of my passion was definitely not about the Marxist revolution, but about something else. It was closer to a consciousness revolution. You change yourself and your entire perception of the world. But this was of course also a part of the Chinese Revolution, which was not just economic or political—but a cultural revolution... Be a realist, demand the impossible was the slogan in Paris in '68. A lack of imagination is not having the imagination to see what's missing. That's exactly what I experienced as a child. We don't have the imagination to see what's missing.[7]

[3] Jean-Pierre Duteuil, *Nanterre, 1965–66–67–68. Vers le Mouvement du 22 mars* (La Bussière, 1988).

[4] Steven L. B. Jensen, ' "Youth enacts society and somebody makes a coup": The Danish student movement between political and lifestyle radicalism', in Axel Schildt and Detlef Siegfried (eds) *Between Marx and Coca-Cola. Youth Cultures in Changing European Societies, 1960–1980* (New York and Oxford, 2006), 224–38.

[5] Ole Vind, 'Pilgrimme og samaritanere', *Superlove* (January 1969), 16 and 'Oprøret og Det ny Samfund', *det ny samfund* 9 (1969), 4–5.

[6] Arthur Koestler, *The Yogi and the Commissar and other Essays* (London, 1945, 1986).

[7] Interview with Ole Vind, conducted by AW, Hillerød, 7 January 2010.

On the other side of the Iron Curtain, in Warsaw, (Stefan Bekier) (b. 1946) was a student at School of Planning and Statistics (now the Warsaw School of Economics), and a member of a group of activist students called the Komandosi or Commandos. His father had been a member of the banned Polish Communist Party in the 1930s and fought with the International Brigades in Spain and the French Resistance before returning to a 'liberated' Poland in 1945 to build socialism there. For them, the communist regimes in Poland and the other People's Democracies of eastern Europe had become bureaucratic and repressive while still claiming their legitimacy from socialist revolution. They asked themselves, how was it possible for discontented students and other young people to have a revolution against regimes that were themselves defined by the ideology of revolution, had the force of the Soviet Red Army standing behind them, and denounced all opposition as counter-revolution? Thus Polish students of the Commando group who came into conflict with the communist regime in March 1968 did not use the word 'revolution' to describe their aims or the reality of their protest and were confused about the way forward. As Stefan Bekier remembers:

> No one was talking about the revolution. It was the revolt. It was the rebellion. The movement. People were talking about the movement. It was a students' movement. For me and for us March was mainly the big upheaval (*zryw*).[8]

THE MODEL OF THE *MAI* EVENTS

For many activists across Europe, May 1968 in Paris was a revolution in the making, and the revolution to be imitated. French students and workers seemed to know what they were doing and had a historical tradition to draw upon. (Bernard Victorri) (b. 1946) was a mathematics student at the École Normale Supérieure, which was the headquarters of the Maoist UJC (ml). The Maoist leadership thought that the revolution would be proletarian and begin in the factories on the outskirts of Paris, but when it erupted in the Latin Quarter Victorri was ready for the barricade fighting:

> May '68 arrived we thought our strategy was correct and that the revolution was about to happen. I was at the École Normale and so in the middle of the Latin Quarter, and I was on the first barricades [in] May... I had been an activist and had been fighting for two years in order to be heard and we arrived at the end of the boulevard Saint-Michel. We raised our voices a bit, there were twenty people, thirty people, a hundred people. We said 'we are going to such-and-such a place'. We were two hundred when we left and we arrived with two thousand—it was mad. There was an absolutely magical side to the mass movement and we had the feeling that we were taking part in history.[9]

---

[8] Interview with Stefan Bekier, conducted by PO, Warsaw, 23 June 2008.
[9] Interview with Anne and Bernard Victorri, conducted by RG, Paris, 28 May 2007. The 'night of the barricades' was 10–11 May 1968. See Jean-François Sirinelli, *Mai 68. L'événement Janus* (Paris, 2008), 145–67.

Following police repression of the student protests, a national general strike was called on 13 May that triggered a wave of factory occupations across France from 14 May. Dominique Grange (b. 1940), a doctor's daughter from Lyon, was older than the normal run of students and in 1968 a successful cabaret singer and TV show hostess. She had little political background but when the Renault car workers went on strike and occupied their factory at Boulogne-Billancourt she went there and sang revolutionary songs from the back of a lorry. She remembers, 'May '68 was something else, a real discovery by workers of the class struggles…ten million workers were on strike, it was the biggest workers' movement in the world, theoretically it was at least a pre-revolution'.[10]

Yves Rocton (b. 1938) was an engineering worker and Trotskyist shop-steward at the Sud-Aviation aircraft factory outside Nantes, which was the first factory to be occupied by its workers on 14 May and held out for a month. He saw 1968 in the context of a historic workers' struggle against capitalism and the police, carried out by men who had been hardened by strikes and by their experience as reluctant combatants in the Algerian War. For Rocton, revolution was something that had to be tasted and given meaning by the collective rendering in their occupied factory of revolutionary songs:

> In 1968 I was thirty and most of my mates were the same age. They were not afraid of a fight. As workers they had already seen strikes, Nantes in 1955 and all that, with paving stones and catapults…It was a factory of two and a half thousand workers, and the guys had hammers and nail guns…But they listened to records, it was a good moment to learn revolutionary songs. Between the pop songs of Yves Montand and old French songs, we sang revolutionary songs like the *Jeune Garde*.[11]

In Britain, the unexpectedly violent anti-Vietnam War demonstration outside the American embassy in Grosvenor Square in March 1968 appeared to herald the arrival of a new form of direct action militancy, although one that seemed to owe little to the politics of class. Nick Wright (b. 1947), whose father had been a communist shop-steward at Vauxhall Motors at Luton and was himself an unwavering member of the Communist Party of Great Britain as well as leader of the sit-in at Hornsey College of Art, played a vigorous part in the demonstration, which he describes in apocalyptic terms:

> in '68 for instance there was the first demonstration in Grosvenor Square…as the mounted police charged across Grosvenor Square my various ultra-left friends scattering to the four winds while the Hornsey Young Communists stood there with their steel banners, like at the battle of Agincourt, confronting the police you know.[12]

---

[10] Interview with Dominique Grange, recorded by RG, Paris, 10 May 2007.

[11] Interview with Yves Rocton, conducted by RG, Fenioux (Deux-Sèvres), 14 May 2008. On events in Nantes see *Cahiers de mai* 1 (15 June 1968); Yannick Guin, *La Commune de Nantes* (Paris, 1969); François Le Madec, *L'aubépine de mai. Chronique d'une usine occupée. Sud-Aviation Nantes 1968* (Nantes, 1988).

[12] Interview with Nick Wright, conducted by JD, Faversham, 23 February 2010.

Although his Young Communists were at the forefront of the battle, Wright did not see this confrontation as revolutionary. According to his Marxist worldview it should be led by workers, and motivated by the clear material interests of the working class:

> A revolution looks like millions of workers on the move...I inhabited a world in which industrial workers were, and big factories were, you know, part of my world you know, I mean I'd worked in a big factory, my family worked in big factories...these were big blocks of workers who were led by, mostly by communists at the rank-and-file level even if they weren't led by communists at the official union level and you know, a revolution looked like workers in action.[13]

Events in Paris two months later, however, convinced some British activists that a revolution was perhaps in the making. Agitprop activist John Hoyland (b. 1941) had visited Castro's Cuba and looked after Rudi Dutschke when he was recovering in London from his assassination attempt in Berlin. He reflected that:

> To say that you thought revolution could and should happen can now seem like, well, we must've been mad and probably we were a bit. But during the May events in Paris for ten days a revolution was very possible. I mean, the students were fighting the police. There were pitched battles every single night. They'd occupied the centre of Paris. And then there was a general strike. The workers went on general strike. I mean, you thought, 'crikey it really is happening'.[14]

Hull University radical Tom Fawthrop (b. 1946), a member of the International Socialists, went to Paris in May 1968 and thought that the Renault and other factory occupations were a vindication of the doctrines of workers' control to which he had already been attracted. Whether they would happen in Britain, however, was another question:

> I already had read some of the tracts, some of the pamphlets which had been published about workers' control, so that was already in my mind. But then when I went to France, so...it's one thing knowing a few intellectuals who are pushing this, and...you go to Paris and you see these ideas already in action, in various forms...In France in particular you had this magnificent solidarity which cut across class lines, in the sense that most students are at least middle-class...I mean, in many countries in the world like Britain the notion of any kind of unity between students and workers is largely an illusion. [laughs] But, it's the Holy Grail, you know, it's the Holy Grail of Trotskyism, but...it usually has no substance.[15]

Paris was of course a magnet for international students, some of whom were political exiles from their own countries. This did not mean that foreign students participated a great deal in the events of May 1968 or even understood what was going on. Greek students who had fled the military coup of 1967 and came to Paris were, for example, often members of the Greek Communist Party which had

---

[13] Wright interview.
[14] Interview with John Hoyland, conducted by JD, London, 25 May 2010.
[15] Interview with Tom Fawthrop, conducted by JD, London, 23 September 2008.

been banned during the Civil War in 1947 and remained outlawed until the end of the dictatorship in 1974. They found it difficult to sympathize with the revolutionism of the Trotskyist, Maoist and anarchist *groupuscules* in France, which had broken with or never belonged to the French Communist Party that was in any case suspicious of movements it did not control.

Giorgios Karambelias (b. 1946) arrived in Paris in 1967 and set up the Antifascist Greek Movement there. On 22 May 1968, with other Greek students, he occupied the Greek pavilion in the Cité Universitaire in Paris to protest against the military dictatorship in Greece and the black flag of the anarchists was hoisted alongside the red flag of the communists. He recalled that members of a Greek Marxist-Leninist group took issue with this departure from revolutionary orthodoxy:

> They said, 'We are not participating because there is a black flag. Remove the black flag and we will consider coming'. They were under pressure too. Certainly their members put pressure on them and after all it was the surrounding atmosphere…but in general those who were organized were the most conservative. It is a paradox but those who participated were those who were not organized.

The ideas and practices of Greek émigré leftists, committed to party discipline, democratic centralism and top-down hierarchy, looked backward, even obsolete, in comparison with those of French and Italian activists, for whom political revolution was only one dimension of a broad social and cultural movement. In this respect, the 1968 movement was a challenge to Greek radicals. They instinctively had more connections with the Italian or French communist parties than with Trotskyists or Maoists. Giorgos Karambelias, who joined the French Maoists, became estranged from many of his Greek comrades:

> To begin with, I think it was very strange to them [other Greeks in Paris]. I mean, perhaps they had a different form of awareness…The slogans, the forms of expression, all these were very strange, for a traditional communist-born organization from Greece…There was a conservatism together with a fear, 'don't mess with it, we are foreigners'.[16]

That said, Greek activists remained much closer than French activists to a revolutionary notion of armed struggle that their parents had practised in the war against Axis occupation and during the Civil War and which seemed to be required again to defeat the military dictatorship. Gerasimos Notaras (b. 1936), a centrist intellectual who became a leading figure of the underground group Dimokratiki Amyna, advocated armed struggle to overthrow the military dictatorship. Arrested in 1967, tortured and imprisoned until 1973, he saw the need for political revolution against oppression as 'self-evident':

> My country was enslaved, thus every citizen had the duty to get rid of this slavery and to get rid of it using any means whatsoever…It was not bizarre that all the people, especially young people who were politicized and had ideological convictions like our

[16] Interview with Giorgios Karambelias, conducted by PV, Athens, 2 July 2008.

circle, thought that the next step was self-evident, when they muzzle you and crush your freedom. You can't just sit down and do nothing.[17]

When Greek activists travelled or fled abroad to more democratic countries, their immediate reaction was to be impressed by how much easier it was to engage in radical political activity where participation and free debate were possible. They thought about how much simpler it was to be a communist in Italy or France. Michalis Tiktopoulos (b. 1946) was a Maoist who fled after the 1967 coup to Bologna to continue his studies and, most importantly, his political activism. He was impressed by the freedom of the press and influence of the left, which highlighted the narrow and doctrinaire approach of Greek activists:

> When I arrived in Italy for the first time, I went to the Feltrinelli bookshop. There was a stand there with several magazines. Three out of four magazines had the hammer and sickle or the red star on their covers. I said to myself: 'Where am I? Am I in heaven? What is going on?' [laughs]...There was a very...narrow understanding what was going on...We were like Jesuits...We were wedded to our ideas and understandings, which I would describe as old-fashioned, actually like those of the Greek Communist Party![18]

In the People's Democracies of central and eastern Europe revolution was difficult to envisage by activists both theoretically, because the rationale of communist states was based on a completed political revolution, and practically, because the Red Army stood behind most of the communist regimes and threatened to intervene if they lost control of their populations. In Poland, some activists argued that the more decent people joined the communist Polish United Workers Party (PUWP), the more likely it was that democratization would follow. In Hungary, similarly, there was a sense that change was more likely to come about by 'working within institutions' rather than by overt confrontation. For these reasons activists might portray protest in favour of greater institutional democratization and meaningful political debate as reform within the system, under the auspices of communist parties and without challenging their ultimate authority. Activism might also take the cultural form of artistic or musical activities that avoided direct confrontation with the state but whose aim to transform power relations or social attitudes had an obvious political meaning.

Although Polish students came into conflict with the communist regime in March 1968, the term 'revolution' was simply not in their arsenal of words or deeds. They knew that action within the bounds of the university might be tolerated, but that a demonstration spilling onto the street would not. Moreover, although as in France and Britain there was a sense among student activists that revolution involved awakening the workers, this was difficult to achieve in a country that officially called itself a workers' state. Jerzy Diatłowicki (b. 1941), a Commando and member of the strike committee at Warsaw University, recalled:

[17] Interview with Gerasimos Notaras, conducted by PV, Athens, 14 April 2009.
[18] Interview with Michalis Tiktopoulos, conducted by PV, Athens, 3 November 2009.

It was our dream [to make contact with workers], because we knew that nothing [was possible without that]. But how were we to reach them? I tell you, there were these silly discussions, ones that revealed the utter isolation of our milieu, its complete isolation. Nobody knew anybody who knew anyone...Yeah, there were endless discussions about it—you know, about having a base. But we were on a hiding to nothing. I mean, it was pathetic and it showed a complete inability to join up the dots...It was dramatic.[19]

Young workers took part in street riots alongside students, but the factories were under the control of older workers who were opposed to strike action. If students came to a factory gate, no one wanted to talk to them. Some students were already working as interns in factories but this did not seem to make the link any easier. (Andrzej Krzesiński)(b. 1947), who was at Warsaw Polytechnic recalled:

Our colleagues also tried to mobilize their people who were doing their internships at various industrial plants. Unfortunately, however, we found out that official propaganda was simply too powerful. After all, in the meantime there had been protest rallies, after which came Gomułka's infamous anti-Semitic speech and those posters 'Zionists to Zion'.[20] None of the workers wanted to even talk with those students who were doing their internships at various plants. We tried many different ways to encourage workers to strike...none of them, literally no one, wanted to respond to our appeal.[21]

One problem was the formal integration of the workers into the socialist state and the effectiveness of its propaganda. Another was that workers had little interest in the students' demands for freedom of speech and civil rights(Jan Wyrowiński)(b. 1947), a student at the Gdańsk Polytechnic, was desperate to build a bridge to the Gdańsk shipyard but soon realized that the workers were not interested in greater democracy:

We wanted them to join us at the rally [at Gdańsk Polytechnic], to have an opportunity of expressing their beliefs along with us. We thought they would support us in matters we regarded as obvious, such as the need for truth in the media. Freedoms which were perhaps less material and more spiritual, that were dear to our heart and which seemed obvious to us. We wanted them to shout with us 'the press is lying', 'more truth', 'democracy'.[22]

In Czechoslovakia, the reforms for which the Polish students fought were steadily conceded during the Prague Spring that followed the appointment of Alexandr Dubček as first secretary of the Communist Party. Czechoslovak students were able

---

[19] Interview with Jerzy Diatłowicki, conducted by PO, Warsaw, 16 November 2009.
[20] The anti-Semitic campaign—under the official banner of 'anti-Zionism'—was launched in June 1967, following the outbreak of Six Day War in the Middle East. Władysław Gomułka condemned Poles of Jewish origin for their alleged sympathy for Israel and denounced them as a 'fifth column'. He repeated those accusations in March 1968 in a speech against protesting students. Activist memory tends to run these two speeches together. See Dariusz Stola, *Kampania antysjonistyczna w Polsce 1967–1968* (Warsaw, 2000).
[21] Interview with Andrzej Krzesiński, conducted by PO, Warsaw, 24 September 2009.
[22] Interview with Jan Wyrowiński, conducted by PO, Warsaw, 8 July 2010.

to operate through official organizations such as the Academic Council of Students in order to promote student freedoms and wider interests. The new political leadership introduced a project of major political and economic changes, society took up the agenda and pushed them forward, perhaps further than the politicians envisaged. The spirit was one of reformism, to improve the system, not to overthrow it: to decentralize the structure of social organizations, to take into account the diversity of individual and group interests, and to allow some internal opposition within the Communist Party. Comparable with western Europe was the degree of 'popular action': a lively public sphere, a sense that individuals could talk, read, meet and travel freely. This might be called 'revolutionary' but only in the sense of transgression, of new ways of thinking and expression.

Although the Prague Spring of 1968 itself was mostly concerned with political themes such as democratization, liberalization, political rehabilitation or the abolition of censorship, some activism was more artistic and cultural than political and developed earlier in the 1960s.[23] It might be an artistic movement designed to transform everyday life, or a parallel, counter-cultural way of subverting a system that was still communist. Cultural activity was nevertheless a form of politics by another name. Although activists are quick to point out that they were not intentionally political, politics was forced upon them.

Milan Knížák (b. 1940) was the founder of a group called Actual art (Aktuální umění) in the early 1960s.[24] He saw himself as a prophet or a guru who wrote detailed scripts for sophisticated rituals, with many instructions for participants. For him and for his team, revolution was not violent and focussed on formal politics but a way of using artistic performance to change social relations and attitudes. They wanted to break down the barriers between art and life, to bring creativity into everyday life in order to change it. Knížák explains:

Our activities were not political but they were inspired by the political way of life that was here. I called them demonstrations, manifestations... They derived from our reality, that was the most important thing. We dissociated ourselves from art for art's sake and wanted to affect everyday life directly.... We were more concerned with social phenomena than with artistic ones. We differed from the West where everything took place in the artistic sphere. We wanted it to be anonymous... in the sense that the art should be anonymous. It meant that a person coming into contact with it should not recognize that it was a piece of art. It was supposed to be a life event. It was clearly provoked by the life here. It was a desire to enter into the social. It was influenced by our experience of living in socialism and our—I stress non-political—dreams about change.[25]

---

[23] Josef Alan et al., *Alternativní kultura. Příběh české společnosti 1945–1989* (Prague, 2001); Pavlína Morganová, *Akční umění* (Olomouc, 1999).

[24] Milan Knížák, *Akce*, photo-documentation (Prague, 2000); idem, *Písně kapely Aktual* (Prague, 2003), idem, *Cestopisy* (Prague, 1990); Petr Volf and Milan Knížák, *Hermafrodit: Rozmluva nadoraz* (Prague, 1998); Milan Knížák, *Aktionen, Konzepte, Projekte, Dokumentationen: Oldenburger Kunstverein, 14. September bis 12. Oktober 1980* (Oldenburg, 1980).

[25] Interview with Milan Knížák, conducted by MČ, Prague, 3 July 2008.

The attitude of another group dating from the early 1960s, the Holy Cross School of Pure Humour without Wit, was somewhat different. Although they might agree about questioning the traditional conception of art, its members consciously distanced themselves from Knížák's programmatic activities. They did not intend to revolutionize society but to subvert its absurdity and to create their own parallel social milieu. They met in pubs, drank beer and planned activities—the name Holy Cross came from the name of the street where the original pub was found. They echoed the Bohemian café societies such as the Dadaists, the Surrealists and a Czech student movement from the 1930s called Recesse.[26] Věra Jirousová (b. 1944), an art historian who graduated from Prague's Philosophy Faculty, remembers that:

> There were two streams of art of action. One of them was Milan Knížák's *Aktual*. I found it very interesting but we made fun of it too…In *Aktual*, there were plenty of people who were my friends, and who needed support…They needed an impulse. I did not need that myself. He [Knížák] was in Nový Svět [a district of Prague, near the castle] while we had the Holy Cross School of Pure Humour without Wit, sitting in little pubs in the Old Town. If Knížák had come there we would have had a laugh. We did things in a spontaneous, creative manner, immediately, not to order: 'Walk down the street and crow'. 'Take off your jacket and throw it off the Charles Bridge'. I don't need to free myself because I am free. That was the difference…All the participants had an equal position during the activities—girls and boys, the painter Honza Steklík had the same status as the two nurses, known as 'Little Giraffes'.[27]

Jan Steklík (b. 1938), an artist and illustrator and member of the Holy Cross School, confirms that while their subversion was not overtly political, the communist political system took an interest in them as artists and obliged them to think politically:

> To be honest, we were not interested in politics that much, rather politics took interest in us and in this way we were obliged to be concerned with politics…I was in *Host do domu* [a literary journal] in 1968, 1969, politics was there even in the Writers' Union…the politics of these times absorbed people even if they had not intended it originally.[28]

REINVENTING REVOLUTION

Apart from countries such as Denmark, where the state successfully defused crisis by largely responding to student demands, at various points in 1968 state authorities clamped down on students' and workers' movements with more or less vigour.

---

[26] Vladimír Borecký, *Odvrácená tvář humoru. Ke komice absurdity* (Prague, 1996).
[27] Interview with Věra Jirousová, conducted by MČ, Prague, 1 January 2009. See also Věra Jirousová, *KŠ—Křižovnická škola čistého humoru bez vtipu*, catalogue (Prague, 1991) and Věra Jirousová, *Jan Steklík*, catalogue (Prague, 1991).
[28] Interview with Jan Steklík, conducted by MČ, Ústí nad Orlicí, 22 May 2010.

The students' protest in Poland was totally suppressed by the end of March. Most of the activists were arrested or subjected to penal conscription into the army. Police terror deterred those who managed to avoid repression from further political activity.[29] Aleksander Smolar (b. 1940), a Commando who left prison in February 1969, described the sense of collapse and the desire to escape reality:

> Our milieu was bruised and shattered. Some people went abroad and still more of them would go in the following months. Others were looking for any kind of job. There was an utterly post-defeat atmosphere. And a party mood too. People drank a lot, had a rich sexual life. A surrogate life. Mechanisms of internal escape.[30]

In France, strikes and factory occupations were largely brought to an end by the Grenelle agreement between the government, employers and trade unions at the end of May. Some pockets of resistance that refused to give up and were defended by student militants led to the death of the *lycée* student Gilles Tautin at the Renault-Flins factory west of Paris on 10 June, while at the Peugeot factory at Sochaux on 11 June, two workers died and 150 were injured.[31] The Trotskyist JCR and Maoist UJC(ml) were banned on 12 June. According to Dominique Grange:

> It was intolerable, awful, we had a feeling that we had been betrayed, screwed by everyone, that there had been a historic betrayal. Some people went back to their old lives easily, but I couldn't. It was as if I had been paralyzed by the force of the change that had taken place inside me, so that I had gone over to the other side. Socially I was on the same side as the people who were involved in the class struggle and I wanted to be involved in it, even against my own class.[32]

The Soviet invasion of Czechoslovakia in August put an end to the Prague Spring. The government was brought to heel and the previous liberalization movement was branded as counter-revolutionary. Knížák emerged to make a gesture of opposition but recalled the futility of considering opposition by force:

> When the Russians arrived we led a campaign against them. I even composed a song, I went round pubs and street-corners and sang: *Russians go home, we don't want you, Russians go home, fuck you.* I have recorded it, later we recorded it and it can be found on the CD *Aktual—Children of Bolshevism.* Later I went to Prague and I took a gun to fight with. I remember meeting a musician Luboš Fišer on a train. I told him, 'Hey, you guy, I'm going...' and I showed him the gun. He ran to the other end of the train. Finally nothing happened, everything seemed to be so normal... The fight was over. I went back.[33]

In the face of state repression, activists had to rethink what revolution now meant. Open, spontaneous action that combined the political and cultural dimensions of revolution became difficult to hold together. Activists who were committed to political revolution were forced in some countries to go underground, switching

---

[29] Krzesiński interview.

[30] Interview with Aleksander Smolar, conducted by PO, Warsaw, 19 February 2009.

[31] Xavier Vigna, *L'Insubordination ouvrière dans les années 68. Essai d'histoire politique des usines* (Rennes, 2007).

[32] Grange interview.

[33] Knížák interview.

from legal to clandestine activity. The organization of revolution became the task of serious networks such as the International Socialists in Britain, GP in France and the Revolutionary Youth Movement in Czechoslovakia. Activists who favoured cultural revolution tended to break away from political concerns and become concerned with lifestyle issues such as communal living, artistic experimentation, feminism and gay rights, inspired by developments in the US or Italy. By the early 1970s the idea of a political revolution provoked by revolutionary minorities was looking distinctly threadbare. It was not that the working classes were apathetic; only that if they moved it would be on their own terms, related less to class struggle than to issues such as the treatment of immigrant workers and working women, housing crises, and environmental and health issues. The focus of these struggles was the community rather than class, and activists learned the ropes of a new community activism, sometimes working within existing institutions, sometimes working in parallel, but seeing revolution not as the seizure of power but as the transformation of power relations.

Cultural and lifestyle revolution

In France, Michel-Antoine Burnier (b. 1942) became one of the prophets of the new cultural revolution. Passionate in his youth about Sartre and the campaign against the Algerian War, he joined the UEC briefly but left in 1965. In 1968 he was involved in a newspaper called *Action*, which spoke for the whole movement rather than for the Marxist *groupuscules*. He developed this attack on the Marxist conception of revolution by means of a magazine called *Actuel*, launched in 1970 with an American flavour and at the cutting edge of cultural happenings:

> We knew that the death of the movement was the *groupuscules*—I knew them, I knew their leaders, I knew that they were mad, I hated the Gauche Prolétarienne, the residue of Maoism. We said to ourselves that we had to undertake a revolution in spirit, which was present in 1968 but which had been stifled by Trotskyism, Maoism, the October Revolution, the Paris Commune, which was all terribly archaic. The real message was that everyone can speak to each other, it's a free democracy, at last people can have sex. Down with bourgeois morality! We secretly said to ourselves, 'this paper will be a machine to kill off the *groupuscules*, the little political factions, we will get them through the revolution in spirit, sexual liberation, music and happenings', and we got them. We killed the revolution... I was very happy with the way things turned out.[34]

In Copenhagen, meanwhile, Ole Vind tried to keep the two dimensions of revolution—political and cultural—together. The New Society Project House was not only a place for drugs, music, social experiments and planning squatter actions, but also for launching political demonstrations such as that against the World Bank. In the summer of 1970 it organized a two-month summer camp in the countryside that was attended by 25,000 residents and 100,000 visitors. The camp marked the peak of

---

[34] Interview with Michel-Antoine Burnier. See also Burnier's memoirs, *A ma fille. Histoire d'un père de cinquante ans qui ne voulait pas avoir d'enfant* (Paris, 1993) and *L'adieu à Sartre* (Paris, 2000).

the importance of the New Society: in 1971 the Project House was closed as an independent user-driven space and taken over by the municipality because of increasing drug problems. Vind considers it as a symptom of the defeat of the efforts to hold together the aspiration of an inseparable political and cultural revolution. He recalls:

> This is the stage where the divisions are evident between those who think it's all about continuing a traditional leftist/Marxist-based project about social change led by the working class…and the flower-power freaks, the hippy crowd, for whom the revolution meant changing their own minds about the world and changing themselves. This [group] had much less room to manoeuvre because it flourished much better in the summer sun. But in meetings it was not quite the same…Song and dance can't be used as arguments in a debate…I remember working to help reconcile the two groups. It was two sides of the same coin…But it didn't work. Much stronger forces were also at work that would prevent us from agreeing in the long run.[35]

Vind continued with the cultural dimension of revolution, experimenting with communal living, teaching in an experimental school and from the late 1970s becoming involved in the environmental movement.

Although cultural revolution might take over from political concerns, in Czechoslovakia the proponents of alternative culture were also forced to retreat. The challenge of cultural subversion required an environment where some dialogue was possible, and this gradually disappeared after the Soviet invasion in August 1968. Any public performance or activity became politicized and thus activists gradually withdrew from the public to the private sphere. There was a gradual attenuation of great collective actions, events and happenings. People grew more dispersed as many of them lost their official jobs and they had to find alternatives. Many artists were dismissed from official art unions and thus lost the ability to work professionally.

Clandestine political revolution

For some activists, government repression meant simply that they would have to organize underground and more effectively, with a view to rekindling revolution for which May 1968 had been only a dress-rehearsal. Where workers had been involved in 1968 they imagined that class war might be revived, especially in heavy industry where the proletariat was concentrated. The outbreak of real revolution was only a matter of time.

Alain Geismar (b. 1939), who as secretary of the lecturers' union SNESup and participant in the 22 March movement, had been one of the key leaders in May 1968. He became convinced that violent revolution was just over the horizon. He co-wrote *Vers la guerre civile* and was one of the founders of the clandestine GP whose aim was 'the fusion of anti-authoritarian revolt and proletarian revolution'.

---

[35] Vind interview.

It would be a revolutionary party in a way that would organize action among the workers and put the 'Stalinist' French Communist Party to shame. He recalls:

> We thought that there were going to be popular uprisings here and there, which would be put down with bloodshed, as at Sochaux or Flins. We thought that the movement would regain momentum and that the Grenelle agreement didn't satisfy all the demands of the workforce...We had witnessed a movement of young, semi-skilled workers against the way work was organized which would provoke movements here and there which would be suppressed by force, and that it was up to us to build a political organization which would enable us to prepare them and ourselves for the massive confrontations that we expected within four or five years.[36]

Jean-Pierre Le Dantec (b. 1943), a graduate of the École Centrale, had been a member of the Maoist UJC(ml), visited the China of the cultural revolution in 1967, and became one of the stalwarts of the GP. Involved in whipping up and sustaining revolutionary fervour, he recalls events in 1970:

> After the formation of the Gauche Prolétarienne, I was appointed editor of its paper, *La Cause du peuple*. This paper campaigned for illegal actions such as the kidnapping of bosses...I remember an article which proclaimed, 'Not one will get out of insurgent Paris alive', talking of the police. Then there was an extraordinary article about what was happening in Northern Ireland. As a result I was arrested for defending arson, sabotage and murder...and got two or three sentences of a year's prison.[37]

The press was one weapon; other tactics included getting jobs in factories in order to incite strike action and spectacular actions to expose the evils of capitalism. Anne and Bernard Victorri joined the Gauche Prolétarienne and went to the heavily industrialized Nord and Pas-de-Calais Départements, whose mining population had a long tradition of strike action and of resistance to German occupation during the Second World War. When sixteen miners were killed in a pit explosion at Fouquières-les-Lens in 1970, they tried to turn proletarian anger against the negligent mining company. Bernard explains how their GP group tried to relaunch class war, resulting for him in a six-month prison sentence.

> There was a fire-damp explosion and we launched a campaign around the theme 'the mining companies kill miners in cold blood'...We stirred up a lot of support but the police crushed it savagely and arrested us on the day of the funeral...About fifty of us were held at the police station. There was a kind of riot, and we battled with the police in the police station. It was quite powerful and violent. When we realized that the miners were not going to follow us we decided on a violent gesture...and threw Molotov cocktails at the offices of the mining company.[38]

[36] Interview with Alain Geismar, conducted by RG, Paris, 29 May 2007. See also Geismar, Serge July and Erlyne Morane, *Vers la Guerre civile* (Paris, 1969) and Geismar, *Pourquoi nous combattons* (Paris, 1970).
[37] Interview with Jean-Pierre Le Dantec, conducted by RG, Paris, 24 April 2007. See also Robert Gildea, James Mark and Niek Pas, 'European radicals and the "Third World": Imagined solidarities and radical networks, 1958–1973', *Cultural and Social History* 8/4 (2011), 455, 460.
[38] Victorri interview.

In Britain, as in France, some activists nurtured the aim of rekindling revolution as some kind of class war, hoping to take advantage of threats of redundancy in some of the traditional industries such as shipbuilding and mining. This required the organization of more centralized, disciplined Marxist groups like the French GP. The International Socialists (IS) were initially quite a broad church, as Sheila Rowbotham (b. 1943) remembers:

> IS seemed the most sensible one to join, because it seemed to have not just sectarian characteristics, it seemed to be more open to working-class people's experience... It attracted a whole generation of young radical people, you know, really, so there were a lot of people with interesting different ideas in IS at that time.[39]

At the end of 1968, however, IS became explicitly Trotskyist, with a firm party discipline. Martin Shaw (b. 1947) explains that as it became more disciplined it became more intolerant of elements like himself who did not cleave to the strict party line:

> IS before 1968 didn't talk about a revolutionary party and after 1968 it did. Before 1968 it had a very loose, decentralized structure; after 1968 [Tony] Cliff introduced the idea of democratic centralism and a more disciplined sort of structure... I didn't see it as a danger at that stage, although some other people did... The tensions and conflicts inside the organization grew and the leadership used organizational means to try and defeat the oppositional tendencies... I didn't like the way in which the leadership manoeuvred and it eventually came to use organizational means to close down opposition. I found myself increasingly marginalized.[40]

Steve Jefferys (b. 1945), former London School of Economics (LSE) radical working on the production lines of Singer and Chrysler in Glasgow and organizer for IS in the Glasgow area, promoted IS's message in support of the totemic workers' occupation to prevent the closure of Upper Clyde Shipbuilders in 1971:

> The IS group flung itself into the activity. There was a period of weeks when we were selling several thousand copies of *Socialist Worker* just on the Clydeside alone. I actually did get a hernia from lifting bales of newspapers. Had to have an operation after that... and we had probably twenty, at different moments, points in time, volunteers coming up to work, doing, to support the local group. I mean effectively because we were supporting the occupation but arguing for more radical policies, we attracted quite a number of members as a result.[41]

In Czechoslovakia, under the new occupation regime, as the government bowed before the Soviet Union, a small minority thought in terms of political revolution. There was a sense that as the mass of the population caved in, it was up to the students to demonstrate their revolutionary potential. In November 1968 a student strike against the Soviet occupation was organised by the Revolutionary Youth

---

[39] Interview with Sheila Rowbotham, conducted by JD, Oxford, 10 June 2009.
[40] Interview with Martin Shaw, conducted by JD, Falmer, 14 November 2008.
[41] Interview with Steve Jefferys, conducted by JD, London, 21 April 2010.

Movement.[42] Jaroslav Suk (b. 1948), a member of the Prague Philosophy Faculty, joined the Movement because he felt that reform was no longer possible. They were, he says, seeking:

> democracy, freedom of speech, human freedom in general and the preservation of social benefits. Not the return to capitalism but a renaissance of socialism. But then, especially after August 1968 we came to the conclusion that it was a dead end... We agreed that this system cannot be reformed and that we want a revolution. [laughs][43]

Suk's laugh betrays the predicament the students were in. On the one hand there seemed no alternative to revolution, and the leaders of the Revolutionary Youth Movement were all arrested and spent time in prison. On the other whatever they indulged in could only be a pale imitation or parody of the Russian Revolution of 1917, which all communist regimes commemorated and on which they had been brought up. Petr Uhl, who had been involved with the UEC in Paris in the mid-1960s and had read Bukharin and Trotsky, had both a serious and a humorous take on revolution:

> I understood the concept of the world revolution that contained three streams: anti-capitalist proletarian revolution, national liberation or national democratic revolution in the third world and a political revolution in the Soviet world where political power will be taken from the bureaucracy. I believed in it much less, we even made fun of it... At the Philosophical Faculty there were cells like Starshij Lejtenant [Senior Lieutenant] or Sergeant Vasya... It was partly parody, partly meant seriously.[44]

Petruška Šustrová (b. 1947), another Prague Philosophical Faculty student, was one of the organizers of the November strike and joined the Revolutionary Youth Movement. She was arrested in December 1969 and spent two years in prison. She takes up the theme of the humorous dimension of the Youth Movement but underlines the additional point that it had only limited support within the student body, most of who fatalistically accepted First Secretary Dubček's agreement to Soviet terms dictated in Moscow:

> We had cells, ours was called Sergeant Vasya, which was of course a joke—we were not that mad about Russia. Another cell in the Philosophical Faculty was called Lev Ackermann aus Böhmen, which sounded intellectual and funny. In my faculty, there were some radicals with opinions close to mine but the majority thought that Dubček was wonderful. Dubček was an important symbol and for me, he failed... When the politicians agreed to legalize the entry of the Warsaw Pact armies, it was no longer an occupation as they became allies. I felt that communists were no longer our allies. Not because they were communists but because they accepted the occupation. Of course I did not know how to oppose them. That is why I welcomed the idea of founding an

---

[42] Jaroslav Pažout, *Hnutí revoluční mládeže* (Prague, 2004); idem, *Mocným navzdory. Studentské hnutí v šedesátých letech 20. století* (Prague, 2008).

[43] Interview with Jaroslav Suk, conducted by MČ, Prague, 15 July 2008.

[44] Interview with Petr Uhl, conducted by MČ, Prague, 17 May 2008. See also Petr Uhl (ed.) *Program společenské samosprávy* (Cologne, 2008), and idem, *Právo a nespravedlnost očima Petra Uhla* (Prague, 1998).

underground organization, suggested to me by Petr Uhl after the November strike, because the legal fight was not possible.[45]

Revolution through community action

Given the difficulty faced by Marxist groups of stimulating revolution as class struggle, other activists began to conceive of revolution in radically different ways. These did not involve class struggle and the seizure of power but focussed on community and the transformation of power relations in everyday life. Paris and the Paris Commune were no longer the model. Marjorie Mayo (b. 1943), who came to community activism through the LSE and social work in London, thought that revolution:

> doesn't have to be a moment with the barricades, I don't think I thought that the barricades are going up in Britain. Well they had gone up in Britain, but not in the sense of the Paris Commune—and look what happened to the Paris Commune. But in the sense that power relations will have to change... before serious progress is going to be made towards a more genuinely democratic and more egalitarian kind of society... community action, like trade union action, is very important, because the issues that people are taking up are important. It matters whether people's housing is improved. It matters if people get access to their welfare rights, just as it matters that they're treated fairly in the workplace. That, of itself, doesn't fundamentally change power relationships, but without that kind of organization and development of solidarity, and development of collective understanding that changes need to be made, you're never going to make them.[46]

The model for this new kind of activism came from the US, where a radical participatory version of community action was evolving in response to the perceived failure of Lyndon Johnson's War on Poverty in urban areas.[47] It also came from Italy, where the revolutionary Lotta Continua movement, founded in 1969 to spread activism from students to youth and factory workers, moved its centre of action from student-worker assemblies in striking factories to the community at large under the slogan, 'take the city' as a whole.[48]

In the UK a form of grassroots urban politics generally labelled 'community action' took root in the early 1970s. For the Camden activist John Cowley (b. 1939), who had witnessed community action in Chicago during two years teaching in the US, community politics offered 'an opening to transform the world and turn it the right way up'.[49] For Australian former anarchist Lynne Segal

---

[45] Interview with Petruška Šustrová, Czech radio, 5–9 March 2007. Sergeant Vasya is a wounded soldier in the 1959 Soviet film *Ballad of a Soldier*. Lev Ackermann is a Russian-sounding take on the medieval German poem *Der Ackermann aus Böhmen*, a dialogue between a ploughman and Death.

[46] Interview with Marjorie Mayo, conducted by JD, London, 30 June 2010.

[47] Peter Marris and Martin Rein, *Dilemmas of Social Reform. Poverty and Community Action in the United States* (London, 1972); Gareth Davies, *From Opportunity to Entitlement: the Transformation of Great Society Liberalism* (Lawrence, KS, 1996).

[48] Luigi Bobbio, *Storia di Lotta continua* (Milan, 1988).

[49] Interview with John Cowley, conducted by JD, London, 22 July 2010.

(b. 1943) the whole nexus of community action in an urban setting entailed 'reclaiming the spaces and places wherever you were. So that might be the nurseries, community centres, youth work...The squatters' movement, tenants' associations'.[50] Squatting in particular became the urban activist's self-help movement of choice. Ron Bailey (b. 1943), of the libertarian socialist organization Solidarity and now a parliamentary lobbyist, spent most of his working life as 'a community shit-stirrer'. He came to prominence in 1969 as the organizer of the occupation of empty houses in Redbridge, in north-east London, which effectively launched the squatting movement. With some 30,000 squatters in London in the early 1970s, squatting was a way to challenge established tenurial relations through 'constructive action':

> 'Constructive...action' for revolutionists is that which empowers people, that which throws away the myths that they need leaders and politicians and bosses and policemen to run their lives for them, that they can't do it themselves, they have to leave it to others. That's constructive action.[51]

Piers Corbyn (b. 1947), then an International Marxist Group (IMG) adherent, had initially dismissed the possibility of squatting himself after eviction from his west London flat ('don't be silly, only hippies do that'), only to become the effective leader of the largest London squat, around Elgin Avenue, and to 'sell' the cause to the IMG:

> I thought squatting in itself was important and we started this view in the IMG that actually the natural trajectory of squatting is expropriation, and it is inherently progressive or revolutionary. We had a lot of opposition to that. 'Oh, Piers, don't be ridiculous. The workplace is what counts'. Blah blah blah blah...Decent housing for all, was our slogan. The IMG liked that. Great stuff. They decided then it was a transitional demand. Housing for all was a transitional demand, i.e. it's got a red tick beside it...Because a transitional demand is one whereby it's reasonable within capitalism to demand it, but capitalism itself cannot grant it, so therefore it's inherently anti-capitalist. So if capitalism granted decent housing, or housing for all, it would collapse. So we'd have a revolution, you see...which was good, because they want revolution, you see.[52]

Inspiration for these movements came partly from Italy. One of the first networks in Britain to be influenced by Lotta Continua was Big Flame, which was formed—initially as a community newspaper—in Liverpool in 1970. Alan Hayling (b. 1947), recently graduated from Cambridge and working for the BBC, found Big Flame 'very attractive to me as being non-sectarian, libertarian, not Leninist, of the people more'.[53] Similarly, Big Flame's appeal to Lynne Segal lay in the fact that:

[50] Interview with Lynne Segal, conducted by JD, London, 22 April 2010.
[51] Interview with Ron Bailey, conducted by JD, London, 15 June 2010.
[52] Interview with Piers Corbyn, conducted by JD, London, 15 June 2010.
[53] Interview with Alan Hayling, conducted by JD, London, 27 July 2010.

it believed in trying to join community and work politics in the place in which you were. It didn't really [do] vanguard leaders. You know it always said, 'We are not the revolutionary party'. We certainly weren't the revolutionary party because there was only a few hundred of us...We had no illusions.[54]

Whereas attempts by revolutionary minorities to mobilize skilled workers in heavy industry showed little result, more success was forthcoming in lighter, more modern industries where the workforce was semi-skilled, female and often immigrant. These had their own reasons for strikes and occupations and were followed rather than led by activists who developed new ideas about community action.

In 1976–8 a protracted battle took place at Grunwick, a film-processing plant in north-west London, where the workforce of mainly Asian women took industrial action to secure trade-union rights. The factory became a fixture of the activist circuit. Marjorie Mayo remembered 'a very good-tempered solidarity with a whole lot of people from the area, and from other areas, going to support these Asian women who had been treated unfairly'.[55] Stephanie Pixner (b. 1945), who had moved from a communist party background to a more eclectic feminism by the 1970s, said:

I was in the Hackney Music Workshop and we would do things like we would write songs and we'd go on demonstrations, we would go to Grunwick's, we would go to tenants' associations or tenants' strikes or whatever and be supportive in that kind of way.[56]

Involving as it did a largely female, immigrant workforce, Grunwick was a model 'Lotta Continua' type of dispute. Big Flame activist Pete Ayrton (b. 1943) thought that it offered 'such a perfect focus for support. Asian women, oppressed at work...They had everything going for them. It was a struggle that a lot of people could support and did support'.[57] Its impact echoed the factory occupations and work-ins by overwhelmingly female workforces in the face of proposed closures at Sexton, Son and Everard, shoemakers in Fakenham, Norfolk, and at Briant Colour Printing in Peckham, south-east London, both in the spring of 1972. They focussed attention both as labour and women's issues and broadened the appeal of feminism from university-educated to working-class women. Sheila Rowbotham, who was involved in the Arsenal Women's Liberation Workshop, reflects:

Women were incredibly active in that period, partly around equal pay, partly about low pay, partly about the right to unionize...After the economic situation got bad, and factories started to be closed, there were these general occupations which often included women like the Briants thing, colour printing...early stuff about Grunwicks actually, before '77, and there was also the Fakenham occupation...and the interesting thing about the Fakenham women occupiers was they were incredibly militant

[54] Segal interview.
[55] Mayo interview.
[56] Interview with Stephanie Pixner, conducted by JD, London, 15 July 2010.
[57] Interview with Pete Ayrton, conducted by JD, London, 5 June 2010.

about their craft skills and sharing their craft skills and continuing their jobs but, they were Tories politically.[58]

In France, Lotta Continua had a particular influence on the Maoist group Vive la Révolution (VLR). This formed at the University of Nanterre after 1968 and set up a 'workers' base' near the Renault factory of Flins, from which further struggles were expected to come. At the same time activists living in nearby communes were experimenting with sexual liberation and published a newspaper, *Tout!*, which became a platform for feminism and gay liberation.[59] In the autumn of 1970 a team from VLR went to Turin to meet representatives of Lotta Continua, who urged them to move on from the factories to 'take the city'. 'Speak out in the street and in the factory' became the new slogan for VLR.[60]

Nadja Ringart (b. 1948) was sent to prison for three months for her part in a VLR attack on the town hall of Meulan near Flins, to highlight the involvement of officials in employers' trafficking of immigrants who lived and worked in atrocious conditions because of their illegal status. Women's prison, she said, made her 'consciously feminist'. As a result, and with her close friend Françoise Picq, also in VLR, she became much more involved in women's issues in the local working-class community, and increasingly in the feminist movement itself:

> With Françoise we started going to see the women in the locality, to talk about contraception and their relationship to their families. Françoise had not yet had her baby. We were not very good talking about education, but contraception and abortion, women's rights, yes. So we drifted away very gently [from VLR].[61]

Meanwhile, sobered after his spell in prison, Bernard Victorri went with Anne and their baby to live at Hautmont in the Sambre valley, which Anne describes as closely imitating Zola's *Germinal*. Their activism changed from class war to community politics and they became part of a network—the Movement for Free Abortion and Contraception (MLAC)—including left-wing doctors, which provided (illegal until 1975) abortions to working women. In a way they had not imagined before, they managed to mobilize support from the working-class community when Anne was sacked from her teaching post in the local school for alleged militancy and began a hunger strike in the local church. She recalls:

> At Hautmont we felt really linked to the masses, even though we had just arrived and knew no one… There was a great popular movement, a sort of mini-'68 at Hautmont. A thousand people came onto the square to talk to us, to complain about the school, to support us… We planned a big demonstration and the CRS [riot police] arrived in

---

[58] Interview with Sheila Rowbotham, conducted by JD, Oxford, 10 June 2009.

[59] Manus McGrogan, '*Tout!* in context, 1968–1973: French radical press at the crossroads of far left, new movements and counterculture', PhD thesis (University of Portsmouth, 2010).

[60] Manus McGrogan, 'Vive la Révolution and the example of Lotta Continua: The circulation of ideas and practices between the left militant worlds of France and Italy following May '68', *Modern and Contemporary France* 18/3 (August 2010), 309–28.

[61] Interview with Nadja Ringart, conducted by RG, Sceaux, 5 June 2007.

buses like an army of occupation. We turned the demonstration into a big meeting and a thousand workers came to the community hall to hear us.[62]

The most eloquent illustration of a shift from class to community action, the switch of influence from *gauchiste* activists from outside to activist workers themselves and the emergence of working-class feminism, were the strikes at the Lip watch-making factory at Besançon in 1973–4 and again in 1976. Threatened by a wave of redundancies the workers struck, occupied the factory and started up the manufacture and sale of watches under workers' control. The movement was driven by a Comité d'Action, representing both unionized and non-unionized workers, one of the leading lights of which was Jean Raguénès, a Dominican priest who ran a local hostel for children at risk and earned a wage in the factory.[63] The committee put pressure on, but also worked with, the shop stewards of the non-communist CFDT union led by Charles Piaget, belying the prejudice of Maoists and Trotsky-ites that trade unions were opposed to grassroots action. A Maoist delegation of the GP visited Lip in June 1973, accompanied by Maurice Clavel, an iconic figure in the Resistance and now involved in their new paper, *Libération*. He saw the Lip strike as a community rather than a class action, was moved by the fraternity of workers in a traditionally Catholic region, and presented the leaders as disciples, calling Piaget Matthew and Raguénès Simon.[64] 'The workers have seized power. Quite simply', said *Libération*.[65]

In August 1973 a police assault retook the factory and forced the workers back into the local community, from which they continued their struggle to be taken back to work. The Lip strike was sustained by 100,000 marchers who descended on Besançon on Saturday 29 September 1973 and by Lip committees that were set up across the country and abroad. Early in 1974 an agreement was reached between the workers and management and work was gradually resumed. The leaders of the GP were very aware of the significance of the strike. Revolution was no longer to be seen as a seizure of power along the lines of the Bolshevik 'Ten Days that Shook the World', but rather a series of local struggles.[66] Moreover, the claim of Marxist activists to teach revolution to workers or peasants was redundant; they had their own interests, their own leaders and their own dynamic. Alain Geismar reflects on the changing meaning of revolution:

> The main risk we ran was that the revolutionary organization found itself in an escalation [of violence] face to face with the police apparatus of the state...Then there was...Lip. We discovered that extremely subversive things were happening in the factories, which did not necessarily lead to a military escalation...the Lip workers had no need of the Gauche Prolétarienne or the Maoists.[67]

[62] Victorri interview.
[63] Jean Raguénès, *De Mai 68 à Lip. Un Dominicain au coeur des luttes* (Paris, 2008).
[64] Maurice Clavel, *Les Paroissiens de Palente* (Paris, 1974). See also Jean Divo, *L'affaire Lip et les Catholiques de Franche-Comté* (Yens-sur-Morges, 2003).
[65] *Libération*, 20 June 1973.
[66] Philippe Gavi, Jean-Paul Sartre and Pierre Victor, *On a Raison de se révolter* (Paris, 1974), 250–5.
[67] Geismar interview.

Lip demonstrated not only the power of the workers but the power of women in the factory and in the community. Women made up 85 per cent of the semi-skilled Lip workforce but the trade-union leadership around Piaget was wholly male and did not take account of issues such as childcare that arose from the strike. Fatima Demougeot (b. 1949), a semi-skilled worker in the Action Committee, relates how from the Lip struggle new issues arose both in the factory and the community, centring on women's rights and women's bodies:

> Until then we were workers who—what shall I say?—discovered our workers' condition, and were mobilized behind a single slogan, the defence of our jobs...Within that there was a single entity, neither man nor woman but a collective life that wove itself around the defence of our jobs. The question of women did not emerge, not at any moment, it occurred only afterwards when the women of the PSU [United Socialist Party] got in touch with the female PSU militants and said, 'a lot of women are involved but we don't see them speak, their needs are not included'...It was only then...that we began to think about our role in the struggle, what it had been like, whether we had spoken, it was really a summing up, but which led us very quickly to 'the unions don't listen to us', 'the men don't listen to us', 'the women's question is not taken on board or analyzed'...We became a force in our own right.[68]

This new confidence among industrial workers was also found in the Baltic shipyards that, as we have seen, did not respond to student agitation in 1968 but later had their own reasons to strike. The presence of sailors who travelled abroad and were more aware of the higher standard of living in western democracies gave rise to open and reflective social networks in the ports. In December 1970 shipyard workers in Gdańsk, Gdynia and Szczecin went on strike, Communist Party buildings were set on fire and the army opened fire on the workers. This time it was the former 1968 activists who remained passive and did not respond to the workers' initiative. This, however, changed in June 1976. The workers again took matters into their own hands and now students, intellectuals and clergy—often the students of 1968 a little further down the line—followed behind, organized in the 'Committee for Workers' Defence' (KOR) to defend workers' rights from the wrath of the state and to communicate their message to activists in the West.

'KOR grew from March', said many former activists of March 1968 who, now in their thirties, were the key organizers.[69] Of its thirty-eight members, thirteen had been involved in protests in March 1968, including the informal leader of the organization, Jacek Kuroń. Doubtless KOR was hardly a revolutionary movement—its activity relied not on urging workers to go onto the streets but on providing victims of repression with legal and financial assistance. But this collaboration between students, intellectuals, priests and workers laid down a marker for what became the Solidarity movement. Mirosław Sawicki (b. 1946), a March activist from the inner circle of Commandos, links Solidarity back to the experience of March 1968 and KOR:

---

[68] Interview with Fatima Demougeot, conducted by RG, Besançon, 21 May 2007.
[69] Jan Józef Lipski, *Komitet Obrony Robotników* (London, 1983); Maria de Hernandez-Paluch, 'Między marcem a KOR-em', *Kontakt* 4/1988.

Many people involved in March became involved in 1976, treating it as a continuity. For them 1976 was something that should have been done much earlier. I mean contact with the working class. KOR derived from such an idea... which showed results in '80 anyway.[70]

Activists in the West were impressed by the stories of the shipyard strikes, KOR and Solidarity. They represented a challenge to the communist authorities at a time when many former 1968 activists were losing their faith in Marxism. They showed the way to a broader oppositional front, including students, intellectuals, clergy and workers. It made particular sense to the workers of Lip, most of whom were from a Catholic background, and also to the activists from the GP and elsewhere who were seduced by the Lip story. Former GP activist Jean-Pierre Le Dantec recalls a meeting with a delegation of Gdańsk workers who came to Lip in 1981. The beacon was shining now from East to West and the Polish workers were being fêted. In the new union, however, it was the former Maoists of the GP, drunk and singing revolutionary anthems, who seemed out of tune as the struggle against state socialism was reaching a climax:

> I remember a meeting at Besançon, the Lip base, where I was with Benny [Lévy], [Alain] Finkielkraut, [Olivier] Rolin, a little team on our side. There were people from Lip including Raguénès and there was a representative from Solidarity. We were in touch with Kuroń, Michnik, those kinds of people... There had been a sort of rapprochement between Wałęsa and the workers of Gdańsk, the ex-opposition of Trotskyist, Marxist origin like Kuroń and Michnik. At the end of the meeting we had a few drinks and started to sing the *Internationale*. The Poles were quite upset to find themselves with people like that.[71]

CONCLUSION

Revolution was always a goal around 1968 although fierce debate raged among activists about what it meant and what was possible. The iconic model of revolution in May 1968 was the combination of student riot and factory occupations that brought France to the brink of crisis and against which other movements measured themselves. Italian activists practised the same union of students and workers but British student activists were unable to build a bridge between anti-war demonstrations and the very traditional image of proletarian struggle they nurtured. Many Danish activists managed to keep political and lifestyle activism in play, while having little contact with working people. Czechoslovak activists built

---

[70] Interview with Mirosław Sawicki, conducted by PO, Warsaw, 27 February 2010. See also Jerzy Holzer, *Solidarność, Geneza i historia* (Warsaw, 1990); Andrzej Friszke, *Opozycja polityczna w PRL 1945–1980* (London, 1994); Ireneusz Krzemiński, *Solidarność, Projekt polskiej demokracji* (Warsaw, 1997).

[71] Interview with Jean-Pierre Le Dantec, conducted by RG, Paris, 27 April 2007. For another account Jean Raguénès, *De Mai 68 à Lip*, 194.

a parallel universe of artistic subversion that, under communist dictatorship, had a political meaning, while some Greek activists exposed to military dictatorship retained a rather archaic model of armed struggle going back to the Civil War.

The suppression of many activist movements in the course of 1968 led to a rethinking of what revolution might mean, and a sharper division between political and lifestyle revolution. Some activists threw themselves into lifestyle activism, seeing political revolution as a dead end or as something to be consciously avoided. Others went down the route of political revolution as a vanguard or with some idea of serving the people, endeavouring to remobilize the workers for class struggle. Many of these were sent to prison for various terms. Increasingly, in the wake of 1968, the idea of revolution as class struggle gave way to that of revolution as community activism. It was generally a response to workers taking action on their own terms at Lip, Grunwick or Gdańsk and eliciting a response from activists. These rethought revolution as a localised struggle rather than centralized activity focussed on national political centres. They now sited themselves in the community and campaigned to change social attitudes and power relations over time rather than suddenly to overthrow the existing order. There were new concerns such as the struggle for women's rights or women's rights as workers. The epicentre of revolution moved from the university quarter of Paris to factories in the suburbs and provinces, and from West to East as Polish workers and intellectuals now showed the way forward to the *gauchistes* of the Left Bank. The Marxist ideal of proletarian revolution was finally displaced.

5

Encounters

James Mark and Anna von der Goltz

That the new radical political, social and cultural movements that emerged around 1968 constituted a global revolt is part of the wider memory of a period in which Marshall McLuhan coined the phrase 'the global village' to describe a more interconnected world with increasing international ties and greater access to the same media.[1] Many activists had championed this notion by showcasing their 'international solidarity' at numerous jointly held events, such as the Vietnam Congress at West Berlin's Technical University in February 1968. In later commemorative publications the 'political family' of 1960s activists was also conceived of in explicitly global terms.[2]

While internationalism was the catchword at the time, the recent 'transnational turn' in historical studies is itself closely intertwined with some of its legacies, a by-product of the rising 'global consciousness' in the wake of 1968—a growth in the number of NGOs, and the emergence of human rights as a global issue.[3] As a result, the period around 1968 is often singled out as one uniquely defined by the links between activists in different countries, the networks they formed and the ideas they exchanged.[4] This is often embedded into a general narrative of 'globalization', a story of technological and economic progress that has led to an ever more enmeshed world.

While a sense of 68er movements as transnational has clearly emerged as a result, the emphasis has primarily been on western and northern Europe.[5] The events in other countries are often viewed as somewhat separate from the western 1968.[6]

---

[1] Marshall McLuhan, *War and Peace in the Global Village* (New York, 1968); cf. June Edmunds and Bryan S. Turner, *Generations, Culture and Society* (Buckingham and Philadelphia, 2002), 5.

[2] Daniel Cohn-Bendit, *Nous l'avons tant aimée, la révolution* (Paris, 1986).

[3] Akira Iriye, 'Transnational history', *Contemporary European History* 13/2 (2004), 213; on transnational human rights activism from the mid-1970s onwards see Sarah Snyder, *Human Rights Activism and the End of the Cold War: A Transnational History of the Helsinki Network* (Cambridge, 2011).

[4] Patricia Clavin, 'Defining transnationalism', *Contemporary European History* 14/4 (2005), 421–39, here 422.

[5] Belinda Davis, Wilfried Mausbach, Martin Klimke and Carla MacDougall (eds), *Changing the World, Changing Oneself: Political Protest and Collective Identities in West Germany and the US in the 1960s and 1970s* (New York and Oxford, 2010); Gerd-Rainer Horn, *The Spirit of '68: Rebellion in Western Europe and North America, 1956–1976* (Oxford, 2008).

[6] Angelika Ebbinghaus (ed.) *Die letzte Chance?—1968 in Osteuropa: Analysen und Berichte über ein Schlüsseljahr* (Hamburg, 2008).

The Prague Spring and Polish March are conceptualized as peripheral 'other '68s'.[7] When they are compared, the different cases are often put side-by-side by virtue of their simultaneity rather than examined in terms of actual transfers and cross-fertilizations.[8] This chapter will attempt to reconcile these different literatures by examining the commonalities and transfers between revolts on both sides of the Iron Curtain.

In doing so, we build on some of the recent trends in Cold War historiography that favour the study of political and cultural convergence and linkages 'across the blocs' over notions of strict bipolarity.[9] This has had a profound impact on interpretations of postwar Europe, particularly since the accession of former Warsaw Pact states to the European Union in 2004. The history of both halves of the divided continent is increasingly being investigated in conjunction. Because the iconic events of the French May and the Prague Spring more or less coincided, 1968 is being discovered and held up as an important—perhaps *the* most important—moment of East–West convergence during the Cold War.[10]

Like other transnational histories, however, such accounts are often quite normative. They seek to remind Europeans of their shared history to foster greater understanding in the present and thereby nurture the process of European integration. Such studies thus offer a somewhat teleological account of the transnational nature of 1968; their 'implicit assumption is that through border crossings and transnational encounters, borders break down'.[11]

This chapter seeks to refine our understanding of the entangled history of 1968 without simply reading the process of European integration backwards or writing 1968 into a neat story of globalization.[12] In particular, it will concentrate on the clash between an imagined transnational experience and the realities of actual encounters in different settings that often forced activists to rethink the meaning (and relevance) of transnationalism in their own struggles. This chapter uses oral

---

[7] cf. Jürgen Danyel, 'Das andere "1968" des Ostens. Prag und Ostberlin', in Martin Sabrow (ed.) *Mythos '1968'* (Leipzig, 2009), 75–94; Jakub Patočka, Jacques Rupnik and Aleksander Smolar, 'L'autre 1968 vu aujourd'hui de Prague et de Varsovie. Table ronde', *Esprit* 5 (2008). The same can be said about the fight of Spanish students against Franco and of Greek activists against the Generals, but this chapter focusses on encounters between East and West.

[8] Martin Klimke, Jacco Pekelder and Joachim Scharloth (eds) *Between Prague Spring and French May 1968: Opposition and Revolt in Europe, 1960–80* (Oxford and New York, 2011); Walter D. Connor, 'Politics, discontents, hopes: 1968 East and West', *Journal of Cold War Studies* 14/2 (2012), 142–53. For a general argument that there was a combined generational revolt in East and West against postwar rationalism, see Charles S. Maier, 'Conclusion: 1968—Did it matter?', in Vladimir Tismaneanu (ed.) *Promises of 1968: Crisis, Illusion, and Utopia* (Budapest and New York, 2011), 412–33.

[9] Patrick Major and Rana Mitter (eds) *Across the Blocs: Cold War Cultural and Social History* (London, 2004); Michael David-Fox, 'The implications of transnationalism', *Kritika: Explorations in Russian and Eurasian History* 12/4 (2011), 887; Patryk Babiracki, 'Interfacing the Soviet bloc: Recent literature and new paradigms', *Ab Imperio* 4 (2011), 376–407; Peter Romijn, Giles Scott-Smith and Joes Segal (eds), *Divided Dreamworlds?: The Cultural Cold War in East and West* (Amsterdam, 2012); Michael David-Fox, 'The Iron Curtain as semi-permeable membrane: The origins and demise of the Stalinist superiority complex', in Patryk Babiracki and Kenyon Zimmer (eds) *Cold War Crossings: International Travel and Exchange across the Soviet Bloc, 1940s–1960s* (College Station, TX, 2013).

[10] Jürgen Danyel, *Crossing 68/89* (Berlin, 2008), 6.

[11] Clavin, 'Defining transnationalism', 423.   [12] ibid., 424.

history and written sources, both to examine individuals (East–West hybrids, border crossers, émigrés) and networks that transcended national boundaries. We investigate how individuals reconciled their (frequently expressed) desire to participate in a broader movement while struggling to negotiate and understand difference. The chapter also deals with trajectories of transnationalism. As we will see, activists fell in and out of love with different ideas of transnational revolt in different phases of their radical careers. Changing political commitments often went hand in hand with refocussing the international imagination and seeking out different linkages with activists from other parts of Europe or the globe.

GAPS IN THE IRON CURTAIN

Although the Iron Curtain remained a powerful barrier to East–West communication, it was increasingly permeable; thus from the mid-1960s until the close of the decade, encounters between western activists and their counterparts in the East—particularly in Czechoslovakia and Hungary—increased, and western culture was much more accessible in everyday life (albeit within strict ideological limits). This did not mean that activists always embraced or identified with the West; nevertheless, politicization might be increasingly tied up with travel or the consumption of culture from beyond national boundaries. Petr Uhl (b. 1941), a member of the Revolutionary Youth Movement in Czechoslovakia, travelled regularly in this period and viewed the gaps in the Iron Curtain as central to his political radicalization. Although in some ways an exceptional case, his biography illustrated the possibilities that existed, especially for those who were prepared to work through ever more relaxed official structures. While the Czechoslovak Youth Organization had enabled Uhl to travel extensively in the countries of the eastern bloc in the late 1950s and early 1960s, he made his first trip to France in 1965. Asked how he had got there, he explained:

> In '64, the party declared that it was possible to travel abroad...if you got a foreign currency bank voucher...or you needed an 'inviter' to declare he would take care of you: mine was Alain Krivine...I had met him whilst camping in Karlovy Vary where I was accompanying a group of Polish exchange students...I spent six weeks in France...It was an essential experience for my Marxist formation...Loaded with French brochures and books I came back to Prague where I pored over them for three years. Then came '68.[13]

Czechoslovakia became one of the most open countries of the region; between 1968 and April 1969, it is estimated that 690,622 citizens travelled to the West, including many students who travelled not only as tourists but in international work camps, for temporary work, on student exchanges, and for fellowships.[14]

---

[13] Interview with Petr Uhl, conducted by MČ, Prague, 17 May 2008. He is probably referring in fact to the Unions des Étudiants Communistes (UEC), which was breaking up at the time.

[14] Jan Rychlík, *Cestování do ciziny v habsburské monarchii a v Československu. Pasová, vízová a vystěhovalecká politika 1848–1989* (Prague, 2007), 83. This compares to 117,704 departures to 'capitalist countries' in 1964 and 154,229 in 1965.

Moreover, western students poured into Prague in 1968: the graffiti on Prague's city walls that summer could be found in Czech, English, French, German, Spanish and Italian.[15]

Uhl himself began a relationship with Sibylle Plogstedt, a West German student, who had spent the summer of 1968 in Prague conducting research on the reconstruction of the Czechoslovak economy. Whereas her fellow travellers from the West German SDS urged her to leave after the invasion of 21 August, Plogstedt still felt drawn to the young Czechoslovaks who supported socialist reform. She recalled:

> I was not ready to return now. I had never witnessed this kind of resistance. I didn't want to miss a single moment. I took to the community of protest like a fish to water. No comparison to what had happened in West Berlin in 1968.[16]

After spending a few weeks as a courier for radical left-wing students from Charles University, she returned to West Germany, but found herself still gripped by what was going on across the border. She returned to Prague in the autumn and became a member of the Revolutionary Youth after she met Uhl. Because of Uhl's political socialization in France, they intuitively understood each other—both politically and sexually. She christened their erotic life 'socialism in one bed',[17] and their intense love affair lasted until they were both arrested and imprisoned in December 1969, and Plogstedt was eventually released to West Germany.

While such long-term relationships between eastern and western activists were by no means the norm, Hungary too opened up in the mid-1960s, albeit with more restrictions than in Czechoslovakia; nevertheless one in forty-five Hungarian students studied in the West in this period; a higher number than elsewhere in the bloc.[18] More importantly perhaps, activists were increasingly exposed to radical (and mainstream) western culture, as the so-called 'Windows to the West' policy was introduced from the mid-1960s onwards. The Party had an ambivalent, but not wholly critical, take on 'progressive forces' in the West.[19] Hungarians could consume cinema that critiqued western capitalism and imperialism, and listen to western beat and folk music; indeed, the songs of western radical popular culture could be translated into Hungarian—such as those of Pete Seeger,[20] Bob Dylan or Latin American political folk. Some cinema of the

---

[15] Richard Ivan Jobs, 'Youth movements: Travel, protest, and Europe in 1968', *American Historical Review* 114/2 (2009), 401.

[16] Sibylle Plogstedt, *Im Netz der Gedichte: Gefangen in Prag nach 1968* (Berlin, 2001), 15.

[17] Ibid., 26.

[18] Arpad A. Kadarkay, 'Hungary: An experiment in communism', *Political Research Quarterly*, 26/2 (1973), 291–2; on opening up for students, see Katalin Somlai, 'Ösztöndíjjal Nyugatra a hatvanas években. Az Országos Ösztöndíj Tanács felállítása', in János Tischler (ed.) *Kádárizmus mélyfúrások* (Budapest, 2009), 273–314; also Csaba Békés, 'A kádári külpolitika, 1956–1968. Látványos sikerek—"láthatatlan konfliktusok"', in idem, *Európából Európába. Magyarország konfliktusok kereszttüzében, 1945–1990* (Budapest, 2004), 237–56.

[19] Gábor Kovács, 'Revolution, lifestyle, power and culture', in János M. Rainer and György Péteri (eds) *Muddling Through in the Long 1960s: Ideas and Everyday Life in High Politics and the Lower Classes of Communist Hungary* (Budapest and Trondheim, 2005), 29.

[20] Interview with György Pór, conducted by JM, Brussels, 13 March 2009.

lifestyle revolution was allowed past the censor, so long as it did not contravene 'socialist morality'. *A Clockwork Orange* was banned, while *Easy Rider* became the biggest international hit of the early 1970s.[21] Bálint Nagy (b. 1949), who flirted with Maoism in the late 1960s before turning to dissidence in the 1970s, remembered the importance of consuming western products gleaned from both official and unofficial sources:

> We listened to radio Free Europe, to Radio Luxembourg... and loads of records came to Szeged [in south-eastern Hungary] across the Yugoslav border, these bakelite things... there was a remarkable thing in the first or second year of college, when there was this Communist Youth camp at Balatonföldvár with these wooden huts, and on the first day we stuck on to the outside walls four large posters of Jimmy Hendrix and Sergeant Pepper's.[22]

Gábor Gyáni (b. 1950), member of the Debrecen University Communist Youth reform movement, and later historian, was sent copies of the *New Musical Express* from Britain on a weekly subscription.[23] György Pór (b. 1944), imprisoned in the main political prison in Budapest in 1968 for involvement in anti-state conspiracy, nevertheless had Jerry Rubin's *Do It*, Abbie Hoffman's *Steal This Book*, along with Che Guevara's *Bolivian Diaries* smuggled into his cell: this became the starting point for his discovery of western 'lifestyle revolution'.[24]

Others noted the parade of international activists who came to Budapest, most notably West German radicals and members of the American New Left who visited György Lukács, alongside the Greek activists who had fled the Colonels' Dictatorship in the late 1960s. For those activists who critiqued really existing socialism from the left, visits to the West could be inspiring in that they provided evidence of an authentic bottom-up democratic leftist culture that contrasted sharply with the seeming sterility of their own official state socialism. István Nemes (b. 1953) was the singer with the Maoist-influenced cultural collective Orfeo, and visited a festival in Italy in 1972. Bologna was mentioned often as a popular destination for official youth delegations:

> We went to Bologna, in '72, it had a great effect on me, seeing the orchestra of the Communist Party, it was a festival organized by the *Unità*, the daily of the Italian CP, people set up little cities, villages, having picnics, cooking for themselves, the main point was that we were all together, it made a big impression on me, the feeling of democracy at the festival, just ordinary people getting together... in the early 1970s we felt a really strong feeling of solidarity with the Italian left, it was a completely different type of leftism to the courtier-leftism found in Hungary.[25]

Whereas some Hungarians had considerable exposure to developments in western Europe, the East German regime was in many respects the least open of the

---

[21] RFE/RL Research Institute, Open Society Archives, Budapest, HU OSA 300-40-2-Box 4. Report February 28 1976.
[22] Interview with Bálint Nagy, conducted by PA, Budapest, 14 November 2008.
[23] Interview with Gábor Gyáni, conducted by JM, Budapest, 27 September 2008.
[24] Pór interview.
[25] Interview with István Nemes, conducted by JM, Budapest, 24 January 2009.

eastern bloc countries when it came to permitting western influences and travel. The regime had literally cemented its rejection of the West with the construction of the Berlin Wall in August 1961. While the first few years after its construction had been characterized by relative openness in the cultural sphere and witnessed artistic experimentation and a thriving youth culture, a large-scale cultural clampdown followed from 1965 onwards that lasted until the early 1970s.[26] The East German authorities began to ban western-inspired music bands, beat groups, films, theatre plays and books. Because East Germany was located furthest west in geographical terms and because East and West Germans shared a language, however, western influences continued to seep into the GDR even after 1961. In spite of being walled in, the GDR was never a hermetically sealed society.[27] The majority of East Germans could receive western TV stations and radio channels. By 1971, 85 per cent of GDR citizens owned a television and viewing western programmes was a widespread habit.[28] East Germans could also travel around most eastern bloc countries without a visa from 1972 onwards. Many had already done so in previous years; East German travel to Czechoslovakia spiked from 50,000 in 1967 to 200,000 in 1968.[29]

Even though they were usually not permitted to travel to the West, many of the East Germans who became active around 1968 had grown up at a time when the inner-German border had been much more porous. Former Trotskyist Thomas Klein explains:

> I was born in 1948...as a Berliner, I internalized both eastern and western experiences, which probably applies to many members of my generation...as a child I spent as much time in West Berlin as in East Berlin.

When 1968 came, this background made him susceptible to both new eastern and western political influences:

> It was a time of great questions, the time when Prague '68 happened, the New Left in the West, the student revolt, the SDS and the first attempts to rediscover the dissident Marxist literature of the 1920s and 1930s that had been banned in the East and forgotten in the West. And therefore I—alongside many others who would go down a different path—belong to the GDR 68ers for whom the Paris May and Prague Spring were the key moments of their political socialization.[30]

Gerd Poppe (b. 1941), a one-time peer of Klein's, describes the political and cultural influences of his childhood as a similar hybrid of East and West. Until he was twenty, he went to West Berlin every week, shopped for books, went to the cinema and sometimes saw three films in one day:

---

[26] Marc-Dietrich Ohse, 'German Democratic Republic', in D. Pollack and J. Wielgohs (eds) *Opposition in Communist Eastern Europe* (Aldershot, 2004), 73–93; Michael Rauhut, *Beat in der Grauzone: DDR-Rock 1964 bis 1972—Politik und Alltag* (Berlin, 1993).

[27] Uta Poiger, *Jazz, Rock, and Rebels: Cold War Politics and American Culture in a Divided Germany* (Berkeley, CA, 2000).

[28] Patrick Major, *Behind the Berlin Wall: East Germany and the Frontiers of Power* (Oxford, 2010), 193.

[29] Ibid., 197.

[30] Interview with Thomas Klein, conducted by AvdG, Berlin, 28 June 2010.

I saw all the Nouvelle Vague films, early Godart, Truffaut and so on. This was all before the Wall was built and therefore I still had these opportunities that those people who were a little younger no longer had. Well, this situation was characteristic for the early sixties... There was a palpable western influence, the music scene, a particular clothing style, all young people wanted Levis and they had these parkas, these military-style ones... Many ran around in those, grew their hair.[31]

Although more than a decade younger than Poppe, Lutz Rathenow (b. 1952) was almost equally exposed to western pop culture and stayed glued to his radio, which received western stations, throughout his teenage years: 'we took a lot of things we couldn't have from the West, via the media... I wanted parts of the hippie, pop and rock culture: the Stones, Jimi Hendrix, Janis Joplin'. In spite of his enthusiasm for western music, however, Rathenow underlines that his upbringing was not entirely dominated by western influences. 'The pattern of socialization is a very West German one under specific East German conditions. And the perspective is a mixed one', he explains. Rather than identifying completely with West German activists of 1968, he discovered:

[common] identity roots, similarities to György Dalos from Budapest, a radical leftist who was imprisoned as a Maoist in Budapest, because he sought to abolish private property... It is a neither a pure eastern nor a pure western perspective. That doesn't just mean the GDR, that means eastern Europe, a piece of eastern European identity.[32]

Although East Germans were for the most part barred from visiting the West from 1961 onwards, westerners frequently travelled east for family and other visits, allowing for relatively easy personal contacts and the exchange of ideas via texts, books, records and other western goods that visitors often brought with them. In March 1968, the East German Security Service (Stasi) reported that one particular group of young people in East Berlin, many of whom would be arrested for protesting against the invasion of Czechoslovakia six months later, received a regular supply of products from West Berlin:

these youths engaged in speculative transactions of studded jeans, parkas [*Amikutten*] and shoes that are being supplied by contacts from West Berlin. These goods stem from the 'Amishop' [sic], West Berlin..., where they can be purchased cheaply. Cigarettes, records and western printed goods are being imported via the same channels and traded among the youths.[33]

Others were politicized through exchanges with visitors from other western European countries. Rupert Schröter (b. 1949) credits a French diplomat's daughter, who could travel freely between East and West Berlin and often smuggled books in her rucksack, with introducing him to the writings of Trotsky and ultimately winning him over to the Trotskyist International.[34] Steffi Recknagel (b. 1950) equally

[31] Interview with Gerd Poppe, conducted by AvdG, Berlin, 11 June 2008.
[32] Interview with Lutz Rathenow, conducted by AvdG, Berlin, 30 April 2010.
[33] See the Stasi files included in Robert Havemann's private papers: MfS, ZAIG, 1454, 15, in *Havemann Archive* (RHG), file RH280. The Stasi probably mistook a West Berlin 'Army Shop' for an 'Amishop'.
[34] Interview with Rupert Schröter, conducted by AvdG, Berlin, 4 January 2010.

remembers the impact a French childhood friend had on her development. They met at 'French camp', comprising young French pupils with ties to the French Communist Party and the trade union CGT, and young East Germans, near Leipzig, while still at school. She befriended a girl from Lyon who returned to the GDR after finishing school to work as a translator for the East German News Agency. They shared a flat and 'that was of course a contact through which much of what was en vogue in France at that time seeped in...It was an important time'.[35]

In some instances, childhood friendships sustained more concrete and long-term political ties. Gerd Poppe, for one, did not have to rely solely on smuggled books to learn about the West German student movement that so interested him, but had a strong and enduring personal link to the West German New Left/Jürgen Holtfreter](b. 1937), a childhood friend from his native Rostock, who had emigrated to the West in 1958, lived in the SDS headquarters on West Berlin's Kurfürstendamm and regularly supplied Poppe with literature. After 21 August 1968 they went to the Czech embassy in East Berlin with about eight other young East Germans to declare their solidarity with Dubček.[36] Holtfreter, whose brothers had remained in the East, remained the go-to guy for a number of different East German political groups when it came to obtaining literature.[37] When he had children in the 1970s, he often smuggled books in their nappies.

THE COMMON STRUGGLE OF A NEW GENERATION?

Given the near-simultaneity of fundamental critiques being levelled against the systems in East and West, often from a New Left perspective, and the extensive and often long-term ties between East and West in this period, it is not surprising that many activists perceived 1968 as a common East–West struggle of a fundamentally new kind. The communist Austrian writer Ernst Fischer, who had attended the infamous Kafka conference at Liblice in 1963, expressed this poignantly in a letter he sent to East German dissident Robert Havemann in June 1968:

> It is indeed a revolutionary year, in Prague and in Paris...In France class struggle, of course, but with new aspects, kindled by young intellectuals like never in the past...These students...represent the essential and steadily growing contradiction of modern industrial society, the contradiction between promise and reality, between the speed of scientific-technical progress and the quickly outdated institutions, the insurrection of fantasy against routine, of consciousness against hypocrisy. And what is happening in Czechoslovakia is no longer class struggle but the fight of the productive and progressive forces against the parasitical ones and those who stifle progress... [I]t is world history we are witnessing. Vietnam, Prague and Paris are, I believe, the dawn of a new development...I wish you and all of us that this movement will become unstoppable.[38]

[35] Interview with Steffi Recknagel, conducted by AvdG, Berlin, 5 January 2010. See above, p. 80.
[36] Poppe interview; interview with Jürgen Holtfreter, conducted by AvdG, Berlin, 25 June 2010.
[37] Interview with Burkhard Kleinert, conducted by AvdG, Berlin, 27 April 2010; interview with Franziska Groszer, conducted by AvdG, Berlin, 7 October 2008.
[38] Ernst Fischer to Robert Havemann, 4 June 1968, in RHG, file RH 022/1.

Nevertheless, such paeans to a joint struggle across the Iron Curtain were often not available to an eastern audience. In Hungary, for instance, Ernst Fischer's *Art and Co-existence*—along with Herbert Marcuse's *One Dimensional Man*, Daniel Cohn-Bendit's *Left-Wing Radicalism* and the Italian New Left's *Il Manifesto*—were restricted reading for the Party elite and never published.[39] Although student protests were widely reported on as evidence of western youth's anti-capitalism and the fragility of political systems to the west of the Iron Curtain, New Left works that asserted that a new global radical youth, rather than the working class, were the new revolutionary agents, were prohibited.[40] Despite this, many elite intellectuals and students were able to obtain copies of New Left works in university libraries, however, and these ideas had some impact. Ágnes Heller (b. 1929) and Mihály Vajda (b. 1935), two members of the 'Budapest School'—the intellectuals that coalesced around György Lukács in Budapest—took from the western New Left the notion that the struggle of a new radical generation could be a common one that transcended the Iron Curtain in the late 1960s. Heller, who was a Party member before 1968, regularly travelled westwards (until her expulsion from the Party following her public criticism of the Soviet invasion of Czechoslovakia) as part of her professional intellectual life:

> In the 1960s, I went out to Germany as part of the sociological institute...I got to know for example Rudi Dutschke, and we had some rather lovely conversations with those who came from a part of the New Left, and you could see a new common atmosphere developing.[41]

Vajda stressed a different point of contact:

> Westerners came here, because Hungary was not hermetically sealed from the outside world. You could know what was going on in the world. You could listen to western radio...we mainly used to meet the young men who came to meet Lukács...from America there was Andrew Arato [a political and social theorist who had been born in Hungary, studied in the US, and returned to Hungary to do research] and János Fekete [another Hungarian-American New Leftist]...and we had a very frequent correspondence [by mail] with them.[42]

Others in the same group experimented with these ideas: György Bence for example, explored the relationship of Marcuse to the New Left student movement, and the student protests as resistance against universities as merely 'specialist factories'.[43] Later, Heller and Vajda emphasized their eventual realization of the deep divides between themselves and the western New Left, and related their encounters with western extremists and terrorist groups in the mid-1970s to illustrate this point. Nevertheless, before this they had seen the potential for a combined assault against

---

[39] List of Closed Circuit Publications, PTI Könyvtár, Leltárkönyvek.

[40] New Left works seem to have been more openly published in Czechoslovakia in this period, especially in student magazines. Jiřina Šiklová, 'Existuje u nás studentská 'New Left'?', *Literární listy*, 3 (21 November 1968).

[41] Interview with Ágnes Heller, conducted by PA, Budapest, 17 December 2008.

[42] Interview with Mihály Vajda, conducted by PA, Budapest, 25 November 2008.

[43] György Bence, 'Marcuse és az újbaloldali diákmozgalom', *Új Írás*, September 1968, 95–102.

the overly bureaucratized, rationalized and alienating forms of political development that, for them, had occurred under both capitalism and communism. They had dismissed the revolutionary potential of the working class and considered them as too successfully integrated into the western European bourgeois capitalist systems during the postwar boom, and too depoliticized and alienated in the East, to operate as authentic carriers of social change.[44] Rather, Heller viewed the western student-led protests as harbingers of a broader resistance against modern industrialized systems that could further develop as youth rebellion on both sides of the Iron Curtain.[45]

Critiquing consumption

Anti-materialism and the notion that consumerism was a form of social control—vital components of western New Left thinking in this period—had the capacity both to undermine and reinforce the notion of a common struggle. After two decades of socialist modernization, an underdeveloped consumer society and contemporary socialist regimes that were increasingly appealing to future promises of consumer satisfaction to justify their existence, it is not surprising that many reformists in the communist bloc were alienated by westerners' seemingly indulgent rejection of their developed consumer societies. According to Miroslav Tyl (b. 1943), a Czechoslovak student leader in 1968:

> We wanted just freedom…they [westerners] fought for a different type of society. My opinion [of the status quo in the West] was deeply positive. I used to say, 'Oh please, your poverty—look at how it seems compared to our poverty, come and visit our agricultural cooperatives and our countryside'. 'Ah, it will be alright soon' [they said]. Or these French [activists], we took a taxi with them [in Prague] and they said: 'Fantastic, great, a city without ads!'. And I said: 'But it is a sad city'.[46]

Nevertheless, anti-consumerism could also provide common ground between western and eastern activists, particularly those attracted to Maoism and the western New Left. They recognized that the West had a more advanced consumer society than they, and hence could inspire them in a struggle that was only just beginning in their countries, as socialist states in the eastern bloc began to embrace materialism and more individualistic forms of consumption in the late 1960s. This was particularly the case in Hungary, where the New Economic Mechanism introduced in 1968 was viewed by some radicals as the victory of 'bourgeois

[44] Heller, *Everyday Life* [first published as *Mindennapi élet* (1970)], (London, 1984), 58.
[45] Open Society Archives, Budapest HU OSA 300-40-2-Box 84. See also György Lukács, *The Process of Democratization*, trans. Susanne Bernhardt and Norman Levine (Albany, NY, 1991), 88. On the cross-bloc linkages in debates over development and modernization, see Jörg Requate, 'Visions of the future: GDR, CSSR and the Federal Republic of Germany in the 1960s', in Heinz-Gerhard Haupt and Jürgen Kocka (eds), *Comparative and Transnational History: Central European Approaches and New Perspectives* (New York and Oxford, 2009), 181-6.
[46] Interview with Miroslav Tyl, from the private collection of Jaroslav Pažout, conducted around 1999.

'consumption' at the expense of revolutionary ideals. Hence western radicals' anti-consumerism could provide them with a welcome language through which to protest. According to Péter Fábry (b. 1949), who was part of the theatre group for the (originally Maoist-influenced) Orfeo collective in Budapest:

> we felt a deep solidarity with them [western student movements], because they also experienced a disproportionate use of force against them, and at the same time we could see in them communal governance, direct democracy, and they wanted to transform universities... [and] we supported their anti-capitalist, anti-consumer society position. There wasn't yet a green movement... we wouldn't accept 'really existing socialism', just as this New Left movement wouldn't accept existing socialist practice [in the West]. Today we can see how really existing socialism was a strong counterbalance for the West; now that it has gone there have been terrible and unforeseeable consequences for the development of the entire capitalist world... the formation of the welfare state was in my opinion the result of the existence of a socialist world system. We have to produce an alternative to socialism which ensures, democratically, wealth and welfare for the majority of society.[47]

Visits to the West, rather than dazzling activists with the possibilities of individualistic consumption, could actually reinforce this impression. Vilmos Heiszler (b. 1947), member of the Communist Youth reform movement, visited Italy in 1969 as part of an official delegation and remembered his shock at the way in which western universities individualized student spaces:

> I remember that in '69 we went to Bologna, and that was a great surprise, they put us up in the university dormitories, and to our great shock, we got single rooms to ourselves... and we said that this wasn't a good thing, because you were separating people out, there was no sense of community, you learn in that environment a good amount of discipline, how to look after one another.[48]

However, others remembered the tensions created by their own desire for a collective socialism that rejected the infiltration of individualistic capitalistic forms of consumption, yet, like those young East Berliners who found ways of smuggling studded jeans and parkas from the West of the city, they found themselves uncomfortably attracted to the symbols of western youth culture. Gábor Révai (b. 1947), who railed against the excessive 'petty-bourgeois' materialism of late 1960s Hungary, recalled his trips to Vienna in this period:

> By the end of high school I began to have relatively long hair... and the other thing was my clothing, and it was an unbelievably big thing to bring in jeans from the West, but by the middle of the sixties you could 'get out' and sometimes it was possible to go to Vienna and bring back some jeans or a hurricane coat. It's awfully difficult to understand today that no matter how left wing you were, those little symbols of the western consumer society had such a large hold over you.[49]

---

[47] Interview with Péter Fábry, conducted by JM, Budapest, 23 January 2009.
[48] Interview with Vilmos Heiszler, conducted by PA, Budapest, 29 October 2008.
[49] Interview with Gábor Révai, conducted by PA, Budapest, 8 October 2008.

A common anti-authoritarian struggle?

For many in the eastern bloc, a sense of broader European or western solidarity was not defined by links to concrete political programmes, but rather by a sense of combined generational revolt in which new attitudes towards hierarchy and lifestyle were the most important determinants of an imagined solidarity: 'The lack of respect that this generation showed their fathers and grandfathers... how they treated particular university professors, the demonstrations, the non-conformist elements', says GDR activist Gerd Poppe.[50] György Dalos (b. 1943), former radical leftist, Maoist and later dissident author, recalled his reaction to the French student protests: 'Now May in Paris—wow! Barricades, red flags and so on, we loved it. Plus they were against every kind of orthodoxy. It was an uprising!'.[51]

For Hungarian-Romanian radical Gáspár Miklós Tamás (b. 1948), growing up in Cluj (Romania) and isolated from 68er movements both in eastern Europe and the West, new forms of radicalism were discovered through the consumption of literature, including that of the New Left—the Austrian *Tagebuch* and *Neues Forum*, the French *Les Temps Modernes* (and *Combat*) and the British *New Left Review*. His father had been part of the workers' movement in the interwar period, had been a party intellectual since 1945 and had become disillusioned after his experience of Stalinism; hence by 1960, when Tamás was seeking political direction, it could not be provided at home. In 1968, however, western lifestyle movements gave him a revolutionary identity that his family could not provide him with politically; French student and intellectual revolt became for him, 'a reply to the mourning of a failed communist movement'.[52] For him, criticisms of sexual repression proposed by French radicals could equally be applied to the stuffy sexual conservatism of communist Romania and even his progressive family:

> it was a very repressed world... sex was supposed to be pretty and sweet, or married and bourgeois... sexual desire couldn't be ugly... I loved it when these attitudes vanished. When I was sixteen girls were always suspicious when alone with a boy, this was humiliating if you were sensitive, boys wanted and girls refused.

He found Paris much more inspiring than Prague in this regard:

> of course there was the Czechoslovak reform movement, [but it] didn't really inspire me. It was perfectly obvious that I was on their side—one had to get rid of the remnants of Stalinism and the Soviet occupation sensibly... but of course they didn't have the revolutionary charisma of Paris and West Berlin and Berkeley and Milan...

Like Tamás, Lutz Rathenow, now a writer and liberal commentator, who was active in the East German peace movement of the 1980s, highlights the important pull of western culture and explains that this was much more important for him than

[50] Poppe interview.
[51] Interview with György Dalos, conducted by PA, Budapest, 17 April 2009.
[52] Interview with Gáspár Miklós Tamás, conducted by JM, Budapest, 5 March 2009.

the political programme of socialist reform. When asked whether the Prague Spring itself played a role, he says:

> It played a role, but not the dominant one...the suppression played a greater role than the Prague Spring itself...the Prague Spring had not convinced me deep down...and the western rock and pop culture was more important...I thought Paris was better. 'Under the paving stones, the beach'—sounds much better. And something like 'He who sleeps with the same woman twice already belongs to the Establishment' [*Wer zweimal mit der selben pennt, gehört schon zum Establishment*]. This West German type of revolution was more interesting than the 1000 or 2000 word manifesto.[53]

Some communist bloc activists noted the inspirational quality of the act of defiance made so powerfully plain in the actions of activists in France and West Germany, even if they disagreed with their political programmes or even found their motivations suspect. According to István Bakos (b. 1943), who played a prominent role in reform movements within KISZ between 1967 and 1970, these movements inspired them to confront university authorities about improving the quality of education, and agitate for greater student representation on university general assemblies and to campaign for institutional autonomy:

> we saw the student uprising in Paris...in many ways it inspired us,...a lot of people, who worked around me, and they knew French well, knew English well, they read about it, and it stimulated our thoughts...at least once a year at the departmental meeting [in the philosophy department at Eötvös Loránd University in Budapest] where the students, the representatives of the teaching body and the leaders of the university were present—and there we could speak out about the issues that concerned all of us.[54]

His successor as leader (and later deputy mayor of Budapest after the collapse of communism) János Atkári (b. 1946), was far more sceptical: 'I saw in the western radical student movements...mainly the children of the elite and was a bit egotistical and self-centred fiddling around'.[55]

Such was also the attitude of many Polish Commandos, an informal grouping of radical students at Warsaw University who would play a leading role in the protests in March 1968; they juxtaposed the struggles they and their Czech and Slovak peers had waged against dictatorship with the struggle for sexual freedom—seeing on the one side real heroism, and on the other hedonistic caprice. 'It seemed to people at that time in Poland to be just a waste of time', said Karol Modzelewski (b. 1937) of the protests in the West.[56] Yet many nevertheless invoked the idea of 'generational solidarity' with young people in America, France, Italy and West Germany, despite a basic mutual miscomprehension. As Seweryn Blumsztajn (b. 1946) recalls:

[53] Rathenow interview.
[54] Interview with István Bakos, conducted by PA, Budapest, 19 November 2008.
[55] Interview with János Atkári, conducted by JM, 12 November 2008.
[56] Interview with Karol Modzelewski, conducted by PO, Warsaw, 18 March 2009.

I had sympathy for those events. And I had a feeling of connection, generational connection, and of their absolute misunderstanding. You know, their attraction to Marxism…That is, we were fighting for what they were rejecting—that was all quite obvious. For us democracy was a dream—but for them it was a prison. So I simply couldn't comprehend their Marxism, their communism, all that leftist ideology of theirs. Those Maoists—wow, that was just pure blather for us. All of it. Nonetheless, I did feel a generational sympathy—that's how I'd label it. I felt there was a bond between us.[57]

The greatest distance was created between activists when they heard that some young western communists and Maoists had supported the suppression of the Prague Spring by Soviet troops. The philosopher Mária Ludassy (b. 1944), who was close to the Budapest School at this time, was dismayed by the lack of protest against the invasion, and noted that Hungarians felt the difference with the western radicals particularly acutely because of their experience of the suppression of reform socialism with the entry of Soviet tanks in 1956:

> PA: Was there some kind of generational connection at a European level?
> ML: I do not think it was important. Paris did not have to endure…Prague—which for us [in Hungary] brought back—even if there were no street battles—1956 and our sense of liberation, and then…somehow our system was the greater of two evils…in France a lot of left wingers 'understood'—and I use the term in quotation marks—that the Soviet intervention [in Czechoslovakia] was necessary. Well, the Trots and Anarchists, perhaps no. But the Maoists, who really accepted the idea that socialism had to be maintained—here in '56, then in Czechoslovakia in '68—although they didn't like the Soviet Union—but that was more important to them [than Dubček]. So in most respects there was not really such a sense of unity.[58]

Anti-Imperialism and the sense of a common struggle

Identification with Third World anti-imperial liberation struggles, particularly the struggle of the Vietnamese against the US, could be an important marker in overcoming fragmentation. Although it took on considerably different meaning in East and West—in the eastern bloc opposition to the war was official socialist policy and was thus more difficult to invoke as a vehicle of protest against the regime—activists often sought to demonstrate their common outlook along these lines. Bettina Wegner (b. 1947), who would become a famous East German songwriter, was arrested after 21 August 1968 for distributing leaflets that not only called for 'Solidarity with Prague' but also warned 'Prague—no second Saigon'.[59] Many other leaflets the Stasi confiscated read 'Don't create a second Vietnam!' or 'Pro Ho-Chi-Minh and Dubček!', thus postulating an explicit link between American 'imperialist aggression' in Southeast Asia and Soviet imperialism in eastern Europe.[60] Members of the Commandos in Poland equally scattered leaflets connecting

---

[57] Interview with Seweryn Blumsztajn conducted by PO, Warsaw, 5 January 2010.
[58] Interview with Mária Ludassy, conducted by PA, Budapest, 1 December 2008.
[59] See the Stasi report on Bettina Wegner in RHG, file RH 173, 385.
[60] See the Stasi report of 17 September 1968, RHG, file RH 173.

the struggles of Vietnam to the fight against Soviet domination in Poland, Hungary and elsewhere.[61]

However, anti-imperialist ideology did not always bring activists together across borders. As Paulina Bren has argued, they were often divided over where to turn for solutions to change their modern bureaucratic societies. Student reformers in Prague—who valued bourgeois democracy over the claims of ultra-leftism—were beginning to advocate a 'return to Europe' as a symbol of democratic values away from the hold of 'Asia' (i.e. the Soviet Union), and saw the 'Third Worldism' of western radicals as off-putting: the 'return to Europe', the slogan of the 'Velvet Revolution' of 1989, was thus already present in the Czechoslovak aspirations of 1968.[62]

Indeed, not all communist bloc activists embraced the idea of a common anti-imperialist struggle against the Soviets and US; for one student who was attracted to the Maoist movement in Budapest remembers that he had believed that support for Dubček against the Soviet Union would mean a weakening of Soviet support for the more important struggle in Vietnam:

> I still have clear memories of looking at a map [of Czechoslovakia] and saying… 'it's not possible… that they will occupy again'. According to one of my friends I was fantasizing about [East German head of state] Walter Ulbricht [who took a hard line on the reform movement and supported intervention] on a white horse in Prague. Now of course this perspective was absurd and two-faced because on one hand we considered the Czechoslovak reform movement as dangerous because it could lead to the weakening of the anti-imperialist front, and could hinder the People's Liberation of Vietnam, but even with the ideological blinkers of that time I could not deny a high level of sympathy for the aspirations of Dubček's attempt at socialism with a human face.[63]

Nevertheless, the language of anti-imperialism, even if it expressed different political positions, could provide a sense of commonality between activists in East and West. Gerd Poppe explains:

> Che Guevara was a point of contact. In general, the Cuban Revolution in the early phase… The figure of Che Guevara, the *Bolivian Diary*, we read that in the East as well. We read it to each other in our groups…. This Bolivian adventure and the African adventure. It was absurd and quite off, but it was impressive that someone attempted a world revolution single-handedly. And for young people also somewhat important. It is these things that established East–West linkages.[64]

Indeed, as Poppe explains, for some activists within the communist bloc, anti-imperialism was more important in establishing solidarity with their western counterparts than forging real contacts with the countries in which these struggles were

---

[61] Franciszek Dąbrowski, Piotr Gontarczyk and Paweł Tomasik (eds) *Marzec 1968 w dokumentach MSW. Tom 1: Niepokorni* (Warsaw, 2008), 822.

[62] Paulina Bren, '1968 in East and West. Visions of political change and student protest from across the Iron Curtain', in Gerd-Rainer Horn and Padraic Kenney (eds) *Transnational Moments of Change: Europe 1945, 1968, 1989*, (Lanham, MD and Oxford, 2004) 127.

[63] Interview with anonymous respondent, conducted by PA, Budapest, 5 October 2008.

[64] Poppe interview.

being fought. In Budapest, for example, ultra-leftists at elite universities who were instrumental in organizing unofficial forms of anti-imperial solidarity were convinced that these were part of a pan-European network, and only later were disabused at the so-called 'Maoist trial' of spring 1968. Nevertheless, they did inspire others; activists in the GDR got wind of the protests in Budapest—via West German activists who visited East Berlin rather than through direct links within the eastern bloc. In January 1968, the Stasi noted that one group of West German visitors had:

> deemed the method of propagating the experiences with the forms and methods of taking on state power of students in other socialist countries...to be most promising in the GDR. In this context they pointed out an alleged act by Hungarian students, who combined participation in a demonstration in favour of Vietnam with the accusation of insufficient activities by their own government in this regard.[65]

Some of the young East Germans present at this meeting, among them Frank Havemann, the son of a famous dissident, followed this advice a few months later. While he boycotted official acts of solidarity with the North Vietnamese at his school, he turned up at an event to mark the new GDR constitution with a poster that read 'Break the solitude of Vietnam'.[66] He and his younger brother Florian also organized Leninist 'subbotniks'—voluntary unpaid shifts in their workplaces—to collect money for the North Vietnamese. Florian used the collectively earned money to buy a bicycle that he donated to the Vietnamese embassy and hoped it would end up loaded with weapons on the Ho Chi Minh trail.[67] Others also used Vietnam as a stick with which to beat the regime, albeit under the cover of embracing official socialist policy.[68]

WEST MEETS EAST—EAST MEETS WEST

Activists in East and West encountered each other in numerous ways in this period: through personal travel, solidarity committees, letter writing and through official youth programmes and congresses. This period thus leaves historians the memories of such encounters, which reveal in nuanced and meaningful forms the ways in which activists on either side of the Iron Curtain attempted to understand the other. Given that some developed new relationships across the East–West divide after the late 1960s, and then experienced the political unification of the continent after 1989, they reflected back on the meanings of their encounters in

---

[65] See the Stasi report about a meeting between eastern and western activists held in East Berlin on 27 January 1968, marked MfS, no. 276/68, in RHG, file RH 280, 9.

[66] See the Stasi's notes on Frank Havemann in RHG, file RH 173, 337.

[67] Florian Havemann, *Havemann: Eine Behauptung* (Frankfurt/M., 2007), 792; on his take on the Vietnam War also 774–5 and 788ff. The Communist Youth in Budapest also organized events to collect money for bikes for North Vietnam in the late 1960s and early 1970s.

[68] See the report of 28 November 1969, marked HA XVIII/5/1, in RHG, file RH 080; Rathenow interview.

their early lives, and the extent to which they represented a continent divided or one in the process of 'coming together'.

Many such encounters between East and West were facilitated through official structures. There were meetings based around anti-imperialist issues, often organized by official socialist bodies with the aim of building global youth solidarity on socialist states' terms. In April 1966, the National Committee of Hungarian Student Organizations held the conference 'We Accuse Imperialism!', which brought together students from fifty-four countries, including those of western Europe; in January 1967, a joint seminar to discuss 'Coexistence and the Third World' was held in Prague, with members of the university committee of the Czechoslovak Youth Union and the West German SDS attending. Nevertheless, western observers often found that Third World solidarity seemed far less important to those on the other side of the Iron Curtain. After visiting Prague in April 1967, French activist Hubert Krivine 'expressed his outrage about the alleged disorientation of Czechoslovak students' with regard to the Vietnam War. He left Czechoslovakia convinced that in this respect 'Czechoslovak students are closer to French fascists'.[69]

The British radical Nick Wright (b. 1947), who came from a Communist Party background and was the leader of a large art school protest in 1968, remembered with similar dismay his encounters with young Prague student reformers when he passed through the city en route to the 9th World Youth Festival in Sofia in the summer of 1968. He considered them to be conservative in outlook, profoundly ill-informed about the situation of workers in the capitalist West—which they appeared to idealize:

> I remember Prague was in absolute ferment. I remember going...down to the Mala Strana where there's people arguing politics in the street...and there's a lecturer from Charles University on a platform...saying that when workers go on strike in Britain they get paid until the strike is over. I said it's bollocks, absolutely...so we got into an argument with this bloke who obviously idealized the West...what struck me about it was the profound ignorance about conditions in the West from people who had completely idealized views...when I first came back I was firmly of the view that the Red Army needed to intervene.[70]

Like Wright, K.D. Wolff (b. 1943), former chairman of the West German SDS, travelled to Sofia in the summer of 1968 as part of an SDS delegation. Wolff remembers having been particularly unimpressed by the Czechoslovak delegates, especially in comparison to the experiences he had elsewhere in northern and western Europe and across the Atlantic:

> you couldn't talk to them...They were stupid. No, really, everywhere you went—in Sweden, in Norway, in England and in America—everywhere they discussed how our

---

[69] Jaroslav Pažout, *Mocným navzdory. Studentské hnutí v šedesátých letech 20. Století* (Prague, 2008), 164. Elsewhere in his work, Pažout notes that part of the Czech student movement did express solidarity with the Vietnamese partisans and protested against American aggression. This aspect is understudied, however.

[70] Interview with Nick Wright, conducted by JD, Faversham, 23 February 2010.

societies ought to change. What's the next step? And here they said 'Freedom of the press! Dubček is our guy!'. Boring, you know. With hindsight I think they were terribly scared, but they didn't say to us: 'We are scared'. They just didn't speak.[71]

Yet not all 'eastern' participants in Sofia shared this idea of a continent divided. The Hungarian former ultra-leftist (and later human rights advocate) Miklós Haraszti (b. 1945) remembers the demonstration in front of the Vietnamese embassy in the Bulgarian capital as an important moment of convergence for western and eastern European activists; his testimony nevertheless reveals the very different possibilities of protest for those on different sides of the Iron Curtain:

> In the summer of 1968 I went to the Muscovite, 'sub-Comintern', pro-Soviet World Youth Congress, specifically for the purpose of making contacts with the western left-wing movements... but the essence was, I went there, and there was a protest in front of the Vietnamese embassy in Sofia, in which all the westerners took part, and, on the basis that 'in the fog everyone is a grey donkey', everyone from the east was there too. I wouldn't have dared to do it back at home. It was on a closed off street... we went in—in 'the American style'—it was from them we had learnt these techniques—at one end of the street there were mounted policemen, and at the other end the street was shut off with a lorry—we couldn't get out. And the horses pulled up, a row of ten in grey workers' uniforms—with gigantic flags in their hands shouting 'Druzhba! Druzhba!', and, as they went, smashed the bones of people who were lying on the ground. So in fact, they had been sent to punish us. People were bleeding. The western student movements then went to their headquarters—I went with them, and watched what they were doing. They got out the mimeograph, and the next morning they produced a lot of leaflets protesting against this and demanded that the organizing committee of the World Youth Congress also protest against it, and tried to collect signatures. Naturally the participants from the east were already removed from the frame.[72]

Nevertheless, many from the west of the Iron Curtain held these stereotypical views of eastern European progressive youth as insufficiently radical and unexciting. Such sentiments were particularly characteristic for a segment of the West German left that would oppose reunification in 1990. As K.D. Wolff explains: 'We did not feel all-German. I still don't feel all-German. I always say that I like Germany so much I would like to have two'. His engagement with the East German 1968 was limited to playing the songs of Wolf Biermann (a famous East German singer-songwriter who was expatriated in 1976 for his oppositional stance) during SDS marches. But he admits that even then they used Biermann's music less to highlight the East German cause than to taunt members of the West German Communist Party (DKP) for whom the treatment of the singer was a touchy subject.

Not all West Germans were as uninterested in East German issues as Wolff, however. Given that some westerners could still travel to East Berlin quickly in

[71] Interview with K.D. Wolff, conducted by AvdG, Berlin, 28 May 2008. For details of Wolff's appearance at the festival that suggest slightly different fault lines than the ones Wolff remembers today, see Martin Klimke, Jacco Pekelder and Joachim Scharloth, 'Introduction', in idem, *Between Prague Spring and French May*, 1.
[72] Interview with Miklós Haraszti, conducted by PA, Vienna, 10 April 2009.

the late 1960s, informally organized meetings took place between leading West German activists of the SDS and some of the most prominent East German dissidents who criticized the regime from the left. Several members of West Berlin's Kommune 1 visited the group around Biermann, the dissident Robert Havemann and the sculptor Ingeborg Hunzinger several times in 1967 and 1968.[73] At one such meeting in January 1968 around thirty-five people were present, among them the dissidents' children and their friends, Rudi Dutschke, as well as the communards Fritz Teufel, Rainer Langhans and Dieter Kunzelmann, who had acquired a high public profile in the West when their plot to attack the visiting US Vice President Hubert Humphrey with pudding was thwarted in April 1967. According to the Stasi, which had an informant at the meeting, the West and East Germans spent several hours comparing the revolutionary situations on both sides of the Iron Curtain. While the eastern hosts had been keen to learn about the western repertoire of protest in the hope of gaining inspiration for their own endeavours, the discussion yielded few overall results—and in some ways mirrored the frustrations expressed by other western visitors to the eastern bloc:

> [They] frequently expressed their disappointment in the helplessness, passivity, and lack of inspiration and in what they perceived as petty bourgeois ideas... They explicitly emphasized the need for action... In this context they underlined the role of gaining influence among young people, especially students and pupils.[74]

Their East German hosts went to great lengths to explain that following a western model—setting up a political organization, demonstrating or seeking publicity for their cause—would not work in the East: 'Due to the differing social conditions in both German states... the forms and methods of activism of the forces agitating against existing conditions had to be different'.[75]

Despite these obvious dissimilarities, however, some of the easterners, among them one young girl who had been present, were impressed by the fervour the western communards displayed. Shortly after the meeting, she sent a letter to Teufel and Langhans, pleading them to come back soon, to supply leaflets and information about Kommune 1, and not to lose patience with their East German counterparts:

> Please don't put your next visit off for too long, because if something is meant to happen here, then, I think, we need your guidance. Don't expect us to pull off a big one overnight... Real enthusiasm has broken out amongst our friends.[76]

---

[73] See the Stasi report of 17 April 1967, RHG, file RH 280, 75.

[74] See the Stasi report about the meeting held on 27 January 1968 marked MfS, no. 276/68, in RHG, file RH 280, 8; see also the long report of 26 February 1968 marked HA XX/1 in the same file.

[75] A Stasi informant summarized Robert Havemann's and Wolf Biermann's position to this effect, ibid., 7. The East Germans present learned about the Hungarian students' stance on Vietnam, discussed above, at the same meeting.

[76] See the letter attached to the Stasi report marked MfS, ZAIG, 1454, in RHG, file RH 280. Although the Stasi records of this particular encounter hint at a controversial, yet still inspirational, exchange between East and West, these files often tend to overemphasize the western influence—to offer 'proof' that opposition in the GDR was not a result of internal contradictions but born out of an external bourgeois-capitalist conspiracy.

This amalgam of enthusiasm for the fervour and provocative gestures of western activists on one hand and on the other scepticism about the chances of emulating their model too closely by 'pulling off a big one' was mirrored elsewhere in eastern Europe. One and a half years earlier, in the autumn of 1966, Czechoslovak student Boja Christovová had begun a correspondence with Roel van Duyn, one of the leading Dutch anarchist provocateurs, the 'Provos', who had also provided inspiration to the West Berlin communards.[77] She styled herself as a 'provo girl', offered herself as their Czechoslovak representative and was not unusual in this regard; Provos received similar letters from Russian, Polish and Yugoslav youth following their calls for an international association of Provos.[78] Nevertheless, van Duyn's suggestions left her wondering whether there were political movements that could truly cross over the Iron Curtain. Their particular style of public provocation would never work in the East, she explained:

> We can't enter the cinema, theatres, public rooms and even hairdressers… You say: provoke! But we can't provoke with our complexion or with our manners. We depend on our society very much. It isn't very difficult to get thrown into prison in our country. And here it means rather more than in yours… Our youth is very afraid!!!![79]

Meeting 'Red Rudi'[80]

As one of the most prolific and iconic West European student leaders—and one who had been raised in the East—East German activists regularly invoked encounters with Rudi Dutschke to illustrate both the strong fascination the western revolt exerted and the differences between East and West—both stylistic and theoretical—that actual encounters laid bare. In a controversial book about his family, first published in 2007, the GDR dissident Robert Havemann's son Florian, who had been arrested after protesting against the invasion in August 1968 and fled to the West in 1971, dedicated a whole chapter to his various meetings with Dutschke. 'There was immediately something akin to love between us, a very great closeness… The love lasted, but the problem with Dutschke was that he only talked nonsense, leftist, stupid 68er nonsense', he wrote.[81]

Rupert Schröter remembers meeting Dutschke in a flat in East Berlin in the early 1970s along similar lines: 'It was a giant palaver. He explained to us why in the West the SPD [Social Democratic Party of Germany] now had to split by all means'. But there was still something about him that attracted Schröter. 'The scorching voice—I took a lot from it'.[82] Franziska Groszer, in whose flat they had met and who befriended Dutschke and remained in touch with him once she had

---

[77] Niek Pas, 'Mediatisation of Provo: From a local movement to a European phenomenon', in Klimke, Pekelder and Scharloth (eds) *Between Prague Spring and French May*, 157–76.
[78] Letter from Boja Christovová to Roel van Duyn, 11 October 1966. Provo Collection IISH Amsterdam.
[79] Christovová to van Duyn, 31 October 1966, ibid.
[80] In Czechoslovak publications of the time, Dutschke was often referred to as 'Rudý Dutschke'—a play on words because Rudý means 'red' in Czech and sounds like Rudi.
[81] Havemann, *Havemann*, 882ff, here 886–7.   [82] Schröter interview.

emigrated to West Berlin, concurs. What he talked about had nothing to do with her own ideas, she explains:

> It was awful chatter and it touched neither my ideas about changing the world nor about the direction in which we were moving. And, I have to say, I only understood half of it. And I still liked him... there were so many other points of contact, we still had an exchange, about ways of living... The debates were highly interesting, but we didn't work jointly on anything theoretical.[83]

Dutschke faced similar difficulties in explaining his political visions to his Czech counterparts, as an article published after his visit to Prague in spring 1968 by the Czech sociologist Jiřina Šiklová illustrates:

> Rudi Dutschke (personally, I liked him) was not very successful with his visions of free, non-restrictive communist society, when he visited Prague during this spring. The arguments of French students and their red flags hanging don't excite our students... I felt sorry for both sides because they restrict each other from confronting their own experience by providing illusions about the possibility of finding solutions on the other side: students from SDS talking about the possibilities and limits of democratic parliamentary systems, ours by revealing real 'socialist practice'.[84]

Despite these difficulties, however, the links remained alive. A delegation of Czech philosophy students visited Dutschke in hospital in West Berlin in May 1968, a few weeks after the right-wing extremist Josef Bachmann had attempted to assassinate him. While there was much overlap in identifying common problems of late industrial society, again little agreement could be achieved concerning the methods to be taken.[85] At the same time, however, Czech activists, like their East German counterparts, continued to be fascinated by Dutschke, numerous articles were published about him in the Czech press, which often highlighted his humanity, exemplified by how lovingly he took care of his child when he visited Prague.[86]

Mourning a western lack of interest

As much as 1968 is presently being promoted as a moment of European convergence, East German activists who invoke East–West encounters often convey a sense of disappointment in what they perceived as a western lack of interest in conditions in the East.[87] Bettina Wegner, who had followed western events with a 'burning heart', soon found that West German activists did not understand the opportunity the Prague Spring presented: 'They were very self-centred. Their own things were important'. She describes a particular incident that looks like a perfect example of activist cooperation across the Iron Curtain at first glance, but actually left her feeling deeply disaffected. After watching West German demonstrators

---

[83] Groszer interview. [84] Šiklová, 'Existuje', *Literární listy* 3.

[85] 'Rudi Dutschke v rekonvalescenci', *Student* 25 (1968) 19/6, cited in Pažout, *Mocným navzdory*, 177–8.

[86] For example, František Černý, 'Rudý Dutschke v Praze', *Reportér* 17 (24 April–1 May 1968).

[87] See Lutz Rathenow, 'Umwege des Aufbegehrens: Beobachtungen am Rande einer politischen Debatte', *Politische Meinung* 378 (2001), 33–4.

being beaten by policemen on television, her partner, Klaus Schlesinger, started to think about how best to aid his western comrades. He raised some money from actors and other wealthy people he knew in the GDR and bought a large number of helmets from a local construction business. Schlesinger had contacts in West Berlin and word spread that anyone who wanted a helmet could come and pick it up at a specific address in East Berlin; Wegner claims that Red Army Faction (RAF) leader Gudrun Ensslin was among those who turned up. Her anger at the westerners' lack of gratitude is still palpable:

> They could have made contact and said 'We'll come visit you more often, invite a few people, we'll exchange ideas'. Noooo! They could have come and said 'We thought it was great that you got us the helmets'...No, nothing...We were with them in our hearts and in '68 we experienced that to our great disappointment they didn't give a shit about us.[88]

Steffi Recknagel (b. 1950) remembers being equally put off after meeting students from West Berlin in a flat in the East despite the fact that the western movement had also been something of an inspiration to her:

> I remember...that they spent the whole evening talking about what was happening at the OSI, the Otto-Suhr-Institut here in West Berlin [the Faculty of Political Science at the Free University]. We rubbed each other up and then I thought 'You idiots! Ok, I mean I understand that you are busy with your own things, but that you aren't at all interested in what is happening on the other side...'—that was disillusioning on one hand and on the other also confirmed that each side had to do its own thing...[89]

She goes on to interpret these memories in the light of the continuing mental distance and problems of understanding between East and West Germans after reunification: 'Each of us was the hub of the universe with one's own problems and issues and in the end a lot of it has remained, to this day. The division was already striking at that time'. This points to a distinguishing feature of East German interviews, in which memories of western 'ignorance' seem especially pronounced. Rather than fostering convergence between East and West, for Recknagel, her encounters actually foreshadowed many of the problems associated with the period post-1990.

Encounters in exile

For those East German activists who, like Steffi Recknagel, eventually fled to the West or were forced to emigrate because of their oppositional stance, the perception that the western struggle differed fundamentally from the eastern one often only fully developed in exile. Being a critic of state socialism in the West meant that activists had to ward off being instrumentalized by right-wing commentators

[88] Interview with Bettina Wegner, conducted by AvdG, Berlin, 2 May 2010. Wolfgang Engler mentions this episode in his *Die Ostdeutschen: Kunde von einem verlorenen Land* (Berlin, 1999), 311–12, but says that it had been RAF members Holger Meins and Astrid Proll who picked up the helmets.
[89] Recknagel interview.

for the anti-socialist cause. Recknagel remembers that once she had fled to the West in the late 1970s she found it extremely difficult to speak about her experiences of imprisonment in the GDR: 'Many of them [i.e. the West German left] didn't like it... Those who spoke openly of their... prison experiences were automatically put in the right-wing corner'.

Even when both parties subscribed to similar political goals, other differences were often palpable. Rupert Schröter, who had run a Trotskyist cell in East Berlin in the 1970s, joined a West German Trotskyist group once he had been released to the West in the late 1970s. While he agreed with his western counterparts politically, he found their style difficult to handle. They did not write well, he says, their language reminded him of the Red Army Faction. The first central committee meeting he attended took place 'in some basement, with fanlights, otherwise just a neon lamp'. He found the whole atmosphere completely stifling and went out to buy a bouquet of flowers that he put on the table to introduce a 'spark of beauty'. After having spent more than a year in prison in the GDR, he thought that 'revolution isn't just about suffering... But they [i.e. the westerners] were really into suffering'.[90]

However, for Hans-Jürgen Uszkoreit (b. 1950), the son of an SED functionary who had been arrested for protesting against the invasion of Czechoslovakia in August 1968, stylistic affinity did not necessarily spell greater convergence either once he had crossed the border and settled in West Berlin after fleeing the GDR in the body of a chemical truck in 1971. While still in the GDR he had felt closely connected to the western revolt, especially its cultural manifestations. Uszkoreit initially chose his new friendship circle based on these cultural affinities: 'I didn't go to parties with members of the Studentenunion [the conservative student organization[91]] but with the ones that looked like me and acted like me'. But the cracks between him and his western lookalikes slowly became apparent:

> But that was precisely where the split was, that precisely those to whom one felt drawn because of their dress, the music, their way of life, their diet, their interests, that there was a glass wall when it came to questions of how one viewed society... even more than that, the whole notion of the responsibility one had in daily life.

He and the other easterners did not buy into what they thought was a 'vulgar' conspiratorial notion of western society, with evil representatives of monopoly capitalism allegedly scheming how to exploit workers. He also thought that westerners idealized the working class:

> This... eventually meant that one grew apart. It worked for a while, one had these gruelling discussions, because one always thought: 'It can't be, we have to converge!'. But we didn't converge. And when things got radicalized in the mid-1970s towards terror, violence... we from the East who had experienced something completely

[90] Schröter interview; eastern activists often highlight how put off they were by 'leftist jargon' in the West; see, Havemann, *Havemann*, 886.
[91] On this aspect see further Anna von der Goltz, 'A polarised generation? Conservative students and West Germany's "1968"', in idem, *'Talkin' 'bout my Generation': Conflicts of Generation Building and Europe's '1968'* (Göttingen, 2011), 195–215.

different said: 'Hey, wait a moment, you still have all the opportunities to do something, why are you so suppressed... you have a press, you can demonstrate... you can
do anything'. That's when one realized that it was a completely different view of society. They were just frustrated, because they marched and shouted and nothing
changed... Anyone watching from another planet would have thought that culturally—
because we wore the same clothes, lived the same way—we were the same. But we
were entirely different.[92]

Stefan Welzk (b. 1942), who fled to West Germany via Bulgaria and Turkey in the
summer of 1968 following a high-profile act of protest against the dynamiting of
Leipzig's University Church in May of that year, shared Uszkoreit's repulsion with
the rhetoric of the West German left, especially in the context of the 'German
autumn' of 1977, when members of the Red Army Faction kidnapped and murdered Hanns-Martin Schleyer, and a Lufthansa plane was hijacked by Palestinian
militants to demand the release of other RAF members and Palestinian militants
held in Turkey: 'It was very unpleasant when they spoke of "isolation torture" [of
RAF prisoners]. We thought...: "They don't know what they are talking about.
Every East German prisoner would long for such conditions"'.

He sympathized with many of the aims of the western left and joined some of
their marches, but often found himself confronted with a radicalism that was profoundly shocking to him. At one demonstration against the ban on left-wing political radicals from employment in the civil service (*Radikalenerlass*) at the University of
Munich he stood next to a 'slim fragile young woman, a beautiful young woman, she
was perhaps twenty and explained to me that the physical destruction of five million
Soviet Kulaks had been a historical necessity. What goes on in these minds?'.[93]

While East German interviewees highlight differences between East and West
particularly adamantly because of continuing problems after reunification, such
accounts are by no means an exclusively German phenomenon. Polish activists
who travelled to France in this period were also often strengthened further in their
belief that the Polish and French 1968s were totally dissimilar events. Czesław
Bielecki (b. 1948), who had stayed in Paris in the early 1970s, remembered his
experiences in the West as having been accompanied by a profound sense of disillusionment, in effect bolstering his own anti-communism:

Those young people and that extreme leftism... It was something I totally disapproved
of; you can say that my trip to the West made my anti-regime attitude turn into some
kind of idealistic anti-communism as I realized there was no other way out. Since
then, I used to say: 'why should I leave Poland to chase communists around the world
if I have my own communists to hand?'... It was horrible to meet a young man somewhere out there in La Défense, at a bus stop, at night—a man who expressed his joy
over the fact that I came from Poland since I came from the country where revolution
had already prevailed, and, using no punctuation marks, he explained to me how
lucky I was and how he hadn't arrived at that yet.[94]

---

[92] Interviews with Hans-Jürgen Uszkoreit, conducted by AvdG, Berlin, 25 and 26 June 2010.
[93] Interview with Stefan Welzk, conducted by AvdG, Berlin, 22 September 2008.
[94] Interview with Czesław Bielecki, conducted by PO, Warsaw, 26 October 2009.

TRAJECTORIES OF TRANSNATIONALISM

As we have seen, transnationalism around 1968 was far from static. Nor did it develop teleologically, with ever closer European and global entanglements emerging continuously from the late 1960s onwards. Instead, activists' changing political commitments often went hand in hand with refocussing their internationalist imagination and seeking changing linkages with activists in other countries over time. This took different forms. While western activists had often ignored the eastern 1968 in the period itself, some western European activists, particularly former Maoists, 'discovered' eastern Europe in the late 1970s and 1980s because it was still seamlessly tied to their fight against 'Soviet imperialism' once other aspects of their struggle had become stale. While this is a particularly prominent story, it is not the only trajectory transnationalism took. For those East European activists who decided to 'march through the institutions' of the communist state, a period of intense engagement with the West and with activists across the Iron Curtain was sometimes followed by the deliberate severing of such ties.

Discovering the eastern European struggle

During the 1980s, former Maoists from western Europe often channelled their energies into human rights activism and began to forge close links with the civil rights activists of Charter 77 and Solidarity in eastern Europe.[95] For West German activist Christian Semler (b. 1938) this represented a new phase of his internationalist commitment. He had already experienced his time in the West German SDS as very internationally focussed, characterized by 'a crazy amount of travelling', and 'spontaneous to-ing and fro-ing of people in different countries who all more or less thought the same thing…And that was very focussed on western Europe'.[96] His early contacts with eastern European activists, however, had been marked by political misunderstandings. Many easterners said to them: 'You are crazy, [protesting] in a democratic state based on the rule of law, against the US—that's our most important ally'.[97]

After the dissolution of the KPD, his Maoist cadre group in 1980, Semler 'discovered' the eastern European struggle. He began to learn Polish, forged a close friendship with Czech dissident Petr Uhl, and covered eastern Europe in the

---

[95] For other accounts of this discovery, see Bent Boel, 'French support for Eastern European dissidence, 1968–1989: Approaches and controversies', in Poul Villaume and Odd Arne Westad (eds) *Perforating the Iron Curtain: European Détente, Transatlantic Relations, and the Cold War, 1965–1985* (Copenhagen, 2010), 215–42; on the connections between anti-colonialism and new West–East solidarities in Europe, see Kim Christiaens, Idesbald Goddeeris and Wouter Goedertier, 'Inspirées par le Sud? Les mobilisations transnationales Est–Ouest pendant la guerre froide', *Vingtième Siècle, Revue d'Histoire* 109 (2011), 155–68; Julian Bourg, *From Revolution to Ethics: May 1968 and Contemporary French Thought* (Montreal, 2007), 243–4.

[96] Interview with Christian Semler, conducted by AvdG, Berlin, 29 August 2008.

[97] He later admitted that the student movement had not understood eastern Europe: Christian Semler, '1968 im Westen—was ging uns die DDR an?', *Aus Politik und Zeitgeschichte* B 45 (2003), 3–5.

taz, a newly founded left-wing daily. Although his life changed fundamentally after the dissolution of the KPD, moving into human rights and supporting eastern European dissident movements flowed quite naturally from Maoist opposition to 'Soviet social imperialism'. One easily recognized former Maoists in the 1980s, he explains, because they suddenly channelled their energies into activities that were directed against the Soviet Union.

Indeed, Helga Hirsch (b. 1948), who had spent ten years in Semler's Maoist party, moved to Poland in 1980 and began an intense engagement with members of the Solidarity movement, even writing her doctoral dissertation about the Polish opposition. Initially, she did not speak Polish, but still somehow managed to communicate with some of the leading Polish activists such as Bogdan Borusewicz, one of the chief organizers of the 1980 strike in the Gdánsk shipyard, whom she met early on. He asked her to get him a printing machine and told her 'that he knew that the Maoists...were better at smuggling than Social Democrats' and therefore trusted her 'to do a good job'.[98] Hirsch felt intensely invested in the Polish cause:

> You know, you are a foreigner. You are a foreigner and it still is a sort of event to which you cannot *not* go...It was very strange, it's not your country, and it's not your topic, but somehow it was my topic and my country despite this.

Hirsch eventually became the East European correspondent of German weekly *Die Zeit*. Since then, there has been growing distance from her Polish friends because she has become increasingly critical of what she perceives as a failure on the part of many Poles to confront their own past critically. Nevertheless, Hirsch still regards her 'eastern European phase' as crucial in her continuous 'search for meaning' because it taught her the value of democracy, albeit belatedly:

> In terms of a basic structure I think a person is stamped...Poland was restitution and still a search for meaning. But there was still something theoretical about it, there was the reworking of what...the Soviet Union had done...or writing this dissertation about the Polish opposition: why is anti-communism not evil? Or, in a different sense, to start appreciating democracy in the first place. That only came as a result.

Polish activists too noted the real and important links that emerged between western activists of 1968 and the emerging Solidarity movement in the late 1970s. Nina Smolar, one of the leading figures of the post-March émigré community in western Europe, drew attention to the fact that among Swedes, Brits, French and Danes it was the 'generation of '68' that undertook the role of couriers most eagerly, transporting books and printing machine parts to Poland—and smuggled manuscripts out of Poland:

> ...that whole horde of wild Maoists, Trotskyists and people from the West's '68—they smuggled books into Poland. And after all, the material from the shipyard in Szczecin, when Gierek met with the workers, those tapes were smuggled out of Poland and to Sweden by our two Trotskyite friends, as they were the most eager. And...when we

---

[98] Interview with Helga Hirsch, conducted by AvdG, Berlin, 30 April 2010.

were in Uppsala then these groups of students, not knowing each other, all arrived in
Poland in cars packed with literature, diverse literature, from…us! The same kind of
thing was happening during the period of Solidarity. Who was most willing and eager
to help? The Trotskyists—because they saw the imperative of struggling against the
dictatorship of the bureaucracy.[99]

In other testimony, especially that from former French Maoists and Trotskyists, the
latter-day 'discovery' of the eastern European struggle against dictatorship was presented more as a rejection of their former radical leftist beliefs as they came to embrace
human rights, the fight against dictatorship, and, for some, solidarity based on a
shared Catholicism. For former Maoist Jean-Pierre Le Dantec (b. 1943) it had been
the anti-imperial struggle in the extra-European world, not within the communist
bloc, that had consumed him around 1968. Jean-Yves Potel (b. 1948), by contrast,
recalled that his interest in eastern Europe had begun in 1968 itself, although on the
basis of a fascination with Trotskyists in the region. For Potel, a meeting at Nanterre
in April 1968 had been a turning point. He found himself 'riveted' by Petr Uhl talking about the 'Open Letter to the Polish Workers' Party' by Jacek Kuroń and Karol
Modzelewski, two dissidents who had recently been arrested in Warsaw.[100] His interest in central Europe was further piqued as he fell ill and spent the year 1969–70 at a
sanatorium outside Grenoble, where a number of sick or exhausted ex-68ers and a
large number of Czech students fleeing repression after August 1968 had taken refuge;
here Potel found a Czech girlfriend. Nevertheless, he conceded that he still found
central European Marxists too 'reformist'—i.e. conceding a central role for parties and
trade unions in the reforming of socialism—for his Trotskyist leanings.[101]

It was only after the ideological transformation of the French left in the mid-
1970s that it became possible to make important new political connections with
68ers from the communist bloc. In 1978, *Le Nouvel Observateur* published an
attack on Third Worldism by former radicals such as Jean-Pierre Le Dantec: 'We
invented the Third World as a myth to help change the world, he confessed, but
now realized that "one barbarism can hide another" '.[102] They discovered the 'awful
truth' about Third World liberation movements that had not resulted in freedom
for oppressed peoples but had degenerated into violence and tyranny in the same
way as communism in the Soviet Union. For them, the moment that epitomized
the end of 'Third Worldism' was the fate of the Boat People fleeing Vietnam after
the fall of Saigon to the North Vietnamese communists in 1975. Michel-Antoine
Burnier, who had been a Young Communist in the 1960s but switched from

[99] Interview with Nina Smolar, conducted by PO, Warsaw, 21 August 2009. On the Polish–
Swedish linkages, see Lars Fredrik Stöcker, 'Eine transnationale Geschichte des geteilten Europa? Die
Brückenfunktion des polnischen politischen Exils in Schweden 1968–1980', in Włodzimierz
Borodziej, Jerzy Kochanowski and Joachim von Puttkamer (eds) *'Schleichwege': Inoffizielle Begegnungen
sozialistischer Staatsbürger zwischen 1956 und 1989* (Cologne, Weimar and Vienna, 2010), 253–74.

[100] Interview with Jean-Yves Potel, conducted by RG, Paris, 16 May 2008.

[101] On French radicals' dislike of eastern European reformism, see Maud Bracke, 'French responses
to the Prague Spring: connections, (mis)perception and appropriation', *Europe-Asia Studies* 60/10
(2008), 1735–47.

[102] Jean-Pierre Le Dantec, 'Une barbarie peut en cacher une autre', *Le Nouvel Observateur* 717, 22
July 1978.

political to cultural revolution after 1968, recalls coming back together with his old friend Bernard Kouchner of *Médecins Sans Frontières*:

> It was only with Vietnam that we did something really culpable, which we tried to repair as best we could…At the time of the Boat People, when Kouchner organized the *L'Île de lumière* boat to go to Vietnam and pull people out of the China Sea, I got going as an activist on the boat straight away, saying that you have to be able to undo what you have done.[103]

Their disillusionment with the 'Third World' was paralleled by a growing fascination with the Second.[104] A recognition of the oppressive characteristics of socialism outside Europe was accompanied by a realization of the authoritarianism of the communist bloc closer to home. Indeed, the 'turn to human rights' by these radicals was in part provoked by the late 'discovery' by French intellectuals of the totalitarian nature of communism following the publication in 1973 of Solzhenitsyn's *Gulag Archipelago*.[105] Internationalism now meant aiding those workers on the other side of the Iron Curtain, who were for them the new heroic anti-colonial fighters, this time against the Soviet master in the name of human rights.[106] Le Dantec recalled that a shared Catholicism rather than Maoist politics sustained these new ties: '…from 1975–6 we supported the dissidents of the eastern bloc, and we established relations between the Lip workers [of Besançon] and the Polish workers of Gdańsk on the basis of Catholicism'.[107]

Potel became decisively interested in eastern Europe in the later 1970s when he had grown disillusioned with Trotskyist notions of revolutionary change. He forged links with the dissident movement around Charter 77 in Czechoslovakia, getting involved with the Committee of 5 January for a Free and Socialist Czechoslovakia. In October 1979, he was sent as a representative of this Committee to the trial of Václav Havel, Petr Uhl and other signatories of Charter 77 and members of the Committee to Defend the Unjustly Prosecuted (the VONS). He was arrested and banned from entering the country until 1989. Potel recalls that:

> I met people who wanted to change things. People who had an approach that was much more ethical and cultural, much less dogmatic. I found myself talking to Christians, to people who had no particular ideology. Generally they hated the terms that I worshipped, such as 'proletariat' or 'internationalism'. That cleared my mind. It was like a thunderbolt.[108]

---

[103] Interview with Michel-Antoine Burnier, conducted by RG, Paris, 11 May 2007. See also Burnier, *Les Sept Vies du Dr Kouchner* (Paris, 2008), 214–31.

[104] Likewise, those Hungarian radicals who had once been fascinated by the Third World but, by the late 1970s, had turned towards dissidence, saw their embracing of liberalism as a 'return to Europe'.

[105] Christofferson, *French Intellectuals Against the Left*, 89–112.

[106] See further Bourg, *From Revolution to Ethics*, 243–4.

[107] Interview with Jean-Pierre Le Dantec, conducted by RG, Paris, 24 April 2007.

[108] Potel interview; see also his publications on this subject: *Procès à Prague. Le V.O.N.S., Comité de Défense des personnes injustement poursuivis, devant ses juges, 22–23 octobre 1979* (Paris, 1980); and Petr Uhl, *Le Socialisme emprisonné* (translated by Antonin Bašta and Jean-Yves Touvais [Potel], notes and presentation by Jean-Yves Touvais) (Paris, 1980). On his own trajectory, see Jean-Yves Potel, *Quand le Soleil se couche à l'Est* (Paris, 1995).

In the summer of 1980, Potel went to Poland in the aftermath of the July strikes at Gdańsk—to do research, much like West German ex-Maoist Helga Hirsch. He ended up meeting many of the same people as she did and remained equally bound to the Polish opposition in the long run:

> I went to Warsaw with a plan to do research on the July strikes for *L'Alternative*. I was in contact with the KOR [Workers' Defence Committee, which led to Solidarity], with Jacek Kuroń and Adam Michnik at Warsaw and Bogdan Borusewicz in Gdańsk... When the strike broke out at Gdańsk on 14 August I was on a pilgrimage at Częstochowa, the biggest Catholic gathering in Communist Poland... It was the beginning of a long story. I stayed at the shipyards, wrote a book,[109] made lots of friends and went back to Poland endlessly until the coup d'état of December 1981... In 1982 I had a daughter, whose mother was an activist in Solidarity and with whom I had a brief relationship.[110]

The 'march through the institutions' and disengagement from the West

Many East German activists who moved towards liberalism and human rights in the 1980s also sought close ties with Solidarity and Charter 77 with the aim of forging an East European dissident network. They continued to invoke 1968 as an important symbol that fostered a transnational sense of understanding: according to an article by several dissidents from across eastern Europe published in the German *samizdat* journal *Grenzfall* it now symbolized that 'democratisation remains the political will of our people'.[111] This pan-Europeanism was not the only trajectory East German 68ers took, however. Another strand existed that remained committed to the project of socialist reform and sought to alter the GDR from within—the eastern version of the 'march through the institutions'.

Among the members of a former East Berlin commune, the 'Kommune 1 East', these two strands are particularly visible.[112] Founding member Franziska Groszer left the commune and slowly engaged in more visible forms of dissidence, eventually emigrated to West Berlin, and forged close ties to both West German leftists and Czechoslovak and Polish dissidents.[113] By contrast, some of the other communards took a different trajectory, which was partly the result of their fascination with the extra-European world and its revolutionary leaders. Klaus Labsch (b. 1948), who had been an 'associated member' of the original commune and later moved into its successor collective remembers that:

---

[109] Jean-Yves Potel, *Scènes de Grève en Pologne* (Paris, 1981); also Jean-Yves Potel, *Gdańsk. La Mémoire ouvrière* (Paris, 1982).

[110] Potel interview.

[111] *Grenzfall* 1–12 (1988), RHG, file PS047/16; *Grenzfall*, 7–12 (1987), RHG, file PS047/11–15.

[112] These two strands are mentioned briefly in Timothy Brown, 'A tale of two communes: The private and the political in divided Berlin, 1967–1973', in Klimke, Pekelder and Scharloth, *Between Prague Spring and French May*, 132–40.

[113] Groszer interview.

Of course we were all unbelievable Castro fans, Castro and Che Guevara were gods for us. And initially we were really shocked that Castro was one of those who supported the Soviet army's invasion…in Czechoslovakia. For us that meant…that we had to think about it. And then we said: '…if a man like Castro supports this invasion explicitly, and says this, then we have to think about it. And perhaps it had really been a counter-revolution that had happened. And what role had the CIA [US Central Intelligence Agency] played? And what had been the real goals of the movement of the Prague Spring and should the Russians just have watched', you know?[114]

Labsch and his fellow communards Erika Berthold, Frank Havemann and Gert Groszer began to engage with the socialist classics and, as a consequence, deliberately turned their backs on the West.[115] As the name suggests, the original 'Kommune 1 East' had been modelled directly on the infamous commune in West Berlin.[116] Labsch remembers having been very impressed by his Kommune 1 contacts:

But we overcame this phase relatively quickly, it didn't fit our conception any more, because we had to distance ourselves from these petty bourgeois protests against their own societies. We wanted something different. We no longer wanted to protest against the GDR, but we wanted to become an integral part of the GDR, a sort of germ cell.

The successor commune abandoned its ideas about anti-authoritarian education and the problems of living collectively and sought to implement what they considered to be a more ambitious political project. In 1970, they set up a new communal flat, which they now labelled 'Socialist Living Collective' rather than 'Commune' in order to make plain its socialist character. At one point they even started burning books by western authors, which came as a profound shock to those housemates and acquaintances who went down a different path.[117] While he is now profoundly embarrassed by the Nazi connotations of 'book burning', Labsch explains that:

This book burning was based on the idea that we wanted to cut off contact with people from the West, we didn't want it any more. Not just because they got on our nerves, but because we wanted to make it official: 'We don't have contact any more! We aren't a GDR branch of Kommune 1!'[118]

In their quest to construct a better socialist society from below, they sought to join the official GDR institutions, such as the Free German Youth (FDJ). The Stasi, however, was initially suspicious of their motives because some of them had been convicted for protesting against the invasion in 1968. In letters they sent to the GDR authorities, the communards went to considerable lengths to document their changing political convictions and to showcase the opportunity their communal way of life presented. Appropriating official socialist discourse, they now

[114] Interview with Klaus Labsch, conducted by AvdG, Berlin, 29 April 2010.
[115] See the Stasi reports marked Verwaltung Gross-Berlin, 30 November 1970, in RHG, file RH 098, 7; and Abteilung XX/2, 10 November 1971, Operative Information Nr. 1378/71, in RHG, file RH 155.
[116] Groszer interview.   [117] Poppe interview; Groszer interview.   [118] Labsch interview.

argued that the commune movement in the West had never posed a real threat to capitalist society and explained that their initial attraction to it had been flawed: 'some youths in the GDR felt compelled to copy this lifestyle' because of the 'manipulation of radio broadcasting and television'.[119] The western influence was a real problem that had to be countered forcefully, particularly in the GDR, another memorandum explained:

> Because the GDR is the socialist state that is geographically furthest to the west, has a state next to it that is one of the most aggressive of Imp.[erialism], in addition the influence of broadcasting, television, and the press of this very state is especially dangerous, precisely because we are all Germans, because the antagonistic contradictions are easier to blur along the lines of 'We are all German!', this means that the delineation has to be very tough and sharp.[120]

They spent the next few years trying to put this demarcation into practice. They left their 'petty bourgeois' professions in favour of jobs in industrial production and spent a considerable amount of time agitating in their factories. They constantly hassled workers to collect money for the North Vietnamese and at one point even attempted to volunteer for armed struggle in Vietnam. Above all, they sought to counter the western influence, particularly the pull of consumerism. Labsch remembers that this sometimes took on comical form: 'I always really disliked the fact that workers in the GDR—of all people—ran around with plastic bags from the West, with adverts on them, these were considered chic... they ironed them at home'. When the GDR authorities produced bags with the official logo of the World Youth Festival of 1973, Labsch and his friends collected these and tried to trade them in at their factories, telling their colleagues: 'Listen, we a have brand new, beautiful plastic bag, we will give you two bags if you give us one of your old battered Nestlé bags'.[121]

While Labsch and his peers were no doubt particularly radical—some became Stasi informants in their quest for the cause—the story he tells of their conscious disengagement from the West is not as exceptional as it may seem. Others who pursued far less radical careers, even some who fled to the West in later years, tell a similar story of considered disentanglement and (re-)focussing on the GDR.[122]

CONCLUSION

As we have seen, the Iron Curtain was far from impenetrable around 1968. Ideas travelled and gave rise to significant revolutionary commonalities across the East–West divide evidenced by important identifications with anti-imperialism, Maoism,

[119] Klaus Labsch, 'Wohnkollektiv, Notwendigkeit oder Notlösung?', RHG, RH 098, 37.
[120] Monika Trautmann/Gert Großer (sic), 'Unsere Absage an Havemann und Biermann', RHG, RH 098, 34.
[121] Labsch interview.   [122] For example, Recknagel interview.

anti-American sentiment and the New Left that could be found among leading intellectuals of the time such as Marcuse, Fischer, Heller and Lukács, and among eastern and western activists. Although anti-Americanism, anti-imperialism and opposition to the Vietnam War took on a different meaning in East and West—as it was a mainstay of eastern European state socialist culture in this period—it could nevertheless be capable of inspiring the young and politicized into activism across the continent.

These linkages transcended the realm of ideas. Activists from both sides of the Iron Curtain encountered each other in numerous ways in this period and sometimes forged lasting ties: through personal travel, solidarity committees, letter writing, and official youth programmes and congresses. Numerous westerners, attracted by the 'ferment' and 'incomparable community of protest' in Prague, travelled eastwards, and young Czechs, East Germans, Poles and Hungarians were fascinated by the charisma and revolutionary playfulness of western activists, such as Rudi Dutschke of the West German SDS.

Yet, it would be overly simplified to infer from these encounters ever closer East–West cooperation—simply to read the story of European integration backwards. As we have seen, East–West encounters around 1968 were often characterized by problems of finding a common political language. While there was often an intuitive cultural affinity, symbolized by shared tastes in music and fashion, political disagreements and embarrassing mutual schooling frequently accompanied real-life encounters. The idea of 'revolution' championed by western activists often carried little clout in socialist east-central Europe, and activists from the eastern bloc regularly accused their western counterparts of 'revolutionary snobbism', criticized their leftist 'jargon', and juxtaposed their own struggle for political freedom with the 'hedonistic' western quest for sexual liberation.[123] 'For us democracy was a dream—but for them it was a prison', as Polish activist Seweryn Blumsztajn observed so eloquently.[124] Others even introduced a somewhat competitive note: according to one-time dissident and author, the Hungarian György Konrád, 'In 1968 revolutionary romanticism was no longer cool in Budapest. Those brand new ideals of western 68ers had made the rounds in the eastern half of Europe twenty years before, in 1948–9'.[125]

However, this desire to emphasize difference in the eastern and western 1968s is in itself a product of contemporary political concerns—just as much as the opposite portrayal of 1968 as a prelude to the unification of Europe after 1989. Although in many ways a useful corrective to a reductionist collective European memory, this overt emphasis on divergence—such as East German activists bemoaning western 'indifference'—writes out many of the commonalities and close ties that had in fact existed.

---

[123] cf. Bren, '1968 in East and West', 124 and 127; Piotr Osęka, '"The people of March": A self-portrait of Poland's generation "68"', in von der Goltz, *Talkin' 'bout my Generation*, 154–5.

[124] Blumsztajn interview.

[125] György Konrád, 'Hatvannyolcasok. A nagyvárosi aszfalt utópiát virágzott', *Magyar Lettre Internationale* 70 (2008).

In some cases, such transnational ties only fully developed after 1968. Many westerners, especially ex-Maoists, 'discovered' eastern Europe belatedly in the 1970s and 1980s. The mutual understanding that, for many, had not been possible around 1968, later thrived in the context of a joint struggle for peace, disarmament and against dictatorship—and this latter-day convergence now also colours memories of earlier East–West cooperation. However, this was not the whole story: the extent to which activists sought, maintained, altered or cut their international ties largely depended on their political outlook. In order to tell a more nuanced and meaningful story of the place transnationalism had in activists' lives we have to take into account the different forms this transnationalism took around 1968—both imagined and real—and follow its trajectories.

6

Spaces

Rebecca Clifford, Juliane Fürst, Robert Gildea, James Mark,
Piotr Osęka and Chris Reynolds

The iconic images of 1968 centre on spaces: street battles in Paris's Latin Quarter and the gaze of portraits of Marx, Lenin and Mao in the courtyard of the liberated Sorbonne; students demonstrating against the Soviet invasion in Prague's Wenceslas Square; or workers in occupied factories proclaiming the victory of workers' control. These images tell their own story of protest and revolt. Yet too often we never get beyond the excited faces of anonymous participants in our attempts to understand the meaning of these demonstrations, occupations and battles for territory.

The life history interview with former activists can offer an understanding of the significance of spaces in the politics of 1968 that images cannot. It provides a subjective understanding of the way certain spaces were invested with symbolic significance, of how individuals became activists through performance in those spaces, and of how relations and mentalities were transformed in the laboratories those spaces became.[1] Moreover, they offer a window into how activists' use of space changed over time. Many who continued their activities after the initial failures around 1968 questioned the utility of the conquest of spaces they once thought it key to inhabit and control, and sought out new areas that reflected their changed views about revolution and alternative culture.

Around 1968 it is possible to detect two broad directions with regard to space. In a first phase there was an offensive movement as protesters debated how to take politics beyond their educational institutions or workplaces into the streets, to challenge power publicly in spaces that were controlled by the state, and to build cross-class alliances. Indeed, 1968 represented an awakening of mass protest after a long period of domestication. For many people, the totalitarian regimes of the 1930s, the horrors of the Second World War and the intense domesticity of the postwar years had stifled alternative public spheres. This challenge was risky even

---

[1] On social space as 'socially produced', see Henri Lefebvre, *The Production of Space* [1974] (Oxford, 1991), 26. On some of these themes see Holger Nehring, 'Demonstrating for "peace" in the Cold War: The British and West German Easter marches, 1958–1964', in Matthias Reiss (ed.) *The Street as Stage. Protest Marches and Public Rallies since the Nineteenth Century* (Oxford, 2007), 275–93.

in the democratic societies of western Europe; in the communist bloc or Mediterranean dictatorships to venture into the streets was to court severe repression. After the initial challenges it was only a matter of time before the state regained control of contested public spaces across Europe. In a second phase, therefore, activists had to reconsider new ways of using space for the continuation or reworking of their agendas. Some activists went underground and operated incognito in spaces such as factories, infiltrating the workforce and seeking to rekindle industrial confrontation. Others, however, sought out spaces away from centres of power in rural and local sites where they hoped to build new laboratories of political and social relations.

OFFENSIVE MOVEMENT: CONTESTING PUBLIC SPACES

France: Contesting power in the city and workplace

The offensive phase of 1968 involved a challenge for control of spaces controlled by university authorities, employers or the state. In France, events were triggered on 22 March 1968 when students occupied the administrative block of the new overspill University of Nanterre outside Paris. Prisca Bachelet (b. 1940), former national student leader then working at the communist-run town hall of Nanterre, was amazed by the new informal style of the meetings of what became the 22 March movement:

> I went along and I was absolutely dumbfounded because they were not like any political meetings I knew. There was no platform . . . everyone was sitting on the floor, people started to speak when they felt like it. There was no order of speakers, no registering to speak, people were not speaking on behalf of their organization, and everything was very heated.[2]

The university authorities closed down the Nanterre campus on 2 May and the next day its students, including Dany Cohn-Bendit, came to the Sorbonne to protest at the closure of their faculty. Riot police entered the Sorbonne to arrest students and took them away in police vans, provoking clashes in the Latin Quarter as students demanded the liberation of their arrested comrades and the reopening of the Sorbonne. These demonstrations culminated on Friday–Saturday 10–11 May in the so-called Night of the Barricades.[3]

Bernard Victorri (b. 1946), a mathematics student at the École Normale Supérieure, broke with the Maoist leadership that had rejected the student revolt and immersed himself in the battle with police for control of the Latin Quarter. His account of his involvement on the boulevards and barricades conveys his personal transformation from student to activist and the way in which he came to view himself as part of the drama of revolutionary French history:

---

[2] Interview with Prisca Bachelet, conducted by RG, Paris, 27 May 2008.
[3] See, for example, Jean-François Sirinelli, *Mai 68. L'Événement Janus* (Paris, 2008), 69–76, 115–23, 145–9; and Chris Reynolds, *Memories of May '68* (Cardiff, 2011), 1–2.

When May '68 arrived we thought…that the revolution was about to happen. I was
at the École Normale and so in the middle of the Latin Quarter, and I was on the first
barricades from the 1st May…I was in the midst of it…We arrived at the end of the
boulevard Saint-Michel. We raised our voices a bit, there were 20 people, 30 people,
100 people. We said 'we are going to such-and-such a place' we were 200 when we left
and we arrived with 2000—it was like *Le Cid.* There was an absolutely magical side to
the mass movement and we had the feeling that we were taking part in history.[4]

The historical significance of the battle was explained further by Jean-Marc Salmon
(b. 1943), a student leader and member of the 22 March movement. Tracing the
route of the 23 May 1968 demonstration on a table napkin in the café where we
met, he links 1968 with the massive strikes that marked the election of the anti-
fascist Popular Front in 1936 and with the Paris Commune of 1871. Sizing 1968
up against these historical symbols, however, he regrets that on his watch the demonstrators did not live up to the exploits of their forefathers by seizing the Hôtel de
Ville (city hall):

JMS: I got involved in the demonstration that left the Gare de Lyon on 23 May. I led
the procession that set fire to the Bourse…We couldn't go to the Hôtel de Ville—
we weren't strong enough, only 2000 people. And no doubt it was defended by
the police…Today I regret not having led a procession to see whether it was
undefended.

RG: But to do what?

JMS: It was the [Paris] Commune, the idea of the Commune. It was where power lay. The
problem with '68 is that apart from the universities we occupied places of work, as in
'36, and the university was also a place of work. But we didn't occupy the sites of power.
The situation would have changed symbolically if we had occupied the sites of power.
So not occupying the Hôtel de Ville was an enormous mistake.[5]

The battle between students and police had already mobilized the workers in a
show of solidarity. A general strike and mass demonstrations on 13 May triggered
a wave of factory occupations that began with the occupation on 14 May at the
Sud-Aviation aircraft factory in Nantes.[6] One of the leaders, Yves Rocton (b. 1938),
a Trotskyist metalworker and trade union leader, recalls how the rally in the city
centre on 13 May in Nantes firmed up class solidarity and put the state on the back
foot, opening the way to factory occupations:

There were more than 10, 15,000 on the place de la Duchesse Anne. That demonstrated the unity of classes…Then the prefecture went up in smoke… The grilles were
breached. Strangely, the guys fell back, but I don't like retreating, so I advanced.
I found myself face to face with a policeman with a firecracker in my hand. It didn't
last long. Luckily he didn't shoot…After that there were Molotov cocktails, all sorts
of things. It was smoking, on fire…As a result the prefect signed a paper freeing the
students and restoring the student union subsidy. For me that was a powerful argument

[4] Interview with Anne and Bernard Victorri, conducted by RG, Paris, 28 May 2007.
[5] Interview with Jean-Marc Salmon, conducted by RG, Paris, 16 April 2008.
[6] Xavier Vigna, *L'Insubordination ouvrière dans les années 68. Essai d'histoire politique des usines*
(Rennes, 2007), 25–87.

when the inter-union committee met the next day…The balance of power meant that action was possible.[7]

Striking workers at the Sud-Aviation plant invaded the factory offices and over-turned conventional power relations by holding the manager hostage for a fort-night and continuing the occupation for a month. Rocton admits that he fully expected a battle with police along the lines of the Algerian War, of which many of the workers were conscripted veterans:

> YR: So, at 2 pm, the inter-union leadership, the workers invaded the management of-fices. Things got very heated. The boss, Duvochel, was in his office…Over 2000 people had occupied the courtyard that led to the offices. It was there that I secured the vote for a total strike and occupation…we were waiting for a phone call to say that the police were coming. But we were alone. The police did not come…We were easily two and a half thousand guys, it was a workers' factory, they had ham-mers and nail guns.
>
> RG: And quite a few had been in the Algerian War?
>
> YR: We were a majority of young men who had been taken on at the same time. In 1968 I was thirty and the great majority were mates of my age. We weren't afraid of a fight.[8]

Although no seat of power was captured in Paris, in Nantes between 23 May and 10 June the town hall fell under the control of a central strike committee of dele-gates of workers' and peasants' unions. This was proclaimed at the time to be 'the beginnings of an autonomous workers' power'[9] and 'the Nantes Commune',[10] al-though Nantes student leader Jean Breteau (b. 1945) was more sceptical about its historical significance:

> In my opinion this is a myth that has been rather overblown by certain interpreters of '68. It was just a regulatory organization, not a soviet. It was made up of delegates from the trade unions not by the strikers. It undertook some regulation, such as over-seeing the supply of the city. Apparently it issued petrol coupons.[11]

The confrontation of French students and workers with the forces of the state in the universities, factories and streets was a model against which movements in Europe often defined themselves. The questions posed in the French case would be raised across Europe in very different political settings: could the university become a space and model for a new form of political organization? Could and should student protestors move beyond the campus to take the streets, centres of power, or attempt to make links with workers in factories? Was violence acceptable or necessary in the taking of these spaces?

---

[7] Interview with Yves Rocton, conducted by RG, Fenioux (Deux-Sèvres), 14 May 2008. On this occupation see François Le Madec, *L'Aubépine de Mai. Chronique d'une usine occupée. Sud-Aviation Nantes 1968* (Nantes, 1988).

[8] Rocton interview. On this occupation, see Le Madec, *L'Aubépine de Mai.*

[9] *Cahiers de mai* no. 1 (15 June 1968), 9–11.

[10] Yannik Guin, *La Commune de Nantes* (Paris, 1969). This interpretation is taken up by Gerd-Rainer Horn, *The Spirit of '68*, 215–16.

[11] Interview with Jean Breteau, conducted by RG, Nantes, 2 April 2008.

Civil rights and challenging space in Northern Ireland

Despite a very different political context, a challenge to the state's control of public space was central to Northern Ireland's experience of protest around 1968. Since the failure of the IRA's (Irish Republican Army) cross-border 'Harvest' campaign in 1962, Northern Ireland had been experiencing a period of relative calm and stability. The province continued to be dominated by a Protestant and Unionist majority but under Prime Minister Terence O'Neill appeared to be making progress towards reducing tensions between the Catholic and Protestant communities. However, the growing desire for equality on one side and the resistance to change from the other would eventually expose deep-seated divisions and pave the way for Northern Ireland's 1968. Here, the taking of new spaces was the project of a movement dominated by Catholics who played a large part in the fight for civil equality in a society divided by class and confession. Indeed, Catholics had only just begun to access free secondary school education under the 1947 Education Act and to arrive at university. Catholic students formed a considerable element in the ranks of those that would link up with the civil rights movement during Northern Ireland's 1968 and take the struggle for equality outside the campus, prepared to confront the Unionists and behind them the British state.

The unsegregated Queen's University Belfast (QUB) was a striking example of a space that enabled students to think about a more utopian organization of society. John Gray (b. 1947), a former People's Democracy (PD) activist whose father was a lecturer at Queen's in the 1960s, called the university a 'cocoon' in which radical ideas could flourish:

> It was the rising expectations created by access to higher education, and in a sense, although I have described Queen's as an extraordinary cocoon, in the midst of the wider society, you were getting a liberal education there. If in fact the society you came from and had to go back to was the complete antithesis of everything your liberal third-level education was teaching you. Well, you know that's certainly one of the triggers.[12]

The university became a space in which the hegemony of the Protestant and Unionist state was discussed and challenged through debate in clubs and societies. Austin Currie (b. 1939), who came from a traditional Catholic family in Coalisland and attended Queen's between 1960 and 1963, explained how he became an activist through political debate in university clubs, which became vehicles for building a new nationalist politics:

> For a time at Queen's you remained inside your ghetto. You went to the Catholic chaplaincy which had a social club and found yourself meeting people of a similar background, but then [it changed]...largely through the debating society...called the Literific...In my second year, there were six of us who founded the New Ireland Society...we organized debates, symposia and lectures, and we put a high emphasis

---

[12] Interview with John Gray, conducted by CR, Belfast, 30 November 2008.

on bringing people from north and south together, and also from people across the divide in Northern Ireland. And it very quickly became the largest university club.[13]

As well as broadening their political horizons, the university space gave students the opportunity to consider their predicament from an international point of view. Former PD activist Brid Ruddy (b. 1950) explains:

> Queen's seemed to have quite a lot of international students. It was the one part of Belfast where you would be mixing with a very diverse range of people. Belfast is a very narrow little provincial city. Yet, people seemed to be coming in from all different parts of the world, so you did have a big mix of people and that was a big influence that whole international involvement of students from everywhere. All the societies at Queen's, a lot of them 'revolutionary student federations', all these international bodies formed in Queen's to support struggles worldwide. I guess for a lot of students that's where the awakening came, because they were becoming involved in international issues and then began to make the link back.[14]

A process that saw such international perspectives converge with local concerns began when the government stepped in to ban republican activity in the universities. When left-wing Irish Republican Party Sinn Féin was banned under the 1964 Special Powers Act, Republican clubs were set up around the province as an outlet for a new strategy based on social agitation. In 1967, the Northern Ireland Minister for Home Affairs William Craig took the decision to ban such clubs.[15] The fact that a Republican club existed at Queen's enabled students to take their protest from the university out onto the streets. Their plight could be linked with the wider emerging civil rights campaign, and they were afforded the opportunity to build bridges to a wider public, including working-class communities.[16] Former PD activist Brid Ruddy explains that the involvement of a broader Catholic constituency than had hitherto been the case made it impossible for the British government to undermine such protests by claiming it was simply the work of core republican activists:

> One of the catalysts for that again was the banning of the republican clubs, and it was Queen's that started up the republican club and again it was banned. Well every time republicanism had been banned, underground families were just completely left to be arrested, locked up with nobody complaining. Now however this was students, this was bringing in the Catholic middle classes. There was a campaign for civil liberties which was going on about the social and economic repression, the discrimination and the gerrymandering. And that allied with the whole political challenge, and again linked to the wider events of 1968, the whole rights issues, people were very aware of America in particular, the civil rights struggles, and the struggles of the students in France.[17]

---

[13] Interview with Austin Currie, conducted by CR, Maynooth, 12 December 2009.

[14] Interview with Brid Ruddy, conducted by CR, Belfast, 31 October 2008.

[15] Bob Purdie, *Politics in the Streets: The Origins of the Civil Rights Movement in Northern Ireland* (Belfast, 1990), 205.

[16] Purdie, *Politics in the Streets*, 205; Peter Gibbon, 'The dialectic of religion and class in Ulster', *New Left Review* 55 (1969), 39.

[17] Ruddy interview.

Students were subsequently present in the first ever civil rights demonstration on 24 August 1968 between Coalisland and Dungannon. However, it was the next march in Derry on 5 October 1968 that would prove pivotal in the development of student activism; signalling for some the beginning of Northern Ireland's 1968 and for others the beginning of almost thirty years of ethno-political violence that became known as the 'Troubles'.[18] Originally planned to start in Protestant territory, this march was served with an official ban. This did not prevent it from going ahead but partly explains why it provoked such a violent reaction from the Royal Ulster Constabulary. It was the brutal repression of this peaceful demonstration that inspired those students present to form the PD at Queen's on 9 October.[19] Bernadette McAliskey (née Devlin) (b. 1947) explains the impact of the Derry march on her:

> I had never been there [Derry] in my life before and I had no reason to be there other than this march was there and I had been on the first march. We had not been allowed as citizens, and we had been told that we were not good enough citizens to congregate in the middle of the town, so off I went to Derry, and I said, well we will see how far we will get today. That was a major event for me.[20]

From the outset the PD sought to take their protest into spaces they were not expected to go. They consistently pushed back these boundaries and challenged the limitations faced as a tactic to expose the discrimination they were trying to overturn. The very march that led to the creation of the PD was a thwarted attempt by students to take their protest against the police brutality of 5 October to Belfast City Hall.[21] On 24 October, students occupied the entrance hall to the Stormont Assembly and on 4 November a second attempt was made to march to Belfast City Hall via Protestant 'unionist-controlled' territory.[22] Referring to the Mexican government's massacre of demonstrating students in Tlatelolco Square on 2 October 1968,[23] McAliskey explains how and why such tactics were so important:

> But they were seats of power, it's like saying why did the Mexicans march on the centre of the city and why did the students take over at the University—they were the seats of power, Stormont was the seat of power, the councils that we used to invade and sit in were seats of government, that's what it was about, the town centres were I suppose the centres, the centres of society, where else would we have gone? But each time we went we reinforced the reality that those places didn't belong to us, that we were excluded from those places.[24]

---

[18] Chris Reynolds, 'The collective European memory of 1968: The case of Northern Ireland', *Études Irlandaises* 36/1 (2011), 73–90; *The Day the Troubles Began* is the title of a BBC documentary looking at 5 October 1968, broadcast on 6 October 2008.

[19] Simon Prince, *Northern Ireland's 68: Civil Rights, Global Revolt and the Origin of the Troubles* (Dublin, 2007), 198.

[20] Interview with Bernadette McAliskey, conducted by CR, Dungannon, 18 July 2009.

[21] Paul Arthur, *The People's Democracy* (Belfast, 1974).

[22] Bernadette Devlin, *The Price of My Soul* (London, 1969), 108–10.

[23] Sarah Stokes, 'Student activism in 1968 in Paris and Mexico City', DPhil thesis (Oxford, 2011).

[24] McAliskey interview.

The struggle for space in Northern Ireland reached a critical point in January 1969, when the PD organized a march from Belfast to Derry, taking their inspiration from the American civil rights march from Selma to Montgomery in Alabama. Despite the insistence of the non-violent credentials of this march, the decision to attempt to pass through 'pieces of Protestant space'[25] meant that it was seen as an invasion of that territory and almost inevitably provoked a violent attack on the cortege by a gang of Unionist vigilantes at Burntollet Bridge on the outskirts of Derry.[26] The battle for space by democratic means reached a dead-end, revealing what PD activists described as the unreformability of the state. John Gray reflects:

> I think the fact of the matter is the Northern Ireland of 1968 had long passed its sell-by date...given the impossibility of adequate change...the only conceivable argument for saying that we shouldn't have done what we did, is to say that rapid change, rapid fundamental change was already under way by peaceful means and you actually prevented it happening for twenty years or thirty years...Well, there weren't any actions in that direction. Therefore some sort of, explosion, upheaval was inevitable. Somebody had to do it and at least People's Democracy gave it a civilized face.

Ultimately, as Ruddy testified, the ambush of the civil rights march at Burntollet exposed the limitations of the non-violent ethos with the upshot an inevitable return to violence:

> I think it changed an awful lot, I do think it changed a lot, and I think it really...the liberal agenda was gone really, it was. We said the Northern Ireland state was unreformable and that crystallized the people into that opinion, people became more...those who were more waffley fell away, and we became then more convinced that you could smash the state, it was all about smashing the state. True violence became more inevitable then.[27]

Poland: Challenging communists in university spaces

The question of the degree to which student protestors could challenge public space was also apparent in the communist bloc, where regimes were even more repressive than the British state. Activists in Poland, Czechoslovakia and Hungary began struggles for greater democracy within universities, fighting for greater autonomy for student organizations. Like their western counterparts, students in the eastern bloc launched movements that explored the boundaries to the spaces that students should be permitted to occupy and control. Yet even protest within the confines of the university represented a major challenge to the system, and revealed the sharp limitations on freedom over space within communist societies.

---

[25] Interview with Paul Bew, conducted by CR, Belfast, 13 February 2009.
[26] Bowes Eagan and Vincent McCormack, *Burntollet* (London, 1969).
[27] Ruddy interview.

The event which triggered the 'Polish March' of 1968 was the rally at Warsaw University to protest against the expulsion of leading student activists. For the student community this was a singular change in the balance of power between communist authorities and students, who had hitherto been permitted discussion groups within the official youth organizations. As Adam Michnik (b. 1946), one of the expelled students, put it:

> We understood then that something was over, that a new stage had begun, and that we had to respond unusually decisively if we were to create a new situation. Otherwise they'd bring the hammer down on us one by one, throw us out of everything, and that'd be that. So, after enormous debate we made up our minds to call a rally, although we were afraid that a public demonstration would force the authorities to reach for radical measures.[28]

Nina Smolar recalled that the idea of students occupying the university also had an American inspiration, taken from the actions of students at Kent University who had a 'sit-in' when the National Guard entered the university: 'They sat down. So we should propagate the idea that in case "something happens" students sit down. And so it was'.[29] The demonstration was called not on the streets but in the heart of the campus, on the square in front of the university library. It was a protest not only against the expulsions but also for the right to protest in communist society, and was attacked by police and thugs.

Rather than calm things down, however, the suppression of the rally triggered student protest throughout the country, in other Warsaw universities and Kraków, Wrocław, Łódź and Lublin in March 1968. Which spaces to contest was at the heart of the student debate. In some university towns they opted to demonstrate within the confines of the university, where they hoped to be relatively immune from police attack. In other cases students decided to take the fight onto the streets—in city squares and in front of party committee buildings—which were entirely controlled by the Communist Party and its forces of order. In most cases, the authorities reacted with extreme brutality, beating protestors with clubs, using water cannons, and sometimes unleashing dogs on demonstrators. This often led to a spiral of aggression that turned demonstrations into riots. Young people built barricades and hurled stones at police.

Given the danger of violent repression, some lecturers and university administrators tried to dissuade the students from going onto the streets. Marcin Rawicz, a student at Warsaw's Academy of Medicine, hoped that if they demonstrated in their white coats they would command respect from the forces of order:

> On Monday [12 March] almost 500 of us gathered at the campus. The main motto was: 'We're gonna show them, we're gonna put on white lab coats and go out into the street, because they won't do anything to us'. I was sitting [in an upper floor window] and strained to hear. It was interesting. When I went out to go to the bathroom,

---

[28] Adam Michnik, Józef Tischner and Jacek Żakowski, *Między Panem a Plebanem* (Kraków 1995), 170.

[29] Interview with Nina Smolar, conducted by PO, Warsaw, 21 August 2009.

a professor of physiology accosted me and said, 'Listen, get this idea of going out into the street out of your head, because they'll simply kill you'.[30]

Eugeniusz Czapiewski, in turn, recalls the attitude of the University of Wrocław's rector:

On March 12 there was a general student rally. Leaders emerged spontaneously... The discussion lasted I'd say two hours and concentrated on the form of our student protest. At one moment an elderly, none-too-tall man with grey hair appeared and presented himself as the rector. It was Professor Alfred Jahn. He pleaded with us passionately not to take our protest out into the street and to remain within the campus walls. Inside the university he guaranteed us full freedom of expression... The rector's opinion tipped the scales, he won everybody over and had their full respect. I can't convey the drama of his words. For the risk that we'd go out on the street was real, but the rector managed to keep us within the university's walls.[31]

The Polish students had very little room for manoeuvre even within the university. The slightest claim for autonomy outside the official student bodies attracted repression and arrest by the authorities. Leszek Sankowski (b. 1945), a member of Warsaw University's strike committee, formed by delegates from all university departments, recalls how their aim was to set up a student parliament that would be a way to engage in dialogue with the authorities for a minimum of autonomy:

Since we couldn't work through the existing organizations, another was necessary. A local one, not a nationwide one... when that committee of department delegates arose, it was to be the seed of a student parliament. It could be seen in various ways, and not only as I saw it. It could be seen not as a group that had political ambitions, but as a group that was questioning the ways things were done, the working formulas of those organizations that were at the university, and was proposing, you know, alternative solutions. A sort of offer to the authorities—that's how it was meant![32]

Stefan Bekier (b. 1946), a student at the School of Planning and Statistics (SGiPS), now the Warsaw School of Economics, remembers that projects for autonomous student organizations were opposed by prudent members of the student body who feared provoking repression:

Our protest rallies lasted throughout that entire week, more or less. We supported the creation of an Intercollegiate Strike Committee in Warsaw. That was a huge step, one we were afraid to take, because everybody was aware [of the risks] of creating a new youth organization—and that's exactly what we were talking about... You know, that instead of the two official youth organizations—ZMS and ZSP—we needed a new organization... I remember I was chosen and sent as a representative of SGiPS to this general intercollegiate meeting of all the committees in Warsaw. It was held at the Politechnika. There someone from the Politechnika tabled that very idea, to create an Intercollegiate Strike Committee. We discussed that at length. I was in favour—others

---

[30] Interview with Marcin Rawicz, conducted by PO, Warsaw, 28 February 2009.
[31] Edward Czapiewski, *Marzec 1968 roku i jego następstwa w moich wspomnieniach* in *Studia i materiały z dziejów Uniwersytetu Wrocławskiego*, vol. 3 (Wrocław, 1994).
[32] Interview with Leszek Sankowski, conducted by PO, Warsaw, 6 April 2009.

were opposed. There were very lively deliberations. But the repressions that ensued led to the rapid collapse of our movement.[33]

Spaces for change within the university were rapidly closed down. Teresa Bogucka (b. 1945), one of leaders of the student Commando group, compares the atmosphere during the sit-in strike at Warsaw University in the last days of March to the heroic but futile Polish defence of the Westerplatte near Gdańsk by an overwhelming German force in September 1939:

> I immediately had this premonition we would lose. Nonetheless, I also had this vision in my mind of Westerplatte—that you fight to the bitter end. I also believed that I had to persist to the end since I had contributed to the fact that people—people otherwise completely unaware of what awaited us—had joined in. I felt I bore responsibility for them. Those are all very unpleasant feelings. So there you have it: they wanted to forge ahead, and I, together with the committee, didn't see any way to extricate ourselves from that. At a certain moment we strove to voice as much as possible before everything would be crushed.[34]

Hungary: The limits of public protest

Unlike Poland or Czechoslovakia, student activists in Hungary did not seek to challenge the state's control of public space in large numbers. However, similar activisms did exist, particularly at elite higher educational establishments such as the Karl Marx University of Economics, the Academy of Fine Art and within the Philosophy Faculty of Eötvös Loránd university in Budapest, and at universities in Szeged and Debrecen, where student activists were increasingly questioning the absence of democracy in their institutions, and were attracted to new models of radical action drawn from Leninism, Maoism or so-called Third World revolutionary movements.[35] Some ultra-leftist radicals were impressed by the public nature of western students' anti-Vietnam demonstrations from 1966 onwards, and the actions of students in Paris in 1968. Indeed, interviewees often presented the challenge to the states' control of urban public spaces, which was widely depicted in the communist youth press, as the most affecting aspect of the western revolt.[36]

Even the revolt of 'ultra-leftists' was cautious, however. It emerged from semi-official or unofficial initiatives within the Communist Youth League's campaigns for anti-imperialist solidarity. Thus, in some instances their own initiatives, such as their rally outside the Greek embassy in spring 1967 to protest against the military dictatorship's arrest of left-wing activist Manolis Glezos, was supported by a state

---

[33] Interview with Stefan Bekier, conducted by PO, Warsaw, 23 June 2009.
[34] Interview with Teresa Bogucka, conducted by PO, Warsaw, 21 January 2009.
[35] On 'Third Worldism' in Hungary, see Robert Gildea, James Mark and Niek Pas, 'European radicals and the "Third World": Imagined solidarities and radical networks 1958–73', *Social and Cultural History* 8/4 (2011), 449–71.
[36] Interview with György Dalos, conducted by PA, Budapest, 17 April 2009.

that encouraged solidarity with Greeks fighting against a US-supported dictatorship. On occasion their protests did contest the state's limited conceptions of solidarity in public spaces, however. In Budapest, students organized unofficial demonstrations, which were eventually cleared by the police, that took place outside the American embassy on 20 July 1966, and in front of the American pavilion at the Budapest International Fair in the same year, where leaflets were distributed and slogans stuck up announcing 'Hands Off Vietnam', and images of America's President Johnson were daubed with paint.[37] These demonstrators were not only criticizing America, but also the lack of real solidarity in the communist bloc and genuine revolutionary ambition at home. As one former radical recalled, the expression of official anti-American anti-imperialist solidarity provided space in which more unofficial threatening protests could develop:

> We took advantage of this official, torch-lit parade they had—the name sounds awful—on Revolutionary Youth Days—on 15 and 21 March...it was at the end of one of these marches to Gellért Hill, and we came back from this before the others, and we paraded to the end of Váci street [the main shopping street in Budapest]...we had the first spontaneous and non-officially sanctioned protest in central Budapest since 1956, which gave me a certain feeling of pride, however absurd it was that we were on Váci street protesting about Vietnam, for anti-imperial solidarity, for the Third World—but there was also the motivation that we were against the new economic [market-based] reform mechanism.[38]

Activists influenced by the Maoist idea of *établissement* went to working-class spaces with the aim of encouraging revolutionary consciousness. For instance, in 1969, István Malgot (b. 1941) founded the influential Maoist-influenced avant-garde theatre, puppetry and music collective Orfeo with other students from the Academy of Fine Arts in Budapest:

> We saw it all around us, that proletarian dictatorship was not the same as proletarian power, that the interests of the party were not those of the working class, we were actively searching for alternatives, we had already flirted with Maoism...not just ideologically, but we were close to that circle who were put on trial, but by the end of 1969 we had gone beyond it...and at that time we started asking the question: what should we do? And we had this idea that we would try puppetry, and with our shows perhaps get much closer to the audience, to the people.[39]

They encouraged workers to take a more critical attitude to the system around them, establishing their music and puppetry centre at a youth club in one of the capital's industrial districts, Kőbánya, taking exhibitions to the industrial district of 'Red' Csepel and performing theatre in factories. They sought to politicize and provoke their audiences, and often attempted to engage them in political debates

[37] Interview with Ferenc Erős, conducted by PA, Budapest, 9 October 2008.
[38] Interview with anonymous respondent, conducted by PA, Budapest, 5 October 2008.
[39] Interview with István Malgot, in István Nánay, 'Az Orfeo-ügy (Fodor Tamás és Malgot István visszaemlékezésével)', *Beszélő* (1998/3).

inspired by their performances once these had ended. Despite their intentions, their main audience remained young intellectuals.[40]

More significant was the fact that many university activists in Hungary decided not to engage in public protest, believing—at least until the early 1970s—that the socialist system in Hungary was experiencing a period of limited democratization that they could best harness working through the institutions of the Communist Youth League. Such groups did not challenge the state's right to control public space, but rather worked within its structures to change university democracy, and later to mobilize for campaigns to address the conditions of workers' hostels in Budapest and social mobility in rural areas.[41] One of leading figures was István Bakos (b. 1943), who headed the Communist Youth committee of the Faculty of Philosophy at Eötvös Loránd in Budapest from 1969:

> There were loads of these public projects that we were hatching, which would lead in the direction of social openness and democracy... [we believed] that everybody should turn to the problems of real life, and just leave politics out of it... Our initiative took shape in such a way that we didn't want the Communist Youth League to be just a façade for party initiatives, but we wanted to create something from our own actions.[42]

They did not, however, seek to build the movement beyond the university or challenge the regime publicly in the streets. Many activists within the Communist Youth deliberately restricted their activities: some believed that the market-based economic reform of the New Economic Mechanism, which gave greater autonomy to factory managers, might lead to greater political autonomy, but feared that 'excessive' public demonstrations of radicalism—in the context of another potentially destabilizing reform experiment in neighbouring Czechoslovakia—might lead to Soviet intervention and an end to all liberalization, as had happened in Hungary in 1956. In this context, few protested when Hungarian troops assisted in the suppression of the Prague Spring in Czechoslovakia in August 1968. Aside from two isolated manifestations of opposition—Hungarian intellectuals Ágnes Heller, Zoltán Tordai, Mária Márkus, György Márkus and Vilmos Sós signing a declaration of protest at the Korčula summer school they were attending in Croatia in

---

[40] Orsolya Ring, 'A színjátszás harmadik útja és a hatalom. Az alternatív Orfeo Együttes kálváriája az 1970-es években', *Múltunk* (2008/3), 244. Interview with Anna Komjáthy, conducted by JM, Budapest, 21 January 2009. Initially Orfeo consisted of a puppetry section, the music group and a theatre. They chose to name their radical culture centre after the Black Panther Angela Davies only after being banned from using 'Che Guevara'; interview with Tamás Fodor, founding member of Orfeo, reproduced in Nánay, 'Az Orfeo-ügy'.

[41] For an account of the student movement that attempts to place it alongside those in Warsaw and Prague, and emphasizes its liberal and republican character, in an attempt to reclaim the story of the Hungarian '68 from ultra-leftist radicals, see Iván Zoltán Dénes, 'Diákmozgalom 1969-ben', *Élet és Irodalom* 52, 31 August 2008. On the absence of challenge in public spaces, see Péter Apor, 'A város mint a lázadás helye: aktivizmus és térhasználat a késő szocialista Budapesten', in Árpád Tóth, István H. Németh and Erika Szívós (eds) *A város és társadalma. Tanulmányok Bácskai Vera tiszteletére* (Budapest, 2011), 22–3.

[42] Interview with István Bakos, conducted by PA, Budapest, 19 November 2008.

August 1968, and the solitary self-immolation of Sándor Bauer on the steps of the National Museum in Budapest[43]—Hungary was politically quiescent in these months, with virtually no other intellectual or public protest against the crushing of the Czechoslovak reform movement.[44]

Although activists' capacity to confront the state's power to control university and public spaces was very different in western Europe and the communist East, some degree of challenge was nevertheless at the centre of all these revolts around 1968. Across Europe, different ideological movements—based around Maoism, civil rights or local autonomy—insisted on challenging spaces of power as a means variously to achieve a workers' revolution, to assert civic dignity, to gain greater political independence or to enable greater democracy within institutions. Moreover, activists commonly were inspired by, or weighed their own revolts up against, challenges to public space elsewhere, whether in Paris, Latin America or American civil rights marches. Furthermore, through the contestation of territory or occupation of space, individuals came to view themselves as activists who were part of history: French 68ers inserted themselves into history at the barricades, seeing themselves as successors to the Paris Commune of 1871, the strikers in support of the anti-fascist Popular Front in 1936, or protestors against the Algerian War. For activists in the communist bloc, by contrast, the memory of defeat and the occupation of space by outside forces—whether the German occupation of Poland or Soviet support in the suppression of the 1956 Hungarian Uprising—played a role in their deliberations over whether to contest public spaces. Across Europe, however, the notion that revolution or revolt could best be accomplished through challenging power directly, and controlling important educational or public spaces, was about to change.

DEFENSIVE MOVEMENTS: THE SEARCH FOR NEW SPACES

The years after 1968 marked a turning away from the public contestation of space in many activists' accounts, especially among Maoists who gave up on political revolution. Jean-Marc Salmon, who went to the University of Vincennes in the autumn of 1968 and joined the GP, wanted to destroy the university before he went to the factories. He relates how clandestine activity became more and more difficult in the face of employer and police repression, how nothing seemed to come from either workers or students. In 1970 he gave up on the idea of revolution altogether:

> JMS: After the first year at Vincennes, when we radicalized the movement a good deal, the message was that the students must leave university and go to the factories...We

---

[43] Open Society Archives, Budapest: HU-OSA 300-40-2 Box 108.

[44] Rudolf L. Tokes, 'Hungarian intellectuals' reaction to the invasion of Czechoslovakia', in E.J. Czerwinski and Jaroslaw Piekalkiewicz (eds) *The Soviet Invasion of Czechoslovakia: Its Effects on Eastern Europe* (New York, 1972), especially 140–1.

were in favour of the destruction of the university and the abolition of wage labour. Since we could not persuade the majority of students about this, we left ourselves. We went to the factories…In '69–'70 we went to Rouen and got work in factories…I was employed in textiles at Elbeuf…I was sacked in June 1970. We spent the summer underground. We were being hunted, the GP was dissolved. We had to find flats to live in…Then in Paris I found that there was nothing left in the student movement. It was just wind, appearances. I said to myself, 'It's finished, there's no hope'. I stopped.

RG: What did you do?

JMS: Nothing. I unwound. I had spent eight years playing with revolution.[45]

In Northern Ireland, for activists from PD, the contestation of spaces where they were supposedly barred had been central to their radicalism. Yet it became clear after the violence that accompanied their marches, and ultimately the killings of Bloody Sunday, that the peaceful occupation of space was no longer an option as guns came to the street. Kevin Boyle, a founding member of PD, explains:

No because I just simply moved away from it. I mean it kind of dissolved itself, it got more and more extreme with fewer and fewer people, as I say I really don't know what happened to its history. For me, my swansong, I think, was the Newry march in '72, after that I was not really as involved in the streets. Indeed there was very little street activity. After Bloody Sunday, the Civil Rights Association was more or less over and so was the PD. There were no more mass demonstrations, the guns and bombs had come out.[46]

Across Europe, protest movements soon discovered the limits imposed by their contestation of places close to power, whether in the university or public urban spaces. The forces of order were always there to protect those sites for the state and ruling party. Following 1968, activists sought out other spaces that could provide vehicles for collective activism. Some activists went underground, working incognito in factories in order to rekindle class war. Others did not think that change would come from old-fashioned proletarian revolution but from new experiments. These might be in private spaces into which they could retreat as a safe haven for small-scale collective dissent. They might be places that could be protected as sanctuaries from external threat from the state and nurtured in a way to produce new relationships and attitudes. This did not mean that there would be no confrontation with the authorities; rather, they were spaces where activists wished to keep power at bay in order to preserve their own communities, values or new radical projects. Below we examine four such experimental spaces that emerged in the early to mid-1970s—in an asylum in Trieste, Italy; on the Larzac plateau in rural southern France; by the shores of Lake Balaton in Hungary; and in the hippie camps of the Gulf of Finland and Baltic states—to illustrate the variety of forms these defensive spaces could take in very different political contexts.

---

[45] Interview with Jean-Marc Salmon, conducted by RG, Paris, 16 April 2008.

[46] Interview with Kevin Boyle, conducted by CR, Colchester, 10 July 2009. On this see also Chapter 10 in this volume.

Trieste asylum, Italy: A new form of revolutionary space

Between 1971 and 1978, in the transformation of the asylum (*manicomio*) in Trieste, north-eastern Italy, we see the efforts of a group of professionals and student volunteers to find practical ways to carry out Gramsci's 'long march through the institutions'. The young psychiatrist who headed the transformation, Franco Basaglia (b. 1924), had been experimenting with therapeutic communities in Gorizia and Parma since 1961, and had become famous for his collectively written book on this experience, *L'Istituzione negata (The Institution Denied)*.[47] He led the transformation of the mental hospital from a prison-like institution to a humane, 'liberated' space, giving some of the utopian visions of the period a concrete shape. Trieste was part of a wider attack on traditional psychiatric institutions, seen in France with the work of Félix Guattari and Gilles Deleuze, in the UK with that of R.D. Laing and David Cooper, and the USA with Thomas Szasz. This was linked to a broader questioning of 'total institutions', led by thinkers such as Erving Goffman and Michel Foucault; in Italy, this interest in circumventing the power of 'total institutions' led to campaigns against prisons, the legal and medical systems, and even the military in the mid-1970s.[48] Trieste was to become the most important example of psychiatric reform in Italy: in 1978, the experiment reached its apex, as parliament passed Law 180 which abolished all psychiatric hospitals in Italy, replacing them with community services.[49] It was to become a model for mental health service reform across the world.

For Basaglia, this project was in part an alternative to wider social revolution. Citing Franz Fanon, who had resigned as a psychiatrist to take up the popular cause, Basaglia concluded that:

> Fanon was able to choose the revolution. We, for obvious reasons, cannot do so...we are forced to live with the contradictions of the system in which we work, creating an institution which we negate, carrying out therapy which we reject, denying that our institutions—which thanks to our activities use subtle and hidden violence—are still functional to the system at large. We are fully aware that this is an absurd gamble, to try and give rights to those who do not have them in a world in which the denial of rights, inequality and death on a daily basis are enshrined in law.[50]

In the early 1970s, hundreds of young volunteers flocked to Trieste from across Europe and the globe.[51] Some ended up there after their renunciation of

---

[47] Franco Basaglia et al., *L'Istituzione negata. Rapporto da un ospedale psichiatrico* (Turin, 1968).

[48] On the various Italian campaigns against 'total institutions', see Giuseppe Cotturri, 'La società della politica istituzionale', *Democrazia e diritto*, special issue: 'Militanza senza appartenenza' (January–February 1986), 7–45.

[49] On the impact of Law 180, see Mario Colucci and Pierangelo Di Vittorio, *Franco Basaglia* (Milan, 2001), 296–314. There is no other country in the world that has a similar law. After Law 180 came into effect, Basaglia left Trieste to take over the running of mental health services in Rome. He died after a brief illness in August 1980.

[50] Franco Basaglia, *Scritti, I, 1953–1968, Dalla psichiatria fenomenologica all'esperienza di Gorizia* (Turin, 1981).

[51] Giuseppe Dell'Acqua, 'Gli anni di Basaglia', in Mario Colucci et al., *Follia e paradosso. Seminari sul pensiero di Franco Basaglia* (Trieste, 1995), 151–5.

political revolution. Klaus Hartung (b. 1940), who had been prominent in the West Berlin student movement, particularly the SDS, related the psychological crisis that followed the collapse of his political revolution:

> People like me, we were left outside. We had nowhere to go. It was an oppressive time. And the psychological crises that were bound up with this, I experienced them as well. I saw that many people really suffered. For many the question was—if you get rid of the whole political vocabulary—the question was for many: 'I can't go on like this, I have ruled out a bourgeois career for myself. What can I...what does my future hold? Where can I start? From which perspective can I work?[52]

The 'self-annihilation' of the movement pained Hartung. He rejected the Marxist-Leninist groups that some of his colleagues joined, and the radicalism of the Red Army Faction. He became involved with Rote Hilfe (Red Aid), a group that offered logistical support to all left-wing radicals in trouble with the law, and became concerned with those 'comrades' who had psychological breakdowns. He rejected an offer from the New Left *Kursbuch* to write about the relationship between psychoanalysis and Marxism, now thinking it nonsensical, and instead started research visiting asylums. He soon realized that he found all psychiatric practice in Germany to be repressive, and began to consider a form of practice in which the patient was not the victim of his own mental crisis but the subject. This would eventually lead him to Trieste, a journey undertaken as a way of rekindling the revolutionary fervour of the late 1960s in a space where the communal and transnational spirit of an earlier age could be reworked:

> There are extreme ruptures that I couldn't have imagined before. On the other hand I see a connection, a search movement. For instance, taking this step of suddenly working in psychiatry, that's a break, isn't it? And on the other hand it was...I was married, had a child, and still lived in this huge communal flat at the clinic...that was '67 all over again! Volunteers came from Spain, from Switzerland, some from Germany, and from Italy...

Carla Prosdocimo (b. 1955), who had been involved in radical politics at her high school and who became a student volunteer in Trieste at eighteen, also viewed Basaglia's experiment as an alternative to political revolution:

> [The Trieste experience] was a practical way to carry out a revolution. Up until [the moment when I first read Basaglia's *The Institution Denied*], my idea of revolution had been shaped by the Italian resistance during the Second World War, but there was something in this model that didn't work, because I had no intention of shooting or of doing anything of the sort, but that was the only model I had, right? But when I discovered [Basaglia's] approach, which was based on practical action, without violence but very radical...this brought things together for me.[53]

Trieste is an excellent example of how spaces could assume deeply *symbolic* meanings. The unreformed asylum was a symbol of social repression; the transformed asylum was a symbol of democracy and equality. Many activists viewed this new form of struggle as one that attacked the remnants of fascism in Italian institutions. Giovanna Gallio (b. circa 1948) had been involved in the occupation of the University of Bologna before coming to Trieste:

> The asylums of the period truly stripped people of their civil rights in a radical way...they didn't have the right to vote...They lost the right to hold property, they lost family rights...In effect, Italian asylums were concentration camps when we opened them up in the 1960s...Italy was a very 'corporative' state, still marked by the corporations inherited from fascism, up until the reform of psychiatric and health services.[54]

Maria Grazia Giannichedda (b. 1948) was in the student movement at the University of Sassari before becoming a volunteer; here she recalls the first time she saw the inside of a *manicomio* (asylum) and the impact this had upon her:

> I loved studying law, and I was very aware of the idea that we belonged to a constitutional democracy, which was built on the struggle of so many people against totalitarianism—this was something serious for me. When I saw [the inside of the asylum] the one image that came to mind was Auschwitz...and I wondered how it was possible that such a place could exist in a constitutional democracy. It was like a prison, and I couldn't accept that people who had committed no crime and who were even said to be ill should be imprisoned like that. I was furious, and I realized that it wasn't possible for me to go to the assembly [in the occupied university] the next day and talk about the struggle to change society—that place had to be changed right away. So, with a group of others, I started going to volunteer in the asylum every day.[55]

Volunteers envisaged that this new space could transform the consciousness of the patients. In Trieste, symbolic changes were prefaced by physical changes as volunteers worked to create an open hospital: locks were removed, bars were taken off windows, front doors were opened; uniforms were done away with, mirrors, combs, brushes and personal objects were introduced; an art workshop was established, as was a café and beauty salon.[56] Patients started organizing among themselves: this led to the creation, in February 1973, of the first work cooperative, with sixty members who cleaned wards, kitchen and grounds, and were paid properly and unionized.[57] For activists, the older institution had reinforced mental illness by turning patients into animals. Earlier forms of record keeping were regarded as impersonal bureaucratic attempts of the psychiatric expert to define his power, and were replaced by 'new patient charts with stories'.[58] Carla Prosdocimo describes her first experience in Trieste, at a moment when Basaglia's experiments were just beginning. She was eighteen and was considering studying medicine when she began volunteering on the ward for *donne agitate* (women considered dangerous):

[54] Interview with Giovanna Gallio, conducted by RC, Trieste, 5 March 2009.
[55] Maria Grazia Giannichedda, conducted by RC, Trieste, 26 June 2008. Giannichedda is referring here to the Sassari *manicomio*, where she volunteered before moving to Trieste in 1972.
[56] Claudio Ernè et al., *Basaglia a Trieste. Cronaca del cambiamento* (Viterbo, 2008), 32.
[57] Giuseppe Dell'Acqua, 'Gli anni di Basaglia', 152.
[58] Prosdocimo interview.

I was very shocked because my idealistic world, in which I was going to become a great prophet of science who could cure all ills, ran up against a reality that had nothing scientific about it: it was the reality of the devastation of these women. Slowly I began to realize that, whether or not they had had an illness to begin with, the real illness was what they had suffered inside the asylum. I had a bit of a crisis after this. I understood that the destruction wrought by the institution was much more significant than that of the illness.

Although it was a local way of making revolution, it nevertheless became a trans-national space that brought together activists and reform psychiatrists from across western and southern Europe, and from South America as well.[59] According to Spanish volunteer Alicia Roig Salas (b. 1944), who had studied medicine and psy-chiatry in Barcelona and then became disillusioned with mainstream methods in Spain:

[There were] congresses, workshops...the majority were international, yes...Robert Castel [French sociologist], Félix Guattari from France, Stanislas, Muriel Caim, from Belgium...Cecilia Marcos from Mexico, David Cooper from England...Eric Woolf, German, Roger Gentis, then Torrubia, Horacio Turrubia, from France too...what was achieved in Italy was *the social movement*...society became involved. It opened up to other professional fields so that they helped the psychiatric reform, the deinstitu-tionalization...It's the only country that has been able to mobilize all these profes-sionals in favour of reform, of psychiatric change.[60]

Lip and Larzac: Rediscovering revolution, locally

In France too, many activists were reconsidering the spaces in which political ac-tivism could be best carried out. The revolutionary strategy of organizations such as the GP came up against both the repressive power of the French state and its own failure to whip up workers who took action in their own spaces and followed their own agenda. Alain Geismar, who spent eighteen months in prison in 1970–1 for reconstituting the banned GP, explains that factory occupation of the Lip watchmakers of Besançon in 1973 and the struggle of the sheep farmers of the Larzac plateau through the 1970s against the extension of a military base demons-trated that new strategies were being generated in new spaces by new kinds of activists:

Then there was the Larzac and Lip. We discovered that extremely subversive things were happening in the factories, which did not necessarily lead to a military escala-tion...There was no need for activists in a place like the Larzac which brought to-gether, as Lip did, all the subversive energy that France could muster. As activists we ran the risk of a provoking a direct confrontation with the state, and that is why we took the decision to dissolve ourselves.[61]

[59] Interview with Franco Rotelli, conducted by RC, Trieste, 5 March 2009.
[60] Interview with Alicia Roig Salas, conducted by NT, Barcelona, 24 March 2009.
[61] Interview with Alain Geismar, conducted by RG, Paris, 29 May 2007.

The Lip workers, who occupied their factory in June 1973 and then set about re-starting production and sales, were a more obvious manifestation of autonomous worker power than the earlier so-called Nantes Commune. They were driven out of the factory by a police attack on 14 August 1973, but resistance simply locked onto the community. Strike leader Charles Piaget (b. 1928) told the workers, 'the factory is not the walls but the workers. It is where they are'. He explained that:

> occupying the factory was an important advantage for us, and when the government occupied it the advantage shifted, of course. We then had to imagine rebuilding the factory in Besançon itself, with some changes, naturally, as it would never quite be the factory. We had one sector in the Janzay gymnasium, where we built partitions, so that the commissions could meet inside...We rebuilt the restaurant in the old fort of Brugey, and we had set up secret workshops in case the factory was ever taken over...Usually when the government occupies a factory and drives out the workers, it's all over, because they are knocked out. But here we were able to bounce back, to show that we weren't knocked out.[62]

The Larzac plateau on the south-west escarpment of the Massif Central became a laboratory for new relationships, ideas and politics that attracted activists from all over France and beyond. It became a symbol of resistance to the aggression of the military state, a symbol whose message was carried to other groups fighting for their land in other parts of the world, and itself becoming a sacred place of pacifist thinking and of reconciliation.[63]

Those sheep farmers who became involved in the Larzac struggle recalled that what they had seen of 1968 on their television sets did not endear them to the students, and that they had been thankful to the French state for restoring order. It was not until Defence Minister Michel Debré announced plans in 1970 to extend a military base that they now found themselves confronted by the power of the state and gradually linked up with *gauchistes* of 1968. Jean-Marie (b. 1938) and Pierre (b. 1943) Burguière were two sons of a farmer and local notable, Léon Burguière, who had been driven by rising farm rents in the north of the Aveyron department to make a new life on the bleak Larzac plateau in 1952. The family was deeply Catholic and both sons had attended seminary and were active in the Jeunesse Agricole Chrétienne (Young Christian Farmers or JAC). Pierre recalls this ideological journey:

> In May '68 we read a certain press, we watched the television. To be honest we did not read left-wing papers...Nothing happened at Millau and at the beginning of the Larzac struggle, when we saw how the media reported the Larzac and what we were doing, we said, 'But they were lying to us, they were lying to us the whole time. They

---

[62] Interview with Charles Piaget, conducted by RG, Besançon, 22 May 2007.

[63] On the Larzac struggle see Michel Le Bris, *Les Fous du Larzac* (Paris, 1975); Jeannette Colombel, 'Résistance du Larzac, 1971–1977', *Les Temps modernes* 371 (June 1977), 1971–2088; Didier Martin, *Larzac. Utopies et Realités* (Paris, 1987); Alexandre Alland, *Le Larzac et après. L'Étude d'un mouvement social novateur* (Paris, 1995); Roger Rawlinson, *Larzac. A nonviolent campaign of the '70s in southern France* (York, 1996); Pauline Vuarin, *Larzac 1971–1981: La Dynamique des Acteurs d'une Lutte Originale et Créatrice* (Paris, 2005); Pierre-Marie Terral, *Larzac: de la Lutte paysanne à l'Altermondialisme* (Toulouse, 2011).

didn't just start lying today'…When Debré talked about the Larzac he said that 'the
crows took a backpack to cross the Larzac', that it was a desert, a French Siberia. That
was a tissue of lies because as he said, there were a number of young farmers who were
setting up there. There was an agricultural revival.[64]

His wife Christiane remembers the growing climate of violence as the army engaged in manoeuvres far from the base, with the aim of intimidating the farmers
and persuading them to sell up and leave:

> There were fights and skirmishes all the time on the land here. The soldiers pushed out
> from the perimeter of their military camp…They came through the hamlets at night
> with their armoured vehicles. They flattened the crops, came in low with helicopters,
> frightened the flocks. They were always on manoeuvre on the plateau.

Such clashes with the army led to a fundamental transformation in the attitude of
sheep farmers towards 68ers. Jean-Marie Burguière recalls:

> We were very strongly against them ['68 movements]. I said, 'They are layabouts. They
> only think about having sex'. My father spoke to me about it. For him it was shocking.
> We said, 'It's disgusting', because we were very modest. We were shocked. Then the
> story of the Larzac came along and we had lots of contact with what were called *gau-
> chistes*…When someone asked my father, 'You, Monsieur Burguière, after all, when
> you see all these *gauchistes*, all these hippies, what do you think?' And my father an-
> swered, 'I don't look at the colour of the hand that is held out to me'. He was right.
> Unfortunately, no fortunately, it was people like that who saved us. Those people, not
> right-wing people.[65]

The Larzac became a nexus of new relations and attitudes through collective
projects and joint campaigns. Sympathy from the government's opponents was
built up by theatrical gestures such as a convoy of tractors to the nearby town of
Rodez on 14 July 1972, and a tractor convoy that headed for Paris in January
1973. This required the help of the farming community on a larger scale and in
particular that of Bernard Lambert (1931–84), a national leader of the JAC from
the Loire-Atlantique who had also served a prison sentence for opposing the Algerian War, campaigned against the war as deputy for Châteaubriant in 1958–62,
had brought out the farmers of Loire-Atlantique to support the students and workers of Nantes in 1968 and had founded the Paysans Travailleurs in 1970. The tractor convoy to Paris was blocked by the authorities at Orléans but the peasants then
changed tactics. Bernard Lambert was instrumental in organizing a huge rally at
Rajal del Guorp (Crow Rock in Occitan) on the Larzac plateau on 25–26 August
1973, at which he famously declared that 'peasants will never again be Versaillais',
a reference to the soldiers, often of rural origin, who had suppressed the Paris
Commune in 1871. The Lip strikers sent a coach of 200 workers to proclaim the
'marriage of Lip and Larzac'. The transformation of the peasantry from a counter-
revolutionary to a revolutionary force was duly performed.

[64] Interview with Pierre and Christiane Burguière, conducted by RG, Le Camper du Larzac,
22 May 2008.
[65] Interview with Jean-Marie Burguière, conducted by RG, La Ferme de l'Hôpital, 21 May 2008.

Photos of the rallies on the Larzac in August 1973 and again in August 1974 show armies of young people, often bare-chested in the sun, swarming across the plateau. This was the coming together of farmers, *gauchistes* and many others who would soon be structured as a constellation of Larzac committees scattered across France and beyond. One of the organizers of these committees was Pierre Vuarin (b. 1948), brought up in Paris but hating school and bourgeois existence. He became a student of agriculture, and was involved in 'long marches' to rally support among the peasants of Brittany and Normandy in 1970–1. He set up an Action Committee for the Larzac at Rodez and joined an autonomous faction of the United Socialist Party (PSU) called the Peasant and Worker Left (GOP):

> I threw myself into involvement with the peasants with a huge amount of energy and had a fantastic time, in particular on the Larzac. I joined the GOP ... and was also on the Larzac Committee. We promoted Larzac committees nationally, with different kinds of people. There were non-violent activists, Occitan nationalists, the GOP, anarchists but also Catholics in the Larzac committees—they were very open. The Larzac committees really got going in '75. They existed before but without any direction. After that there was coordination at the national level.[66]

Back on the Larzac plateau the struggle moved from defending land against encroachments by the army to liberating it through the occupation of farms that had been sold to the army by landowners. A group of conscientious objectors to military service moved in to take over land that had been sold to the army by landowners who were not part of the campaign. Christian Rocqueirol (b. 1954), who was too young to have taken part in 1968 but refused to do military service in 1973, came to the Larzac in 1975. He describes a stand-off with the army that was ready-made for the media:

> We occupied the farm of Cavaillès in October '76. Another farm that had been sold to the army ... The Larzac peasants set us up—each of them gave us a sheep to build up our flock. At the beginning we had forty sheep which came from twenty different farms. So we occupied this farm but on the third or fourth day the army expelled us ... They built a fortified camp surrounded by barbed wire and we built a wooden house just outside the barbed wire ... Between '76 and '81, when the matter was settled, we cohabited with the army. They had a watchtower in a tree and watched us all day ... We pastured the sheep on land that the army could not keep an eye on. Because they were focussed on the buildings they couldn't keep track of the land ... Journalists from the national media came to see us—the soldiers were surrounded by sheep.[67]

Towards the end of the campaign the farmers of the Larzac returned to the offensive, taking the struggle to the seat of power in Paris. A score of farmers marched the 700 kilometres to the capital in November–December 1978, joined by a huge crowd as they reached the outskirts. Two years later, in November 1980, eighty sheep farmers and their families took the symbolic fight fully into

---

[66] Interview with Pierre Vuarin, conducted by RG, Paris, 12 May 2008.
[67] Interview with Christian Rocqueirol, conducted by RG, Saint-Sauveur du Larzac, 23 May 2008.

enemy territory by camping for five days on the Champ de Mars, the historic site of military reviews, before they were moved on. The farmers and activists of the Larzac are keen to explain that theirs was one the few protests in the 1970s to end successfully. When François Mitterrand came to power in 1981 he cancelled plans to extend the military base. As a result of the struggle, however, the Larzac farmers acquired a much wider vision and saw it as their mission as a symbol of resistance to return the solidarity that had been shown to them through supporting other groups worldwide struggling to defend their land. One people with whom the peasants and activists of the Larzac forged a particular bond were the indigenous Kanaks of New Caledonia, who were fighting for independence against the French state and French settler population.[68] A group of Larzac activists visited New Caledonia, advising the Kanak leader Jean-Marie Tjibaou and Yéwéné Yéwéné on the need for non-violent struggle, and welcomed them to the Larzac plateau. These struggles opened the Larzac sheep farmers to the wider world; Christiane and Pierre Burguière explain:

> CB: The Larzac was bound to return the solidarity it had received in support. We had to pay back that solidarity where we were asked to, whether in local struggles or international ones...
>
> PB: We feel that we have changed in many ways. We are more open to the problems of the world, and more rebellious too, as there are things that we cannot tolerate...

Balatonboglár chapel, Hungary: Discovering separate spaces in the eastern Bloc

Every summer from 1970 to 1973, the neo avant-garde artist György Galántai (b. 1941) organized a series of exhibitions in a small disused Roman Catholic chapel and its grounds in the village of Balatonboglár on the south shore of Lake Balaton.[69] It was an important centre for avant-garde art at a point of great creativity in Hungary, developing over three years into a site for exhibitions, theatrical and poetry performances, happenings, concerts and lectures. Such private retreats— which acted as artistic communities or communes or both—situated far from seats of power, emerged across the bloc. In central Bohemia, in the disused industrial 'barracks' of northern Bohemia, and in the abandoned houses of the rural Sudentenland from which Germans had been expelled after the war, Czech radicals set up rural communes, and artistic and underground communities.[70] In Hungary, communes

---

[68] Interview with Daniel and Nobue Ishii Darras, conducted by RG, Cap d'Ase, Larzac, 23 May 2008.

[69] Owing to the excellent archive 'Artpool' that Galántai built up from 1979 onwards, it is also one of the best documented alternative spaces of late socialist Hungary. For an in-depth account, see Júlia Klaniczay and Edit Sasvári (eds) *Törvénytelen avantgárd. Galántai György balatonboglári kápolnaműterme 1970–1973* (Budapest, 2003).

[70] Knížák and the Aktual group obtained a house in a small village near Mariensbad; Vratislav Brabenec (b. 1943), who had been a member of the Holy Cross School of Pure Humour, lived in a commune in an ex-farm in central Bohemia that was an important rehearsal site for the underground group *Plastic People of the Universe*, whose eventual arrest in part provoked Charter 77.

were established by both the Maoist-influenced cultural collective Orfeo and young radical Catholics in rural locations around the Danube Bend. There were also some in Budapest, such as the Péter Halász commune theatre on Dohány street.[71] The Soviet case is discussed below. In Hungary, the existence of such separate private spaces of alternative culture was in part the result of the political ascendency of reform liberalizing communists from the late 1960s through to 1973, some of whom recognized the political utility of removing troublesome culture into parochial, (semi-)private settings.[72] These forms of cultural defence—in which communities searched for limited forms of cultural or personal autonomy—prefigured the much more political dissident movements that emerged in the late 1970s, which took up the idea of living apart from power as they asked eastern bloc societies to live 'in truth', in political and moral communities that insulated themselves from the political structures and values of the socialist state.

Its founder Galántai was not himself linked to the radical movements that had emerged in the late 1960s. He recalls that he disliked not only their leftism but also their seeming attempts to provoke the state. His own identity was neither dissident nor rebel: rather, the memory of the violence of the 1956 Uprising still loomed large for him, and he considered provocation inadvisable:

> There were Maoists...but I wasn't very sympathetic to them, I didn't want to deal with politics...I was never a dissident...I never looked for trouble, I didn't look for it in '56 either, I was never opposed (*ellenséges*)...I never ever provoke the police. I'm a peace-loving guy. There is the phrase, 'if they throw stones, throw bread back'. Well, if they threw stones, I didn't even throw bread back.[73]

Rather, he wanted to create a space for freedom that could be tolerated. Galántai became frustrated with the Communist Youth League, where genuine cultural creativity was not possible. While others sought to work through it, or reform it, from 1968 he looked to find another space for his experimentation:

> I was a member of the Communist Youth League but nothing happened there, and I wouldn't have dared to do anything myself...at the Young Artists' Studio—a Communist Youth organization...I tried to be active, but they didn't care about it...So if I was to do something outside the party structures, as things turned out at Balatonboglár, then there could be trouble from it. So I had to do it in some kind of controlled supervised way...there had to be some kind of interaction with the party, with power that was basically omniscient.

He viewed the space he established at Balatonboglár as a defensive one, apart from society, and which could be designed so as not to be directly dangerous to the

---

[71] In Poland, hippies set up communes in rural areas (e.g. Bieszczady mountains), but there was little link with the activists of March 1968. On rural activism in Hungary, see Apor, 'A város', 23.

[72] On this removal into the private, see, on Czechoslovakia, Paulina Bren, 'Weekend getaways: The chata, the tramp and the politics of private life in post-1968 Czechoslovakia', in David Crowley and Susan E. Reid (eds) *Socialist Spaces: Sites of Everyday Life in the Eastern Bloc* (Oxford, 2002), 123–40.

[73] Interview with György Galántai, conducted by JM, Budapest, 23 January 2009.

188 *Being an activist*

authorities. His project reflected common ideas about the role of the 'underground' in this period, pithily expressed in Béla Hap's *A Silent Hungarian Underground*:

> What is Underground? It is an artistic movement which neither supports nor attacks the establishment, but remains outside it. Any attack on the establishment would acknowledge its existence... It wants to be a form of unidentifiable, unanalysable, ungraspable, and incorruptible outsider art. PRIVATE ART.[74]

Despite this attempt at distance, from 1971 Galántai was increasingly subjected to a campaign of official harassment towards his exhibitions at the chapel, as the community was seen to overstep the acceptable boundaries of private expression. From 1972, their exhibitions became increasingly provocative, as the chapel displayed pieces that had been banned in Budapest. The chapel was eventually closed down by the authorities in 1973 as part of a wider clampdown on autonomous activity from a newly resurgent conservative wing of the elite.

Some attendees, however, were frustrated by what they saw as a closed, elite, defensive space in which the dominant culture was not publicly confronted. László Najmányi (b. 1946), who would become the singer in Hungary's first major punk band in 1977 and would be expelled from the country, remembered his frustrations with the narrow intellectual circles who attended, eventually turning to a musical form that he hoped would provoke Hungarian working-class youth:

> I was invited there twice to Balantonboglár in '72 and '73, I did first a solo performance in which people were allowed to ask me questions but I answered with a tape using answers that were pre-recorded. Later on I learnt that around that time John Cage did the same thing... For me it was a very depressing experience because we got out of Budapest, but the same people were sitting in the audience. So for a very long time I had this recurring nightmare that I look down and the same people are sitting there.[75]

This rural artistic retreat attracted a wide range of attendees over four summers. It was, in limited ways, a transnational space, in that it provided avant-garde artists from Vojvodina, in northern Yugoslavia, with a place to interact with the Hungarian avant-garde.[76] It brought together artists from different traditions and generations, from abstract painters such as Imre Bak to more conceptual figures such as Tamás Szentjóby who were influenced by happenings, Fluxus and situationism. It was also a countercultural space that promised a summer lifestyle of alternative art, sex and marijuana. It attracted the former ultra-leftists such as György Pór (b. 1944) and Miklós Haraszti (b. 1945) whom Galántai had previously been distanced from. Pór attended the Balatonboglár chapel during its last two summers and was present, and arrested, when it was closed by the authorities in 1973. His story illustrated both the shift from political to cultural

---

[74] Quoted in Amy Brouillette, 'Remapping *Samizdat*: Underground publishing and the Hungarian avant-garde, 1966 to 1975', MA thesis (Central European University, 2009).
[75] Interview with László Najmányi, conducted by JM, Budapest, 26 January 2009.
[76] Interview with Bálint Szombathy, conducted by JM, Budapest, 13 November 2008.

revolution, and the way in which a figure like himself—who represented unacceptable political revolution—could disrupt the rules that allowed separate private dissenting cultural spaces:

> I was shut away for twenty months [in 1968]—the trial [for what the state called 'Maoist conspiracy'] was the wakeup call for everybody in the sense of leading to a critical investigation of one's own beliefs...So what we needed was not a political revolution [but one in] social life where oppression exists and needs to be liberated through a deeper cultural transformation—thus activism and resistance were no longer about creating a new party. It was mostly in the cultural scene in '69/'70, early seventies, most of my friends were philosophers, sociologists and the artistic avant-garde...there was one play that I just enjoyed so much...about the French student movement of '68, in a 'cave theatre', and there was one moment in that play when the French students were chanting 'down with the police state!' and I remember that we were standing up and chanting with the actors. It caught the attention of the police and they didn't like me there—they said that I was inciting just by my presence...I went to the Balatonboglár chapel with Szentjóby and Haraszti was there...it was a commune and so we were sleeping together in the big room when one night I woke up to a lot of noise and dogs barking and I opened my eyes...there was an article which tried to compromise the artistic avant-garde by saying that the event was attended by criminals, and naming me...I wanted to make their machinations transparent, so I took [them] to the Budapest court, and lost. And then I took it to the next level, the Supreme Court.

Soviet Union: The discovery of separate spaces

A similar trajectory of moving from public, open spaces to more separate enclaves can be observed in relation to a very different group: the Soviet hippie movement. Initially, the hippies had followed in the trail of early subcultures such as the Teddy-Boy-like *stiliagi* and chose to occupy very central spaces in their respective cities. In the Soviet capital that meant Pushkin and Maiakovskii squares on Gorkii street and the Psichodrom (a courtyard in front of the old building of the Moscow State University). Here their presence clashed with the official understandings of these spaces as sites at the very centre of Moscow, and hence the Soviet Union, and loaded with symbolic meaning for the Bolshevik regime. Maiakovskii Square had been the focal point for rebellious, intellectual youth in the early 1960s, when young poets recited regime-critical poems to an audience of young bohemian intellectuals.[77] Pushkin Square served as the assembly point for Moscow dissidents for their annual demonstration. Visibility was the mantra of those seeking change in the 1960s.

The Soviet hippies followed the birth of the dissident movement close at heel and partly originated from the same groups and networks. When, on 5 December 1965, the dissident movement was born by staging its first demonstration in support

---

[77] For more detail, see Juliane Fürst, Piotr Osęka and Chris Reynolds, 'Breaking the walls of Privacy: How rebellion came to the street', *Cultural and Social History* 8/4 (2011), 505.

of the writers Seniavskii and Daniel on Pushkin Square, a future hippie leader was among them. She came out of the wider circle surrounding a young beatnik community named SMOG—an ironic acronym for the Russian 'The Youngest Organization of Geniuses'. Yet the hippie community that emerged in the late 1960s did not see itself as a continuation of these bohemian rebels, but preferred to think of itself as part of a global phenomenon. They drew inspiration from newspaper articles in the Soviet press, photos in the TASS (Telegraph Agency of the Soviet Union) windows, and loopholes provided by personal contacts, not least because many of the early set of hippies were children of very privileged backgrounds. Their slang, their clothes and their music, which was dominated by the Beatles, Rolling Stones and Pink Floyd, marked them as a part of a wider community of youngsters in search of a better form of life and a more interesting form of living.

Yet initially the Moscow hippies copied some of the repertoire established by earlier nonconformists—and in some cases such as the Psichodrom and the Maiakovskii Square, they took over these very same spaces.[78] To see and to be seen was part and parcel of the hippie lifestyle: they relished the indignation they caused among passers-by and were keen to proselytize their new message of peace and love by singing songs and engaging passing youth in conversation.[79] In 1969, there came a first mass demonstration when 150 hippies went barefoot across the centre of Moscow, coming within spitting distance of the Kremlin. Sasha Zaborovskii remembers:

> It was quite spontaneous. We went up to Maiakovskii Square and there some decided that we needed to have a demonstration because it was the Day of the Tank Driver. And then somehow a thought appeared—remember our tanks in Prague. And then we decided to go barefoot—the devil knows why . . . maybe because the American hippies went barefoot.[80]

The ambition of some to organize proper hippie demonstrations had begun. On 1 June 1971, the Moscow hippies planned to stage a demonstration against the Vietnam War in front of the American embassy in Moscow, erroneously believing that the Soviet regime would support their anti-capitalist display (or as some other versions say, falling victim to a cleverly staged provocation). The initiator of the demonstration was Iura Buriakov, nicknamed Sontse or Sunny, possibly working together with the national security agency, the KGB, or, according to other testimony, honestly believing in the possibility of staging hippie politics under the anti-American umbrella of Soviet foreign policy.[81] The date was not coincidental.

---

[78] Whether this was a conscious or unconscious decision cannot be established due to the death of some of the early decision-makers within the hippie movement.

[79] Interview with Sasha Zaborovskii, conducted by JF, Moscow, 14 July 2010.

[80] Zaborovskii interview.

[81] On KGB collaboration, see the interview with Sergei Lishenko (Baske), conducted by JF, Moscow, July 2010 and with Sergei Batovrin, conducted by JF, New York, May 2011; on this 'honest belief', see the interview with Vladimir Soldatov, conducted by JF, Moscow, 15 June 2010 and with Vladimir Wiedemann, conducted by JF, London, May 2011.

The Day for the Defence of Children was a fixed spot in the Soviet calendar. It was adopted by the hippies who liked to celebrate themselves as 'flower children', yet also represented an opportunity to do what their American peers did: demonstrate against the war in Vietnam. Sontse held such authority among the hippies that many followed him to the demonstration, often spontaneously and without much thought to its political implications. In the event all participants were arrested at the gathering point for the demonstration. A few were subsequently sentenced to fifteen days' incarceration, a number of them were expelled from the university and quite a few suddenly drafted into the army. The Soviet state had made clear that it would not tolerate hippies in the middle of its most prestigious academic institution.

Yet the hippie movement proved to be robust and a new generation appeared at the established hippie hang-outs, even though the Psichodrom, the site of the 1971 arrests, went into rapid decline. In the mid-1970s a new ideologically minded, younger set of hippies took over, who were far more mobile, and connected across republics, than previous generations. They also introduced a different direction to hippie spatial politics, very consciously searching for places where they were shielded from outside interference. The idea of a summer camp was first realized near Leningrad, on the Gulf of Finland, in 1976. Taking advantage of the more liberal climate of the Baltic republics, the next year saw a camp in Vitrupe in Lithuania, which ended with all participants being kicked out of the republic altogether. The following year Misha Bombin invited his friends to Gauja, a place near Riga and near his own house: this remote, yet easy to reach location was to become the home of the Soviet hippie summer camps until 1992, when Latvia became a foreign state for the majority of once-Soviet hippies.

The idea of a rural retreat was not new to either the global or the Soviet hippie community. A *samizdat* item published by the hippie Tsen Baptist in 1973 refers to Drop City in Colorado, which is credited with being one of the first rural hippie communes in the world and had been featured in the Soviet journal *Sovetskaia Arkhitektura*.[82] Yet the generation that made up the readership of this pamphlet seems to have done little to create a Soviet version of this vision, if one does not count the numerous trips to the south and in particular the Crimea. According to Misha Bombin, helicopters destroyed a first attempt to create a more permanent camp there.[83] Then there were several attempts to create a commune among those hippies who had almost permanent contact with each other via the *sistema*—the loose federation of hippies that, according to Misha Bombin and Gena Zaitsev, had become a 'state within a state'.[84] With true communal life an impossibility in a KGB-ruled state, Bombin opted for a summer camp, which took place for the first time in 1978. Unlike the early trips down to the Crimea, when people went to famous spa towns such as Gurzuf and Koktebel, Gauja distinguished itself because

[82] Private Archive Volodia Terplishev.
[83] Interview with Misha Bombin, conducted by JF, Riga, 9 April 2009. Interview with Gena Zaitsev, conducted by JF, Luga, May 2009. There were attempts at communal life in Leningrad and the surroundings of Moscow. Most were very short-lived.
[84] Bombin interview.

of its remoteness and natural beauty. The Soviet hippies turned their back on their usual stomping ground of the big cities and searched for 'conversation with those who thought like them'. They felt that they had truly created something special—a kind of hippieland, where 'they all felt well. And when all had to leave, many cried and did not want to leave, because they said that something like this was never going to happen again'.[85]

CONCLUSION

In the years around 1968, rebels sought to contest power in university and public spaces. While in western democracies it was possible to mount this challenge in the streets and workplaces, in the state-socialist East there was much less room for manoeuvre. By the early 1970s, these same rebels were often looking to new sites to enable new forms of radical experiment. Although political context ensured that there were differences in uses of space, activists in both western Europe and the communist bloc moved into local—often rural or parochial—defensive spaces in which new forms of revolution or alternative culture could be tried out, hopefully distant from the gaze of the state. These new sites often brought together rebels from a variety of ideological traditions who otherwise might not have worked together and afforded them the opportunity to invent alternative social models, lifestyles or cultures; in some cases, these also became transnational spaces that both created real links across borders and created new forms of solidarity. Despite their marginal locations, these spaces could shape very powerful movements: the Trieste experiment helped the cause of psychiatric reform in Italy, the Larzac protestors both defeated the French military and forged new kinds of peasant solidarity, and in the eastern bloc new experiments with separate artistic and lifestyle communities prefigured the later challenge of political dissident culture.

[85] Bombin interview.

7

Drop-outs

John Davis and Juliane Fürst

An observant visitor to Leningrad in the early 1980s would have found some curious graffiti on the walls of the Kazan Cathedral. It said 'Long live the commune Yellow Submarine'. As it happened, the graffiti lasted a lot longer than the commune to which it referred, even though it, like the commune, eventually fell victim to the cleansing effort of the Leningrad authorities.[1] Similarly, a 'hippie tourist' reading the walls of the Villa Road squat in Brixton, south London, in 1976 would have learned that 'in the not too distant future, wars will no longer exist, but there will still be Lambeth Council'.[2] In this case half, at least, of the squat would outlive the graffiti and resist the attempts of the London Borough of Lambeth to destroy it; some houses in Villa Road continue to be squatted today.

London and Leningrad are not often compared in studies of '1968'. But the protest idiom generated in the late 1960s was transnational, even crossing the Iron Curtain, as many of the chapters in this volume demonstrate. A focus on the alternative scene in Leningrad and London reveals parallel nonconformist cultures, propelled by similar sentiments and based on a shared sense of what it meant to be young, free and different. The squats and communes of London and Leningrad show that, local political and societal differences notwithstanding, the spirit of the late 1960s had gone global, creating feelings, attitudes and experiences among youth that were peculiar to time rather than place. Yet, this exploration of alternative lifestyles on two different sides of the Cold War world is not a story of imitation—indeed the trickle of information that crossed the Iron Curtain was far too thin to allow for complete assimilation to the West—but rather an attempt to distil what many interviewees have called 'something in the air': the dynamics that created new alternative spaces for youth, but also those that eventually pulled it apart.

We are looking here at a form of dissent, which rested upon the development of alternative modes of living. It was less overtly assertive than the protest march or demonstration; indeed it was characteristically self-contained and even introverted. This was the case in the East, where anybody living outside the officially sanctioned

---

[1] Interview with Feliks and Marina Vinogradov, conducted by JF, St Petersburg, 8 June 2009.
[2] *The Villain* 17, September 1976. The twenty-five issues of *The Villain* used for this essay are in the possession of Mr Christian Wolmar, whom we would like to thank for making them available to us.

norm existed under the constant observation of authorities who instinctively equated cultural nonconformity with political dissent. But it was also true in different ways for the West, where conventional society was frequently unsympathetic to the mores and some of the behaviour associated with lifestyle radicalism. Alternative lifestyles in the USSR were subjected more severely to state repression—which could range from simple disapproval to arrest and/or forceful incarceration in prisons or psychiatric hospitals. But even in London, squatter communities lived in the justified fear of heavy-handed action to evict them, likely to lead to violence if they resisted. In both communities, therefore, there was an underlying sense of living under siege, generating a degree of tension and introversion, which in turn affected the way in which these lifestyle experiments played out.

As will become apparent, Leningrad and London had more in common in the long 1970s than is ordinarily imagined. Both played host to a band of disaffected youngsters who explored various avenues of living in a world alternative to the one that they saw as the dominant mainstream. Their motivation and strategies of creating difference demonstrate the same desire to put distance between their world and 'normal' society, which they considered to have sold out, be corrupted or browbeaten by either the forces of capitalism or those of socialism. Both scenes existed against a background of a new type of music, art and political thinking, which rose to prominence in the West around 1968. The fact that the Leningrad commune was only created in 1977 does not place it outside the 'spirit' of 1968, but highlights that 1968 should be less understood as a chronological marker and more as a shorthand for a bundle of cultural and social forces that were unleashed in the late 1960s in Europe (and not only western) and North America and continued to reverberate around the world for quite some time.

This chapter will thus—by way of a detailed double case study of two remarkable 'alternative' hotspots in Leningrad and London—make a strong case for an extension of our understanding of the term 1968: both chronologically and geographically. It will also highlight that, contrary to common perception, much of 1968 did not happen on the street, but that some of its most interesting spaces could be found hidden away from the public eye. It was in the closed spaces of communes and squats that much of the discussion of what the 1968 'protest' and 'counterculture' was supposed to mean and effect within larger society was continued and battled out. And it was in these spaces that the destructive and divisive aspect of these discussions became most visible, tearing apart the very communal structures that were to symbolize 'alternativity' and gradually burying the spirit of 1968 under conflict and division.

LIVING ON THE EDGE

In the 1970s London and Leningrad were melting pots, with ethnically diverse populations of various backgrounds and incomes. Each had a pulsating cultural and artistic life and each was a magnet for young people looking for entertainment, enlightenment and difference. While nonconformist life in Leningrad was more underground, it was by no means invisible or unimportant. The café Saigon on the corner of Nevsky and Liteiny Prospekt was a daily assembly point of the city's alternative scene, encompassing musicians, artists, writers, professional dissidents and whoever else was curious to get a glimpse of its coffee-sipping, chain-smoking clientele. The city was bustling with semi-legal rock concerts, awash with the circulation of all kinds of *samizdat* and home to several iconoclastic non-conformist artistic groups. London, of course, was regarded in the 1960s as the hub of cultural modernity in the western world. Its creative industries drew in the products of Britain's newly expanded higher education system, including a generation of student radicals, with the effect that as the capital's more ephemeral 'swinging city' image dissipated, it became instead a focal point for attempts in Britain to apply both lifestyle and political radicalism beyond the campus.

The Yellow Submarine commune was founded in 1977 on the outskirts of Leningrad in a wooden house from the pre-revolutionary era. Communal life was nothing new to a city that even in the 1970s had a large proportion of communal apartments, whose enforced nature, however, had little of the communal spirit envisaged by the youngsters who put together the Yellow Submarine. Its very name suggests its inhabitants' desire to be separate from the mainstream—locked away in a little, yellow enclosed space navigating the black ocean of Soviet life. Its eclectic population ranged from hippies to neo-Marxists, from girls escaping their dominant mothers to drifters looking for a place to live, from married couples to bachelors, who, at least in theory, were ready for 'free love'. Its core was made up of two couples living upstairs on the first floor and two bachelors on the ground floor, who were supplemented by a never-ending stream of more or less permanent visitors.

On the upper level Feliks Vinogradov (b. 1957) and his pregnant wife Marina (b. 1958) constituted the heart of the commune. Feliks Vinogradov came from a privileged family background rich in Party members, with a father working for border control and thus the KGB. Marina was friends with both Aleksandr Skobov (b. 1957), main inhabitant of the ground floor, and Tatiana Komarova (b. 1958), who was less 'communally' inclined, but saw in the commune a chance to escape conflicts with her mother. She soon became the companion of Andrei Antonenko (b. 1958), a friend of Feliks from university who had been, until recently, a Komsomol activist and youth journalist (who had got into trouble with the authorities over some risqué joke in the faculty's wall newspaper). She was also in intimate contact with another sometime commune inhabitant nicknamed Lupus, who joined Skobov on the ground floor. Alexandr Skobov was a classic political hothead who even at school had advocated a new anti-bureaucratic revolution. Skobov saw the commune as the nucleus of a new world order. For the early part of the commune the ground floor was also home to Igor Mal'skii, who also came from a family of privileged Party members with his father working in the top echelons of the Party organization in Moldovia. Skobov also made the commune the base for political adventures with old school friends. Andrei (b. 1957) and his girlfriend Irina also at times joined the commune, while his political ally Arkadii Tsurkov (b. 1957) and his girlfriend Irina Lopotukhina (b. 1958), though sceptical of communal life, spent much time there producing a neo-Marxist, anarchist journal.

London similarly attracted the unattached young. Indeed, London's housing shortage was the result not of a deficiency of houses but of a rising number of households, reflecting the influx of young singles into the 'swinging city'. In contrast to Leningrad, informal or irregular housing was widespread in 1970s London where, in a period of acute housing shortage, the squatter population was said to number around 30,000. Though London's squatter population consisted mostly of the homeless, housed in short-life accommodation by arrangement with local authorities, there was always a radical fringe that squatted unofficially, seeking not only to house themselves but also to effect a political protest or a countercultural experiment.

Just as in Leningrad, the residents of unlicensed London squats ranged from those who wanted little more than a roof over their heads to those who believed that by preserving the physical fabric of inner-city areas it would be possible to revitalize a working-class neighbourhood, those who sought to turn their need for housing into an opportunity for escapist or hedonistic experiences, those who sought to create new forms of countercultural community and those who sought to subvert 'the system'.

The squat at Villa Road, Brixton, emerged in the summer of 1973.[3] It was much larger than the Yellow Submarine commune, occupying a whole street and involving some 200 people at its peak—a peak that really ended in the summer of 1977 when the south side of the street was demolished, though some houses continue to be squatted today. The houses in Villa Road had been acquired by the local authority—Lambeth Borough Council—to create a new park. Open space was in short supply in inner London, but affordable housing was still scarcer, and resentment at the destruction of serviceable houses by a public authority provided the political basis for the squat. Villa Road was thus a 'contested space' in a way that the Yellow Submarine house was not. The motives behind the squat were, though, similar to those of the Leningraders: the need for a roof over their heads, an eagerness to challenge and to ridicule authority—easier to do openly in the UK than in the USSR—and a desire to develop an alternative mode of living.

CREATING A DIFFERENT SPACE

Both communities were formulated on the desire to be 'different'—to 'drop out' from the mainstream. They both saw their enclosed space as something more than just an abode, but as a place in which a new and different form of living could be enacted. Hence, despite the inherent difference in motivation to occupy an empty house for free or rent a private home for a certain amount of money, much of what people in London and Leningrad had to say about why they formed their respective collectives highlights the same sentiments. They looked down on 'squares' (normal people), they dreamed of being the beginning of a new order, they valued

---

[3] The Villa Road squat was the subject of Vanessa Engle's film *Property is Theft* in the series 'Lefties', shown on BBC4 on 8 February 2006.

freedom (yet were not always quite clear from what), they set themselves and their spaces apart in physical appearance, they strove for a certain sound to their lives and they considered themselves spiritually superior to those they had left behind. Yet the very goal of 'living differently'—valued so highly by this generation—created new structures, ostensibly rejecting older values, but also building up new norms, rules and constraints to freedom.

The idea of setting up a commune had initially seemed outlandish to the young Leningrad students involved. Antonenko remembers: 'The very first discussion happened on the bus, when somebody said: "Would it not be nice to live somewhere?". And then we talked immediately about something else because it was all so unrealistic. And then it somehow grew'.[4]

Yellow Submarine had been anticipated by an earlier commune that had sprung up casually next to the university—a squat of students living illegally in the basement space reserved for a local courtyard caretaker. Among them was Marina Vinogradov's uncle. She recalls how she had been fascinated and horrified by the arrangement:

> And there was this interesting space, almost a commune. We started to assemble there and to look what was going on in his place...It was almost not a living space. There was only gas and water and cockroaches...Lots of rooms, worn-out furniture—in general it was difficult to live there.[5]

The squat was soon dismantled by the Soviet police on the grounds that most of its residents lacked a Leningrad registration, yet its beguiling atmosphere lingered on in the minds of its visitors. Despite its dirt, it seemed to offer a more honest way of life than that within normal Soviet society. Marina remembers that it was this sentiment that drove her away from her usual surroundings and into the arms of the commune:

> I formed somehow a strong anti-communist outlook, maybe because all children comprehend lies at a certain level and for me it was that they said one thing in the radio and in school, but did everything differently. And this truth of life, which you can see and judge and all these lies around, made me feel like this [makes a sign of sickness]. I had a strong desire to get out my family and go into the commune—to a place that was free.[6]

Feliks, Marina and Skobov set out to make the old, wooden house they had found a space that was 'free'. An unusual space by its very nature (it was one of the last old, private wooden houses left in Leningrad), they made its interior reflect their mindset.

Yellow Submarine was, of course, named after one of the more surreal Beatles songs and the spin-off psychedelic animation. Antonenko admitted that none of them had seen the *Yellow Submarine* film, but claimed that their aesthetics were 'just like that'.[7] Feliks painted the walls of the upstairs kitchen with big, red strawberries

---

[4] Interview with Andrei Antonenko, conducted by JF, St Petersburg, 10 June 2009.
[5] Feliks and Marina Vinogradov interview.
[6] Feliks and Marina Vinogradov interview.
[7] Antonenko interview.

after another Beatles song, *Strawberry Fields Forever*. Skobov decorated his room with a Che Guevara poster and a militant Jesus depiction. To render its autarchic nature even more pronounced, a logbook and logo were created, soon to be joined by a communal constitution. The commune became a bolthole, separate from a world that was seen with a mixture of contempt and suspicion. Antonenko speaks of 'a locking in from the inside—that was one step towards freedom'. As Tatiana Komarova recalls:

> We said then that it was a kind of inner emigration. We could not leave the country. But we organized ourselves a society that was separate from general society. We lived by our laws and among our people and with the rest we only communicated as necessary, we went to the university and so on.[8]

This inner emigration was paradoxically achieved by an orientation to a world far away from their home: the West. At least for some members of the commune, it was the markers of the West that were to distinguish them from the rest of Soviet society: jeans, music and a sense of freedom. And yet, this West, while so very real in its sound (via records and tapes) and feel (via the treasured items of clothing—jeans) existed mainly in the heads of the Yellow Submarine members, none of whom had ever been abroad. This 'imaginary West' proved a very useful tool of differentiation, yet its limitations as a basis for life in the Soviet Union soon became apparent in the commune.

The residents of Yellow Submarine had knowingly set up a community apart from its surroundings; the occupiers of Villa Road were less clear-sighted in their escapism. Part of the motivation for the politicized squatters was the belief that a bureaucratic and insensitive approach to housing policy by public authorities was eviscerating traditional working-class neighbourhoods; as Nick Wates (b. 1951), leader of the Tolmers Square squatters in Camden, put it: 'houses were being deliberately left empty and allowed to run down and that was running the whole community down'.[9] Squatters hoped to run together the lifestyle aim of 'living differently' and the political objective of protecting a working-class community. In the words of the libertarian socialist Paul Atkinson (b. 1949), himself a Lambeth squatter in the early 1970s:

> You'd got the feeling, definitely the feeling, that it's a political action … squatting an empty house and doing it up a little bit and using it, and seeing that as kind of joining a, some kind of a community, probably quite idealized actually, but by doing that you're making a statement…[10]

Central to the squatter ethos, therefore, was the belief that squatters had common interests with the working-class community around them. In November 1976 the Villa Road squat launched its 'Agitvan' to tour the streets of Brixton in order 'to make people realize what we are doing in the street'.[11] The need to reach out to the neighbours was felt to be paramount:

[8] Interview with Tatiana Komarova, conducted by JF, Munich, 2 May 2011.
[9] Interview with Nick Wates, conducted by JD, Hastings, 3 March 2009.
[10] Interview with Paul Atkinson, conducted by JD, London, 9 July 2010.
[11] *Villain* 19, November 1976.

we can't really be surprised that so many people who are basically in the same situation as us, fall such easy prey to the sort of shit which the established media peddle about us. But without this outside support, we can't realistically hope to survive.[12]

In Brixton, though, the usual difficulties faced by squatters seeking to integrate with working-class neighbours were accentuated by the changing ethnic composition of the local community. As Patrick Day (b. 1946) acknowledges:

I think that was the sadness that where we were in the middle of Brixton, we were basically a bunch of white middle-class kids. OK, there were also some pikeys [travellers or Roma], but that was...we reached the pikeys but we couldn't reach the black Londoners and that was when you could realize that ok, it wasn't perfect, it was ok for a bit of gayness for a bit of dope-smoking, and going on demos, but we weren't actually really integrating.[13]

The squat's introversion was enhanced by the barricades erected to deter eviction attempts by Lambeth Council. They were painted 'rather colourfully', as Pete Cooper (b. 1951) recalled,[14] but they hardly brought the squatters closer to those around them.

By necessity, then, the Villa Road squatters were drawn into the attempt to 'enjoy each other a lot better than anaesthetised people in boring council estates or 2-up 2-down Acacia Avenue'.[15] 'To me, living in Villa Road means something more than just squatting and living on Social Security', wrote one resident in the squat newspaper, *The Villain*:

It means living amongst people who are trying to set up alternatives for themselves, and anyone else who can no longer accept what Society offers or is doing to itself; alternatives for instance housing and ways of living with people, education, community care, sex attitudes, work and technology.[16]

'It was suddenly like being in love with a community', Patrick Day remembers, 'lots of people who I really felt...you know, you could talk politically to and who were attractive'.[17] People occupied Villa Road for varying reasons, but all sought to escape 'the days of isolation in this big city'. As the squat took shape, forming its own institutions, they became increasingly anxious not to be evicted, 'to live in low grade housing alone, without the help and support, friendship and love of the community'.[18]

During the five years or so that the squat was at its strongest, this community became increasingly self-sufficient. The street had its own informal economy, largely supported by benefit payments from the Department of Health and Social Security. As Day remembers:

---

[12] Anon., 'Villa on the road', *Villain* 21, December 1976.
[13] Interview with Patrick Day, conducted by JD, London, 22 April 2009.
[14] Interview with Pete Cooper, conducted by JD, London, 15 July 2010.
[15] Jimmy (no. 42), 'Villa Road is more than just houses (to me)', *Villain* 24, 20 June 1977.
[16] Steve Bythesea, 'For me—Villa Road', *The Villain* 21, December 1976.
[17] Day interview.
[18] Colin (no. 20), 'An acknowledgement to two years' struggle', *Villain* 18, October 1976.

one of the things about Villa Road...was like there would be people there whose probably main activity of the week would be to get their GIRO cheque cashed, which would involve possibly a half a mile walk into Brixton but somebody would have to take them in a van.

But residents' contributions apparently kept the street fund in modest surplus.[19] From 1975 the squatters maintained a food cooperative, drawing on the newly relocated Covent Garden fruit and vegetable market at Nine Elms, and a street café, perennially loss-making but sustained by a voluntary levy on users.[20] A medical service was provided by Day and his future wife Maureen, both qualified GPs: 'for the small price of a smoke', Maureen wrote, 'a choice of top ranking physicians is on your very own doorstep'.[21] A women's group formed in the street, at least during the winter of 1975–6, reading collectively canonical texts such as Lessing's *Golden Notebook* and contemplating forming a study group and a 'self-teaching massage group'.[22] The street's few children benefited from an adventure playground and occasional children's parties.[23] Three street carnivals took place in 1975–7, while the squat community was large enough to support them.[24] In 1975 a musical cooperative was mooted, 'to pool ideas, equipment and knowledge right across the board from musical theory to instrument construction and repair'.[25] At least three bands were formed by the Villa Road occupiers. Pete Cooper played electric violin in the longest-lived of them, the appropriately named Cuckoo's Nest.[26]

This micro-civil society produced a newspaper, *The Villain*, edited by the journalist and squatter Christian Wolmar (b. 1949), and parodied liberal democracy—rather as the Yellow Submariners parodied Soviet institutions—through house and street meetings. Day remembers house meetings lapsing into procedural paralysis:

> There were only three women. So, house meetings never progressed beyond item A, which was 'this meeting cannot possibly be quorate because it's not fair and equal. So therefore all your other questions—fuck off, where's the brown rice? Who's got the pie? I'm off to a house where there's more women', you know, what could you do?[27]

Street meetings were allegedly dominated by the politicos—'your "Chosen Few" who talk in a dogmatic way as if they had swallowed the English dictionary arseways'.[28] Cooper acknowledges that 'there were some people...who'd thought about it in advance and knew exactly what they wanted to argue for and so they'd be probably...be more likely to be persuasive and carry the meeting', and accepted

[19] Day interview; accounts in *Villain* 13, June 1976 and 27, August 1977.
[20] Interview with Christian Wolmar, conducted by JD, London, 23 January 2009; *Villain* 1, 3 January 1976; 'Do we want the caff?', *Villain* 8, 10 April 1976.
[21] Day interview; Maureen (no. 31), 'Villa Road medical services?', *Villain* 25, 14 July 1977.
[22] *Villain* 1, 3 January 1976.
[23] Invitation to one in 1976 in Christian Wolmar's papers.
[24] Villa Road chronology in *Villain* 24, 20 June 1977; 'Hey! Let's start de karnival', *Villain* 11, 22 May 1976.
[25] Nick (no. 66), 'Street music. A history of Villa Road bands', *Villain* 27, August 1977.
[26] Cooper interview.
[27] Day interview.
[28] Mary McKeon (no. 23A), 'I'm not satisfied with our community policy at the moment. Are you?', *Villain* 14, July 1976.

that he was one of them, but believed that 'there was always a sense that the whole street was behind us in any actions and participation was extremely good'.[29]

Yellow Submarine and Villa Road were, therefore, communities that could function and subsist. Neither was ever entirely secure, but each was sufficiently stable to provide a foundation on which to explore the implications of 'living differently'.

THE MEANING OF DISSENT

Difference and autarchy were thus at the heart of both the Villa Road and the Leningrad communes, even if their respective specific lifestyles, circumstances and ideologies differed quite markedly. Rebellion in a socialist country necessarily contained a good deal of idealization of the West, while those in the capitalist West were keen to apply anti-capitalist, socialist principles to their life. However, in the wider sense both communities saw themselves as 'dissenters' from what they considered the norms of their respective countries. More interesting than dwelling on the East/West difference is the analysis of the conflicts that soon ensued within these two collectives. They not only reflect the difficulty of a large number of people trying to forge a collective life, they also expose the limits of the protest and countercultural idiom that had swept across Europe in the wake of 1968. Both collectives soon ran into trouble when their values of 'freedom', 'difference' and 'equality' were put to the test.

In the Yellow Submarine the realization soon set in that while they did not want to be like 'squares', meaning normal people, they also felt not quite at one with the stream of fellow nonconformist visitors, who started to seek out the commune and brought with them drugs, chaos and more relaxed moral values. Even Skobov, who was frequently chided about his own alcoholic and slovenly lifestyle, complained in the logbook about the state of the commune after visitors had had a party in the absence of any of the inhabitants.[30] As the commune became wilder and attracted more strangers, Antonenko developed more general feelings of concern, expressed when he describes the fate of the cat Dissa, routinely fed on gin and vodka:

> The fate of this cat was horrible, because on Saturdays it was fed wine from a teaspoon. The cat did not become an alcoholic, but she went a bit crazy...she jumped, ran, clawed...Because there was a huge number of people all the time and she did not know any more, who was her owner...[31]

This sense of 'things getting out of control' also pervades the accounts of other commune members and regular visitors. Irina Lopotukhina, who typed the illegal journal produced on the ground floor, remembers a growing stream of visitors and all-night, all-day parties, to the point that the communal life resembled a permanent invasion.[32]

---

[29] Cooper interview.   [30] Logbook.
[31] Antonenko interview.
[32] Interview with Irina Lopotukhina, conducted by JF, El Kfad, 3 August 2011.

The problem of outside visitors, however, soon took second rank to that of conflicts arising within the commune itself. At the heart of this was nothing less than the why and what for of the commune itself and the ensuing debates conducted in meetings, the logbook and even mock trials demonstrating that the ideas of freedom and collectivity could be interpreted very differently. The top floor was keener on preserving what they had established, as a clandestine locus for alternative living in a hostile society, while the ground floor saw the commune as the hotbed of revolution. It believed in a certain order of things, which included stable relationships and regular contributions to the kitty, and considered the ground floor irresponsible and wild and excessively promiscuous. The top floor also conducted semi-tongue-in-cheek meetings and trials, in which they censored Skobov for his lifestyle and condemned Mal'skii for his dishonesty. Both found themselves excluded for anti-social behaviour—in Skobov's case only temporarily. Mal'skii left the commune after he had been accused of theft.[33] Money was chronically tight and questions of the common kitty led to further tensions over lifestyle and collective codes of behaviour. All of the top-floor inhabitants remember the time when Skobov finished off a preprepared dinner all by himself while his fellow commune members were at the cinema.

The most serious disagreements, however, ensued over differing interpretations of what their lifestyle represented and where they fitted in, in relation to both Soviet society and global counterculture. Feliks and Marina Vinogradov considered hippie life to stand for world peace and their dress to symbolize freedom. Hippiedom was thus connected to more abstract ideals of resistance and liberation. Specifically this meant resistance to political engagement and liberation from the duties of normal Soviet citizens. Feliks remarks that while 'a Soviet citizen went to work in the morning, he [Feliks] went out to cut wood', while Marina declared that their freedom was 'that we did not have to march any further with the pioneers and *komsomolites*'. She concluded that 'we simply did not want to live the Soviet way of life, it was distasteful to us'.[34]

The West looms large in Feliks's view of himself, the commune and the wider world. His so-called pop posters, which he produced and which adorned the upper part of the commune, reflected his views and preoccupations at the time. America, the fabled land, appears in them in the form of items of denim: 'Everything was linked in our minds. Therefore jeans were associated with freedom and freedom with the United States'. Brezhnev appears as a tank (referencing the events in Prague in 1968), while a row of numbers symbolizes events of the time: '11' represents 11 September 1973, when Allende was overthrown by American-backed Putschists in Chile, '72' stands for pacifism, '68' for May and '67' for the six-day war in Israel. A mild-faced woman represents the Czech idea of 'socialism with a human face', while a brain in jeans reiterates the notion of jeans as liberators.[35] This did not mean that Feliks was devoid of missionary zeal. He saw himself in the service of creating a parallel world—and thus akin to a private revolution:

[33] Lopotukhina interview.
[34] Lopotukhina interview.
[35] Feliks and Marina Vinogradov interview.

Let's remember that our goal was the multiple metamorphosis and foundation of a so-called 'parallel society'…Are we in agreement or not that we differ significantly from 'squares'?…and what our mutual relations are concerned. From time to time one feels some hostility based on nothing…and then remember that our common goal was self-perfection and education of oneself and those close to us. And also, if we differ from the masses, then one has to see this in our manner of behaviour and in our external look. You can accuse me of 'socialism' and in pursuit of cheap popularity, but this is what we need.[36]

However, not everybody in the commune was convinced whether exterior markers of fashion should constitute the limits of their dissent. Upstairs and downstairs differed in their take on the commune's purpose. As Antonenko recalls:

We tried to achieve the best possible self-perfection and character-building, yet declared our desire to build these in an introverted society. Yet some like Skobov wanted to use this space of freedom to enlarge this freedom to cover the whole of the Soviet Union. That was inevitable.[37]

Skobov, who emerges in interviews and in the logbook as the most political voice in the commune, was not content to stop at fashion and lifestyle as markers of revolution. He still mocks the views of his friend Feliks and those like him who:

by hippiedom…only understood the wearing of a standard prescribed uniform of jeans and certain attributes, and anyone who did not wear this, he [Feliks] called not a person, but a 'square'. As he then said: 'only jeans and pay will bring us democracy'.

Those downstairs were not content with departing from convention: they wanted to change normality on a grand scale. Skobov explains laconically:

There was an idea of some kind of nonconformist lifestyle, which was understood quite differently by different people. Because I did everything to surround myself with critically minded and more socially active people, in order to have at least some kind of perspective for some kind of collective action. And the majority was more inclined to the idea of dropping out from mainstream society in order to be less involved in society but also in order to have society less involved in them.[38]

Skobov's critique of the Soviet system drew largely from Marx and Lenin (as has been the case for political underground groups in the Soviet Union for decades), yet he and his co-conspirators Andrei Reznikov (who sometimes lived in the commune), and Arkadii Tsurkov, who discussed politics there, tried to find a new socialist framework of reference, more akin to what was labelled the 'New Left'.[39] Skobov considered the events in Chile in 1973 the equivalent of the Prague Spring for the older generation: 'a spark of hope that there was a better alternative within socialism—one with a human face'.[40] On the possibility of a future revolution he admits his youthful enthusiasm:

[36] Logbook.
[37] Antonenko interview.
[38] Interview with Aleksandr Skobov, conducted by JF, St Petersburg, 7 June 2009.
[39] Skobov interview; interview with Andrei Reznikov, conducted by JF, St Petersburg, 5 June 2009; interview with Arkadii Tsurkov, conducted by JF, St Petersburg, 3 August 2011.
[40] Skobov interview.

Is there an alternative to the capitalist system?...I want to believe there is. How real-
istic that is and when it will come into existence—I cannot say now, but in my youth
I believed very strongly that something better could happen tomorrow, the day after
tomorrow...And I believe until today that if you are not allowed to speak, you are
allowed to shoot.[41]

In July 1978 the logbook again chronicles disputes, with Skobov calling the upstairs the 'higher people'. The upstairs in turn responded with a 'letter to the reader'
and a spoof radio transmission from the 'free upstairs' (in itself a joke on the CIA-
funded Radio Free Europe). While a playful parody, this pun went straight to the
heart of the matter. Marina, Feliks and the upstairs believed that a free life in the
commune could only be achieved if people followed 'the rules of the game', while
Skobov and Mal'skii downstairs likened these rules to the suppression of freedom
in Soviet society. Skobov rebuked his colleagues in the logbook:

You pride yourself in your independence from official ideology. But in reality you live
imprisoned by the tenets of this ideology, in particular the Soviet idea of collectivism.
Real collectivism, based on the need of the individual to live in association with other
individuals, is only possible when the collective respects the right of every one of its
members, only then living together is not a burden.

For Skobov freedom meant to follow his political instincts and that meant producing his underground journal *Perspektivy*. The upstairs watched with horror, fully
aware that the journal pushed them over the edge of nonconformism into Soviet
illegality. Yet Skobov proved unstoppable. The upstairs retreated into itself. Antonenko, possibly the most sympathetic upstairs member towards the political
activities of the ground floor, later mused that the divisions within the commune
had indeed reflected the character of the people who founded it: 'the demands of
communal life were particularly strong on people who were not very communal by
mentality. That is to say on individualists'. The very individualistic act of living
differently in a society that valued conformism attracted people reluctant to submit
to communal rules, yet the commune offered their best chance to escape into
difference.

The Villa Road squatters were spared the more severe ideological dilemmas facing
the Yellow Submarine residents. If conservatism existed in Villa Road it remained
silent: 'politics' meant the politics of the left. With the squatters at war with a Labour-
controlled council in Lambeth, backed by what some of them considered 'the most
reactionary Labour government ever',[42] the 'politics of the left' meant the politics of
the far left, beyond the Labour Party. Several of the Villa Road squatters professed
revolutionary aims and Day remembers the radical academic-turned-journalist
Nick Anning as 'fairly full-on IMG and a little bit of an authority, I think, over
some of the Lefties'. The International Marxist Group (IMG) was the most sympathetic of all the formal far-left groups towards squatting. Piers Corbyn of the
Elgin Avenue squatters claims to have persuaded them to shed the assumption that

[41] Skobov interview.
[42] Untitled and anonymous article, *Villain* 24, 20 June 1977.

squatting was merely an expression of hippie escapism by convincing them that the squatters were making a 'transitional demand', i.e. a demand that was reasonable to make but that capitalism could not afford to grant: 'So if capitalism granted decent housing, or housing for all, it would collapse. So we'd have a revolution, you see. So...which was good, because they want revolution, you see'.[43]

Of our interviewees, Pete Cooper was initially the most clearly committed to the IMG view—that 'bourgeois property should be expropriated by the masses and a squatting-like occupation was a form of class struggle'.[44] Christian Wolmar says '[I] would have considered myself on the extreme left, you know, beyond the Labour Party', but he remained suspicious of the recognized sects: 'whenever I got near a Socialist Worker I hated them and I thought you know, I thought they were authoritarian, far too serious, incoherent in what they're actually trying to do'.[45] Patrick Day was the most eclectic, though still clearly on the radical left. He recalls:

the Communists [at Glasgow University] used to call me a confused liberal, but I think that went with the sort of...I was just curious...I didn't do the party line but I'd sort of hang around the odd...keep up to date with...and when the demos were on I was sort of around.[46]

What they all shared—and shared with most of the political activists in the street—was a commitment to community action, hardened by the practical experience of conflict with the council. This engendered an impatience with those forms of radical sectarianism that appeared impotent in practice. Cooper remembers:

a group of libertarian socialists who lived across the road...They were very much...seemed to be involved with...they were...had political discussions but they never seemed to do anything...[47]

The politics of the squat became sharply focussed on the housing question and broader domestic issues:

Individually and as a group squatters from Villa Road have been involved in large numbers on the Grunwick picket lines, on the anti-National Front demonstrations, like Lewisham, at the Firemens' [sic] strike benefits, on the CACTL[48] demonstrations, with the All Lambeth Squatters (old and new), with the Squatters Action Council and the All London Squatters, and with local squatting struggles at St Agnes Place and Heath Road. The connections have been made with other non-housing struggles.[49]

The large internationalist campaigns that had characterized late-1960s radicalism rather faded from view: 'of course I was against the Vietnam war', Wolmar recalls, 'but it was more kind of more a bit of fun rather than any great commitment to the cause, to be honest'.[50]

[43] Interview with Piers Corbyn, conducted by JD, London, 15 June 2010. See also, p. 124.
[44] Cooper interview.   [45] Wolmar interview.   [46] Day interview.   [47] Cooper interview.
[48] Campaign Against the Criminal Trespass Law, i.e. the attempt to make the squatting of empty properties a criminal offence.
[49] Anon., 'The politics of squatting in Villa Road', *Villain* 27, August 1977.
[50] Wolmar interview

Some worried that community action was ideologically shapeless. 'In the next *Villain*', an anonymous contributor wrote in the autumn of 1977, 'someone might care to unravel Villa Road's class-unconscious, woolly concept of "community"'.[51] In the event no further issues of *The Villain* appeared, and the concept remained unelucidated. Whatever the ambiguities, though, tensions in Villa Road arose less from political difference than from the more fundamental conflict between those who sought to change society and those who sought to escape society and find themselves.

Others denied the dilemma. In a 'political' squat such as Villa Road, it was claimed, the very act of belonging to a community that saw itself as a standing protest against housing shortage and stood in a state of near-permanent conflict with the local authority was political in itself:

> No matter what our individual attitude to politics is, our existence as a squatting community puts all our activities in a political context. Even total rejection of street meetings or political involvement or the community is a political action.[52]

Those who considered squatting a political act were reluctant to see it as primarily individualistic. The tension was demonstrated starkly in Villa Road as a result of the emergence of first one then two houses devoted to the therapeutic practice of primal screaming. Number 12 Villa Road was occupied by a group of screamers, led by Jenny James, author of the book *Room to Breathe*. James, after a decade devoted to conventional left-wing politics, had been induced by a friend's suicide to consider the impact of personal repression. Convinced that 'it's not all out there—it's also inside', she had become a devotee first of Wilhelm Reich, then of the Californian advocate of primal screaming, Arthur Janov.[53] One of the group explains:

> Like most squatters, the occupiers of no 12 had 'taken the problem of housing into their own hands'. But they're also using the freedom this has given them to explore the problems of personal relationships, thereby taking their *whole* lives out of the hands of 'experts' like doctors, psychiatrists, civil servants, ministers of religion and social workers...To allow yourself more emotional freedom [they felt] you need help. You need friends, you need places where you can laugh or cry or scream or hit cushions etc. to *express* your feelings rather than repress them...[54]

A 'therapy room' was established in the house. Cooper, initially sceptical of the screamers, became one of its habitués:

> they called it a therapy room, which was just covered with mattresses on the floor and the walls, actually and there were drapes and lots of cushions, so there was a lot of beating things and emoting loudly and shouting. Basically the idea was that that would put you in touch with your feelings, your true feelings and oddly you did sometimes find you were really furious about something that had seemed quite irritating,

[51] *Villain* 27, August 1977.
[52] Anon, 'Villa Road—a class analysis', *Villain* 16, 8 August 1976.
[53] Interview with Jenny James in Engle's film *Property is Theft*.
[54] *Villain* 2, 'Special Colour Supplement', 17 January 1976.

but when you actually started putting it energetically, that's ... you were really furious about it and that often would lead, would trigger childhood memories. So there was a sort of quasi-Freudian dimension to it that you would say 'Actually ...', you'd realize 'Actually it's not you I'm frustrated with, it's my mother at the age ... when I was one and a half because she wouldn't feed me when I wanted to be fed ...' or something.[55]

The screamers' analysis of repression extends to a critique of the far-left politics that Cooper had previously practised:

We felt I think that ... well ... that the way that leftists behaved and the way they were as people was often very stiff, very kind of repressed, very ... they disavowed their own personal feelings and I certainly, during my most Trotskyist phase, felt as if I was becoming a bit of a robot.

Wolmar, who repelled an attractive female honey-trap from no. 12, suggests that 'Villa Road was divided into two factions ... us and the politicos on one side and the primal screamers on the other'.[56] This reflected a distinction between the advocates of personal reclamation and those whose politics made them resist diversions from the attack on capitalism. In July 1977, after the demolition of no. 12 and the departure of its inhabitants, *The Villain* carried a forceful anonymous critique of primal therapy, arguing that 'you haven't changed a whole system just by changing your head':

However much the primal commune tries to become a closed circle, however much it pleads it only wants to be left alone, it exists just the same in a real and definite world. It acts and is acted upon. Capitalism in crisis creates victims, it creates the material and psychological conditions where people get so abused they feel the need to turn to something like primal therapy ... In many ways they're direct descendants of the 1960s ideology that if it feels right, then it must be right, so go ahead and do it and you'll end up in the right place because that's just the way it's gonna have to be. The 1970s have shown that it's just as easy to end up in some very wrong places. Self-proclaimed libertarian movements of this kind are easy pickings for capitalist society.[57]

Dropping out, it was argued, could not be cost-free.

DECLINE, END AND LEGACIES

Four Villa Road residents acknowledged in the final issue of *Villain* that 'living behind barricades for so long had a very detrimental effect on people's spirit'.[58] The street's hippies 'all seemed to bugger off as soon as the barricades went up and "it was all too heavy man"', Cooper recalls, but the experience of living under siege deterred even those who were not out-and-out hedonists but declined 'to go

[55] Cooper interview.
[56] Wolmar interview.
[57] 'Whose Revolution?', *Villain* 25, 14 July 1977.
[58] Liz (no. 25), Gilly (no. 25), Tony (no. 13) and Kevin (no. 7), 'The state of Villa Road', *Villain* 27, August 1977.

through a Custer's Last Stand routine with the bailiffs and the police'.[59] 'I suppose towards the end', Wolmar remembers, 'I realized that I couldn't really live the rest of my life like this'.[60] An awareness that the squat was becoming harder to live in undermined the appetite of most squatters for conflict and made possible the deal eventually done with Lambeth Council in 1978, by which the north side of the street was left unmolested in return for the evacuation and demolition of the south side.

Yellow Submarine ended more suddenly. Ominous signs were already visible in August 1978 when commune members noticed men observing the house. Men in grey asked to check residents' passports and registration documents. Yet it was only in October that the KGB pounced, arresting Skobov on the 16th and Tsurkov on the 31st. By then the first floor had left—tipped off by Feliks Vinogradov's father.[61] That the commune had already become the stuff of legend is shown by the rumours that started circulating in Leningrad's underground. Irina Lopotukhina heard that uniformed men had broken in at night, shone their torches in the faces of the sleepers and abducted Feliks and Marina before the KGB dissolved the commune. The writer Vadim Nechaev reported that in August the KGB had brought the commune under control when a man turned up declaring that he was now in charge (probably referring to the passport incident). After Nechaev's emigration to Paris in October 1978 the story reached the information department of Radio Liberty and thus the West.[62]

What explained this sudden end? Was it, as the first-floor residents maintain, Skobov's politics that destroyed the commune? Were they betrayed? Lopotukhina attributes their discovery to the indiscretions of the commune's transient hippie visitors.[63] Or was Skobov himself damagingly indiscreet, as Antonenko suspects:

> You know, we have always related sceptically towards Skobov as a revolutionary. Already because of his personal traits. You could not do revolution in the USSR as you did in 1968 in France. This was only possible in the underground. Skobov thought he was an excellent conspirator, but in essence his skills were proselytizing and agitating. He would tell everybody in a beer bar about his plans. This would not be so bad, except in every beer bar at least one person was an informer.[64]

Or was the end caused by internal rifts and the realization that communal life was not sustainable? While some like Marina were more optimistic about communal life, others such as Antonenko were more philosophical. The logbook, the get-together, the whole idea of 'life on a yellow submarine' had been one big parody of the system, yet the system did not appreciate jokes. Antonenko concludes that 'It was in the end clear that this story was to end like this. The games were over and now one had to pay for these games'.[65]

---

[59] Anon, 'Why I want rehousing', *Villain* 18, October 1976.
[60] Wolmar interview.
[61] Skobov interview and Feliks and Marina Vinogradov interview.
[62] Open Society Archives, Budapest, Hu OSA 300-80-1-45.
[63] Lopotukhina interview.
[64] Antonenko interview.   [65] Antonenko interview.

Skobov and Tsurkov suffered especially. Tsurkov received eight years in prison; Skobov was detained in a psychiatric hospital until 1981. Yet the others never quite re-entered normal society. All went through numerous interrogations. Feliks and Marina were roughed up on the second anniversary of the 4 July unrests—mainly because they were still wearing their beloved denim. Reznikov was repeatedly arrested, threatened and framed—supposedly by Vladimir Putin himself—in a fake incident involving an attack on an elderly lady.[66] Andrei Antonenko and Tatiana Komarova split up. Antonenko was reduced to working in the Leningrad Public Library—a job he got via his mother. Lopothukhina found her own voice after the arrest of her boyfriend Tsurkov. She married him in prison and became a leading human rights activist in Leningrad. Some years later she was arrested for disseminating political anecdotes. Skobov also remained political, joining an illegal trade union after his release from hospital. After being rearrested and sent to the camps, upon his release he became a critic of Yeltsin and Putin. Shortly after being interviewed for this book, he was photographed being arrested at a demonstration in St Petersburg.

LINKS AND MEANINGS

'1968', interpreted as the variegated radical movements of the late 1960s, prompted a wide variety of ideologies, lifestyles and cultural activities. And, as this chapter has argued, it would be wrong to assume that the Iron Curtain blocked the transmission of countercultural influences from West to East. Hippie communities existed from Danzig to Valdivostok, the New Left emerged as a new political (underground) force in the eastern bloc and rock music made the Iron Curtain vibrate. The Yellow Submarine was motivated by the same desire for freedom and individual space as Villa Road. Communal life, so despised in its communist form, experienced a renaissance among a new generation, who took it as a form of resisting and not conforming to the state. Both spaces provided a new form of self-expression for young people and a new way of thinking about state and individual—and as such informed their participants' thoughts and actions long after their communal and squatting days.

The nonconformist communities that we have studied in London and Leningrad were both influenced by the central messages of 1968—reaction against political authority and experimentation in alternative modes of living. Each faced the problem of reconciling the two. In each case the business of challenging bourgeois convention, whether through sex and drugs or through primal screaming, threatened to become so hedonistic or solipsistic as to impede the political project of changing society. Tension grew and divisions formed between upstairs and downstairs in Yellow Submarine, between politicos and primal screamers in Villa Road. In neither case were these tensions and divisions exclusively responsible for the failure of the experiment in collective living, but in both places they helped to sour the experience,

[66] Reznikov interview.

making still more difficult the business of living in permanent conflict with the public authorities.

Unsurprisingly, the penalties for nonconformism were greater in the Soviet Union than in the UK. Where the Yellow Submarine residents faced arrest, imprisonment, spurious psychiatric treatment or simple state brutality, Wolmar pursued his journalistic career and Day his medical career after Villa Road, while Cooper has made a living from his music, teaching and writing about the fiddle. At the same time, our English interviewees were less certain of the lasting significance of their social experiment than were our Russian subjects. 'It was an exciting time you know…', Wolmar recalls, 'there was a ferment of ideas and discussion but, as I say, within a slightly idealistic context that never, never quite worked itself out'.[67] The squatter experiment of the 1970s would appear dated even a decade later. As Cooper acknowledges:

> we weren't living a life that we proposed as a model for society as a whole. But I suppose…it was a bit of an open question what society would be like in the future. No one knew, we were just on this tide that suddenly came to a bit of a halt in 1979 when Margaret Thatcher was elected.[68]

By contrast, ten years after Yellow Submarine was closed down, Leningrad was in the euphoric grip of Perestroika. Experimental culture and new forms of social living flourished. It is no coincidence that the most famous Leningrad squat of this time, Pushkinskaia 10, was not only a hub for young artists, but also the place where the Yellow Submarine was officially commemorated for the first time. An exhibition in 1997 showed Feliks's posters and honoured the pioneers of communal life in Leningrad. The nonconformists of the post-Soviet years made a definite link between the new times and the nonconformist experiment of the late 1970s. The former members of the 'Submarine' also felt that their commune played a role in shaping Soviet history. As Skobov, always the most idealistic, puts it:

> We were keeping some form of fire alive. A fire that could have under different circumstances—not by our will and with our strength—developed into a huge bonfire. I have even then…considered my activity as keeping this fire until better times. The fire has to be kept alive. You need to throw in some sort of wood.

---

[67] Wolmar interview.   [68] Cooper interview.

8

Faith

Péter Apor, Rebecca Clifford and Nigel Townson

It is often assumed that the movements surrounding 1968 were innately secular in nature. Indeed, the 1960s are often remembered as a time of rapidly increasing secularization, as adherents began to turn away from religious institutions that seemed out of step with the modern world.[1] The slide into secularization, however, was not the only challenge facing these institutions in and around 1968: official religious bodies were also touched by the waves of protest that marked the period, as radical believers questioned the authority of church hierarchies. Radical Catholic activism, in particular, was at the fore of protest in Mediterranean Europe, and was evident behind the Iron Curtain as well. This chapter analyses the nature and extent of religious radicalism around 1968 by focussing primarily on Catholic activism in France, Italy and Spain in the West, and Hungary in the East. In the Mediterranean countries, militant Catholicism furnished a salutary apprenticeship for activists in a wide variety of movements, ranging from student politics and extreme left-wing parties to neighbourhood associations and trade unions. It also represented a formidable wellspring of protest in its own right, as radical Catholics sought to transform not only their church but also their societies from within. Such overt radicalism was not possible in the eastern bloc countries, where religious leaders were under state surveillance and were careful to avoid political activities and positions. Dissident religious groups did gain strength in this period, however, and they constituted a significant part of the '1968' experienced behind the Iron Curtain. We also examine—though to a lesser extent—Protestant activism in both East and West. Many sectors of Protestantism, like Catholicism, were radicalized during the 1960s; like their Catholic counterparts, radical Protestants did not limit their activism to the church but strove to change the society around them. Rejecting the path of secularism, religious activists found powerful ways to tie protest to belief.

This chapter focusses on activists who engaged in religious protest—women and men who worked within faith-based communities and organizations to change the world around them, to change themselves, and to try to change their churches as institutions. It does not explore the stories of those who defined themselves as believers but who were involved in secular protest movements. We focus here predominantly on Catholic activists, not because other religious institutions went

---

[1] For a comparative overview of the 'crisis' in both the Catholic and Protestant churches in the 1960s, see in particular Hugh McLeod, *The Religious Crisis of the 1960s* (Oxford, 2007), ch. 1.

unchallenged in this period, but because left-wing Catholic radicalism was such a significant aspect of 1960s protest in Europe, and one that has been almost completely overlooked by historians.[2] For the same reasons, we have deliberately concentrated on activist networks that questioned aspects of faith or church hierarchies (in western Europe) or that worked against state-enforced atheism (in the socialist bloc)—militant reactions *against* dissident left-wing religious protest were also part of the activism of this period, but this is not our focus here.[3] Nor do we tackle Jewish or Muslim left-wing militancy during this period; although a number of former activists interviewed for this project defined themselves as having a Jewish or Muslim religious identity, none saw their own activism in terms of challenging the hierarchies of religious organizations. For this reason their voices are not included here (although readers will find them elsewhere in this book), but we note that this is an area that calls out for further research.[4]

Our comparative analysis is based principally on interviews with activists themselves, and concentrates on the subjective, personal experience of religious activism. Interviewees were drawn from a wide range of networks: Catholic trade unions, dissident journals, base ecclesial communities, the youth and worker sections of Catholic Action, the worker-priest movement, and clandestine religious communities in eastern Europe. The Protestant activists interviewed were involved with youth groups, inter-church oppositional networks and the conscientious objection movement.

In understanding the relationship between these radical religious communities and 1968, one must see '1968' not as a single year, but as a longer period characterized by a willingness, on the part of radical groups, to question authorities and to work towards flattening or overcoming social hierarchies. Many of the groups and communities we focus on existed well before 1968, and some were already experiencing a slow process of increasing radicalization from the 1950s onwards.[5] However,

[2] The question is overlooked, for example, in Gerd-Rainer Horn, *The Spirit of '68: Rebellion in Western Europe and North America, 1956–1976* (Oxford, 2007) and Martin Klimke and Joachim Scharloth (eds) *1968 in Europe: A History of Protest and Activism, 1956–1977* (Basingstoke, 2008).

[3] An example of reactionary religious protest in this period is the Italian organization Comunione e Liberazione (CL), formed by university students in Milan in 1969 with the goal of wooing young people away from dissident left-wing Catholic groups. CL members particularly rejected the exploration of Marxist ideas that characterized left-wing Catholic protest in Italy and elsewhere. See Sandro Bianchi and Angelo Turchini, *Gli estremisti di centro. Il neo-integralismo cattolico degli anni '70: Comunione e Liberazione* (Florence, 1975); and Dario Zadra, 'Comunione e Liberazione: A Fundamentalist Idea of Power', in Martin Marty and R. Scott Appleby (eds), *Accounting for Fundamentalisms: The Dynamic Character of Movements* (Chicago, 1994), 124–47.

[4] We are not aware of any historical research that looks specifically at dissident Jewish or Muslim religious radicalism in this period in the countries studied here. On the US, see Terry Anderson, *The Movement and the Sixties: Protest in America from Greensboro to Wounded Knee* (Oxford, 1995), 268 and 382–3.

[5] On the development of progressive Catholic circles in France and Italy in the 1950s, see Gerd-Rainer Horn, *Western European Liberation Theology: The First Wave, 1924–1959* (Oxford, 2008). For Spain, see Feliciano Blázquez, *La traición de los clérigos en la España de Franco. Crónica de una intolerancia (1936–1975)* (Madrid, 1991); William, J. Callahan, *The Catholic Church in Spain, 1875–1998* (Washington, DC, 2000); Guy Hermet, *Los católicos en la España franquista. I. Los actores del juego político* (Madrid, 1985) and *Los católicos en la España franquista. II. Crónica de una dictadura* (Madrid, 1986); and Frances Lannon, *Privilege, Persecution, and Prophecy: The Catholic Church in Spain 1875–1975* (Oxford, 1987), 224–5 and 246–53.

the wave of protest that marked the late 1960s in Europe accelerated this process, as religious radicals saw in the student and worker movements a struggle to transform society that ran parallel to their own efforts. For some, 1968 was indeed a watershed year, marking a moment when religious activists protested alongside secular ones, and, in some cases, split away from the official church.

How and why did individuals turn to Christian activism? To what degree was this commitment shaped by developments within the churches, and to what extent by changes within society at large? What did it mean to be a radical Christian activist in a democratic country, in a right-wing dictatorship, or in a country of the eastern bloc? This chapter seeks to explore these central questions, focussing on the ways in which radical Christians entered activism, on the nature and scope of their activist commitments, and on the place of their stories within a broader history of 1968 in Europe. In terms of participatory structures, language, ideology, involvement with the marginalized and the working class, and the influence of international events such as the Vietnam War and the Chinese Cultural Revolution, faith-based activist networks shared much in common with their secular counterparts, reminding us that religious radicalism was very much a part of Europe's 1968.

FORGING RELIGIOUS REBELS

Why were individuals drawn into religious radicalism? In the narratives of former activists from the Mediterranean countries, the memory of social and economic divides and injustices figures prominently. The majority recall that they were propelled into activism by a sense of outrage over the growing and highly visible gap between rich and poor that was one of the fruits of the economic miracle of the 1950s and 1960s. In Spain, France and Italy, the economic boom of the *trente glorieuses* had led to dramatic internal migration, bringing people from impoverished rural areas to crowd into the under-serviced and isolated working-class neighbourhoods that ringed the large industrial cities.[6] For activists from middle-class backgrounds, the shock of the first encounter with the terrible living conditions in these shanty towns could be a powerful incentive to seek out more equitable ways of living, and radical Catholics placed equality for rich and poor at the fore of their activities. It is true that these encounters between middle and working class often inspired activists in secular movements as well (see Chapter 1, 'Awakenings'), but these were particularly significant for those involved in faith-based activism, marking a shift away from traditional religious notions of charity towards an idea of social justice. Francisca Sauquillo (b. 1943) played a prominent role in student politics in Madrid during the early 1960s, and worked on behalf of the clandestine

---

[6] On the economic miracle and internal migration in Italy, see Paul Ginsborg, *A History of Contemporary Italy: Society and Politics, 1943–1988* (London, 2003), ch. 7. On the *trente glorieuses* in France, see Jean and Jacqueline Fourastié, *D'une France à une autre. Avant et après les Trente Glorieuses* (Paris, 1987). On the economic boom in Spain, see Pablo Martín Aceña and Elena Martínez Ruiz, 'The golden age of Spanish capitalism: Economic growth without political freedom', in Nigel Townson (ed.) *Spain Transformed: The Late Franco Dictatorship, 1959–75* (Basingstoke, 2010), 30–46.

Christian trade union, the Alternativa Sindical de Trabajadores (AST, Alternative Union of Workers). She recalls that she underwent 'a change' in 1966, the year she became a practising lawyer, because of her work in the shanty towns of Madrid with internal migrants. Many of these people came to the capital in search of work, but some were trying to flee from the Francoist authorities on account of their trade union or political activities:

> I went to the outlying districts of Madrid. And...there were 30,000 shacks, basically of the people that had come from Extremadura and Andalucía, that is to say entire villages that had come during the 1950s, had got off the train, and had begun to build the shacks...I opened a practice there, and began to get to know a very different reality, a reality not only to do with the persecution of the trade unions, but also with how people lived. People who had had to become internal refugees, shall we say, that is to say, emigrants, having abandoned the village of Martos in Jaén, having abandoned many places in order to come to Madrid because they were persecuted.[7]

Jean Lecuir (b. 1939), the son of an engineer who was brought up in Neuilly, a well-to-do suburb of Paris, was active in the JEC, the Catholic students' organization that entered into open conflict with Church hierarchies during May 1968.[8] Lecuir clashed with religious authorities over the Church's official stance on the Algerian War. He became sensitized to a completely new world, that of the working class and the labour movement, through his involvement in the Catholic journal *La Lettre*:

> Coming from Neuilly and from a fairly privileged school and university background, for me *La Lettre* was a place where I found people who were engaged with the working-class world. I found out about the worker-priests. I knew they existed, but it was not the same thing as going to a mass in a flat in the Paris suburbs, as I did.[9]

Those from working-class backgrounds were often drawn into activism by their own experience of injustice or isolation in impoverished suburbs. Carlo Consigli (b. 1941) moved with his family to a working-class suburb of Florence known as the Isolotto in 1954. As a teenager, he became involved with a radical youth group that formed around dissident priest don Enzo Mazzi in the community, and later played an instrumental role in helping to establish the Isolotto as Italy's first non-aligned Catholic *comunità di base*, or base ecclesial community.[10] Consigli recalls that the newness of the hastily built suburb made it a fertile environment for

---

[7] Interview with Francisca Sauquillo Pérez, conducted by NT, Madrid, 1 September 2009.

[8] Jean-Paul Ciret and Jean-Pierre Sueur, *Les Étudiants, la Politique et l'Église. Une Impasse?* (Paris, 1970); Denis Pelletier, *La Crise Catholique. Religion, Société, Politique en France, 1965–1978* (Paris, 2005), 33–77.

[9] Interview with Jean Lecuir, conducted by RG, Toulouse, 29 April 2008.

[10] On the development of the base ecclesial community movement in Italy, see Mario Cuminetti, *Il dissenso cattolico in Italia, 1965–1980* (Milan, 1983); Roberto Beretta, *Il lungo autunno. Controstoria del Sessantotto cattolico* (Milan, 1998); and Silvano Burgalassi, 'Dissenso cattolico e comunità di base', in F. Traniello and G. Campanini (eds) *Dizionario storico del movimento cattolico in Italia, 1860–1980, I.2* (Turin, 1981), 278–84.

radical approaches to religion, as there were no established customs to protect, and not even a common language between the migrants who had poured into the area from southern Italy and the Istrian Peninsula:

> [When we moved to the Isolotto] there were no streets, there was nowhere to meet, there was nowhere to discuss things... There was nothing. It was a *terra di missione*. There were people who were extremely poor, people who came from the south... just think: everyone spoke a different dialect, people spoke Sicilian, and it took an extraordinary effort to find commonalities. This was a significant stimulus [towards the creation of an open religious community], this need to find a common language and culture.[11]

Spanish priest Pedro Requeno (b. 1944) was born into a working-class family near Madrid. His parents were proud of his entry into the priesthood because: 'The priest was seen, well, as a way of escaping the poverty in which they had lived. The priest was a figure, not just their son, because they were going to be 'the parents of Don...'.[12]

Upon leaving the seminary in 1967, Requeno regarded himself as a Francoist, having voted for the dictator in the referendum of 1966.[13] He soon changed. He was sent to work as a parish priest in the working-class town of Getafe on the outskirts of Madrid, then undergoing rapid industrial and urban expansion. It was above all the daily reality of life in Getafe that made him become an activist. As he recalls, he was moved by:

> The actual reality that I saw there, how the people lived. In such a way that this made me recover, then, my own history. My own history; that is to say, seeing these boys with whom I was working, their families, the exploitation that they suffered, the general situation, no? This made me say, 'well, but I belong to this world, to this world, which is the working-class world'... The seminary, above all, had helped to de-class [me], not to be conscious of this class.

The concept of community was also vital in attracting people to activism. Some were drawn to the base ecclesial communities that were partly inspired by the movement that had spread throughout Latin America in the 1950s and 1960s, while others simply sought a more communal way of living, particularly within emerging urban and suburban environments where a sense of community had yet to form.[14] In both cases, activists hoped to create a fusion of their collective ideals and their spirituality. In France and Italy, members of base communities often attempted to bridge the divide between Catholics and non-Catholics, or between the working and middle classes, in an endeavour to create more egalitarian and less hierarchical social environments. These experiments often included reaching out to working-class communists, who had invariably given up on the Church

---

[11] Interview with Carlo Consigli, conducted by RC, Florence, 9 May 2008.
[12] Interview with Pedro Requeno Regaño, conducted by NT, Madrid, 25 July and 28 August 2009.
[13] On the referendum of 1966 on the new Organic Law of the State, see Stanley Payne, *The Franco Regime 1936–1975* (London, 2000), 513–15.
[14] On the development of the base ecclesial community movement in Latin America, see Anthony Gill, *Rendering unto Caesar: The Catholic State in Latin America* (Chicago, 1998), 37–8.

altogether. Sergio Gomiti, assistant priest in the Isolotto community, recalls that one of his goals was 'to break down the barriers that divide non-believers from believers, non-practisers from practisers... and communists from Christian Democrats'.[15] Carlo Consigli elaborates on this point:

> In '59, when the Officine Galileo [a local factory] went on strike and the workers had nowhere to meet, we had them meet in the church. This shows that the church wasn't simply a place for the liturgy, but the space itself was important, as it gave people the chance to be together, to work together... Consider that at that time... the Church excommunicated communists, so how could one dare to speak to a communist? They were excommunicated, they weren't supposed to enter a church, it was terrible. But we spoke to them, this dialogue was important to us, we rejected those party divisions.[16]

Another salient motive for becoming an activist was a conviction that the traditional channels of the church were insufficiently responsive to the needs of both the rank-and-file clergy and the laity. Many activists felt suffocated by the hierarchical structures that dominated their churches, and aspired not only to a more accountable church, but also to a more open environment in which the clergy and laity could freely debate ecclesiastical interpretations. For some activists, the appeal of these radical groups was precisely that they provided the opportunity to explore, discuss and challenge religious teachings in an uninhibited fashion. Luciana Angeloni (b. 1939) joined the youth discussion group in the Isolotto when she moved to Florence in 1959. She remembers the thrill of reading the Bible herself, rather than having it interpreted for her through a priest:

> [This] was really important to me: this group of young people who studied the Bible together. In the church in the village where I came from, you couldn't read the Bible yourself, it was prohibited because... the Bible was considered a dangerous book: it could lead to Protestantism. And in the culture of my village then, Protestantism was seen as an absolute taboo... But this group of young people took this book in hand and they weren't afraid of Protestantism, they took this book in hand to revisit it, to understand what it was. And at the beginning this really surprised me, but [through it] I experienced a sort of mental awakening that I welcomed.[17]

The situation was somewhat different in eastern Europe, and particularly in Hungary, where clerical authorities were under strict state control and could not take overtly political positions. Like their western counterparts, religious activists in the East also sought a more just, equal and moral society, but they tended to articulate these objectives in spiritual terms, rather than political ones. From the 1950s onwards, the state framed the persecution of clerics and religious activists in political terms, accusing them of counter-revolutionary propaganda, conspiracy against the state, or serving western imperialist interests. Religious organizations and associations

---

[15] Interview with Sergio Gomiti, conducted by RC, Florence, 21 April 2008. On the tensions between Catholics and communists at the local level in Italy in this period, see David I. Kertzer, *Comrades and Christians: Religion and Political Struggle in Communist Italy* (Cambridge, 1980), 2–7 and 98–107.

[16] Consigli interview. On the interaction between the Isolotto community and the Officine Galileo, see Comunità dell'Isolotto, *Isolotto. 1954–1969* (Bari, 1969), 113–19.

[17] Interview with Luciana Angeloni, conducted by RC, Florence, 5 May 2008.

were dissolved and banned on the basis of their alleged 'anti-democratic' (meaning anti-communist) activities. As a consequence, most of those involved in religious activism avoided political issues and terminology, and steered clear of participation in dissident groups.[18]

Religious radicals in the East thus had to seek subtler means of expressing opposition. One delicate method of criticizing communist society was to stress continuities with pre-communist religious organizations, such as the Hungarian Regnum Marianum community, originally founded in 1896, to promote youth education and an everyday spirituality, officially registered with the Vatican in 1902, and banned by the state in 1951.[19] Risking persecution, priests from the community decided to continue their activities after 1951, which involved organizing youth groups and summer camps, disseminating religious literature and experimenting with new forms of religious practice: embracing 'religious beat' music, holding masses in the forest and incorporating elements of new spiritual visions from abroad (such as the Italian Focolare and the French Taizé movements). Many activists were arrested and jailed in trials in 1961, 1965 and 1971. Partly as a consequence, the younger generation of lay community members began to assume a more active role as youth trainers, organizers and leaders. The Regnum Marianum had an ambivalent relationship with the Catholic authorities: on the one hand, it was keen to emphasize its faithfulness to mainstream Catholicism; on the other hand, its leaders tended to criticize the clerical establishment in Hungary for their ineffective measures in building bridges between the devout and society as a whole. The Hungarian Church hierarchy, while appreciating Regnum Marianum's commitment and effort, saw its radicalism as a constant danger to the pact between the state and the Church, which officials were inclined to believe was the guarantee for the survival of the Hungarian Catholic Church itself.[20]

Those involved in Regnum Marianum recall that, like their western counterparts, they were drawn into activism out of discontent over conventional Church practices. Here, however, they expressed their discontent in terms of religious, rather than social, criticism. László Diószegi (b. 1947), a priest and youth activist in the Regnum Marianum, describes his journey into activism in terms of a drive to preserve spiritual Christian values. Diószegi, born into a religious middle-class family, became one of the leading members of a group of young priests who, in the early 1970s in Hungary, began to experiment with new methods of reaching out to lay

---

[18] On Poland, see Andrzej Paczkowski, *Pól wieku dziejów Polski 1939–1989* (Warsaw, 1995). On Romania, see Anca Maria Şincan, 'Mechanisms of state control over religious denominations in Romania in the late 1940s and early 1950s', in Balazs Apor, Péter Apor and E.A. Rees (eds) *The Sovietization of Eastern Europe, New Perspectives on the Postwar Period* (Washington, DC, 2008), 201–12. On Yugoslavia, see Mateja Režek, 'Cuius regio eius religio: The relationship of communist authorities with the Catholic Church in Slovenia and Yugoslavia after 1945', in ibid., 213–33. On Hungary, see Csaba Szabó, 'Die totale Kontrolle der römisch-katholischen Kirche Ungarns in der Phase des real existierenden Sozialismus (1945–1989)', in Katharina Kunter and Jens Holger Schjorring (eds) *Die Kirchen und das Erbe des Kommunismus* (Erlangen, 2007), 317–33.

[19] János Dobszay, *Így—vagy sehogy! Fejezetek a Regnum Marianum életéből* (Budapest, 1991), 10–16, 76–85.

[20] On the broader context of the relationship between the Catholic Church and the communist state in Hungary, see Csaba Szabó, *Die katholische Kirche Ungarns und der Staat in den Jahren 1945–1965* (Munich, 2003), and Ferenc Tomka, *Halálra szántak, mégis élünk* (Budapest, 2005).

people, using religious beat music, discussion groups and youth festivals. Diószegi stresses that spiritual commitment itself could be a form of protest under a communist state:

> Since our fathers were involved in all these show trials, accused of conspiracy against the state, we avoided discussions that dealt explicitly with society, social issues and justice. We did not worry about whether what we were doing shaped society or affected the regime, but we did say that if the state was founded on atheism and we weren't atheists, then the state could not regard us as its supporters... So it was an incredibly good thing that the natural inclination of youth to revolt and to oppose could be channelled in a positive direction, since we opposed the regime, opposed atheism, opposed communism, opposed everything that was mandatory in that world. I didn't become a [Young Communist] pioneer. It was mandatory, but despite that I didn't become one. I fulfilled my oppositional desires, not by living against something, not by denying something, but in a positive struggle for values.[21]

IDEAS AND INFLUENCES

The Second Vatican Council

A vital aspect of Catholic radicalization in this period was the Second Vatican Council of 1962–5, which was a major catalyst of change within world Catholicism. The reforms introduced by the Council had far-reaching, if not revolutionary, implications for the Church. They drastically reconfigured relations within Catholicism by overturning the clergy's monopoly on the liturgy, by championing 'the apostolate of the laity', by extending a hand to other religions and even to non-believers, and by accepting that the Church was constituted not just by the clergy but by all believers, 'the people of God'.[22] This had wide-ranging implications for relations between the ecclesiastical elite and the rank-and-file clergy, as well as for those between the representatives of the Church and the laity.

By introducing such concepts into Church doctrine, the Council not only gave radicals an enormous fillip, but also accelerated the process of radicalization. The outcome was an extraordinary tumult of activity as radicals everywhere laboured to put the Vatican's ground-breaking strictures into practice. New journals, study groups and communities sprouted up in France, Italy, Spain, Hungary and elsewhere as the Church's renewed temporal and spiritual mission was

---

[21] Interview with László Diószegi, conducted by PA, Budapest, 1 December 2008.

[22] On the importance and impact of the Second Vatican Council see the useful overview in McLeod, *Religious Crisis*, ch. 4. On France, see Emile Poulat, *Une Eglise ébranlée. Changement, conflit et continuité de Pie XII à Jean-Paul II* (Paris, 1980) and Denis Pelletier, *La Crise catholique. Religion, société et politique en France, 1965–1978* (Paris, 2005). On Spain, see Blázquez, *La traición* ch. 6 and 7; Callahan, *The Catholic Church*, 501 and 509–34; Hermet, *Los católicos en la España franquista. II.*, chs. 6 and 7; Frances Lannon, *Privilege, Persecution, and Prophecy*, 224–5 and 246–53. On Italy, see Guido Verucci, *La Chiesa nella società contemporanea* (Bari, 1988), ch. VII, and Cuminetti, *Il dissenso cattolico in Italia*, part II, chs. 1 and 2.

ardently embraced by progressive Catholics.[23] For individual activists, the Council could represent a turning point in their lives, as it either led them into activism or else deepened their already existing radicalism. Francisca Sauquillo went to a conventional, upper-class Catholic school in Madrid before going to university to read law in 1961, a year that was to change her life forever:

The change, for me, came about in the year in which I arrived at the university, where I plunged into the Christian communities...I'm talking about 1961, right when the Second Vatican Council begins, which affected me deeply [the Council actually began in 1962]. The two encyclicals: the encyclical *Mater et Magistra*, because it opened a new horizon for me in terms of the subject of labour relations, and the encyclical *Pacem in Terris*, because it also changed my mentality...During the university years I believed a lot in the Church that was emerging from the Second Vatican Council, which was a Church, from my point of view, that wanted to liberate the world from injustice.[24]

In East as well as West, the progressive spirit of the Council had a pronounced effect on activists. Győző Somogyi (b. 1942) was active as a worker-priest in Budapest between 1968 and 1975, when his 'avant-garde' approach to religious practice led him into conflict with both state and Church authorities. Banned from the priesthood, he turned his energies to the fledgling Hungarian ecology movement in the late 1970s, becoming a leading artist and environmental activist. At the time of the Council, he was a young seminarist and he recalls the vibrant atmosphere it generated:

I was a seminarist during the Vatican Council...first, everyone believed that celibacy would be abolished. So people said our generation would marry. Then, having Hungarian instead of Latin, this was such a great change since we had started studying in Latin, classes and exams were in Latin. Then the vernacular and the new liturgy appeared, and then these hippie-like new Christian ideas, so we all began our clerical careers in an animated and excited atmosphere.[25]

Excitement over the reforms introduced by the Council sometimes propelled activists into direct conflict with local Catholic authorities, who did not necessarily embrace its progressive spirit. Some radical groups managed to thrive in this atmosphere of confrontation; others were forced to moderate their stances, or to abandon the official Church altogether. Guy Goureaux (b. 1930) was a physics lecturer who moved to the new University of Nantes in 1962. Appalled by the grip of the Catholic Church on private education, and its alliance with big employers, he set up a Cercle Jean XXIII the following year, which in time gathered 800 members. He recalls that the conflict between the leaders of the discussion group and the local bishop spurred their radicalism onwards:

When John XXIII took office, it was fantastic for us. We were euphoric about the Council...We set up the Cercle Jean XXIII, which became one of the defining elements of Christianity in Nantes, but which the bishop refused to recognize...Several

[23] Feliciano Montero, *La Iglesia: De la colaboración a la disidencia (1956–1975)* (Madrid, 2009), ch. 2; Laura Serrano Blanco, *Aportaciones de la Iglesia a la democracia, desde la diócesis de Valladolid. 1959–1979* (Salamanca, 2006), ch. 3; Cuminetti, *Il dissenso cattolico in Italia*, part II, ch. 2.

[24] Sauquillo interview.

[25] Interview with Győző Somogyi, conducted by PA, Salföld, 7 November 2008.

times he asked me, 'Would you like a chaplain?'. And I said to him, 'I am not asking for a chaplain. We have forty theologians who come from all over France to join our discussions. We don't need a chaplain. We are grown-ups and can manage on our own. All the priests from Catholic Action in the diocese were upset because we circumvented them. We had more or less set up a popular theological university, if you like.[26]

Radicals were not always so successful, however, in their battles with conservatives at the local and national levels. Members of Florence's Isolotto community warmly embraced the changes proposed by the Council, sometimes taking these changes further than the architects of Vatican II had envisioned. Using up the idea that the Church was the 'people of God', lay members of the community, encouraged by parish priest Enzo Mazzi, held general assemblies, wrote their own catechism, and participated in the running of religious services. The community began to run into conflict with the conservative archbishop of Florence from the time of Vatican II onwards and the situation came to a head in 1968. When don Mazzi and his parishioners wrote a letter of solidarity to a group of Catholic students who had occupied the cathedral in Parma in the autumn of that year, the archbishop de-manded that Mazzi either retract the letter or resign. Community members refused to give up their priest, tensions between the community and the archbishop's office escalated, and in early 1969 Mazzi's supporters were locked out of the church build-ing. Forced out of the church both physically and institutionally, they took the collective decision to recreate themselves as Italy's first Christian base community, Catholic in terms of self-identity but not aligned with the Vatican.[27] Giancarlo Zani (b. 1935), a member of the Isolotto's youth discussion group and a founder of its after-school programme for impoverished children, recalls both the youth group's excitement over the utopian vision of the Second Vatican Council, and their sense of betrayal as conservative hierarchies within the Church clamped down on at-tempts to bring the Council's more progressive recommendations to fruition:

For us [the Council] was an enormous sign of hope, an enormous sign of hope because it was exactly what we had been wanting and hoping for: to be able to have a different Church, an innovative Church that would be capable of dealing with the problems of humans and society rather than the Church of the last 2000 years, the historical church disconnected from reality. And our hope grew bigger and bigger and as the Council's decrees began to come out, we read them and studied them and we were excited. And we dreamed of great things, and this was...the rupture, see? This hope was never realized.[28]

In Spain, the conservative backlash against Vatican II was even more pronounced. Between 1966 and 1969 the Spanish hierarchy strove to make the Church's reforms compatible with the 'National Catholicism' that had been the bedrock of the

---

[26] Interview with Guy Goureaux, conducted by RG, Paris, 9 June 2007. See also Guy Goureaux, *Le Cercle Jean XXIII. Des Catholiques en liberté. Nantes, 1963–1980* (Paris, 2004).

[27] On the history of the Isolotto community and their split from the official Church, see their col-lectively authored texts, *Isolotto. 1954–1969* (Bari, 1969), and *Isolotto sotto processo* (Bari, 1971). See also Sidney Tarrow, *Democracy and Disorder: Protest and Politics in Italy 1965–1975* (Oxford, 1989), 200–16.

[28] Interview with Giancarlo Zani, conducted by RC, Florence, 10 May 2008.

relationship between the Church and the Franco dictatorship since 1939.[29] Leonardo Aragón, who in 1964 joined the JEC Catholic student group and a few years later became the European and then world president of the organization, vividly recalls the hierarchy's battle against the apostolic associations and other groups. Those bishops in charge of Catholic Action:

> declared us, we could say, 'undesirables'. We no longer had any judicial status. The Church ceased to recognize us. But we carried on, eh. We would meet where we could. The situation, as a result, was a much more difficult situation, but this occurred in Madrid and at the national level. The JEC practically exploded, disappeared, because they wouldn't accept the type of approach that we had. So we kept going and even held a semi-clandestine national meeting or two. We held a meeting in Murcia, I remember, because we thought it was the safest place.[30]

Many radicals not only resigned from their posts but even left the Church altogether. Feliciano Montero, a JEC activist at the time, remembers that:

> many activists reach the conclusion that their option is a fundamentally political and trade unionist option, and that the least important thing is Catholic Christian identity or living it. If, furthermore, it's rejected within the very Church, well then 'goodbye and good riddance'.[31]

Dialogues with Marxism

In western Europe, being a radical Christian often meant engaging with the ideas of Marxism, in part because of the Marxist milieu that predominated in working-class, student and other circles, and in part because Marxism's critique of capitalist society echoed many of the concerns of progressive Christians. Most radicals found Marxism theoretically useful but spiritually impoverished. Some, such as the French Dominican Paul Blanquart, sought a synthesis of Christianity and Marxism that would provide the revolution with spiritual meaning:

> I was Marxist in an independent spirit. With regard to religion, I approached it with a critical stance needed to... to free up the experience of faith itself. So it was a well-developed cohabitation, and yet at the same time, I felt that theoretical Marxism was not enough to lead a movement of social liberation.[32]

---

[29] On the youth and worker sections of Catholic Action, see José Castaño Colomer, *La JOC en España (1946–1970)* (Salamanca, 1978); Javier Domínguez, *Organizaciones obreras cristianas en la oposición al franquismo* (Bilbao, 1975); Feliciano Montero, *Juventud Estudiante Católica 1947–1997* (Madrid, 1998); Feliciano Montero, *La Acción Católica y el franquismo: Auge y crisis de la Acción Católica Especializada en los años sesenta* (Madrid, 2000); and Montero, *La Iglesia*, 158–166. On the showdown with the Church hierarchy, see Blázquez, *La traición*, 165–6; Callahan, *The Catholic Church*, 519–23; Hermet, *Los católicos en la España franquista. II*, 344–7; Lannon, *Privilege, Persecution, and Prophecy*, 235–7; and Montero, *La Iglesia*, 168–70 and 229–39.
[30] Interview with Leonardo Aragón Marín, conducted by NT, Madrid, 14 April 2008.
[31] Interview with Feliciano Montero García, conducted by NT, Madrid, 15 December 2008.
[32] Interview with Paul Blanquart, conducted by RG, Paris, 15 May 2007. On the synthesis of Christianity and Marxism, see also Blanquart's memoirs, *En Bâtardise. Itinéraires d'un Chretien marxiste, 1967–1980* (Paris, 1981).

In the more liberal environment fostered by the Second Vatican Council, many radical Catholics were convinced that their doctrines chimed with the leading tenets of Marxism. Key thinkers, such as Italy's don Lorenzo Milani—whose book *Lettera ad una professoressa* (*Letter to a Schoolteacher*) was one of the iconic texts of the Italian 1968—popularized these ideas by drawing on the language of Marxism to explore and explain the marginalization of the poor in contemporary society.[33] This blend of Marxist and Catholic thinking often struck activists as naturally compatible. The Spanish worker-priest Mariano Gamo (b. 1931) adopted Marxist ideas 'without any kind of internal conflict',[34] and Francisca Sauquillo remembers that as a student she saw no contradiction between calling herself both a Marxist and a Catholic:

> The 'God the Saviour', the Catholic doctrine of those five years at university, predominated, we could say. As a result, I didn't think of the contradiction between Marxism and Catholicism, but believed that there could be a very real compatibility between being a Marxist of dialectical materialism and believing that there existed a prophetic figure such as that of Jesus...In short, this God helped the poor. It fitted, eh...Well, I didn't see the contradiction...Marxist methodology was a good ideology for analysing society, no? So I began to realize that those that were atheists, or came from the republican world or the communist world, were not my enemies, but that my enemies were rather the capitalists and, above all, those who were fascist.[35]

Leonardo Aragón takes a more pragmatic approach:

> Marxist theory, both from the point of view of the economy and of sociology, helped a lot in analysing reality...It wasn't a question of being Marxist or not, but a question of seeing what was useful to me. And insofar as it was useful to you in order to analyse reality, just as—I insist—it remains so today in many aspects, why were we not going to use it?[36]

Other activists defended an accommodation between Marxism and Catholicism while maintaining that there were still fundamental divergences. For Julio Lois (b. 1935), who knew and admired the leading liberation theologist Gustavo Gutiérrez and was a founder member of the liberation-inspired 'Christians for Socialism', there was a definite tension between the 'Christian' goals of socialism and the dialectical materialism of Marx:

> It seems to me that it was convenient and that it continues to be convenient to show that one can be Christian and at the same time assume the socialist vision of reality...But we never linked—never linked—the theological reflection with what we could call the 'materialistic analysis' or the 'materialist conception' of Marxism. Because it was obvious that this was not on. That is to say, one cannot be a dialectical materialist in the most explicit Marxist sense and, at the same time, a believer.[37]

---

[33] Robert Lumley, *States of Emergency: Cultures of Revolt in Italy from 1968 to 1978* (London, 1990), 82–3. Many of the Italian activists interviewed for this study trace the roots of their radicalism to Milani's ideas.

[34] Interview with Mariano Gamo Sánchez, conducted by NT, Madrid, 26 July 2009.

[35] Sauquillo interview.

[36] Aragón interview.

[37] Interview with Julio Lois Fernández, conducted by NT, Madrid, 22 June 2009. See also his books, *El Dios de los pobres* (Salamanca, 2007), *La cristología de Jon Sobrino* (Bilbao, 2007), and *Teología de la liberación: opción por los pobres* (Madrid, 1986). On the debate between Christianity and

In eastern Europe, the relationship with Marxism was necessarily different, as activists identified Marxism as the official language of the atheist state. This did not mean, however, that all activists on the other side of the Iron Curtain rejected Marxism out of hand; some recall that they saw ways in which the very language of Marxism could be turned into a tool to criticize official ideology. The memory, however, is an ambivalent one, complicated by the later efforts of individuals to distance themselves from all aspects of communist thinking. Győző Somogyi recalls that he flirted with Maoism, but that his explorations of Marxist thought were ultimately 'damaging':

> This was the golden age of Maoism . . . we had vague and idealized images, we were not aware of the horrors and merciless cruelty of the Cultural Revolution in China and what damage it did to humankind, particularly to the Chinese. At the time it looked like a daring way of thinking in opposition to the USSR, beating communist ideology with its own weapons, by using its own phraseology, turning its own ideas against it. I liked it very much as there were no words or arguments, especially important for those educated in a Marxist spirit . . . Christianity does not speak about politics. Therefore, you simply stammered about political topics. I know it was very damaging to me that I read a lot of Marxist works, and their terminology shaped my thinking. [I have had] a decade-long conscious and stubborn effort to get rid of it somehow.[38]

The Chinese Cultural Revolution was not the only alternative communist model that activists in the East turned to; some looked closer to home. Heiko Lietz (b. 1943), a Protestant vicar in East Germany who supported dissident youth and created a nationwide network for conscientious objectors, felt that Czechoslovakian leader Alexander Dubček's 'socialism with a human face' matched his own convictions:

> It was a very exciting model . . . I was more than interested in it, for me it was a matter of transcending social praxis on the basis of my theological approach. And therefore I was a real advocate of the idea that it would be possible to build a society beyond capitalism, beyond profit, beyond economic and financial interests.[39]

For many Christian radicals, the blend of Marxism and spirituality found in Latin American liberation theology was particularly significant. Although liberation theology was directly inspired by the Second Vatican Council and then developed among the Catholic communities of Latin America in the 1960s, even Protestant activists recall the power of its influence.[40] West German

---

Marxism within Spain, see Jesús Aguirre et al., *Cristianos y Marxistas: Los problemas de un diálogo* (Madrid, 1969); Daniel Francisco Álvarez Espinosa, *Cristianos y Marxistas contra Franco* (Cádiz, 2002); Guy Hermet, *Los católicos en la España franquista. I. Los actores del juego político* (Madrid, 1985), 151–61 and 353–5; Montero, *La Iglesia*, 196–9; and Reyes Maté, *Pueden ser 'rojos' los cristianos?* (Madrid, 1977), as well as the journal *Iglesia Viva* 52–53, July–October 1974, 60, November–December 1975, and 66, November–December 1976.

[38] Somogyi interview.
[39] Interview with Heiko Lietz, conducted by AvdG, Schwerin, 28 April 2010.
[40] On the origins and development of liberation theology, see Gustavo Gutiérrez, *A Theology of Liberation: History, Politics, and Salvation* (Maryknoll, NY, 2000). On its impact, see Daniel H. Levine, 'Assessing the impacts of liberation theology in Latin America', *The Review of Politics* 50/2 (1988), 241–63.

Protestant vicar Wolfgang Schiesches (1931–2010) was a member of the *Celler Konferenz*, an oppositional network of inter-church socialists founded in 1968–9 that included both Protestants and Catholics. The group aimed to overcome traditional ecclesiastical hierarchies by building new church structures from below, and Schiesches recalls the potency of liberation theology in this context:

> According to liberation theology there is a connection between the gospel and solidarity (*Kameradschaft*) between brothers and sisters. When we pray to our Father we are all brothers and sisters. And that's a completely new type of theology, to which those who want to cash in their pension the traditional way respond with a lack of understanding and indignation.[41]

Some looked to liberation theology, and to the model of the revolutionary Latin American priests that preceded it, for political inspiration as much as for spiritual guidance. Paul Blanquart recalls the important influence of radical Colombian priest Camilo Torres, who became a guerrilla fighter and was killed in 1966. Torres was his inspiration for the idea that priests should also be revolutionaries:

> I had a particular relationship with Cuba, because I was invited to the congress of intellectuals held there in early '68, January '68. I met three Latin American priests there, who intended to write a declaration, and it happened that I wrote the text and they signed it, and this text was taken up by Fidel Castro in his closing speech. The text said that... we supported Cuba in the difficult situation of her blockade, and that we understood that Marxism was part of that movement, but that Christian faith also had something to contribute, and we used the example of Camilo Torres... We stated that priests should become revolutionaries.[42]

In Hungary too, the revolutionary activism of Latin American priests had an influence in progressive Catholic circles, although this was complicated by the fact that the official press endorsed developments in Latin America. István Deák, who led a youth group within the Regnum Marianum community, remembers that he found a reflection of his own social concerns in the issues confronted by Latin American liberation theologians, and that in this sense he accepted the official reading of the situation in Latin America. However, Deák insists that while the position of the authorities was shaped by political ideology, his was motivated by Christian morality:

> There was a priest called Ortega. We read the poems that he wrote against social injustice. We took for granted the official depiction of the situation in Latin America, and we agreed that things really were no good there—but from the perspective of Christian morality and ethics [rather than politics].[43]

[41] Interview with Wolfgang Schiesches, conducted by AvdG, Bremen, 23 February 2010. See also his *Aufbruch der Freiheit* (Bremen, 1972), which elaborates on the theoretical foundations of his faith and includes discussions of Marx and Mao.
[42] Blanquart interview.
[43] Interview with Istvan Déak, conducted by PA, Budapest, 19 February 2009.

BEING A RELIGIOUS ACTIVIST

What did it mean to be a religious activist in and around 1968? Like those involved in the secular protest movements of the period, religious radicals sought to change themselves, change their relationships with others, change their communities, and ultimately to change the world they lived in. Their activism, however, had a vital additional component, as they sought to change the relationship between individual, community and faith, and in most cases to change the church itself as an institution. New forms of evangelization, often enabled by Vatican II, were eagerly pursued by radicals in an effort to reduce the many barriers between the clergy and the laity, in the hopes of transforming the traditional relationship between the individual, the church as an institution and the very concept of faith.

Transforming space

The transformation of key physical spaces, in particular the parish priest's house and the local church itself, was a significant first step towards activism in many radical communities. Radical clergy broke with tradition either by opening their homes to community use, or by choosing to live outside church property altogether. The opening of the presbytery not only broke down divisions between the clergy and lay members of the community, but could also transform community life by providing a space in which radical social projects could be carried out. Mira Furlani (b. 1937), a key participant in the experience of the Isolotto community, recalls that one of the first radical social experiments carried out in the Isolotto was the opening of a 'casa famiglia' in the presbytery, where abandoned children living in orphanages were taken in and raised by female community members. While priest Enzo Mazzi converted the basement of the presbytery into his living quarters, the living space intended for the priest was transformed into a 'family home':[44]

> The presbytery was two storeys [and was] the most beautiful house in the Isolotto. For don Mazzi, it seemed like an affront to those who didn't have houses, or who had tiny houses where seven, eight, nine, ten people were living together. So one day he asked me if I'd consider using the presbytery to welcome either children or elderly people. He then asked me to be a foster mother to these children... So that's how the first 'casa famiglia' began.[45]

Perceptions on both sides of the ecclesiastical divide were altered when priests chose to live outside church property, as Julio Pérez Pinillos discovered when he moved into 'a normal house... where ordinary people live': 'Your mental make-up is clerical, from the clergy, from a clergy that is removed from society, no? So, by going in there, logically, you go in so as to become just one more person'.[46]

---

[44] The idea of the 'casa famiglia' was inspired by similar experiments in the older Nomadelfia religious community, established by don Zeno Saltini in the 1930s; see Antonio Saltini, *Don Zeno: Il sovversivo di Dio* (Modena, 2003), 53–60.

[45] Interview with Mira Furlani, conducted by RC, Florence, 8 May 2008.

[46] Interview with Julio Pérez Pinillos, conducted by NT, Rivas Vaciamadrid, 19 April 2010.

The space of the local church itself could also be transformed by religious radicals, with an eye to erasing the physical barriers that separated clergy from laity. For some, these changes to the church structure were eagerly adopted after the Second Vatican Council, which had recommended that the altar of a church be turned around so that the priest would face his parishioners during services, rather than having his back towards them. Other communities introduced these changes even before Vatican II. Carlo Consigli recalls that the transformation of the interior of the Isolotto parish church was one of the community's first radical acts, taken at the end of the 1950s. The turning of the altar was accompanied by a parallel reading of the liturgical service in both Latin and Italian, another change that presaged Vatican II:

> Normally the priest had his back turned to the people, but we turned the altar around, so he could see us…We [lay people] were really involved, because as you know, normally the priest speaks in Latin, but the people don't understand a word of Latin. So we said to ourselves 'let's play the part of *altoparlanti*, we'll stand behind [the parishioners], they won't see us, and the priest will speak in Latin and we'll speak in Italian so that the people will be able to understand'…So the altar was [in the middle of the church], and the pews were all around, and there were two platforms [behind] and that's where we stood…Things change if the change is concrete. Ideas are all very well and good, but they aren't worth much if things don't really change.[47]

Such physical changes were not necessarily confined to the interior of the church. Some priests took the decision to build their own churches from scratch, thereby marking a complete rupture with the past. In the late 1960s, Pérez Pinillos's church in the working-class district of Vallecas in Madrid was 'built by the people from the area. This was amazing because they felt that they were the builders of their own church'.[48]

The stark simplicity of the new structure was rooted in the community's decision that, as the builders of the church put it, 'the school has needs, the area too, that should be prioritized before the needs of the temple'. Even the name of a church could reflect these shifts towards a more egalitarian environment. A sign over the entrance to Mariano Gamo's makeshift church in the area of Moratalaz outside Madrid stated that it was a *Casa del pueblo de dios* (House of the People of God), a reference to the Second Vatican Council's definition of the Church as 'the people of God', but also a seditious play on '*Casa del pueblo*', the name given to a local socialist branch before the Civil War.

In eastern Europe, where public space was tightly controlled by the state and priests were excluded from public roles other than services within their churches, religious activists sometimes turned to the countryside in search of a partial retreat from state surveillance. Activists in the Regnum Marianum regularly held training programmes in outdoor camps, provided masses and other religious services in the woods, and organized meetings of group leaders in the hills surrounding Budapest. Priests associated with the group worked in rural villages to put together underground

[47] Consligli interview. [48] Pérez Pinillos interview.

religious networks, such as the 'Borókás' meetings that were held on a farm near Budapest and that brought together various illegal or semi-legal Christian spiritual groups during the 1970s, or the Christian youth festivals that began to take place in the village of Kismaros in 1971.[49] This retreat to the outdoors furnished occasional opportunities for establishing transnational contacts. Károly Elek, an important youth leader in the Regnum Marianum, remembers that the Regnum Marianum youth group used outdoor spaces to meet with Polish religious activists, who were under even greater police surveillance than their Hungarian counterparts:

> [István Deák, Regnum Marianum youth group leader] was on really good terms with the Poles, and we went hiking on a very long road, it was more than 100 kilometres long, with a Polish group that was parallel to ours, but they had to be very careful as they were constantly observed by the secret police. So it was very secret, but nonetheless we met almost every day... they were doing the same things as us. But they were subjected to more control. We made the same camp. They had an altar which they had constructed and we used it, as we knew its location, for the mass.[50]

Transforming relationships

These changes to places of worship were physical manifestations of the transformation of relationships and roles within these communities. Not only did priests make efforts to cast off the outward signs of status, but lay people assumed powerful new voices and roles. The shift in the balance of power between the two resulted in a more participatory and collective atmosphere within the Church. This new environment could be seen in the nature of Bible study and discussion groups, in which lay people took the initiative in interpreting Church teachings and linking them to contemporary social issues. Many interviewees place this empowering experience at the heart of their personal stories of activism, recalling that the marriage of spiritual and political issues in these discussion groups sharpened their engagement in both spheres. Danilo Lotti (b. 1929), who began to participate in a Bible discussion group in the Isolotto community in the early 1970s, when the community had separated from the official Church and was holding its weekly mass in the public square outside the parish church, remembers the excitement of finding himself in an environment where even the disturbing aspects of the Bible were freely discussed and interpreted by lay people:

> I came in the evenings at nine, to read the Bible, which we did freely, and everyone gave their own interpretation. We'd even [talk about] the parts we couldn't stomach. In the Bible you read that the Hebrews, when they occupied a city, would kill everyone there, children, animals, etc. And it struck me that this was a bit like Vietnam,

[49] István Kamarás, *Lelkierőmű Nagymaroson: Religiográfia* (Budapest, 1989); János Dobszay, *Mozaikok a Regnum életéből a hetvenes évektől napjainkig* (Budapest, 1996), 15–21.
[50] Interview with Károly Elek, conducted by PA, Budapest, 9 January 2009.

where the archbishop of New York had blessed the napalm bombs that were going to bombard Vietnam.[51]

Within a dictatorship such as Spain, Bible study could even serve a pointedly subversive function. In discussing Moses's Exodus from Egypt, for instance, Mariano Gamo likened the Franco regime to the 'Pharaonic dictatorship', while members of his study group were urged to 'adopt the Exodus atitude, that is to say struggle against the tyranny of whatever "pharaoh" is in power'.[52] Nor was it only lay people who benefitted from the opportunity to interpret Biblical teachings in their own way. Pedro Requeno learned much from the contemporary reading of the Gospel by the youngsters that he dealt with: 'To go from life to the Bible and then from the Bible back to life again, well, in my case this was taught to me by youngsters that didn't have much education, much culture, but they'd understood this'.[53]

Radical priests also approached the sacraments in a more accessible and less hierarchical fashion. In an effort to empower and engage the laity, Pedro Requeno would break with tradition by explaining ceremonies such as baptism to parishioners in their own home, thereby aiming to create a greater 'closeness': 'When we went to people's homes the people felt that they were "playing at home" more and that they had more freedom, then, to express themselves, to say what they felt about the Church, negative experiences that they'd had'.

Mariano Gamo's rebellious spirit led him to put the words of a catechismal song that he had written himself to the music of the Internationale:

> Poor of the World
> Join in Fellowship
> Make the Earth the Kingdom of the Lord
> Make the Earth the Kingdom of Love

Once Franco died in 1975 and the Internationale became much more widely known, the youngsters that had studied the catechism under Mariano Gamo were convinced that 'they've copied our catechism song'![54]

In many radical religious communities, popular assemblies were also introduced towards the end of the 1960s to break down further the divide between priest and parishioners. These popular assemblies were influenced by similar developments in the student and workers' movements, and they sought to address contemporary social issues as much as religious ones. In the Isolotto community, for example, at a large assembly held to mark Easter 1967, the focus of discussion was ostensibly the papal encyclical *Populorum Progressio*, but debate in fact concentrated on the horrors of the Vietnam War.[55] In dictatorial Spain, assemblies could have a markedly

[51] Interview with Danilo Lotti, conducted by RC, Florence, 21 April 2008. On the pro-war stance of Cardinal Spellman of New York, see Hugh McLeod, *Religious Crisis*, 144–5.

[52] Interview with Mariano Gamo Sánchez, conducted by NT, Madrid, 2 August 2009.

[53] Requeno interview.

[54] Gamo interview.

[55] Archivio storico della Comunità dell'Isolotto, assembly transcriptions, 'Assemblea sulla "Populorum progressio" enciclica di Paolo VI', 21 April 1967. The Isolotto community held weekly

subversive function and sometimes attracted unwanted attention from the authorities. The assemblies held by Mariano Gamo after mass on Sunday, which were open to believers and non-believers alike, broached subjects as diverse as the celibacy of the clergy, the invasion of Czechoslovakia and the failure of a local housing scheme. An assembly in late April 1968 on the significance of May Day resulted in the church being surrounded by the white vans of the police (popularly known as the 'milkvans'):

> What do we do? So people intervened etc., 'No, we stay here'. The dominant feeling is that 'we remain here until the bishop comes to get us out'... After half an hour, the auxiliary bishop appeared, who had already spoken to the police, of course... And when we left, the bishop left at the head of everyone.[56]

This peaceful outcome notwithstanding, such gatherings were an overt challenge to the power and legitimacy of the Franco dictatorship. Mariano Gamo was treading a very dangerous line. Indeed, following an assembly in early 1969 that addressed the question of the state of national emergency, he was arrested by the police and imprisoned for three years in a special jail set up for the clergy. The archbishop took advantage of Gamo's absence not only to raze his makeshift church to the ground, but also to replace his like-minded assistant.

Protestant activists were concerned with many of the same fundamental issues as their Catholic counterparts. They also struggled to reduce the separation between clergy and laity, to develop a less hierarchical religious community, and even to do away with conventional forms of evangelization altogether. In East Germany, radical vicar Heiko Lietz recalls that he felt compelled to fight the hierarchical nature of the Evangelical-Lutheran Church from the inside:

> I was no longer willing to work in these structures of inequality between ordained vicars and the laity. I wanted to tear down the walls between the clergy and the laity— based on fundamental, biblical ideas of the New Testament. I said the Church is too far removed from Jesus' idea of the first primitive community; it's become an institution with hierarchies. And I wanted to tear this down.[57]

Lietz was not so much interested in reforming or radicalizing the established modes of evangelization as rejecting them completely:

> I never evangelized in the sense that I said: You have to be baptized! I wasn't interested in that, in making up the numbers. I didn't work to make up the numbers. Nor to fulfil a particular idea of the church, but I always had the feeling that I was close to my master Jesus. What matters happens in the streets and squares... democracy in the streets and squares. The place where life happens is in the streets and squares and not in enclosed spaces.

---

assemblies following the mass from 15 April 1965 onwards; see Comunità dell'Isolotto, *Isolotto. 1954–1969*, 74–5.

[56] Gamo interview.

[57] Lietz interview.

Transforming the self

For radical members of the clergy, the first steps towards an activist lifestyle often focussed on the elimination of outward, physical signs of ecclesiastical status and authority: in order to diminish the distance between themselves and the faithful, they abandoned liturgical vestments and insisted that they were addressed informally by parishioners. Julio Pérez Pinillos recalls that he shied away from the use of the formal mode of address in Spain—*usted*—and favoured the informal *tú*. 'Dialogue was always *tú* to *tú*... I've always done that. From *tú* to *tú*'. Like other radical priests, he also insisted that the use of 'don' before his name was dropped, so that he was simply known as 'Julio' among his parishioners.[58]

The public struggle by activists to transform their churches and their communities invariably had far-reaching consequences for their *private* lives. The personal lifestyles of many priests were revolutionized by their activism. Pedro Requeno lived communally with other priests in an ordinary flat in the working-class town of Getafe near Madrid, and he recalls that: 'Our house was an open house. We had the keys in the front door and the house was a place where kids, youngsters, married couples could meet'.[59]

Requeno paid a high price for his new-found activism as his lifestyle did not meet the expectations of his parents:

> The great hope of my parents was to have a son that was a priest because this would also mean a certain rise in their social standing. And they came once, only once, to Getafe. My first year as a priest. They arrive, they see the house, and their world collapses. A house, well, full of second-hand furnishings, of bunk beds from Caritas, of different coloured chairs and above all a house full of kids, so that they had to find a place there, in the corner, and [they saw] that I was not 'Don Pedro' but 'Perico'. I was known as 'Perico the Priest' in Getafe, no? Others called me 'The communist Priest'.

The change in circumstances was too much for Requeno's parents. 'My mother left crying', he recalls. Disillusioned, his parents never returned. His new-found lifestyle 'created tensions' within the family, his father reproaching him: 'You've been a priest for I don't know how long, and yet you still have a scooter, but here Don So-and-so and Don Thingeyme have their own cars... This *pueblo* is turning you into a communist'.

Some of the lifestyle options embraced by Catholic activists presented an even more fundamental challenge to the Church. Having fallen in love with a woman at the Ericcson factory, Julio Pérez Pinillos decided that he wanted to get married but still remain a priest. The bishop of Vallecas at the time was the well-known left-winger Alberto Iniesta, who later fell out of favour with the Vatican. Pérez Pinillos vividly remembers the advice given him by the bishop:

> If you believe that you are called to this, then a priest can be married. Someone has to begin. If you believe yourselves called, think it over well. I dare not say 'no' to you. It's going to be a very hard road. Very long.[60]

---

[58] Pérez Pinillos interview.   [59] Requeno interview.   [60] Pérez Pinillos interview.

The support offered by the bishop left Pérez Pinillos feeling 'liberated'. The upshot was that:

> We got married in the church, but without the Church. In the temple, but without the official rituals. Without a priest to preside, without papers to sign. Everyone that knew us, whether from the factory or the places that I had passed through as priest, we called these people to say to them: 'We're going to get married. So that you know that it's another step'.

In 1978, Julio became co-founder and first president of the Movement for Optional Celibacy, later being elected leader of the International Federation. He was very clear about how he managed to achieve all of this:

> You've got to do something. You've got to do something, knowing that the historical processes don't change at the speed you want them to. But you have to know how to be part of them. And I'm aware, I'm aware that I'm in a path-breaking movement.

Arguably the most radical form of Catholic militancy—and one which had the most dramatic consequences for the public and private lives of its adherents—was that of the worker-priests. Not only did worker-priests make a clear and committed effort to change both the Church and society, but they also strove to change themselves and every aspect of their lifestyle. The worker-priest movement originated in France during the Second World War, inspired by the efforts of Young Christian Workers (JOC)-associated chaplain Henri Godin to halt the de-Christianization of working-class France by recasting working-class communities as missionary territory.[61] Worker-priests entered factories and took up manual jobs, approaching their mission by living and labouring alongside manual workers who had turned away from the Church (and often towards the Communist Party). However, as the Cold War deepened, the worker-priests walked an ever thinner line: the act of 'going to the people' within the factory environment brought the worker-priests into the heart of the PCF's stronghold, and by the early 1950s some in the Catholic hierarchy feared that contact with communists had too often spilled over into sympathy for Marxism. Pope Pius XII banned the worker-priests in 1954, thus bringing the first wave of the movement to a close.[62]

As part of the progressive changes brought in by the Second Vatican Council, the ban against the worker-priests was lifted in 1965, and this allowed a second wave of the movement to develop and flourish.[63] Like their predecessors, the

---

[61] With Yvan Daniel, Henri Godin authored *La France: pays de mission?* (Paris, 1943)—a book that Gerd-Rainer Horn has called 'the single most influential book publication of its kind in francophone Europe'. The book inspired the creation of the Mission de France and fuelled the growth of the first wave of worker-priests. See Horn, *Western European Liberation Theology*, ch. 5.

[62] On the first wave of the worker-priest movement, see Oscar L. Arnal, *Priests in Working-Class Blue: The History of the Worker-Priests (1943–1954)* (New York, 1990) and Emile Poulat, *Les Prêtres-ouvriers. Naissance et fin* (Paris, 1999).

[63] See the prologue by Pedro Carasa to José Centeno García, Luis Díez Maestro and Julio Pérez Pinillos (eds) *Curas obreros: Cuarenta y cinco años de testimonio 1963–2008* (Barcelona, 2009), 18–19. On the worker-priests in Spain, see Julio Pérez Pinillos, *Los Curas Obreros en España* (Madrid, 2004) and Esteban Tabares, *Los Curas Obreros, su compromiso y su espíritu* (Madrid, 2005).

second wave of worker-priests broke with the distinctive profile of the priest by divesting themselves of the clothes, language and living quarters traditionally associated with the clergy, and forfeiting their earnings from the Church. Renouncing the traditional role, privileges and income of a priest for the life of an ordinary worker was a matter of principle for worker-priests. As Pedro Requeno insists, 'something which is fundamental to evangelization is the incarnation: living with, and like, the people'.[64] Similarly, Julio Pérez Pinillos is adamant that:

> No evangelization is serious if it doesn't start from how one lives one's life…And we discover God discovering the human being. That's the way. Don't get sidetracked. It's not a question of reading many more things, it's not a question of much more study…This is the change that takes place and the reference, the reference, is the working-class world, which I didn't know. So, get immersed in the world of the working class.[65]

The worker-priests' approach was also a matter of practicalities: it was extremely difficult to reach out to people that had long since rejected the Church without going to them and living among them. Requeno claims that 'Only from within and by sharing and living as the people live could we evangelize a reality such as the working-class one'.

The worker-priests' insistence on a degree of autonomy meant that they were both part of and separate from the Church. By eliminating a whole raft of social and ecclesiastical barriers between the clergy and the laity, the worker-priests can be regarded in many respects as the culmination of the anti-hierarchical, collective, integrative ideals inherent in radical Catholicism.

Within or outside of the church?

Choosing to operate in a liminal space that was both within and outside of the church was not possible for all Christian radicals. In seeking to change their churches, activists—both Catholic and Protestant—often had to make a decision as to whether or not they were willing to break with the official church altogether. Most hoped to change the church from within, but some ultimately reached a point where they had to choose between the desire to pursue utopian goals, and the rules and constrictions imposed by the church as an institution. Some found ways to work within the official church without compromising their ideals; others were driven out, and here some regional differences are apparent. In Spain and France, the base communities, which were inspired by liberation theology, emerged out of the crisis of Catholic Action in the late 1960s. These new communities found it possible to follow radical agendas while remaining within the official church.[66] Julio Lois, who was a promoter of the base communities

---

[64] Requeno interview.   [65] Pérez Pinillos interview.
[66] For groups that *were* striving to create a 'parallel' church, see Blázquez, *La traición*, 186–7 and 219–20 and, for a local example, Serrano Blanco, *Aportaciones de la Iglesia a la democracia*, 361–80 and 410–22.

in Spain, stresses that 'we never spoke of a "parallel Church"'. On the contrary, the base communities:

> have always insisted on the necessity of remaining within the Church and of defending a legitimate pluralism within the Church and of defending dialogue as an essential element and of protesting against any attempt at homogeneity because there is a legitimate pluralism: not only is there one, but there has to be one of interpretations. Consequently the base communities have never tried to form a 'Church apart'.[67]

Similarly, Julio Pérez Pinillos always defended the necessity of striving for change within the Church:

> Always from within. There have been offers: 'Why don't you join the Protestant Church?'. No. I'm in my house. I want to debate in my house. What I want is for my house to be more open. Like the Greek Church, with which, in the last instance, there are certain parallels. And no, no. I'm in my house. Neither am I interested, nor is my house any better than the other. I have the right to be in my house and this man has the right to be in his. It's my house which I believe has to be cleaned. My wife, the same. This, always from within. From within. From within and at the pace that's possible.[68]

In France, the base community movement also remained largely within the fold of the Church. Its motto was 'a Church in solidarity with human liberation'. One of its leading lights, Philippe Warnier, undertook a survey of forty base communities in 1981 and showed that 80 per cent had a priest in their ranks, which enabled them to celebrate the eucharist.[69] One of the members of the journal *La Lettre*, which took a stance that was to the left of the base community movement, said of Warnier: 'He was a friend, but also an adversary...because for him it was all about loyalty to the Church. The Church. In the end he was ordained a deacon'.[70]

In Italy, the base community movement was formed out of a rupture between community and Church, a situation that was brought to a head by the events of 1968. Communities such as the Isolotto had been pursuing increasingly radical spiritual and social goals for some time before 1968, but as universities, factories and other institutions began to be paralyzed by mass protests, religious radicals began to extend gestures of solidarity to students and workers—and Church authorities began to seek to rein in rebellious priests. Urbano Cipriani (b. 1940), who first became involved in the Isolotto community in 1966 when he was a young social sciences teacher, recalls that the situation in 1968 was 'explosive':

> In '68 they were worried because of the general crisis, right? It wasn't only us that the Roman Church was worried about...If you put the parishes alongside the factories and the schools, it was an explosive mixture.

---

[67] Lois interview.   [68] Pérez Pinillos interview.
[69] Phillipe Warnier, *Nouveaux Témoins de l'Église. Les Communautés de base* (Paris, 1981), 76–87. See also Philippe Warnier, *Le Phénomène des communautés de base* (Paris, 1973); J.M. González-Ruiz, 'Genèse des communautés de base en contexte ecclésial', *Lumière de Vie* 99 (1970), 43–59; and Pelletier, *La Crise Catholique*, 112–31.
[70] Interview with anonymous respondent, conducted by RG, Paris, 25 May 2007.

When the community was forced to choose between keeping their priest, Enzo Mazzi, and staying within the Church, they took the collective decision to leave the Church and to form an independent base community, a move that spurred the creation of other non-aligned base communities in Italy. Isolotto members recall, however, that they never wanted or intended to split with the official Church. Cipriani affirms that 'Enzo [Mazzi] was always very careful to define [the community] as existing within the Church, because he profoundly believed that it was possible to change the Church from the inside'.[71]

In eastern Europe, where radical religious groups suffered state persecution, conflicts with the official Church did sometimes arise, but no permanent rift with Rome was possible in such a precarious political situation. While some groups in Hungary, such as the radical Catholic 'Bokor' community, occasionally sought open confrontation with Church authorities, this was not an option for those groups that hoped to operate under the wing of the official Church. For those in the Regnum Marianum, official Catholic doctrine and mainstream Catholic practice were unquestionable components of their religious identity: they considered themselves to be radical *because* they were stubborn defenders of true Catholicism. Regnum Marianum youth group leader Julianna Hajba (b. 1947), who was among the first female leaders of the community, recalls that this strict allegiance to the official Church was sometimes difficult to maintain in practice:

> The relationship between the community and the official Church was not really unclouded. So, we had—but the Fathers always took it very seriously, particularly Father Gábor László, who used to say that the Church was our mother. And you shouldn't say anything bad to your mother. There are times when you are not well cared for, when your mother is in a bad mood. To put it simply, positions against the Church were not allowed at all. One could criticize individuals or their expressions, but anti-Church positions were not tolerated.[72]

Those in the East who felt compelled to question Church hierarchies often paid a heavy price. The efforts of the East German vicar Heiko Lietz to 'tear down the walls between the clergy and the laity' eventually led to 'a massive conflict with my Church'. He was suspended from his pastoral duties in 1979, and dismissed from the Church altogether the following year. As he recalls:

> There was a real conflict and at least outwardly I was the one who lost out. I was suspended from duty, or rather asked to be suspended but wanted to keep working for the Church, but the Church refused. And then I became unemployed.[73]

1968

For religious radicals in the West, the movements of 1968 were a spur to greater involvement not only with religious matters, but also with social and political issues in

[71] Interview with Urbano Cipriani, conducted by RC, Florence, 19 April 2008.
[72] Interview with Julianna Hajba, conducted by PA, Budapest, 25 February 2009.
[73] Lietz interview.

the wider world. In Bremen, Wolfgang Schiesches, who had made it a priority to work with and for young people in his parish, protested alongside young activists during the tram riots of 1968, during which youths clashed with police over the raising of public transport fares. In Paris, Paul Blanquart co-wrote an appeal to Christian students, asking them to participate fully in the events of May: 'I asked Christian students to take full part in the movement, to wipe away our horrible nineteenth century…to wipe away the reactionary past…to get rid of the rift between Christianity and the working class'.[74]

Blanquart was later involved in the action committee of the 13th *arrondisement* in south-east Paris, and donated money from the committee to striking workers at the Panhard factory. Dominican priest Jean Raguénès was likewise inspired by the events of May 1968 in France, opting to join the workers' movement and to become involved with the iconic strike at the Lip watch factory in Besançon in 1973:

> It was not enough for me to 'go to', to help and succour, but to 'be with', to struggle in solidarity with the excluded, to forge a class consciousness with them, and to accompany them every day in their fight for liberation.[75]

In Spain, Italy and France, activists were often involved in the growing workers' movement through the Catholic trade unions, some of which radicalized far more quickly than their communist and socialist counterparts. Olivier Rolin (b. 1947), who was a secular activist in the Maoist GP, recalls that during the strike at the Lip watch factory, it was the Catholic workers of the Confédération Française Démocratique du Travail (CFDT, the Catholic trade union), who, in collaboration with Jean Raguénès, were at the fore of protest:

> The fact that the greatest, most inventive strike, the one that was closest to a kind of workers' control, was led by workers who were not in the CGT [the Confédération Générale du Travail, the communist trade union]…but were in the CFDT, many of whom were Christians and who were inspired by a Dominican priest…that confirmed that we were right to question ourselves, that the Gauche Prolétarienne was doubtless not the right tool to develop revolutionary struggles, if a Dominican father and a few old Christian workers could do better than us young Maoists.[76]

In Italy, both the Catholic union, the Confederazione Italiana Sindacati Lavoratori (CISL, Italian Confederation of Workers' Trade Unions) and the Associazioni Cristiane Lavoratori Italiani (ACLI, Italian Association of Christian Workers), a Catholic workers' advocacy group, were involved in the mass workers' movement of 1968–9.[77] Leda Cossu (b. 1947), who worked in a textile factory on the

---

[74] Blanquart interview.
[75] Jean Raguénès, *De Mai 68 à Lip. Un dominicain au couer des luttes* (Paris, 2008), 108.
[76] Interview with Olivier Rolin, conducted by RG, Paris, 4 May 2007.
[77] On the CISL and the ACLI in the 1960s, see Gian Primo Cella, Paola Piva and Bruno Manghi, *Un sindacato italiano negli anni sessanta. La FIM-CISL dall'Associazione alla classe* (Bari, 1972); Guido Baglioni (ed.) *Analisi della CISL. Fatti e giudizi di un'esperienza sindacale* (Rome, 1980); Gino Bedani, *Politics and Ideology in the Italian Workers' Movement* (Oxford, 1995); and Sergio Turone, *Storia del sindacato in Italia* (Bari, 1976), 404–16.

outskirts of Venice and who was very active in her quickly radicalizing local branch of the ACLI, recalls that the ACLI provided a platform for workers and students to come together, to learn from each other and to become involved in each other's causes:

> This ACLI group brought together all these people from a very cultured Catholic world with the Catholic world coming from the factories. This was the experience of the ACLI...we ran cultural events with conferences and real vocational training seminars of fifteen days in which we workers went together with these cultured speakers, like [Catholic student leader] Marco Boato, we went to the mountains and we did vocational training.[78]

In Spain, many of the clandestine trade unions, such as the AST, the Unión Sindical Obrera (Workers' United Union) and, above all, the Comisiones Obreras or Workers' Commissions—which became the single most important source of opposition to the dictatorship—were solely or jointly founded by Catholics.[79] As a worker-priest at the Swedish firm Ericsson, Julio Pérez Pinillos helped establish a Workers' Commission there:

> It's nice to see how a trade union is born, no? Together, we were seeing, first at the grassroots level, that one has to adopt a different, much freer union model. And one has to coordinate things, not via the official [Francoist] delegates, because they are of another ideology, but via the delegates that we were getting for ourselves. As a result, the Commissions were formed.

The illegal trade unions drew on the support of the Church, as Pérez Pinillos relates:

> The union meetings in which I was involved, which were still clandestine, many of the meetings were held in the churches. In this respect, I had a certain advantage because, as a priest, I knew this bloke or that one, so [I'd ask] 'will you let us use the church?', and an ever higher percentage said yes. As long as we were discreet, that it wasn't obvious, and so on.[80]

The anti-Francoist activity of radical Catholics was not limited to the trade union sphere alone.[81] Catholics were involved in student politics not only by means of the relevant section of Catholic Action, the Juventud Estudiantil Católica (Catholic Student Youth), but also as founders of one of the two most important student bodies of the 1960s, the Popular Liberation Front (FLP). The Juventud Estudiantil Católica, along with other Catholic Action worker and youth sections, was considered such a threat by the Church hierarchy that it unleashed a full-scale onslaught against them in the late 1960s. Radical Catholics in Spain also fought against the Franco

---

[78] Interview with Leda Cossu, conducted by RC, Venice, 31 March 2009.

[79] On the Catholic unions in Spain, see Guy Hermet, *Los católicos en la España franquista. I.*, 203–7 and Montero, *La Iglesia*, 164–6.

[80] Pérez Pinillos interview.

[81] On the Catholic contribution to the anti-Francoist opposition in general, see Blázquez, *La traición*, 131, 140 and 179–80; Callahan, *The Catholic Church*, 505; Hermet, *Los católicos en la España franquista. II.*, 408–10; and Lannon, *Privilege, Persecution, and Prophecy*, 235.

dictatorship by trying to strengthen civil society through the creation and promotion of neighbourhood associations.[82] In 1968, José Molina, a Catholic member of the Maoist ORT who eventually became vice-president of the Federation of Neighbourhood Associations in Madrid, was a founding member of the first neighbourhood association in the working-class district of Vallecas in Madrid, which was created to fight an expropriation order on 12,000 dwellings. 'From that moment on,' he recalls, 'a neighbourhood associational movement was launched. We saw that there were some extraordinary possibilities there to organize people, to introduce ideas, to create struggle, social movements etc.'.[83] This was not down to the efforts of the ORT alone, as Molina recognizes:

> The Church has been fundamental for the development of certain social movements, certain movements and struggles...because it gave us legal cover, because it lent us the churches, because it provided resources. Yesterday a priest was commenting to me that he had very compromising documents in his sacristy, for example, hidden there to avoid a police search, because you knew that the police were not going to go in there, right?

As testimony like this demonstrates, radical Catholics not only participated in the movements and struggles of 1968 in their own right, but they also worked alongside and in coordination with secular groups, even those inspired by anti-religious ideologies such as Maoism. This marks a remarkable coming together of oppositional forces in and around 1968, and demonstrates that religion and faith had real roles—practical, theoretical and spiritual—to play in the movements of the period. Yet we continue to think of 1968 as wholly secular. It is true that the 1960s, a decade of unprecedented economic prosperity for the western world, is generally viewed as an age of rampant secularization. Hugh McLeod goes so far as to claim that these years marked 'a rupture as profound as that brought about by the Reformation', and that they 'set the stage for the rest of the century' where the process of secularization is concerned.[84] The social and political militancy of Catholics and Protestants in western and eastern Europe alike does not so much disprove the secularization thesis as provide a salutary corrective to it. Religious activists on both sides of the Iron Curtain were struggling in the 1960s and 1970s to bridge the ever growing gulf between the exigencies of an urban, industrial and modern society, and what they considered the increasingly irrelevant approach of the traditional churches. The upsurge in radical religious activism may therefore be seen as a response to the advancing secularization of postwar Europe, and its very success during these years qualifies the dominant narratives of 1968. In seeking to bridge the divide between modern society and the sometimes out-of-step traditional

[82] On the church's contribution to the rebuilding of civil society under the Franco dictatorship, see the revisionist articles of Pamela Radcliff: 'La Iglesia católica y la transición a la democracia' in Carolyn Boyd (ed.) *Religión y política en la España contemporánea* (Madrid, 2007), 209–28; and 'Associations and the social origins of the transition during the late Franco regime', in Townson (ed.) *Spain Transformed*, 140–62. See also her excellent book, *Making Democratic Citizens in Spain: Civil Society and the Popular Origins of the Transition, 1960–78* (Basingstoke, 2011).
[83] Interview with José Molina, conducted by NT, Madrid, 1 June 2010.
[84] McLeod, *The Religious Crisis*, 1–2.

churches, not only did Catholic and Protestant activists alike adapt the language and practices of the wider student and worker movements, but they also collaborated closely with them. Religious activists forged their own trade unions, student organizations, communities, journals, discussion circles and other groups. The sheer scale of this religious rebellion inevitably challenges us to rethink '1968' as an inherently secular moment of transformation.

9

Gender and sexuality

Rebecca Clifford, Robert Gildea and Anette Warring[1]

The utopian projects of the late 1960s and early 1970s involved an interrogation of the existing scope of politics, as well as a desire on the part of activists both to change the world and change themselves. Activists began to draw explicit connections between subjective desires and external change. The slogan 'the personal is political', which originated in the women's liberation movement that was developing in the USA in the late 1960s was taken up by activists in many countries.[2] It opened the possibility of including domestic and sexual aspects of life within the political project. It also legitimized critiques of personal relations, which had been silenced within both the social democratic and Marxist traditions of left-wing politics. The transformation envisaged within the commonly used term 'liberation' involved the whole of human existence and being; it was at once collective and individual.[3]

This led the way to a fundamental challenging of gender roles for many women and men involved in 1968. Given the centrality of issues of gender and sexuality to the period, there has been surprisingly little work by historians that focusses on 1968 and gender, yet even studies that pass these issues over tend to recognize that challenges to received gender roles—linked to the emergence of second-wave feminism—were among the most significant legacies of 1968.[4] There has been a sizeable amount of work that examines the links between the student and New Left movements and the emergence of second-wave feminism, both in terms of the positive skills and ideas that women took away from an initial political apprenticeship

[1] We are very grateful to Sheila Rowbotham for her comments and advice on drafts of this chapter.

[2] The phrase 'the personal is political' was first used as the title of an essay by feminist activist Carol Hanisch, published in 1970 in Shulamith Firestone and Anne Koedt's *Notes from the Second Year: Women's Liberation*. However, the idea has older origins and can be found in particular in the work of sociologist C. Wright Mills, who discussed the intersection of public and personal issues in his 1950 *The Sociological Imagination*—a work that had a profound influence on New Left circles in the 1960s.

[3] Jeffrey Weeks, *The World We Have Won: The Remaking of Erotic and Intimate Life* (London, 2007). On silences in Marxist traditions, see Anne Phillips, 'Marxism and feminism', in Feminist Anthology Collective (eds) *No Turning Back: Writing from the Women's Liberation Movement, 1975–80* (London, 1981), 90–8. For an exploration of how gay activism challenged left-wing political traditions, see Lucy Robinson, *Gay Men and the Left in Postwar Britain: How the Personal got Political* (Manchester, 2007).

[4] Recent exceptions are Sara M. Evans, 'Sons, daughters and patriarchy: Gender and the 1968 generation', *American Historical Review* 114/2 (April 2009), 331–47, and Lessie Jo Frazier and Deborah Cohen (eds) *Gender and Sexuality in 1968: Transformative Politics in the Cultural Imagination* (New York, 2009).

in earlier social movements, and in terms of the negative ways in which they experienced sexism and subjugation in practice within these movements.[5] In focussing on the experiences of women who later took up the feminist cause, however, this work tells only a part of the broader story of how female activists experienced and remember 1968. It also overlooks men's responses to and memories of challenges to gender roles in this period.

It is our contention that both women and men engaged with, and wrestled with, the concept of the personal as political. Interviewees often struggle to articulate a fundamental paradox at the heart of this issue: changing modes and forms of gender and sexual identity were experienced, and are remembered, as being at once profoundly liberating and at the same time oppressive, hurtful or constraining. The combination of the political and the intimate, however, often meant different things for women and men. Many women, as Sheila Rowbotham has observed, faced the challenge of taking forward the 'heady utopianism' of 1968 while questioning its male-centric 'r-r-revolutionary bombast'.[6] Male activists, by contrast, may have tussled with the need to integrate intimate life into politics and to enter a new world of emotions. This chapter seeks to explore the ways in which former activists narrate, or struggle to narrate, their subjective remembrance of these conflicts and paradoxes. It focusses on activists from Denmark, France and Italy; because the study of gender and 1968 is an emerging area of scholarly interest, we have kept our geographical focus narrow with the aim of offering a starting point in what will, we hope, become a far more expansive historiographical discussion in years to come.

The conflicts and contradictions explored here have several facets, and this chapter looks at four key issues found among them. First, in what ways did sexual liberation mean different things to men and women? Second, was gender equality part of political liberation, or was it something more complicated? Could activists change the world and change themselves at the same time, or would they ultimately have to choose between one and the other? Third, if women and men chose to prioritize the search for a more equal relationship between the sexes, could they do this together or would it require men and women to work separately? Fourth, what was the relationship between male and female separatism and sexual orientation? Under what circumstances did female separatism imply lesbianism and the men's movement gay rights?

SEXUAL LIBERATION AND INEQUALITY

The promise of liberation—political, sexual, social, personal and otherwise—was an extremely powerful aspect of the protest movements that emerged around 1968, and

[5] The bulk of this work focusses on the United States. See in particular Alice Echols, *Daring to be Bad: Radical Feminism in America, 1967–1975* (Minneapolis, MN, 1989); Sara M. Evans, *Personal Politics* (New York, 1979); and Doug McAdam, *Freedom Summer* (New York, 1988). For a comparative overview of Britain and the US, see David Bouchier, *The Feminist Challenge: The Movement for Women's Liberation in Britain and the USA* (New York, 1984).
[6] Sheila Rowbotham, '1968: Spring-board for women's liberation', in Karen Dubinsky (ed.) *'New World Coming': The Sixties and the Shaping of Global Consciousness* (Toronto, 2009), 257–65.

both women and men recall the thrill experienced as they explored freer social relations and more direct political participation. Nadja Ringart (b. 1948), the daughter of Polish- and Russian-Jewish immigrants brought up in Catholic and conservative provincial France, who became active in VLR and in the women's movement, recalls a diffuse and barely articulated sense of revolt against social and political conformity:

> NR: Society was completely stifling...I was in revolt against morality, I think. You can't imagine what it was like. I had the idea that liberty was a fundamental value in my itinerary, even more than equality.
> RG: But political liberty or cultural or sexual?
> NR: Sexual, personal, political, everything, the self-determination of peoples. Things about which no doubt I didn't reflect on much.[7]

Lia Migale (b. 1949), who was active in the student movement at the University of Rome and who played a central role in the Roman branch of the extra-parliamentary left organization Lotta Continua, places freedom at the centre of her thoughts on 1968. This was a personal and sexual freedom that even found expression in the wearing of clothing that challenged codes of propriety, such as the miniskirt. She speaks of a tension between the sense of liberation that young women experienced as they broke away from conservative modes of behaviour, and the limitations placed on this freedom by the inequality that existed between women and men within the student movement:

> For me personally, '68 was...freedom, meaning the realization of the concept of freedom...We came from a world that was full of restrictions for girls, in terms of modes of comportment, of a lack of freedom of expression. I'm not talking only about sexual freedom, although that was...for someone coming from the provinces, innocent, that was more of a problem than anything else. I had lots of issues with sexual freedom but...well, just think of miniskirts! I had a miniskirt that came up to here! [laughs] There were lots of things that had to do with comportment, but these things led to new ways of thinking, and this led us to think about inequality. Because after all, what sense is there in having freedom but not being able to use it?[8]

This tension between the excitement of newly discovered freedoms and the limits placed on these freedoms crops up frequently in interviews with women. For many women, the 'liberation' discovered in the student movement could be utopian and emancipating, and yet at the same time complicated, limiting and even abusive. This was particularly true of sexual liberation.[9] Lucia Motti (b. 1950), who skipped classes as a high school student to spend her days at the occupied university of Bari in southern Italy, explains that sexual freedom involved a double standard for men and for women. For women it could mean being able to challenge familial and social conventions, while for men it may have meant easy access to women, who often felt pressured into sexual activity:

[7] Inteview with Nadja Ringart, conducted by RG, Sceaux, 5 July 2007.

[8] Interview with Lia Migale, conducted by RC, Rome, 4 December 2008.

[9] The fact that many women found the changes wrought by the sexual revolution to be both liberating and at the same time exploitative is often overlooked by historians of the period; for a brief analysis that does address these contradictions and complications, see Luisa Passerini, *Autobiography of a Generation: Italy, 1968* (Middletown, CT, 1996), 95–100.

[High school] didn't mean anything to me because I was truly convinced that we were changing the world, that a huge revolutionary process was taking place, and thus my final exams were really the least of my problems. I had another problem in that period that was harder for me to solve: '68 was, even in the south [of Italy]—and it is really important to say this—it was a moment of great sexual liberation, of great sexual freedom, perhaps with its own problems because we didn't realize how we were being used as women. This freedom was real to us, but for men it might only have been a way to use us in a more liberal way. I had a relationship that lasted for a year and a half, and I was hugely afraid of getting pregnant.[10]

While the availability of the contraceptive pill made some difference to sexual liberation, it did not provide all the answers.[11] Commitment to political revolution in extreme-left circles was supposed to come above all else; personal feelings and emotions were sacrificed to this higher good. The rejection of emotions could thus become another weapon in the armoury of male persuasiveness. Rosetta Stella (b. 1951), who was involved in the student movement at the University of Rome, recalls the strange contradiction between the discovery of her own sexual desire and the 'revolt against feelings' that was part of the world of far-left politics that she immersed herself in as a university student:

Another experience that I had in '68 was the discovery of my own sexual desire. This was very important in '68, there was the sexual revolution, let's call it that. It happened in a disorganized fashion...and with a certain amount of excess that didn't...that didn't contribute to real sexual liberation, let's say. I discovered the pill, because in those years...and of course it was all hidden from my parents; keep in mind that at home I was a perfect little daughter, but then outside the home all this stuff happened. [laughs] The pill, and then...a sexual education that was fairly aggressive, with this revolt against feelings, meaning that everything sentimental was considered to be wrong because real revolutionaries don't have feelings.[12]

She then illustrates the extremes to which this 'revolt against feelings' could be taken, and suggests that it nonetheless provoked the beginnings of a feminist understanding of herself and her body:

One of my friends, her boyfriend was in the hospital because he'd been in an accident, and when he was getting out of the hospital my friend said, 'listen, I have to ask you something. I've got my period, and given that he's getting out of the hospital, he's going to want to make love. Could you do it in my place, as I can't?' [laughs] And so what happened? I didn't do it, but I had to think about it. You couldn't just say 'no', you had to think about it and there was some mental work involved in finding a way

[10] Interview with Lucia Motti, conducted by RC, Rome, 24 June 2008.
[11] Dagmar Herzog, *Sexuality in Europe: A Twentieth-Century History* (Cambridge, 2011), 136–46. For a more detailed case study, see her 'Between coitus and commodification: Young West German women and the impact of the pill', in Axel Schildt and Detlef Siegfried (eds) *Between Marx and Coca-Cola: Youth Cultures in Changing European Societies 1960–1980* (New York, 2006). It is important to keep in mind that the situation regarding the legality and availability of contraception was different across Europe. Legal restrictions on contraception or on the dissemination of contraceptive advice were in force until 1955 in Denmark, 1967 in France and 1971 in Italy.
[12] Interview with Rosetta Stella, conducted by RC, Rome, 8 December 2008.

to say no. This is an extreme example, but the positive element was the fact that you discovered your body, your own desire, you discovered pleasure, and all this stuff that was later so important in terms of a feminist awakening and your own sense of self.

The attitude of some male revolutionaries is typified by Romain Goupil (b. 1951), a Trotskyist belonging to the JCR, a campaigner against the Vietnam War and one of the founders of the Comités d'Action Lycéens (CAL), which recruited support in high schools. He explains that the Trotskyists saw themselves as heirs to the Bolsheviks, and that this pleasure in political prowess fed easily into the possibility of sexual conquest:

We had great pleasure as leaders or authority figures going into those *lycées*, to spread propaganda or hold debates or make speeches, creating the CAL or Vietnam Committees. In the same organization, in a group of thirty, there might be fifteen girls and fifteen boys. There was rivalry between the boys for those fifteen girls, each one of whom was prettier or more desirable than the last...At that time there were a lot of love stories, in a platonic sense, flirting...with girls who were absolutely magnificent.[13]

Some male activists were less comfortable with the prevailing revolutionary model. Patrick Viveret (b. 1948), a Nanterre student and member of the subversive March 22nd movement who was also a member of the JEC, was critical of the way in which some Trotskyists combined political bullying and seigneurial rights over female members of the organization:

I was struck by the number of men who used revolutionary ideology to persuade young women to have sex with them, saying that if they refused it was because of their petit-bourgeois morality. In some extreme left-wing groups it was a caricature. The double speciality of the [Trotskyist] Alliance des Jeunes pour le Socialisme was the defenestration of their enemies and the *droit de cuissage* over any women who entered their group.[14]

CHANGING THE WORLD, CHANGING ONESELF

Although the personal was becoming political, the twin goals of changing oneself and changing the world were not always easy to hold together. Many activists were extremely creative and determined in maintaining this balance, but there were several key issues that drove a wedge between personal and political goals. One was the question of different interpretations of sexual liberation, which sometimes concealed the issue of sexual inequality. Another was the use of a consciously abstract and theoretical Marxist ideology that shaped debate in so many activist groups. It was defined, constructed and monopolized by young male activists, leaving no space for other voices. Many activists—women especially, but also men—felt

[13] Interview with Romain Goupil, conducted by RG, Paris, 24 May 2007.
[14] Interview with Patrick Viveret, conducted by RG, Paris, 15 May 2008. Under feudalism, the *droit de cuissage* was the (mythical) seigneur's right of the first night with women who married in his manor.

voiceless within these groups. They recall that there was no room for them to speak
at political meetings, and they remember the complex and contradictory sensation
that they at once belonged to the group, and yet were marginalized and alienated
within it. This sense of alienation was one of the key roots of the women's
movement.[15]

Maria Paola Fiorensoli (b. 1947) moved from Turin to Rome in 1968 and entered the university there, where she quickly became caught up in the student
movement. She later redirected her activism towards feminism, and she describes
how her frustration over the disjuncture between belonging and marginality within
the student movement led to her joining a women-only collective within the
occupied university. She recalls that what characterized the period for her was 'a
sense of unanimity, a sense of being recognized', and yet at the same time she felt
sidelined as a woman:

> There was a sense of co-participation, going to the assemblies. But that's where the
> road to the feminist collectives began, because at the assemblies, you have to put all
> these factors together to understand: a small number of women, a tiny number with
> little preparation, you had to throw yourself right into the fray. You'd put your name
> on the list to speak, but you'd never speak! First there would be this *compagno* [male
> comrade], and then this one and this one and this one, and the chance for a *compagna*
> [female comrade] to speak never came. You want to know how the [women's] collec-
> tives were formed? It was like this. Out of rage that you were never allowed to speak
> in the student assemblies...In the huge crowd of the lecture theatre, squashed in the
> middle of that mass of people, it was always 'hey, I'm thirsty, go and get me some
> water! Hey, I'm hungry, go and get me a sandwich!'. We did it at first, because it was
> something that we'd been taught to do. It was only a bit later that you said 'go and get
> it yourself!'

She then describes a day that sticks particularly in her mind, when her friend Lucia
had put her name on the list to speak in an assembly. She found herself running up
against the assumption that even in radical movements men's role was public and
women's supportive:

> When Lucia's turn arrived, the man after her started to speak immediately, and so
> Lucia started to cry. And the whole assembly began laughing, because women cry,
> they're stupid, they can't talk about politics, they turn red, right?... How could you
> make them understand that they were discriminating against you? They discrimi-
> nated against you, they wouldn't let you speak because you were a woman. How
> could you make them understand? We spent hours at the mimeograph machine,
> making pamphlets, and yet you counted for nothing, for nothing. So if you want to
> know how the collectives formed, that's how mine formed...It was a process of
> protest within the movement...within a group that you nonetheless felt you be-
> longed to.[16]

---

[15] Luisa Passerini observes that this contradictory sense of belonging and marginality can itself be a
product of memory, which 'introduces a discourse of exclusion and extraneousness for those women
who appeared to be at the center of the movement and its leadership'. See Passerini, *Autobiography of
a Generation*, 144–8.

[16] Interview with Maria Paola Fiorensoli, conducted by RC, Rome, 11 December 2008.

Like Fiorensoli, Karen Syberg (b. 1945) experienced the encounter with the student movement and the Marxist milieu in her university as tempting and liberating, but also as marginalizing and oppressive. She felt like an outsider, and recalls sensing that nothing she knew was of any use in this context, a feeling exacerbated by the fact that men dominated political meetings and discussions in study groups:

> We were a group of women. We were all talented girls in high school, right. When we started studying at university, we felt that…certainly in comparative literature, but in other subjects as well, that it was someone else who defined what was right. And once you'd figured it out, the truth changed, so there was that feeling of being defined from the outside and constantly rushing to catch up on what was right, your skills, your knowledge etc., both politically and professionally. It was very gendered. Men were the ones who did the defining. This is largely what we opposed initially in the first round. In other words, this is how *we* define it, which is also what shocked the men.[17]

Together with about a dozen female students, inspired by the American radical feminist group Redstockings, she began participating in feminist demonstrations on the streets of Copenhagen in the spring of 1970, and was one of the founders of the umbrella organization Rødstrømpebevægelsen (Redstocking Movement) that went on to become the largest and most powerful feminist organization in Denmark.[18]

Another Danish activist, Birgitte Dud (b. 1944), dedicated herself to combining socialist and gender politics despite sometimes feeling ambivalent about how best to balance the two. After being involved in leftist and student politics for several years, she joined a local Maoist feminist group affiliated with the Redstocking Movement in 1971 because she felt attracted by the women's movement. However, a growing interest in bringing personal experiences into her activism prompted her to leave the group when it broke with the Redstocking Movement in order to give priority to class struggle. Here she recalls the difficulties in reconciling the personal with the political in this context:

> I didn't feel the need to examine myself very often, but at the same time I was constantly drawn into it, into a place where we examined ourselves and talked about personal development, private things and relationships, and how to make relationships work and such, as well as talking about authority and jobs and families and childhood stories and how our mothers had lived…I was strongly aware of both issues…and socialist consciousness or…you could say consciousness about the class struggle or class awareness. Even though I didn't come from a working-class family my socialist consciousness was strong. It was also very much a part of the Redstocking

---

[17] Interview with Karen Syberg, conducted by AW, Svensmarke, 5 January 2011.
[18] On the Danish Redstockings, see Drude Dahlerup, *Rødstrømperne. Den danske Rødstrømpebevægelses udvikling, nytænkning og gennemslag 1970–1985*, vol. 1 & 2 (Copenhagen, 1998); for an overview in English, see Lynn Walter, 'The Redstocking Movement: Sex, love, and politics in 1968', in Anna Clark (ed.) *The History of Sexuality in Europe: A Sourcebook and Reader* (Oxford, 2011), 297–316. On the American Redstockings, see Alice Echols, *Daring to be Bad*, ch. 4, and Ellen Willis, 'Radical feminism and feminist radicalism', in Ellen Willis, *No More Nice Girls: Countercultural Essays* (Middletown, 1992), 117–50.

Movement. But there were also quite a lot of people who were indifferent to what was
going on and who were there mainly out of self-interest.[19]

A sense of exclusion was brought about not only by the dominance of Marxist
ideology, but also by the cult of the genuine revolutionary who subordinated the
personal to the political, and the emotional to the reasoned, in the quest for
proletarian revolution.[20] Private life was seen to be a distraction and a luxury. Some
women, for a time, managed to achieve this subordination, but rarely for long.
Anne Victorri (b. 1949), who took her *baccalauréat* in 1968, threw in the option
of further study to follow her boyfriend, Bernard Victorri, a mathematician from
the École Normale Supérieure, into the GP. She and Bernard worked in a succession of grim factories in the industrial north of France in an attempt to rekindle
proletarian revolution. Their Maoist superior obliged them to marry in order to
satisfy the alleged requirements of 'proletarian love', since workers were seen to
distrust 'hippies'. Having got married, however, they were immediately required to
live apart out of commitment to revolution. Bernard was arrested for a Molotov
cocktail attack on the offices of a mining company and went to prison. Anne Victorri recalls the strength of the Maoist spirit of sacrifice in the cause of revolution
that steamrollered over her needs as a young wife and mother:

> I lived some very grim, hard years, but it was the spirit of sacrifice which ruled...That
> was the Maoist idea, the spirit of sacrifice, they kept repeating it, a word which con-
> stantly returned to our vocabulary, constantly, constantly, constantly. Our private life
> was completely cut off by everything else...Our daughter was born and the first time
> she saw her father was in La Santé prison.[21]

Giovanna Gallio (b. 1950) was involved in the student movement at the University
of Bologna before redirecting her energies towards the fight to reform and ultimately abolish psychiatric institutions, a movement that was an important out-
growth of 1968 in Italy.[22] Gallio recalls that, when she was only twenty years old,
she found herself caught between her young family and her commitment to revolutionary politics, unable to balance the personal and the political aspects of her life:

> At the age of twenty I had two children, one right after the other, just at the very
> moment that I was discovering my revolutionary identity...I had become the leader
> of a political group that I had formed, and I went along with my little just-born baby
> to hand out leaflets in front of the shoe factories. Just think about the effort it took, to

[19] Interview with Birgitte Due, conducted by AW, Copenhagen, 8 December 2010.
[20] On the power of this image of the revolutionary and the ways in which it affected both women
and men, see Lessie Jo Frazier and Deborah Cohen, 'Talking back to '68: Gendered narratives, participatory spaces, and political cultures', in Frazier and Cohen (eds) *Gender and Sexuality in 1968*,
145–72; and Rebecca Clifford, 'Emotions and gender in oral history: narrating Italy's 1968', *Modern
Italy* 17/2 (2012), 209–21.
[21] Interview with Anne and Bernard Victorri, conducted by RG, Paris, 28 May 2007.
[22] On the 'democratic psychiatry' movement in Italy and its connection to 1968, see Maria Luisa
Boccia, 'Psichiatria democratica. Riformatori e riformati', *Democrazia e diritto* 1 (January–February
1986), 151–9, and Aldo Agosti, Luisa Passerini and Nicola Tranfaglia (eds) *La cultura e i luoghi del '68.
Atti del convegno di studi organizzato dal Dipartimento di Storia dell'Università di Torino* (Milan, 1991),
22–3. See also Chapter 6, pp. 179–82, in this volume for further details.

do all that simultaneously. I had a baby that had just been born, and naturally I arrived at the brink of suicide because I was…I was skinny, weak, at the end of…it was an enormous expenditure, one trauma after another because a mother needs to stay in one place to raise her child in the first year, and instead all this happened, and caused a colossal amount of trauma. My children grew up in a period in which motherhood was negated. I was a child myself at the time, I had children who were like toys, I hardly even knew how to treat them.[23]

Whereas many women describe feeling marginalized within the student movement and the New Left because they were women, some men also recall that they lacked a voice in these groups, either because they could not or did not want to articulate the necessary Marxist theory, or because they felt ambivalent about the culture of *machismo* that often flourished in revolutionary circles. Roland Castro (b. 1940), an architecture student, became involved in the Maoist UJC(ml). Its leaders were philosophy students, pupils of the Marxist guru Louis Althusser at the École Normale Supérieure in Paris. Castro, who after the collapse of the UJC(ml) in 1968 became a founder and leader of the 'soft' Maoist VLR group, confides that he felt inadequate in the pre-68 radical movement because he was not an intellectual but approached revolution intuitively:

I was very reticent…I had a rather special status in the Union of Communist Youth because I was not at the rue d'Ulm, not at the École Normale Sup. I was at the Beaux Arts…and they fascinated me with their knowledge…they were able to handle Marxist thought scientifically, it was nothing to do with revolutionary passion. Being at the Beaux Arts, I was more on the intuitive side. They manipulated me because I was ordinary, I was funny. I was not a keeper of the scriptures, I was a bawdy monk in their church system.[24]

VLR, which combined agitation among workers and communal living, was a lively experiment in combining political and lifestyle activism. Castro recalls that:

It was about 'living' the revolution, not 'making' it. It was the sexual revolution, a cultural revolution, a revolution in all fields of social life…We were leaving sociological Marxism…It was a criticism of collectivism. We were already anti-totalitarian.

This attempt to combine political and sexual revolution did not ultimately work out within VLR, however. Françoise Picq (b. 1944), a member of VLR's women's group, explains how the group ruptured in 1971 over the issue of sexual liberation, discussed in its magazine, *Tout!*, when women members argued that it concealed an unequal power relationship:

We began to attack the concept of sexual liberation that was being developed around *Tout!*…We wrote a piece called 'Your sexual liberation is not the same as ours', which was written by the women as a group…We said that given [power] relations between men and women, women have always been in a situation of being dominated. They haven't had access to their own desires, but submitted themselves to men's desires. So

---

[23] Interview with Giovanna Gallio, conducted by RC, Trieste, 5 March 2009.
[24] Interview with Roland Castro, conducted by RG, Paris, 9 May 2007.

our quest for liberation was to know our own desires and to build relationships that were not relationships of power.[25]

Some men also felt uncomfortable with the way in which masculinity was constructed through overt sexual power and the use of abstract theory, and decided to break away from conventional revolutionary organizations to form men's groups.[26] The women's movement was an important catalyst for the formation of men's movements in countries such as Britain, Denmark and the other Scandinavian countries, and men's groups in France, Italy and Holland.[27] Danish activist Hans-Otto Loldrup (b. 1948), the founder of the Danish men's movement, describes his rejection of the denial of personal experience within the Marxist mindset that he encountered at university in the first half of the 1970s:

> It was that whole system that I found atrocious and male-dominated... The whole idea [behind the men's movement] was that it was a break with the role of men at the university, where... personal experiences and one's own feelings about this or that are always ignored, because everything has to be analysed at a higher level and fit into a conceptual framework that is out of touch with reality. I attacked this vehemently.[28]

When he subsequently published his critique in a newspaper and invited men to get in touch, he received 150 letters and organized a meeting with the purpose of forming men's groups. 'In that way', he recalls, 'we initiated the Copenhagen version of the men's movement':

> This is why we launched the group Rødsokkerne [Red Socks], because some of the activities took place simultaneously with the debate days that the women's rights movement had on campus. This also encouraged men to examine themselves a little. But I would say that the commotion concerning the social conventions of men was already in play and not the result of what was happening. Suddenly there was a platform where meetings could be held to have discussions, so it got quite big all of a sudden.

The Danish men's movement adapted the Redstockings' equation of gender and class struggle, formulating it as 'Men's struggle is class struggle. Class struggle is men's struggle'. Just how to prioritize these two aims, however, was a problem. Two

---

[25] Interview with Françoise Picq, conducted by RG, Paris, 27 April 2007. On this see also Françoise Picq, *Libération des femmes. Les années-mouvement* (Paris, 1993); Manus McGrogan, '*Tout!* in context, 1968–1973: French radical press at the crossroads of the far left, new movements and counterculture', PhD thesis (University of Portsmouth, 2010), 101–4; and Julian Bourg, '"Your Sexual Revolution is not Ours": French feminist "moralism" and the limits of desire', in Frazier and Cohen (eds), *Gender and Sexuality in 1968*, 85–113.

[26] On the Swedish men's movement, see Helena Hill, *Befria mannen! Idéer om förtryck, frigörelse och förandring hos en svensk mansrörelse under 1970-och tidigt 1980-tal* (Umeå, 2007). On the Danish men's movement, see Laura Pérez Skardhamar, *'Det private er politisk—en analyse af et kollektiv, ø-lejre og mandebevægelse i de lange halvfjerdsere i Danmark* (Roskilde, 2010).

[27] We are not aware of any historical research that looks at men's groups in France and Italy. However, documents from the time attest to their existence: a letter in the private archive of Hans-Otto Loldrup, from Georges Por to Hans-Otto Loldrup, dated 15 March 1977, describes contacts between men's groups in Denmark and southern Europe.

[28] Interview with Hans-Otto Loldrup, conducted by AW, Copenhagen, 4 January 2011.

positions emerged, that of the so-called 'class fighters' and that of the 'psychos' who were much more interested in feelings and emotions. Finn Westermann (b. 1946), who joined the men's movement at its inception, tried to keep both goals in play:

> I probably wouldn't have distinguished between those things, as I believed that we should have some sort of socialism, but I wasn't one of those people who thought that if we could just have socialism, then things would probably change. I didn't believe in that. I saw it as two parallel battles that should be fought, and that's probably because I saw how many of those men who called themselves socialists acted... They didn't have the faintest idea about gender policy, many of them didn't... And they thought that we had to fight the other battle first, and then we could always take the other one up later, right... But, you can keep telling yourself that you're the one that has to change and then not see that perhaps there are structural factors that must also change in society.[29]

By the 1980s the social movements initiated by 1968 were becoming more focussed on the personal and individual aspects of change. Hans-Otto Loldrup abandoned a long struggle to combine the personal and political and ended up leaving the movement in the mid-1980s because he felt that the personal had overwhelmed the political. Changing the world no longer seemed to be a consideration:

> Well, I think in fact that I was kind of caught between a rock and a hard place by wanting to pursue what I described before about starting with something personal and then you could well end up in a class struggle, who knows?... The reason I left the men's movement many years later, at a later stage, was because of a growing sense of frustration about people coming in with these types of problems and never moving on. I think that it would've been interesting if personal private problems were used to analyze and talk about how things could be different, and then this resulted in moving up a level and getting something done so that things changed. But at that point I thought we had turned into a bunch of narcissistic whiners who complained about how hard everything was and patted each other on the back and where not a damn thing happened.[30]

Although men's groups were most significant in Scandinavia, Britain also had a flirtation with the men's liberation movement. Paul Atkinson (b. 1949), who was involved in the so-called libertarian Marxist organization Big Flame (which patterned itself on the Italian group Lotta Continua), like Loldrup, saw the challenge of feminism and women's groups as an invitation to men to begin to think about the personal and emotional dimension of politics:

> I mean separatist feminism, I just felt very defensive about [it] and reacted to [it] in various ways: 'all men are rapists', that kind of stuff. It kind of got to me. But I knew more women like Sheila [Rowbotham], socialist feminists, and women who on the whole liked men. Though they had trouble with men, they liked men, they were largely, usually heterosexual, not necessarily. So it felt to me then, although it was a big challenge, it felt like that kind of feminism was an invitation to do something with my own sort

---

[29] Interview with Finn Westermann, conducted by AW, Smørum, 21 December 2010.
[30] Loldrup interview.

of emotional sensibilities and so on…For men, the women's movement actually le-
gitimizes that project in a way that it's quite difficult for men, among themselves, to
legitimize…and the heart of it for me was the invitation from the women's movement
to men to engage in an emotional politics as well as an external politics.[31]

Atkinson helped to found a men's group, Red Therapy, which combined
elements of therapy and political consciousness-raising. This led to thinking
about the patriarchal system, and how it affected men as well as women. That
said, he recalls that feminists did not always take at face value the redemption
of the new man:

> I think we spent a lot of time, my men's group, the men I knew spent a lot of time
> thinking about how to get out from under feeling guilty into being able to think in a
> more open way about how patriarchy works as a system. So, a lot of women didn't like
> that very much. There were a lot of arguments about that, really, about how… is this
> men just trying to recapture their ground by producing theories that put us all in the
> same boat? [laughs] You know, 'we're all in the same boat, we're all as much victims of
> patriarchy as you are', or is there something legitimate and important to add to what
> feminism is saying, you know?[32]

CHANGING TOGETHER OR CHANGING SEPARATELY?

As the first wave of student and radical politics began to break up in the early
1970s, women and men began to explore the issues of gender equality and sexual
politics in different ways, through new types of communities and organizations.
Some tried to bring the political and personal together on a day-to-day basis in
communes, with varied success. Some women left their New Left groups en masse
to explore feminism, which might initially have included a few male fellow-travel-
lers, but soon became separatist.[33] Feminist separatism challenged some men to
rethink a great deal about their relationship with feminist women, their own
thoughts about personal politics and difference, and their own desire to explore
separatist environments. Some of these experiments also raised the question of
sexual preference. For some women, feminism ultimately implied lesbianism,
while for some men revolution implied gay rights.
    One space in which men and women together could challenge patriarchal soci-
ety, gender inequality and traditional gender roles was the commune. Patrick
Viveret, who had criticized the sexual politics of the Trotskyists, spent most of the
1970s working for the socialist press and living in a commune, having thought a
great deal about the gender organization of society:

---

[31] Interview with Paul Atkinson, conducted by JD, London, 9 July 2010.
[32] Atkinson interview.
[33] On the complexities of feminist separatism, see Eileen Bresnahan, 'The strange case of Jackie
East: When identities collide', in Barbara Ryan (ed.) *Identity Politics in the Women's Movement* (New
York, 2001), 183–96.

I lived in a commune for ten years, but I remember that for six months we read about and discussed all the experiences of communes that we knew both in France and abroad to discover the principal errors not to make. Among these errors was a certain idealism about loving relationships and the question of children, believing that children could belong to the community and that parental ties would easily dissolve, or that everyone could make love with everyone else, that it was healthy and posed no problems. Those were things we identified as not being obvious.[34]

Experimenting with communes created ways of living that differed from that of conventional nuclear families.[35] The goal was an equal distribution of power with no fixed social or gender roles. Niels Frölich (b. 1945) was involved in many different kinds of political activism while living in the Danish commune Brøndby Strand from 1970 to 1973. He recalls that:

> It was a continually recurring discussion. All that. It was always an issue. And I think we really made an effort to divide things up correctly, I mean, equally. But it was never perfect, of course. Gender issues popped up all the time, I will say fortunately... Even though it was perhaps not obvious to us, it was part of the spirit of the times to challenge the old ways of living, whether it made people cry or not; and it did. It was highly educational in a really good way.[36]

Despite their good intentions, men's educational progress could be too slow for women in these communal environments. Pia Søndergaard (b. 1945), who joined a squat commune with high expectations, moved out after a year because of its lack of seriousness, lack of gender equality and the absence of the help she needed as a single mother. What she found missing in the commune she discovered instead in the women's movement:

> Of course it was the men who were in charge... [We discussed] men and women's relationships and opportunities, but I don't really think that we came to any conclusions that really made an impression on me... I also think it was pretty obvious that what we had going on wouldn't change much in society, and it was really, it was just a bunch of ramblings. Hash, you know... Well, those were the things that I thought I found answers to in the women's movement, you know. People were receptive to each others' arguments there. There was solidarity, yes. I think it was... you could say that this is where the real answers came from about all the things we would do differently. We helped each other, we supported each other, we were in solidarity, we were in solidarity. We didn't run off with each other's boyfriends.[37]

Sometimes the break between feminists and communes or mixed revolutionary groups was gradual and amicable. Feminists might continue relationships either with men sympathetic to the feminist cause or with men who were revolutionary leaders and 'alpha' males, or indeed with both. Having discovered that sexual liberation was

---

[34] Viveret interview.

[35] John Davis and Anette Warring, 'Living utopia. Communal living in Denmark and Britain', *Cultural and Social History* 8/4 (2011), 511–28. For a study of gender relations in communes that focusses on the US and on the experiences of men, see Tim Hodgdon, *Manhood in the Age of Aquarius: Masculinity in Two Countercultural Communities, 1965–83* (New York, 2007).

[36] Interview with Niels Frölich, conducted by AW, Albertslund, 13 February 2009.

[37] Interview with Pia Søndergaard, conducted by AW, Aarhus, 4 February 2009.

about power, Françoise Picq was able to combine feminism with simultaneous relationships with two kinds of men, one a leader of VLR, the other a so-called *gentil*:

> After the editorial meetings of *Tout!* we used to go to a nearby restaurant called *Chez Mohammed*... There were two rooms and all the women were in one room but there were two or three men on the editorial committee who had no problem with the women and whom we called the *gentils*. There was no power issue with them but a little rivalry because they had amorous relations with certain women who might also have amorous relations with the leaders... I experienced a great period of sexual liberation, with complicated relationships at times. The best time for me was when I was seeing two men and was respected because when one of them said, 'I'll see you this evening or tomorrow', I said, 'I will have to see'.[38]

In other cases, the break of feminists with revolutionary organizations could be violent. In Italy, tensions between men and women in extra-parliamentary left-wing organizations began to boil over in the early to mid-1970s, as the influence of the growing women's movement led female members to challenge the sometimes sexist policies and behaviour of their male comrades, and to form their own sub-groups that excluded men.[39] Lia Migale recalls that, by the mid-1970s, ideological differences within the extreme-left organizations 'were far less important than divisions between men and women', divisions that began to cause 'incurable ruptures'. Indeed, tensions between men and women led, in some cases, to physical violence and to the collapse of entire organizations. In 1975, male members of Lotta Continua's *servizio d'ordine* physically attacked female members who were participating in a women-only march for abortion rights in Rome, an incident that was one of the key factors leading to the mass exodus of women from the organization in 1976.[40] Migale, who was among those attacked at the march, explains how she later challenged her male comrades to explain themselves:

> Well, I asked them, I said 'You've been working with me for a whole year, we've talked together every day, how did this idea ever get in your heads?'. And they responded, 'We don't know why we did it, we did it without thinking or really understanding.' And it was a huge... it was a moment of intense emotion. Now you can hardly believe that it ever happened. From that point onward, there was a period of intense emotion in Lotta Continua... The breakdown between men and women had become overwhelming.[41]

In their own separate feminist groups women overcame the way they felt gagged at male-dominated *gauchiste* meetings, and found a new language and a new set of

[38] Picq interview.
[39] Tensions between male and female members of extra-parliamentary left organizations were particularly notable in the Italian case. See Camilla Pozione, *Breve storia del movimento femminile in Italia* (Rome, 1978), 250–1, 283.
[40] On the violence that erupted between men and women in Lotta Continua, which led to the collapse of the organization, see Mariella Gramaglia, 'Affinità e conflitto con la nuova sinistra', *Memoria. Rivista di storia delle donne* 19–20 (1987) 19–37. Lia Migale herself has written a useful account of her experience in Lotta Continua: see the chapter by Migale in Giulietta Ascoli (ed.) *La parola elettorale. Viaggio nell'universo politico maschile* (Rome, 1976), 174–228.
[41] Migale interview.

tools for exploring their identity through consciousness-raising.[42] Many feminists use the terms *prise de parole/presa di parola*, 'speaking out' (literally, a seizing of words), to describe their discovery of the power of their own voices. Paola Mastrangeli (b. 1946), who was active in a Roman feminist collective, recalls the first time that she attended the collective's regular weekly meeting and experienced a consciousness-raising session first-hand:

> I listened to the others speak; they were speaking of the body, of orgasm, of...but with a sense of liberation and almost of abandon, of pleasure; it was almost erotic...There was...madness, creativity, gaiety, strength. And most importantly, my loneliness, my worries, that feeling I had of being...uncomfortable in situations, that sense that I couldn't find myself in history—it was gone! It was gone![43]

Women's separatism was not only a retreat into a women's haven, but could be assertive in its rejection of traditional female stereotypes. When women created their own segregated spaces, cut their hair, and abandoned make-up and feminine clothes, it was part of a liberating but also confrontational strategy. Karen Syberg of the Danish Redstockings recalls that there was an element of deliberate provocation in the ways in which members of her women-only commune dressed and acted:

> KS: Just our appearance. Three of us moved into the first women's commune, which we called 'cunt cave', also just to provoke people, you know. Vibeke Vasbo and someone named Lone Christensen and me. Going to the pub in the evening was like a sport for us. When the three of us traipsed in the door at the Drop Inn, there was total silence.
>
> AW: So you were looking for a fight?
>
> KS: Yes, one that we instigated. And if we sat down at a table across from a bunch of left-wing men, the conversation died instantly.
>
> AW: Did you think that they were afraid of you?
>
> KS: Yeah, they were. And they've even said so later. And that was also the point...emasculation.
>
> AW: That's how you saw it?
>
> KS: We studied psychoanalysis and stuff like that.
>
> AW: So you consciously worked out what you were going to say?
>
> KS: Our approach was deliberately provocative.

When some men responded aggressively, she saw this as 'a confirmation that what we did was right', although she remembers that 'there were also other nice leftist men' who thought it was 'quite all right'.

PERSONAL LIBERATION AND SEXUAL IDENTITY

The women's movement of course was not a unified bloc. It was divided between radicals, liberals and socialists, and between feminists who remained in heterosexual

---

[42] In Italy as elsewhere in Europe, women's groups readily adopted the practice of consciousness-raising, learned from their American counterparts, in the early 1970s. See Anna Rossi-Doria, 'Ipotesi per una storia che verrà', in Teresa Bertilotti and Anna Scattigno (eds), *Il femminismo degli anni Settanta* (Rome, 2005), 1–23.

[43] Interview with Paola Mastrangeli, conducted by RC, Rome, 25 November 2008.

relationships, and those who argued that separatism necessarily involved the rejection of sexual relations with men.[44] Significant among the latter in France was the Psychologie et Politique (Psych et Po) collective, which emerged from a women's study group at the University of Vincennes and was led by the charismatic Antoinette Fouque. The group considered that women were enslaved by a male symbolic order and must 'expel the penis from their heads'.[45] Françoise Picq, who endeavoured to keep the various strands of the women's liberation movement together through her 'Thursday group' of feminists, was opposed to the hegemonic pretensions of Psych et Po, and uses the same anti-Stalinist language to describe it as Maoists and Trotskyists had used against the mainstream Communist Party:

> Psych et Po became quite closed and adopted Stalinist tactics, with trials and purges. It defined itself against others by building a mythical image of feminism. That was the Stalinist side. We wanted to debate, to be able not to agree. We didn't want to just parrot, we didn't want purges, a compulsion to be a certain way, sectarianism, rules that couldn't be changed. For example, lesbianism was a must.[46]

Many feminist groups that started life as inclusive women-only collectives, where heterosexuals and lesbians were equally welcome, fragmented over time along lines of sexuality and sexual preference. The 'gay-straight split' within the women's movement grew out of developments in the US, but affected feminist groups in Europe deeply, sometimes ushering in their demise.[47] Julienne Travers (b. 1930) was among the founding members of Rome's largest feminist collective, the Movimento Femminista Romano, also known as the Pompeo Magno group because they met in a rented flat on via Pompeo Magno.[48] The group was known for welcoming both lesbian and heterosexual women, and its diversity and openness were its key strengths. However, after many years of working together, tensions began to develop between lesbians and straight women within the group, and the collective finally collapsed as its members turned on each other. The breakdown of what had been a fruitful, decade-long collective project was enormously painful for all involved:

> A lot of harrowing things happened in those years, that's why I say... the lovely things I remember and I feel wonderful about them, but the bad things are really bad and hard to think about. And also hard to think about because it's all over, it's all finished and it also finished off the feminist movement... It was a very gradual thing, somehow around '78, it began to sort of creep forward and it was like... 'there are women here who are lesbians and we are discriminated against inside Pompeo Magno'. This is a terrible accusation, because we were there just to do the exact opposite, you

---

[44] Kristina Schulz, 'The women's movement', in Martin Klimke and Joachim Scharloth (eds) *1968 in Europe* (Basingstoke, 2008), 281–93. On these divisions in the French case see Françoise Picq, *Libération des femmes. Les années mouvement* (Paris, 1993), 190–230; and Claire Duchen, *Feminism in France: From May '68 to Mitterrand* (London, 1986), 27–46.

[45] Antoinette Fouque, *Women: The Pioneer Front of Democracy* (Paris, 1995).

[46] On this conflict see the Association du Mouvement pour les luttes féministes, *Chronique d'une imposture. Du Mouvement de la Libération des Femmes à une marque commerciale* (Paris, 1981).

[47] On the tensions that emerged between lesbian and heterosexual women in the feminist movement in the mid-to-late 1970s, see Sara M. Evans, *Tidal Wave: How Women Changed America at Century's End* (New York, 2003), 122–3.

[48] On the history of the Pompeo Magno collective, see Centro di Documentazione del Movimento Femminista Romano, *Donnità. Cronache del movimento femminista romano* (Rome, 1976).

know?... Gradually, it was just like a snowball, it started very small and got bigger and bigger and finally it was like 'you think we're dirty', really heavy insults and... then the hostility got so bad that some women dropped out because they couldn't face it, you know. And I thought 'well, it just can't be true', and then finally I realized that it really was, the thing went too deep... After ten years [it collapsed]. Instead of having a lovely festival, you know, a party to celebrate... that's how it went.[49]

In Denmark, Birgitte Due progressed from the Redstocking Movement to the lesbian movement. She is adamant that she was still happy to associate with heterosexual feminists both personally and politically, but it was not easy. She felt torn by the continual conflicts between heterosexual and lesbian feminists and lost close friends:

> A megalomaniac notion simultaneously appeared that it might be best if the women's movement were lesbian, because women were together all the time, right, and a conflict arose with the Redstockings... Many heterosexuals felt that the lesbians were going to steal the show... We needed to define all the good things about being a lesbian... Being made invisible in the women's liberation movement, the fact that we were also lesbian was ignored; well, the movement was perceived as heterosexual. And among the lesbians who were there, many of them also thought that since we're women and we're fighting for women's liberation, and we're striving to give women the best opportunities possible, then maybe the best choice is to be a lesbian, because then we would be with women all the time... There was the same schism, no matter where I went in the political landscape. I was part of a powerful schism involving lesbians and feminism.[50]

After living for many years as a heterosexual and being politically active on the Danish left wing, Birthe Marker's (b. 1936) encounter with the new women's movement in 1970 led to a break with heterosexuality. She left her husband and children and became a guiding force of the Danish lesbian movement. Like the Gay Liberation Front, it differed from pre-existing homophile organizations dedicated to social equality, such as the Alliance of 1948, in that it linked sexual liberation to fundamental changes in society:[51]

> Those of us from the women's liberation movement had a different... we had nothing to do with gays, with the Alliance. We were feminists, lesbian feminists, we were not gay... Our stories were different. Our interests were different. We had no common interests. They were men, and we were women. It's crystal clear. Well, there are some people that can't understand it, which means we should look at it again, which is why I think that using the term queer is currently so predominant and why I see it as a defeat for the feminist movement's mindset today.[52]

In France, gay activism burst onto the scene with Guy Hocquenghem's FHAR. It claimed to be revolutionary, overthrowing in a very public and dramatic way generations of hostility to homosexuality.[53] Jean Le Bitoux (1948–2010), then a student in Nice, recalled reading the FHAR's manifesto in the twelfth edition of the magazine *Tout!*:

[49] Interview with Julienne Travers, conducted by RC, Rome, 3 December 2008.

[50] Due interview.

[51] On the Danish gay and lesbian movements, see Vibeke Nissen and Inge Lise Paulsen, 'Handling gi'r forvandling—klip af homobevægelsens historie i Danmark', *Lambda Nordica* 2–3 (2000).

[52] Interview with Birthe Marker, conducted by AW, Copenhagen, 22 November 2010.

[53] See Guy Hocquenghem, *Le Désir homosexuel* (Paris, 1972, 1977 & 2000) and his posthumous autobiography, *L'Amphithéâtre des morts* (Paris, 1994).

I discovered an incredible thing, a convergence of my revolutionary convictions and my secret. That is, the emergence or revolt of something as intimate as your sexual preferences which are not those of others... I discovered militant friendship. Until then I had not had sex, I did not even know how to masturbate. I think that I only just avoided psychiatric hospital or suicide... I began to piece together the bits of my political convictions and the story of my body.[54]

He nevertheless fell out with Guy Hocquenghem, who was lionized by an older generation of homosexual activists such as René Schérer, who had been his teacher at the École Normale Supérieure, over what Le Bitoux saw as his spectacular and self-seeking political style:

challenging social conventions, insolence, provocation. He was always close to the *grandes folles* of the FHAR. He was their idol. He was never my idol. He was an old cowboy. He did everything on his own, and made a personal career out of it. But something was missing. Not everyone was at the École des Beaux Arts screaming and having sex parties on the top floor.

Le Bitoux founded his own gay magazine *Gai pied* in 1979, and was indebted to Michel Foucault for the title, which plays with 'to have it away' (*prendre son pied*) as a gay, 'wasp's nest' (*guêpier*) and to 'take your pleasure from the wasp's nest'. Le Bitoux was disappointed that Foucault himself refused to have an interview with him declaring his homosexuality in the first issue, and regretted that Foucault never 'came out' as a homosexual himself, lest it undermine his claim to be a universal intellectual:

Six months before he had given me a long interview on homosexuality. That interview had a long history. At the last moment he telephoned me and said, 'No. If I come out too explicitly on the question of homosexuality, people will call me a homosexual philosopher. I will be ghettoized and only be allowed to talk about homosexuality'. I continue to think that he still has lots to say about that.

Daniel Defert (b. 1937), who was Foucault's partner for over twenty years, taught philosophy at the University of Vincennes and was a member of the GP. He echoes the point that while a minority of homosexuals were ready to campaign for gay rights, many saw the risks of being defined by their homosexuality:

The *Gai pied* people wanted him to write, 'Yes, I am gay', but Foucault hated that kind of declaration of identity. He always considered it to be a police interrogation question to which gays subscribed. He always said that you had to invent what gay means and not simply declare it... The idea of belonging to a group like the FHAR was against Foucault's ideas.[55]

[54] Interview with Jean Le Bitoux, conducted by RG, Paris, 10 April 2008. See also Le Bitoux's autobiography, *Citoyen de la Seconde Zone* (Paris, 2003); and Frédéric Martel, *Le Rose et le Noir. Les Homosexuels en France depuis 1968* (Paris, 2000), 27–58 and 185–94.
[55] Interview with Daniel Defert, conducted by RG, Paris, 17 April 2008. On Foucault's biography see David Macey, *The Lives of Michel Foucault* (London, 1993).

CONCLUSION

Perhaps more than any other set of issues opened up by 1968, issues of gender and sexuality illuminate the dramatic scope of the utopian projects of the period, as well as the magnitude of the rifts engendered by those projects. In experimenting with concepts of sexual and personal liberation, and in trying on a range of non-traditional gender roles, women and men opened up a world of possibilities for re-constructing their own lives and the lives of others around them. At the same time, however, these stories lay bare the difficult nature of such experiments. Women and men struggled, often in very different ways, with the complications and contradictions inherent in wedding the personal and political. For many women, whether or not they actively embraced feminism, the route to a political understanding of personal experience entailed a fundamental break with dominant discourses of femininity. For many men, integrating the intimate and private into their political understanding equally meant a break with received notions of masculinity.

At both the individual and the collective level, there were myriad stumbling blocks on this path. The project of 'liberation' could be at once emancipating and oppressive. The tension between the desire to change oneself and the hope of changing the world could be unsustainable, even destructive. Both women and men could feel marginalized or voiceless in groups dominated by well organized and highly articulate revolutionaries. As women and men pushed their experimentation with gender and sexual identities further, collective projects splintered and were sometimes torn apart. Male and female activists separated and violence between them was not unknown. For many former activists, it remains difficult to discuss these rifts.

Memory plays a powerful role here. The many ways in which these experiments echo down the years of an individual life are evident in these life history narratives. Interviewees' reflections on past struggles with gender issues are often the fruit of many decades of thoughtful consideration and reconsideration. Each stage in the life history allows the previous one to be reread and reinterpreted: through discovering a sense of belonging in the women's movement, for example, a speaker 'realizes' her own voicelessness in the student movement. The personal and collective discoveries made through experiments with gender and sexuality thus have powerful, long-term consequences for the speaker's own life story and for her or his sense of self, both then and in the present. In memory, the importance of the political projects of 1968 sometimes fades, but the importance of challenges to gender and sexual identities remains a vibrant thread that weaves through a speaker's life story, as compelling and relevant now as it was then.

10

Violence

Robert Gildea, Gudni Jóhannesson, Chris Reynolds
and Polymeris Voglis

Young people who became involved in radical activism around 1968 were often inspired by the role model of an idealized revolutionary. This revolutionary might be a Bolshevik of 1917, a fighter from the Spanish Civil War, a French or Greek resister, Italian partisan, Latin American guerrilla or Palestinian *fedayeen*. Struggles for liberation against colonialism and imperialism in the Third World in the 1960s conferred a certain exoticism on revolutionary violence. In 1968 the heroic model was the street-fighting man, hardened by conflict with police or right-wing groups, possibly wearing a motorcycle helmet, adept at throwing paving stones or Molotov cocktails. In the 1970s and 1980s, as student protests died down, a minority of revolutionaries with international connections took the road of 'armed struggle', planting bombs, kidnapping or even killing powerful individuals who represented multinational capitalism, imperialism or militarism. There was what sociologist Michel Wieviorka has called 'the rapid loss of legitimacy of violence'.[1] These revolutionaries lost the heroic aura and were regarded simply as terrorists. Activists who were involved in 1968 and subsequent events are keenly aware of the danger of being labelled as a terrorist, have placed distance between themselves and the idea of violence, or construed their violence in less threatening ways. Some activists, meanwhile, went to the other extreme and consciously adopted a quite different model, that of the non-violent revolutionary, taking as icons the likes of Gandhi or Martin Luther King. This might be both for strategic reasons, to retain control over an ongoing protest movement and to prevent violent elements breaking away, or in order to win the battle for the support of public opinion. The tension between these three kinds of violence and non-violence are very evident in activists' narratives.

'Strictly speaking', says Isabelle Sommier, 'there are no activist documents explicitly concerned with the legitimation of violence, as if recourse to violence was "natural" and obvious for every revolutionary'.[2] This of course is incorrect, as the

---

[1] Michel Wieviorka (ed.) *Violence en France* (Paris, 1999), 27.
[2] Isabelle Sommier, *La Violence politique et son deuil. L'après 68 en France et en Italie* (Rennes, 2008), 53.

writings of Ulrike Meinhof for one attest.[3] For our purposes, the oral testimony of activists also contains a great deal of soul-searching about the legitimacy of violence, an issue that has haunted activists for the past forty years. Protest and revolution might imply recourse to violence, but it has also left a legacy of guilt. Therefore activists navigate this issue sometimes imaginatively, sometimes with difficulty, defending some manifestations of violence and distancing themselves from others. They may argue that some violence was purely rhetorical or symbolic, to achieve status or headlines, rather than real, involving casualties. They may justify the destruction of property while disqualifying violence against individuals as terrorism. They may seek to legitimize violence in terms of the historical analogy of resistance to oppression or struggles for liberation, or by linking it to the *Zeitgeist* of the 1960s or 1970s.

The activists and networks for this chapter are not drawn from the core European countries of Italy and West Germany, which engendered the Red Brigades and Red Army Faction and about which a great deal has been written.[4] They are drawn instead from France and the European periphery: from democratic Iceland and Northern Ireland to dictatorial Spain and Greece.[5] The first section explores tensions in the construction of competing role models by and for activists—as the idealized revolutionary, the terrorist and the non-violent campaigner—and touches on the gendering of role models. A second section introduces a comparative element and asks whether activists found it easier to defend violence in parts of Europe living under dictatorship than in those living under democracies. It asks whether national boundaries mattered, and how activists in countries that had very different experiences of left-wing violence explained the different choices they made. A final section explores divisions between activists in the same country over violent and non-violent tactics that are brought to consciousness when former activists recall these debates in the present.

---

[3] Sarah Colvin, *Ulrike Meinhof and West German Terrorism: Language, Violence, and Identity* (Rochester and New York, 2009).

[4] See for example Donatella della Porta, *Social Movements, Political Violence and the State. A Comparative Analysis of Italy and Germany* (Cambridge, 1995); Jeremy Varon, *Bringing the War Home: The Weather Underground, The Red Army Faction and Revolutionary Violence in the 60s and 70s* (Berkeley, 2004); Sarah Colvin, *Ulrike Meinhof and West German Terrorism*; David Crawford, review of Wolfgang Kraushaas (ed.) 'Die RAF und der linke Terrorismus', *Journal of Cold War Studies* 9/4 (2007), 160–4; Raimondo Cantanzaro (ed.) *The Red Brigades and Left-Wing Terrorism in Italy* (London, 1991); Martha Crenshaw, *Terrorism in Context* (University Park, PA, 1995); Holger Nehring, 'The era of non-violence: "Terrorism" in West German, Italian and French political culture, 1968–1982', *European Review of History* 14/3 (2007), 343–71; David Moss, *The Politics of Left Wing Violence in Italy, 1969–1985* (New York, 1989); Peter Katzenstein, *Left-Wing Violence and State Response: United States, Germany, Italy and Japan, 1960s–1990s* (Cornell, 1998).

[5] For France see Sommier, *La Violence politique et son deuil* and Wieviorka, *Violence en France*. For Iceland, see Gestur Gudmundsson and Kristín Ólafsdóttir, *68. Hugarflug úr vidjum vanans* (Reykjavík, 1987); Leifur Reynisson, 'Ímyndunarraflid til valda. Barátta 68-kynslódarinnar fyrir betri heimi', *Sagnir* 19 (1998), 60–9; Gudni Jóhannesson, *Óvinir ríkisins. Ógnir og innra öryggi í kalda strídinu á Íslandi* (Reykjavík, 2006); Ólafur Ormsson, *Byltingarmenn og bóhemar* (Reykjavík, 2009). For Northern Ireland, see Henry Patterson, *Ireland since 1939. The Persistence of Conflict* (Dublin, 2006); Alan O'Day (ed.) *Political Violence in Northern Ireland: Conflict and Conflict Resolution* (London, 1997); W.H. Van Voris, *Violence in Ulster. An Oral Documentary* (Massachusetts, 1975). For Greece, see Mary Bosi, *Ellada kai tromokratia. Ethnikes kai diethneis diastaseis* (Athens, 1996); and George Kasimeris, *Europe's Last Red Terrorists. The Revolutionary Organisation 17 November* (London, 2000).

CONFLICTING ROLE MODELS FOR ACTIVISTS

The idealized revolutionary who stood as a role model for activists of 1968 embodied the violence of the barricade fighter or guerrilla. This revolutionary might be a Communard of 1871, a Bolshevik of 1917, a republican of the Spanish Civil War, a French Resistance fighter, a Red Guard of the Chinese Cultural Revolution or a Latin American guerrilla hero. The cult of heroes was highly gendered, and female activists tended to have a preference for leaders of social movements such as labour activists, whose effect depended on popular pressure such as strike action rather than armed struggle. The historical dimension was also important: the appeal of contemporary figures such as Che Guevara might be counterbalanced by other figures and moments that are firmly located in a revolutionary tradition that confers legitimacy.

Romain Goupil (b. 1951), a young Trotskyist and one of the organizers of the CAL in Paris, claims a long revolutionary heritage for the revolt of high-school students against the Vietnam War and the repressive school system:

> We were the heirs of eternal revolt and we did not understand why our parents had stopped. We wanted to have a revolution as it happened in Russia. We were the direct heirs of 1917...We built barricades as if we had always built barricades. As if we were in 1830, 1848, 1871, 1968. The only thing to do was to build barricades, that was it. We all saw ourselves as insurgents.[6]

Female activists had a rather different litany of role models, women who advocated social movements and social transformation rather than revolutionary violence. Prisca Bachelet (b. 1940) was inspired by Rosa Luxemburg's emphasis on the mass strike,[7] while Annette Lévy-Willard, who broke with VLR over the question of violence, was inspired by the American anarchist Emma Goldman: 'She was like my grandmother...An anarchist, Jewish, who was interested in contraception. A formidable story and life'.[8]

Greek activist Anna Filini was enthusiastic about Che Guevara as a Third World thinker. Unfortunately what her counterparts wanted from Che was his legitimation of clandestine violent action, and this was a cause of rupture between them:

> I very much liked Che Guevara's speeches. In Algiers he had given a very good talk on the economic development of the Third World. I believed that his thought was very broad...The groups I had contact with also fastened on Che's model, but believed that groups in Greece should act in a completely military and clandestine way. When I realized this, I was scared, I didn't want it, so I broke away.[9]

[6] Interview with Romain Goupil, conducted by RG, Paris, 24 May 2007.
[7] See Chapter 4.
[8] Interview with Annette Lévy-Willard, conducted by RG, Paris, 6 June 2007. See also Annette Lévy-Willard and Cathy Bernheim, *L'Epopée d'une anarchiste* (Paris, 1979), a translation and adaptation of Emma Goldman's *Living my Life*.
[9] Interview with Anna Filini, conducted by PV, Athens, 29 February 2008.

Barricade-fighting and mass movements were one thing; deliberate and planned revolutionary violence was another. Some historians talk about the 'decomposition of *gauchisme*', the shift from 'years of hope' to 'days of rage', or from 'days of dreams' to 'days of lead'.[10] Activists who flirted with violence after 1968 when the struggle against the state became more intense are aware of the need to justify their actions. Olivier Rolin (b. 1947) who headed the Nouvelle Résistance Populaire (NRP)—the military wing of the Maoist GP—is keen to call their strategy one of 'illegalism rather than violence'. In addition he explains that their task was not to undertake violence themselves but to reawaken class consciousness among the masses who had gone back to work after 1968 and to encourage *them* to revolt:

> My role in the division of labour, after '68, when the Gauche Prolétarienne existed, my role was to be a kind of... I have to return to a point of doctrine, if I may... The task of the Gauche Prolétarienne was a kind of pedagogy of illegalism. We thought that the springs of illegality, of war, of guerrilla action were in the heart of the masses, but they had rusted... We had to awaken their courage and audacity to overthrow bourgeois law. Illegalism rather than violence.[11]

The defence of violence is much more difficult for Jean-Marc Rouillan (b. 1952), whose activist career took him in the 1980s to Action Directe, which was held responsible for the assassinations of arms exporter General Audran and Renault boss Georges Besse, and who has been in prison since 1987.[12] He confidently uses the term 'armed struggle' rather than 'illegalism' and argues that at the time it was an integral part of the revolutionary process from the US to the Middle East. He regrets that in contemporary France hostility to violence as terror has been focussed onto the Action Directe 'gang of four' who have been demonized by the media and politicians, even by repentant revolutionaries who draw a firm line between what they were doing as heirs of 1968 and what Rouillan himself did, which they say had nothing to do with the spirit of 1968:

> Armed struggle was part and parcel of the revolutionary movement. We talked about the Black Panthers or the Weathermen in the United States, or about other movements like the Palestinians or the phenomenon of guerrilla war, and found it quite natural. But I understand the media and political importance of four prisoners like us, and how the whole story of 1968 has been rewritten around our trial. We have been seen as an aberration, that we had come afterwards, that we had never been part of the *gauchiste* movement... Action Directe was four people who killed for no apparent reason, or rather because they were evil. It was in their blood. In Germany they were called psychopaths, a handful of psychopaths.[13]

---

[10] Wieviorka, *Violence en France*, 24; Todd Gitlin, *The Sixties: Years of Hope, Days of Rage* (New York, 1987); Hervé Hamon and Patrick Rotman, *Génération I. Les Années de Rêve. II. Les Années de Poudre* (Paris, 1987–8).

[11] Interview with Olivier Rolin, conducted by RG, Paris, 4 May 2007. See also the arguments he advances in Antoine Liniers [pseudonym] 'Objections contre une prise d'armes', in François Furet, Antoine Liniers and Philippe Raynaud, *Terrorisme et Démocratie* (Paris, 1985), 137–224.

[12] On Action Directe see Alain Hamon and Jean-Charles Marchand, *Action Directe. Du Terrorisme français à l'Euroterrorisme* (Paris, 1986); and Roland Jacquard, *La Longue Traque d'Action Directe* (Paris, 1987).

[13] Interview with Jean-Marc Rouillan, conducted by RG, Marseille, 17 April 2008. 'They' refers to the German Red Army Faction whose violence was used to demoralize Action Directe by association.

Another place where debates about models of political resistance were very intense was Northern Ireland. Activists in the civil rights movement of the 1960s and in the student-based People's Democracy (PD), which emerged in 1968, are acutely aware of the overshadowing of 1960s-style protest by the onset 'The Troubles'— the long war between republican and loyalist paramilitaries and the British state— and about their possible responsibility for this. Austin Currie (b. 1939), a Catholic deeply involved in the Civil Rights Association, wonders whether he would have become an activist if he could have anticipated the decisions and events that led to those Troubles:

> I asked myself that question. I do ask myself the question that had I known in '68 that actions I was going to take could lead to directly or indirectly to 3000 people losing their lives, would I have gone ahead? And of course the answer is no, I wouldn't have. But then how was I to know? And I mean, what happened was as a result of hundreds maybe thousands of people taking individual decisions as to what they were going to do etc. But I don't think anyone asked the question. If you'd known so many people were going to lose their lives, one would say no, I'd think. Certainly I would say I would reconsider it.[14]

To insulate themselves from later accusations of culpability, activists of the Civil Rights Association lay claim to the legitimacy of non-violence. They argue that they were linked to a different tradition, inspired less by 1968 in Paris and Prague than by both the American civil rights campaign and the non-violent campaigns of Gandhi. As Ivan Cooper (b. 1944) explains:

> We saw the impact of Gandhi and we saw the impact of Martin Luther King and this non-violent approach and that's precisely the reason why we adopted that stance...I remember we particularly studied what had happened in Prague and what had happened in France and Germany as well, but as regards major influence, the major influence was Martin Luther King and Gandhi. The whole theme of non-violence was a major factor for the Derry citizens' action committee...Not European, it felt linked to the whole thing in the American civil rights movement.[15]

The fact that violence was not avoided is explained by many former Northern Ireland activists in terms of the logic of the sectarian divide between Catholic Nationalist and Protestant Unionist, and in particular by the repressive nature of the British state, whose pretence to democratic governance seemed to be laid aside in the Irish context.

Bernadette McAliskey, née Devlin (b. 1947), placed the blame for the descent into violence squarely at the door of the British state. After the repression meted out to Catholic Nationalists by the British on Bloody Sunday 1972, she says that it no longer made sense to argue for non-violence. Although she herself had not been involved in any killing she had supported the republican war and therefore ran the risk of being 'mistaken as an apologist for terrorism':

---

[14] Interview with Austin Currie, conducted by CR, Maynooth, 16 February 2010. See also Austin Currie, *All Hell will Break Loose* (Dublin, 2004).
[15] Interview with Ivan Cooper, conducted by CR, Derry, 15 May 2009.

I think up until '72 and Bloody Sunday was I think where my trajectory was set in stone... I'm not saying I was right or wrong, I'm saying that that trajectory for me was set on Bloody Sunday. I took a conscious decision... I have never killed somebody and I have never been a party to actively setting somebody up. I think we all have been a party to the war in whatever way you look at it but I consciously set off the table an argument against and any attempt to ideologically argue against taking up arms against the state from '72... People would say then you became an apologist for terrorism, I would argue against that but the fact that I would be considered or mistaken as an apologist for terrorism was the least of my worries and that is a big shift.[16]

In France, the descent into extreme violence was largely avoided except in the case of Action Directe, and the violence of organizations such as the GP diminished rather than increased in the early 1970s. One reason for this was the challenge and relative success of non-violent popular movements such as the Lip factory strike of 1973–4 in Besançon and the struggle of activists against the extension of a military base on the Larzac plateau on the Massif Central. On the Larzac, non-violence was developed as a rationale and strategy both by the local sheep farmers whose lands were threatened by the army and by outside activists, many of whom had a history of conscientious objection to military service. A history of opposition to the Algerian War brought together religious figures with those who had been liable for military service during that dirty war. Robert Siméon (b. 1941), a Paris typesetter of communist persuasion, was imprisoned in 1962–3 for refusing to serve in the Algerian War, and joined a group called Non-Violent Civic Action. Through this he met Lanza del Vasto, a former disciple of Gandhi, who headed the ashram-like Arche community, a few miles to the south of the Larzac. Coming to the nearby Causses as a shepherd, Siméon linked Lanza and the Larzac farmers:

I knew the Arche community because Non-Violent Civic Action had campaigned against house arrest orders during the Algerian War and had helped draft-dodgers to organize. I went to see them from time to time... The Arche community was founded by Lanza del Vasto. He wanted to promote the teaching of Mahatma Gandhi in the West, in some way... We organized the first demonstration on 9 May 1971. It was joined by the Arche community, peasant activists from around here, political militants and ecologists, although they weren't called that at the time.[17]

Two of those peasant activists were sheep farmers Pierre (b. 1943) and Christiane (b. 1946) Burguière, who describe the two-week fast led at Easter 1972 by Lanza del Vasto among the sheep farmers of the Larzac plateau to convert them to the doctrine and practice of non-violence:

[16] Interview with Bernadette McAliskey, conducted by CR, Dungannon, 18 July 2008. See also Bernadette Devlin, *The Price of my Soul* (London, 1969).
[17] Interview with Robert Siméon and Brigitte Cadot Siméon, conducted by RG, Millau, 20 May 2008.

CB: He conquered us straight away, because we finally felt sustained by someone. He was like a beacon, because we were completely in the dark and he showed us what to do...He said, 'It is up to you to find forms of action that are attractive to public opinion, try to widen your campaign through the support of public opinion'.

PB: He said this to us, 'As far as violence goes, you don't have any weapons, and you will find yourselves confronted by a power that will crush you'. Very quickly we found that non-violence was an extraordinary defensive strategy.[18]

The heroic model of the revolutionary that was so current in 1968 was thus marginalized by the descent into terrorism and civil war. Some activists escape this by laying claim to the discourse and practice of non-violence. Others, however, who clearly engaged in violent activities at the time but who later returned to the political mainstream, have developed euphemistic strategies for talking about the violence in which they did engage.

JUSTIFYING POLITICAL VIOLENCE

Activists who saw themselves in the late 1960s as revolutionaries have subsequently been torn between the model of the idealized revolutionary—the guerrilla or street fighter—and the fear of being demonized as a terrorist. The influential sociologist Michel Wieviorka has argued that 'terrorism is an extreme, decomposed and very particular form of anti-social movement'. Whereas a social movement involves the masses and has some kind of utopian ideal, terrorism, he argues, engages only the self and has no utopian ideal, only 'fanatical purity'.[19] In the years since their activism, the legitimacy of violence practised by any other actor than the state has diminished further, and hence they are now pressured to make sense of their former attachment to violence in new ways. On the one hand they boast about the violent actions in which they were involved in order to raise their status as revolutionaries, and to distinguish themselves from despised politicians. On the other hand they distance themselves from any potential accusation that they inflicted harm on individuals. They distinguish between violence against people, which may not be legitimate, and violence against things, which is. They also distinguish between symbolic violence, which is theatrical and has a propaganda function, and real physical violence. Lastly, they often explain violence in terms of a relationship to a historic past or to the violence of the contemporary context.

Talking about violence serves a rhetorical function, to distinguish revolutionaries as such from conventional parties of the left committed to the ballot box. In Greece the question of the revolution and the violent overthrow of the established political elites was considered by the extreme left as a major demarcation line between itself and the old left of the Communist Party and the EDA, who were accused of accommodation with the status quo. In the mid-1960s Antonis

---

[18] Interview with Pierre and Christiane Burguière, conducted by RG, Le Camper du Larzac, 22 May 2008.

[19] Michel Wieviorka, *Sociétés et Terrorisme* (Paris, 1988), 17–22.

Sotirakos (b. 1946) chose to join a Trotskyist group rather than the established left (EDA) on ideological grounds:

> What did I like more [in the Trotskyists]? The EDA were damned pen-pushers, you couldn't stand them. You follow me? We wanted to change the society... The confrontation was rather ideological. We raised questions about the transformation and the overthrow of the state. At that time the EDA believed in the principle of the peaceful transition to socialism. The confrontation was around this question. We wanted the revolution here and now. Perhaps some may still want it. [laughs][20]

Similarly, economics student Jean Bijaoui (b. 1946) explains that an attack on the right-wing exhibition in Paris promoting the USA's role in Vietnam in April 1968 was also a way of drawing a line between the *gauchistes* and the conventional left, in particular the French Communist Party, which many leftists blamed for not squarely supporting the 1968 protest movement of which it was not in control:[21]

> You have to put that back in context. At the time that kind of [violent] action had been completely forgotten on the left, among the progressive forces, and had been confiscated by fascists. Smashing things up, getting into fights, that happened in the '30s but no longer. The French Communist Party never did things like that, except within their own organization, against the *gauchistes*, they knew how to do that. With our feeble means we tried to get that kind of action back onto the agenda. It was difficult, we were starting from zero.[22]

While wanting to portray themselves as revolutionaries, activists often deploy the idea of symbolic violence, which is contrasted with real physical violence. Symbolic violence is visual and theatrical, designed to expose hidden oppressions in society, to subvert and caricature existing hierarchies, to break with the blind routine of everyday life, or to sharpen class consciousness. It is a way of communicating their revolutionary cause to the media and the public. Even if the violence is real, activists still continue to defend it as a media exercise.

In the summer of 1969 a few members of Æskulýdsfylkingin, an Icelandic Marxist-Leninist youth brigade that had broken from the socialist People's Alliance, tried to blow up an abandoned barracks on one of the US bases that stood on Icelandic soil. Although their homemade time bomb failed to detonate, the attempt received considerable attention in the national press. Two years later, the Icelandic police discovered that five members of the brigade had stolen dynamite tubes and planned either to kidnap the American ambassador to Iceland or to blow up some installations at the US base at Keflavík or a Swiss-owned aluminium smelter nearby. The group was arrested before the dynamite was used but news of the theft and descriptions of 'terrorist' intentions made the national headlines.[23]

---

[20] Interview with Antonis Sotirakos, conducted by PV, Athens, 12 May 2009.
[21] On the PCF and 1968 see André Barjonet, *La Révolution trahie* (Paris, 1968) and Danielle Tartakowsky, 'Le PCF en mai–juin 1968', in René Mouriaux, Annick Percheron, Antoine Prost and Danielle Tartakowsky (eds) *1968: Exploration du mai français. II Acteurs* (Paris, 1992), 141–63.
[22] Interview with Jean Bijaoui, conducted by RG, Paris, 10 April 2008.
[23] Gudni Jóhannesson, *Óvinir ríkisins*, 251–62, 281–5.

Since the dynamite had been stolen in the small town of Kópavogur, the radical group was mockingly branded 'Kópamaros' after the legendary Tupamaros guerrillas in Uruguay. Some of the 'Kópamaros' group probably delighted in being compared to the Tupamaros. One of them later recalled that the comrade who persuaded him to take part in the operation had taunted him by saying, 'Do you just want to be a "café-commie?"'. The same activist nevertheless made clear that the group would never have carried out the 'empty talk' of kidnappings or explosions, and that they had engaged in symbolic violence that had only propaganda value.[24] Birna Thórdardóttir (b. 1949), a former activist of the Brigade, says that 'terrorism' was not on their agenda:

> No, that wasn't our scene. But we talked quite a bit about this... because the means has a great bearing on the ends... That was our decision at any rate, the decision of the majority—that the ends don't justify the means. It isn't like that. Let's say we had intended to kill some company director or bank director, to kill him to set an example that this professional class should be wiped out or something, someone who behaves like that. I say and said 'no' because that would turn us into the sort of people who can never accomplish anything good.[25]

Even in Greece, where military dictatorship was a reality, the Elliniko Dimokratiko Kinima group planted bombs in power distributors and in front of buildings but claimed that they did not target individuals, even when these belonged to the repressive apparatus of the military dictatorship, such as the army and the police. Dimosthenis Dodos (b. 1948), a member of that group, explains the thinking behind the bomb they set off on 22 December 1968:

> There was a plan to select targets that did not risk human lives... In the gendarmerie-school headquarters in Makrygianni [in Athens] there was a sentry. We opened a hole in the thick wall, it was so thick that we put the 'package' forty to sixty centimeters inside the wall and six to seven meters away from the sentry. Nobody was hurt, not even the sentry was injured or anything. We had decided that we will not harm people, that we take all precautions so that no one would get hurt, and that decision shaped our turn to 'dynamic', so to speak, actions.[26]

Bombs were described by activists as a form of 'armed propaganda'. As such, it was felt to have more impact on the media than tracts or clandestine newspapers. A leaflet against the dictatorship would go unnoticed by the press, whereas even a small bomb would attract the attention of the media, especially the foreign press that was hostile to the dictatorship. Dimosthenis Dodos continues:

> These [bombs] triggered... a climate that was created by the [media] stations. The foreign press wrote 'Explosions in Athens! Explosions in Athens', and generally speaking it was much more effective in creating the image that something went wrong in

[24] Interview with an anonymous member of the Socialist Youth Brigade and 'Kópamaros'.
[25] Interview with Birna Thórdardóttir, conducted by GJ and K. Björnsson, Reykjavík, 16 August 2008.
[26] Interview with Dimosthenis Dodos, conducted by PV, Thessaloniki, 23 June 2008. For the activities of the Elliniko Dimokratiko Kinima and Dimosthenis Dodos see Vasilis Filias, *Ta axehasta kai ta lismonimena* (Athens, 1997), 171–5.

Athens. I have to say that the journalists themselves, the foreign correspondents, more or less backed the whole story. For instance they reported two bombs, when in reality there were two petrol-filled bottles. Thus, the step from the paper, the hand-out, to something that will make more noise was easier, simpler. Generally, it was considered to be more productive, more effective than anything else.[27]

In France, similarly, activists are on the one hand keen to claim revolutionary credentials but on the other they wish to avoid the accusation that, like terrorists, they put human lives at risk. Bernard (b. 1946) and Anne (b. 1949) Victorri enter into a conversation about their revolutionary past that sets up a tension between their claims of revolutionary bravado and their desire to minimize the significance of violence. After the collapse of the strike wave of 1968 Anne and Bernard joined the Maoist GP and became involved in campaigns to rekindle revolution among the industrial workers of northern France. Following the deaths of sixteen miners in a fire-damp explosion on the northern French coalfield in December 1970, a GP commando launched an attack on the offices of the mining company that they held to be criminally responsible for the deaths. Bernard begins by boasting of his violent actions but Anne insists that they were purely symbolic and Bernard himself then concedes that the violence used was minimal in both its intention and its effects:

BV: We threw Molotov cocktails at the mining company offices at Henin-les-Tars... We undertook more and more violent actions. On one occasion I was at Roubaix—as I was one of the leaders in the Nord I always had to be in the front line in all the actions.

AV: They were spectacular actions, not violent actions, you see. We weren't in Italy. They were symbolic actions, very symbolic, like throwing paint pots over those female supervisors.

RG: But what about the Molotov cocktails?

BV: It's the only one we threw. It didn't set fire to much, although it could have set fire to the mine... We never...

AV: Took the risk of killing.

BV: Or even of seriously injuring anyone. For example in the coal mines it was an attack, arson, which could have killed people. But we went to check the place out, to be sure that nobody was there—not even a tramp—in the company offices. We took lots of risks to be sure that the fire, which we would have liked to be more spectacular, only burned a bit of parquet flooring.[28]

Extreme actions might also be legitimated by reference to the ambient climate of violence in the 1960s and 1970s, or by comparison to previous historic resistance to oppression, including foreign occupation, which had previously resulted in liberation and was therefore defensible.

In Greece, one of the arguments of activists who took to violence was that it was simply part of the contemporary climate, not least in the lead-up to the military coup in 1967. Antonis Sotirakos (b. 1946), a student at the Business School, says that the atmosphere at universities in 1966 was 'very violent' because of the

---

[27] Dodos interview.
[28] Interview with Anne and Bernard Victorri, conducted by RG, Paris, 28 May 2007. See also Chapter 4 109, 120, 126–7.

imminence of a *coup d'état* and the aggression of extreme-right students. In his own school:

> AS: There were *mêlées*, and I mean really a lot of beating. I remember once, it was a little before the dictatorship, there was a student assembly, it must have been in the Alhambra theatre. The theatre was completely ruined, nothing was left. Even the returning officer who was there to supervize the assembly was beaten.
>
> PV: Why is this? How do you explain the violence of the confrontation at the time?
>
> AS: There isn't…such were the times then. I mean, the left was rising, and the right wouldn't let you rise. When I was a student the things were at that point, on that threshold.[29]

In the 1960s Greek activists used historical analogies such as the Greek Revolution or resistance against German occupation in order to legitimate their struggles to bring about revolutionary change in Greece.[30] Their goal was not just to overthrow the dictatorship and restore parliamentary democracy, but to set a revolution in motion. Interestingly, activists interviewed much later rarely seek to establish the legitimacy of their actions in the revolutions of the revolutionary past but talk only about overthrowing the dictatorship. While it is acceptable to speak of some traditions of violence, such as resistance to German occupation in the Second World War and struggles for national independence, in other cases the spectre of terrorism has evacuated the revolutionary imagination.

Reference to resistance to German occupation and Nazi persecution has widely been seen by 1968 activists to confer legitimacy on their struggles. While De Gaulle, the man of 18 June 1940, remained in power, it was difficult for activists to invoke the Resistance against him, but after his fall in 1969, and as state repression increased, activists argued that their struggles were completing the wartime work of the Resistance, and former heroes of the Resistance mobilized to defend them. Jean-Pierre Le Dantec, editor of GP's paper, *La Cause du Peuple*, who was tried and sent to prison in 1970 for inciting violence, explains how they were continuing the unfinished work of the French Resistance:

> Our thought at the time was that we were a new resistance. The process of resistance had never been completed in France. After the end of the war the forced alliance of Gaullists and communists had frozen issues, consigned them to the cupboard. The police had never been properly de-Petainised.[31]

Charles Tillon, wartime leader of the Francs Tireurs et Partisans, wrote to Le Dantec's father: 'Emotion overcomes me when I think of your son who has taken up my fight in a world where everything is more difficult…great things belong to his generation'.[32] After he left prison and decided on a more open and democratic struggle Le Dantec met Maurice Clavel (1920–79), the so-called 'liberator of Chartres cathedral', and together they laid a wreath at the Monument to the Resistance at Mont Valérien on 18 June 1971.

---

[29] Interview with Antonis Sotirakos, conducted by PV, Athens, 12 May 2009.
[30] See Chapter 3.
[31] Interview with Jean-Pierre Le Dantec, conducted by RG, Paris, 24 April 2007. See also his memoir, *Les Dangers du Soleil* (Paris, 1978).
[32] Le Dantec interview. Sciences Po, Centre d'Histoire, fonds Tillon, Tillon to Denis Le Dantec, n.d. [October 1970].

Jean-Marc Rouillan, who went down the road to terrorism that the GP pulled back from, related 'the very powerful mythology of resistance we got from all those films about clandestine operations'. That said, growing up in Toulouse, he was more impressed by stories of the contribution of those Spanish republican exiles who fled to France after defeat in the Civil War, and continued their struggles against the Franco regime:

> There were a lot of Spanish exiles in Toulouse, which was the capital of the govern-ment in exile until '46–'47... Besides, Toulouse was liberated by Spanish guerrillas in '44 and most of the *maquis* in the region were made up of Spaniards or veterans of the International Brigades who had been held in concentration camps along the fron-tier... The people I looked to and admired were old Spanish guerrillas who refused to surrender and remained guerrillas till the end.[33]

Changing tack, Rouillan also argues that the violence of Action Directe germi-nated not only as a continuation of the Spanish Civil War but also in an atmos-phere in which even the rock music was violent. Explaining that his first encounter with the police was his arrest at the Isle of Wight festival in 1970 for carrying dope and fighting Hell's Angels he says:

> I was very much influenced, not by American music but the music of Swinging London. I was really keen on making music, the electric guitar. The more I think back on that time, and see the videos, I feel a violence contained in old pieces by Van Mor-rison or the Yardbirds. A violence which exploded in '68. When you listen to *My Generation* by the Who there are some very aggressive words and you sense that this generation is going to cause problems.[34]

Rouillan's purpose here is to contest the argument of many former activists, in-cluding those of the GP, that Action Directe were the 'monstruous children' of 1968, were too young to participate in the cultural movement of '68 and did not understand the passion for liberation on all fronts.[35] Here, by contrast, he is keen to demonstrate that Action Directe emerged from the mainstream of 1968 and was part of its legacy.

Whereas French radicals attracted to violence remembered the role of the resist-ance to German occupation in the Second World War and Spanish resistance to Franco, in Northern Ireland there was a tension between civil rights activists seek-ing a democratic way forward and revolutionary activists who were prepared to use violence. Civil rights activists deliberately avoided making reference to the ghosts of violent struggle in their history, which they hoped would not be awoken through their activism. The Irish revolutionary past seemed both too close and too painful. Instead they sought legitimacy from more peaceful periods of national struggle. Paul Bew (b. 1950), a member of People's Democracy, looked hopefully to a new

---

[33] Interview with Jean-Marc Rouillan, recorded by RG, Marseille, 17 April 2008. See also his mem-oirs, Jean-Marc Rouillan, *De Mémoire (1). Les Jours du début: Un automne 1970 à Toulouse* (Marseille, 2007) and *De Mémoire (2). Le Deuil de l'innocence: Un jour de septembre 1973 à Barcelone* (Marseille, 2009).
[34] Rouillan interview.
[35] Sommier, *La Violence politique et son deuil*, 195–6.

version of the Springtime of Peoples in 1848 or to a utopian socialism antedating its corruption by the Bolshevik Revolution and Soviet communism:

> Well, I mean, in '68 I thought this was fantastic. Look I thought this was another 1848 or whatever coming all over again—rebirth of the European revolutionary tradition and basically what I believed was, alright we had the Russian revolution but the idea of socialism had been as it were stymied by the idea, concept of Stalinism, that it was possible, you know…We all believed this: we all believed that as it was an unfortunate path that socialism had been pushed down into by the Russian Revolution. We were now re-emerging and there were new historic opportunities in place. It was a fairly spectacular delusion.[36]

Austin Currie described how he used the historical parallel of the 'New Departure' in the late nineteenth century, when constitutionalists and revolutionary Fenians came together in a united front on the Irish question, as a means to legitimate the non-violent approach in 1968:

> I had seen a certain historical precedent…In the 1880s what was described as the New Departure was the relation to the Irish Parliamentary Party, the Fenian brotherhood and the Land League [that] had come together in what was described—it didn't last that long—was described as the New Departure. Well in two speeches in Armagh in 1967 I had referred to the necessity for a new, an updated 'new departure'. So I was conscious of the necessity of trying to maintain a mass movement but at the same time make it quite radical.[37]

That said, Paul Arthur (b. 1945), another key member of PD, recalled that violence was a curse of Irish history and that though it might be repressed for a time, it would inevitably return. He relates the unheeded advice of Irish academic, writer and politician Conor Cruise O'Brien (1917–2008) about the 'frozen violence' under the surface of Irish history:

> I recall Conor Cruise O'Brien coming to Belfast and giving a lecture and he advised us very strongly against getting involved in direct action. And he said that you know, you may well consider yourself to be non-sectarian but what you have to remember is that sectarianism is just beneath the surface, that what we have in Northern Ireland is what he called a form of frozen violence and that could break out anytime into real violence and that what started as a non-sectarian movement would drift in the sectarian direction. And in all of that he was absolutely correct but we didn't see it that way.[38]

INTERNAL DEBATES ABOUT VIOLENCE

The narratives of activists rehearse not only their arguments legitimating violence, but they also describe moments in the past when activist comrades clearly

[36] Interview with Paul Bew, conducted by CR, Belfast, 13 February 2009. See also Paul Bew, *Ireland: The Politics of Enmity 1789–2006* (Oxford, 2009).
[37] Currie interview.
[38] Interview with Paul Arthur, conducted by CR, Bangor NI, 13 February 2009. See also Paul Arthur, *The People's Democracy 1968–73* (Belfast, 1974).

disagreed over the use of violence. There is a comparative dimension here: the justification of violence was easier for activists who were living under dictatorship, while for those in democracies it was less defensible. Some activists insist on a national exceptionalism, so that French activists, for example, are keen to point out that they did not go down the same path to terrorism as West German or Italian activists. Interviews can nevertheless replay conflicts between activists in the same country and even the same organization, who came into conflict over violence, and the account still reveals the intensity of feeling and sense of betrayal experienced at the time.

In Iceland, while the majority of the Æskulýdsfylkingin brigade members disliked or ridiculed all ideas about 'terrorist' actions on home soil, they nevertheless argued that elsewhere conditions might call for such efforts in the class struggle. Thus the brigade supported resistance to the Greek military dictatorship, establishing contacts with political exiles from Greece, and resistance to the Franco dictatorship. Erlingur Hansson (b. 1950) a long-serving member of the brigade, opposed violence in Iceland but argued that it was 'understandable that those who were opposed to the government in Spain would resort to such extreme measures'.[39] Similarly, some brigade members defended the motives of the Red Brigade in Italy and the Baader-Meinhof group in West Germany. The artist and activist Róska (Ragnhildur Óskarsdóttir) lived for extended periods in Italy with her Italian husband and was a member of the Lotta Continua. When she was in Iceland in the early 1970s and took part in debates within the brigade, comrades such as Vernhardur Linnet (b. 1944) later recalled that she was 'extensively trained out there in the wildest left and anarchism in Rome'. Róska criticized the group for its timidity, while Linnet reflected that 'She naturally wanted to go a lot further in operations, perhaps in a way more in the vein of urban guerrilla warfare, but we were of course very traditional and set in our classical Icelandic approach'.[40]

At the other end of Europe, in Greece, the 1967 military coup removed any hesitations regarding the use of violence as a means of opposition to the dictatorship. People who had never thought about the use of violent means before the coup now espoused it as perfectly legitimate. Discussion among opposition groups was not whether the use of violent means was justified but rather whether it was appropriate, that is, capable of sparking a mass protest movement against the dictatorship. Nikos Manios (b. 1947), a member of the armed group Kinima 20is Oktovri (20 October Movement), which planted bombs in military trucks (30 March 1970), television vans and the statue of the US President Harry Truman (both actions on 26 November 1970), says that before the arrest of this group in October 1971 he was convinced that they were on the verge of a mass uprising, after which the rationale for activist violence would cease:

> We had written a long, good text arguing that we were witnessing a new era, in which a mass student movement would emerge and that this thing should make us reconsider

---

[39] Interview with Erlingur Hansson, conducted by GJ and K. Björnsson, Reykjavík, 8 October 2009.
[40] Interview with Vernhardur Linnet, conducted by GJ, Reykjavík, 10 October 2009.

our practice. And that we would anyway do one more action and perhaps, perhaps one more impressive action and then we would stop...A new cell was set up that would do mass work and wouldn't be involved at all [in violent actions]. They wouldn't see any guns or bombs.[41]

The other legitimating factor for the use of violence was the struggle against dictatorship. With the fall of the military regime in 1974 and the passage to parliamentary democracy Nikos Manios explains that violence was no longer on the agenda:

> It is one thing to use guns because I don't have any other means of expression, because the bombs were armed propaganda, and it is a different thing when I am allowed to speak. On this question, we, as an organization, were consistent. We showed this consistency right after the fall of the dictatorship. We had a meeting when the regime changed to discuss whether there was any point to continue like this, the Kinima 20is Oktovri as a semi-legal, semi-illegal organization. What do we have to offer to Greek society, when we were free to say anything we wanted? We decided that we didn't have anything to offer. We dissolved it [the organization].[42]

The argument that violence was used to trigger mass action was used as much by French activists as Greek ones. As if to rebut Wieviorka's description of terrorism as an 'anti-movement', French Maoists are keen to argue that their actions were closer to social movements in that they took their revolutionary cues from the masses and would not lead the masses to violence if there was no spontaneous desire for it. Olivier Rolin argues that the goal of the GP was always to serve the people and to take signals from them. If the people did not revolt it was not the task of the Maoists to act without them:

> We did not see ourselves as an avant-garde, but as a simple tool at the service of popular revolt. This gave us no right...to announce the main stages on the forward march towards revolution. In our folly there was perhaps an element of reason. If we had had another theory, perhaps, we might have taken the road they took in Italy or Germany. But we did not have that thought.[43]

Maren Sell (b. 1945), who went from Germany to Paris in September 1968 and joined the Maoist GP, throws light on the different approaches to narratives of violence among French and West German activists. Because French activists, she argues, felt confident in mass support, which had manifested itself both in 1968 and during the wartime struggle against Nazi occupation, they saw their violence as a way of exposing political and social oppression, which would stimulate popular revolution. In West Germany, however, some of her German friends became involved in the RAF or Baader-Meinhof group because history had taught them that the workers, who had not resisted Nazism, would not now resist bourgeois democracy, and that they therefore had to be taught to be violent:

> That was probably the intrinsic difference between the Germans and the French. In France there had been a general strike in '68 and the activists thought that they could trust the people. It was a people which had resisted Nazism. In Germany history

---

[41] Interview with Nikos Manios, conducted by PV, Athens, 13 October 2009.
[42] Manios interview.   [43] Rolin interview.

taught activists that they could not have confidence in the people... So their armed struggle remained separate from the people... They thought that the more they escalated violence the more they would radicalize the people.[44]

That said, even French activists were divided over the question of violence. This can be seen at the end of May '68, when some Maoists thought that the bloody clash between striking workers who refused to return to work and the police pointed the way to class war, which had to be organized, while others did not want any part in escalating the violence. Yves Cohen (b. 1951), a member of the UJC(ml), had been a friend of the *lycée* student Gilles Tautin, who died during the battle at the car factory of Renault-Flins on 10 June 1968. In 1970, as a member of the GP, he returned to work incognito at the Peugeot factory of Sochaux, where two workers had been killed on 11 June 1968. There, if anywhere, insurrection was due to break out:

We had been involved at Sochaux, 'factory number 1', on 11 June, and so had the workers, who had come from their homes that day with guns, took up arms. It seemed to us that the beginning of an armed insurrection was possible and that is why the police had pulled back on 11 June. Later I learned that on the bosses' side too they were arming themselves and had grenades left over from the Algerian War.[45]

Other Maoists, however, while seeking greater solidarity with the workers had no desire for violent action. Roland Castro describes in dramatic terms the moment he broke with Benny Lévy, leader of the GP, over the action in support of the workers of Flins in June 1968. Significantly, Castro's argument against Benny Lévy turned on the contradictory maxims of Mao that a single spark can provoke revolution but that cadres have to be sure of the revolutionary potential of the workers or peasants before inciting them to action:

That shit Benny Lévy, he ordered me to kill a policeman... He asked me to go, he asked me... there were workers at Flins, one of our men was at Flins, and he said simply, 'if you think that everything is ready, a spark can set fire to the prairie and sometimes you must not hesitate to kill'... So we asked at the door of the factory and in the bars, 'What would you think if we organized an ambush against the cops?' And the next day hardly any workers turned up... Since then people don't speak to me about Benny Lévy and I never spoke to him again.[46]

Activist thinking about violence, of course, was not limited to how ready for revolution were the working class or peasantry in Europe. It might be that the collapse of the strikes of 1968 suggested that European workers were not prepared for real conflict. But the European workforce consisted of increasing numbers of immigrants from the 'Third World', more exploited, more marginalized, less organized and potentially more volatile than European workers. Moreover, models of revolution were provided by the anti-imperialist struggles of the 'Third World' revolution, not only

[44] Interview with Maren Sell, conducted by RG, Paris, 21 April 2008. See also her fictionalized account of those years, *Mourir d'absence* (Paris, 1978).
[45] Interview with Yves Cohen, conducted by RG, Paris, 9 May 2008.
[46] Interview with Roland Castro, conducted by RG, Paris, 9 May 2007.

in Cuba or Latin America, China or Vietnam, but also the Palestinian struggle that came to world view after the Black September repression of 1970 in Jordan.

In this context the GP built a bridge to North African Arab immigrant activists angered by events in the Middle East, through so-called Palestine Committees that sought to mobilize immigrant workers in ghetto-like areas such as the Goutte d'Or district of north-east Paris, where the tensions that had torn France apart during the Algerian War had never quite died down. Support for the Palestinian cause reached crisis point, however, when the Palestinian Black September group took Israeli athletes hostage at the 1972 Munich Olympics and killed eleven of them. For the GP, Olivier Rolin recalls that this manifestation of Arab violence was a turning point for many of the GP who were of Jewish origin:

> The centre of gravity of armed action in the 1960s was Cuba or the Latin American guerrilla movements. After that it was Palestine...For many of us, who were ashamed of France's collaboration [with the Third Reich], anything that looked like anti-Semitism was absolutely repugnant to us, and so we—me in any case—frankly had no sympathy for the Palestinian *groupuscules*...I know that the FNLP [Popular Front for the Liberation of Palestine] suggested joint action and we refused. We were I think the only extreme-left group in Europe to condemn the Munich attack.

By contrast, some North African activists in the Palestinian committees sought greater autonomy from the GP and set up their own Mouvement des Travailleurs Arabes (MTA) or Arab Workers' Movement. The MTA took a completely different view of the incident, based on the worldwide climate of state and revolutionary violence. For example, Abdel Majid Daboussi (b. 1944), a Tunisian economics student of Muslim origin and active in both the Palestinian committees and the MTA, says that:

> Benny Lévy and I'm not sure who else read a communiqué to denounce the attack...Our analysis at the time was quite simple. They took Israeli athletes hostage to demand the liberation of Palestinian prisoners. The massacre was done by the German army...Taking hostages to liberate prisoners was a tactic in Latin America, worldwide. For us there was no problem if the aim was to free prisoners, especially if they were activists. So there was a total rupture and we went our own way.[47]

The shift of the leadership of the Third World from communist China to the Palestinians caused problems for the GP but not for the MTA or for more extreme activists such as Jean-Marc Rouillan who founded Action Directe in 1977. He points out that he was always keen to build 'transnational' links to other activist groups and claims that they were acting not as terrorists isolated from the masses but on behalf of the masses in Third World countries:

> I have always tried to bring in a transnational dimension, either in Europe or with the Palestinians or Lebanese or combatants from other countries. I think that one of the main tasks of revolutionaries here is to support the revolution of those masses who are potentially revolutionary today. That is, the masses of the Third World. That I understood quite quickly.[48]

---

[47] Interview with Abdel Majid Daboussi, conducted by RG, Paris, 26 May 2008.
[48] Rouillan interview.

Even before Action Directe was formed, however, Rouillan justified the use of violence in the struggle against the brutal Franco dictatorship that brought together Basque, Catalan and French activists on either side of the French–Spanish border in the MIL.[49] This was smashed by the Spanish authorities and one of its members, Puig Antich, was garrotted in March 1974. Jean-Marc Rouillan explains how the survivors set up a new group, the Groupes d'action révolutionnaire internationalistes (GARI) or Internationalist Revolutionary Action Groups, to avenge this judicial murder. He explains that revolutionary violence was a response to state violence and in particular the need to continue the combat of fallen comrades:

> We crossed the frontier [to France] and built up an armed organization with armed groups to save people from execution, as happened at the time of the Burgos trial [in 1970]. When this harsh repression set in, with this execution and torture, we experienced a profound change... There are some things which tip you over and become irreversible... There is no way back. It is almost romantic... For a political activist vengeance means continuing the fight on behalf of the comrade who has fallen.[50]

From the MIL to the GARI and thence to Action Directe, Jean-Marc Rouillan became increasingly isolated both from fellow activists who did not wish to follow him and indeed from elements of 'the masses' who might have lent their support. References to the support of the masses of the Third World rang increasingly hollow. Michel Camilleri (b. 1952), who had been a *lycée* student with Rouillan in Toulouse and a member of the GARI, left Action Directe in 1982 because he thought it had lost touch with popular movements:

> At the time we wanted to link up a bit more with popular movements. In particular there were miners' strikes, things like that. We thought that it was a good time to melt back into them, or if we could not do that, to disappear as a group, then to try to support them. A month later we were arrested.[51]

In Greece, some activists advanced a similar defence of violence, arguing that their armed struggle for national liberation against the US-backed Colonel's Dictatorship was linked to and justified by similar armed struggles for national liberation in the Third World. One of these groups was the Laiki Epanastatiki Antistasi (People's Revolutionary Resistance), which was responsible for bombs in trucks of an American company (9 July 1971) and in the basement of the US embassy in Athens (29 August 1972). The declaration of the group in 1971 reads:

> We believe in armed resistance. The main strategic goal of the struggle, that is the violent overthrow of the system and the takeover of the power by the people, show the one and only path that such a struggle can take: the armed people's resistance, as a basic form of struggle, as a strategy to take over power and not simply as a means to exert pressure... The path of the armed resistance has developed in a different form

[49] Sergi Rosès Codovilla, *Le MIL: une histoire politique* (La Bussière, 2007); Antoni Segura and Jordi Solé (eds), *El FONS MIL: Entre el record i la historia* (Catarroja/Barcelona, 2006).
[50] Rouillan interview.
[51] Interview with Michel Camilleri, conducted by RG, Toulouse, 28 April 2008.

in each country, the peoples of Asia, Africa and Latin America had to liberate themselves from the predatory exploitation of American imperialism, the peoples' worst
enemy.[52]

As in France, however, some Greek activists thought that the path to armed struggle left activists increasingly isolated. The question of violence was controversial in
opposition circles. Anna Filini initially believed that armed struggle against the
dictatorship was meaningful, but later she had second thoughts, fearing that these
groups were becoming increasingly isolated and lacked popular support. She left
the circles that supported violence and went on to establish a new political group,
the EKKE. She explains:

> I have to admit that I was deeply involved, I knew things that scared me. I lived with
> a question always in my head: are we risking our lives? Of course we risked our lives!
> It was a persistent question for many people, for many Greeks, right? It was this press-
> ing question that made many people disappear, not that they were killed. This dilemma
> hindered the development of the right political forces. That's how I see it in hindsight.
> These groups became very isolated and I believe that some of them did harm. Perhaps
> in Greece they were more spontaneous. There they were spontaneous in the beginning
> but... When a movement doesn't develop these things end up in... bleak, dangerous,
> undemocratic things.[53]

VIOLENCE AND NON-VIOLENCE

In some cases, the debate was not simply between activists who were more or less
sure of the validity of violence, but between activists who were prepared to consider violence and those who were positively committed to a philosophy of non-
violence. This might be for ethical reasons and Gandhi, Martin Luther King and
Nelson Mandela were regularly cited as role models. Equally, however, non-violence
might be defended for tactical reasons by core groups who wanted to avoid a direct
confrontation with the state that they could not win, and also to retain control of
movements against outsiders who were more prone to inciting violence. Here we
will compare two cases, that of Northern Ireland, where the path of non-violent
opposition to Unionist rule was attempted in 1968 but did not succeed, and that
of the Larzac in southern France, where the strategy of non-violent resistance by
sheep farmers to the extension of a military base did succeed. In each case, the
recollections of activists show that violence and non-violence was a matter of intense debate at the time.

In Northern Ireland tensions emerged between the veterans of the civil rights
movement who were strongly committed to non-violence and the ethics of Martin
Luther King and the younger, student-based movements that became PD and were
inspired by the anti-Vietnam War struggles and May 1968 in Paris. The first Civil

---

[52] 'Declaration of the Laiki Epanastatiki Antistasi', *Epithesi* 1 (15 September 1971), 15.
[53] Filini interview.

Rights march on 24 August 1968 from Coalisland to Dungannon exposed the difficulties faced in reconciling these two elements.[54] Austin Currie of the Civil Rights Association explains:

> We had held two meetings in Coalisland to organize the march and we had taken certain definite decisions. One was that no banners except for the civil rights banner would be carried and secondly that anybody who attempted to cause trouble would be restrained, and this crowd arrived from Belfast. They had been I think earlier in the day to some sort of anti-Vietnam protest or whatever and they had these posters and banners with them. And they were told in no uncertain terms, 'You're not carrying those', which caused a bit of trouble... there was an element there that had to be controlled.[55]

The Queen's University Belfast students formed PD in October 1968. Situated on the fringes of the Civil Rights Association it aimed to force the British state into reform. In January 1969, following a series of demonstrations, protests and provocative acts, it forged ahead with a controversial 'long march' from Belfast to Derry that ended in violence at Burntollet Bridge. Despite the insistence by some activists of this march being modelled on the non-violent 1965 civil rights march in Alabama from Selma to Montgomery, Denis Haughey (b. 1944), a former founder member of the Civil Rights Association and Social Democratic Labour Party (SDLP) politician, saw it as deliberately provocative towards the Unionists and British state and a step too far:

> We thought it was good that there were students who were sufficiently concerned about the whole thing to take part. It wasn't until the PD was set up and then proposed the march from Belfast to Derry that we began to think; 'now this is risky, this is dangerous'. Because we had been walking a fine line. You know you create a level of agitation, you create... maybe you even bring some level of violence on yourself, but you don't set out deliberately to stir up violence. And you avoid risky demonstrations and you avoid areas where there was a lot of volatility.[56]

Bernadette McAliskey, one of the leading lights of PD, argues that though the protest was based on the Selma march it was intended to challenge the government and would carry on in a straight line through Protestant and Unionist areas if they lay in the path of the march:

> There was not doubt that it was based on the Selma march, the posters very much reflected that and that was the thinking-and like the Selma march it was intended to challenge the government to protect the rights of the people knowing that the government wouldn't... Now the government did not ban that demonstration, that was a lawful march and the government therefore had a statutory obligation to allow it to take place and to protect it... We could have diverted off our path and stayed where Fenians were allowed to go just as the Selma march could have diverted off the straight road and stuck [to] the places were black people were allowed to go, the Belfast to Derry march went up the straight road to Derry and that was the whole point, it

---

[54] Austin Currie, *All Hell will Break Loose*, 101–08.
[55] Currie interview.
[56] Interview with Denis Haughey, conducted by CR, Cookstown, 13 May 2009.

wasn't that there was a conscious decision taken to trail your coat somewhere where you had no need to be. It was the direct route.[57]

While loss of control of protest by the Civil Rights Association meant that violence was not avoided in Northern Ireland, the case of the Larzac plateau in France was rather different. After 1970 the plateau was threatened by the extension of a military base, and became the site of a national, if not international, campaign to preserve the local sheep-farming community from the expansion of a site that for them represented aggressive militarism. Many activists from the outside were former *gauchistes* in search of another confrontation with the state, which had now shifted from the streets of Paris to *la France profonde*.[58] The sheep farmers of the plateau, however, took an oath of solidarity and non-violence under the inspiration of Lanza del Vasto who led a fast on the Larzac at Easter 1972. Pierre Burguière recalls how Lanza demonstrated the futility of direct confrontation with the state and the propaganda power of appearing as victims:

> He said, 'you don't have weapons, and you will find yourselves up against a military power that can crush you'. We discovered that non-violence was an extraordinary defence method. We just had to adapt it to our struggle. We realized that in the eyes of public opinion we needed to appear as the martyrs and victims of totalitarian power. In ten years I only once saw a man lose his cool and throw a punch at a *gendarme*.[59]

Unlike in Northern Ireland, the advocates of non-violence maintained control of the situation, welcoming the support of outside activists but adamant that since they would take the brunt of any government repression of protest they should keep the whip hand deciding tactics and impose the non-violent approach. Pierre Burguière explains that:

> Of the 107 sheep farmers 103 signed an oath to say that they would never leave, whatever means were used to expel them. That was always the heart of the struggle, the reference...So when people suggested—there were people who arrived bringing explosives, and others who said, 'you could blow something up there'...or 'We could do this at the weekend', we would say, 'fine but stay here on Monday, Tuesday, Wednesday, and take the consequences'. Then they said, 'But we have to go back to work'. And we said, 'When you agree to take the consequences we can do something together, because we have to take responsibility every day'.[60]

The struggle against the extension of the military base on the Larzac was related to wider protest movements against nuclear power in the 1970s, some of which did not avoid violent confrontation with the state.[61] In August 1977 demonstrators clashed with the government over plans to build a nuclear super-reactor at Malville, near Grenoble. On this occasion local protesters were overrun by outside activists

---

[57] McAliskey interview.   [58] See above, pp. 126–9.   [59] Burguière interview.
[60] Burguière interview.
[61] See Andrew Tompkins, '"Better active today than radioactive tomorrow!" The transnational opposition to nuclear energy in France and West Germany, 1968–1981', DPhil thesis (University of Oxford, 2013).

whose actions provoked a number of casualties; which in turn allowed the government to clamp down severely on the campaign. Hervé Ott argues that this kind of confrontation was to be avoided at all costs on the Larzac:

> The paper *La Gueule Ouverte* called for a big demonstration but offered no organization. It was disrupted by troublemakers who came from all over. One *gendarme* was killed, another had his hand blown off by a grenade or something. That did for the anti-nuclear movement for some time. It was catastrophic. Giscard decided to push on at whatever price. He was promoting nuclear power and would not give up...that incident set us back twenty years.[62]

CONCLUSION

In their accounts of activism, former 1968 militants are torn between a number of competing models or scripts of resistance. The first is the heroic model of the idealized revolutionary, a second that of the non-violent guru or civil rights campaigner, and a third, favoured by some female activists, that of the leader of a mass movement. One model to be avoided was that of the gun-toting terrorist. Activists who are drawn to the heroic model of the revolutionary need to avoid any association with terrorism by demonstrating that they inflicted no harm on innocent people.

Activists spend a good deal of time and effort justifying violence. Rhetorically, violent pronouncements were used to distance themselves from compromise politics. The danger of appearing as terrorists meant, however, that they mobilize a repertoire of arguments to explain their violence. They argue variously that it was 'illegalism' rather than violence, that the violence was symbolic rather than real, that it was aimed at property rather than people, that it was the product of the current climate or *Zeitgeist*, or that it was the continuation of a legitimate historical struggle.

Powerful debates took place between activists across Europe and within individual countries. There was a sense that violence against dictatorships such as Spain and Greece was easy to justify, but more complicated in the context of democracies. Activists with transnational connections argued that violence might be justified by the exceptionalism of the political and historical context in one country but not in another. Activists were divided over the question of whether the masses in their own countries were ready for revolution or whether they should be bringing revolutionary violence 'back home' from Third World countries.

Finally, there were clashes between those who were prepared to consider violence because of the repressive nature of the state and those who argued that direct confrontation with the state should be avoided. This articulated a battle within the activist camp for control of the protest movement and the breakthrough or otherwise of violence often depended upon which school of activists managed to impose its strategy on its rivals, as the divergent cases of Northern Ireland and the Larzac demonstrate.

---

[62] Interview with Hervé Ott, conducted by RG, Le Cun du Larzac, 24 May 2008.

PART III

MAKING SENSE OF ACTIVISM

11

Reflections

James Mark, Anna von der Goltz and Anette Warring

This book is largely based on individual stories—stories in which our interviewees have packaged their memories of 1968 as they have sought to make sense of their activism in the years since. In this sense, the oral history interview is a dialogue between the past and present. In recent years, questions of memory and shifting national discourses and collective representations of 1968 in the context of changing political settings have become autonomous subjects of scholarly inquiry.[1] Furthermore, social movement theorists have investigated the consequences of activism and its impact on the individual life course in political, personal and professional terms, and have mapped those who had been active in the years around 1968 particularly closely.[2] Rather than studying the memory of 1968 from the top down or generating statistical data about the trajectories our interviewees took, this chapter looks at how they have given meaning to their activism over time.[3] Interviews are full of individual musings, re-workings and re-elaborations, and this chapter brings these to the fore to explore more fully what our interviewees now think they did around 1968 and what they have done since.[4]

In doing so, we follow some of the most interesting and sophisticated recent scholarship on this period. Kristin Ross, for one, has shown that the meaning of 1968 cannot easily be reduced to history without the concurrent study of the trajectories activists took. Her investigation of *May '68 and its Afterlives* focussed on the new meanings former activists, and their critics, inscribed onto

---

[1] See, for example, Albrecht von Lucke, *68 oder neues Biedermeier: Der Kampf um die Deutungsmacht* (Berlin, 2008); Ingo Cornils and Sarah Waters (eds) *Memories of 1968: International Perspectives* (Bern, 2010); Chris Reynolds, *Memories of May '68: France's Convenient Consensus* (Cardiff, 2011).

[2] Marco G. Giugni, 'Personal and biographical consequences', in David A. Snow, Sarah A. Soule and Hanspeter Kriesi (eds) *The Blackwell Companion to Social Movements* (Oxford, 2004), 489–507. Earlier studies of US activists include James M. Fendrich, 'Keeping the faith or pursuing the good life: A study of the consequences of participation in the civil rights movement', *American Sociological Review* 42 (1977), 144–57; Jack Whalen and Richard Flacks, *Beyond the Barricades: The Sixties Generation Grows Up* (Philadelphia, 1989); and Paul Berman, *A Tale of Two Utopias. The Political Journey of the Generation of 1968* (New York, 1996) on how for many radicals their 'leftist utopia' was transformed into a belief in a 'liberal utopia'.

[3] For another attempt at this, see Rebecca E. Klatch, *A Generation Divided: The New Left, the New Right, and the 1960s* (Berkeley, Los Angeles and London, 1999), chs. 8 and 9.

[4] cf. Alessandro Portelli, 'What makes oral history different?', *History Workshop* 12 (1981), 96–107; on the role of stories in making and remaking identities see Charles Tilly, *Stories, Identities and Political Change* (Oxford, 2002).

the event in the context of changing political constellations in France.[5] Her argument was that any history that attempts to reconstruct the political world of 1968 needs to unpick the reformulations of its meaning that have obscured our capacity to understand it. To this end she reconstructs the movement and the multiple discourses that have attempted to refashion—or often belittle it—in the years since.[6]

While we build on Ross's approach in some important respects, we do so without her more political intention to recover the political programme of 1968 and shape it to mobilize in the present. Whereas she sought to rescue 1968 from later re-workings—which she saw as a plot to sanitize it and thus render it powerless—we investigate these recurring re-elaborations in their own right, as windows into different meanings of political activism rather than as conscious ploys to divert from past errors. As spaces in which former radicals trace the relationship of their own lives to the positive and problematic legacies of activism, life stories do not just echo official discourses but also cut through them in important respects.

In many life stories, the boundaries between the individual autobiography and the sense of collective achievement were dissolved: the successes (and failures) of individual lives were delivered alongside an appreciation of what they had produced collectively.[7] Indeed, Luisa Passerini, an activist in, and one of the best-known writers on, 1968, asserted in her *Autobiography of a Generation: Italy, 1968* that it was only a sense of generational belonging and collective storytelling that had given her the strength to produce her own account of those years: 'If I had not heard the life stories of the generation of '68, I would not have been able to write about myself; those stories have nourished mine, giving it the strength to get to its feet and speak'.[8] As the sense of a '1968 generation' has emerged—in many European countries this process seems to have begun sometime in the late 1970s[9]—so the representatives of this era have come to evaluate their own lives in terms of what their generation has given to the development of politics and society both nationally and globally. This chapter explores how these individual life stories and collective representations of 1968—both celebratory and condemnatory—are interwoven in nuanced and meaningful ways.

[5] Kristin Ross, *May '68 and its Afterlives* (Chicago and London, 2002).

[6] For more on these re-workings, see Kostis Kornetis, 'Introduction: 1968–2008: The inheritance of utopia', *Historein* 9 (2009), 7–20; Luisa Passerini, 'The problematic intellectual repercussions of '68: Reflections in a jump-cut style', in *Historein* 9 (2009), 21–33; Sarah Waters, 'Introduction: 1968 in memory and place', in Cornils and Waters (eds) *Memories of 1968*, 1–22.

[7] This is a common feature of autobiographical narratives, see Sigrid Weigel, 'Generation, Genealogie, Geschlecht', in Lutz Musner and Gotthart Wunberg (eds) *Kulturwissenschaften* (Vienna, 2002), 164.

[8] Luisa Passerini, *Autobiography of a Generation: Italy, 1968* (Middletown, CT, 1996). 124.

[9] Anna von der Goltz (ed.) *'Talkin' 'bout my Generation' Conflicts of Generation Building and Europe's '1968'* (Göttingen, 2011).

CELEBRATING THE LEGACIES OF 1968?

Kristian Riis, a Danish activist (b. 1941), was engaged in intense and multi-faceted forms of political activism in the 1960s and 1970s before he became the secretary-general of a voluntary social organization in 1990. Towards the end of the interview, he highlights his personal contribution to creating a more democratic society in Denmark, which he frames as part of a collective story:

> If we look at the lives of these key people since, we see a mixture of having a meaningful job, either socially or as lawyers or high-school teachers or... in the public sector, where you think you make a difference... Because there are so damned many of us who've ended up doing good things in our lives, but never been directors. Well, yes, I became secretary-general, so I'm one of those who did hold a high position... but in a strange way I ended up being the leader, and, of course, I became that in a place where the main battle is about spreading influence in democratic forms.... So I have no doubts that I am one of the main reasons we have senior citizens' councils in Denmark... And there's no doubt that people like me have exercised a lot of political influence, but in decentralized structures.[10]

Riis was not alone in this assessment. Jeffrey Weeks (b. 1945), a British gay rights activist and historian of sexuality, tells a story that weighs the outcomes of the radicalism of the 1960s in similar terms. As a mainstream Labour Party supporter, Weeks had 'felt quite detached from the radicalism of '68 because it didn't mean anything to me'. What was meaningful about 1968 for Weeks would be the recasting of radical politics in the years that followed to provide new opportunities for individual and collective efforts to effect meaningful social change:

> I think the critical achievement of those movements... was to develop this sense of agency, of being able to remake your own lives... for those of us who lived through gay liberation, and I think the same is true of my friends in the women's movement, it was a transformative moment, because the intense excitement, the sense of collective experience, the sense that anything was possible, made it necessary to change your own lives, to rethink what we were about, and to put all the fragments together to create ourselves as whole people... The politics, the revolutionary politics, in a sense is almost peripheral, in retrospect... So the moment of '68 and the immediate aftermath, is for me that moment of agency rather than the more exciting political arguments of the time... I don't look back nostalgically to that 1968 moment. I actually see it as having opened up possibilities, which are still continuing.[11]

The title of Weeks's most recent book, *The World We Have Won*, expresses his sense that 1968 was less a transient utopian moment to be endlessly lamented than the source of durable social gains, achieved by grassroots action and retained in the face of subsequent political reaction.[12] Like Weeks, many interviewees—even those who had doubts about aspects of their former engagement—emphasize that this period of radical commitment led to very positive social and cultural changes.

[10] Interview with Kristian Riis, conducted by AW, Copenhagen, 4 April 2009.
[11] Interview with Jeffrey Weeks, conducted by JD, London, 17 June 2010.
[12] Jeffrey Weeks, *The World We Have Won: The Remaking of Erotic and Intimate Life* (London, 2007).

Their personal narratives thus mirror some of the dominant themes in popular memory and the historiography of 1968 that often portray the 'cultural revolution' as one of the defining features and legacies of this period.[13]

In particular, activists often explain that their generation fostered the democratization of European societies, although the meaning of such a claim is very different depending on political context. In western European democracies, for example, activists seldom present themselves as successful political revolutionaries but rather, like Weeks, as vanguards of social liberalization and democratization, long-term processes that had led to greater gender equality, sexual liberation, a less authoritarian society, freer social conventions and more open dialogue, flatter organizational structures, and a less hierarchical education system.

Such narratives of 'democratization' and 'liberalization' were not necessarily confined to the national arena. Sheila Rowbotham (b. 1943), the British socialist feminist writer and campaigner, first began to connect women's politics to radical politics in 1968, inspired by that year's equal pay movement in Britain and by a high-profile campaign by the wives of Hull trawlermen to secure greater safety for their husbands at sea. After forty years spent promoting gender politics and writing gender history, she now sees her generation's achievement as not simply domestic or even European—but global:

> We thought we were trying to change all of society in Britain, and society did change, but often not as we imagined, but then the women's movement did have an impact far beyond our imaginings because it affected women in so many different countries, in really severe circumstances, like Iran and…women organizing around environmental issues in Africa…South Korea, we couldn't possibly have really quite grasped that. We knew that there were anti-imperialist movements but…we didn't envisage that there would be such amazing international impetus that keeps sort of going on even though the women's movement in Britain is not so much around any more.[14]

Some self-identified '68ers' from the former Warsaw Pact states similarly interpret 1968 as a moment that was instrumental in opening up a world beyond the Eastern bloc. Hungarian activists frequently present themselves as *the* generation that helped their country 'return to democratic European values', and often make sense of their biographies by linking their attraction to global revolt in the late 1960s and the return of their country to the arms of the West after 1989.[15] Gábor Demszky (b. 1952), who became liberal mayor of Budapest after 1990, offers an eastern European perspective on the 'cultural revolution' when he explains that 1968 both for him and for his country meant a turn to liberal western culture. He constructs a linear historical narrative that connects the beginnings of Hungarians' identification with Western revolt in the late 1960s with the later achievement of entry into the European Union in 2005:[16]

---

[13] Arthur Marwick, *The Sixties: Cultural Revolution in Britain, France, Italy, and the United States, 1958–1974* (Oxford, 1999).

[14] Interview with Sheila Rowbotham, conducted by JD, Oxford, 10 June 2009.

[15] For this linking of 1968 to 1989, see Vladimir Tismaneanu, 'Introduction', in idem (ed.) *Promises of 1968: Crisis, Illusion, and Utopia* (Budapest and New York, 2011), 8, 16–18.

[16] For a longer discussion, see Péter Apor and James Mark, 'Mobilising generation. The idea of 1968 in Hungary', in von der Goltz (ed.) *Talkin' 'bout my Generation*, 97–9.

1968 historically was the beginning of an anti-authoritarian period, and in my own personal history it had a very powerful effect on my entire life...'68 brought a real change, after that the world turned to a more cultured and fortunately more westernized direction, and it was already neither necessary nor possible to live or think in these older ways, it was the end of the eastern Soviet system and the intelligentsia could no longer think in their terms. Our young heroes of '68 were Daniel Cohn-Bendit in Paris, Rudi Dutschke in Berlin, Tom Hayden and Abbie Hoffman in the US...[17]

Gáspár Miklós Tamás (b. 1948), a dissident journalist and intellectual who stood for the liberal Free Democrats in the first post-communist elections in 1990, even presents 1968 as a great trans-European breakthrough that united a new generation of East and West against the 'grumbling', stiff morality and Victorian stuffiness that characterized both capitalist and communist Europe. 1968 meant that young Europeans everywhere could be simultaneously fashionable *and* radical politically:

> The generation of my parents grumbled constantly...we were the first 'un-grumblers' and I mean, there really used to be this constant quarrelling and telling off...this new rebellion appeared on the horizon...it was...an answer to the unhappiness of my parents' generation [who] were all in mourning because of the...unimaginable losses the communists went through in the war...this revolution started with the youth and it was trying to get rid of the Victorian repressiveness of both the social democratic and the Bolshevik movements. I wasn't then practicing free love—that came much later—I was a perfectly puritanical monogamist young person but I was very glad that it was happening in theory...this was exactly what we wanted: a combination of social revolution and personal liberation. Of course it seemed that...we can grow up as a generation that could be 'normal'—who could at once not be 'square' and at the same time not betray the great cause and not break the great radical traditions.[18]

Tamás presents 1968 as the beginning of a struggle that is still incomplete; the fight for a more tolerant, less nationalistic, more liberal and westernized society still remains unfinished in many parts of Hungary 'untouched by 1968'. His life story is therefore placed in the context of an ongoing struggle for liberalization and democratization that has only been partially realized with the collapse of communism in 1989:

> ...we live in a much, much, much, much more agreeable world and that's thanks to '68...I can feel it particularly in the large sections of this [Hungarian] society...that are somehow very definitely pre-'68, I still dislike heartily, I don't like harsh, macho, racist, boring drunk subcultures. But I am tolerant of it...I can sit with a former friend whose milieu is nationalist right-wing petit-bourgeois. But you know, but still to this very day, if I think what's the difference [between us] it is '68, that's the difference. We won't wear our clothes the same way, we don't sit the same way, we don't light our pipes the same way, and especially we won't address women the same way—all this 'csókolom'—'I kiss your hand'...I can feel this [dividing] line, I can feel it.

---

[17] Gábor Demszky, ''68-as vagyok', *Index* (17 July 2008). Available at <http://index.hu/velemeny/olvir/dg68/> (accessed 1 August 2010).

[18] Interview with Gáspár Miklós Tamás, conducted by JM, Budapest, 5 March 2009.

Other activists from the former communist bloc also highlight that 1968 led to the triumph of democracy, albeit in a subtly different way. They celebrate their role in criticizing the socialist dictatorship and thus in helping to overcome it in 1989. Their stories are therefore often 'autobiographies of democratization' in which they write themselves into the story of the collapse of communist dictatorship.[19] In some instances, these stories are even juxtaposed explicitly with the legacies of the western 1968. In 2001, Werner Schulz, a former peace activist and Green Party MP from East Germany, goes as far as accusing the West German left of 'fate envy' (*Schicksalsneid*). Whereas the West German left's utopian ideas of revolution had failed in 1968, the East German 68ers had played a decisive role in bringing down a repressive dictatorship by peaceful means in 1989, an outcome that West German activists envied, Schulz claims.[20]

In the former East Germany such accounts typically emphasize the long-term and spiralling state suppression that eventually led to more widespread opposition within the GDR. Seen from this angle, 1968 becomes a significant milestone on the path to the GDR's collapse and thus an important prelude to 1989.[21] East German activist Gerd Poppe (b. 1941), for one, writes his experiences of the late 1960s into a broader story of a slowly evolving, yet almost teleological struggle for democracy in the GDR. One of the most prominent civil rights activists of the 1980s, and one of the relatively few who pursued a successful political career in the Green Party after 1990, he traces his critical stance towards state socialism back to his childhood. He admits that he sought inspiration in ideas of socialist reform until the late 1970s. Towards the end of that decade, however, Poppe, like many others around him, came to the conclusion that only publicly visible activism would make a real difference. The 1980s were the high point of his oppositional activities. He and his circle discovered new topics, such as the environment and human rights, and started to take over the activist repertoire of other East European dissidents, most notably the *samizdat*, which he thinks was successful in creating a small but viable independent public sphere that helped to lend greater coherence to the dissidents' cause. Poppe emphasizes the evolutionary character of his own trajectory when he says that:

> no one ever turns up and says 'Now I'm a revolutionary!', but these things happen step by step as a result of the limitations placed on one's biography that become less and less bearable. And the more you found like-minded people who have had similar experiences, the more you exchanged ideas up until this moment when we took a stand and said 'Now we have to set up these oppositional groups'.[22]

[19] On the writing of 1989 as the culmination of 1968, see Luisa Passerini, 'The problematic intellectual repercussions of '68', in Historien 9 (2009) 23. See also the framing of the meaning of 1968 in Stefan Garsztecki 'Poland' and Jan Pauer 'Czechoslovakia' in Martin Klimke and Joachim Scharloth (eds) *1968 in Europe: A History of Protest and Activism* (New York, 2008); Tismaneanu (ed.) *Promises of 1968*, especially Part Two; see also Osęka, Apor and Mark, and Matějka in von der Goltz, *Talkin' 'bout my Generation*.
[20] 'Kein '89 ohne '68', *Der Spiegel* 12 (2001), 57.
[21] Some scholars have also interpreted the demise of the GDR as a 'collapse in instalments' of which 1968 was one: Armin Mitter and Stefan Wolle, *Untergang auf Raten: Unbekannte Kapitel der DDR-Geschichte* (Munich, 1993).
[22] Interview with Gerd Poppe, conducted by AvdG, Berlin, 11 June 2008.

Organized dissidence was thus the culmination of his trajectory. Poppe feels vindicated by the mass protests of 1989 and considers his activism a decisive contributing factor to the collapse of state socialism. They kept up the pressure and hollowed socialism out from within the GDR, he explains. Although he is not uncritical of reunified Germany, he condemns all those who nurture nostalgia for state socialism. He thinks that one has to 'to show real, real, real commitment to democracy, despite all the problems it has. And I see problems as well and have always seen them'. Despite the Federal Republic's shortcomings, for Poppe an unequivocal commitment to parliamentary democracy remains the logical outcome of an activist biography that spans nearly forty years.

While both activists from the West and East thus celebrate the positive long-term legacies of 1968, especially those that remained on the left sometimes consider these a double-edged sword. They argue that 1968 gave power to a range of economic and political processes that had, in fact, inhibited democratic development. British activist Hilary Wainwright (b. 1949), a socialist and feminist, and editor of the independent magazine *Red Pepper*, was 'totally' affected by the May events as a student in 1968. With hindsight she is concerned that the forces released then eventually gave shape to new forms of economic individualism that would later swamp the left, particularly during the financial crisis that emerged from 2008:

> I think that being directly involved gave one an incredibly important sense of the possibilities of change [and] the potential fragility of the established order. I mean, one also learnt about its resilience, its authoritarianism when under threat, but you also could see the potential of creative popular action...Also looking back, one can see the flaws...in our...over-optimism about the potential of fluid movements. I think we didn't really address the questions of institutional consolidation and development of the innovations that we made. And I think in a sense that made the ideas of '68 very vulnerable to all kinds of sort of appropriation and dispersion...Because one's got to recognize that...it was also the beginnings of a sort of financialization of the economic system, the expansion of credit and financial facilities which also became a source of innovation, and, at the same time, an incubator of crisis...so there's a lot of unfinished business.[23]

Like Wainwright, West German activist Olaf Dinné (b. 1935) emphasizes that although 1968 contributed to the destruction of authoritarian values, there were negative side effects that 'swamped' contemporary societies. In 1959, he had founded the Lila Eule, Bremen's first jazz club, which soon became a space for political discussions, subversive music and independent film screenings, eventually counting Rudi Dutschke and some of the members of Kommune 1 among its guests. He gave up on building an anti-Vietnam War movement in a city with few students in the late 1960s and instead turned his attention to local causes, successfully campaigning against the construction of an inner-city motorway. Dinné has since been involved in similar causes at a local level, fusing his professional ideas

---

[23] Interview with Hilary Wainwright, conducted by JD, London, 27 July 2010.

about sustainable architecture with a deep suspicion of international investors. He argues that his role in creating a subculture in Bremen eventually led to gentrification 'by the backdoor':

> If I were asked 'Would you do it again?', then I'd say 'I contributed significantly to the destruction of values', the ones that existed, which in the end I think are positive. The notion of community played a big role in '68, I held all that in very high esteem, but observed that it all went out of the window because of the increasing individualization and self-realization which became the fashion. And for this reason there was an incredible wave of innovation that now swamps cities in the shape of gentrification. I'm partly responsible for this shit. And I therefore consider it my task to erect a shield against the whirlwind I helped to sow. That is how I see my fate.[24]

The impact of '1968' on sexual liberation and gender equality is often the subject of activists' accounts, although not always in an unequivocally positive sense. They talk about how painful divorces, jealousy and unstable conditions for raising children were woven together with a powerful feeling of liberation from a narrow-minded sexual morality and an oppressive ideal of womanhood. They also highlight that this liberation had some negative long-term effects. Danish feminist and socialist Karen Syberg (b. 1945) points to current social trends such as the separation of sex and love and the conflicting requirements both men and women are subject to in order either to be considered successful, or to perceive themselves as successful. According to Syberg, this was the result of both developments she helped set in train, and the backlash against them she believed began in the 1980s. Syberg was a pioneer in the Danish women's liberation movement. In the spring of 1970, she was among the founders of the feminist movement Rødstrømpebevægelsen (the Redstockings), participating in spectacular events during the movement's highly prolific first year. Later, she was a key figure in the nascent Marxist women's studies. Although she underlines that her core values have remained the same, some social developments have prompted her to look back critically at previous positions and to 'clarify some things where I think our views were quite simplistic in retrospect':

> Sexual liberation, what exactly is it about? You also become more knowledgeable about issues such as abortion. I support abortion on demand, because the alternative is surely worse. You can choose between fetal death and a grown woman's death, but today we know more about what a fetus is compared to back then when we said it was 'just a blob of snot'... But take a look at what sexuality is like today, where an old granny like me gets pretty disgusted at the way girls behave, I must say. But we're the ones who set the trend. Now it's, how can I describe it?... sex and love, I get the impression, are completely separate issues for many people. Scoring a guy has nothing to do with whether or not you could imagine being with him for months... I doubt that that's going to be much fun...[25]

[24] Interview with Olaf Dinné, conducted by AvdG, Bremen, 27 December 2009.
[25] Interview with Karen Syberg, conducted by AW, Svensmarke, 5 January 2011.

According to Syberg the meaning of sexual liberation has shifted:

> We were brought up in the '50s to be nice girls, you know, so it was a huge relief and we didn't have to be afraid of getting pregnant; we could just hop into the sack with a guy, if we felt like it. That was awesome. So in that way I absolutely understand young women today. In reality, it most likely has to do with the fact that they have nothing to compare it with. For us it was the contrast to being brought up as nice girls, while for them it happens in a void, a kind of meaninglessness. But that's how I look at it. You can't be sure that it's like that for them. Regardless, this is one thing that we undeniably set in motion.

Just as some western European interviewees refrained from providing clear-cut celebratory accounts of the legacies of their activism, many radicals in the former communist bloc also hesitated to offer an unequivocally positive assessment of what 1968 produced. 1989 was an important caesura in European history as a whole, but the date plays a more important role as a structuring device in eastern European accounts than in those of western activists—with the exception of westerners who supported one of the pro-Soviet communist parties. Especially those eastern activists who remained on the left challenged the idea that 1968 could be associated with the post-1989 political settlement without difficulty. They rejected the contemporary dominant European narrative that links 1968 with the 'victory of 1989'—as expressed above. For them, 1968 was about the defeat of a repressive bureaucratic authoritarian leftist state and the creation of a new authentic progressive socialism; hence—from their perspective—1989, which ushered in late capitalism and neoliberalism, cannot be considered a victory. Rather, 1968 is conceived of as a lost moment during which there was a possibility to create a democratic socialism. For them, the defeat of this vision in 1968—with the suppression of the Prague Spring and other reformist movements in the communist bloc—foreshadowed 1989 in a different way: it became a prelude to another defeat of a true socialist vision.

Thomas Klein (b. 1948), an East German ex-Trotskyist who now advises the ex-communist *Die Linke*, experienced the GDR as a repressive state, but still considers himself as a left-wing socialist. After 1989, he became a historian, writing books on GDR history and its left-wing opposition, partly to show that opposition and dissent were not just liberal and democratic, but often connected to left-wing socialist traditions.[26] In the interview, he challenges what he calls the 'memory cartel' that controls what can be said about GDR history in general and the links between 1968 and 1989 in particular. For him both moments were defeats for a leftism he has never seen realized. Like Poppe, Klein believes that his opposition contributed to the collapse of communism, but, contrary to those who embraced the new system, nevertheless sees '89 as a defeat: 'We belonged to the vanquished of the autumn revolution even though we helped to spark it', he explains. Yet he

---

[26] Leonore Ansorg, Bernd Gehrke, Thomas Klein and Danuta Kneipp, *'Das Land ist still—noch!' Herrschaftswandel und politische Gegnerschaft in der DDR (1971–1989)* (Cologne, 2009); Thomas Klein, *Frieden und Gerechtigkeit: Die Politisierung der unabhängigen Friedensbewegung in Ost-Berlin während der 80er Jahre* (Cologne, Weimar, Vienna, 2007).

reflects on how he had failed to win over others with a true alternative vision of society, and that many former dissidents who had once resisted one extreme now fail to resist another:

> That people who used to show their bravery by standing up against the political bureaucratism of the GDR and other things, who took many risks, that they observe the obscenities of really existing capitalism with indifference is a reason for me to keep my distance.[27]

Like Klein, former East German pastor Heiko Lietz (b. 1943), who was politicized around 1968 and became one of the proponents of the 1980s peace movement, thinks that the links between 1968 and 1989 are ambiguous at best. He initially joined the Green Party after 1989, but soon left and ran a community bureau in Schwerin near the Baltic coast. Lietz sees 1989 as a defeat after his post-'68 struggles:

> Well, in '89 there were moments when I had the feeling that there was a brief glimpse of paradise…In that moment the door was ajar for a moment and…I peered through it…and thought there is a room where it could all become reality. And with every day…that passed I noticed that many didn't enter this room…There was a door to freedom and we just ended up in the room next door—the Federal Republic. Ok, the tapestry is a bit nicer and so on. There are also many things that are sort of acceptable, but it has little to do with my vision.[28]

Still a devout Protestant who is critical of the church hierarchy, he explains that late capitalism and neo-liberalism have nothing to do with his vision of taking God's kingdom seriously. Nevertheless, remembering 1968 is still vital for him—a powerful reminder of the need for 'revolution no. 2'.

For Gáspár Miklós Tamás, too, remembering former radical commitments is regarded as necessary to critique the neo-liberal present. Tamás repudiated his earlier leftist and anarchist positions in the 1980s when, as a dissident, he rejected the 68er western New Left for what he perceived to be their unjustifiable pro-Soviet stance, and embraced liberalism, Reagan and the power of the free market as necessary ideologies to destroy state socialism. In his account, the leftist traditions laid down around 1968 offered no political solutions for him in this period. Yet, unlike many other former dissidents, he revived his former leftist radicalism in new forms in the late 1990s. Faced with what he perceived to be the disastrous consequences of global capitalism on Hungarian society, he began to repent his earlier ideological detour; he abandoned professional politics in 1994, went abroad 'to collect himself', recovered his late 1960s engagement with Marx and began to give public support to trade unions and the green movement. In this new guise he was one of the most prominent promoters of the 'memory of 1968' in Hungary at the fortieth anniversary in 2008.[29] He recounts this shift thus:

Interview with Thomas Klein, conducted by AvdG, Berlin, 28 June 2010.

[28] Interview with Heiko Lietz, conducted by AvdG, Schwerin, 28 April 2010.

[29] Gáspár Miklós Tamás, 'Augusztusi Nap', in Maja and Reuben Fowkes (eds) *Forradalom szeretlek: 1968 a művészetben, a politikában és a filozófiában* (Budapest, 2008); 'El ne merd olvasni!', *Élet és Irodalom* LII. 20, 16 May 2008.

And so I became Marxist when I was 56 or 57 years old. I didn't come to it totally uninitiated, so it was not a 'conversion', but something that had accompanied me throughout my life since the 1960s...I have the most banal bad conscience about the transformation of history [i.e. the way we transformed Hungary after 1989] and I am perhaps the only public person to have said publicly that we were mistaken and I am sorry...at all these conferences they were asking, 'why don't the East Europeans love democracy?'. 'Is it their non-liberal past and their authoritarian traditions that made them despise democracy so much?'. I attended many conferences in Washington and I had the effrontery to think about it and it turned out these people were much less authoritarian...—they just didn't like to be ill without a doctor and they didn't like it when they couldn't buy nice food for their children, it was not so complicated. They were just poor and impoverished and humiliated and there was a new rhetoric of competition in which they were also considered losers, incompetent, lazy bums. That disgusted me and to think that I was part of that establishment that spewed forth that kind of shit fills me with deep shame...[30]

Many interviewees thus write their own lives into broader collective stories of the achievements and failures of the '1968 moment'—and often do both in the same account. Some celebrate the democratization of institutions and gender and sexual liberation that were part of an ongoing revolution that has still to run its course; in eastern Europe some former radicals tell stories of resistance that link their radical challenges to dictatorship with the eventual establishment of liberal democracy in their countries. Yet in both East and West this assessment is often double-edged: their struggles, they believe, unleashed forces of consumerism, individualism and sexual liberation whose effects are not wholly positive. Others are even less convinced that they should recall their lives in a way that links their former activist energies with a celebration of the present, arguing that '1968' represented a defeat for an alternative non-market-based vision of society, meant an absence of progressive, social equitable alternatives available when communism did collapse in 1989, and ushered in a new form of rampant individualism that they perceive as a necessary underpinning for a newly powerful global capitalism.

RETHINKING ACTIVISM

Life histories of 1968 activists not only write the individual biography into a wider story of collective success or failure; they are also accounts in which the regular rethinking, and reassessing of earlier social, cultural or political radicalism is central. As such, they are often very *reflexive* personal histories: respondents not only speak about what they did, but also relate the process of trying to make sense of the meaning of their former commitments, as their activism later evolved, declined or came to a halt. The frequency of such a form of autobiographical narrative is in part a reflection of our own methodology; we employed a technique which required

---

[30] Tamás interview.

respondents to make their lives comprehensible to an interviewer—often from a different generation whom, the interviewee might assume, was shaped politically in different ways. Indeed, we explicitly asked how they reflect now on their former politics at the end of interviews if they had not done so already.

Even given this, the frequency with which interviewees produce personal narratives that interweave important life changes with reconsiderations of the meanings of their earlier activism is striking. Faced with shifts—the collapse of their radical energies, changing political allegiances, professional careers, or children—or with new public discourses on the radicalism of the 1960s, whether internally from the left or, often more importantly, from demonization from the right—former activists recount how they attempted to rethink their pasts.

For some, it was an important shift in their lives that they remember as prompting them to rethink the meaning of their earlier commitments. Italian feminist Liliana Ingargiola, who dedicated many years of her life to the women's movement, realized in the early 1980s that she had lost the thread of her personal life in the collective experience of militant feminism:

> In '83 I decided to take a deep look at myself...at my life...And so it seemed to me that...the question 'Where am I politically?' that my female friends were asking themselves, was also something that I could ask of myself, 'Where am I personally?'. I was thirty-five or thirty-six years old, and thus at an age that has a particular significance for a woman. I wasn't married, I didn't have children, I'd never thought about having children...I decided to go back to school, but I fell into a sort of crisis of my own destructuralization. Indeed, I ended up having to go into analysis because I was panicking, I could hardly walk, this [life change] was so huge for me that I had this type of reaction. So I went into analysis, and I tried to find a path for myself in this new life, which was also an isolated life because, in order to allow myself to study, I'd lost my political role, my social role.[31]

Others present the regular re-evaluation of one's personal past as a necessary task in order to ensure that progressive politics remained relevant and vital. For some interviewees, this was particularly important because, in their estimation, the left had failed to adequately think through their former commitments, and in doing so had allowed their political opponents to do it for them; thus, they explain, the right had been allowed to develop a powerful hold over the way in which their lives were presented—and often demonized—in the public sphere. Such is the position of the Dane Morten Thing (b. 1945), who was involved in a wide variety of political activism and was primarily known for being a member of the editorial staff of the influential Danish magazine *Politisk Revy* (*Political Review*) from 1969 to 1981. He argues that in the mid-1990s, when former 68ers—including himself—were aggressively attacked in the media, the right attempted to close down the possibility that activists could intelligently present their former positions and reconsider them; rather, as he puts it, 'The right wing's ban on thinking rests on the formal demand for regret. There are specific words you have to say. The regret has to

---

[31] Interview with Liliana Ingargiola, conducted by RC, Rome, 29 November 2008.

appear in the acceptance of *their* grammar'. He argues that this frightened many former leftist activists away from 'the complicated work of re-considering [their] own story', something he on the other hand considers important: 'I think a critical re-consideration of our past would be profitable for the left in the future. First of all it is necessary to ourselves'.[32]

For others, the desire of 68ers regularly to rethink the autobiography is also deeply rooted in the nature of the revolt itself, whose speed of development and intensity forced activists to make, and remake, sense of events from the moment they were happening. Klaus Hartung (b. 1940), a former member of the West Berlin SDS and now a retired journalist, emphasizes that they were constantly reformulating their beliefs from the outset of their political engagement, ever keen to develop their ideas further and to distance themselves from previous mistakes. Doing this was almost an obsession of the student movement, he says. He talks about 'life as a permanent cataclysm (*Umwälzung*)' and thinks that this explains why the West German left was so fixated on chronicling its own endeavours. Hartung himself began to write about the legacies of 1968—or ''67' as he calls it with reference to the killing of student Benno Ohnesorg on 2 June 1967 at the hands of a West Berlin policeman—in the early 1970s. By the mid-1970s, he had real regrets about the political 'excesses', the fragmentation of the West German left, the political destructiveness of the Maoist K-Groups, and his own flirtation with violence; these considerations eventually led him to recreate 'his '67' in Trieste in 1976, where he spent four years as a volunteer in Basaglia's anti-psychiatry experiment. He describes both his own and the left's trajectory in the 1970s as a 'giant search movement' to find ways to return to, and also rethink in new settings, the original impetus of ''67'. His desire regularly to rethink earlier life experiences in order to reconstitute activism in the present is a feature of many 68er autobiographies:

> I went to Italy in '76 and for me— I still see it like this today—for me Trieste was really a kind of continuation of '67. There was something like an anti-institutional struggle. They didn't just dissolve the psychiatric hospital, but during this process of dissolution new institutions were being built, which, in their turn, had to be overcome. The question was always 'Aren't we just setting up another mental asylum?'. Because in the end communal flats (were) really tiny mental asylums, you know.[33]

In the remainder of this chapter, we chart the journeys that activists took after their initial radical engagements around 1968, and assess some of the ways in which they attempt to make sense of their former political and personal lives in the face of new pressures and experiences. In the first sections, we consider how two important life changes—entry into professional careers and the decline in experimentation with communal living—provoked former activists to reflect on the meaning of their earlier engagement, and, in some cases, re-work it for a new present. In the

---

[32] Interview with Morten Thing, conducted by AW, Copenhagen, 12 February 2009; Morten Thing, 'Inkvisitionens hærgen: venstrefløjens historie', *Solidaritet* 22, 2000, 12–21.
[33] Interview with Klaus Hartung, conducted by AvdG, Berlin, 5 January 2010.

final sections, we reflect on how activists respond to the ways in which 1968 has been remembered in different political contexts, assessing the ways in which they seek to reframe and recover the meaning of their experiences in light of both the political right's demonization of their activism and their own critiques of their former political and moral commitments.

Professionalizing activism

Many young activists later became journalists, lawyers, human rights activists, psychologists, teachers, academics and researchers, childcare and social workers, and, in some instances, business people.[34] The moments at which their public activism began to compete with, or even be replaced by, a fuller involvement with professional life are often presented as important staging posts at which they began a process of rethinking the meaning of their earlier activism. On one hand, radicals might face the charge from former colleagues that they had 'sold out' by taking 'refuge in institutions'. On the other, individuals themselves had to determine whether to bring their radical energies into their chosen profession. These decisions drew upon many considerations: new critiques of their earlier activist periods, their assessments of the power of protest, their attempts to accommodate activism with the demands of parenthood, and their judgements as to how best to embed their values into deep-rooted professional and political structures where they could have a long-lasting impact on the development of society. Some view their careers as the direct continuation of a struggle that they began in an earlier radical period; others are convinced that the transition from public to professional activism gave them the power to change lives around them in more concrete ways, or view themselves as part of movements to revolutionize professions in a way that embedded long-term social and cultural change. Yet this is not true for all: some understand their 'retreat into professionalism' as an attempt to depoliticize themselves and distance themselves from their activist past. These decisions were often not merely due to individual choice, but reflected broader possibilities and meanings of activism in the professional sphere that varied across professions and across countries and political systems.

For some, entry into the professional world is viewed as the direct continuation of earlier activism. Indeed, for the former West German activist Peter Schleuning (b. 1941), now a distinguished emeritus professor of musicology, his professional and political interests were combined even during his most active years. He was a member of the musical protest group Red Note, which became a regular fixture of the anti-nuclear protests in Wyhl in the early 1970s. The band saw bridging the gap between the local winegrowers and the Freiburg students who rallied against the construction of a nuclear power plant as one of its main tasks and this was reflected in its musical canon; they not only played re-worked songs of socialist composers from the 1920s (Hanns Eisler, Bertolt Brecht), but also

---

[34] On their notable concentration in teaching or helping professions, see Giugni, 'Personal and biographical consequences', 494

adapted old German folk songs to resonate with the local population. Schleuning does not see his music as a sphere to which he eventually 'retreated' after becoming 'disillusioned' with his activist commitment. On the contrary, he portrays his professional life as inextricably bound to his activism. He is convinced that his music nurtured his activism and made it more effective. However, he faced the charge that he had 'sold out' and chosen the 'cushy' path. Given such accusations, former activists sometimes felt the need to defend their careers as having enabled a more effective form of activism than just 'standing in front of factories', or they emphasize how they did not become 'institutionalized' or ensnared by the temptations of careerism:

> ... contrary to other people it was always very important to me... in spite of *and* because of my political ideas and activism that I continued my professional stuff. Musicology and playing the flute helped me tremendously in the future, because I could use it professionally and in my political activities and elsewhere. I could do things. Other people just stood in front of factories and handed out leaflets, which I don't seek to condemn. Some of them eventually dropped out, did other things and... my advantage was that I passed all the exams and that I knew my stuff. And I could apply it. Many people thought that that was quite cushy.[35]

He explains that his political beliefs fed into and shaped his academic interests, as he sought to make the study of music more accessible and 'democratic'. His research interests—old folk music, the political aspects of the works of composers such as Bach, Beethoven, the role of nature and the environment in eighteenth-century music, the music of Mendelssohn's sister Fanny Hensel—all reflect his former beliefs and commitments.

As a former chairman of the West German SDS, K.D. Wolff (b. 1943) is one of the best-known West German activists of 1968. Like Schleuning, he sees his entry into the professional world not as straying from the path of revolution, but rather as the transfer of ideas of rebellion into the publishing world, to revolutionize the editing process of literary works. Wolff now runs the successful and distinguished publishing house Stroemfeld in Frankfurt. He began his publishing career in the late 1960s, working for several independent publishing houses that put out the writings of the New Left. In the context of the hunt for members of the terrorist RAF, police pressure on these outlets grew within Germany, and Wolff decided to set up Stroemfeld across the border in Basel in 1979. By then, he was keen to do something original. Their first big project—which was completed only recently—was a multi-volume, painfully annotated edition of the works of German romantic poet Friedrich Hölderlin that lay bare his many re-workings of the original text for the first time:

> We wanted to do something new. Something that was linked to our interests and dreams. And we no longer wanted to just instrumentalize ourselves... And Hölderlin was perfect... We could find links to the revolutionary movement around 1800. That failed as well, you know. And we saw that we could do something that did not just

---

[35] Interview with Peter Schleuning, conducted by AvdG, Bremen, 22 December 2008.

have to do with the 'power question', but something that arose from our own work and that would make a real difference, within ourselves and society…We practically turned the whole editorial sciences upside down …[36]

Dane Kristian Riis (b. 1941) also tells a story that links his initial activism with his later professional work. He presents his life as a consistent engagement with different kinds of activism that all promoted democratization through encouraging the feedback of users, and decentralized and flatter organizational structures. He does not perceive his transition from full-time political activist to father and professional as a rejection of older concerns but as a natural continuation of them in different spheres. In 1975, he took up a part-time job at the Huset (The House), which was a centre for cultural and political activism in Copenhagen. It had been founded by Det ny Samfund (The New Society) and became more professionalized and 'managed' during the 1970s, but was still collectively run and shaped by its users. His appointment at Huset was part of this semi-professionalization. Riis was fired in 1981 because of conflicts and in the following years he had a turbulent work life engaging in lots of different cultural activities, fuelled by both his energetic entrepreneurship and generous unemployment benefit. He considers 1985 to be the most important turning point. He got a job in a local council organizing activities for elderly people, which later landed him a job as general secretary for the organization of voluntary social work. He more or less ceased his political activities but considers his various posts as 'jobs marked by activism'. This shift was not based on a critique of the full-time activism that had previously subsumed his entire life—as is the case for other activists—but rather was understood a natural turning point related to the formation of his family. His former activism and involvement was transformed into a job where he thought he could promote and realize many of his ideas and political aspirations:

> And I can see that the idea of user involvement is something I've taken with me when I do voluntary social work…There are core values that mean something, even today. This is why you, for example, shouldn't define people's lives without allowing them to have a say. And that's what I've brought with me; you shouldn't bloody make policies on ageing without having a forum where you can enter into dialogue with the elderly, the people who will be affected. And I think then, that one of the things I'm most proud of is actually making laws on user involvement in nursing homes, because I'm truly convinced by the idea that the most disadvantaged elderly can have an influence on their institutions…And that comes from the youth rebellion. It would have been inconceivable without us.[37]

Although Morten Thing also frames his narrative of his transformation of full-time activism into intellectual work as a continuation, he distinguishes between his earlier period of acting politically as an activist and his later life as a political intellectual. As the son of a Jewish mother and a former leader of a resistance sabotage organization, both of whom had left the DKP after 1956, he entered

[36] Interview with K.D. Wolff, conducted by AvdG, Berlin, 28 May 2008.
[37] Riis interview.

political activism very young, explaining that 'beyond our parents' break with the DKP we were under an obligation [to commit to] a political project'. His first independent political act was participating in the marches organized by CND, followed by a deep involvement in the different socialist parties, the student revolt and the movement against the Vietnam War. Crucially, he became part of the editorial staff of the influential Danish leftist magazine *Politisk Revy* in 1969, although he remained a full-time activist until 1972. At this point, he abandoned the Venstresocialisterne (Left Socialists), in part because he started to have doubts about Leninism and because he decided to finish his studies: 'Then *Politisk Revy* became very much what I was doing as a political activist. So the writing and acting politically in that way very much replaced the activism'. Today Thing is employed as a research university librarian, has a doctoral degree in history and literature, a long career as a debater behind him, and is the author of books and articles about the history of communism, Jewish history and various other topics, including pornography, Zionism and the Palestinian question. In 1981 he stopped editing *Politisk Revy*, obtained a research grant a year later, and had a second child and twins within the space of two years:

> The activist or political practice sort of started to hang together because of the criticism of the Danish Communist Party, which politically was very topical at the end of the 1970s, when I was writing my first book... Of course it continued being political, but it also became very much a part of my own lifelong project because I started to research 'what I am'... But I actually think that, well besides I have had political intellectual work. Well, I played a part in creating *Giraffen* [*The Giraffe*, a left-wing magazine in the 1990s]. And I have been writing a lot in *Social Kritik* [*Social Critique*]. All in all I considered that I had two ways of writing [as scholar and as debater]. I don't think these roles were contradictory. But it was two different ways of doing things. And I think it has been that way all the time, but in a way I never really got back to being an activist. The left wing started to change greatly. So my research took over. Research and the children took over, didn't they?[38]

Thing's autobiographic narrative takes the form of continuous reflections on socialist ideas and practice. For him, his scholarly research is both closely intertwined with his personal identity work, and is understood as a kind of political practice designed to encourage public debate about leftist activism, especially in the context of the right's attacks on former activists, including himself.

The meaning of professionalization in different lives was shaped not only by individual choice but also by the possibilities for activism that were provided both publicly and within the professional sphere; nowhere is this more apparent than for those living under the very different conditions of the communist bloc. Some Hungarian activists present their entry into the professional world as a greater rupture with the public activism than those elsewhere. Following a period of some tolerance for radical activity in the late 1960s and early 1970s, a conservative backlash within the Party elite in 1973 saw increasingly punitive clampdowns on the

---

[38] Thing interview.

expression of independent activist behaviour and the exile of prominent figures such as radical György Pór, Situationist artist Tamás Szentjóbi and sociologist Iván Szelényi who were considered to have overstepped ideological boundaries in either their public activities or professional work. Many of the young student radicals of the late 1960s were experimenting with new ways of working, or the possibility of entering the professional workplace, in the early to mid-1970s. The beginnings of a career thus frequently required a reassessment of activism: some searched for professions in which they could continue the issues of social concern that had once motivated their once semi-tolerated public activism, while others saw it as a radical step of rejecting their past politicized identities that now were pointless in a political system they increasingly felt could not be changed.

Judit Gáspár (b. 1946) wished to continue her radical identity in new settings, and searched out a space where she could express those social concerns that had once animated her activism, but the possibilities for which were increasingly closed down in public. She had become a supporter of what the state termed 'Maoism', was kicked out of university in 1968, and began to work in the Ganz factory in Budapest as a sociologist in the ergonomics section. This was her first and only attempt to use her professional position to assert her revolutionary ideas: she tried to conduct research within the factory that explored the possibility of workers' democracy, and was involved in various projects to encourage workers to question their own position within the enterprise. She was eventually fired for spreading what was considered oppositional material. She later became a prominent psychoanalyst and promoter of 'free association' techniques. The turning point for her was her attendance at the radical sociological seminars in the early 1970s led by András Hegedűs, the former communist prime minister. Then, rejecting the political sphere as a space in which social transformation could be enabled, she decided to train as a psychologist. She explains that she had given up on the revolutionary potential of the proletariat in the factory, so turned her professional attention to those workers who had achieved social mobility but had psychological difficulties:

> they [factory workers] weren't really opponents of the regime [which she had hoped they would be], it was really painful to me that we couldn't ever get them to protest. But for me, I became a psychologist and I have remained so until today... a good deal of my psychoanalytic practice deals with the suffering of first generation intellectuals. A very difficult business...[39]

She lived in a commune between 1971 and 1974 as she went through her training, and then worked in a psychiatric unit in Pesthidegkút. Despite knowing some of the members of the nascent democratic opposition in the late 1970s, she decided not to resume her former political activism: the intellectual radicalism and social concern that her career allowed her to express were more important. However, she often found herself in conflict with the state owing to her experimental practice.

---

[39] Interview with Judit Gáspár, conducted by PA, Budapest, 11 March 2009.

Another former Hungarian Maoist views his entry into the professional world as a radical act of depoliticization in a world in which meaningful political change was impossible. He had originally seen his decision to study economics at the prestigious Karl Marx Economics University in Budapest as a socially progressive choice; he relates how, in the mid-1960s, he wanted to contribute to reforming the socialist economy and society in an environment in which economists could be meaningfully interested in sociology and social renewal. He also notes the freer intellectual atmosphere that allowed his own, less officially approved radicalism to develop: he helped organize a semi-official Vietnam Solidarity Committee, anti-imperialist demonstrations and a network of radical so-called 'Maoist' students as part of a radical 'Marxist-Leninist' alternative. Yet his eventual choice of career as an economist is presented as the result of a growing realization that political action was pointless. This was based on two major events, he notes. First, the trial of those colleagues with whom he had been involved in formulating socialist alternatives; these developments convinced him that political action was an impossibility, and he, along with disillusioned colleagues, began their journey into a professional career of scholarship as a way of escaping politics:

> The basic turning point was, when one's ambitions changed. It's probably attributable to the so-called Maoist conspiracy—and the [official] movement against our university group and its members—when it turned out that there had been an informer in our cells. Basically it's down to that, three of us who had broad connections with this, all three of us turned to scholarship, and at least until 1990 we didn't even try to deal with politics.[40]

The second was his reaction to the suppression of the Prague Spring: although he had not always identified with its reformers, he nevertheless presents the entry of Soviet troops into Czechoslovakia as representing the end of his real interest in political change:

> It meant that 'after August' [i.e. 1968], it was clear that political actions were not compatible with the norms of the system, and from this point of view the system didn't give you any hope…it was utterly irrelevant what I thought about Vietnam, communism, the Soviet Union, imperialism or anything else.

Unlike Gáspár, he did not try to bring his formerly radical identity into his work, but rather saw his career as a way of depoliticizing himself. His professional study of economics was no longer viewed as part of a programme to change socialism from within; rather, his decision to avoid politically relevant research topics emerged from both a political disillusionment and a desire to protect himself from politicized attacks by the regime:

> I didn't explicitly follow any kind of political activity; if you like, I witnessed it all from my 'ivory tower'. Because I decided that here, with what was here, I couldn't deal with many themes in a scholarly way, as one was required to mock and ridicule capitalism, therefore…there was only a single thing that you could really deal with in a scholarly

[40] Interview with anonymous respondent, conducted by PA, Budapest, 5 October 2008.

way: earlier economic theories. Now it wasn't something that was really important in the course of 'socialist construction'...but at the same time it guaranteed me some academic tolerance...so I began to deal with earlier history....

Rethinking experiments with intimate life

Expanding politics and blurring the boundaries of the private and the public, the personal and the political, was at the very heart of different forms of communal living around 1968.[41] Reflecting on such all-consuming activities features prominently in the accounts of former communards. Many activists' autobiographical narratives chart a journey from growing up in conventional nuclear families with fixed gender roles, a bigoted sexual morality and authoritarian upbringing, through a phase of experiments with new forms of living, sexuality and social relations to a return to nuclear families more or less renewed as a result of 1968.

As was the case with many activists, it was a combination of family experiences and the anti-psychiatric criticism of the nuclear family that motivated Danish activist Hatla Thelle (b. 1947) to move into the commune 100 Blomster (Flowers), whose name was inspired by the Chinese Cultural Revolution, in 1969. 'We saw the family as the bogeyman' and our 'goal was that everyone would truly share everything. And everything should be open, and you had to talk about it', she explains. Thelle, who has a degree in sinology and now works at the Danish Centre for Human Rights, began studying psychology in 1967 and quickly became involved in the student riots. She lived in various communes until she started a nuclear family with her new husband in 1980, a trajectory many activists share. While she was living in a commune, she nevertheless believed that she would live this way permanently.

Together with the other communards of Brøndby Strand, which Thelle had joined to live with her boyfriend, Morten Thing, she was involved in the movement against the Vietnam War, wrote pieces that were 'critically enthusiastic' about China in the influential magazine *Politisk Revy* and participated briefly in the feminist women's liberation movement. She and Morten had a child at the same time as another couple in the commune, and in both Brøndby Strand and a collective they lived in even after they had divorced, they tried to put the shared parenting ideal into practice. Thelle's memories of communal life are mostly positive, even though she stopped participating in it after ten years:

> It was really, really good for me...I don't know why they all have to confess their sins and things like that. I think it was right and I think we've all learned immensely from it. I think that society actually learned something from it, too. Fundamentally, I think that it was a really good thing. We tried a lot of things...That means you could say that many of us have returned, in reality, to the nuclear family, but I think we've done it in an extremely well-thought-out way. I don't think there are any of us with unfulfilled dreams.[42]

---

[41] John Davis and Anette Warring, 'Living utopia. Communal living in Denmark and Britain', *Cultural and Social History* 8/4 (2011), 511–28.
[42] Interview with Hatla Thelle, conducted by AW, Copenhagen, 26 January 2009.

Yet, even such positively framed histories usually contain sub-narratives about conflicts, difficulties and failures, which are integrated into a broader story of life as a long learning process. Hatla Thelle refers to conflicts about gender and personal relations, about dominance and 'being collective' enough, which together with shifting love affairs, jealousy and political disagreements are recurrent themes in the narratives of other former communards. Like Thelle, however, most do not distance themselves from the politicization of intimate relationships and the general quest to realize equality and community through communal living and practising radical democracy, the equal distribution of power, resources and work, openness about emotions, sexuality and social relations, and a freer attitude towards the body and physical closeness. Instead, they often refer to the difficulties in putting their vision into practice. Thelle, for one, invokes her socialization when she explains that she returned to the nuclear family because she felt exhausted after having lived in a commune for so many years:

> We've gone back to it [the nuclear family] because it fits our emotional patterns...with what we can live with, right? Well, at that time we could, but when we got older, we couldn't. Living closely together with so many people wasn't possible. I don't think it's possible because you didn't grow up with it...I can remember clearly that I just simply didn't want to. And I was damn angry most of the time. And I can remember when I met Palle [her new partner] and we became lovers, and we expected a child straight away and things like that, then I remember that it was quite clear to me: no more collective...I pictured, well, a small kitchen table and...modest surroundings. Manageable, and not always having to commit oneself, because [in the commune] you always had to get to know the new people coming in, and some people left and others had problems. I didn't want to do it any more.

While Hatla Thelle emphasizes that some of their ideas had been difficult to realize, her former husband, Morten Thing, goes further in reformulating what politicizing the personal actually meant. In his account he uses his experiences about how emotional conflicts were transformed into political conflicts in a commune he joined after Brøndby Strand to critique ideas about expanding politics and politicizing intimate relations in general:

> One way to understand why communal living failed is realizing that we perhaps considered it as too political. And were not capable enough of talking openly about it, organizing different personalities in the same community, that it is difficult for all people in all circumstances, both in marriages and companies and things like that...it was very poor, what were able to bring into this. Well, such as 'you are not communal enough' and things like that.[43]

He now thinks that this is why the psychological make-up and personal relationships of its members were the deciding factors in whether or not living in a commune actually worked.

Reflecting on the experiences and wellbeing of the children that lived in a commune is a pivotal theme in accounts of many former communards. While the

---

[43] Thing interview.

ideal of shared parenthood is rejected principally by all today, the memories are
more diverse and often ambiguous. After years of practising shared childcare in
different communes, both Hatla Thelle and Morten Thing ended up establishing
nuclear families with new partners and new children. Although they both opted to
follow a different model in the long run, their memories of bringing up their children communally are not entirely negative, as demonstrated in Thing's narrative.
On the one hand it 'involved lots of changes in the children's lives with all these
shifts we made'. On the other hand they think 'that the children benefited a lot
from having known all these grown up people' and emphasize that the emotional
ties between the adults and children of the Brøndby Strand commune, where the
children were born, have lasted to this day.

Pia Søndergaard (b. 1945) in contrast feels that, as a single mother with an
infant, she did not get the help and support she needed while living in the Danish
commune of Anholtsgade. Anholtsgade was a squat commune and, unlike Brøndby
Strand, it was not formed by a pre-existing group of friends but by individuals
motivated by opposition to urban renewal. In order to escape her biological family,
Pia had studied in West Germany between 1966 and the summer of 1968 and had
been part of the radical student milieu that had contacts to people around later
RAF terrorists Andreas Baader and Ulrike Meinhof. Finding her life in Germany
increasingly difficult and dangerous, she returned to Denmark after being injured
by the police during the 'Easter riots' of 1968. Back in Denmark, she continued
her political activities. Abandoned by her son's father, a West German activist, she
agreed to move into the commune, but quickly realized that the decision-making
processes and division of labour did not live up to her ideals of equality and solidarity. Her story revolves around examples of gender inequality: 'it was the men
who ruled'. They left household tasks undone in order to attend political meetings;
divorced fathers let her watch their children when they had them; and the men
believed that the sexual revolution meant that women should be sexually available
at all times, seeing them as middle-class prudes if they turned them down:

> Sexuality was a big issue. People had sex wherever and with whomever. And there was
> alcohol; there was hash. These factors had quite a big influence on life, I think. When
> the guys came home from the pub, for example, they were really horny, you know, and
> they assumed that the women should...I had a hard time coping with this view of
> women...as someone who should just be readily available. At one point, I started
> locking my door...I wasn't prepared to be at their disposal sexually. I wanted to decide
> about my own body. And whom I would have sex with.[44]

Disappointed expectations about what she believed would be a substitute for her
authoritarian, insensitive and uncaring family were central for her:

> We were overtaken by daily life and our own backgrounds and by how complex life
> really was...There was a hard, heartless attitude. It was like there was no empathy; we
> were pretty tough on each other...We thought we were driven by reason, but in real-
> ity it was our likes and dislikes. And of course our emotions that controlled things.

---

[44] Interview with Pia Søndergaard, conducted by AW, Århus, 4 February 2009.

She shares Thelle's perception that the communards' own socialization process was a significant obstacle for realizing radical changes in domestic life. Similar to Thing, she points out that personal and emotional relationships were crucial to whether one's memories of experimenting with communal living and the politicization of people's private lives were positive or negative. Søndergaard moved out of the commune and became active in the women's liberation movement, where she found the solidarity and warmth she had lacked at Anholtsgade. She gradually cut back on her activism but kept her ties to Germany. She had become close friends with Rudi and Gretchen Dutschke, who lived in Denmark from 1971 onwards, and she was present when Dutschke died on Christmas Eve 1979. After the end of the decade and once she had got married, however, she ended her involvement in politics.

Not all activists turned their back on this way of life. Peter Gäng's (b. 1942) colourful political trajectory saw him evolve from being a full-time activist and fervent anti-Vietnam War campaigner in the West German SDS to becoming a construction worker, followed by a successful career as a Buddhist scholar and business coach. While his professional commitments have changed frequently over the last forty years, he has lived in the same commune since the early 1970s. Some of its members left over time, but three of the original communards still share a spacious apartment on the top floor of a large block of flats in Berlin Kreuzberg: Peter Gäng, his long-term partner, as well as another woman.

Like Morten Thing, Gäng is convinced that emotional chemistry and a shared outlook on life are much more important than political conformity in making communal life work. The Kreuzberg communards share all their income and brought up one woman's son together, whom Gäng considers his own even though he is not the biological father. They had also raised the daughter of another woman who eventually left the commune because she no longer felt comfortable having joint finances. Gäng explains that, like those of Brøndby Strand, the two children of this Kreuzberg commune think of each other as brother and sister and share many positive memories of their upbringing—even though they have chosen to set up nuclear families themselves.

Gäng's account of living communally is a far cry from popular representations of 1960s communes as centres of free love and hedonism; while he and his long-term partner have had a monogamous relationship, they have shared all other aspects of their lives with the other communards.[45] Gäng's idea of communal living pivots on providing a support network, both emotionally and financially, and in this spirit they jointly took care of two of Gäng's elderly relatives before their deaths. This explains why he remains highly critical of the nuclear family, albeit without his former missionary zeal:

> It [communal living] was simply the alternative to the bourgeois nuclear family. And of the bourgeois nuclear family: firstly, all of us knew what it was, because we

---

[45] Our respondents do not include people who lived in extreme experiments as e.g. the Vienna Friedrichshof commune formed by disciples of Wilhelm Reich.

had all grown up in such a thing...And on the other hand the fact that it is a way of living that is not sustainable. Well...to my great surprise it still works, but at the time I was certain that a communal form of living is really the best thing one can imagine. I still think that, but today I don't think that everybody ought to see this. It turns out that not everybody recognizes it. It's just—today at my age—this notion that you live in a family with father, mother, two children, the children then go off somewhere and either father or mother dies and the other one remains...I think this is an appalling notion![46]

The British lifelong anarchist Clifford Harper (b. 1949) shares this emphasis on the continuing social relevance of communal living, especially in terms of integrating different generations. The son of a free-spirited mother whose innate anti-authoritarianism was sharpened in the restrictive context of a grammar school education, he interested himself in communal living as a means of expressing his lifelong hostility to formal social structures and institutionalization. His first commune, in deepest rural Cumbria, was established not only as an experiment in collective living but also as a reception centre for escapees from mental hospitals. Harper himself, though, rejected both the escapism and the discomfort of rural Cumbria and, having failed to re-ignite revolution in Paris in 1969, established a new commune at Eel Pie Island, in the Thames near Twickenham. This ambitious collective experiment enjoyed an idyllic beginning in the autumn of 1969, but, dominated by junkies, eventually collapsed eighteen months later. Harper spent much of the 1970s in a series of London squats, finding squatter communities more 'outward', less introverted, than communards, before moving into housing association accommodation. The bruising experience of social disintegration at Eel Pie Island left him permanently aware of the problems associated with collective living, but he has never abandoned the ideal, and has recently become more conscious again of its advantages:

Lately my thinking has changed quite a bit about it all, because lately I've become ill...And I've become old...And I've also become poor. And that's changed my attitude towards collective living, because if I was living collectively a lot of the troubles I've got, I wouldn't have...The answer is I think we should live collectively. I think living in groups is really a much better way of doing it. Particularly if you're ill or incapable...There should be all ages together.[47]

While Harper consciously decided to abandon the communal way of life but has since reappraised it, other ex-communards would not consider reviving their former experiments, but nevertheless experienced the process of leaving the collective behind as painful.

Former Danish communard Birgitte Due (b. 1944) acknowledged that she was in need of a more peaceful life after having been active virtually full-time for more than two decades. Due had become politically involved early on, taking part in the Danish student riots and the anti-Vietnam War movement in the 1960s and

---

[46] Interview with Peter Gäng, conducted by AvdG, Berlin, 29 April 2010.
[47] Interview with Clifford Harper, conducted by JD, London, 12 May 2009.

devoting herself entirely to feminist activism in the women's liberation and lesbian movements in the 1970s. She lived in various communes with communal property rights and open attitudes towards sexual relations, one of which was a female folk high school that the women's movement established, a self-contained feminist society. In the late 1980s, Due finished training as a therapist, which she considered to be a natural extension of the women's movement's 'therapeutic touch'. She became a self-employed therapist and is no longer politically active. While this was her decision, she did not find swapping life in a community with one determined by individual responsibility easy:

> It's a completely different life; it's a life that's very different to the life of an activist. I lived in the context of a commune for years and I missed, I greatly missed being part of a fellowship—a community process—when I suddenly worked alone with clients and had sole responsibility for supervision. Being a part of a group that creates something together and has ideas and inspires each other and suchlike. I have that to some degree because I also do things with other colleagues, but daily life is just completely different. I missed it on the one hand but got, on the other hand, a sense of peace, some time for self-contemplation and the space to calm down and let my nervous system settle down, because it had been highly tense for all those years... Like a thousand other people I lament the fact that we don't have the same amount of community spirit in our lives now... I'm not the only one who suddenly lives much more separately from others.[48]

For Franziska Groszer (b. 1945) leaving East Berlin's Kommune 1 Ost, which she and her husband Gert had set up with another married couple in early 1969, was unambiguously a huge relief. She and Gert had married and had two children soon after finishing school, but quickly encountered marital problems that they hoped to overcome in a communal flat with their friends Frank Havemann and Erika Berthold. Franziska recalls the first few months of this living experiment—fairly exceptional in East Germany with its state-controlled housing market—very fondly:

> For a few months it was just fun, it was fun to do joint activities with the other adults and the children, to sit in the kitchen in the evening... it was the first time we sat around in this kind of circle and really talked about ourselves, about our parents, about our fantasies, ideas, and to think about ourselves collectively and individually. That was an intense, very intense, and fun period... And well, it didn't last very long, because the men went off in a completely different direction... and I became an enemy of the state in my own house... an incredibly dismal situation.[49]

This was as much a personal as a political breach about the question of whether one should try and change the GDR by embracing state socialism and 'marching through the institutions' or by continuing more open dissidence, which was Franziska Groszer's choice. By this stage, she had a new partner and recalls the period during which she searched for a new place to live as painful for both her children and herself:

---

[48] Interview with Birgitte Due, conducted by AW, Copenhagen, 8 December 2010.
[49] Interview with Franziska Groszer, conducted by AvdG, Berlin, 7 October 2008.

It lasted for roughly another six months during which I spent more or less time there, tried to get my own flat, partly stayed with other friends—with the children and without the children. A really, really, dismal situation, and I still ask myself today, well, I don't ask myself, but I am angry that I didn't have the insight to say, for the sake of the children alone, 'sod yourselves, this is my flat' and chucked them out...I'm still angry that I did that, because I exposed my children, who were still very young, to a lot of instability...because I was so unhappy, and there was no calm anywhere, no resting place...that was quite terrible.

Although Franziska Groszer clearly has many regrets about this time, these centre around the disintegration of relationships and the political breach that opened up within the group. Few activists rejected, in principle, the communal way of life; however, at some point, most of our interviewees chose not to go on living this way. For some, having children was the primary trigger, for others it came after having lived communally with their children for many years. The late 1970s, when youth rebellion and political activism on the left were generally waning, were a key moment. Many of the activists who had lived a communal life in the 1960s and 1970s had got older, finished their studies and had children. While it is difficult to establish an unambiguous causal link between the commune movement's cycle and the life stage of the activists involved, some convergence can be identified. The number of communes declined in the late 1970s and looking back at the experiences of experimenting with politics and different lifestyles determined the mood. It was at this point that a number of activists first published books about their experiences.[50]

Rethinking radical commitment

Politics was not only personalized in communal flats, but the boundaries were blurred when activism subsumed individuals' entire lives, when personal conflicts were transformed into political ones and vice versa, and when critique and self-criticism were practised in political groups based on the model of 'cultural revolution'.[51]

Like many ex-communards, former activists, who had been part of one of the manifold close-knit networks of different brands of Marxism-Leninism that emerged in western Europe in the wake of 1968, began to chronicle and reflect back on their experiences when these groups began to disintegrate in the late 1970s.[52] Today, few western activists believe that agitating in these radicalized groups was the best way to bring about meaningful political change—after all, the

---

[50] See e.g. Niels Westerberg et al., *Livsstykker* (Copenhagen, 1979); Anette Steen Pedersen and Morten Thing, *Far, mor, børn—14 samtaler om familien i krise* (Copenhagen, 1979); and Poul Berendt, *Bissen og Dullen. Familiehistorier fra nutiden* (Copenhagen,1984).

[51] On life in West German K-Groups and their political beliefs see Andreas Kühn, *Stalins Enkel, Maos Söhne: Die Lebenswelt der K-Gruppen in der Bundesrepublik der 70er Jahre* (Frankfurt/M. and New York, 2005); on the intricacies of Norwegian Maoist groups see Terje Tvedt (ed.) *(ml): en bok om maoismen i Norge* (Oslo, 1989).

[52] Autorenkollektiv, *Wir warn die stärkste der Partein...Erfahrungsberichte aus der Welt der K-Gruppen* (Berlin, 1977).

political revolution they had envisaged never occurred. Even those who remain convinced that their radical phase was a good thing in principle often concede that they lacked a sense of perspective towards the outside world. In turn, activists who came to reject their radical commitment still feel the need to explain what had once fuelled their—seemingly futile—endeavours. They thus highlight the intensity of life in radical groups or invoke the allure and sense of purpose and security their radicalism provided to make sense of the longevity and depth of their political dedication.

French activist Anne Victorri (b. 1949) had been part of the Maoist GP in the early 1970s. She sacrificed the chance of a university education and a conventional marriage to the revolution, and got involved with her husband Bernard in trying to raise the industrial working class of northern France to revolt while bringing up two small children. After they abandoned revolutionary activity it seemed impossible to return to their previous lives in Paris so they emigrated to Canada. Coming back to France in 1984 she put her children into an experimental school and became a children's librarian. Her account veers between regrets that she was young and naïve and a desire to keep the faith and remain loyal to comrades and causes:

Sometimes I think it was yesterday...I don't repudiate anything, I love what I was, I love that commitment. We were totally bound up with the masses. We were mistaken about almost everything, there were things that didn't make any sense. But politically I would sometimes like to have the sort of naïveté I used to have, the Manichean view of good and bad, left and right. Now my thoughts seem to be more complicated and more difficult to express...I think that when you are fifteen or twenty, to want to change the world is...I continue to think that it is rather good.[53]

Roland Castro (b. 1940), who founded VLR after 1968, was a 'soft' Maoist rather than the 'hard' variety of the GP, and dissolved VLR when it started to pull itself apart over questions of political violence and sexual politics. A graduate of the École des Beaux Arts, he developed a career as an architect after spending seven years in therapy with Jacques Lacan, and persuaded President Mitterrand to underwrite his 'Banlieu 89' project to transform run-down inner cities. He retained from his communist past the idea of collective projects that could make life more humane, but rejected what he saw as the Maoist idea that human nature could be altered to create beings who were entirely committed to revolution:

I have remained a communist in that I believe that you can do things together...I still have the idea that you can change society but I now think that while people can grow you can't change them. Changing men, no thank you, Mr Mao Tse-Tung, I'm not with you, I'm not going there. I am up for doing things, and for changing society with people who are, as Malraux said, 'miserable heaps of little secrets'...I think that one reason I dissolved VLR was that I realized that at the end of the day you cannot change people.[54]

Christian Semler (b. 1938), formerly a prominent member of the West German SDS, spent the entire 1970s as a leading and full-time functionary of the Maoist KPD. The

[53] Interview with Anne Victorri, conducted by RG, Paris, 28 May 2007.
[54] Interview with Roland Castro, conducted by RG, Paris, 9 May 2007.

anti-bureaucratic and popular thrust of the Maoist revolution appealed to him; like Anne Victorri and Roland Castro, he is adamant that he would never 'join the choir of condemnation'. Semler found life as a full-time functionary enriching in many ways, but nevertheless questions the extent of his radical commitment and the human toll it took. He admits that 'It led to a really strong narrowing of my horizon. Before then I was interested in many more things'. Many of his fellow Maoists had played musical instruments before joining the cadre group, Semler recalls, but stopped prac-tising because of their ever intensifying political commitment. Friendships outside the groups and family relationships became increasingly hard to maintain:

> That is a real drama. I'd had a relatively large circle of friends and…ending these rela-tionships was already the norm in the late 1960s. My mum died as early as '74 and I'd just about kept in touch with her…we strongly lacked any perspective on human relationships. That was the case with everyone.[55]

Other ex-radicals reject their former selves much more forcefully and structure their stories around their desire to 'atone'. Tissy Bruns (b. 1951), now a well-known editor of the left-liberal German daily *Tagesspiegel*, was a highly committed activist in the newly founded West German Communist Party for nearly twenty years, first as a leading functionary of the party's student wing, MSB Spartakus, which dominated West German university politics in the 1970s, and later as a writer for the German Communist Party-financed *Deutsche Volkszeitung*. Bruns now emphatically rejects her former beliefs and describes herself as politically 'moderate to the core'. Nevertheless, she still understands what had attracted her to one of the 'political sects'. She remembers the 1970s as a really strange mixture of a life without rules and of 'revolutionary discipline'. Bruns describes the members of these radical groups as extremely ambitious, often working seventy-hour weeks and trying to outdo each other in showcasing their commitment to the revolution-ary cause. This was less the result of the particular brand of Marxism-Leninism the German Communist Party espoused—you 'were where your friends were', she explains—as of the close-knit community and unified worldview the party offered:

> I think that in my case one of the sources of this gigantic error was the deceptive intel-lectual promise that one held the philosopher's stone, the universal formula, in one's hand. And to apply a theory to everything that both explains things and guides you…[56]

While she still recognizes the seductiveness of her past convictions—the 'idea that one really knew the true essence of life'—she now considers this deeply problematic, because it killed the original 'critical spirit' of 1968, which she still considers positive:

> …because you start to make reality fit the theory…which is intellectually seductive…It becomes terrible at the point—which we soon reached—when you start to disregard as unimportant…concrete human rights in the name of an abstract, better world.

---

[55] Interview with Christian Semler, conducted by AvdG, Berlin, 29 August 2008.
[56] Interview with Tissy Bruns, conducted by AvdG, Berlin, 18 December 2009.

Although Bruns had doubts long before the collapse of communism in 1989, she explains that it took until then to cut her ties with the German Communist Party because she had already gone incredibly far in the name of the Party. She only left when she had a child and frames her post-activist years as driven by a desire to right her previous wrongs. Although she discusses what she refers to as a 'gigantic error' very openly, Bruns refuses to draw 'moral lessons' from it, which, she fears, would vindicate her past choices indirectly. Instead, she explains that she feels a fundamental 'life sadness' of both a 'selfless and selfish kind'. The selfless kind stemmed from 'really having made mistakes...That was the case...My head, my mind, and my heart say that'. The selfish part arose from the fact that, 'I could have done so many other, better things with all that time'.

Like Tissy Bruns, the Danish activist Charlotte Christiani (b. 1949) points to the lack of critical reflection at the time and argues that it ultimately contributed to the left's defeat. Contrary to Bruns, however, Christiani does not think that this omission was the result of ideological commitment and the 'unified worldview' it provided, but believes that their extremely high level of activity simply left little time to reflect. Christiani was awakened politically during a stay at an American university in 1968 where she encountered the hippie culture and protests against the Vietnam War. After returning to Denmark, she dedicated herself intensely to activism concerned with labour unions and housing policy. She lived in various communes and was a member of the Kommunistisk Forbund (Communist Alliance), which prioritized political activism in the workplace and ideological schooling. In addition to her studies and a full-time job and raising children later on, she maintained an extremely high level of activity; hence, experiencing exhaustion is a recurrent theme in her narrative:

> Life at that time was insanely impulsive, extraordinarily intense and hectic. For me, there was too little time for reflection. I didn't even really realize that taking time for reflection was important...Everything happened so quickly and you always had to consider: Does it matter...Is it true...Does it matter...Does it matter now? Is there time to think about it? No, there isn't. You have to make a decision now...Life always seemed to consist of making insanely quick decisions...Actually it would've been possible to get something totally different out of the left in Denmark if we'd been more visionary or if we'd perhaps taken more time to reflect than I had, I think...Things went too fast, the movement and the time.[57]

Like Christian Semler, discussed above, West German Helga Hirsch (b. 1948) spent the entire 1970s in the Maoist KPD. She is now a liberal journalist and, in 2010, ran the press operation for the first presidential campaign of former East German dissident Joachim Gauck, who was finally elected in 2012. Hirsch is very critical of her former ideological convictions, is in contact with few of her former peers, and stresses the futility of her activism; she relates how she often rose before dawn to sell 'four or five' copies of the Party newspaper. Like many others, she brings up the toll her radicalism took on her relationships with people outside

---

[57] Interview with Charlotte Christiani, conducted by AW, Århus, 3 February 2009.

the Party. She invokes this sense of being out of sync with a 'normal' lifecycle to explain what sustained her commitment to the cause over time:

> I sometimes ask myself...what kept us together for so long? And I think that even though I didn't like the others, or some of the others, at least I couldn't lose them, it was stronger than a family. In a way...the ones who left—and that kept me from leaving until the end—no longer had anyone. We—well, I at least—didn't have a job, others had a job. But I didn't know any normal people...I was also afraid to [interact] with normal people, because at my age—I was in my mid-thirties—they had jobs, they had children. I never desperately wanted a child, but perhaps that would have been different if the situation had been different. Well, I wasn't normal.[58]

Hirsch explains that this form of politics as community provided much-needed assurance at a time when most other relationships had disintegrated:

> We were really an in-group. And everyone knew exactly—and perhaps in a perverse sense that's also a form of security—I knew exactly what the line was on a particular day, what I was allowed to say...this represents a limitation, but also security.

Given the unequivocal failure to bring about the political revolution they once envisaged, many western activists struggle to make sense of one-time beliefs that often defined much of their lives for several years, if not decades. They thus invoke the 'intensity' and 'density' of this period, emphasize the self-perpetuating nature of their beliefs, and regularly liken their commitment to that of acolytes of religious sects.

Although operating in fundamentally different conditions, numerous radicalized and often small and clandestine Marxist-Leninist groups also existed in eastern Europe. Typically set up after the reformist movements of 1968 had been crushed, they continued to criticize socialist regimes from the left. Although these were fuelled by a similarly radical commitment to their cause and their members shared many experiences with their western counterparts—including the juggling of professional and political commitments, flirtations with violence, and the severing of relationships outside the group—the overall meaning East European activists give to their radicalism differs considerably from western accounts. Instead of foregrounding their flawed thinking and dogged radicalism, they are able to write their activities into a broader story of opposition and anti-dictatorship struggle—and thus to convey that these had served a purpose that made some of the absurdities and personal difficulties their radical commitment had produced more tolerable.

Like her West German counterparts, Monika Palm (b. 1951), a trained psychotherapist who had been part of a clandestine Trotskyist network in East Germany in the 1970s, emphasizes the 'density' of this period with multiple professional and political commitments. She equally references the impact her political beliefs had on her private life, eventually leading to the disintegration of her marriage. The relationship with her husband no longer worked because of her political commitment. 'You cannot conspire behind your partner's back', she concedes.

---

[58] Interview with Helga Hirsch, conducted by AvdG, Berlin, 30 April 2010.

Despite the heavy toll it took on her personal life, Palm describes her growing radicalism as almost inevitable, as having emerged organically from a series of encounters with state repression that had begun at an early age. She finally joined a small conspiratorial circle of committed Trotskyists in East Berlin in the early 1970s. While her western counterparts often emphasize the 'ideological blinders' of that period and bemoan their lack of 'critical reflection', Palm portrays her Trotskyism as something she went into consciously and with her eyes wide open: 'Joining means exposing myself to danger. Prison is likely...I made this decision and said, "Yes, I will go down this path"'.[59]

After most of her fellow Trotskyists had been imprisoned in 1976, Palm felt increasingly trapped and became even more radicalized as a result. She considered taking up the armed struggle and began to think seriously about stocking weapons. She is clearly relieved that her pregnancy and the birth of her son Lew in 1980 'saved' her from seeing this through. While having a child was no doubt a decisive moment that made her reassess her political activities, her narrative of spiralling radicalization ends very abruptly with her emigration to West Germany in 1981. Since then, she has focussed on her work as a psychotherapist and finds herself increasingly convinced that individual 'energy' and personal harmony, not politics, provide the keys to a fulfilled life. Because Palm's account of her radical commitment—including her flirtation with violence—is framed as anti-dictatorship struggle, there seemed to be no place for it once she had left the GDR.

The subtly different ways in which activists make sense of their former radical commitment in eastern and western Europe come even more clearly to the fore in the narrative of Rupert Schröter (b. 1949), the unofficial leader of Palm's Trotskyist cell. Unlike her, he joined a clandestine Trotskyist cell within the SDP once he had been released from GDR prison and arrived in West Berlin in the late 1970s. Born into a family of leading GDR functionaries, Schröter had been introduced to Trotsky's writings by a French diplomat's daughter after he had become disillusioned with socialist reality in the GDR. While many western ex-radicals invoke the inflexibility of their ideological corset, Schröter relates how Trotsky opened up a world beyond state socialism. The writings gave him a language to criticize the regime and a lens through which to study 'where the socialist experiment had taken a wrong turn'. This was empowering: 'I needed a theory' that 'gave me the right' to want different things, Schröter explains.

He no longer subscribes to Trotskyism and concedes that he had been extremely radical and 'overly ideological' in the 1970s, but still maintains that GDR Trotskyists asked the right kinds of questions of state socialism. Schröter still understands what attracted him to these ideas, but when talking about his experiences with West German Trotskyism in the late 1970s and 1980s his account veers towards those of repenting westerners such as Tissy Bruns or Helga Hirsch. While he interprets his East German Trotskyist phase as part of a broader—and explicitly 'heroic'—struggle against a repressive dictatorship, his account of his latter phase is embedded in a

[59] Interview with Monika Palm, conducted by AvdG, Berlin, 7 January 2010.

narrative of dogged western radicalism and left-wing dogmatism that served little purpose and was terribly 'misanthropic'. Schröter describes the western Trotskyists thus:

> A difficult club, a difficult club, increasingly also in terms of its membership, the kinds of people who joined—proper pathological types, including myself. Well, I had my heroism—but others [joined] who could tell at first glance fulfilled orders and everything, [and had] a sort of bureaucratic character.[60]

In the 1980s he clearly still believed that Trotskyism served a purpose in a liberal democracy—he remained a committed member until the mid-1980s when he was expelled from his group for wanting to form a separate faction. Yet, he now calls joining a West German cell his 'biggest regret' and thinks that he 'brainwashed' himself:

> I cannot say how it happened and it seemed extremely depressing to me. I only really opted for resistance at the end... I have to admit today... I myself wonder... how far this kind of auto-brainwashing can go... Because that's what it took. They didn't come everyday to lock you up and brainwash you... You had to actively participate in this brainwashing.

Only 1989 brought the final realization that 'socialist development' was over, and Schröter spent the next ten years working for a Social Democratic politician in Brandenburg, a period he remembers most fondly. Once the GDR had ceased to exist, Trotskyism—which for Schröter had always been tied up with a quest to critique and eventually undermine the East German dictatorship—no longer had any role to play.

While Schröter's account no doubt provides a particularly powerful illustration of the ways in which individual choices are framed by the wider political meanings attached to particular types of activism in East and West, activists from elsewhere in Eastern Europe also legitimize their former membership of radical groups as having been driven by a desire to undermine socialist regimes. The Hungarian radical György Pór (b. 1944), for one, did not need to distance himself from his Marxist-Leninist political past as he also understood it as a form of opposition to state socialism. Pór was inspired to found a small 'pure' Marxist-Leninist party with underground cells in the mid-1960s. He presents his most directly political period as a form of legitimate opposition to an overly bureaucratized system that had abandoned the best interests of the workers:

> the influence of Karl Marx... deepened when I started studying his writings and... [I] experienced a sharp contrast between what he envisioned and the Hungarian reality... So that was my first conscious articulation of my opposition to the system... That was also when Mao mobilized the Red Guards against the Party and state bureaucrats and privileges [in the Chinese Cultural Revolution]—that was something much more aligned with the original high ideals [of socialism]—again I didn't know anything about the reality of the Red Guards... many people couldn't really understand that later when I told them about my life.[61]

---

[60] Interview with Rupert Schröter, conducted by AvdG, Berlin, 4 January 2010.
[61] Interview with György Pór, conducted by JM, Brussels, 13 March 2009.

Despite understanding his 'Maoist'[62] phase as a legitimate critique of state socialism, Pór still needed to make sense of this intense period of political activity in other respects, because he had later rejected his radicalization. The twenty-month imprisonment, which had followed his conviction as a subversive 'Maoist' in a trial in Budapest in spring 1968, is presented as the moment when he fundamentally rethought himself as a political creature. First, he began to reflect on the impossibility of creating political change in state socialist Hungary 'from below'. Second, following an engagement with American countercultural writers, he began to see direct political action as a very limited form of expression and instead focussed his energies on raising 'critical consciousness'. In 1974, he was expelled from Hungary and became a sociology lecturer at the University of Vincennes in Paris. By the late 1970s, he had not only withdrawn from politics but had also become critical of intellectualism, and—like Monika Palm after her move to West Germany—found himself primarily interested in the 'inner journey'; Pór travelled to an ashram in India in 1979, before returning to France to open a meditation centre. Although he consciously sought to repress the memory of his political radicalism in Hungary in order to remake himself, Pór nevertheless believes that it marks his present in important ways. In the later stages of his life, he worked to reform public institutions so that human beings would be able to realize their 'creative capacities'. He connects this fascination with the struggle for both institutional and psychological freedom and creativity to his earlier radical politicization:

> Friends who knew me in different stages... frequently told me they just don't understand it, but for me there has been a line throughout these different changes and that was about increasing freedom... In the first half of my life my primary concern was political freedom: being free from a repressive regime. And in the second half, I have been less concerned with freedom from something but rather freedom for realizing our highest potential... now I don't have to fight against an oppressive system [but] there is still the tyranny to defeat, the tyranny of the mind, the tyranny of the ego...

Thus not all former eastern European radicals feel that their radical critiques served little or no purpose in the West or after 1989, but, for the most part, they endow their erstwhile radical commitment with meaning by framing it as part of the struggle against dictatorship—a feat much more difficult to accomplish for activists from western Europe whose radicalism failed to ignite a political revolution.

Repentance for supporting state socialism and Maoism

As we have seen, after ending their involvement in what were often tight-knit and conspiratorial groups, many activists felt the need to address their former radicalism in one way or another in their testimonies. While these reflections were in part driven by activists themselves, those who had supported European state socialism or Chinese Maoism also had to react to *being accused* publicly, particularly from the right. The renewed intensification of the Cold War and the conservative revival embodied by Margaret Thatcher, Helmut Kohl and Ronald Reagan in the 1980s meant that

---

[62] Pór himself rejected the label that the state attached to him.

powerful totalitarian discourses already linked western European individuals' radical left-wing commitments to complicity with dictatorship and violence. Following the collapse of eastern European socialist regimes in 1989 and the Tiananmen Square massacre of the same year, former activists across the continent were attacked more than ever before. In the 1990s, when the news regularly featured revelations about human rights abuses in the former eastern bloc, this erupted into contentious public disputes. In Denmark, for instance, the question of 'Who did they support?' [63] during the Cold War was pivotal in the right's general offensive against the left in the middle of the 1990s, a campaign that intensified after the formation of a right-wing government in 2001 that started 'a cultural struggle against 1968'. Despite the fact that the left had been very divided over the question of support for 'really existing socialism', it was accused *en masse* of treason, or at the very least of having acted as a useful idiot for the communist dictatorships.[64] During the 1990s and 2000s the Danish parliament conducted historical and judicial inquiries that investigated, variously, whether the Danish Security and Intelligence Service had illegally recorded legal leftist political activities and sought to establish the character of these group activities and the so-called external and internal threats during the Cold War. The issues they raised were highly controversial and sparked much public debate.[65] In reunified Germany the fact that many on the West German left had not supported reunification in 1990 provided critics on the right with particularly powerful ammunition to accuse the left of an underlying identification with state socialism. In addition, the arrival of a new left-wing party, the PDS (the successor organization to the former state socialist party of East Germany) on the electoral map fuelled conservative fears of a 'red scare' from within—an alliance between Social Democrats, Greens and ex-Socialists. 'Towards the future, but not in red socks' was a particularly memorable line from a Christian Democratic election poster of 1994 that exemplified the tendency to paint all left-wing groups with the same brush.[66]

While in no small measure sparked by attacks from the right, the notion that former sympathies with Maoism or state socialism needed to be addressed was also part of internal critiques that radicals felt as they began to rethink their activism and political commitments in later decades. In particular, it was former western

---

[63] It was the title of a book edited by the right-liberal Bertel Haarder, who was minister during several right-wing governments. Bertel Haarder (ed.) *Hvem støttede de?* (Copenhagen, 1999). See also Bent Blüdnikow (ed.) *Opgøret om den kolde krig* (Copenhagen, 2003); Adam Holm and Peter Scharff Smith, *Idealisme eller fanatisme? Opgøret om venstrefløjen under den kolde krig* (Copenhagen, 2003). For a brief analysis of the debate see Morten Bendix Andersen and Niklas Olsen, 'Arven fra 68', in Morten Bendix Andersen and Niklas Olsen, *1968. Dengang og nu* (Copenhagen, 2004), 9–28.

[64] Besides the ideological attacks, rightists demanded that former members of the DKP who had come to occupy prominent positions in the Danish media—such as Bjørn Erichsen, the manager of the Danish Broadcasting Corporation (DR) 1996–2002, and Jacob Mollerup the chief editor of the newspaper *Information*—should be fired.

[65] See Nikolaj Petersen, 'Kampen om Den Kolde Krig i dansk politik og forskning', *Historisk Tidsskrift* 109/1 (2009), 154–204.

[66] See also in late 1980s, Bernard Kouchner, *Le Procès de mai*, Roland Portiche and Henri Weber, TF1, 22 May 1988. On the demonization of French 68ers through television 'trial', see Reynolds, *Memories of May '68*, 20–1. Also Ross, *May '68*, especially ch. 3.

European radicals who had idealized state socialism or Maoism who found their former attachments much harder to deal with: later in their lives they admitted their ignorance of the crimes of the eastern bloc, and more commonly sought to address what they now often considered ethical or moral lapses in their earlier political commitments. Some western German activists of this type tell their life story as one of eventual repentance for their support for what they now consider unjustifiable 'totalitarian ideologies'. In particular, they often reflect on the fact that they failed to channel their energies into undermining the GDR dictatorship—or, in some cases, glorified 'really existing socialism'.

Former SDS activist Klaus Hartung, for one, references the 'German question' as a particularly complex and problematic subject for former West German activists. Having lived mostly in Berlin since the 1960s, he thinks it is 'shameful that the Wall existed' for as long as it did and that it never became a focus of their activism, despite the fact that they lived in close physical proximity to it. 'What could we have done?', he asks rhetorically, emphasizing their powerlessness. Hartung further admits that he only realized the importance of the Prague Spring much later and only captured slowly how much of a rupture the Warsaw Pact's invasion had represented. The invasion should have cured him of any illusions about the socialist experiment, he is now convinced, but it did not. 'In reality, our story was over then'.[67]

Katja Barloschky (b. 1954), now the chief executive of a service provider in the employment sector, finds it even more difficult to make sense of her actual endorsement of 'really existing socialism'. A member of the national leadership committee of the German Communist Party's student wing MSB Spartakus in the 1970s and 1980s and a leading and committed party functionary until 1989, Barloschky describes herself as one of those who 'remained until the bitter end'. She finds the longevity of her convictions—by the time she left the Party she had been a member for more than half her lifetime—particularly difficult to come to terms with.

Barloschky explains that even before 1989, she had experienced the rigid Marxist-Leninist doctrine espoused by the West German Communist Party as inflexible and contradictory. She discovered feminism in the 1980s—no more than a 'secondary contradiction' according to the Party line—felt inspired by Gorbachev's *Perestroika*, but also found it increasingly difficult to abstain from criticizing the Soviet Union after the catastrophe in the nuclear reactor at Chernobyl in 1986. She set up a faction within the Party that sought its renewal via a 'Third Way'. It was sidelined by the Party leadership, but she remained part of the Communist Party until 1989, when, following the fall of the Berlin Wall in early November, the whole group, consisting of several hundred members, left jointly. Barloschy felt a mixture of 'relief, happiness and shame' at the time and spent the next five years deliberately and publicly defining herself as an ex-West German Communist Party member.[68] 'It was my skinning process. It was necessary', she explains. It took her another five years to grasp the true extent of Stalinism:

[67] Hartung interview.
[68] Among others, see the article about the difficulties the West German left faced after the collapse of the Wall in which she features as a prominent case study: 'Lieber rot als tot', in *Die Zeit* 45/2 (November 1990).

The dimension and social psychological dimension of the whole process and the tragic relationship to the history of my people, of my country... This question: Why did it happen? Why did I, unlike many others, not decide to leave the Party after Biermann's [a singer and famous East German dissident] expatriation in 1976?[69]

Like several of her peers, Barloschky says that having 'stood for something that was so entirely wrong' made her incapable of getting involved in party politics once more. Since leaving the Party, she has often been asked to consider running for office for either the Social Democrats or the Greens, but finds herself imprisoned by her past 'errors'. 'I can't do it, to stand up in the front row once more and say: "But now I know what's right again!" '.

While reunification may have led West German members of the old communist left to question particularly strongly their former glorification of state socialism, Danish activists of similar political colours were no less vocal about repenting for their past 'errors' after 1989. Michael Kjeldsen (b. 1954), in a newspaper feature entitled 'I was wrong', became part of an intense debate on the left in the mid-1990s about its former relationship with so-called 'real socialism'. Having been a prominent member of the Danish Communist Youth, the communist student organization, KOMM. S., as well as a member of the Communist Party itself later on, Kjeldsen had unquestionably demonstrated his active support of Soviet communism. He had been born into a wealthy bourgeois family and describes himself as a 'conservative revolutionary' who had never been attracted by the youth rebellion's anti-authoritarian cultural activities. Early on, he leaned towards the left, but later explained that his commitment to communism as the one true ideology derived from his anger over the Vietnam War and the coup in Chile, his own personality and an existential crisis resulting from his father's suicide in 1970. He published analyses defending the invasions of Hungary, Czechoslovakia and Afghanistan. His break with communism began with Gorbachev, whom he followed closely. Doubt began to creep in after both his experiences working as a home carer and his new political activities and historical studies that did not fit in with the party's analyses. He also read, for example, Kautsky's critique of Lenin, and Sakharov. Like Barloschky, he experienced the break as a long and painful process that lasted four to five years and ended with his resignation in early 1990:

And during that period I started asking myself distressing questions about whether I was still a communist or whether I was becoming a reformist... While reading Sakharov's *My Country and the World*... I said that it was like receiving a blow, well, we've been supporting the wrong people. We should have sided with Sakharov, and not, not with Brezhnev. And, in a way, I openly expressed my change in loyalty... It's partly that you've supported murderous regimes and it becomes increasingly clear, and you can take [the film] *The Lives of Others* and the Stasi and things like that... You were able to see something idealistic in something that wasn't. But then again I went into it with my eyes wide open, because if you deliberately choose to be a Leninist, you

---

[69] Interview with Katja Barloschy, conducted by AvdG, Bremen, 21 June 2010. Wolf Biermann was a songwriter who was stripped of his GDR citizenship for his 'nonconformist communism' while on tour in West Germany in 1976. Many prominent intellectuals protested.

accept, in a way, that being hard on the class enemy is okay. That's basically the whole spirit of proletarian dictatorship. But then somehow you get derailed when what you believe is a minor detail turns out to be of gigantic proportions, right.[70]

Unlike many of his former Danish political allies, the break from Soviet communism led him to distance himself far from the left, and today he describes himself as politically eclectic: a conservative social democratic when it comes to the welfare state; a foreign policy neoconservative; and a hardliner on immigrant policy. The history of Kjeldsen's life story revolves around understanding the strong pull of Soviet communism both generally and for him personally, combined with a clear rejection of what he calls the 'totalitarian temptation'. He derives meaning from the moral aspects of his story in the obligation he now feels to contribute to public debate and to make the conflict between democracy and communism a pivotal part of his teaching and research:

> Somehow or another it's *Schuld abtragen* [to work away at one's guilt], as they say in German. So try to make amends, try to make it a research topic. Somehow, maybe I can show that I've learned something from my own experiences, I would say. I don't know how much we can learn from history, but I think, at least, that I've experienced something that I personally would like to avoid repeating.

Indeed, some former radicals did try to recover the positive impulse for social change that Maoism or other forms of ultra-leftism had inspired, and sought only to critique the excesses of those ideologies that had led to violence: they would not demonize their former commitments as such. French activist Bernard Victorri (b. 1946) was a member of the French Maoist GP who spent a period in prison for political violence in 1970/71. Having burned his boats in France he emigrated with his wife Anne to Canada for eight years, before returning to France in 1984 to rebuild his academic career as a professor of linguistics. Reflecting on his past, he distinguishes between the high ideals to which he still holds and the mistakes he made with regard to political violence:

> Today I would not support that kind of politics, particularly that violent politics that threatened lives and things, even though we never went as far as killing anyone. We subverted things a bit, but I don't regret it at all because we did it in good faith, for an ideal that I have never renounced, an ideal of happiness and humanity. [71]

He explains that the Maoist model of cultural revolution had been an illusion and that it had led only to lies and violence on the part of the state. That said, he is clear that the generation of 1968 of which he was at the vanguard was driven by the fear of betraying high ideals and compromising with reality, the very sin of which their parents were guilty:

> We gave the impression that communism provided a solution, but we deceived ourselves completely with Maoism and what was happening in China. We contributed to what is worst about politics, that is, official lies. I am rather ambivalent about the

---

[70] Interview with Michael Kjeldsen, conducted by AW, Roskilde, 31 January 2011.
[71] Interview with Anne and Bernard Victorri, recorded by RG, Paris, 28 May 2007.

effect of our struggles. There were positive sides and very negative sides. I don't have any regrets personally about having taken part in this venture and I feel that today when I criticize certain left-wing attitudes I am not a traitor. On the contrary I have continued in a straight line. What strikes me most about our generation which experienced '68, where you find the *bobos* [bourgeois bohemians] who are in the same situation as us, is that you find that most of them are fairly lucid about the state of France and [also] continue to be on the left or extreme left out of loyalty, for fear of betrayal…Why? Because through the '68 period we said, 'our parents betrayed us, our parents who had been resisters have become old farts (*vieux cons*)'. The dread of becoming old farts like our parents was something that marked out our generation.

There are clear regional divides in the way in which former activists make sense of their former commitments. For those who had lived in western democracies the re-forging of the left required a very explicit moral critique of past failings, either to distance themselves from former positions or to remake relevant leftist positions in the present. Activists who had worked as radical leftists in the socialist East, by contrast, avoided moral critiques in favour of far less ambiguous, and often positive, narratives that, as we saw in the previous section, linked their past leftism with the eventual defeat of dictatorship and European unity. This was despite the fact that many had faced similar accusations of complicity as those in the West following the fall of communism in 1989. In the Czech Republic, following the adoption by parliament of a law in spring 1993 that declared the communist regime per se to be criminal, the press commonly reacted by declaring that '68ers' of the Prague Spring had not 'repented' and were still marked by a 'criminal stigma'.[72] In both Hungary and Poland, activists who had become (mainly liberal) dissidents in the 1980s were now attacked for once being radical leftists who despite their later anti-regime activity had earlier operated in the same ideological universe as the socialist state; moreover, it was believed that due to this heritage they had gone soft on the anti-communist struggle by letting former communists into the new post-communist political system in the Round Table talks of 1989.[73] In Hungary, this accusation was re-ignited in 1994, when the Free Democrats, a new party consisting in some significant part of 68ers who had become liberals in the 1980s, formed a governmental coalition with the communist successor party.[74] In Germany, members of the ex-communist PDS, which appropriated the idea of 'democratic socialism' and included many former 'reform socialists' socialized politically around 1968, were similarly vilified.

Those who had turned to liberalism, human rights activities in an unofficial sphere, had emigrated before 1989, or had abandoned their political activism

[72] Ondřej Matějka, '"We are the generation that will construct socialism". The Czech 68ers between manifest destiny and the mark of Cain', in von der Goltz (ed.) *Talkin' 'bout my Generation*, 133.

[73] On this characterization of the Polish March '68, see Piotr Osęka, 'The people of March', in von der Goltz (ed.) *Talkin' 'bout my Generation*, 157–8; also James Mark, *The Unfinished Revolution. Making Sense of the Communist Past in Central-eastern Europe* (New Haven, CT, 2010), ch. 1. This accusation emerged very soon after the transition in Hungary; for an example, Unsigned, 'Apák és Fiúk [Fathers and Sons],' *Magyar Fórum*, 31 March 1990, 2.

[74] See Péter Apor and James Mark, 'Mobilizing generation. The idea of 1968 in Hungary', in von der Goltz (ed.) *Talkin' 'bout my Generation*, 111–112.

altogether faced little difficulty in claiming a heroic role as resisters of the previous regime. Crucially, however, those whose radical energies did not lead them towards clearly identifiable dissidence, but led them to work *for* the regime in the 1970s and 1980s also had to tell an intelligible story of how they had got from 68er rebellion to engaging actively with state socialism.

Klaus Labsch (b. 1948), who had been part of a loose oppositional circle in East Berlin in the late 1960s, from which several prominent émigrés and liberal dissidents would emerge, followed a very different trajectory from 1970 onwards. While some of his former peers grew increasingly sceptical of state socialism and would eventually opt for publicly visible opposition, Labsch and his inner circle became convinced that the true path to socialist reform lay in 'marching through the institutions' of the socialist state. They invested considerable energy into persuading the socialist authorities that their transformation was real and that they were no longer 'enemies of the GDR'. Labsch was finally allowed to join the Party in 1975, began to study philosophy, wrote his doctoral dissertation, and landed a job as a teaching and research assistant in the Department of Marxism-Leninism of Berlin's Humboldt University. At one point, he was approached and agreed to work for the Stasi, East Germany's security service—the ultimate marker of complicity in German public discourse. When he voluntarily 'confesses' his role as an informant for the regime towards the end of the interview, Labsch pre-emptively addresses some of the accusations he expects this admission might prompt:

> The hard core of the commune [in which Labsch lived] ... was persuaded to cooperate with the Stasi, including myself. And I can talk about it well, quite well. But the argument will probably raise your alarm bells because I can't listen to it myself: 'Well, I did it, but I didn't hurt anyone'. But I have to say one thing, to explain the following: ... I don't know if it's just embarrassing or if one can understand it somehow— ... it seemed to us to be the final token of trust that these people who had been on our case for years, who controlled us, always, around the clock, and who mistrusted us enormously—partly rightly so—that these same people now came to us and asked whether we wanted to join them. That really knocked our socks off.

Being approached by the Stasi was thus an important milestone for Labsch; he points out that he was persuaded to cooperate on the basis that the Stasi could avoid having to arrest radical left-wing critics of the GDR with his help. Labsch felt unable to turn them down because someone had to do the 'dirty work' in constructing true socialism—a project he was radically committed to. His doubts about the reformability of socialism had grown towards the end of the 1980s, but the final realization that the system was fatally flawed only came in 1989. Things had:

> got worse year by year, this problem of still clinging to the basic idea and to say that it really is a great thing, the liberation of mankind ... But the situation got worse, continuously worse, that means that the pressure to justify also grew. The ridiculous policy that was pursued made us feel physical pain, sometimes. But we lacked the courage, the strength and perhaps also the conviction to say: 'Now we will stop'.[75]

---

[75] Interview with Klaus Labsch, conducted by AvdG, Berlin, 29 April 2010.

While he had looked down on members of the party hierarchy before 1989, he later became convinced that they had been much 'cleverer'; whereas he had remained a socialist idealist, they had not had any illusions about the system's reformability—a 'bitter realization'.

Labsch thus makes sense of his former choices by divorcing the GDR regime from his own socialist idealism—he had simply been wrong in assuming that one could contain the other. While he now regrets that he hurt individual people, he considered 'marching through the institutions', including the Stasi, part of a long quest for a 'socialist utopia' that ultimately turned out to have been misguided and naïve but one that, he insists, had nevertheless been motivated by honourable ideals.

Other East European activists who decided to work for the socialist regimes after 1968 tell their life story as one in which they dismantled dictatorship from within. In Hungary, where the system ended through Round Table discussions between the communists and the opposition in 1989, those late 1960s reformers and radicals who made their way within the regime could also claim that they prepared the way for a peaceful transition to liberal democracy. Tamás Bauer (b. 1946) was one such individual whose life path led him to cross over both the official reformist and dissident spheres. In the mid-1960s he was part of unofficial anti-imperialist solidarity and reform Communist youth movements. He was then excited by the possibility of democratizing socialism, was attracted to the economic field as the best way of achieving this, and was in the Czechoslovak capital during the Prague Spring (in the summer of 1968 he began to learn Czech, in part so he could communicate with reformers there). He graduated in 1968 and joined the Institute of Economics in Budapest as a professional economist and supported the marketization of the socialist economy. However, he was a critic of the regime, who had been kicked out of the Party in 1974, and had turned towards liberalism with the suppression of Solidarity in Poland in 1981. In the following years, he also became close to dissident circles, publishing (under a pseudonym) in their underground journal *Beszélő* (*The Speaker*). Nevertheless, he continued to play an important role—which he is still proud of—as part of an economic technocratic elite who had made Hungary the most effective economy in the eastern bloc. He presents himself as a technocrat whose successes in economic reorganization strengthened the hand of reformers within the Party, which eventually led them to a facilitating role in the quiet negotiated 'system change' of 1989. Thus he argues that 1968 led both to the creation of a liberal opposition (who eventually rejected socialism and leftist alternatives) and also to a strong reform wing within the Party who embraced economic change: it was these two parties who negotiated the system away at the end. Bauer himself had a foot in both camps, and views himself as an ideologically disillusioned critic who still worked to make the system function as best it could from within:

> I was a child of communist parents, I was a convinced communist, but step by step I realized that infeasibility of its economics—'68 and the occupation of Czechoslovakia was the first step, then '81 was the *coup de grâce* with Solidarity [in Poland] when it became unambiguous that the system was unreformable...but still in the 1980s

socialism, the Party, and the leadership of the Soviet Union were a given, and I didn't see any political opportunity to eliminate the system of state property, so within this framework you had to think about how to make the economy more efficient and socially acceptable, to make the system more democratic. That was the real question.[76]

Nevertheless, he dismisses the transition to liberal capitalism as a 'fucked up process' full of missed opportunities to complete a comprehensive liberalization or marketization of the economy. His earlier attachment to leftist alternatives is something that he feels no need to reject: rather, it provided him with an economic language with which he could continue to advocate reform to the regime, while also providing him with a critical intellectual faculty that eventually led to the embracing of liberalism. Both of these strands allow him to link his own life trajectory to the eventual victory over dictatorship in 1989.

Former ideological attachments are also often less problematic for those who were part of Maoist or far leftist groups under southern European authoritarian regimes as their commitments could be presented as resistance against dictatorship and hence part of a story of democratization. One such activist was José Luis Gómez Navarro, who had been Madrid secretary-general of the Maoist Workers' Revolutionary Organization.[77] In 1974, he travelled to Beijing to plead for financial support for their struggle against Franco and succeeded through convincing Chinese communists to allow them to establish a small company to import Chinese petrol into Spain that would secretly fund their underground organization. When Franco died in November 1975 and his regime collapsed, Gómez Navarro abandoned Maoism; yet for him, there was no need for a moral critique of his past. Rather, there was simply a realization that in the new democratic Spain his former political attachments made no sense as revolution was an impossibility, and, he increasingly believed, unnecessary:

> I lasted in the Workers' Revolutionary Organization until '75. When I saw that democracy was coming or was on the way, I began to think that with this type of thought we hadn't understood much about the country. And so I abandoned all activism...I saw that we didn't understand Spanish society. And that the chances for a revolution were zero. It was that clear. The subsequent evolution made you question deeper things, no? But what I thought is that the revolutionary possibilities—of the type of revolution of which we were thinking—were nil...We had a theory that Spain was different to Europe, not because we wanted it to be, but because it was, and that, as a result, there were possibilities of carrying out a revolution here. But there came a moment in which you say: 'Well, we were wrong,...We're somewhat different to Europe, but only a little'. As a result, the possibilities of a revolution did not exist.[78]

Indeed, the absence of moral critique of his former leftist commitments—which we found so strongly in the West German and Danish examples above—was

[76] Interview with Tamás Bauer, conducted by PA, Budapest, 5 March 2009.

[77] Other Maoist interviewees from the Workers' Revolutionary Organization—such as José Sanroma Aldea and Francisca Saquillo—connect their struggle before 1975 with the achievements of the democratic transition of the mid-1970s even more powerfully than Gómez Navarro.

[78] Interview with José Louis Gómez Navarro, conducted by NT, Madrid, 11 March 2010.

reinforced by the positive connections he drew between his Maoist past and his present as a businessman. Gómez Navarro is convinced that his clandestine Maoist activism, the torture that he suffered once he was arrested, the time that he spent in jail, and the military service with the paratroops that he was forced to undergo by the Francoist authorities, all shaped his character and prepared him for his life as an international business consultant working in difficult circumstances:

> I value it. I believe that for me, me personally, I've learnt a lot, personally. It has forged my character and personality... I lead a very atypical life, very atypical, because for years I've been acting as a consultant for Spanish companies outside Spain. What does it give me? I've dedicated many years—and I continue to do so—to analysing political risk in countries with political risk, above all in the cases of Latin America and China. For many years, for Spanish companies... In terms of endurance, in terms of analysis, in terms of taking on alone a severe company crisis that could imply many things... and not to get nervous... I would not have been able to do it without the experience [of activism]. For certain.

CONCLUSION

As we have seen, grand narratives of '1968' exist in all the countries studied here. Albeit to varying degrees, '1968' has become a battlefield for 'memory politics' and competing political identities across Europe, and the ferocity of these battles shows no signs of abating in the twenty-first century. Although shaped by national debates and discourses, the competing public representations of 1968 can be divided into broad categories with relative ease across the continent: celebratory accounts, for the most part, highlight the emancipatory impetus of the late 1960s and attribute positive legacies to this era of revolt, be it broader social, cultural and political changes or the eventual undermining of both right- and left-wing dictatorships. Condemnatory accounts, by contrast, emphasize a general 'destruction of values', the 'legitimation of political violence' or an unhealthy political 'romanticism' and 'radicalism'. Moreover, former activists are faced with accusatory narratives from several other (political) directions: accusations of 'selling out', of 'treachery' because of having supported various forms of left-wing dictatorship, and of inadvertently accelerating some of the negative features of capitalism. Life stories are clearly framed by these debates, and former activists frequently address these themes more or less directly. Rather than being easily grouped into those who 'kept the faith' and still celebrated 1968 unequivocally and those who had 'sold out', 'repented' of their deeds or 'rejected' their former commitments entirely, however, we found that the accounts our interviewees produced often escaped neat categorization. To be sure, interviewees wrote their own lives into broader collective stories of the achievements and failures of the '1968 moment', but they often did both in the same account. Dividing them entirely along present political lines would create similar difficulties. As this chapter has demonstrated, present political concerns have a powerful effect on how a life story is told and which aspects of past commitment are emphasized to the interviewer. Yet, individual choices and experiences do not always fit into a tight political corset. Rather, the interview is a space in which interviewees seek to make their individual life path meaningful—the stories they generate are windows into the meaning-making processes through which wider public discourses, former and present political beliefs, as well as individual experiences with activism are integrated into a more or less coherent whole and understanding of self. This chapter has been an attempt to investigate these complex and highly nuanced stories on their own terms. In doing so, we have sought to shed fresh light on the meaning(s) of '1968', its personal and political legacies, and the powerful resonance this period continues to carry in the present.

Conclusion: Europe's 1968

Robert Gildea and James Mark

At the heart of this book is the contention that a revolt that took place across a continent divided not only by diverse national cultures but also into different political systems—liberal democracies in the West and North, the communist bloc to the East and right-wing dictatorships in the South—is nevertheless worth examining as a pan-European phenomenon. Unlike most accounts of 1968 in Europe, which limit themselves to the study of national cultures and view the East and South as experiencing 'other 1968s', this work has investigated the similarities and differences in ideas of activism, revolt and rebellion across a continent. One must note that although there was consciousness of the revolt as an event with European characteristics, most radicals were equally national *or* global in their outlooks. Nevertheless, this study has sought to detect patterns in the playing out of activism beyond national borders, to discover how far there were *real* encounters and interactions between networks of activists across Europe, and to uncover the extent to which radicals *imagined* themselves to be part of the same struggle, whether continental or global, against such targets as fascism, imperialism, authoritarianism and conventional society and morality. Lastly, we have examined how far a European 1968 has been constructed in memory, and the extent to which activists have re-worked the transnational and national meanings of their activism over time.

ANTI-IMPERIALISM

In making sense of their revolt, activists across Europe were inspired by the example of the anti-colonialist and anti-imperialist revolts that ripped through Latin America, Africa and Asia in the late 1950s and 1960s. Greek activists supported the struggles of their countrymen in Cyprus against British colonialism. French activists were shaped by the long struggle of Algerian nationalists against the French state and colonists, by the threat of military service to put down the Algerian revolt and stories of torture used against Algerian rebels. The success of the Castro's revolution in Cuba, the legend of the Chinese Cultural Revolution and the struggle of the North Vietnamese against American imperialism were all inspirations to young activists across Europe and were causes that in some cases brought them together. According to East German activist Gerd Poppe (b. 1941):

> Che Guevara was a point of contact. In general, the Cuban revolution in the early phase... The figure of Che Guevara, the *Bolivian Diary*, we read that in the East as well. We read it to each other in our groups... It is these things that established East–West linkages.[1]

For all the commonalities in the discovery of anti-imperialism by activists across Europe, its significance was understood very differently in various contexts: it could equally become inspiration for a nationally specific struggle as an expression of a new internationalist consciousness. Greek leftists who quit their country after the installation of the US-backed Colonels' Dictatorship in 1967 often noted this shift, from their earlier embracing of anti-colonialism as a nationalist ideology aimed at freeing Greece from the pernicious effects of western imperialism to a new internationalist anti-imperialism they discovered in exile that embraced the struggles of the Vietnamese and others alongside their own. In the communist bloc, matters were complicated by the fact that regimes were officially anti-imperialist; some activists were socialized into solidarity with Third World anti-imperialist movements at school and university, but nevertheless found ways of turning its language back against the regime. Members of the Polish Commando group, for instance, recalled how they invoked the struggle of Vietnam against US hegemony as code for their own national fight against Soviet imperialism. By contrast, radical Catholics in southern Europe were especially moved by the guerrilla struggles in Latin America that made heroes of priests such as Camilo Torres, and sought to bring their liberation theology to Europe.

COMING TO TERMS WITH THE SECOND WORLD WAR

For many activists, coming to terms with the memory of the Second World War and its aftermath was a central part of how they now understood their journey into radical political activity. This was particularly the case in those parts of western Europe that had experienced Nazism and fascism, where activists frequently interpreted their formative clashes with the institutions—churches, the military, and, most commonly, educational institutions—as the result of an older generation's incapacity to address the problematic legacies of the Second World War after 1945 in their construction of the postwar democratic state. For these activists, patriarchy might be understood as a legacy of the inhumanity of bombing; the degrading numbering of workers at factories as the unresolved legacy of the concentration camp, or the authoritarian structures of schooling as the remnants of fascism. Sometimes the threat of a revival in fascism—as in France during the Algerian War, in Italy, or in Greece under the military dictatorship—led activists to see their radicalism as a new form of anti-fascist resistance; for some, this was viewed as an

---

[1] Interview with Gerd Poppe, conducted by AvdG, Berlin, 11 June 2008.

imitation of their own parents' heroism during the war. In other cases, it could be seen as a compensation for the failures of their parents; in particular, in the case of Spanish, Greek or Jewish activists, their activism was often understood as a redressing of the defeats of an older generation whose hopes of a 'brave new world' had been dashed by losing civil wars or in the Holocaust.

It was not only the legacy of war, but the betrayal of the settlement that emerged from its aftermath, that moved activists. They might express disappointment both with the dashed hopes of new liberal democratic or communist regimes after 1945 and—even if their parents had fought in resistance movements—with the failure of their mothers or fathers to continue the struggle for those 'brave new worlds'. Particularly strongly felt was the betrayal of communist parties that were no longer perceived to be the carriers of radical change but had compromised with Franco in Spain, refused in France to condemn the atrocities committed in Algeria, or, in the eastern bloc, represented a form of sclerotic, bureaucratic, authoritarian and inflexible communism that suppressed any leftist alternatives. Activists who came from communist families in west, east and south of the continent would pay homage to the leftist traditions of their parents while seeking to distance themselves in order to take up the struggle for the new worlds that had eluded the generation that had come before them.

TRANSNATIONAL ENCOUNTERS

This book also explores the extent to which activists were engaged in an interconnected struggle, both in the sense of real encounters and networks, and in terms of participating in the same imagined revolution. Dramatic manifestations of student solidarity across Europe included the Vietnam Congress held in West Berlin in February 1968, which brought together mostly Trotskyist delegates from across Europe, and the BBC programme *Students in Revolt* in June 1968, which brought together students from Europe, the US and Japan. Before and after these events activists criss-crossed Europe: oral interviews have given us insights into the complexity and detail of these linkages. British activists went to Paris in May 1968 to observe or participate in a revolution that they wished to see in their own country. French activists went to Turin to meet Lotta Continua. Activists from Berlin, France, Spain, USA and India visited the Danish commune Skovkilde. Moreover, the Iron Curtain was not impenetrable in this period. Western students visited Prague and Budapest in the lead up to 1968. Czech activist Petr Uhl was invited to Paris by Alain Krivine in 1965 and flirted politically with the Union des Étudiants Communistes; Hungarian Marxist revisionist philosopher Ágnes Heller travelled to West Germany and met Rudi Dutschke. Western communist youth engaged with their eastern bloc comrades at summer camps on the other side of the Iron Curtain, while Hungarian reform communist youth activists recalled trips to the communist strongholds of northern Italy. The Dutch counterculture Provo movement had its supporters in the East, although they might complain of their inability to use the provocative methods their western counterparts could. Links with the southern Mediterranean dictatorships were important too. The exposure of Greek radicals forced into exile after the assumption of power by the Colonels to revolt across both eastern and western Europe made them the transnational force par excellence of the European 1968. Spanish anarchists travelled to support networks in France, Italy, Belgium and Britain; indeed, meetings with exiled Spanish anarchists and republicans at summer camps in Switzerland, or in Toulouse, were vital moments that shaped the activism of French radicals Jean-Pierre Duteuil and Jean-Marc Rouillan, among others. In some cases activists travelled further and were inspired to bring forms of radicalism home to Europe: French and Spanish radicals went to Mao's China to witness the Cultural Revolution and obtain a Chinese blessing for their nascent Maoist movements; left-wing Catholics visited Latin America and met liberation theologians such as Gustavo Gutiérrez, while Paul Blanquart contributed to Castro's speech at the Cuban Congress of Intellectuals in January 1968. Links to American activism were both imagined and real: the example of the civil rights movement was crucial to those fighting for civil equality in Northern Ireland, while the black power movements were an inspiration to Northern Irish Trotskyites, the Hungarian Maoist-influenced cultural collective Orfeo and to Action Directe in France, among others. Direct links with the USA were particularly important for new forms of gender activism as French feminists travelled across the Atlantic for inspiration, and American feminists brought their new movements to Europe: Julienne Travers, for instance, was a founding member of the Pompeo Magna feminist group in Rome.

DEBATING REVOLUTION

Even when such real linkages were less in evidence, activists often imagined that they were part of the same international revolutionary movement. They had overlapping aims and ambitions, were inspired by the same heroes and causes, and used space in similar ways. New Left activists in both West and East saw themselves as alienated from and opposed to bureaucracy, technocracy, capitalism and consumerism that seemed prevalent both in explicitly capitalist states and formally socialist states that seemed to be going down the road of 'goulash socialism'. A Marxist analysis of urban and rural poverty, economic exploitation, class struggle and revolution was the common currency of many activists, although this might be substituted among some by a radical religious image of a more equal, more communitarian and spiritual society. Activists had in their minds an idealized image of the heroic revolutionary, which might be a Paris Communard, a Bolshevik from 1917, a Polish wartime resistor or a Latin American guerrilla. Activists all over Europe saw themselves as supporting revolutionary movements of national liberation against colonialist power and imperialism in Latin America, Africa and Asia and were keen to use the dynamic and example of these movements at home. Even a group in democratic Iceland—the Kópamaros—saw itself as imitating the violent urban guerrilla actions of the Uruguayan Tupamaros. Across Europe, activists made similar use of space in developing their revolutionary offensives and setting up laboratories of new social relations. Movements began in the universities across Europe, but then pushed into the streets, challenging the state for control of symbolic spaces and coming into conflict with the forces of order.

The 'revolution' of which activists talked was broad in scope and somewhat flexible. It could mean both political and cultural revolution. The first involved changing the political order to achieve greater democracy or equality, building a bridge if possible to that idealized motor of revolution, the working class, and contemplating the use of violence if necessary. Cultural activism might involve transforming social relations and attitudes through music, literature, art or fashion, subverting traditional gender relations or sexual morality, a revolution in consciousness or releasing unconscious desires. The term 'cultural revolution' was itself ambiguous, referring both to the Chinese model of 'revolution within the revolution'—a new version of communist revolution based on mass participation rather than party rule—or the much wider lifestyle revolution.

Whereas forms of political revolution might divide activists in dictatorships and democracies, cultural revolution in its broadest sense tended to bring together activists from all parts of Europe. Activists from the communist bloc often had access to western culture, with its diet of rock music, and could get hold in one way or another of books, records and clothes from the West. Levi jeans and long hair were a universal marker of discontented youth even in the most anti-capitalist circles. As Gábor Révai (b. 1947), a one-time Hungarian leftist radical remembers:

> By the end of high school I began to have relatively long hair...and the other thing was my clothing, and it was an unbelievably big thing to bring in jeans from the West, but by the middle of the '60s you could 'get out' and sometimes it was possible to go to Vienna and bring back some jeans or a hurricane coat. It's awfully difficult to understand today that no matter how left wing you were, those little symbols of the western consumer society had such a large hold over you.[2]

Artistic movements were a vehicle of criticism and transgression in the East even more than in the West. Radicals in Franco's Spain too, such as Juan Aranzadi (b. 1949), remembers vividly the cultural revolution of that era that ran alongside their political activism:

> Everything entered, not only the anti-imperialist struggle in Vietnam but also the hippies...Nothing appeared strange to anyone. I began, for a period, to go to Formentera [to embrace] the mysticism of lysergic acid, ideas along the lines of Timothy Leary...The belief in the esoteric potential of the joint, to think that the family and marriage were outdated institutions that were never going to return ever, no? All this vital amalgam that was my life along with 200,000 neuroses...All this defined what was—at least, in a certain environment—the vital climate of Madrid, the situation between '69 and '75, which is when this social tide became general and spread even more.[3]

---

[2] Interview with Gábor Révai, conducted by PA, Budapest, 8 October 2008.
[3] Interview with Juan Aranzadi Martínez, conducted by NT, Madrid, 21 April 2010.

There were of course significant differences in the way revolution was imagined and practised between North and South and western and eastern Europe, structured by very different political and ideological conditions. Yet there was plenty of room for debate and for change, so that differences apparent at one point might dissolve with the passage of time. Activists in the East were often unhappy with the term 'revolution' because it was the official ideology of communist regimes and any opposition, as in Hungary in 1956 or Czechoslovakia in 1968, was branded counter-revolutionary. Stefan Bekier (b. 1946) recalls that in the student protests of March 1968 in Poland:

> No one was talking about the revolution. It was the revolt. It was the rebellion. The movement. People were talking about the movement. It was a students' movement. For me and for us 'March' was mainly the big upheaval (*zryw*).[4]

Activists in the West often affected a revolutionary superiority. They regarded activists in the East as having a petty-bourgeois concern for democracy and lacking the ability to rouse the working classes to revolt. Looking back in the late 1970s, Rudi Dutschke, as one of the few western European activists who regularly visited the communist bloc, reflected on how these assumptions had led him to dismiss the 'eastern European '68'. The defeat of the Prague Spring, which had by then become the symbol for the end of the possibility of a reformed socialism, now seemed to him a much more important legacy of that year:

> I have very little to say about May '68 in France: in the first place, because I happened to be in the hospital, but above all because, in retrospect, the great event of '68 in Europe was not Paris, but Prague. But we were unable to see this at the time.[5]

In turn, some activists within the communist bloc could not understand western revolutionaries' obsession with Marxism, the bitter realities of which they were experiencing. Polish activist Seweryn Blumsztajn (b. 1946) relates these differences, but nevertheless concedes that they did not eliminate a sense of generational solidarity:

> I had a feeling of connection, generational connection, and of their absolute misunderstanding. You know, their attraction to Marxism...That is, we were fighting for what they were rejecting—that was all quite obvious. For us democracy was a dream—but for them it was a prison. So I simply couldn't comprehend their Marxism, their communism, all that leftist ideology of theirs. Those Maoists—wow, that was just pure blather for us. All of it. Nonetheless, I did feel a generational sympathy—that's how I'd label it. I felt there was a bond between us.[6]

There were also great variations between different countries in the amount of social space that existed for political activity. May '68 in France was defeated first by shock elections that gave a landslide to the ruling Gaullist party, then by the

---

[4] Interview with Stefan Bekier, conducted by PO, Warsaw, 23 June 2008.
[5] Jacques Rupnik interview with Rudi Dutschke, 'The misunderstanding of 1968', *Transit* 35 (Summer 2008), reproduced at <http://www.eurozine.com/articles/2008-05-16-dutschke-en.html>.
[6] Interview with Seweryn Blumsztajn, conducted by PO, Warsaw, 5 January 2010.

banning of revolutionary organizations. Repression in Poland after March 1968 or in Czechoslovakia after August 1968 was much more severe. Prison sentences were meted out and revolutionary groups in both East and West went underground. In France, the GP became a clandestine organization, although it maintained a democratic arm, the Secours Rouge. Following the destruction of the Prague Spring, Petr Uhl (b. 1941) and his friends set up a Revolutionary Youth Movement in Czechoslovakia, but under such repressive circumstances it could only be a parody of revolutionary movements and its leaders were soon rounded up. Activists in the dictatorships of Spain and Greece also felt that they had little room for manoeuvre at home and were stunned by how much easier it was to be an activist in France or Italy. Greek Maoist Michalis Tiktopoulos (b. 1946) who fled to Italy after the 1967 military coup recalls, 'I went to the Feltrinelli bookshop... Three out of four magazines had the hammer and sickle or the red star on their covers. I said to myself: "Where am I? Am I in heaven?"'.[7]

Activists in different parts of Europe had different views of violence. In the western democracies violence was an option, although its use radically divided activists one from another. Under the Mediterranean military dictatorships 'armed struggle' was more commonly part of the repertoire. In the communist bloc, dictatorship was so all-pervasive that political violence was simply not an option. György Pór (b. 1944), who was sentenced in spring 1968 after setting up a clandestine 'authentic' Marxist-Leninist party in communist Hungary, recalled:

> our intention was to understand... how we could create a better world... there was one sentence in one of our political pamphlets where we said that we want to change the system by any means; but that never included acts of terrorism... In the Marxist tradition, terrorism is not favourably looked upon, but rather seen as a set of isolated individual acts that cannot replace the class struggle... And we had the Red Army in our backyard so even if we had wanted to, we wouldn't have had a chance of gaining power with guns.[8]

Although much activism was grounded in Marxism, an important thread of radicalism also derived from religious faith, both Catholic and Protestant. These activists were critical both of the conservatism of their churches and of inequality and injustice in society. In the West, many religious radicals entertained a dialogue with Marxism, drawn towards it by its analysis of economic exploitation and class struggle. They became involved in conflicts alongside students and workers, seeking to give revolution a spiritual dimension. In the East, Marxism had been appropriated by the regimes and was less obvious as a critical tool. Religious radicals under communism were less keen to criticize their hierarchies that were themselves subject to persecution by the atheistic state and less keen to become involved in politics since under official atheism the clandestine cultivation of spirituality was itself a manifestation of opposition. In both western countries such as France and in eastern bloc countries such as Poland and Hungary, activists of a Jewish

---

[7] Interview with Michalis Tiktopoulos, conducted by PV, Athens, 3 November 2009.
[8] Interview with György Pór, conducted by JM, Brussels, 13 March 2009.

background were often in evidence. This may be seen as evidence of a Jewish Bundist or Jewish Bolshevik tradition, or as a reaction against being condemned to hide from persecution or to blend silently into postwar society.

Perhaps the greatest point of convergence for activists between different parts of Europe was the cultural version of revolution. Lutz Rathenow (b. 1952), who was active in the East German peace movement of the 1980s, highlights the important pull of western culture and explains that this was much more important for him than the political programme of socialist reform. When asked whether the Prague Spring itself played a role, he says:

> It played a role, but not the dominant one...—the suppression played a greater role than the Prague Spring itself...the Prague Spring had not convinced me deep down...and the western rock and pop culture was more important...I thought Paris was better. 'Under the paving stones, the beach'—sounds much better. And something like 'He who sleeps with the same woman twice already belongs to the Establishment'. This West German type of revolution was more interesting than the 2000-word manifesto [written by Czech reformist writer Ludvík Vaculík in 1968].[9]

RETHINKING REVOLUTION

Ideas of revolution were not only flexible, but were also in constant flux. This was never more the case than after European states came down on the 'first wave' of revolution in 1968 and obliged activists to rethink what kind of brave new world they wanted and how they would achieve it. New critiques of Marxism, activist practice and revolution would lead to new forms of radical action centred on gender and community activism, and the ideological drift of some activists away from the left.

Issues of gender and sexuality became a central site for revolution, especially after 1970. These currents were strong in western Europe but much weaker in both the eastern bloc—where women's liberation to work was official policy—and in the southern European dictatorships—where revolution continued to be understood mainly as the struggle against repressive state power. Making sense of gender radicalism in the contemporary interview often involved a critique of 1968 itself. Individuals presented their journeys into gender activism not only as a revolt against authoritarian patriarchal societies, but as an escape from the late 1960s cultures of radicalism that still embodied the worst elements of this patriarchy: the ideological monopoly exercised by male leaders of radical groups, the machismo, the sexual possessiveness, the absence of a politics of emotion and a spirit of sacrifice that always put proletarian revolution before personal questions. Gender activism was often presented as the product of debates that went far beyond national settings. Daniel Defert (b. 1937), a former Maoist who was also Michel

---

[9] Interview with Lutz Rathenow, conducted by AvdG, Berlin, 30 April 2010.

Foucault's partner, recalls the French feminist Antoinette Fouque arriving like a messiah on the plane to Paris in the early 1970s:

> I remember Antoinette Fouque arriving from England. She was a friend, we had studied together. I was going to fetch Foucault at Orly...and Antoinette Fouque arrived at the same time, on the same plane. And she said, 'I am bringing the revolution from England'. It was feminism.[10]

Sexual liberation was not simply the discarding of conventional family expectations and social morality. Activists across western and northern Europe wrestled with a variety of questions, such as whether they could pursue political revolution at the same time as feminism, whether men could be involved in feminist movements and whether feminism required lesbianism. Danish activist Birgitte Due (b. 1944) found herself pulled towards different political identities, and then between heterosexuality and lesbianism:

> I was constantly drawn into it, into a place where we examined ourselves and talked about personal development, private things and relationships, and how to make relationships work and such...I had been strongly aware of...socialist consciousness or...you could say consciousness about the class struggle or class awareness...This was a schism for me, and then another schism happened. Hmm, what year was it? Maybe '72–'73? Because for the first time I fell in love with a woman.[11]

Meanwhile some men began to question whether the ideal of the heroic revolutionary was the only model for radical politics and wondered whether they should learn from feminist politics. Men's movements developed in the UK, Netherlands, Scandinavia, France and Italy but little elsewhere. In Britain, Paul Atkinson (b. 1949) reflects:

> it felt like that kind of feminism was an invitation to do something with my own sort of emotional sensibilities and so on...For men, the women's movement actually legitimizes that project in a way that it's quite difficult for men, among themselves, to legitimize...the heart of it for me was the invitation from the women's movement to men to engage in an emotional politics as well as an external politics.[12]

Another subject of change was the nature of revolution itself. The idea that revolution would come from the factory working class, and with violent class struggle, as Marx had predicted, had lost much credibility by the mid-1970s. The emerging agenda was to transform social relations peacefully, over time, and at the local and community level, through practical projects: squatting in properties blighted by development plans, campaigns around women's health issues, such as abortion, as well as campaigns in the workplace now seen as the hub of the community. This coincided with the search for new spaces away from the reach of the state where experiments in social action could be undertaken. The locus of struggle moved to specific sites that often took on an iconic significance:

---

[10] Interview with Daniel Defert, conducted by RG, Paris, 7 April 2008.
[11] Interview with Birgitte Due, conducted by AW, Copenhagen, 8 December 2010.
[12] Interview with Paul Atkinson, conducted by JD, London, 9 July 2010.

Lip and Larzac in France, Grunwick and Fakenham in Britain, Christiania in Denmark, Isolotto and Porto Marghera in Italy, Gdańsk in Poland. These new sites embodied a shift from 'top-down' activism by leftists whose aim was to stimulate activism among workers or peasants, to 'bottom-up' activism by workers and peasants in defence of their livelihoods and against the power of the state, who began to educate students and intellectuals in the practice of resistance, if not revolution. Although seemingly more parochial, these sites did not necessarily mean that activism had become less transnational: they were sometimes places that attracted an international following—such as the Larzac plateau in France where activists protested against a planned military base, or in Basaglia's democratic psychiatric hospital at Trieste—or whose struggles—as at Gdańsk in Poland—were to attract international support and solidarity. Transnational inspirations were refocussed too: British and French community activists increasingly looked to similar experiments such as Lotta Continua in Italy, or to community organization in the US, particularly in Chicago.

Some activists came to reject their radical leftism completely: a development that opened up the possibility of forging new East–West transnational links. Activists in the communist bloc often felt that western activists were indifferent to their fate after the Soviet invasion of Czechoslovakia in August 1968. By the end of the 1970s and early 1980s, however, revolutionary leadership in Europe moved to the shipyards of the Polish Baltic and the intellectuals who were now defending the workers, and developed new transnational resonances. This corresponded to a decline in the star of Marxism and the growing interest of former Marxists in the West in the dissident movements in the communist bloc, first the Charter 77 movement in Czechoslovakia, then the Solidarity movement in Poland. Jean-Yves Potel (b. 1948), formerly a French Trotskyist, attended the trial of Václav Havel, Petr Uhl and other signatories of Charter 77 in Prague in 1979 and recalls a damascene experience:

> I met people who wanted to change things. People who had an approach that was much more ethical and cultural, much less dogmatic. I found myself talking to Christians, to people who had no particular ideology. Generally they hated the terms that I worshipped, such as 'proletariat' or 'internationalism'. That cleared my mind. It was like a thunderbolt.[13]

Yet this reconfiguration of activism did not always lead to new transnational linkages. Those dissidents fighting the communist state could find the western New Left's language disingenuous and see them as useful idiots for the Soviet Union. Likewise, those in eastern Europe who remained on the left sometimes gave up on their transnational dreams around 1968 and decided to work through the institutions of the communist state. Much of the internationalism of the Greek activists in exile fell away after 1974 as many returned to Greece or turned inwards to their own community.

---

[13] Interview with Jean-Yves Potel, conducted by RG, Paris, 16 May 2008.

EUROPE'S 1968: BETWEEN MEMORY AND HISTORY

Oral history gives us access to the processes through which former activists in the present make sense of their pasts in the light of new political and cultural developments that have the potential to reshape how they see their great moment of rebellion. Across Europe, peaking in the early 1990s, former 68ers were demonized for their participation in what was framed as an irresponsible revolt. They could be cast as communist collaborators after the system fell in the East, as useful idiots for the Soviet Union, or for being responsible for a disastrous cultural counter-revolution that undermined the values of western civilization.

Dominique Grange (b. 1940), protest singer and former Maoist, interviewed during the 2007 French presidential campaign during which Nicolas Sarkozy promised to liquidate the heritage of 1968, speaks for an embattled minority of former 68ers who continue to campaign for the values of that moment against powerful voices that seek to demonize them:

> I don't know what will happen next in this society that Sarkozy is promising us. What I know is that he wants to forbid us hope when he says, 'I want to liquidate the heritage of May '68 …'. He ended his speech by saying that the 68ers did not amount to much (*c'était pas grand-chose*), but I don't feel that we did amount to very little, even if we were not… even if we weren't the spearhead—that was the workers… I have already written a song about it… *Les pas grand-chose.*[14]

Despite their demonization by the right across Europe, former activists have found many ways to celebrate the legacies of 1968. This was particularly the case in the former eastern bloc, where after the Berlin Wall came down it became possible to construct a narrative in which a struggle for freedom and democracy in 1968 reached its natural conclusion in 1989. *Transit 68/89*, a publicly funded joint German-Czech research project from 2008, highlighted the teleological narrative arc between 1968, the emergence of dissidence and the collapse of communism. This argument was particularly strong for those radical leftists who had become liberally minded dissidents. Gábor Demszky (b. 1952), who became liberal mayor of Budapest between 1990 and 2010, connects 1968 and the collapse of communism in 1989 and highlighted his own role in its downfall:

> '68 brought a real change, after that the world turned to a more cultured and fortunately more westernized direction, and it was already neither necessary nor possible to live or think in these older ways, it was the end of the eastern Soviet system.[15]

Activists also celebrate their struggle for the democratization of institutions, the broadening of social opportunity, and the granting of rights and status to previous marginalized groups, as important legacies of their revolt. Even in Northern Ireland, after the horror of over thirty years of sectarian conflict and questions of how much responsibility to lay at the doors of those who were active in 1968, the peace

---

[14] Interview with Dominique Grange, conducted by RG, Paris, 10 May 2007.
[15] Interview with Gábor Demszky, conducted by PA, Budapest, 2 December 2008.

process and a gradual return to political normalcy has made it possible for 1968 activists to connect themselves to narrative of the struggle for civil rights and to seek a rightful place for Northern Ireland in broader western accounts of democratization.

There were other ways in which a broader European—or western—1968 was constructed in the memory of the participants. Radical Catholics, for instance, whose social activism as worker-priests or community workers often long outlived other forms of revolutionary activity of the period, refer back to a sense of social sympathy and action that was engendered in activists across Europe and beyond. According to Spanish Catholic activist Leonardo Aragón (b. 1945):

> In relation to what we could call the 'immediacy', the 'immediacy' of '68, one never loses the feeling of affection (*simpatía*). It lasts. Despite the fact that, now, politically, many of the things that, at that time, I simply accepted, I couldn't accept now. But my *simpatía* remains... What was done in that period had its internal logic, and not only the French May, but the Spanish '68, the German '68, the English '68 and the '66 and '67 in California. This had a context and this had an origin and this had a *raison d'être*. And this, then, received the *simpatía* of all the youth of that period.[16]

Likewise for Klaus Hartung (b. 1940), former leading member of the Berlin Socialist German Student Union, and later volunteer in Basaglia's anti-psychiatry experiment in Trieste (1976–80), '68 can still be celebrated as it gave activists the sense that they could change society, even if their movement had led to ideological excesses:

> And all in all I would say, with hindsight, that I can be entirely grateful—and I am—for the period of '67/'68. This experience, that you can *do* something, is irreplaceable. And I really had this. I was helpless before... My feeling was that in this society, which I didn't experience as pleasant, everything is already decided, everything has been decided. I could only become a frustrated professor. I pictured myself as someone who has to plough through secondary literature with frustration and grim determination. And I couldn't see myself doing this... So in a sense I am really proud of this time and what I did. And on the other hand I see all the big, big mistakes and the blindness—in part an inevitable blindness.[17]

Not all accounts are so celebratory. Across Europe, activists who have remained on the left often mourn '1968' as a lost moment. They argue that the defeat of '1968' meant the end of alternative non-market-based visions of society, an absence of progressive, socially equitable alternatives available when communism collapsed in 1989 and had ushered in a new form of rampant individualism that they perceived as a necessary underpinning for a newly powerful global capitalism. British activist Hilary Wainwright (b. 1949) regrets that the 68ers failed to get to grips with many of the institutional obstacles to reform at the time and fears that possibilities for change are now radically limited:

---

[16] Interview with Leonardo Aragón, conducted by NT, Madrid, 14 April 2008.
[17] Interview with Klaus Hartung, conducted by AvdG, Berlin, 5 January 2010.

Looking back, one can see the flaws, you know, in our over-optimism about the potential of fluid movements, you know. I think we didn't really address the questions of institutional consolidation and development of the innovations that we made…Now the sort of financial crisis is making it impossible for many of the desires that '68 produced to be met within the system.[18]

Thus alongside the triumphalist story that beats a path from 1968 to 1989, there is the story of missed opportunity and defeatism that holds that the flames lit in 1968 have all but been extinguished. Despite this, some refuse to mourn. Former Maoist, the Spaniard Juan Aranzadi (b. 1949), still celebrates the glorious defeat of his revolution:

I believe that the principal characteristic of May '68 is that it was a kind of spectacle that embodied all the goals from the French Revolution until then. And this type of apocalyptic climate, of surrealist utopia, I believe that not only *I* lived it but also my generation. I have a magnificent memory… of jail, a magnificent memory of the clandestine life, which took place, well, in a more or less miserable housing estate in Vallecas [a working-class area of Madrid]…What in strictly objective terms could be considered 'sacrifices for the Revolution' for me was quite the opposite, I want to say. I would do it again, even knowing that I would fail… I'm tremendously content and satisfied to have lived in that climate and to have lived that experience during that time.[19]

---

[18] Interview with Hilary Wainwright, conducted by JD, London, 27 July 2010.
[19] Interview with Juan Aranzadi Martínez, conducted by NT, Madrid, 21 April 2010.

Networks consulted

CZECHOSLOVAKIA

Aktuální umění (Actual Art)
Hnutí revoluční mládeže (Revolutionary Youth Movement)
Křižovnická škola čistého humoru bez vtipu (Holy Cross School of Pure Humour without Wit)
Literární noviny (Literary Journal)
Trampové (Tramps)

DENMARK

Anholtsgade kollektivet (Anholtsgade commune)
Brøndby Strand kollektivet (Brøndby Beach commune)
Det ny Samfund (The New Society)
Kvindefronten (Women's Front)
Lesbisk Bevægelse (The Lesbian Movement)
Mandebevægelsen (The Men's Movement)
Rødstrømperne (The Redstockings)
Venstresocialisterne (Leftist Socialists)

FRANCE

22 Mars (22 March)
Action Directe (Direct Action)
Centre Révolutionnaire d'Initiatives et de Recherches (Revolutionary Initiatives and Research Centre)
Cercle Jean XXIII (John XXIII Circle)
Clubs de Loisirs et d'Action de la Jeunesse (Youth Leisure and Activity Clubs)
Comité de Base pour l'Abolition du Salariat et la Destruction de l'Université (Base Committee for the Abolition of Wage Labour and the Destruction of the University)
Comités Palestine (Palestine Committees)
Front Homosexuel d'Action Révolutionnaire (Revolutionary Homosexual Action Front)
Front Universitaire Antifasciste (Antifascist University Front)
Gauche Prolétarienne (Proletarian Left)
Groupe du Jeudi (Thursday Group)
Intersyndicale de Nantes (Inter-union Committee of Nantes)

```
```

Les 'Italiens' (The 'Italians')
Jeunesse Agricole Chrétienne (Christian Young Farmers)
Jeunesse Communiste Révolutionnaire (Revolutionary Communist Youth)
Jeunesse Étudiante Chrétienne (Young Christian Students)
La Lettre (The Letter)
Larzac activists
Lip Comité d'Action (Lip Action Committee)
Mouvement de Libération des Femmes (Women's Liberation Movement)
Mouvement des Travailleurs Arabes (Arab Workers' Movement)
Mouvement Ibérique de Libération (Iberian Liberation Front)
Mouvement Rural de la Jeunesse Chrétienne (Christian Youth Rural Movement)
Organisation Communiste Internationaliste (Communist Internationalist Organization)
Psych et Po (Psychology and Politics)
Secours Rouge (Red Aid)
Union des Étudiants Communistes (Union of Communist Students)
Union des Jeunesses Communistes (marxiste-léniniste) (Union of Marxist-Leninist Communist Youth)
Union Nationale des Étudiants de France (French National Union of Students)
Vive la Révolution (Long Live Revolution)

GERMANY (DEMOCRATIC REPUBLIC)

'Eintopp', 'Kramladen' ('Hotpot', 'General Store')
Bausoldaten (Conscientious Objectors)
East Berlin children of dissidents and intellectuals
Kommune 1 Ost, Samariterstraße (Commune 1 East, Samariterstraße)
Ostberliner Trotzkisten (East Berlin Trotskyists)
Sozialistisches Wohnkollektiv (Socialist Living Collective)
Wochenend-Kommune Stahnsdorf (Stahnsdorf Weekend Commune)

GERMANY (FEDERAL REPUBLIC)

Activists from Bremen
Anti-AKW Aktivisten Wyhl (Wyhl Anti-nuclear Activists)
Kommunistische Partei Deutschlands (Aufbauorganisation) (German Communist Party (Assembly Organization))
Marxistischer Studentenbund Spartakus (Spartakus Marxist Student League)
Sozialistischer Deutscher Studentenbund (Socialist German Student League)

GREAT BRITAIN

Eel Pie Island communards
Essex Road Women's Centre
International Marxist Group
International Socialists
London School of Economics student radicals

Shrubb Farm communards
Villa Road squatters

GREECE

Antifasistiko Kinima Elladas (Anti-fascist Movement of Greece)
Dimokratikes Epitropes Antistaseos (Democratic Committees of Resistance)
Dimokratiki Amyna (Democratic Defence)
Dimokratiki Neolaia Lambraki (Lambrakis Democratic Youth)
Elliniko Dimokratiko Kinima (Greek Democratic Movement)
Eniaia Dimokratiki Aristera (United Democratic Left)
Epanastatiko Kommounistiko Kinima Elladas (Revolutionary Communist Movement of
    Greece)
Kinima 20is Oktovri (20 October Movement)
Neolaia EDA (Youth of the United Democratic Left)
Panellinio Apeleftherotiko Kinima (Panhellenic Liberation Movement)

HUNGARY

Balatonboglár Group
Budapest Marxist-Leninist Party/so-called 'Maoists'
Budapesti iskola/Új baloldal/Lukács-óvoda (The Budapest School/New Left/The 'Lukács
    Kindergarten')
Dissenting Catholics/Regnum Marianum
KISZ Communist Youth League Reform Movement
Orfeo
Vietnámi Szolidaritási Bizottság (Vietnam Solidarity Committee)

ICELAND

'Kópamaros' (Kopamaros)
Fylkingin (Revolutionary Socialist League, later Revolutionary Communist League)

IRELAND (NORTHERN)

Northern Ireland Civil Rights Association
The People's Democracy
Young Socialist Alliance

ITALY

Circolo Culturale Montesacro (Montesacro Cultural Circle) (associated with Il Manifesto)
Comunità dell'Isolotto (dissident Catholics)
Movimento Femminista Romano (Roman Feminist Movement)

Porto Marghera industrial workers
Volunteers and staff from Trieste's mental hospital

POLAND

Komandosi (The Commandos)
Uczestnicy strajku na Politechnice Warszawskiej (Warsaw University of Technology
    Strikers)
Uczestnicy strajku na Uniwersytcie Jagiellońskim (Jagiellonian University Strikers)

SOVIET UNION

Fontanka (Fontaka Canal, St Petersburg)
Kaunas hippies
Leningrad hijackers
Refuseniks
Riga hippies
Saigon
Systema
Systema 1970s
Systema Sontse (Sun System)
Yellow Submarine

SPAIN

Acción Católica Especializada (Specialized Catholic Action)
Curas obreros (Worker-priests)
Frente de Liberación Popular (Popular Liberation Front)
Organización Revolucionaria de Trabajadores (Revolutionary Workers' Organization)

Bibliography

I. PRIMARY SOURCES

a. Interviews

Aggelopoulos, Venios, PV, Athens, 2 December 2008.

Angeloni, Luciana, RC, Florence, 5 May 2008.

Anonymous member of Socialist Youth Brigade and Kópamaros, GJ, Reykjavík, 12 January 2006.

Anonymous respondent, AvdG, Bremen, 13 November 2008.

Anonymous respondent, PA, Budapest, 5 October 2008.

Anonymous respondent, RG, Paris, 25 May 2007.

Antonenko, Andrei, JF, St Petersburg, 10 June 2009.

Aragón Marín, Leonardo, NT, Madrid, 14 April 2008.

Aranzadi Martínez, Juan, NT, Madrid, 21 April 2010.

Arthur, Paul, CR, Bangor (N. Ireland), 13 February 2009.

Atkári, János, JM, Budapest, 12 November 2008.

Atkinson, Paul, JD, London, 9 July 2010.

Ayrton, Pete, JD, London, 5 June 2010.

Bachelet, Prisca, RG, Paris, 27 May 2008.

Bailey, Ron, JD, London, 15 June 2010.

Bakos, István, PA, Budapest, 19 November 2008.

Barloschky, Katja, AvdG, Bremen, 21 June 2010.

Batovrin, Sergei, JF, New York, May 2011.

Bauer, Tamás, PA, Budapest, 5 March 2009.

Behnke, Klaus, AvdG, Berlin, 3 May 2010.

Bekier, Stefan, PO, Warsaw, 23 June 2009.

Bertelli, Gualtiero, RC, Mira, 19 March 2009.

Bew, Paul, CR, Belfast, 13 February 2009.

Bielecki, Czesław, PO, Warsaw, 26 October 2009.

Bijaoui, Jean, RG, Paris, 10 April 2008.

Blanquart, Paul, RG, Paris, 15 May 2007.

Blumsztajn, Seweryn, PO, Warsaw, 5 January 2010.

Bogucka, Teresa, PO, Warsaw, 21 January 2009.

Bombin, Misha, JF, Riga, 9 April 2009.

Boyle, Kevin, CR, Colchester, 10 July 2009.

Breteau, Jean, RG, Nantes, 2 April 2008.

Bruns, Tissy, AvdG, Berlin, 18 December 2009.

Bujwicki, Bernard, PO, Białystok, 17 July 2010.

Burguière, Jean-Marie, RG, Larzac, 21 May 2008.

Burguière, Pierre and Christiane, RG, Larzac, 22 May 2008.

Burnier, Michel-Antoine, RG, Paris, 11 May 2007.

Bury, Carola, AvdG, Bremen, 22 June 2010.

Camilleri, Michel, RG, Toulouse, 28 April 2008.

Castro, Roland, RG, Paris, 9 May 2007.

Christiani, Charlotte, AW, Aarhus, 3 February 2009.

Cipriani, Urbano, RC, Florence, 19 April 2008.

Cohen, Yves, RG, Paris, 9 May 2008.

Consigli, Carlo, RC, Florence, 9 May 2008.

Cooper, Ivan, CR, Derry, 15 May 2009.

Cooper, Pete, JD, London, 15 July 2010.

Corbyn, Piers, JD, London, 15 June 2010.

Cossu, Leda, RC, Venice, 31 March 2009.

Cowley, John, JD, London, 22 July 2010.

Currie, Austin, CR, Maynooth, 16 February 2010.

Daboussi, Abdel Majid, RG, Paris, 26 May 2008.

Dalos, György, PA, Budapest, 17 April 2009.

Darras, Daniel and Nobue Ishii Darras, RG, Larzac, 23 May 2008.

Day, Patrick, JD, London, 22 April 2009.

De Gennaro, Pietro, RC, Rome, 11 December 2008.

De Zárraga Moreno, José Luis, NT, Madrid, 2 June 2010.

Deák, Istvan, PA, Budapest, 19 February 2009.

Defert, Daniel, RG, Paris, 7 April 2008.

Demougeot, Fatima, RG, Besançon, 21 May 2007.

Demszky, Gábor, PA, Budapest, 2 December 2008.

Diatłowicki, Jerzy, PO, Warsaw, 16 November 2009.

Dinné, Olaf, AvdG, Bremen, 27 December 2009.

Diószegi, László, PA, Budapest, 1 December 2008.

Dodos, Dimosthenis, PV, Thessaloniki, 23 February 2008.

Dodziuk, Anna, PO, Warsaw, 7 September 2009.

Dollé, Jean-Paul, RG, Paris, 15 May 2007.

Due, Birgitte, AW, Copenhagen, 8 December 2010.

Duteuil, Jean-Pierre, RG, Paris, 27 May 2008.

Eckert, Rainer, AvdG, Leipzig, 24 June 2010.

Elek, Károly, PA, Budapest, 9 January 2009.

Erős, Ferenc, PA, Budapest, 9 October 2008.

Fábry, Péter, JM, Budapest, 23 January 2009.

Fawthrop, Tom, JD, London, 23 September 2008.

Filini, Anna, PV, Athens, 29 February 2008.

Fiorensoli, Maria Paola, RC, Rome, 11 December 2008.

Frölich, Niels, AW, Albertslund, 13 February 2009.

Furlani, Mira, RC, Florence, 8 May 2008.

Galántai, György, JM, Budapest, 23 January 2009.

Gallio, Giovanna, RC, Trieste, 5 March 2009.

Gamo Sánchez, Mariano, NT, Madrid, 26 July and 2 August 2009.

Gäng, Peter, AvdG, Berlin, 29 April 2010.

Garí Ramos, Manuel, NT, Madrid, 4 June 2010.

Gáspár, Judit, PA, Budapest, 11 March 2009.

Gáti, Tibor, PA, Budapest, 20 October 2008.

Geismar, Alain, RG, Paris, 29 May 2007.

Giannichedda, Maria Grazia, RC, Trieste, 26 June 2008.

Glynos, Giorgos, PV, Athens, 18 May 2009.

Gómez Navarro, José Luis, NT, Madrid, 11 March 2010.

Gomiti, Sergio, RC, Florence, 21 April 2008.

González González, Miguel, NT, Madrid, 6 May 2010.

Goupil, Romain, RG, Paris, 24 May 2007.
Goureaux, Guy, RG, Paris, 9 June 2007.
Grange, Dominique, RG, Paris, 10 May 2007.
Gray, John, CR, Belfast, 30 November 2008.
Groszer, Franziska, AvdG, Berlin, 7 October 2008.
Grumbach, Tiennot, RG, Paris, 18 April 2008.
Gyáni, Gábor, JM, Budapest, 27 September 2008.
Hajba, Julianna, PA, Budapest, 25 February 2009.
Hansson, Erlingur, GJ, Reykjavík, 8 October 2009.
Haraszti, Miklós, PA, Vienna, 10 April 2009.
Harper, Clifford, JD, London, 12 May 2009.
Hartung, Klaus, AvdG, Berlin, 5 January 2010.
Haughey, Denis, CR, Cookstown, 13 May 2009.
Hayling, Alan, JD, London, 27 July 2010.
Heiszler, Vilmos, PA, Budapest, 29 October 2008.
Heller, Ágnes, PA, Budapest, 17 December 2008.
Hirsch, Helga, AvdG, Berlin, 30 April 2010.
Holtfreter, Jürgen, AvdG, Berlin, 25 June 2010.
Hoyland, John, JD, London, 25 May 2010.
Illg, Jerzy, PO, Warsaw, 17 February 2010.
Ingargiola, Liliana, RC, Rome, 29 November 2008.
Jeffreys, Steve, JD, London, 21 April 2010.
Jirousová, Věra, MČ, Prague, 1 January 2009.
Karambelias, Giorgios, PV, Athens, 2 July 2008.
Katsoulis, Elias, PV, Athens, 18 January 2008.
Kavvadia, Maria, PV, Athens, 12 May 2009.
Kiss, Mihály, JM, Budapest, 29 January 2009.
Kjeldsen, Michael, AW, Roskilde, 31 January 2011.
Klein, Thomas, AvdG, Berlin, 28 June 2010.
Kleinert, Burkhard, AvdG, Berlin, 27 April 2010.
Knížák, Milan, MČ, Prague, 3 July 2008.
Komarova, Tatiana, JF, Munich, 2 May 2011.
Komjáthy, Anna, JM, Budapest, 21 January 2009.
Kounalakis, Petros, PV, Athens, 21 October 2009.
Krzesinski, Andrzej, PO, Warsaw, 24 September 2009.
Labsch, Klaus, AvdG, Berlin, 29 April 2010.
Lampronti, Maurizio, RC, Florence, 17 April 2008.
Le Bitoux, Jean, RG, Paris, 10 April 2008.
Le Dantec, Jean-Pierre, RG, Paris, 24 April 2007.
Lecuir, Jean, RG, Toulouse, 29 April 2008.
Lévy-Willard, Annette, RG, Paris, 6 June 2007.
Lietz, Heiko, AvdG, Schwerin, 28 April 2010.
Linnet, Vernhardur, GJ, Reykjavík, 10 October 2009.
Lishenko (Baske), Sergei, JF, Moscow, July 2010.
Lityński, Jan, PO, Warsaw, November 25 2009.
Lois Fernández, Julio, NT, Madrid, 22 June 2009.
Loldrup, Hans-Otto, AW, Copenhagen, 4 January 2011.
Lopotukhina, Irina, JF, El Kfad, 3 August 2011.
Lotti, Danilo, RC, Florence, 21 April 2008.

Ludassy, Mária, PA, Budapest, 1 December 2008.
Manios, Nikos, PV, Athens, 13 October 2009.
Mariti, Germano, RC, Porto Marghera, 16 March 2009.
Marker, Birthe, AW, Copenhagen, 22 November 2010.
Maroulakou, Despoina, PV, Athens, 6 December 2008.
Mastrangeli, Paola, RC, Rome, 25 November 2008.
Matsas, Sabbetai, PV, Athens, 26 January 2009.
Mayo, Marjorie, JD, London, 30 June 2010.
McAliskey, Bernadette, CR, Dungannon, 18 July 2009.
Migale, Lia, RC, Rome, 4 December 2008.
Modzelewski, Karol, PO, Warsaw, 18 March 2009.
Mohedano Fuertes, José María, NT, Madrid, 7 June 2010.
Molina Blázquez, José, NT, 1 June 2010.
Montero García, Feliciano, NT, Madrid, 15 December 2008.
Motti, Lucia, RC, Rome, 24 June 2008.
Nagy, Bálint, PA, Budapest, 14 November 2008.
Najmányi, László, JM, Budapest, 26 January 2009.
Nemes, István, JM, Budapest, 24 January 2009.
Notaras, Gerasimos, PV, Athens, 14 April 2009.
Ott, Hervé, RG, Le Cun du Larzac, 24 May 2008.
Pala, Giovanna, RC, Rome, 2 December 2008.
Palm, Monika, AvdG, Berlin, 7 January 2010.
Paraskevopoulos, Theodoros, PV, Athens, 30 September 2009.
Pereña García, Francisco, NT, Madrid, 26 May 2010.
Pérez Pinillos, Julio, NT, Rivas Vaciamadrid, 19 April 2010.
Piaget, Charles, RG, Besançon, 22 May 2007.
Picq, Françoise, RG, Paris, 27 April 2007.
Pixner, Stephanie, JD, London, 15 July 2010.
Poppe, Gerd, AvdG, Berlin, 11 June 2008.
Pór, György, JM, Brussels, 13 March 2009.
Portelli, Alessandro, RC, Rome, 12 December 2008.
Potel, Jean-Yves, RG, Paris, 16 May 2008.
Prosdocimo, Carla, RC, Trieste, 23 March 2009.
Rachtan, Piotr, PO, Warsaw, 24 June 2009.
Rathenow, Lutz, AvdG, Berlin, 30 April 2010.
Rawicz, Marcin, PO, Warsaw, 28 February 2009.
Recknagel, Steffi, AvdG, Berlin, 5 January 2010.
Requeno Regaño, Pedro, NT, Madrid, 25 July and 28 August 2009.
Révai, Gábor, PA, Budapest, 8 October 2008.
Reznikov, Andrei, JF, St Petersburg, 5 June 2009.
Riis, Kristian, AW, Copenhagen, 4 April 2009.
Ringart, Nadja, RG, Sceaux, 5 June 2007.
Ringer, Adam, PO, Warsaw, 25 July 2009.
Rocqueirol, Christian, RG, Saint-Sauveur du Larzac, 23 May 2008.
Rocton, Yves, RG, Fenioux (Deux-Sèvres), 14 May 2008.
Roig Salas, Alicia, NT, Barcelona, 24 March 2009.
Rolin, Olivier, RG, Paris, 4 May 2007.
Rotelli, Franco, RC, Trieste, 5 March 2009.
Rouillan, Jean-Marc, RG, Marseille, 17 April 2008.

Rowbotham, Sheila, JD, Oxford, 10 June 2009.
Ruddy, Brid, CR, Belfast, 31 October 2008.
Salmon, Jean-Marc, RG, Paris, 16 April 2008.
Sankowski, Leszek, PO, Warsaw, 6 April 2009.
Sanroma Aldea, José, NT, Madrid, 1 June 2010.
Sauquillo Pérez, Francisca, NT, Madrid, 1 September 2009.
Sawicki, Mirosław, PO, Warsaw, 27 February 2010.
Schiesches, Wolfgang, AvdG, Bremen, 23 February 2010.
Schleuning, Peter, AvdG, Bremen, 22 December 2008.
Schröter, Rupert, AvdG, Berlin, 4 January 2010.
Segal, Lynne, JD, London, 22 April 2010.
Sell, Maren, RG, Paris, 21 April 2008.
Semler, Christian, AvdG, Berlin, 29 August 2008.
Senik, André, RG, Paris, 3 April 2007.
Shaw, Martin, JD, Falmer, 14 November 2008.
Siméon, Robert and Brigitte Cadot Siméon, RG, Millau, 20 May 2008.
Skobov, Aleksandr, JF, St Petersburg, 7 June 2009.
Smolar, Aleksander, PO, Warsaw, 19 February 2009.
Smolar, Nina, PO, Warsaw, 21 August 2009.
Soldatov, Vladimir, JF, Moscow, 15 June 2010.
Solé Sugranyes, Jordi, NT, Barcelona, 16 May 2010.
Somogyi, Győző, PA, Salföld, 7 November 2008.
Søndergaard, Pia, AW, Aarhus, 4 February 2009.
Sotirakos, Antonis, PV, Athens, 12 May 2009.
Stamatopoulou, Christina, PV, Athens, 2 November 2007.
Steklík, Jan, MČ, Ústí nad Orlicí, 22 May 2010.
Stella, Rosetta, RC, Rome, 8 December 2008.
Streese, Jörg, AvdG, Bremen, 27 February 2010.
Suk, Jaroslav, MČ, Prague, 15 July 2008.
Syberg, Karen, AW, Svensmarke, 5 January 2011.
Szombathy, Bálint, JM, Budapest, 13 November 2008.
Taborri, Massimo, RC, Rome, 11 December 2008.
Tamás, Gáspár Miklós, JM, Budapest, 5 March 2009.
Thelle, Hatla, AW, Copenhagen, 26 January 2009.
Thing, Morten, AW, Copenhagen, 12 February 2009.
Thórdardóttir, Birna, GJ, Reykjavík, 16 August 2008.
Tiktopoulos, Michalis, PV, Athens, 3 November 2009.
Torricini, Gioietta, RC, Florence, 5 May 2008.
Travers, Julienne, RC, Rome, 3 December 2008.
Trencsényi, László, PA, Budapest, 15 January 2009.
Tsaousidis, Klearchos, PV, Thessaloniki, 25 May 2009.
Tsiokos, Nikos, PV, Athens, 24 June 2009.
Tsurkov, Arkadii, JF, St Petersburg, 3 August 2011.
Tyl, Miroslav, interview from the private collection of Jaroslav Pažout (c. 1999).
Uhl, Petr, MČ, Prague, 17 May 2008.
Uszkoreit, Hans-Jürgen, AvdG, Berlin, 25 and 26 June 2010.
Vajda, Mihály, PA, Budapest, 25 November 2008.
Vasileiadis, Damianos, PV, Athens, 22 December 2007.
Victorri, Anne and Bernard, RG, Paris, 28 May 2007.

Vind, Ole, AW, Hillerød, 7 January 2010.
Vinogradov, Feliks and Marina, JF, St Petersburg, 8 June 2009.
Viveret, Patrick, RG, Paris, 15 May 2008.
Vuarin, Pierre, RG, Paris, 12 May 2008.
Wainwright, Hilary, JD, London, 27 July 2010.
Wates, Nick, JD, Hastings, 3 March 2009.
Weeks, Jeffrey, JD, London, 17 June 2010.
Wegner, Bettina, AvdG, Berlin, 2 May 2010.
Wegner, Claudia, AvdG, Berlin, 24 June 2010.
Welzk, Stefan, AvdG, Berlin, 22 September 2008.
Westermann, Finn, AW, Smørum, 21 December 2010.
Wiedemann, Vladimir, JF, London, May 2011.
Witaszewski, Włodzimierz, PO, Warsaw, 30 April 2010.
Wolff, K.D., AvdG, Berlin, 28 May 2008.
Wolmar, Christian, JD, London, 23 January 2009.
Wright, Nick, JD, Faversham, 23 February 2010.
Wyrowiński, Jan, PO, Warsaw, 8 July 2010.
Zaborovskii, Sasha, JF, Moscow, 14 July 2010.
Zaitsev, Gena, JF, Luga, May 2009.
Zani, Giancarlo, RC, Florence, 10 May 2008.
Zwoliński, Marek, PO, Warsaw, 25 November 2009.

b. Archival sources
Christovova, Boja, 'Letter to Roel van Duyn, 11 October 1966', Provo Collection IISH (Amsterdam).
Comunita dell'Isolotto, 'Assemblea sulla "Populorum progressio" enciclica di Paolo VI', Archivio storico della Comunita dell'Isolotto (21 April 1967).
Robert-Havemann-Gesellschaft, Berlin (RHG):
RHG 022/1
RHG 080
RHG 098
RHG 155
RHG 173
RHG 280
RHG PS047
Open Society Archives, Budapest: HU OSA 300-40-2 Boxes 4, 21, 53, 84, 108; HU OSA 300-80-1-45.
A Politikatörténeti Intézet Levéltára, Budapest: PIL 289/2/55; PIL 289/3/193.

II. SECONDARY SOURCES

Abellán, José Luis (ed.), *El exilio español de 1939*, 6 vols (Madrid, 1976–8).
Abellán, José Luis, *De la guerra civil al exilio republicano, 1936–1977* (Madrid, 1983).
Abrams, Lynn, *Oral History Theory* (Abingdon and New York, 2010).
Aceña, Pablo Martín and Elena Martínez Ruiz, 'The golden age of Spanish capitalism: Economic growth without political freedom', in Nigel Townson (ed.), *Spain Transformed: The Late Franco Dictatorship, 1959–75* (Basingstoke, 2010), 30–46.

Agosti, Aldo, Luisa Passerini and Nicola Tranfaglia (eds), *La cultura e i luoghi del '68. Atti del convegno di studi organizzato dal Dipartimento di Storia dell'Università di Torino* (Milan, 1991).

Aguilar, Paloma, *Memory and Amnesia: The Role of the Spanish Civil War in the Transition to Democracy* (Oxford, 2000).

Aguirre, Jesús, K. Rahner, L. Lombardo-Radice, J. Girardi, M. Machovec, G. Mury, J. B. Metz, L. Althusser, M. Sacristán and J. L. L. Aranguren, *Cristianos y Marxistas. Los problemas de un diálogo* (Madrid, 1969).

Alan, Josef and Tomáš Bitrich, *Alternativní kultura. Příběh české společnosti 1945–1989* (Prague, 2001).

Alland, Alexandre, *Le Larzac et après. L'Étude d'un mouvement social novateur* (Paris, 1995).

Allerbeck, Klaus, *Soziologie radikaler Studentenbewegungen* (Munich, 1973).

Álvarez Espinosa and Daniel Francisco, *Cristianos y Marxistas contra Franco* (Cádiz, 2002).

Anderson, Terry, *The Movement and the Sixties: Protest in America from Greensboro to Wounded Knee* (Oxford, 1995).

Ansorg, Leonore, Bernd Gehrke, Thomas Klein and Danuta Kneipp, *'Das Land ist still— noch!' Herrschaftswandel und politische Gegnerschaft in der DDR (1971–1989)* (Cologne, 2009).

Apor, Péter, 'A város mint a lázadás helye: aktivizmus és térhasználat a késő szocialista Budapesten', in Árpád Tóth, István H. Németh and Erika Szívós (eds), *A város és társadalma. Tanulmányok Bácskai Vera tiszteletére* (Budapest, 2011), 15–25.

Apor, Péter and James Mark, 'Mobilizing generation: The idea of 1968 in Hungary', in Anna von der Goltz (ed.), *'Talkin' 'bout my Generation': Conflicts of Generation Building and Europe's '1968'* (Göttingen, 2011), 99–118.

Arnal, Oscar L., *Priests in Working-Class Blue: The History of the Worker-Priests, 1943–1954* (New York, 1990).

Arthur, Paul, *The People's Democracy 1968–73* (Belfast, 1974).

Ascoli, Giulietta (ed.), *La parola elettorale. Viaggio nell'universo politico maschile* (Rome, 1976).

Association du Mouvement pour les luttes féministes, *Chronique d'une imposture. Du Mouvement de la Libération des Femmes à une marque commerciale* (Paris, 1981).

Autorenkollektiv, *Wir warn die stärkste der Partein... Erfahrungsberichte aus der Welt der K-Gruppen* (Berlin, 1977).

Babiracki, Patryk, 'Interfacing the Soviet bloc: Recent literature and new paradigms', *Ab Imperio* 4 (2011), 376–407.

Baglioni, Guido (ed.), *Analisi della CISL. Fatti e giudizi di un'esperienza sindacale* (Rome, 1980).

Barjonet, André, *La Révolution trahie* (Paris, 1968).

Basaglia, Franco, *Scritti. Vol. I: 1953–1968. Dalla psichiatria fenomenologica all'esperienza di Gorizia* (Turin, 1981).

Basaglia, Franco, Agostino Pirella and Salvatore Taverna, *L'Istituzione negata. Rapporto da un ospedale psichiatrico* (Turin, 1968).

Bascetta, Marco and Andrea Colombo (eds), *Enciclopedia del '68* (Rome, 2008).

Bedani, Gino, *Politics and Ideology in the Italian Workers' Movement* (Oxford, 1995).

Behnke, Klaus, *Stasi auf dem Schulhof. Der Missbrauch von Kindern und Jugendlichen durch das Ministerium für Staatssicherheit* (Berlin, 1998).

Behnke, Klaus and Jürgen Fuchs, *Zersetzung der Seele. Psychologie und Psychiatrie im Dienste der Stasi* (Hamburg, 1995).

Békés, Csaba, *Európából Európába. Magyarország konfliktusok kereszttüzében, 1945–1990* (Budapest, 2004).

Bence, György, 'Marcuse és az újbaloldali diákmozgalom', *Új Írás* (September 1968), 95–102.

Bendix Andersen, Morten and Niklas Olsen, 'Arven fra 68', in Bendix Andersen and Niklas Olsen, *1968. Dengang og nu* (Copenhagen, 2004), 9–28.

Berend, Iván T., *The Hungarian Economic Reforms 1953–1988* (Cambridge, 1990).

Berendt, Poul, *Bissen og Dullen. Familiehistorier fra nutiden* (Copenhagen, 1984).

Beretta, Roberto, *Il lungo autunno. Controstoria del Sessantotto cattolico* (Milan, 1998).

Berman, Paul, *A Tale of Two Utopias: The Political Journey of the Generation of 1968* (New York, 1996).

Bertaux, Daniel, *Biography and Society: The Life History Approach in the Social Sciences* (Beverly Hills, CA, 1981).

Bertaux, Daniel, *Le Récit de vie* (Paris, 1997).

Besnaci-Lancou, Fatima, *Les Harkis dans la colonisation et ses suites* (Paris, 2008).

Bessel, Richard and Dirk Schumann, 'Introduction: Violence, normality, and the construction of postwar Europe', in Richard Bessel and Dirk Schumann (eds), *Life after Death: Approaches to a Cultural and Social History of Europe during the 1940s and 1950s* (Cambridge, 2003), 1–14.

Bew, Paul, *Ireland: The Politics of Enmity 1789–2006* (Oxford, 2009).

Bianchi, Sandro and Angelo Turchini, *Gli estremisti di centro. Il neo-integralismo cattolico degli anni '70: Comunione e Liberazione* (Florence, 1975).

Biess, Frank, 'Introduction', in Frank Biess and Robert G. Moeller (eds), *Histories of the Aftermath: The Legacies of the Second World War in Europe* (Oxford, 2010), 1–10.

Blanquart, Paul, *En bâtardise. Itinéraires d'un Chrétien marxiste, 1967–1980* (Paris, 1981).

Blázquez, Feliciano, *La traición de los clérigos en la España de Franco. Crónica de una intolerancia (1936–1975)* (Madrid, 1991).

Blüdnikow, Bent (ed.), *Opgøret om den kolde krig* (Copenhagen, 2003).

Bobbio, Luigi, *Storia di Lotta continua* (Milan, 1988).

Boccia, Maria Luisa, 'Psichiatria democratica. Riformatori e riformati', *Democrazia e diritto* 1 (January–February 1986), 151–9.

Boel, Bent, 'French support for eastern European dissidence, 1968–1989: Approaches and controversies', in Poul Villaume and Odd Arne Westad (eds), *Perforating the Iron Curtain: European Détente, Transatlantic Relations, and the Cold War, 1965–1985* (Copenhagen, 2010), 215–42.

Boeschoten, R. V., T. Vervenioti, E. Voutyra, V. Dalkavoukis and K. Mbada (eds), *Mnimes kai lithi tou ellinikou emfyliou polemou* (Thessaloniki, 2008).

Borecký, Vladimír, *Odvrácená tvář humour. Ke komice absurdity* (Prague, 1996).

Bosi, Mary, *Ellada kai tromokratia. Ethnikes kai diethneis diastaseis* (Athens, 1996).

Bouchier, David, *The Feminist Challenge: The Movement for Women's Liberation in Britain and the USA* (New York, 1984).

Bourg, Julian, *From Revolution to Ethics: May 1968 and Contemporary French Thought* (Montreal, 2007).

Bourg, Julian, ' "Your sexual revolution is not ours": French feminist "moralism" and the limits of desire', in Lessie Jo Frazier and Deborah Cohen (eds), *Gender and Sexuality in 1968: Transformative Politics in the Cultural Imagination* (New York, 2009), 85–113.

Bourseiller, Christophe, *Les Maoïstes. La folle histoire des gardes rouges français* (Paris, 1996).

Bracke, Maud, 'French responses to the Prague Spring: connections, (mis)perception and appropriation', *Europe-Asia Studies* 60/10 (2008), 1735–47.

Bravo, Anna, *A colpi di cuore. Storie del Sessantotto* (Rome, 2008).

Bren, Paulina, 'Weekend getaways: The chata, the tramp and the politics of private life in post-1968 Czechoslovakia', in David Crowley and Susan E. Reid (eds), *Socialist Spaces: Sites of Everyday Life in the Eastern Bloc* (Oxford, 2002), 123–40.

Bren, Paulina, '1968 in East and West: Visions of political change and student protest from across the Iron Curtain', in Gerd-Rainer Horn and Padraic Kenney (eds), *Transnational Moments of Change: Europe 1945, 1968, 1989* (Lanham, MD and Oxford, 2004), 119–35.

Bresnahan, Eileen, 'The strange case of Jackie East: When identities collide', in Barbara Ryan (ed.), *Identity Politics in the Women's Movement* (New York, 2001), 183–96.

Brouillette, Amy, 'Remapping *Samizdat*: Underground publishing and the Hungarian avant-garde, 1966 to 1975', MA thesis (Central European University, 2009).

Brown, Timothy, 'A tale of two communes: The private and the political in divided Berlin, 1967–1973', in Martin Klimke, Jacco Pekelder and Joachim Scharloth (eds), *Between Prague Spring and French May 1968: Opposition and Revolt in Europe, 1960–80* (Oxford and New York, 2011), 132–40.

Burgalassi, Silvano, 'Dissenso cattolico e comunità di base', in F. Traniello and G. Campanini (eds), *Dizionario storico del movimento cattolico in Italia, 1860–1980, I.2* (Turin, 1981), 278–84.

Burnier, Michel-Antoine, *A ma fille. Histoire d'un père de cinquante ans qui ne voulait pas avoir d'enfant* (Paris, 1993).

Burnier, Michel-Antoine, *L'Adieu à Sartre* (Paris, 2002).

Burnier, Michel-Antoine, *Les Sept Vies du Dr Kouchner* (Paris, 2008).

Callahan, William J., *The Catholic Church in Spain, 1875–1998* (Washington, DC, 2000).

Cantanzaro, Raimondo (ed.), *The Red Brigades and Left-Wing Terrorism in Italy* (London, 1991).

Carabott, Philip and Thanasis Sfikas (eds), *The Greek Civil War: Essays on a Conflict of Exceptionalism and Silences* (London, 2004).

Castaño Colomer, José, *La JOC en España (1946–1970)* (Salamanca, 1978).

Caute, David, *Sixty-Eight: The Year of the Barricades* (London, 1988).

Cella, Gian Primo, Paola Piva and Bruno Manghi, *Un sindacato italiano negli anni sessanta. La FIM-CISL dall'Associazione alla classe* (Bari, 1972).

Centeno García, José, Luis Díez Maestro and Julio Pérez Pinillos (eds), *Curas obreros: Cuarenta y cinco años de testimonio 1963–2008* (Barcelona, 2009).

Centro di Documentazione del Movimento Femminista Romano, *Donnità. Cronache del movimento femminista romano* (Rome, 1976).

Černý, František, 'Rudý Dutschke v Praze', *Reportér* 17 (24 April–1 May 1968).

Chinello, Cesco, *Sindacato, Pci, movimenti negli anni sessanta. Porto Marghera–Venezia 1955–1970*, vol. 2 (Milan, 1996).

Christiaens, Kim, Idesbald Goddeeris and Wouter Goedertier, 'Inspirées par le Sud? Les mobilisations transnationales Est–Ouest pendant la guerre froide', *Vingtième Siècle. Revue d'Histoire* 109 (2011), 155–68.

Christofferson, Michael Scott, *French Intellectuals Against the Left: The Antitotalitarian Moment of the 1970s* (New York, 2004).

Chytilek, Roman and Jakub Šedo (eds), *Volební systémy* (Brno, 2004).

Ciret, Jean-Paul and Jean-Pierre Sueur, *Les Étudiants, la politique et l'Église. Une impasse?* (Paris, 1970).

Claussen, Detlev, 'Chiffre 68', in Dietrich Harth and Jan Assmann (eds), *Revolution und Mythos* (Frankfurt am Main, 1992), 219–28.

Clavel, Maurice, *Les Paroissiens de Palente* (Paris, 1974).

Clavin, Patricia, 'Defining transnationalism', *Contemporary European History* 14/4 (2005), 421–39.

Clifford, Rebecca, 'Emotions and gender in oral history: Narrating Italy's 1968', *Modern Italy* 17/2 (2012), 209–21.

Close, David (ed.), *The Greek Civil War, 1943–1950: Studies of Polarization* (London, 1993).

Cohn-Bendit, Daniel, *Nous l'avons tant aimée, la révolution* (Paris, 1986).

Cohn-Bendit, Daniel, *Forget '68* (Paris, 2008).

Colombel, Jeannette, *Les Murs de l'école* (Paris, 1975).

Colombel, Jeannette, 'Résistance du Larzac, 1971–1977', *Les Temps modernes* 371 (June 1977), 1971–2088.

Colucci, Mario and Pierangelo Di Vittorio, *Franco Basaglia* (Milan, 2001).

Colvin, Sarah, *Ulrike Meinhof and West German Terrorism: Language, Violence, and Identity* (Rochester and New York, 2009).

Communist Party of Greece, 'On the side of the Egyptian people who fight for independence', 31 October 1956, *Communist Party of Greece, Official Texts 1956–1961* (Athens, 1997), 111–12.

Comunità dell'Isolotto, *Isolotto. 1954–1969* (Bari, 1969).

Comunità dell'Isolotto, *Isolotto sotto processo* (Bari, 1971).

Confino, Alon and Peter Fritzsche, *The Work of Memory: New Directions in the Study of German Society and Culture* (Urbana, IL, 2002).

Connor, Walter D., 'Politics, discontents, hopes: 1968 East and West', *Journal of Cold War Studies* 14/2 (2012), 142–53.

Cornils, Ingo and Sarah Waters (eds), *Memories of 1968: International Perspectives* (Bern, 2010).

Cotturri, Giuseppe, 'La società della politica istituzionale', *Democrazia e diritto*, special issue 'Militanza senza appartenenza' (January–February 1986), 7–45.

Crane, Susan, 'Writing the individual back into collective memory', *American Historical Review* 102/4 (1997), 1372–5.

Crawford, David, review of Wolfgang Kraushaar (ed.), 'Die RAF und der linke Terrorismus', *Journal of Cold War Studies* 9/4 (Autumn 2007), 160–4.

Crenshaw, Martha, *Terrorism in Context* (University Park, PA, 1995).

Csizmadia, Ervin, *A magyar demokratikus ellenzék (1968–1988)*, 3 vols (Budapest, 1995).

Csoóri, Sándor, *Kubai napló* (Budapest, 1965).

Csoóri, Sándor, 'Közel a szülőföldhöz', *Kortárs* 4 (2004), 17–24.

Cuhra, Jaroslav, 'KSČ, stát a římskokatolická církev', *Soudobé dějiny* 2–3 (2001).

Cuminetti, Mario, *Il dissenso cattolico in Italia, 1965–1980* (Milan, 1983).

Currie, Austin, *All Hell will Break Loose* (Dublin, 2004).

Czapiewski, Edward, *Marzec 1968 roku i jego następstwa w moich wspomnieniach* in *Studia i materiały z dziejów Uniwersytetu Wrocławskiego*, 2 vols (Wrocław, 1994).

Dąbrowski, Franciszek, Piotr Gontarczyk and Paweł Tomasik (eds), *Marzec 1968 w dokumentach MSW. Tom 1: Niepokorni* (Warsaw, 2008).

Dahlerup, Drude, *Rødstrømperne. Den danske Rødstrømpebevægelses udvikling, nytænkning og gennemslag 1970–1985*, 2 vols (Copenhagen, 1998).

Daniel, Yvan and Henri Godin, *La France: pays de mission?* (Paris, 1943).

Danyel, Jürgen, *Crossing 68/89* (Berlin, 2008).

Danyel, Jürgen, 'Das andere "1968" des Ostens: Prag und Ostberlin', in Martin Sabrow (ed.), *Mythos '1968'* (Leipzig, 2009), 75–94.

Dard, Olivier, *Voyage au cœur de l'OAS* (Paris, 2011).

David-Fox, Michael, 'The implications of transnationalism', *Kritika: Explorations in Russian and Eurasian History* 12/4 (2011), 885–904.

David-Fox, Michael, 'The Iron Curtain as semi-permeable membrane: The origins and demise of the Stalinist superiority complex', in Patryk Babiracki and Kenyon Zimmer (eds), *Cold War Crossings: International Travel and Exchange across the Soviet Bloc, 1940s–1960s* (College Station, TX, 2013).

Davies, Bronwyn and Susanne Gannon (eds), *Doing Collective Biography: Investigating the Production of Subjectivity* (New York, 2006).

Davies, Gareth, *From Opportunity to Entitlement: The Transformation of Great Society Liberalism* (Lawrence, KS, 1996).

Davis, Belinda, 'New Leftists and West Germany: Fascism, violence, and the public sphere, 1967–1974', in P. Gassert and A. E. Steinweis (eds), *Coping with the Nazi Past: West German Debates on Nazism and Generational Conflict 1955–1975* (New York and Oxford, 2006), 210–37.

Davis, Belinda, 'A whole world opening up: Transcultural contact, difference and the politicization of New Left activists', in Belinda Davis, Wilfried Mausbach, Martin Klimke and Carla MacDougall (eds), *Changing the World, Changing Oneself: Political Protest and Collective Identities in West Germany and the US in the 1960s and 1970s* (New York and Oxford, 2010), 255–73.

Davis, John and Anette Warring, 'Living utopia: Communal living in Denmark and Britain', *Cultural and Social History* 8/4 (2011), 511–28.

de Hernandez-Paluch, Maria, 'Miêdzy marcem a KOR-em', *Kontakt* 4 (1988), 20–7.

Debray, Régis, *La Révolution dans la Révolution* (Paris, 1967).

Debray, Régis, 'Marxism and the national question', *New Left Review* (September–October 1977), 25–41.

Dell'Acqua, Giuseppe, 'Gli anni di Basaglia', in Mario Colucci et al., *Follia e paradosso. Seminari sul pensiero di Franco Basaglia* (Trieste, 1995), 151–5.

Della Porta, Donatella, *Social Movements, Political Violence and the State: A Comparative Analysis of Italy and Germany* (Cambridge, 1995).

Demszky, Gábor, '68-as vagyok', *Index* (17 July 2008), <http://index.hu/velemeny/olvir/dg68/> (accessed 1 August 2010).

Dénes, Iván Zoltán, 'Diákmozgalom 1969-ben', *Élet és Irodalom* 52 (31 August 2008).

Devlin, Bernadette, *The Price of my Soul* (London, 1969).

Dinné, Olaf, Jochen Grünwaldt and Peter Kuckuck (eds), *Anno dunnemals. 68 in Bremen* (Bremen, 1998).

Divo, Jean, *Lip et les catholiques de Franche-Comté* (Yens-sur-Morges, 2003).

Dobszay, János, *Így—vagy sehogy! Fejezetek a Regnum Marianum életéből* (Budapest, 1991).

Dobszay, János, *Mozaikok a Regnum életéből a hetvenes évektől napjainkig* (Budapest, 1996).

Domínguez, Javier, *Organizaciones obreras cristianas en la oposición al franquismo* (Bilbao, 1975).

Dreyfus-Armand, Geneviève and Jacques Portes, 'Les Interactions internationales de la guerre du Viêtnam et mai 68', in Dreyfus-Armand et al. (eds), *Les Années 68. Le temps de la contestation* (Paris, 2000, 2008), 31–68.

Duchen, Claire, *Feminism in France: From May '68 to Mitterrand* (London, 1986).

Duteuil, Jean-Pierre, *Nanterre, 1965–66–67–68. Vers le Mouvement du 22 mars* (La Bussière, 1988).

Duteuil, Jean-Pierre, *Mai 68. Un mouvement politique* (La Bussière, 2008).

Ebbinghaus, Angelika (ed.), *Die letzte Chance?—1968 in Osteuropa: Analysen und Berichte über ein Schlüsseljahr* (Hamburg, 2008).

Echols, Alice, *Daring to be Bad: Radical Feminism in America, 1967–1975* (Minneapolis, MN, 1989).

Eck, Werner (ed.), *Prosopographie und Sozialgeschichte: Studien zur Methodik und Erkenntnismöglichkeit der kaiserzeitlichen Prosopographie* (Cologne, 1993).

Edmunds, June and Bryan S. Turner, *Generations, Culture and Society* (Buckingham and Philadelphia, 2002).

Egan, Bowes and Vincent McCormack, *Burntollet* (London, 1969).

Engerman, David, 'The Second World's Third World', *Kritika* 12/1 (2011), 183–211.

Engler, Wolfgang, *Die Ostdeutschen: Kunde von einem verlorenen Land* (Berlin, 1999).

Ergas, Yasmine, 'Tra sesso e genere', *Memoria. Rivista di storia delle donne* 19–20 (1987), 11–18.

Erll, Astrid and Ann Rigney (eds), *Mediation, Remediation, and the Dynamics of Cultural Memory* (Berlin, 2009).

Ernè, Claudio, *Basaglia a Trieste. Cronaca del cambiamento* (Viterbo, 2008).

Evans, Sara M., *Personal Politics: The Roots of Women's Liberation in the Civil Rights Movement and the New Left* (New York, 1980).

Evans, Sara M., *Tidal Wave: How Women Changed America at Century's End* (New York, 2003).

Evans, Sara M., 'Sons, daughters, and patriarchy: Gender and the 1968 generation', *American Historical Review* 114/2 (April 2009), 331–47.

Eyerman, Ron and Andrew Jamison, *Music and Social Movements: Mobilizing Traditions in the Twentieth Century* (Cambridge, 1998).

Fendrich, James M., 'Keeping the faith or pursuing the good life: A study of the consequences of participation in the civil rights movement', *American Sociological Review* 42 (1977), 144–57.

Fietze, Beate, '1968 als Symbol der ersten globalen Generation', *Berliner Journal für Soziologie* 3 (1997), 365–86.

Filias, Vasilis, *Ta axehasta kai ta lismonimena* (Athens, 1997).

Fink, Carol, Philipp Gassert and Detlef Junker (eds), *1968: The World Transformed* (Cambridge, 1998).

Førland, Tor Egil, 'Introduction to the special issue on 1968', *Scandinavian Journal of History* 33/4 (2008), 317–25.

Fouque, Antoinette, *Women: The Pioneer Front of Democracy* (Paris, 1995).

Fourastié, Jean and Jacqueline, *D'une France à une autre. Avant et après les Trente Glorieuses* (Paris, 1987).

François, Étienne, Matthias Middell, Emmanuel Terray and Dorothee Wierling (eds), *1968: Ein europäisches Jahr?* (Leipzig, 1997).

Frank, Robert, 'Imaginaire politique et figures symboliques internationales: Castro, Hô, Mao, et le "Che"', in Geneviève Dreyfus-Armand, Robert Frank, Marie-Françoise Lévy and Michelle Zancarini-Fournel (eds), *Les Années 68. Le temps de la contestation* (Paris and Brussels, 2000), 31–47.

Fraser, Ronald, *1968: A Student Generation in Revolt* (London, 1988).

Frazier, Lessie Jo and Deborah Cohen (eds), *Gender and Sexuality in 1968: Transformative Politics in the Cultural Imagination* (New York, 2009).

Frei, Norbert, *1968: Jugendrevolte und globaler Protest* (Munich, 2008).

Frisch, Michael, *A Shared Authority: Essays on the Craft and Meaning of Oral and Public History* (Albany, NY, 1990).

Friszke, Andrzej, *Opozycja polityczna w PRL 1945–1980* (London, 1994).

Fuchs, Eckhardt and Benedikt Stuchtey (eds), *Across Cultural Borders: Historiography in Global Perspective* (Lanham, MD, 2002).

Fürst, Juliane, Piotr Osęka and Chris Reynolds, 'Breaking the walls of privacy: How rebellion came to the street', *Cultural and Social History* 8/4 (December 2011), 493–512.

García Alcalá, Julio Antonio, *Historia del Felipe (FLP, FOC y ESBA). De Julio Cerón a la Liga Comunista Revolucionaria* (Madrid, 2001).

Garí, Manuel, 'El "Felipe": una historia por escribir', in José Manuel Roca (ed.), *El proyecto radical. Auge y declive de la izquierda revolucionaria en España (1964–1992)* (Madrid, 1993), 123–32.

Gavi, Philippe, Jean-Paul Sartre and Pierre Victor, *On a raison de se révolter* (Paris, 1974).

Geismar, Alain, Serge July and Erlyne Morane, *Vers la guerre civile* (Paris, 1969).

Geismar, Alain, *Pourquoi nous combattons* (Paris, 1970).

Geismar, Alain, *Mon mai 68* (Paris, 2008).

Geppert, Dominik, *The Postwar Challenge: Cultural, Social, and Political Change in Western Europe, 1945–58* (Oxford, 2003).

Gibbon, Peter, 'The dialectic of religion and class in Ulster', *New Left Review* 55 (1969), 20–41.

Gilcher-Holtey, Ingrid (ed.), *1968: Vom Ereignis zum Gegenstand der Geschichtswissenschaft* (Göttingen, 1998).

Gilcher-Holtey, Ingrid, *Die 68er Bewegung: Deutschland–Westeuropa–USA* (Munich, 2001).

Gildea, Robert, James Mark and Niek Pas, 'European radicals and the "Third World": Imagined solidarities and radical networks 1958–73', *Cultural and Social History* 8/4 (2011), 449–71.

Gill, Anthony, *Rendering unto Caesar: The Catholic State in Latin America* (Chicago, 1998).

Ginsborg, Paul, *A History of Contemporary Italy: Society and Politics, 1943–1988* (London, 2003).

Gitlin, Todd, *The Sixties: Years of Hope, Days of Rage* (New York, 1987).

Giugni, Marco G., 'Personal and biographical consequences', in David A. Snow, Sarah A. Soule and Hanspeter Kriesi (eds), *The Blackwell Companion to Social Movements* (Oxford, 2004), 489–507.

González-Ruiz, J. M., 'Genèse des communautés de base en contexte ecclésial', *Lumière de Vie* 99 (1970), 43–59.

Goureaux, Guy, *Le Cercle Jean XXIII. Des Catholiques en liberté. Nantes, 1963–1980* (Paris, 2004).

Gramaglia, Mariella, 'Affinità e conflitto con la nuova sinistra', *Memoria. Rivista di storia delle donne* 19–20 (1987), 19–37.

Green, Anna, 'Individual remembering and collective memories: Theoretical presuppositions and contemporary debates', *Oral History* 32/2 (2004), 35–44.

Green, Anna, 'Can memory be collective?', in Donald Ritchie (ed.), *Oxford Handbook of Oral History* (Oxford, 2011), 77–95.

Greenblatt, Stephen, *Will in the World: How Shakespeare became Shakespeare* (London, 2004).

Grele, Ronald, 'Private memories and public presentation: The art of oral history', in Ronald Grele (ed.), *Envelopes of Sound* (New York, 1991), 254–60.

Gudmundsson, Gestur and Kristín Ólafsdóttir, *68. Hugarflug úr vidjum vanans* (Reykjavík, 1987).

Guin, Yannick, *La Commune de Nantes* (Paris, 1969).

Gutiérrez, Gustavo, *A Theology of Liberation: History, Politics, and Salvation* (Maryknoll, NY, 2000).

Gyáni, Gábor, 'Keleti és nyugati hatvannyolc: különbözőség és egység', *Mozgó világ* 8 (2008), 29–34.

Haarder, Bertel (ed.), *Hvem holdt de med?* (Copenhagen, 1999).

Hage, Julien, 'Sur les chemins du tiers monde en lutte: Partisans, Révolution, Tricontinental', in Philippe Artières and Michelle Zancarini-Fournel (eds), *68. Une Histoire collective, 1962–1981* (Paris, 2008), 86–93.

Halbwachs, Maurice, *On Collective Memory* (Chicago, 1992 [1950]).

Hamilton, Paula and Linda Shopes (eds), *Oral History and Public Memories* (Philadelphia, PA, 2008).

Hamon, Alain and Jean-Charles Marchand, *Action Directe. Du terrorisme français à l'Euroterrorisme* (Paris, 1986).

Hamon, Hervé and Patrick Rotman, *Génération. Tome I: Les Années de rêve, Tome II: Les Années de poudre* (Paris, 1987–8).

Havemann, Florian, *Havemann: Eine Behauptung* (Frankfurt am Main, 2007).

Hazareesingh, Sudhir, *Le Mythe gaullien* (Paris, 2010).

Heine, Hartmut, 'La contribución de la "Nueva Izquierda" al resurgir de la democracia española, 1957–1976', in Josep Fontana (ed.), *España bajo el franquismo* (Barcelona, 2000), 142–59.

Heller, Ágnes, *Everyday Life* (London, 1984).

Herberg, Miguel, *La guerra de España y la resistencia española (Entrevistas con Julio Álvarez del Vayo, 1974)* (Madrid, 2009).

Herf, Jeffrey, *Divided Memory: The Nazi Past in the Two Germanys* (Cambridge, MA, 1997).

Hermet, Guy, *Los católicos en la España franquista*, 2 vols (Madrid, 1985 and 1986).

Herrerín, Ángel, *La CNT durante el franquismo. Clandestinidad y exilio (1939–1975)* (Madrid, 2004).

Herzog, Dagmar, 'Between coitus and commodification: Young West German women and the impact of the pill', in Axel Schildt and Detlef Siegfried (eds), *Between Marx and Coca-Cola: Youth Cultures in Changing European Societies, 1960–1980* (New York, 2006), 261–86.

Herzog, Dagmar, *Sexuality in Europe: A Twentieth-Century History* (Cambridge, 2011).

Hill, Helena, *Befria mannen! Idéer om förtryck, frigörelse och förandring hos en svensk mansrörelse under 1970-och tidigt 1980-tal* (Umeå, 2007).

Hocquenghem, Guy, *Le Désir homosexuel* (Paris, 1972).

Hocquenghem, Guy, *L'Amphithéâtre des morts. Mémoires anticipées* (Paris, 1994).

Hodgdon, Tim, *Manhood in the Age of Aquarius: Masculinity in Two Countercultural Communities, 1965–83* (New York, 2007).

Holm, Adam and Peter Scharff Smith, *Idealisme eller fanatisme? Opgøret om venstrefløjen under den kolde krig* (Copenhagen, 2003).

Holzer, Jerzy, *Solidarność, Geneza i historia* (Warsaw, 1990).

Hong, Young-Sun, ' "The Benefits of Health Must Spread Among All": International solidarity, health, and race in the East German encounter with the Third World', in Katherine Pence and Paul Betts (eds), *Socialist Modern: East German Everyday Culture and Politics* (Ann Arbor, MI, 2008), 183–210.

Horn, Gerd-Rainer (ed.), *1968 und die Arbeiter: Studien zum 'proletarischen Mai' in Europa* (Hamburg, 2007).

Horn, Gerd-Rainer, *The Spirit of '68: Rebellion in Western Europe and North America, 1956–1976* (Oxford, 2008).

Horn, Gerd-Rainer, *Western European Liberation Theology: The First Wave, 1924–1959* (Oxford, 2008).

Horn, Gerd-Rainer and Padraic Kenney, *Transnational Moments of Change: Europe 1945, 1968, 1989* (Lanham, MD and Oxford, 2004).

Iatrides, John O. and Linda Wrigley (eds), *Greece at the Crossroads: The Civil War and its Legacy* (University Park, PA, 1995).

Inglehart, Ronald, *The Silent Revolution: Changing Values and Political Styles among Western Publics* (Princeton, NJ, 1977).

Iriye, Akira, 'Transnational history', *Contemporary European History* 13/2 (2004), 211–22.

Jacquard, Roland, *La longue traque d'Action Directe* (Paris, 1987).

Jamison, Andrew, *Social Movements: A Cognitive Approach* (Cambridge, 1991).

Jensen, Steven L. B., ' "Youth Enacts Society and Somebody Makes a Coup": The Danish student movement between political and lifestyle radicalism', in Axel Schildt and Detlef Siegfried (eds), *Between Marx and Coca-Cola: Youth Cultures in Changing European Societies, 1960–1980* (New York and Oxford, 2006), 224–38.

Jirousová, Věra, *Jan Steklík*, catalogue (Prague, 1991).

Jirousová, Věra, *KŠ—Křižovnická škola čistého humoru bez vtipu*, catalogue (Prague, 1991).

Jobs, Richard Ivan, 'Youth movements: Travel, protest, and Europe in 1968', *American Historical Review* 114/2 (2009), 376–404.

Jóhannesson, Gudni, *Óvinir ríkisins. Ógnir og innra öryggi í kalda stríðinu á Íslandi* (Reykjavík, 2006).

Joly, Danièle, *The French Communist Party and the Algerian War* (Basingstoke, 1991).

Jørgensen, Thomas Ekman, 'The Scandinavian 1968 in a European perspective', *Scandinavian Journal of History* 33/4 (2008), 326–38.

Juchler, Ingo, *Die Studentenbewegungen in den Vereinigten Staaten und der Bundesrepublik Deutschland der sechziger Jahre. Eine Untersuchung hinsichtlich ihrer Beeinflussung durch Befreiungsbewegungen und -theorien aus der Dritten Welt* (Berlin, 1996).

Juliá, Santos (ed.), *Víctimas de la Guerra Civil* (Madrid, 1999).

Juliá, Santos, *Historias de las dos Españas* (Madrid, 2006).

Juliá, Santos (ed.), *Memoria de la guerra y del franquismo* (Madrid, 2006).

Kadarkay, Arpad A. 'Hungary: An experiment in communism', *Political Research Quarterly* 26/2 (1973), 280–301.

Kalter, Christoph, *Die Entdeckung der Dritten Welt* (Frankfurt am Main, 2011).

Kamarás, István, *Lelkierőmű Nagymaroson: Religiográfia* (Budapest, 1989).

Kaplan, Karel, *Stát a církev v Československu v letech 1948–1953* (Brno, 1993).

Kasimeris, George, *Europe's Last Red Terrorists: The Revolutionary Organisation 17 November* (London, 2000).

Katzenstein, Peter, *Left-Wing Violence and State Response: United States, Germany, Italy, and Japan, 1960s–1990s* (Ithaca, NY, 1998).

Kertzer, David I., *Comrades and Christians: Religion and Political Struggle in Communist Italy* (Cambridge, 1980).

Klaniczay, Júlia and Edit Sasvári (eds), *Törvénytelen avantgárd. Galántai György balatonboglári kápolnaműterme 1970–1973* (Budapest, 2003).

Klatch, Rebecca E., *A Generation Divided: The New Left, the New Right, and the 1960s* (Berkeley, Los Angeles and London, 1999).

Klein, Thomas, *Frieden und Gerechtigkeit: Die Politisierung der unabhängigen Friedensbewegung in Ost-Berlin während der 80er Jahre* (Cologne, Weimar and Vienna, 2007).

Klimke, Martin, *The Other Alliance: Student Protests in West Germany and the United States in the Global Sixties* (Princeton, NJ, 2010).

Klimke, Martin and Philipp Gassert (eds), *1968: Memories and Legacies of a Global Revolt* (Washington, DC, 2009).

Klimke, Martin and Joachim Scharloth (eds), *1968 in Europe: A History of Protest and Activism, 1956–1977* (Basingstoke, 2008).

Klimke, Martin, Jacco Pekelder and Joachim Scharloth (eds), *Between Prague Spring and French May: Opposition and Revolt in Europe, 1960–80* (New York and Oxford, 2011).

Knížák, Milan, *Aktionen, Konzepte, Projekte, Dokumentationen: Oldenburger Kunstverein, 14. September bis 12. Oktober 1980* (Oldenburg, 1980).

Knížák, Milan, *Cestopisy* (Prague, 1990).

Knížák, Milan, *Akce* (Prague, 2000).

Knížák, Milan, *Písně kapely Aktual* (Prague, 2003).

Koestler, Arthur, *The Yogi and the Commissar and Other Essays* (London, 1986 [1945]).

Konrád, György, 'Hatvannyolcasok. A nagyvárosi aszfalt utópiát virágzott', *Magyar Lettre Internationale* 70 (2008).

Koopmans, Ruud, *Democracy from Below: New Social Movements and the Political System in West Germany* (Boulder, CO, San Francisco and Oxford, 1995).

Kornetis, Kostis, 'Student resistance to the Greek military dictatorship: Subjectivity, memory and cultural politics', PhD thesis (European University Institute, Florence, 2006).

Kornetis, Kostis, 'Introduction: 1968–2008: The inheritance of Utopia', *Historein* 9 (2009), 7–20.

Kornetis, Kostis, ' "Everything links?" Temporality, territoriality and cultural transfer in the '68 protest movements', *Historein* 9 (2009), 34–45.

Kovács, Gábor, 'Revolution, lifestyle, power, and culture', in János M. Rainer and György Péteri (eds), *Muddling Through in the Long 1960s: Ideas and Everyday Life in High Politics and the Lower Classes of Communist Hungary* (Budapest and Trondheim, 2005), 27–52.

Kraushaar, Wolfgang, *Achtundsechzig: Eine Bilanz* (Berlin, 2008).

Krohn, Claus-Dieter, 'Die westdeutsche Studentenbewegung und das "andere Deutschland"', in Axel Schildt, Detlef Siegfried, and Karl-Christian Lammers (eds), *Dynamische Zeiten, Die 60er Jahre in den beiden deutschen Gesellschaften* (Hamburg, 2000), 695–718.

Krzemiński, Ireneusz, *Solidarność, Projekt polskiej demokracji* (Warsaw, 1997).

Kühn, Andreas, *Stalins Enkel, Maos Söhne: Die Lebenswelt der K-Gruppen in der Bundesrepublik der 70er Jahre* (Frankfurt am Main and New York, 2005).

Kundnani, Hans, *Utopia or Auschwitz: Germany's 1968 Generation and the Holocaust* (London, 2009).

Lagrou, Pieter, *The Legacy of Nazi Occupation: Patriotic Memory and National Recovery in Western Europe, 1945–1965* (Cambridge, 2000).

Laiz, Consuelo, *La lucha final: los partidos de la izquierda radical durante la transición española* (Madrid, 1995).

Langhans, Rainer, *Ich bin's—Die ersten 68 Jahre* (Berlin, 2008).

Lannon, Frances, *Privilege, Persecution, and Prophecy: The Catholic Church in Spain 1875–1975* (Oxford, 1987).

Le Bitoux, Jean, *Citoyen de la Seconde Zone* (Paris, 2003).

Le Bris, Michel, *Les Fous du Larzac* (Paris, 1975).

Le Dantec, Jean-Pierre, *Les Dangers du soleil* (Paris, 1978).

Le Dantec, Jean-Pierre, 'Une barbarie peut en cacher une autre', *Le Nouvel Observateur* 717 (22 July 1978).

Le Madec, François, *L'aubépine de mai. Chronique d'une usine occupée. Sud-Aviation Nantes 1968* (Nantes, 1988).

Lefebvre, Henri, *The Production of Space* (Oxford, 1991 [1974]).

Levine, Daniel H., 'Assessing the impacts of liberation theology in Latin America', *The Review of Politics* 50/2 (1988), 241–63.

Lévy-Willard, Annette and Cathy Bernheim, *L'Epopée d'une anarchiste* (Paris, 1979).

Light, Alison, *Mrs Woolf and the Servants* (London, 2007).

Liniers, Antoine, 'Objections contre une prise d'armes', in François Furet, Antoine Liniers and Philippe Raynaud (eds), *Terrorisme et Démocratie* (Paris, 1985), 137–224.

Lipski, Jan Józef, *Komitet Obrony Robotników* (London, 1983).

Lizcano, Pablo, *La generación del '56: La Universidad contra Franco* (Madrid, 2006).

Lois Fernández, Julio Lois, *Teología de la liberación: opción por los pobres* (Madrid, 1986).

Lois Fernández, Julio Lois, *El dios de los pobres* (Salamanca, 2007).

Lois Fernández, Julio Lois, *La cristología de Jon Sobrino* (Bilbao, 2007).

Lukács, György, *The Process of Democratization*, trans. Susanne Bernhardt and Norman Levine (Albany, NY, 1991).

Lumley, Robert, *States of Emergency: Cultures of Revolt in Italy from 1968 to 1978* (London, 1990).

Macey, David, *The Lives of Michel Foucault* (London, 1993).

Magyar Ifjúság, 'The intellectual youth', *Magyar Ifjúság* (30 January 1970), 3–4.

Maier, Charles S., 'Conclusion: 1968—did it matter?', in Vladimir Tismaneanu (ed.), *Promises of 1968: Crisis, Illusion, and Utopia* (Budapest and New York, 2011), 407–9.

Major, Patrick, *Behind the Berlin Wall: East Germany and the Frontiers of Power* (Oxford, 2010).

Major, Patrick and Rana Mitter (eds), *Across the Blocs: Cold War Cultural and Social History* (London, 2004).

Margadant, Jo Burr (ed.), *The New Biography: Performing Femininity in Nineteenth-Century France* (Berkeley, CA and Los Angeles, 2000).

Marino, Giuseppe Carlo, *Biografia del Sessantotto* (Milan, 2005).

Mark, James, *The Unfinished Revolution: Making Sense of the Communist Past in Central-Eastern Europe* (New Haven, CT, 2010).

Marris, Peter and Martin Rein, *Dilemmas of Social Reform: Poverty and Community Action in the United States* (London, 1972).

Martel, Frédéric, *Le Rose et le Noir. Les Homosexuels en France depuis 1968* (Paris, 2000).

Martin, Didier, *Larzac. Utopies et réalités* (Paris, 1987).

Marwick, Arthur *The Sixties: Cultural Change in Britain, France, Italy, and the United States, c. 1958–c. 1974* (Oxford and New York, 1998).

Marzec 68. Referaty z sesji na Uniwersytecie Warszawskim w 1981 roku [*March '68. Papers from the session at the University of Warsaw in 1981*] (Warsaw, 2008).

Maté, Reyes, *Pueden ser 'rojos' los cristianos?* (Madrid, 1977).

Matějka, Ondřej, ' "We are the Generation that will Construct Socialism": The Czech 68ers between manifest destiny and the Mark of Cain', in Anna von der Goltz (ed.) *'Talkin' 'bout my Generation': Conflicts of Generation Building and Europe's '1968'* (Göttingen, 2011), 118–39.

Mausbach, Wilfried, 'America's Vietnam in Germany—Germany in America's Vietnam: On the relocation of spaces and the appropriation of history', in Belinda Davis et al. (eds), *Changing the World, Changing Oneself* (New York and Oxford, 2010), 41–64.

Maynes, Mary Jo, Jennifer L. Pierce and Barbara Laslett (eds), *Telling Stories: The Use of Personal Narratives in the Social Sciences and History* (Ithaca, NY, 2008).

Mazower, Mark (ed.), *After the War was Over: Reconstructing the Family, Nation, and State in Greece, 1943–1960* (Princeton, NJ, 2000).

McAdam, Doug, *Freedom Summer* (New York, 1988).

McGrogan, Manus, '*Tout!* in context, 1968–1973: French radical press at the crossroads of far left, new movements, and counterculture', PhD thesis (University of Portsmouth, 2010).

McGrogan, Manus, 'Vive la Révolution and the example of Lotta Continua: The circulation of ideas and practices between the left militant worlds of France and Italy following May '68', *Modern and Contemporary France* 18/3 (August 2010), 309–28.

McLeod, Hugh, *The Religious Crisis of the 1960s* (Oxford, 2007).

McLuhan, Marshall, *War and Peace in the Global Village* (New York, 1968).

Mead, Margaret, *Culture and Commitment: A Study of the Generation Gap* (New York, 1970).

Michelers, Detlef, *Draufhauen, Draufhauen, Nachsetzen! Die Bremer Schülerbewegung, die Straßenbahndemonstrationen und ihre Folgen 1967/70* (Bremen, 2002).

Michnik, Adam, Józef Tischner and Jacek Żakowski, *Między Panem a Plebanem* (Kraków, 1995).

Mitter, Armin and Stefan Wolle, *Untergang auf Raten: Unbekannte Kapitel der DDR-Geschichte* (Munich, 1993).

Moeller, Robert, *War Stories: The Search for a Usable Past in the Federal Republic of Germany* (Berkeley, CA, 2001).

Montero, Feliciano, *Juventud Estudiante Católica 1947–1997* (Madrid, 1998).

Montero, Feliciano, *La Acción Católica y el franquismo: Auge y crisis de la Acción Católica Especializada en los años sesenta* (Madrid, 2000).

Montero, Feliciano, *La Iglesia: de la colaboración a la disidencia (1956–1975)* (Madrid, 2009).

Morganová, Pavlína, *Akční umění* (Olomouc, 1999).

Moss, David, *The Politics of Left-Wing Violence in Italy, 1969–1985* (New York, 1989).

Moyn, Samuel, *The Last Utopia* (Cambridge, MA, 2010).

Muñoz Soro, Javier, 'La reconciliación como política: memoria de la violencia y la guerra en el antifranquismo', *Jerónimo Zurita* 84 (2009), 113–33.

Naimark, Norman, 'The persistence of the "postwar": Germany and Poland', in Frank Biess and Robert Moeller (eds), *Histories of the Aftermath: The Legacies of the Second World War in Europe* (New York and Oxford, 2010), 13–29.

Nánay, István, 'Az Orfeo-ügy. Fodor Tamás és Malgot István visszaemlékezésével', *Beszélő* 3 (1998).

Nehring, Holger, 'Demonstrating for "peace" in the Cold War: The British and West German Easter marches, 1958–1964', in Matthias Reiss (ed.), *The Street as Stage: Protest Marches and Public Rallies since the Nineteenth Century* (Oxford, 2007), 275–93.

Nehring, Holger, 'The era of non-violence: "Terrorism" in West German, Italian, and French political culture, 1968–1982', *European Review of History* 14/3 (2007), 343–71.

Nehring, Holger, ' "Generation", modernity and the making of contemporary history: Responses in West European protest movements around "1968" ', in Anna von der Goltz (ed.), *'Talkin' 'bout my Generation': Conflicts of Generation Building and Europe's '1968'* (Göttingen, 2011), 71–94.

Neubert, Ehrhart, *Geschichte der Opposition in der DDR 1949–1989* (Berlin, 1997).

Neuschwander, Claude, *Patron, mais...* (Paris, 1975).

Nissen, Vibeke and Inge Lise Paulsen, 'Handling gi'r forvandling—klip af homobevægelsens historie i Danmark', *Lambda Nordica* 2–3 (2000).

O'Day, Alan (ed.), *Political Violence in Northern Ireland: Conflict and Conflict Resolution* (London, 1997).

Ohse, Marc-Dietrich, 'German Democratic Republic', in D. Pollack and J. Wielgohs (eds), *Opposition in Communist Eastern Europe* (Aldershot, 2004), 73–93.

Olick, Jeffrey K. and Joyce Robbins, 'Social memory studies: From 'collective memory' to the historical sociology of mnemonic practices', *Annual Review of Sociology* 24 (1998), 105–40.

Ormsson, Ólafur, *Byltingarmenn og bóhemar* (Reykjavík, 2009).

Osęka, Piotr, 'The people of March', in Anna von der Goltz (ed.), *'Talkin' 'bout my Generation': Conflicts of Generation Building and Europe's '1968'* (Göttingen, 2011), 137–62.

Paczkowski, Andrzej, *Pół wieku dziejów Polski 1939–1989* (Warsaw, 1995).

Papathanasiou, Ioanna, *I neolaia Lambraki sti dekaetia tou 1960. Arheiakes tekmirioseis kai autoviografikes katatheseis* (Athens, 2008).

Pas, Niek, 'Mediatisation of Provo: From a local movement to a European phenomenon', in Martin Klimke, Jacco Pekelder and Joachim Scharloth (eds), *Between Prague Spring and French May* (New York and Oxford, 2011), 157–76.

Pasetto, Egidio and Giuseppe Pupillo, 'Il gruppo "Potere operaio" nella lotta di Porto Marghera: primavera '66–primavera '70', *Classe* 3 (1970), 95–119.

Passerini, Luisa, *Autobiography of a Generation: Italy, 1968* (Middletown, CT, 1996).

Passerini, Luisa, 'The problematic intellectual repercussions of '68: Reflections in a jump-cut style', *Historein* 9 (2009), 21–33.

Patočka, Jakub, Jacques Rupnik and Aleksander Smolar, 'L'autre 1968 vu aujourd'hui de Prague et de Varsovie. Table ronde', *Esprit* 5 (May 2008).

Patterson, Henry, *Ireland since 1939: The Persistence of Conflict* (Dublin, 2006).

Payne, Stanley G., *The Franco Regime 1936–1975* (London, 2000).

Payne, Stanley G., *Civil War in Europe 1905–1949* (Cambridge, 2011).

Pažout, Jaroslav, *Hnutí revoluční mládeže* (Prague, 2004).

Pažout, Jaroslav, *Mocným navzdory. Studentské hnutí v šedesátých letech 20. století* (Prague, 2008).

Pelletier, Denis, *La Crise catholique. Réligion, société et politique en France, 1965–1978* (Paris, 2005).

Pérez Pinillos, Julio, *Los Curas Obreros en España* (Madrid, 2004).

Pérez Skardhamar, Laura, 'Det private er politisk': en analyse af et kollektiv, ø-lejre og mande-bevægelse i de lange halvfjerdsere i Danmark (Roskilde, 2010).

Petersen, Nikolaj, 'Kampen om Den Kolde Krig i dansk politik og forskning', Historisk Tidsskrift 109/1 (2009), 154–204.

Phillips, Anne, 'Marxism and feminism', in Feminist Anthology Collective (eds), No Turn-ing Back: Writing from the Women's Liberation Movement, 1975–80 (London, 1981), 90–8.

Piaget, Charles, Lip. Charles Piaget et les Lip racontent (Paris, 1973).

Picq, Françoise, Libération des femmes. Les années mouvement (Paris, 1993).

Piton, Monique, C'est possible! (Paris, 1975).

Pizzorno, Alessandro, Colin Crouch, Manuel Castells, Luciano Cappelletti, Ralf Dahrendorf, Donatella Della Porta and Marcos Kaplan (eds), Lotte operaie e sindacato. Il ciclo 1968–1972 in Italia (Bologna, 1978).

Plogstedt, Sibylle, Im Netz der Gedichte: Gefangen in Prag nach 1968 (Berlin, 2001).

Poiger, Uta, Jazz, Rock, and Rebels: Cold War Politics and American Culture in a Divided Germany (Berkeley, CA, 2000).

Polletta, Francesca, It Was Like a Fever: Storytelling in Protest and Politics (Chicago, 2006).

Pons Prades, Eduardo, Guerrillas españolas, 1936–1960 (Barcelona, 1977).

Portelli, Alessandro, 'What makes oral history different?', History Workshop 12 (1981), 96–107.

Portelli, Alessandro, The Death of Luigi Trastulli: Form and Meaning in Oral History (New York, 1991).

Portelli, Alessandro, 'Philosophy and the facts', in Alessandro Portelli (ed.), The Battle of Valle Giulia: Oral History and the Art of Dialogue (Madison, WI, 1997), 79–88.

Portelli, Alessandro, 'Introduzione', in Francesca Cerocchi et al. (eds.), Un anno durato de-cenni. Vite di persone comuni prima, durante e dopo il '68 (Rome, 2006), 5–14.

Potel, Jean-Yves, Procès à Prague. Le V.O.N.S., Comité de Défense des personnes injustement poursuivis, devant ses juges, 22–23 octobre 1979 (Paris, 1980).

Potel, Jean-Yves, Scènes de grève en Pologne (Paris, 1981).

Potel, Jean-Yves, Gdańsk. La Mémoire ouvrière (Paris, 1982).

Potel, Jean-Yves, Quand le soleil se couche à l'Est. La fin du système soviétique (Paris, 1995).

Poulat, Emile, Une Eglise ébranlée. Changement, conflit et continuité de Pie XII à Jean-Paul II (Paris, 1980).

Poulat, Emile, Les Prêtres-ouvriers. Naissance et fin (Paris, 1999).

Powell, Charles, 'The United States and Spain: From Franco to Juan Carlos', in Nigel Townson (ed.), Spain Transformed: The Late Franco Dictatorship, 1959–75 (Basingstoke, 2010), 227–47.

Powell, Charles, El amigo americano. España y Estados Unidos: de la dictadura a la democracia (Barcelona, 2011).

Pozione, Camilla, Breve storia del movimento femminile in Italia (Rome, 1978).

Preston, Paul, The Spanish Holocaust: Inquisition and Extermination in Twentieth Century Spain (New York, 2012).

Prince, Simon, Northern Ireland's 68: Civil rights, Global Revolt and the Origin of the Troubles (Dublin, 2007).

Psarrou, Eleni-Nelly, 'The Greek diaspora in eastern Europe and the Former Soviet Union', in J. Blaschke (ed.), Immigration and Political Intervention. Vol. II: Diasporas in Transition Countries (Berlin, 2004).

Purdie, Bob, Politics in the Streets: The Origins of the Civil Rights Movement in Northern Ireland (Belfast, 1990).

Radcliff, Pamela, 'Associations and the social origins of the transition during the late Franco regime', in Nigel Townson (ed.), *Spain Transformed: The Late Franco Dictatorship, 1959–75* (Basingstoke, 2010), 140–62.

Radcliff, Pamela, 'La Iglesia católica y la transición a la democracia', in Carolyn Boyd (ed.), *Religión y política en la España contemporánea* (Madrid, 2007), 209–28.

Radcliff, Pamela, *Making Democratic Citizens in Spain: Civil Society and the Popular Origins of the Transition, 1960–78* (Basingstoke, 2011).

Raguénès, Jean, *De mai 68 à Lip. Un Dominicain au coeur des luttes* (Paris, 2008).

Raschke, Joachim, *Soziale Bewegungen. Ein historisch-systematischer Grundriss* (Frankfurt and New York, 1985).

Rathenow, Lutz, 'Umwege des Aufbegehrens: Beobachtungen am Rande einer politischen Debatte', *Politische Meinung* 378 (2001), 33–4.

Rauhut, Michael, *Beat in der Grauzone: DDR-Rock 1964 bis 1972—Politik und Alltag* (Berlin, 1993).

Rawlinson, Roger, *Larzac: A Nonviolent Campaign of the '70s in Southern France* (York, 1996).

Requate, Jörg, 'Visions of the Future: GDR, CSSR and the Federal Republic of Germany in the 1960s', in Heinz-Gerhard Haupt and Jürgen Kocka (eds), *Comparative and Transnational History: Central European Approaches and New Perspectives* (New York and Oxford, 2009), 181–6.

Révész, Sándor (ed.), *Beszélő évek. A Kádár-korszak története* (Budapest, 2000).

Reynisson, Leifur, 'Ímyndunaraflið til valda. Barátta 68-kynslódarinnar fyrir betri heimi', *Sagnir* 19 (1998), 60–9.

Reynolds, Chris, *Memories of May '68: France's Convenient Consensus* (Cardiff, 2011).

Reynolds, Chris, 'The collective European memory of 1968: The case of Northern Ireland', *Études Irlandaises* 36/1 (2011), 73–90.

Režek, Mateja, 'Cuius regio eius religio: The relationship of communist authorities with the Catholic Church in Slovenia and Yugoslavia after 1945', in Balázs Apor, Péter Apor and E. A. Rees (eds), *The Sovietization of Eastern Europe: New Perspectives on the Postwar Period* (Washington, DC, 2008), 213–33.

Righart, Hans, 'Moderate versions of the "global Sixties": A comparison of Great Britain and the Netherlands', *Journal of Contemporary European Studies* 6/13 (1998), 82–96.

Ring, Orsolya, 'A színjátszás harmadik útja és a hatalom. Az alternatív Orfeo Együttes kálváriája az 1970-es években', *Múltunk* (March 2008), 233–57.

Robinson, Lucy, *Gay Men and the Left in Postwar Britain: How the Personal Got Political* (Manchester, 2007).

Roca, José Manuel (ed.), *El proyecto radical. Auge y declive de la izquierda revolucionaria en España (1964–1992)* (Madrid, 1993).

Romijn, Peter, Giles Scott-Smith and Joe Segal (eds), *Divided Dreamworlds?: The Cultural Cold War in East and West* (Amsterdam, 2012).

Rosès Codovilla, Sergi, *Le MIL. Une histoire politique* (La Bussière, 2007).

Ross, Kristin, *May '68 and its Afterlives* (Chicago and London, 2002).

Rossi-Doria, Anna, 'Ipotesi per una storia che verrà', in Teresa Bertilotti and Anna Scattigno (eds), *Il femminismo degli anni settanta* (Rome, 2005), 1–23.

Rouillan, Jean-Marc, *De mémoire. Tome I: Les Jours du début. Un automne 1970 à Toulouse, Tome II: Le Deuil de l'innocence. Un jour de septembre 1973 à Barcelone* (Marseille, 2007–9).

Rousso, Henri, *The Vichy Syndrome: History and Memory in France since 1944* (Cambridge, MA, 1991).

Rowbotham, Sheila, *Edward Carpenter: A Life of Love and Liberty* (London, 2008).

Rowbotham, Sheila, '1968: Springboard for women's liberation', in Karen Dubinsky (ed.), *'New World Coming': The Sixties and the Shaping of Global Consciousness* (Toronto, 2009), 257–65.

Rucht, Dieter, Barbara Blattert and Dieter Rink, *Soziale Bewegungen auf dem Weg zur Institutionalisierung. Zum Strukturwandel 'alternativer' Gruppen in beiden Teilen Deutschlands* (Frankfurt and New York, 1997).

Ruiz, Julius, *Franco's Justice: Repression in Madrid after the Spanish Civil War* (Oxford, 2005).

Ruiz, Julius, *El terror rojo* (Madrid, 2012).

Rupnik, Jacques, interview with Rudi Dutschke, 'The misunderstanding of 1968', *Transit* 35 (Summer 2008), <http://www.eurozine.com/articles/2008-05-16-dutschke-en.html>.

Rychlík, Jan, *Cestování do ciziny v habsburské monarchii a v Československu. Pasová, vízová a vystěhovalecká politika 1848–1989* (Prague, 2007).

Saltini, Antonio, *Don Zeno. Il sovversivo di Dio* (Modena, 2003).

Samuel, Raphael (ed.), *Miners, Quarrymen, and Saltworkers* (London, 1977).

Sauvageot, J., A. Geismar, D. Cohn-Bendit and J.-P. Duteuil, *La Révolte étudiante. Les animateurs parlent* (Paris, 1968).

Schaffer, Simon, Lissa Roberts, Kapil Raj and James Delbourgo, *The Brokered World: Go-Betweens and Global Intelligence, 1770–1820* (Sagamore Beach, MA, 2009).

Schiesches, Wolfgang, *Aufbruch der Freiheit* (Bremen, 1972).

Schildt, Axel and Arnold Sywottek (eds), *Modernisierung im Wiederaufbau: Die westdeutsche Gesellschaft der 50er Jahre* (Bonn, 1993).

Schleicher, Hans-Georg and Ilona, *Special Flights: The GDR and Liberation Movements in Southern Africa* (Harare, 1998).

Schneider, Peter, *Rebellion und Wahn—Mein 68. Eine autobiographische Erzählung* (Cologne, 2008).

Schulz, Kristina, 'The women's movement', in Martin Klimke and Joachim Scharloth, *1968 in Europe* (Basingstoke, 2008), 281–93.

Scott, Joan W., Cora Kaplan and Debra Keates (eds), *Transitions, Environments, Translations: Feminisms in International Politics* (London, 1997).

Segura, Antoni and Jordi Solé Sugranyes, *El FONS MIL. Entre el record i la historia* (Barcelona, 2006).

Seidman, Michael, *The Victorious Counterrevolution: The Nationalist Effort in the Spanish Civil War* (Madison, WI, 2011).

Sell, Maren, *Mourir d'absence* (Paris, 1978).

Semler, Christian, '1968 im Westen—was ging uns die DDR an?', *Aus Politik und Zeitgeschichte* B45 (2003), 3–5.

Seregni, A., *El antiamericanismo español* (Madrid, 2007).

Serenelli-Messenger, Sofia, '1968 in an Italian province: Memory and the everyday life of a New Left group in Macerata', in Ingo Cornils and Sarah Waters (eds), *Memories of 1968: International Perspectives* (Bern, 2010), 348–51.

Serrano Blanco, Laura, *Aportaciones de la Iglesia a la democracia, desde la diócesis de Valladolid 1959–1979* (Salamanca, 2006).

Serrano, Secundino, *Maquis. Historia de la guerrilla antifranquista* (Madrid, 2001).

Shepard, Todd, *The Invention of Decolonization: The Algerian War and the Remaking of France* (Ithaca, NY and London, 2008).

Siegfried, Detlef, 'Understanding 1968: Youth rebellion, generational change, and postindustrial society', in Axel Schildt and Detlef Siegfried (eds), *Between Marx and Coca-Cola: Youth Cultures in Changing European Societies* (Oxford, 2006), 59–81.

Šiklová, Jiřina, 'Existuje u nás studentská "new left"?' *Literární listy* 3 (21 November 1968).

Simon, Catherine, 'Les pieds-rouges, hors de l'histoire officielle', in Philippe Artières and Michelle Zancarini-Fournel (eds), *68. Une Histoire collective, 1962–1981* (Paris, 2008), 158–65.

Şincan, Anca Maria, 'Mechanisms of state control over religious denominations in Romania in the late 1940s and early 1950s', in Balázs Apor, Péter Apor and E. A. Rees (eds), *The Sovietization of Eastern Europe: New Perspectives on the Postwar Period* (Washington, DC, 2008), 201–12.

Sirinelli, Jean-François, *Mai 68. L'Événement Janus* (Paris, 2008).

Slobodian, Quinn, *Foreign Front: Third World Politics in Sixties West Germany* (Durham and London, 2012).

Snyder, Sarah, *Human Rights Activism and the End of the Cold War: A Transnational History of the Helsinki Network* (Cambridge, 2011).

Somlai, Katalin, 'Ösztöndíjjal Nyugatra a hatvanas években. Az Országos Ösztöndíj Tanács felállítása', in János Tischler (ed.), *Kádárizmus mélyfúrások* (Budapest, 2009), 273–314.

Sommier, Isabelle, *La Violence politique et son deuil. L'après 68 en France et en Italie* (Rennes, 2008).

Steedman, Catherine, *Landscape for a Good Woman* (London, 1986).

Steen Pedersen, Anette and Morten Thing, *Far, mor, børn–14 samtaler om familien i krise* (Copenhagen, 1979).

Stefanidis, Ioannis, *Stirring the Greek Nation: Political Culture, Irredentism and Anti-Americanism in Postwar Greece, 1945–1967* (Aldershot, 2007).

Stein, Louis, *Beyond Death and Exile: The Spanish Republicans in France, 1939–1955* (Cambridge, MA, 1979).

Stöcker, Lars Fredrik, 'Eine transnationale Geschichte des geteilten Europa? Die Brückenfunktion des polnischen politischen Exils in Schweden 1968–1980', in Włodzimierz Borodziej, Jerzy Kochanowski and Joachim von Puttkamer (eds), *'Schleichwege': Inoffizielle Begegnungen sozialistischer Staatsbürger zwischen 1956 und 1989* (Cologne, Weimar and Vienna, 2010), 253–74.

Stokes, Sarah, 'Student activism in 1968 in Paris and Mexico City', DPhil thesis (University of Oxford, 2011).

Stola, Dariusz, *Kampania antysjonistyczna w Polsce 1967–1968* (Warsaw, 2000).

Sturges, Paul, 'Collective biography in the 1980s', *Biography* 6/4 (1983), 316–32.

Symes, Ronald, *The Roman Revolution* (Oxford, 1939).

Szabó, Csaba, *Die katholische Kirche Ungarns und der Staat in den Jahren 1945–1965* (Munich, 2003).

Szabó, Csaba, 'Die totale Kontrolle der römisch-katholischen Kirche Ungarns in der Phase des real existierenden Sozialismus (1945–1989)', in Katharina Kunter and Jens Holger Schjorring (eds), *Die Kirchen und das Erbe des Kommunismus* (Erlangen, 2007), 317–33.

Szőke, Zoltán, 'Magyarország és a vietnami háború, 1962–1975', *Századok* 144/1 (2010), 47–98.

Tabares, Esteban, *Los Curas Obreros, su compromiso y su espíritu* (Madrid, 2005).

Tackett, Timothy, *Becoming a Revolutionary: The Deputies of the French National Assembly and the Emergence of a Revolutionary Culture, 1789–1790* (Princeton, NJ, 1996).

Tamás, Gáspár Miklós, 'Augusztusi nap', in Maja and Reuben Fowkes (eds), *Forradalom szeretlek: 1968 a művészetben, a politikában és a filozófiában* (Budapest, 2008).

Tarrow, Sidney, *Democracy and Disorder: Protest and Politics in Italy 1965–1975* (Oxford, 1989).

Tartakowsky, Danielle, 'Le PCF en mai–juin 1968', in René Mouriaux, Annick Percheron, Antoine Prost and Danielle Tartakowsky, *1968. Exploration du mai français. Tome II: Acteurs* (Paris, 1992), 141–63.

Terral, Pierre-Marie, *Larzac. De la Lutte paysanne à l'Altermondialisme* (Toulouse, 2011).

Thing, Morten, 'Inkvisitionens hærgen: venstrefløjens historie', *Solidaritet* 22 (2000), 12–21.

Thompson, Paul, *The Edwardians: The Remaking of British Society* (London, 1975).

Thomson, Alistair, 'Memory and remembering in oral history', in Donald Ritchie (ed.), *Oxford Handbook of Oral History* (Oxford, 2011), 96–111.

Thonfeld, Christoph, 'Memories of former World War Two forced labourers: An international comparison', *Oral History* 39 (2011), 33–48.

Tilly, Charles, *Stories, Identities, and Political Change* (Oxford, 2002).

Tismaneanu, Vladimir (ed.), *Promises of 1968: Crisis, Illusion, and Utopia* (Budapest and New York, 2011).

Tokes, Rudolf L., 'Hungarian intellectuals' reaction to the invasion of Czechoslovakia', in E. J. Czerwinski and Jaroslaw Piekalkiewicz (eds), *The Soviet Invasion of Czechoslovakia: Its Effects on Eastern Europe* (New York, 1972), 139–57.

Tomka, Ferenc, *Halálra szántak, mégis élünk* (Budapest, 2005).

Tompkins, Andrew, '"Better active today than radioactive tomorrow!" The transnational opposition to nuclear energy in France and West Germany, 1968–1981', DPhil thesis (University of Oxford, 2013).

Trentin, Bruno, *Autunno caldo. Il secondo biennio rosso 1968–1969* (Rome, 1999).

Turone, Sergio, *Storia del sindacato in Italia* (Bari, 1976).

Tvedt, Terje (ed.), *(ml): en bok om maoismen i Norge* (Oslo, 1989).

Tyl, Miroslav, interview from the private collection of Jaroslav Pažout (c. 1999).

Uhl, Petr, *Le Socialisme emprisonné*, trans. Antonin Bašta and Jean-Yves Touvais [Jean-Yves Potel], ed. Jean-Yves Touvais (Paris, 1980).

Uhl, Petr, *Právo a nespravedlnost očima Petra Uhla* (Prague, 1998).

Uhl, Petr (ed.), *Program společenské samosprávy* (Cologne, 2008).

Van Voris, W. H., *Violence in Ulster: An Oral Documentary* (Cambridge, MA, 1975).

Varon, Jeremy, *Bringing the War Home: The Weather Underground, the Red Army Faction, and Revolutionary Violence in the Sixties and Seventies* (Berkeley, CA and London, 2004).

Verucci, Guido, *La chiesa nella società contemporanea* (Bari, 1988).

Vidal Sales, José Antonio, *Maquis. La verdad histórica de la 'otra guerra'* (Madrid, 2005).

Vigna, Xavier, *L'Insubordination ouvrière dans les années 68. Essai d'histoire politique des usines* (Rennes, 2007).

Vilanova, Mercedes, 'Oral history and democracy: Lessons from illiterates', in Donald Ritchie (ed.), *Oxford Handbook of Oral History* (Oxford, 2011), 65–74.

Vind, Ole, 'Oprøret og Det ny Samfund', *det ny Samfund* 9 (1969), 4–5.

Vind, Ole, 'Pilgrimme og samaritanere', *Superlove* (January 1969), 16.

Vinen, Richard, 'The poisoned madeleine: The autobiographical turn in historical writing', *Journal of Contemporary History* 46 (2011), 531–54.

Voglis, Polymeris, *Becoming a Subject: Political Prisoners during the Greek Civil War* (New York, 2002).

Volf, Petr and Milan Knížák, *Hermafrodit: Rozmluva nadoraz* (Prague, 1998).

von der Goltz, Anna (ed.), *'Talkin' 'bout my Generation': Conflicts of Generation Building and Europe's '1968'* (Göttingen, 2011).

von Lucke, Albrecht, *68 oder neues Biedermeier: Der Kampf um die Deutungsmacht* (Berlin, 2008).

von Plato, Alexander, Almut Leh and Christoph Thonfeld (eds), *Hitler's Slaves: Life Stories of Forced Labourers in Nazi-Occupied Europe* (Oxford, 2010).

Vuarin, Pauline, 'Larzac 1971–1981. La dynamique des acteurs d'une lutte originale et créatrice' (Thofter's thesis, University d Paris I, 2005).

Walter, Lynn, 'The Redstocking movement: Sex, love, and politics in 1968', in Anna Clark (ed.), *The History of Sexuality in Europe: A Sourcebook and Reader* (Oxford, 2011), 297–316.

Warnier, Philippe, *Le Phénomène des communautés de base* (Paris, 1973).

Warnier, Philippe, *Nouveaux témoins de l'Église. Les communautés de base* (Paris, 1981).

Waters, Sarah, 'Introduction: 1968 in memory and place', in Ingo Cornils and Sarah Waters, *Memories of 1968: International Perspectives* (Bern, 2010), 1–22.

Weeks, Jeffrey, *The World We Have Won: The Remaking of Erotic and Intimate Life* (London, 2007).

Weigel, Sigrid, 'Generation, Genealogie, Geschlecht', in Lutz Musner and Gotthart Wunberg (eds), *Kulturwissenschaften* (Vienna, 2002), 161–90.

Werner, Michael and Bénédicte Zimmermann, 'Beyond comparison: *Histoire croisée* and the challenge of reflexivity', *Theory and History* 45 (2006), 30–50.

Wernicke, Günter, 'The World Peace Council and the antiwar movement in East Germany', in Andreas W. Daum, Lloyd C. Gardner and Wilfried Mausbach (eds), *America, the Vietnam War, and the World* (Cambridge and New York, 2003), 299–320.

Westad, Odd Arne, *The Global Cold War: Third-World Interventions and the Making of Our Times* (Cambridge, 2005).

Westerberg, Niels, Dorte Møller, Merete Ipsen, Niels Ole Finnemann and Jette Sandal, *Livsstykker. Fem historier fra det nye venstres almanak* (Århus, 1979).

Whalen, Jack and Richard Flacks, *Beyond the Barricades: The Sixties Generation Grows Up* (Philadelphia, 1989).

Wierling, Dorothee, 'Generations as narrative communities: Some private sources of public memory in postwar Germany', in Frank Biess and Robert Moeller (eds), *Histories of the Aftermath: The Legacies of the Second World War in Europe* (New York and Oxford, 2010), 102–22.

Wieviorka, Michel, *Sociétés et terrorisme* (Paris, 1988).

Wieviorka, Michel (ed.), *Violence en France* (Paris, 1999).

Willis, Ellen, *No More Nice Girls: Countercultural Essays* (Middletown, CT, 1992).

Wiszniewicz, Joanna, *Życie przecięte. Opowieści pokolenia Marca* (Wołowiec, 2008).

Wolin, Richard, *The Wind from the East: French Intellectuals, the Cultural Revolution, and the Legacy of the 1960s* (Princeton, NJ, 2010).

Zadra, Dario, 'Comunione e liberazione: A fundamentalist idea of power', in Martin Marty
    and R. Scott Appleby (eds), *Accounting for Fundamentalisms: The Dynamic Character of
    Movements* (Chicago, 1994), 124–47.
Zemon Davis, Natalie, *Women at the Margins: Three Seventeenth-Century Lives* (Cambridge,
    MA, 1995).

Index

Index

Index

Printed and bound by CPI Group (UK) Ltd, Croydon, CR0 4YY